Using Assessment Results for Career Development

7th Edition

Debra S. Osborn

Vernon G. Zunker

Executive Editor: *Lisa Gebo*
Acquisitions Editor: *Marquita Flemming*
Assistant Editor: *Jennifer Walsh*
Technology Project Manager: *Inna Fedoseyeva*
Marketing Manager: *Caroline Concilla*
Marketing Assistant: *Rebecca Weisman*
Advertising Project Manager: *Tami Strang*

Project Manager, Editorial Production: *Christy Krueger*
Print Buyer: *Nora Massuda*
Permissions Editor: *Sarah Harkrader*
Compositor: *Hoby Corp.*
Cover Designer: *Irene Morris*
Printer: *Thomson West*

Printed in the United States of America
1 2 3 4 5 6 7 09 08 07 06 05

For more information about our products, contact us at:
Thomson Learning Academic Resource Center
1-800-423-0563

For permission to use material from this text or product, submit a request online at
http://www.thomsonrights.com
Any additional questions about permissions can be submitted by email at
thomsonrights@thomson.com

Thomson Higher Education
10 Davis Drive
Belmont, CA 94002-3098
USA

Library of Congress Control Number: 2005934284

ISBN 0-534-63279-3

Table of Contents

Preface

> Pleasure in the job puts perfection in the work.
> —Aristotle

Finding a pleasurable career is the main reason why people seek career counseling. But this isn't the only factor people consider: they may also want to find work that takes into account their aptitudes or skills, interests, values, knowledge, and/or needs. Regardless of the career theory used, career counselors help people to organize information about themselves as one component of effective career decision-making.

We believe the following areas of knowledge to be critical for professionals who want to utilize inventories as a part of career counseling: knowledge of how to incorporate career testing into the career counseling session, an understanding of basic statistics for interpreting test results, knowledge of specific tests, and knowledge of ethical issues surrounding testing. The decision of if, when, and how to incorporate testing into the counseling session is addressed in Chapters 1 and 2, where we provide a model of how to incorporate testing, whether standardized or non-standardized, into the career counseling session. In Chapter 3, measurement concepts and basic statistics are covered. Chapters 4 through 9 illustrate how to use the results of ability tests, achievement tests, interest inventories, personality inventories, value inventories, and career development inventories. Chapter 10 describes the use of card sorts in counseling, while Chapter 11 covers the use of computer-assisted career guidance programs and online career testing. Chapter 12 covers the use of assessment instruments especially designed for people with disabilities and people who are academically disadvantaged. Chapter 13 covers the use of non-standardized self-assessment devices in career exploration. How to combine various assessment results in counseling is described in Chapter 14, and ethical issues related to career testing are covered in Chapter 15.

We describe and review individual tests and provide sample protocols that may be used by career counselors. These reviews cover a description of the instrument, its purpose, some technical information, where to find other extensive reviews, and case studies. Our principal motive in writing this book has been to provide counselors with a tool for understanding how to use a variety of inventories in counseling. The case studies offer examples of how each instrument can be introduced and how the results can be interpreted. Each chapter also features a list of suggested activities and questions so that readers may apply the information to practical situations.

In this seventh edition, we have made a few changes, the most obvious one being in authorship order. Additional changes include a chapter on ethical issues and testing, a new appendix outlining career tests by age level, an incorporation of international inventories, and a section on online career testing. Yet despite these modifications, our vision for this text remains the same: to provide a practical tool that will arm counseling professionals with the information necessary to effectively choose, administer, and interpret inventories within career counseling.

Acknowledgments

We wish to acknowledge the people in our lives who have helped make the writing of this seventh edition a reality. We are grateful to the many students and colleagues who offered words of encouragement and wisdom as we were putting these pages together, including our reviewers Jodi Caldwell-John, Georgia Southern University; John Carey, University of Massachusetts, Amherst; Jennifer Smirnoff, The University of Toledo; Gregory Garske, Bowling Green State University; and Ann Carter-Obayuwana, Howard University.

I, Debbie, would also like to thank Vern Zunker, for providing me with the opportunity and encouragement to be the primary author for this seventh edition. In addition, I would like to thank some very special people at Florida State University who have believed in me, encouraged me, and offered me valuable guidance throughout my educational and professional career: Dr. Robert Reardon, Dr. Jim Sampson, Jr., Dr. Janet Lenz, and Dr. Gary Peterson. Thanks to my husband, Keith, and our daughters, Sarah and Savannah, for their love, unwavering belief in me, and constant encouragement. Finally, a special thank you to my parents, Verna and Bob Norris, and my grandmother, Esther Norris, for their love and support.

I, Vern, am most grateful to my wife, Rosalie, who encouraged, prodded, and kept her vivacious sense of humor throughout the entire writing of this text. Without her encouragement, the entire project would have been less meaningful.

Debra S. Osborn
Vernon G. Zunker

Using Assessment Results for Career Development

1 Interpreting Assessment Results

"I need to figure out what major I should choose." "I've been in this career for most of my life – I think I'm ready for a change." "I have a degree in education and have been a teacher for several years – what else can I do besides teach?" "I get so confused when trying to make a career decision. It's hard to know where to start." "Can you give me that test that will tell me what I should be?" These statements are representative of what career counselors hear from students and clients who need or want some clarity on their career goals, and see taking a career assessment as a means of achieving that clarity. Career testing is usually an integral part of career counseling, whether the purpose is to identify interests and prioritize careers, discover negative thinking that might be hindering the career decision-making process, or to aid in the brainstorming of other career options. In order to help individuals evaluate and make decisions about their careers, some type of assessment, whether formal or informal, standardized or non-standardized, is often desirable.

Regardless of the theoretical approach of the counselor, a common activity in which those providing career counseling often engage is that of administering and interpreting the results of an assessment to a client or a student. The purpose of this book is to review a variety of such inventories, provide basic information about the psychometric properties of these tools, and demonstrate how the results of such inventories might be used in practice. This book begins where courses in assessment and appraisal methods usually end. Instead of emphasizing the procedures used for standardizing tests and inventories and the methods used to develop them, this book illustrates the use of assessment results. The material is presented with the assumption that the reader has a substantial foundation in tests and measurements. In each chapter, we review representative examples of tests, inventories, and self-assessment measures and explain how results are used.

Fictitious cases further illustrate the use of many of these instruments. These cases resemble actual counseling encounters that we have had or that counselors we have supervised have had. The cases do not include descriptions of the entire information-gathering process and all counseling encounters. In each case, we have included only the material relevant for illustrating the use of assessment results. All standardized assessment instruments mentioned in this book are listed in Appendix A, along with the names and addresses of the publishers.

Various approaches to assessment interpretation have been reported in the literature since Parsons's (1909) seminal work. The trait-and-factor approach advocated by Parsons and later by Williamson (1939, 1949) and reviewed by Prediger (1995) was straightforward—it matched individual abilities and aptitudes with the requirements of a job. Parsons originally defined these requirements as "conditions of success." Does the person's abilities and aptitudes line up with what it takes to be successful in this particular job? This approach has been drastically modified over the years toward considering, for example, many different individual characteristics and traits. In other words, individuals are being encouraged to consider many aspects of themselves in the career decision-making process, including their abilities, interests, personalities, values, needs, hobbies, past work and leisure experiences, and total lifestyles. In fact, more emphasis is being placed on integrating all life roles in the career counseling process. Specifically, individuals are encouraged to evaluate the effect work roles will have on other roles such as family, civic, and leisure roles.

This broad approach has been accompanied by computer scoring, online administration of valid (and not-so-valid nor reliable) tests, new assessment instruments, and economic and societal changes, which have all complicated the issues of measurement and certainly the interpretation and use of assessment results. Computerized reports provide an almost unlimited amount of assessment information. The introduction of new measuring instruments and the refinement and revitalization of established tests and inventories provide further information to the career counselor. In addition, new technology has created a variety of new occupations, and the changing economic conditions and restructuring of organizations have caused many individuals to search for new, different occupations

(Drucker, 1992). The stereotypes of the breadwinner father and the homemaker mother have undergone significant modification. Women will continue to enter the labor force at a rate faster than men, and with 61.6% of U.S. women working in 2012, will comprise 47.5% of the entire workforce in 2012 (Toossi, 2004).

The look of the labor force will be older, with workers ages 55 and older projecting to have a growth rate that is almost 4 times the growth rate of the entire labor force (Toossi, 2004). The variety of clients may include a former executive who is a victim of downsizing in an organization, a homemaker and divorcee who is entering the work force for the first time, a high school dropout, an undecided college student, and a graduate who is unable to find an appropriate career path. Special instruments have also been developed for individuals who are disadvantaged or who have disabling conditions. All these factors have made it necessary for counselors to reevaluate how they can most effectively use assessment results.

In this chapter, we provide a general background for interpreting assessment results. First, we discuss assessment as a diagnostic and predictive tool, assessment as a means of comparing an individual with criterion groups, and the developmental use of assessment results. Second, we discuss norms—when to use them, what kind to use, and how much weight to give to them. Third, we describe the interpretation of score profiles. Fourth, we review the limitations of one-shot counseling. Finally, we provide a preview of the following chapters, which illustrate the use of assessment results in specific situations.

Use of Assessment Results

Assessment results are counseling tools for fostering career exploration and serving as a springboard for deeper discussion. All theories, systems, and strategies underscore the inclusive and complex nature of the career choice process. Using assessments should fit within the counselor's career theory. For example, see Table 1-1 for a sample of how assessments might fit in with Cognitive Information Processing theory (Peterson, Sampson, Reardon & Lenz, 2002). Other examples might include aptitude testing for Parson's approach, values/needs and work environment testing for Person-Environment Correspondence theory, values inventories and card sorts for Brown's Value-Based Holistic model, and interest inventories for Holland's RIASEC theory. Even the more person-centered or developmental approaches include an opportunity for assessment – whether using standardized tests or directive questioning. For example, Super's concept of career maturity might be tested with the Career Maturity Inventory, and other portions of his archway model might be tested with various values, interests and skills inventories.

Table 1-1	Testing related to CIP theory	
Cognitive Information Processing	**Domain**	**Type of Testing**
	Knowledge Domain	Interest, Values, Skills
	Decision Making Domain	Decision Making Abilities
	Executive Domain	Negative career thoughts, vocational identity, career beliefs, self-esteem

As a counselor, the decision to use an inventory shouldn't be random, or because you're not sure what else to do. There should be a reason for testing, and that reason should stem from the career theory of the counselor. Tied to that reason should be a goal or desired outcome for what the test will provide. The goal or outcome should also stem from the career theory of the counselor.

In addition, counselors should consider the cultural background of a client when engaging in career counseling and career testing. Flores, Spanierman and Obasi (2003) identify a four stage linear model for culturally appropriate career assessment (see Figure 1-1). In addition, Leong and Hartung (2000) encouraged counselors to consider cultural validity (how valid an instrument is for specific cultures) and cultural specificity (how cultural variables such as language and world view impact the assessment process) when selecting an assessment.

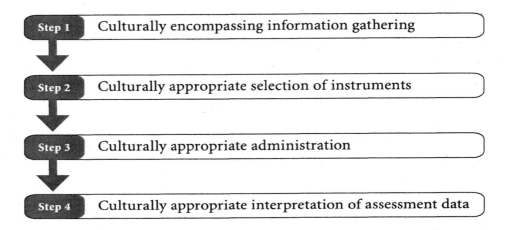

Figure 1-1

As with culturally appropriate career counseling, culturally appropriate career assessment should be synonymous with general career assessment. That is, career assessment (and career counseling, for that matter) that is culturally enriched is beneficial for all clients. To self-assess cultural competencies, a counselor might complete Ward and Bingham's (1993) Multicultural Career Counseling Checklist, which includes a section on exploration and assessment.

The process of deciding is indeed complex and unique for each individual, dependent on cognitive factors and the social structure of the individual's milieu. Individuals evaluate their choices internally by considering values, interests, achievements, and experiences and externally by seeking acceptance and approval within the work environment. Individuals must deal with self-doubts concerning the appropriateness of their choices in the process, making a careful examination of cognitive and affective domains. The significance of choosing a career parallels other major choices in an individual's life; assessment results can provide useful information in the career decision-making process.

How, when, and whether to use assessment results are decisions shared by the counselor and the client. These decisions are based primarily on evaluation of the purpose for using measuring instruments. Can assessment results provide the information sought, and is that information relevant for the decisions that are to be made? This principle is followed when using assessment results for individuals as well as for groups. Tests are not to be given indiscriminately, and the same tests are not to be given routinely to everyone. Individuals in different phases of career development have different needs, which must be considered when determining whether to use assessment procedures. One individual may need assistance in developing an awareness of her interests; another may need to clarify his values so he can establish priorities. Personality conflicts may be a deterrent for another individual who is considering a job change. Yet another may need assistance in clarifying her expectations about work in general.

A careful analysis of the purpose for using measurement devices would answer these questions: When in the career decision-making process is the most strategic time to introduce assessment? What are the alternatives the individual is considering? Does the information provided by the test correspond to the requirements of the particular jobs or training programs under consideration? Or, if a group is being counseled, will the results from the inventory introduce pertinent information for group discussion?

Because career exploration follows paths determined by individual needs, the use of assessment results in career counseling will vary and should be geared toward meeting specific objectives. Later chapters show how the use of assessment results in counseling can be designed to meet individual objectives. In this chapter we discuss assessment in a general way as a diagnostic and predictive tool, as a means of comparing an individual to criterion groups, and, most important, as relevant information for fostering career development over the life span.

Some overlap in the use of measuring instruments may occur; for example, a diagnostic test may be used to predict performance. However, a diagnostic test used to determine treatment for deficiencies might not be useful in predicting how well an individual will perform on a specific job. Likewise, a test used to predict performance might not be useful for determining treatment or for comparing an individual with criterion groups. For each client, a counselor must decide what kind of tests or inventories to use.

It should be noted that counselors are scientists as well as educators and artists. As a scientist, the counselor is making observations, asking investigative questions, forming hypotheses and making interventions based on what the client says and the client's non-verbals. What the client "says" could be in the form of dialogue or via an assessment. All the information that a counselor gathers during a traditional "talk" session can also be seen as assessment results – and formal assessment results should always be viewed in light of what has been discussed and observed during counseling sessions. As an educator, the counselor provides current, relevant information and tools for making good decisions. As an artist, the counselor joins with the client in creating a promising career path.

Diagnostic Uses of Assessment

Achievement and aptitude assessment results, in particular, are often used to evaluate individual strengths and weaknesses in order to determine preparedness and potential for training and for beginning work. The identification of skills and aptitudes may broaden the individual's options for careers and education. In the same sense, the assessment of academic and skill deficiencies may help identify the need for treatment, remedial training, or skill development.

Jake, a high school senior, was among a group of students participating in career exploration with his high school counselor. During the initial interview, Jake told the counselor that he wanted to go to college but that he had many interests and was not sure which one to pursue. Also, he expressed concern about his ability to succeed academically in college. After further discussion, the counselor and Jake agreed that he would complete an aptitude battery. The assessment results identified several academic strengths and a few specific deficiencies. Next, Jake and the counselor spent several sessions relating Jake's strengths to career fields and college majors that might be explored. Finally, they reviewed the curricula of nearby colleges and decided, in light of Jake's academic deficiencies, which remedial courses he might take during his freshman year. By the end of counseling, Jake, though still not decided, had narrowed his ideas about a career choice. Moreover, he indicated that he felt positive about his initial academic plan.

Interest, value, personality, and career inventories can also be used diagnostically. Typically, these measures are used to raise an individual's level of self-awareness and to indicate to counselors when clients are lacking in self-awareness or have views of themselves that are inconsistent with assessment results.

Predictive Uses of Assessment

Assessment results may also be used to predict future academic and job performance. The probability of performing well on a job, in a training program, or in an educational program is relevant information on which to base further exploration. However, currently available ability measures primarily provide broad measures of an individual's experience and ability at the time of testing (aptitude tests), whereas achievement tests assess present levels of developed abilities. What is vitally needed is a measure of the occupational significance of abilities—that is, how important it is to have certain abilities to perform successfully in specific occupations. Until we have more data about prediction of occupational success and prediction of training and occupational performance, we should limit these references to more general terms in the counseling dialogue.

Herb wanted to know whether he could qualify for a machine operator's job in a local industrial plant. Fortunately, Herb's counselor had worked closely with the personnel division at the plant and, in fact, had assisted in gathering data for selection and placement. As a result, the counselor administered the test that had been used to develop cutoff scores for a variety of jobs in the plant. Herb's score was sufficiently high for him to qualify for a machine operator's job. In this case, Herb was provided with information that helped him evaluate his chances of meeting the requirements of a specific job.

Noelle decided that she would like to attend the local community college. However, she was concerned about her chances of being a successful student in that college. Her counselor had developed an expectancy table (see Chapter 3) based on test scores and grades earned at the college by students who had attended the high school from which Noelle was graduating. Noelle agreed to take the test used in the study, and the counselor was able to assess her chances of getting a C or better at the college. The prediction of success based on local data was vitally important in Noelle's career exploration.

When assessment results are used to predict subsequent performance, the counselor should ensure that relevant predictive validity has been established for the tests that are used. For example, a test used to predict job performance should have a previously established high correlation with performance criteria for that job. Likewise, tests for predicting academic performance should be used only when relevant expectancy tables have already been established. Predicting academic performance is illustrated in Chapter 3 with the use of an expectancy table, and predicting job performance is discussed in Chapter 4 with the use ability tests.

Comparative Uses of Assessment

Comparing one's personal characteristics (abilities, interests, values) with those of criterion groups is a stimulating part of career exploration. For example, it can be enlightening for individuals to compare their interests with the interests of individuals in certain occupational groups. The similarities and differences found can encourage discussion of the relevance of interests in career exploration.

The Strong Interest Inventory is an example of an interpretive report that compares an individual's interests with those of people in a wide range of occupations. Although an individual may be pleased to find that her interests are similar to those of social science teachers, she should also be encouraged to pay attention to interests that are similar to those of other occupational groups.

Developmental Uses of Assessment

Career development as a continuous process is enhanced by relevant assessment results used to increase awareness of career exploration opportunities over the life span. Learning to link measured aptitudes, interests, and values to work requirements and lifestyle preferences are good examples of using assessment results to foster career development. Meaningful assessment during all phases of career development involves the diagnostic, predictive, and comparative use of assessment results.

At the elementary school level, for example, a career development objective focus may center on increasing self-awareness by relating assessed personal characteristics to broad expectations of future work. A career development objective at the junior high school level stresses measured likes and dislikes and their influence on positive self-concepts. At the high school level, students should understand the interrelationship between educational achievement results and work requirements.

The college student is challenged with assessing personal aptitudes and preferences when determining a major or a career. The career development objective for an adult in career transition requires an evaluation of learned skills from previous work and leisure experiences in determining a new and different career direction. For the older adult, measured interests and leisure activities, skills needed in part-time or volunteer work, and assessment of established values are relevant developmental uses of assessment results. In all the examples of career development objectives, assessment results provide vital information for enhancing individual growth. The career counselor needs to be aware of a wide range of assessment instruments to meet individual needs at various stages of career development.

Guidelines and qualifications for testing activities have been delineated by professional organizations, including the National Career Development Association (http://www.ncda.org), the National Board of Certified Counselors (http://www.nbcc.org), American Counseling Association (http://www.counseling.org/resources/codeofethics.htm), and the Association for Testing in Counseling (http://www.aac.uc.edu/aac/Resources/resources.html). Appendix C includes the ethical codes of several of these organizations. Any counselor who will be using an inventory or test should be familiar with the guidelines put forth by these organizations. The most common guidelines include these: reviewing the validity and reliability of the instrument, being aware of your boundaries of competence (only give and interpret tests that you are qualified for and have had experience giving and interpreting), providing an orientation in which you describe how the test results will be used and stored (including confidentiality and test security), considering whether the test is appropriate for your client, explaining all test limitations, obtaining informed consent, ensuring that any advertising that your school or agency puts out about the test is accurate and not misleading, following standardized instructions, and providing correct and easy to understand interpretations.

In addition, the casebook put out by the American Psychological Association (1993) outlines seven factors of responsible test use:

1. Assessment should be comprehensive, integrating test scores with personal history.

2. Test administrators should ensure that the selected test is used properly at all stages.

3. The person interpreting the test must have adequate knowledge of basic psychometric and statistical principles.

4. Test interpretation should occur within the context of correct psychometric knowledge, and test limitations should be acknowledged and taken into consideration.

5. Before interpreting the test, scores should be double-checked for accuracy.

6. Tests should be interpreted with respect to the normative data provided.

7. Verbal interpretations of test scores should be correct and easy to understand.

The role of assessment in career development counseling has also been emphasized by the National Occupational Information Coordinating Committee (NOICC, 1992) in national guidelines suggested for student and adult career development competencies. The NOICC guidelines were revised in 1996. While that office is no longer in existence, the National Career Development Guidelines continue and are currently being updated. Zunker (2005) has a summary of career development competencies by area and level. Some examples of specific competencies in which the developmental use of assessment results can be the major focus are as follows:

1. For the elementary school student
    Competency: Knowledge of the importance of self-concept.
    The student will:

    *   Identify personal interests, abilities, strengths, and weaknesses
    *   Describe ways to meet personal needs through work

    Competency: Awareness of the benefits of educational achievement.
    The student will:

    *   Identify personal strengths and weaknesses in academic areas
    *   Identify academic skills needed in several occupational groups
    *   Describe school tasks that are similar to skills essential for job success

2. For the junior or middle school student
    Competency: Knowledge of the influence of a positive self-concept.
    The student will:

    *   Describe personal likes and dislikes

    Competency: Knowledge of the benefits of educational achievement to career opportunities.
    The student will:

    *   Describe individual strengths and weaknesses in school subjects
    *   Describe the skills needed to adjust to changing occupational requirements
    *   Describe the importance of academic and occupational skills in the world of work
    *   Describe how aptitudes and abilities relate to broad occupational groups

3. For the senior high school student
    Competency: Understanding the influence of a positive self-concept.
    The student will:

    *   Demonstrate an understanding of how individual characteristics relate to achieving personal, social, educational, and career goals
    *   Identify and appreciate personal interests, abilities, and skills

    Competency: Understanding the relationship between educational achievement and career planning.
    The student will:

    *   Describe the relationship of academic and vocational skills to personal interests
    *   Demonstrate transferable skills that can apply to a variety of occupations and changing occupational requirements

4. For the adult
    Competency: Skills to maintain a positive self-concept.
    The adult will:

    *   Identify skills, abilities, interests, experiences, values, and personality traits and their influence on career decisions
    *   Determine or clarify career and life goals based on a realistic understanding of self
    *   More specific suggestions for developmental use of assessment results are included in Chapters 4, 5, 6, 7, and 8.

International Career Testing

While many of the popular career inventories in the United States have been translated into languages other than English, there is a dearth of research reporting the reliability, validity and normative findings for use of these instruments in other countries. Volume 50 of the Career Development Quarterly is a special issue about career counseling in Asia. Some off the articles address the issue of career testing. Leung (2002) identified four factors impacting career testing in Hong Kong: (1) the lack of an official Chinese translation of popular U.S. inventories; (2) the inventories are too expensive; (3) lack of research proving the reliability and validity of the inventories for the different communities within Hong Kong; and (4) the occupations and structure of occupations that are presented either as part of the inventories or as a result of taking such inventories doesn't match the occupations and occupational structure of Hong Kong.

In Taiwan, Chang (2002) described that for centuries, test results were used to classify people into occupations, and people would follow the career path that was suggested by these results. This highlights a difference in philosophy. We believe one assumption about testing in general is that the purpose is to expand, not narrow, a person's career options. Counselors may find it difficult to change a mindset that has been the reality for decades. This relates back to the validity and reliability information. Knowing that a client from Taiwan probably puts a great deal of faith into test results, test developers must ensure that the test meets the highest psychometric standards. Chang also described that the government controls testing, funding and staff. Without government assistance, developing test norms is difficult to accomplish. Chang also outlined the issues of test security, test over-exposure and conditions of testing as factors that are slowing the development of computer-assisted career guidance in Taiwan.

The issue of international career testing is one that is just beginning to gain some attention. At this point in time, we can identify the following concerns, based on the articles above:

- Translation does not equate with cultural applicability
- Occupations, work tasks and occupational structures of the U.S. are not generalizable to those of other countries
- Validity and reliability must be established for each inventory. It is incorrect to assume that because a test has high validity and reliability in the U.S., that it will demonstrate the same in other countries.
- The costs associated with test training, purchasing tests, software or licenses can be prohibitive.
- The philosophy of how a career choice is made, the power of career tests, and who is in control of making career decisions for individuals may need to be addressed before an inventory is selected.

While many counselors may not see themselves as counseling in another country, in today's global workplace, it is very easy to see how a counselor who engages in online career counseling might very well have a career counseling client who is from another country. Another common situation is with providing career counseling to international students who hope to return to work in their home country. It is then that these issues and others (i.e., ethical issues regarding online counseling) become more pertinent.

Norms

The usefulness of assessment results in career counseling is determined by the types of norms available. In using norms, the counselor should keep the following questions in mind: When should norms be used? What kind of norms should be used? How much weight should be given to norms? Norms represent the level of performance obtained by the individuals (normative sample) used in developing score standards. Norms can thus be thought of as typical or normal scores. Norms for some tests and inventories are based on the general population. Other norms are based on specific groups such as all 12th-grade students, 12th-grade students who plan to attend college, left-handed individuals, former drug abusers, former alcoholics, or individuals with physical disabilities.

The organization of norm tables varies somewhat from test to test. For example, the manual for the Self-Directed Search lists separate norms for males and females by adult, high school, and college level for the six corresponding Holland types (Holland, Powell, & Fritzsche, 1994). The Adult Basic Learning Examination (Level III) provides norms for adults by sex, age, race, last grade completed, and median Stanford Achievement Test (SAT) score.

The normative sample description is critical to the test's effective use. In some manuals, only a brief description is given, leaving counselors to assume that their clients resemble the normative population.

Others, such as the Kuder Occupational Interest Survey, provide specific definitions of normative groups. Such detailed descriptions of persons sampled in standardizing an inventory provide good data for comparing the norm samples with client groups. In many instances, more information would be useful, such as score differences between age and ethnic groups and between individuals in different geographical locations. The more descriptive the norms are, the greater their utility and flexibility.

When using norms, counselors must carefully evaluate the population from which the norms have been derived to determine whether that population resembles their clients in background and individual characteristics. We would not want to use norms derived from a sample of Puerto Ricans in the Northeast to advise a group of Chinese students on the West Coast. However, norms derived from Puerto Ricans in the Northeast are more appropriate for use with Puerto Ricans living elsewhere in the country than are general-population norms.

National norms, sometimes referred to as general-population norms or people-in-general norms, are usually controlled in the sampling process to be balanced in geographical area, ethnicity, educational level, sex, age, and other factors. National norms may be helpful in determining underlying individual characteristics and patterns. For example, an individual whose measured values suggest only an average need for achievement compared with that of business executives and entrepreneurs may exhibit a moderately high need for achievement when compared with people in general. This information suggests an underlying or secondary need for achievement that might not otherwise have been clarified. The identification of lower-order yet important personal traits affords greater depth for career exploration.

In many instances, national norms should not be used. National norms based on a sample of 12th graders are of little value in predicting success in a particular university; appropriate norms would be those derived from students who have attended the university under consideration. Likewise, norms based on a general population are not useful in predicting success in a certain job at a local factory. Selection and placement in an industry are usually based on norms derived from workers in a specific occupation or work setting.

Because operational and educational requirements vary from one location to another, using local norms is recommended. For example, you will recall that, for predicting Noelle's chances of being successful in a particular college, the counselor had collected data from former students of Noelle's high school to develop the norms.

Local norms are also useful for job placement. Although more weight can be given to local norms than to general norms and local norms should be developed whenever possible, counselors usually do not have the necessary time and resources to devote to such projects. Most counselors must rely on the published norms furnished in test and inventory manuals. Most of the counseling cases discussed in later chapters illustrate the use of assessment results with published norms.

Score Profiles

In early counseling approaches, the profile served as the primary tool for making one-shot predictions of vocational choice (Goldman, 1972; Prediger, 1980). Choices were considered definite and irreversible (Cronbach, 1984). Currently, the score profile is considered as only one source of information on individual characteristics.

To make assessment results as meaningful as possible, computer-generated narrative reports are increasingly being used as supplements to the profile. The computer interprets the score results in narrative form according to a planned program, and these narrative reports are often sent directly to students and parents. Because score profiles alone do not always stimulate individuals to explore careers, supplementary materials and follow-up exercises are needed to complement the interpretation process (Prediger, 1980). Although supplements to profiles may prove helpful in stimulating career exploration, the counselor should not completely abandon the role of interpreting the profile. In fact, the potential for increasing the number and variety of computer-generated score interpretations in the future is almost a mandate for counselors to sharpen their skills in this respect.

Regardless of the format of the score profile, three important principles of interpretation must be retained: (1) differences between scores should be interpreted with caution, (2) profiles should be interpreted with concern for the influence of norms, and (3) scores should be expressed in ranges rather than in points.

Differences Between Scores

Caution must always be used when interpreting differences between scores on a profile. Small score differences are meaningless and should be attributed to chance effects. Clients may be tempted to make much more of small score differences between subtests than is plausible. But one should not eliminate second-, third-, or fourth-order measured interests and consider only highest measured interests in career exploration. Likewise, when interpreting the score profile from a general abilities test, one should not consider only a career in mathematics because the score in mathematics was a few percentile points higher than the other scores. To point a person narrowly to a slightly higher measured characteristic is counterproductive in developmental counseling. (Score differences are discussed further in Chapters 3 and 4.)

Relation of Norms to the Shape of a Profile

An individual's profile must be carefully interpreted in light of the norm reference group. The position of scores on a profile (its shape) is determined by the norms used. For example, Manuel, who is interested in architecture, has taken the Differential Aptitude Test. His score profile compared with that of men in general suggests that his general abilities are high enough for him to consider college. To obtain a reliable estimate of his chances of success in a school of architecture, his scores were compared with norms derived from architecture students. The shapes of the profiles were quite different. When Manuel's scores were plotted against those for men in general, all were considerably above average. When compared with scores of architecture students, most of his scores were in the average range. This profile gives a much more valid estimate of his chances for success in a school of architecture than does the general profile. Whenever possible, score profiles used for predicting performance should be compared with those of competitors (Cronbach, 1984).

Scores as a Range

On some score profiles, results are reported as points on a scale; on others, scores are reported as a range that includes the error of measurement of each test. The range may be represented on a percentile graph by a bar, line, or row of x's, with the obtained percentile at the center. The purpose for this is to show where a person's true score might actually be. For example, if a person was praised or criticized, or was feeling unusually good or bad just prior to completing an inventory, the inventory might not reflect the person's real or true score. Showing a range reflects the individual's true score more accurately than does the single-point method.

Because career development is a continuous process, the score profile provides information from which only tentative decisions need be made. These decisions, not being binding or irreversible, provide information on which to base a further study of individual characteristics. Therefore, the range is more appropriate as a reference for individual decisions than is a single point. Because we are usually not able to obtain precise measures in career exploration, the error of measurement should be considered for all scores recorded as a single point on a scale.

Using Holland's Codes for Interpretation

According to John Holland (1997), individuals are attracted to a given career by their particular personalities and numerous variables that constitute their backgrounds. Although Holland's work is centered on the development of interest inventories and their interpretation, his concepts are also related to skills, abilities, attitudes, and values that will be discussed in many of the following chapters. It is therefore important to introduce the basic assumptions of his theory (Holland, Powell & Fritzsche, 1994, pp. 5–6):

1. In our culture, most persons can be categorized as one of six types: realistic, investigative, artistic, social, enterprising, or conventional.
2. There are six kinds of environments: realistic, investigative, artistic, social, enterprising, and conventional.
3. People search for environments that will let them exercise their skills and abilities, express their attitudes and values, and take on agreeable problems and roles.
4. A person's behavior is determined by an interaction between his or her personality and the characteristics of the environment.

Central to Holland's theory is the concept that one chooses a career to satisfy one's preferred personal modal orientation. For example, a socially oriented individual prefers to work in an environment that provides interaction with others, such as a teaching position. A mechanically inclined individual, however, might seek out an environment where the trade could be quietly practiced and one could avoid socializing to a great extent. Occupational homogeneity—that is, congruence between one's work and interests—provides the best route to self-fulfillment and a consistent career pattern. Individuals out of their element who have conflicting occupational environmental roles and goals will have inconsistent and divergent career patterns.

A brief explanation of Holland's personal styles and occupational environments follows. For a more complete explanation, see Zunker (2005).

Many of the following chapters refer to Holland's types and codes, and, in fact, some of this information will be repeated for a better understanding of his typology. For in-depth coverage, read Holland's book about his theory (1997) and the many research articles that support his occupational types.

Table 1-2	Holland Personal Styles	
Type	**Personal Style**	**Occupational Environments**
Realistic (R)	R types prefer concrete versus abstract work tasks, work outdoors in manual activities, and like to work alone or with other realistic people.	Most occupations are blue-collar ones, such as plumber, electrician, and service occupations.
Investigative (I)	I types prefer to work in an environment where one is required to use abstract and analytical skills, are somewhat independent, and are strongly oriented to accomplishing tasks.	Many scientific professions require high levels of education and are intellectually oriented, such as chemist, biologist, and researcher. Examples of other investigative occupations are laboratory technician, computer programmer, and electronics worker.
Artistic (A)	A types include imaginative and creative individuals who value aesthetics, prefer self-expression through the arts, and are rather independent and extroverted.	Some occupations included in this category are sculptor, artist, designer, music teacher, orchestra leader, editor, writer, and critic.
Social (S)	S types are very concerned with social problems, prefer social interaction, are religious, participate in community service, are interested in educational activities, and prefer working with people. There is a strong orientation toward working with others and using interpersonal skills.	Occupational categories in this group include those in education, such as teacher, school administrator, and college professor. Others are social worker, rehabilitation counselor, and professional nurse.
Enterprising (E)	E types are extroverted, aggressive, adventurous, dominant, and persuasive and prefer leadership roles. Their behavior is also characterized as goal-directed, and they like to coordinate others' work.	Occupational categories are managerial, including workers in charge of production and in various sales positions.
Conventional (C)	C types are practical, well controlled, sociable, and rather conservative. They prefer structured tasks and are comfortable when working with details.	Occupations include office and clerical workers, accountant, bookkeeper, receptionist, teller, and key-punch operator.

One-Shot Counseling

People have different expectations for career counseling. Some take a realistic approach and expect to spend considerable time in individual study and in counseling encounters. Others expect counselors to analyze their assessment results and prescribe a career in one counseling session (Cronbach, 1984; Prediger, 1980). To illustrate this second kind of expectation, imagine yourself as a counselor in the following two cases.

Ying, a high school senior, drops by the counseling office one week before graduation and tells the counselor that he would like to know what major he should select for his first summer session in college: "I would like to take the test that will tell me what to major in." As Ying sees it, the test holds the key to his future.

Ann, a second-semester college sophomore, makes an appointment in the college counseling center during mid-semester break. She explains, "I would like to take those tests that will tell me what career I should choose so I can register for the courses next semester." She has an entire half-day to make this decision!

Often, in more subtle ways than these, parents and students expect one-shot assessment interpretations to resolve the issue of career choice, as if believing that tests have a mystical power to foretell the future. The pressure to declare a major or a career immediately is demonstrated best by college students right before a holiday – when they are headed home and will be expected to have an answer for the question, "So, what are you majoring in?" Some clients may very well have high expectations of what psychological tests can do—that is, solve their problems. From that frame of reference, a counselor's major responsibility is to test clients and place them in the right job, major or career path.

The limitations of one-shot counseling are apparent. First, in career exploration, many decisions are tentative; one-shot counseling approaches give just the opposite impression. Second, there is little opportunity to confirm the decisions based on assessment results. One-shot counseling does not provide for follow-up through observation, continuous discussion of assessment results, or retesting. Third, a one-shot counseling approach affirms the individual's desire to make decisions without devoting time to gathering information and considering alternatives. There is little opportunity to develop a systematic method of decision making. In effect, the client is seeking the counselor's approval to approach career decision making from a single throw of the dice without considering alternative information.

Ideally, the use of assessment results should be only one phase of career exploration. Individual characteristics measured by tests and inventories should be only one facet considered in the career decision-making process. Assessment results should be combined with background information for making career decisions over the life span. Counselors and clients can then periodically verify or reevaluate assessment results along with other material and experiences in the continuous process of career development. In the next chapter, we'll explore models other than one-shot counseling for using assessment results in career counseling.

Preview of this Book

A model for using assessment results described in Chapter 2 is illustrated by a contrived counseling case found on pages 16-20. Other case studies in Chapters 3 through 14 are excerpts of the model and are used primarily to illustrate the use of a variety of assessment instruments.

Chapters 4 through 12 review a variety of tests and inventories selected because they are widely used or provide innovative methods of presenting score results or both. They are representative of the tests and inventories available. For a general evaluation of tests, consult the following references: A Counselor's Guide to Career Assessment Instruments, 4th ed. (Kapes & Whitfield, 2002) and The Mental Measurements Yearbook.

Each review in this book follows approximately the same format and provides the following information: purpose of the instrument, description of subtests, description of reliability and validity studies when appropriate, description of profile and score results, and method for interpreting the results. Case studies illustrate how the instruments may be used for career development. The cases demonstrate the use of assessment in career counseling with clients ranging in age from high school youths to middle-aged adults.

Finally, Chapters 4 through 8 provide suggestions for the developmental use of assessment results that are based on the National Career Development Guidelines.

Summary

Computerized narrative reports, the refinement and revitalization of tests and inventories, societal changes, and new technology have caused counselors to reevaluate the use of assessment results in career counseling. As a diagnostic tool, assessment results identify individual strengths and weaknesses. As a predictive tool, assessment results forecast the probability of performing well on a job or in a training/educational program. By comparing an individual to criterion groups, assessment results are used to stimulate career exploration. Throughout this book, we emphasize using assessment results to build competencies for career development.

Norms should be carefully evaluated to determine whether the population sample resembles the client in background and individual characteristics. Whenever possible, local norms should be developed. More weight can be given to norms that are established on the basis of successful performance in a particular educational/training program or an occupation than to general norms.

The score profile is the primary tool used to interpret assessment results. When using the score profile, the counselor must be cautious in interpreting differences between scores, must carefully evaluate the norms used, and must consider scores as ranges rather than as points on a scale.

Expectations of career counseling differ. Some clients expect a one-shot counseling encounter to answer the questions of career choice. One-shot counseling provides little opportunity for developing methods of decision making.

Questions and Exercises

1. What kind of norms should be used to predict an individual's chances of getting a C grade or better at a certain community college? Explain your answer.

2. How can national norms be most effectively used in career counseling? What are the limitations?

3. What kinds of tests are most often used for diagnostic purposes? Explain.

4. Describe one circumstance where assessment may be used as (a) a diagnostic tool, (b) a predictive tool, and (c) a means of comparing an individual with a criterion group.

5. How would you answer the request of Ying, the high school senior used as an example of one-shot counseling?

6. What type of activities might you have students and adults engage in to assess and develop their level of career competency?

2 A Conceptual Model for Using Assessment Results

Career counseling is both an art and a science. Deciding if, when and how to incorporate career testing into the process can be complicated, involving factors such as the client's needs and the reason/desired outcomes for testing. A counselor might choose to have a client complete an inventory as part of their session, or as an activity for the client to complete outside of the session and to bring for discussion at the next meeting. With many inventories being online, it is plausible that clients might come to their first session with results in hand from a reliable, or in some cases, a questionable virtual inventory.

A recent (2005) online search in the Mental Measurements Yearbook yielded over 400 test results for the word "interests" alone. If you did a search on abilities, skills, values, or decision, you'd add substantially to that list. The ever-increasing number of sophisticated assessment instruments requires that career counselors continually upgrade their skills in using assessment results to meet the demands of a wide range of individuals. With the multitude of available inventories on the market, career counselors are challenged to understand and apply the statistics associated with test data into meaningful information.

As an integral component of the career counseling process, assessment is also changing and growing in complexity. For instance, computer-assisted career guidance programs and online testing have grown in popularity. Career service providers must be aware of potential errors and misleading results or inappropriate interpretations of computer-generated statements or results from a questionable inventory or career quiz that was taken virtually. In the next section of this chapter, the counselor's responsibilities associated with using standardized assessment instruments will be emphasized, along with suggestions for improving the general use of assessment instruments.

We recognize from our current perspective that the use of assessment results for career counseling have gone through significant changes that are thoroughly discussed in a number of textbooks, including Zunker (2005). No doubt the use of assessment for career counseling will make further changes in the 21st century, along with advances in technology and refinement of career counseling models. In the next paragraphs, we offer a brief summary of a conceptual perspective of promoting career development through assessment.

In early counseling approaches, assessment results were used primarily as analytical and diagnostic instruments (Prediger, 1995). A general transition from trait-and-factor approaches in career counseling practices to an emphasis on life stages and developmental tasks has created a different perspective for counselors using assessment results. For instance, in career decision-making approaches, assessment results are considered as only one facet of information the counselor uses with other sources of information about a client; more importantly, the client becomes an active participant in the career search. Other factors to consider, based on career theory, have included self-esteem, the impact of negative thinking on career decision-making, and values, among others. Thus, assessment results are used to stimulate dialogue about important issues involved in finding an occupational fit, and they are used to encourage individuals to evaluate themselves, including their self-concepts and their self-efficacy development. In essence, assessment results are used as a tool to promote career exploration, identify barriers to decision making, and enhance discussion, rather than serving as the primary or sole basis for decisions.

The increasing complexity and diversity of assessment results suggest the need for a systematic model that will permit counselors to make an effective analysis of the assessment procedures and results appropriate for specific counseling needs. This chapter discusses a conceptual model for using assessment results in career counseling, followed by suggestions for how counselors can improve and sharpen their skills when using standardized assessment measures. In addition, we present a rationale for using assessment results before discussing the use of a model in individual counseling. Finally, we illustrate how the model can be used to stimulate career exploration among groups.

Rationale

In this model, the use of assessment results is conceptualized as a learning process emphasizing the development of self-knowledge. Identification and verification of individual characteristics are the main information provided by assessment results. This information is used with other information in career decision making. Although assessment results are used in a variety of ways (as discussed in Chapter 1), career counselors are encouraged to look beyond the score report to facilitate meaningful learning experiences that will enhance self-awareness and lead to effective career exploration and ultimately, successful career decision making.

Thus, assessment results should be only one kind of information used in career counseling. Testing and interpreting score reports should not dominate the counseling process. Other factors, such as work experiences, grades, leisure activities, skills, and attitudes toward work, should receive equal attention. Assessment results are best used when they can contribute information that is relevant within this overall context.

The process is complex in that individuals must consider their own values, interests, aptitudes, and other unique qualities in making decisions. Although the method of career decision making is a relatively easily learned skill, one's application of the scheme involves considering one's complex and unique characteristics. The process usually begins when an individual recognizes a need to make a decision and subsequently establishes an objective or purpose. Then the individual collects data and surveys possible courses of action. Next the individual uses the data in determining possible courses of action and the probability of certain outcomes. Estimating the desirability of outcomes centers attention on the individual's value system. The final step involves individual decisions that require specific courses of action. Possible outcomes should be specified and evaluated for optimal fit with an individual's personal characteristics. Individuals with the same objectives will undoubtedly reach decisions by different paths based primarily on personal values and self-knowledge.

Brown (2002) reviewed other examples of decision models. Some models specifically use assessment results to identify and clarify individual characteristics in order to enhance the decision process. For example, Sari, a high school senior, is attempting to decide which college to attend. She collects information concerning entry requirements, costs, faculty/student ratios, academic programs, and other data from five colleges. Using assessments of her skills and abilities, she weighs her chances of being accepted by the colleges under consideration and the probability that she will be able to meet academic requirements at those institutions.

In determining a major at the college chosen, Sari considers results of value inventories. These are among the questions she asks herself: "How much do I value a high salary? And if I do value a high salary, which college major would most likely lead to a high-paying job?" Value assessment is essential for making satisfactory decisions here. After Sari selects an institution and major, she once again evaluates the possible outcomes of the decision. In sum, decision making requires the client's self-knowledge of abilities, interests, values, relevant past experiences, and the application of this knowledge to the consideration of alternatives.

Information is a key variable in making an effective career decision (Peterson, Sampson, Reardon, & Lenz, 2002). For Sari, tests that measure scholastic aptitude and achievement were used with other data such as earned grades to make adequate predictions. These assessment results provided support information that is not easily attained by other means, such as through interviews or from biographical data. Assessment data have the distinct advantage of stimulating discussion of specific individual characteristics that can be linked to educational and occupational requirements.

Preparing the Counselor for Using Assessment Results

Throughout this book, we urge the counselor to inform each client about the purpose of testing and how the results match the goals set out by the counselor and the client. Thus, the counselor must be well informed about each measurement instrument used in career development counseling. Appendix B contains "The Code of Fair Testing Practices in Education" that each counselor should carefully review and follow for test selection. In addition, the following are some more strategies for learning about measurement instruments:

1. Take the instrument yourself.

2. Administer the instrument to a friend or colleague. Practice explaining the purpose of the instrument.

3. Look for any flaws in how the instrument is administered.

4. Learn to interpret the instrument by going over the results with a friend or colleague. Practice going over the interpretive report and seek additional information to make scores more meaningful.

5 Thoroughly read the professional manual.

A Model for Individual Counseling

The effective selection and implementation of assessment devices in career counseling can best be attained by using a conceptual model. Such a model provides a systematic method for establishing the purpose of testing and the subsequent use of assessment results. To be operationally effective, a model must be flexible enough to meet the needs of a wide variety of individuals in different stages of their lives. In essence, a model should provide guidelines that are applicable to individuals at all educational levels, in all population groups, of both sexes, and of all ages.

Drawing from the works of Cronbach (1984), Anastasi (1988), and Super, Osborne, Walsh, Brown, and Niles (1992), Zunker has conceptualized a model for using assessment results in developmental career counseling as having four major steps. As shown in Figure 2-1, these steps are analyzing needs, establishing the purpose of testing, determining the instruments, and utilizing the results. The process is cyclical and continuous. One may return to the first step during career exploration, after a period of being employed, or after completing an educational/training program. For example, an individual who is exploring careers has discussed general interests with a counselor and, after reviewing occupational requirements, has identified a need for an assessment of abilities.

An individual who is dissatisfied with her current career wishes to begin the process anew and to select a different career based on her increased understanding of needs that are not being met. After completing a training program for licensed vocational nurses, another individual has decided that this occupation is not what he wants; he wishes to meet with a counselor to analyze why he is dissatisfied and to reassess his career decision. Because career development is a continuous process, assessment may prove to be useful at any point in the life span. See Zunker (2005) for more information on the use of assessment results with career counseling models. Super and colleagues (1992) consider career maturity to be an important index to an individual's readiness for making career decisions. In an assessment model labeled the Career-Development Assessment and Counseling model (C-DAC), Super and colleagues suggest that expressed preferences, such as interest inventory results, should be viewed as basic status data or level of career maturity.

Other measures, such as value inventories and life role importance questionnaires, should be used as moderator variables in the career counseling process. The basic logic underlying this approach is to measure developmental stages according to Super's (1990) scheme and the individual's tasks or concerns to determine the client's needs plus his or her readiness to make career commitments. With this information and additional data gathered through interview and self-reports, counselors can determine developmental counseling intervention strategies for each client. Developmental strategies are thus suggested throughout this text.

Analyzing Needs

To ensure that a counselor is on an effective course for meeting individual needs, a needs analysis may be accomplished by using interviews, a biographical data form, education and work records, or a combination of these methods. The underlying goal is to encourage client participation. Clients who recognize their needs are likely to participate actively and enthusiastically in all phases of preparing for and using assessment results. For example, when Beth recognizes that she needs a structured approach for career exploration, she can be shown how assessment results can assist her.

Likewise, when Raj recognizes the need for help in predicting his chances of success in an educational program, he should be motivated to do his best. Thus, the first key to effective use of assessment results is the counselor's skill in aiding the client in identifying needs and in relating needs to the purpose of testing.

The following four objectives are designed to assist the counselor in identifying needs: establish the counseling relationship, accept and adopt the client's views, establish lifestyle dimensions, and specify the needs. Accomplishing these objectives may take more time than the initial interview.

To establish a counseling relationship is to foster a sense of trust and mutual respect. To accomplish this goal, the counselor communicates a sincere desire to help the client, provides hospitality by being

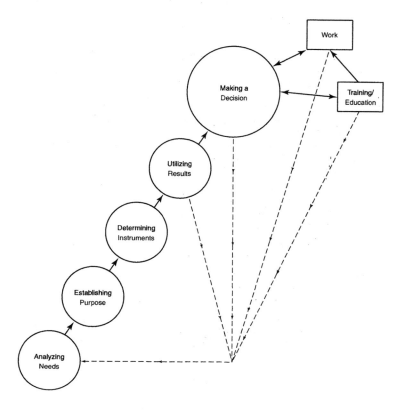

Figure 2-1

friendly, arranges for personal introductions of staff members, and is on time for the appointment. A warm, friendly atmosphere is particularly essential during the initial interview. Every attempt should be made to communicate to the client that he or she has the counselor's undivided attention.

To launch the initial counseling session, the counselor may start with a simple question: "What brings you by today?" The counselor listens for clues to continue the session. Although individual needs vary, the counselor should attempt to answer some of the following questions: What are the client's expectations of career counseling? Where is the client in the career decision-making process? Are tests indicated or contraindicated? Will the client be willing to invest the time necessary for career counseling? Does the client understand the counselor's role and his or her own role as a client? What is the client hoping to achieve by the end of this meeting? Are these goals realistic, and do they match with the services provided by the counselor's setting?

Establishing the relationship also means acknowledging the diversity of both the counselor and the client. This may include racial, ethnic or cultural differences, but may also include religious viewpoints, geographic differences, sexual orientation or disability. Counselors should acknowledge and incorporate the individual attributes of each client throughout all the stages of counseling, including establishing a relationship, understanding core issues and the client's world views, choosing inventories and interventions, and in closure. Appropriate self-disclosure can be a way to begin this conversation.

COUNSELOR: Kenya, maybe as a way to get started, it might help if we learn a little bit more about each other's backgrounds and what's important to us. What do you think?

KENYA: Yes, I'd like that.

COUNSELOR: Well, I grew up in Daytona Beach. I have a younger brother and sister. My parents are older, and live about 5 hours away. Most of my family is from the south, and has a strong value for family. I'm married and have two young girls, ages three and five. I guess what's really most important to me right now is spending time with my family – and having work that allows me to do that. I'm finding now that my parents are aging, that I miss them more, and wish that I had more time to spend with them. I think a lot about how we might arrange things so we can be closer. I've got advanced degrees in career counseling, and have been doing that for about 10 years. How about you?

KENYA: As you were talking, I saw some things that are similar in our stories. My family is most important to me. I know that I can choose any career that I want, but really, I don't want a career that is going to take me far away from my parents and my sisters and aunts. I would feel lost without them. I see them everyday, and we get together on weekends. I really listen to them when they give me advice – especially advice from my grandmother. She's almost always right, and is very wise. Everyone says I should get out on my own, and make my decisions, but that doesn't sound all that exciting to me. I like my life now. I just want to figure out what I can do as a career that will help me provide for my family.

Through this opening discussion and self-disclosure, the counselor made it safe for Kenya to share some of her values of inter-dependent decision making. This leads into the second step, accepting and adopting the client's views.

To accept and adopt the client's views requires that the counselor recognize that individuals are unique and have the right to their own commitments, self-awareness, and priorities. The counselor's role here is to assist clients in becoming aware of their viewpoints and in recognizing how their viewpoints can affect their career decision making. Paying attention and exploring the role of culture in the client's worldviews are also a vital part of this process. The following questions may be used to structure this part of the counseling session:

- Does the client have realistic expectations about the world of work?
- Has the client experienced discrimination? What impact do those experiences have on his/her current perspective about career choice?
- What is the client's level of sophistication in regard to career considerations?
- Has the client established short-term and long-term goals?
- How committed is the client to his or her viewpoints?
- Would value clarification be helpful?
- What stereotypes and biases does the counselor have that may impact his or her counseling approach?

Because career decisions can greatly influence an individual's style of life, the counselor should attempt *to establish the dimensions of lifestyle* when identifying needs. Place of residence, work climate, family responsibilities, use of leisure time, leadership opportunities, financial needs, mobility, and the desire to contribute to society are dimensions of lifestyle that warrant considerations in career decision making.

For example, consider an individual who expresses a strong orientation toward achieving financial independence and yet is exploring careers that may not be suitable for meeting this objective. The counselor can encourage this individual to clarify priorities for lifestyle, and through this process realistic alternatives and options can be developed. Questions such as these help establish lifestyle dimensions:

- Does the client recognize how career choice will affect lifestyle?
- Has the client set lifestyle priorities?
- Would an interest, value, or personality inventory help this individual clarify needs?
- Would it help to bring in family members or spouses/partners in this discussion?
- Are there significant discrepancies between lifestyle dimensions and the needs most likely to be met by the careers under consideration?

Finally, *to specify needs*, the counselor can maximize the client's participation by using statements and questions such as these:

- "Tell me more about your desire to explore interests."
- "You mentioned earlier that you are interested in knowing more about your aptitudes."
- "Can you explain how you could meet your personal goals by selecting this career?"
- "What is it about this kind of job that makes it interesting?"
- "How would you describe an individual who chooses jobs that help others?"
- "Would you like to know more about your interests?"
- "How do the needs of your family play a part in this career decision?"
- "Would you like to bring in a family member or others as we talk about your needs, your family's needs, and the community's needs?"

As the client states needs, the counselor summarizes and records the statements for later use in reinforcing the purpose of testing. After doing a needs analysis, counselor and client may decide that assessment is not needed. Individuals seek career counseling for a variety of reasons. For example, an individual who has decided on a job may come to a career counselor for educational/training information, rather than for testing. Individuals who have given considerable thought to selecting a career and have narrowed their choices to a particular field are probably best served by providing them with both an opportunity to discuss that field and sources of information about it.

Establishing the Purpose

Following the needs analysis, the counselor and client decide on the purpose of testing. Both should recognize that testing cannot be expected to meet all identified needs. As stated in Chapter 1; testing can be used for diagnosis, prediction, and comparing individuals with criterion groups. The results can be used to stimulate further study of individual characteristics relative to potential career choices. In some instances, the purpose of testing is to answer a specific question, as in predicting chances of success in a training program or an occupation. In other instances, the purpose of testing may be less specific, as in establishing a direction for career exploration for an individual who is floundering. In cases such as this, where the purpose of testing is less tangible, the counselor may be tempted to prescribe a battery of tests without obtaining the client's agreement on the purpose of the tests. To avoid this pitfall, the counselor should establish the policy of explaining the purpose of each measuring instrument selected and making sure that the results of the testing relates to either the overall or specific goal(s).

The purpose of each test and inventory should be explained in terms that the client can comprehend. For example, the purpose of an interest inventory may be explained to a high school student as follows: "This inventory will help us identify your interests. We can then compare your interests to the interests of groups of individuals in certain jobs." A high school student who is in the process of determining which college to apply to and who has inquired about an aptitude test will find the following explanation appropriate: "These test scores will give us some idea of your chances of making a C or better at the college you are considering." The purpose of a test may have to be explained in simple terms to an individual who has a limited educational background: "This achievement test will show us how well you can read, spell, and do arithmetic problems. We can use the scores to help us choose a job or a training program for you." In all instances, to make assessment results meaningful, we should attempt to relate the purpose of testing to the needs the client has identified (Cronbach, 1984). The client should also be made aware of how assessment results are used with other data in the career decision-making process. The following dialogue illustrates how a counselor can accomplish these objectives.

COUNSELOR: As you will recall, we agreed to record your needs for information, materials, programs, and tests. Let's review our comments on testing possibilities. Do you remember any of the testing needs agreed on?

CLIENT: Yes, I want to take an interest inventory.

COUNSELOR: Do you remember why?

CLIENT: I am not sure about what I want to do. I believe knowing more about my interests would help in choosing a career.

COUNSELOR: Do you recall specifically how the results of an interest inventory would help the career decision-making process?

CLIENT: Yes, I believe that I will be able to compare the interests of people in different occupations with my own interests.

COUNSELOR: Go on.

CLIENT: This will give me information about personal traits that I can use with other things I've learned about myself.

Determining the Instruments

A considerable amount of literature has accumulated concerning the selection of measuring instruments. The central consideration is meeting the standards for educational and psychological tests established by professional organizations such as the American Counseling Association (1995) and the American Psychological Association (2002). As you will recall, this book is to be used following or in conjunction with courses on tests and measurements. Therefore, technical methods of evaluating measuring instruments for selection will not be covered. However, readers are referred to Chapter 15 and Appendix

C for ethical issues and standards for testing. Of particular concern is choosing tests that are free from bias and are culturally fair.

Practitioners must be thoroughly familiar with the basic standards of test reliability and test validity before an effective evaluation of tests can be made. The types of reliability and validity that should be established for a test are determined by the purpose and use of the test. A review of the procedures for determining and comparing different types of reliability and validity may be found in several texts, including Anastasi (1988), Cronbach (1984), Drummond (2004), Kaplan and Saccuzzo (1993), Zunker (2005), and Whiston (2000).

In this book, we concentrate on tests of ability and achievement and on inventories that measure career development, interests, personality, and values. Ability tests can also be used to determine assignment to appropriate remediation levels. Achievement tests aid the counselor in evaluating educational strengths and weaknesses.   More specifically, these tests can be used to select appropriate remedial educational programs and other educational intervention strategies such as skills training. Career maturity inventories are used to assess vocational development in self-awareness, planning skills, decision-making skills, and other equally important variables. Interest measures, long associated with career counseling, provide a means of comparing an individual's interest patterns with those of reference groups. Personality inventories provide clues to individual traits that influence behavior. Value inventories also reflect individual traits; these tests identify value constructs that influence behavior. Results from interest, personality, and value inventories promote discussion of the client's relationship to the working world and the satisfaction the client may derive from a career.

In the chapters that follow, each of the test categories mentioned here is discussed in detail.

Using the Results

Because individual choice patterns are unique and can be influenced by economic conditions and experiences over the life span, assessment use varies greatly. More than likely, individuals will find that assessment results can assist them at various stages of their lives, particularly in clarifying needs and in developing self-awareness. Contemporary thought places considerable importance on the individual's responsibility for finding satisfaction in the ever-changing world of work. This concept was succinctly stated by Shakespeare in *Julius Caesar*: "The fault, dear Brutus, is not in our stars, but in ourselves, that we are underlings."

The use of assessment results in career counseling should be carefully calculated and systematically accomplished through established operational procedures. In general, assessment results identify individual characteristics and traits, which in turn point to possible avenues for career exploration. The counselor and the client discuss potential career fields using assessment results to facilitate the dialogue.

Beyond this pragmatic and operational procedure for using assessment results are considerations that place testing and the use of test results in perspective—that help clients use test results to view themselves as total persons. So far, we have dealt with some specific uses of assessment, and in the chapters that follow we illustrate these uses in detail. In all this reporting and confirming of assessment data, counselors are in effect helping clients build and generate a broad concept of themselves as total persons. Counselors segregate and clarify individual differences to help them formulate plans for the present and lay the foundations for planning in the future. Clients integrate their individual traits and characteristics to stabilize their sense of direction in an ever-changing society.

The concept of career development as being continuous over the life span suggests that individuals change. There is, therefore, a tentativeness to many career decisions. One consistency in career decision making is a conceptual framework that provides for in-depth and effective use of assessment results because classifying an individual's traits will always involve, at least to some extent, the measuring instruments available at the time.

Hopefully, counselors have been cautious and thorough in their review of the appropriateness of a specific test for a given client – especially clients from culturally diverse backgrounds, or any client who does not fit the normative sample for a given test. If the test is appropriate, then the counselor can have some degree of certainty that the results are valid. Culturally competent counselors should interpret test results in light of the client's cultural background.

Using the Model for Individual Counseling: A Case Example

The following counseling case illustrates the use of a conceptual model using assessment results in a senior high school counseling center. Each step in the model is illustrated by dialogue between counselor and client and by occasional notations made by the counselor. Standardized assessment instruments used in this case were not identified. In later chapters, other counseling cases describing the use of models employing assessment results are described, citing specific standardized assessment instruments.

In the following illustration of the conceptual model, both major and minor components of the model are identified to demonstrate a sequential order of events. Notations and dialogue between counselor and client were created for the purpose of illustration.

Amy, a self-referred 17-year-old Hispanic female high school senior, reported to the counseling center that she was undecided about plans after graduation. She filled out a questionnaire and was introduced to Gretchen, her counselor.

Step 1. Analyzing Needs

A. Establish the counseling relationship

COUNSELOR: Amy, I'm Gretchen, welcome to the Counseling Center. I believe you have met Carla, our secretary, who will help us with appointments and records. Please call either one of us if you need any information as we go along. My office is the first door to the left, here. Please come in and have a seat.

After a brief discussion of current events, the counselor explained the order of procedures and assured Amy of client confidentiality. The counselor shared some of her personal background and invited Amy to do the same. Amy shared that she was a first generation American, and that at times, she felt somewhat torn between "the old ways" and the "new way." Her parents had always stressed the importance of a good education, and not taking for granted the opportunities before her. While they were generally supportive of any career path she might choose, there was an unspoken emphasis on being "successful". The conversation shifted easily to Amy's indecision concerning her plans after high school.

AMY: I'm not even sure I'm ready to go to college. I don't know what I want to be and I can't decide about a major. All my friends have this settled, but not me. I don't want to disappoint my family. They have been saving for my college since I was born. I don't want to waste my time or their money by making a bad choice.

The counselor assured Amy that the counseling center could help her make these decisions. The counselor continued to build the relationship by not immediately challenging the family values, but by saying, "You're right. This is an important decision, and you want to make the best choice that you can." Gretchen also informed Amy of their career counseling time commitment of five to six counseling sessions with some additional time for testing, if appropriate. The counselor also established a counseling goal by asking Amy if she could make a table that compared her ideas about possible majors/careers with those of her parents and family.

B. Accept and adopt the client's views

The counselor encouraged Amy to discuss her academic background, general interests, leisure and work experiences, and values. Amy informed the counselor of her previous work experience, which consisted of two months as a swimming instructor and four months as an assistant program director in a home for the elderly. Amy indicated that she liked both jobs.

COUNSELOR: Could you explain how the experiences of these two jobs might influence your future choice of a career?

AMY: Well, I never thought about it, but I do enjoy working with people. I like to teach, also, but I don't believe I would like to be a school teacher.

COUNSELOR: I would be interested in knowing how you've come to those conclusions.

AMY: I'm not sure I could handle all the discipline problems that teachers have to deal with. Besides, I want to do other things helping people. I really enjoyed the work I did with the elderly.

Amy continued to express interests and aspirations while the counselor made the following notations:

- Good rapport has been established
- Amy feels free to express herself
- Likes working with people
- Has some limited exposure to careers
- Has developed tentative expectations of the future, but needs help in clarifying interests
- Some pressures to make a "wise" choice, and not disappoint others
- Family influence and input highly valued

C. Establish the dimensions of lifestyle

COUNSELOR: Now, let's take a look at the future. In fact, I would like you to project yourself into the future. For example, think about where you would like to live five or ten years from now and what kind of leisure activities such as travel you would like.

AMY: Okay, let me see (pause) . . . Hmm, someday I would like to be living in an apartment on my own, of course, with my own car right here in the city, I think. I would like to have a nice place, but I really don't want a fancy car, just a fairly new one. I guess one of the most important things to me is having good clothes and being able to eat out in nice restaurants. I also like to travel. I've been overseas on vacation with my parents, and I would like to go back some day. About money . . . I want enough to be able to do these things.

COUNSELOR: That's a good start, Amy. We will be discussing lifestyle preferences again. I think we can sort out more specific aspects of your lifestyle choices and how they may influence career decisions in one of our future sessions.

During the course of the counseling session, the counselor thought that the following assessments might be helpful:

1. Measure of college aptitude — Information for predicting success in selected colleges.

2. Measure of interests — General interest patterns are needed to stimulate dialogue about future goals. Specific interests will be used to link college majors with potential careers.

3. Measure of lifestyle preferences — Lifestyle measures will introduce another dimension for consideration in the decision-making process.

4. Invite Amy's parents in for discussion of their vision for their daughter's career path.

The counselor's overall goal was to provide Amy with relevant information that could be used in the decision-making process.

Step 2. Establish the Purpose

COUNSELOR: Our discussion has been very productive and, before you leave today, let's summarize some of the needs you have expressed. One of the first topics we discussed was your indecision about college. Remember you questioned whether you should attend or not.

AMY: Yes, that's right. Maybe I was just blowing off steam; I know I should probably go to college. Really, it's not an option. I will be going – I just want to know why I'm going.

COUNSELOR: Would you like to take an aptitude test to see how prepared you are for college?

AMY: Yes . . . okay . . . (pause) . . . I did take one of the required exams for college a few months ago.

COUNSELOR: Good, we probably have the results in our files and we can use these to help us with our decision. I'll check the files and if we need another test, I'll let you know at our next appointment.

(Amy nodded approval.)

COUNSELOR: Another need you mentioned is choosing a college major.

AMY: Yes, I don't really know what I want to do. I've had subjects I like, but nothing grabs me.

COUNSELOR: One of the things we discussed was comparing the options you're considering with options your parents see for you. You can extend that to family members as well. After all, they've seen you develop through the years and have a much more thorough view than I do or any inventory. That being said, we do have several interest inventories that might confirm some of your choices and suggest new ones. Would you like to take one?

When Amy agreed to complete the table, and also that an interest inventory would be fine with her, the counselor turned her attention to the last of the list of indicated needs—lifestyle preferences.

COUNSELOR: Today I also asked you to project yourself into the future and you were able to express some of your goals. Do you think it would be helpful to further clarify your lifestyle preferences?

AMY: That's something I really haven't thought about very much. I think it might help, but I'm not sure just how.

COUNSELOR: Okay, that's a good question. Let me briefly explain that career and lifestyle are closely related. For example, your career choice will determine to some extent the kind of lifestyle you will have in the future.

One illustration involves the financial returns you get from a job. Remember, you said you wanted a new car, to have the opportunity to travel to Europe, and to have a nice apartment. In order to be able to have and do these things, you will need a job that provides the necessary resources.

AMY: I see. Well, yes, I probably should talk more about my future.

After the counselor was certain that Amy understood the purpose of each assessment instrument, an appointment for the next counseling session was set.

Step 3. Determine the Instrument

The counselor discovered that Amy had taken a nationally administered college aptitude test and the results were on file in the counseling center. Composite scores indicated that Amy was well above the national norm for college-bound students. These test scores were current and could be used to predict chances of making a C or better at several colleges, so the counselor decided that another aptitude test was unnecessary.

The counselor chose an interest inventory providing measures of general and specific occupational interests. The goal was to stimulate discussion of general interests and to verify preferences Amy had previously expressed. Moreover, the counselor's primary objective was to stimulate dialogue that could help Amy clarify her interests. Finally, the counselor chose a lifestyle measure that would assess Amy's preferences for a variety of lifestyle factors. The counselor was particularly interested in assessing Amy's preferences for work achievement and leadership, work environment, and leisure orientation. As with the interest inventory, the counselor's objective was to stimulate discussion to help Amy clarify values and lifestyle preferences.

Step 4. Use the Results

During Amy's next appointment, the interest inventory and lifestyle preference surveys were administered. After they were scored, the results of these inventories and aptitude tests were carefully reviewed by the counselor during pre-interpretation preparation. The counselor made notes on several items she felt would stimulate discussion. For example, on the interest inventory, she made a notation that Amy had a very high score on the general occupational theme—social—and on such specific occupations as social worker and guidance counselor.

Highest scores on the lifestyle preference survey were educational achievement, work achievement, and structured work environment. The counselor was particularly interested in having Amy link lifestyle preferences to high-interest occupations and general occupational themes. Priorities for lifestyle preferences would be used to introduce another dimension of Amy's values in the decision-making process.

Finally, the counselor obtained studies of students' expectancies of making a C or better at several community colleges and universities. This information would provide an index to predict Amy's chances of matriculating at several two- and four-year institutions of higher learning.

The counselor began the utilization-of-results session by explaining the purpose of the college aptitude test Amy had taken. The scores were explained as follows.

COUNSELOR: Since you have said you want to go to college, we will interpret your scores by using National College Bound Norms. These norms are derived for students who have indicated that they intend to enroll in a college or a university. Your total score places you in the 86th percentile among college-bound students. This means that 86 out of 100 college-bound students who took the test scored lower than you did and 14 out of 100 scored higher than you did.

AMY: Wow! That's better than I thought I would do on that test. Does this mean that I could do okay at City College?

The counselor was able to answer Amy's question by referring to an expectancy table that had been provided by City College. On the basis of Amy's total test score, the counselor was able to inform Amy that her chances of making an overall C average during her freshman year at City College were very good. The counselor was also able to point out the chances of making a C or better in specific courses offered to freshmen at City College. These data not only provided an index for predicting Amy's chances of matriculating in City College, but also could be used for suggesting an academic major.

The counselor's next step in using assessment results was to outline the organization of scores on the interest profile. She explained the various scales on the test, including general occupational interest scores and scores on specific occupations. The scores were interpreted as follows.

COUNSELOR: Amy, you scored in the high category on the general occupational theme—social. People who score high on this theme like to work with people, share responsibilities, and enjoy working in groups. Do you feel that this is an accurate representation of your interests?

Using this procedure, the counselor encouraged Amy to discuss other scores on the general occupational theme part of the profile. Likewise, this procedure was used to enhance the discussion of scores measuring specific occupations. Then the counselor asked Amy to share the table she had completed. Amy shared that there was a lot of agreement with her own ideas as well as that with her family, and even some friends, about what career options might be best for her. Some of the options included teaching, counseling, nursing, human resource development and hospitality. Amy was encouraged to jot down occupations of interest for further exploration in the career library and on the computerized career information system. A discussion of lifestyle orientation related to interests helped Amy crystallize her projections of future needs and desires.

Step 5. Make a Decision

Amy decided that she should pursue a college education. She decided to attend City College and tentatively major in human resource development, an area that met her interests and values, and also was within the prestige and "success" level expected by her family.

Stimulating Career Exploration in Groups

In the early 1970s, a new concept of education emerged that emphasized career development, attitudes, and values as well as traditional outcomes of career choices (Hoyt, 1972). The career education concept is a comprehensive one that focuses on relationships between traditional education programs and the world of work. The major objective of career education is to prepare individuals for living and working in our society (Zunker, 2005). The impact of career education programs on career counseling has not been fully determined, although a meta-analytic study of 50 articles demonstrated that structured career counseling groups and career workshops are effective as interventions (Whiston, Brecheisen, & Stephens, 2003). But there is little doubt that career education programs will increase the need for counselors to turn to group procedures when using assessment results to stimulate career exploration because of demands on their time and the ratio of students to counselors.

The model for using assessment results proposed in the previous section can easily be adapted to groups. The same steps apply. However, methods used in applying the model may have to be altered. For example, a needs analysis can be accomplished through group discussion or as part of a screening inventory, with each individual noting his or her own needs. Some will find that testing is not necessary at this point in their career development. Those who decide that testing is appropriate will move to the next step of establishing the purposes of testing. After purposes are identified, different types of tests and inventories can be selected. Small groups may be formed for administering the tests and sharing results. Individuals or entire groups may then go back to the first step, to reestablish needs, at any time in career exploration.

A modification of the model for groups could include the following procedures: introduce the concepts of career development; explain the use of assessment; introduce the types of measuring instruments; interpret the results; and introduce support material. Interest inventories are especially effective in promoting group discussions and are usually less threatening than aptitude or achievement tests seem. However, other types of measuring instruments can also be used effectively to generate activities for groups. The following example illustrates the use of an interest inventory in a classroom setting.

Ms. Alvarez, a high school counselor, was invited to a high school class that was working through a career education program. She was asked to present the types of measuring instruments available and to explain how the students could use the career resource center. Before the presentation, Ms. Alvarez asked the teacher's permission to introduce the steps in career decision making and to make some comments on the basic elements of career development. As she presented this material, she emphasized the purpose and use of assessment results.

The students requested that an interest inventory be administered. Afterward, the counselor explained how to interpret the score profiles. Ms. Alvarez spent considerable time answering individual questions concerning the results. The counselor emphasized that interests are one of the important considerations in career decision making.

Following the interpretation of results, the counselor introduced the next step in the career decision-making process. Some of the students decided to take additional tests and inventories. Others took different courses of action. Several decided to collect information about selected careers in the career resource center, and some members of the group chose to visit work sites.

In this case, interest inventory results stimulated students to generate further activities within the framework of a decision-making model. This example illustrates the importance of clarifying the role of assessment within a career decision-making model. The counselor emphasized that career decision making involves a sequence of steps and support materials. By placing assessment in proper perspective, the counselor was able to enhance the group's usage of assessment results.

Summary

Assessment results can be effectively used to enhance the development of self-knowledge. Within a career decision-making model, assessment results are used to clarify individual characteristics and to generate further activities. The decision to include an assessment should be a mutually agreed-upon choice that ties into the client's goal(s) for career counseling. A model for using assessment results has the following steps: analyzing needs, establishing the purpose of testing, determining the instruments, and utilizing the results. Clients should be actively involved in all steps of the model, which may be used for individual or group counseling.

Questions and Exercises

What evidence can you give for the rationale that assessment results are used to enhance self-awareness? Using an example, illustrate how the model for using assessment results described in this chapter is cyclical.

1. Why is the model of using assessment results only one part of the career decision-making process?

2. Why might it be necessary to retest an individual after two or three years?

3. How are assessment results used in the total-person approach to career decision making?

4. Describe how and when you would incorporate the assessment model into the career counseling theory you follow and your career counseling approach.

5. How would you address issues of diversity into a model of career assessment and career testing?

6. How do you believe traditional test results might complement information gained from open-ended questioning and active listening (or vice versa)?

3 Some Measurement Concepts

In this chapter, we discuss several measurement concepts and methods of interpreting assessment results to help improve the career counselor's skill in the selecting and using standardized instruments. Later chapters will make numerous references to the material in this chapter in describing specific tests and inventories. Generally, the information found in this chapter is contained in separate chapters in most textbooks. We have combined this information here to provide, first, an overview of the common elements used in assessment interpretation, second, the information necessary for comparing the strengths and weaknesses of currently used methods of score reporting, and third, definitions of measurement concepts for easy referral.

The first section of this chapter emphasizes methods of interpreting assessment results. Specifically, we describe the normal bell-shaped curve and then discuss percentile equivalents, standard scores, grade equivalents, and criterion-referenced measures. The second section discusses important measurement concepts: standard error of measurement, standard error of differences between two subtests, and expectancy tables.

Transformation of Scores

Bell-Shaped Curve

Two of the most prominently used methods of interpreting assessment results are percentile equivalents and standard scores. To obtain an understanding of the relationship between these two reporting procedures, refer to the well-known normal, or bell-shaped, curve in Figure 3-1. M represents the mean, or midpoint (50th percentile), with 4 standard deviations on each side of the mean.

Starting at M, go to the right to +1 standard deviation and note the percentile equivalent of 84 (in rounded numbers). Likewise, go to the left of M to −1 standard deviation and find the percentile equivalent of 16. You will notice that other percentile points can be obtained for each standard deviation. Understanding the relationship of percentile equivalents to standard deviations and their relative positions on the bell-shaped curve helps interpret test scores. For example, a percentile score of 98 is 2 standard deviations from the mean. A score equal to 2 standard deviations below the mean is approximately at the 2nd percentile.

Referring to Figure 3-1, you can see also that a GATB score of 120 is 1 standard deviation above the mean, or at the 84th percentile. An ACT score of 25 is at the same relative position. These two scores are not to be regarded as equal. The standard scores for each test were developed using samples from different populations, and each test may be quite different in content. However, two standard scores can be compared by their relative position under the normal bell-shaped curve. For example, an ACT score of 25 is at the same relative position within its reference group as a GATB of 120.

It's useful at times to compare an individual's score to where the majority of the scores lie. For example, +1 or -1 standard deviation from the mean will capture approximately 68% of the variance. (To obtain the 68%, you add the 13.59% that is contained within -1 standard deviation and the 13.59% that is contained within +1 standard deviation). People whose scores are closest to those of the norm group will score within + or − 1 standard deviation from the mean. As you move out further from the mean, the frequency of people scoring in that range becomes fewer. For example, one of the qualifications of being labeled as gifted is an intelligence quotient of 130 or higher. The mean for most intelligence tests is 100, and the standard deviation is 15. So, to meet that criteria for giftedness, a person would need to score 2 standard deviations above the mean. If you learn that a person's score is 2 or 3 standard deviations above or below the mean, you conceptually know that their score is outside of what the normal scores typically are.

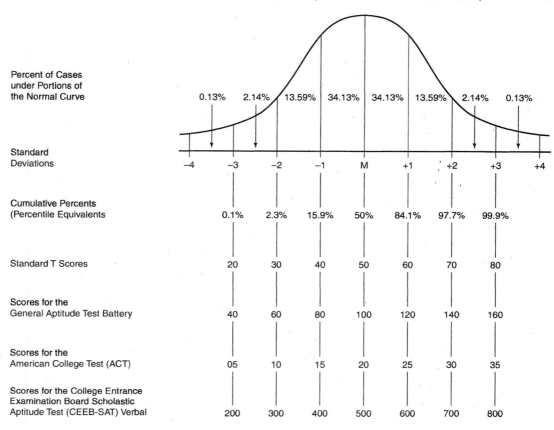

Percent of Cases under Portions of the Normal Curve: 0.13% 2.14% 13.59% 34.13% 34.13% 13.59% 2.14% 0.13%

Standard Deviations: −4 −3 −2 −1 M +1 +2 +3 +4

Cumulative Percents (Percentile Equivalents: 0.1% 2.3% 15.9% 50% 84.1% 97.7% 99.9%

Standard T Scores: 20 30 40 50 60 70 80

Scores for the General Aptitude Test Battery: 40 60 80 100 120 140 160

Scores for the American College Test (ACT): 05 10 15 20 25 30 35

Scores for the College Entrance Examination Board Scholastic Aptitude Test (CEEB-SAT) Verbal: 200 300 400 500 600 700 800

Figure 3-1

This isn't necessarily bad. For example, a person 3 standard deviations above the mean on career decidedness is someone who has a very clear sense of what they want to do. However, someone who is 3 SDs above the mean on dysfunctional thinking has some major internal barriers to making decisions.

Using Figure 3-1 and a GATB score of 63, you can determine the exact percentile equivalent. Here's the process:

1. First, you need to find the 1% increase between 60 and 80. These numbers aren't chosen arbitrarily. 60 lies at -2 standard deviations, and the next GATB number reported is 80, which lies at -1 standard deviation. 63 lies in between those numbers. Three steps are required to find the 1% increase, including:

    a. Find how many numbers lie between the range for the observed score.

    • 80 - 60 = 20

    b. Calculate the difference between the standard deviations around the observed score.

    • 15.9 - 2.3 = 13.6

    c. Divide the SD difference by the number of integers between the range surrounding the observed score to determine the 1% increase.

    • 13.6 / 20 = .68

    d. Multiply the 1% increase to the number that you want to increase the score by. This will give you the percentage increase to add to the lower percentage (in this case, 60).

    • We want to get to 63, and we already know the percentile for 60. We need to move up from 60 to 63, or by 3. So, we multiply .68 by 3.

    • .68 * 3 = 2.04

e.   Determine the percentile equivalent.

- The percentile equivalent for 60 is 2.3.

- To gain the percentile equivalent for 63, you'd add 2.04 to 2.3.

- 2.3 + 2.04 = 4.34

f.   Double-check your answer. We know that a GATB of 65 = 5.7 percentile. If our calculations are correct, when we multiply .68 times five and add that to 2.3 we should get 5.7 (.68*5 = 3.4 + 2.3 = 5.7).

Percentile Equivalents

In Figure 3-2, a typical test profile is constructed to depict percentile equivalents. Note the heavy line representing the midpoint and the thinner lines representing the 25th and 75th percentiles, the average range for this particular achievement test. The difference in scores between the 25th and 75th percentiles is not as great as may appear. Refer to the bell-shaped curve in Figure 3-1 and notice that to move several percentile points within the average band does not take as great a performance as it does to move the same number of percentile points beyond the 75th percentile. Thus, the counselor needs to be cautious when interpreting differences in scores within the average range; the difference in performance within this range may not be as significant as it appears.

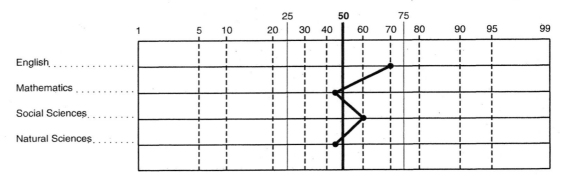

Figure 3-2

Percentile equivalents are direct and relatively easy to understand, which is a primary reason for their popularity. However, it is important to identify the norm reference group from which the percentile equivalents have been derived. Norm-referenced tests can be based on local, state, regional, or national data or on data for selected groups such as all seniors (nationally) who are attending college or all college seniors in the western region of the United States. One of the problems is with the interpretation of percentile equivalents. People tend to interpret a 45% as failing, or a 95% as an "A". We attach labels to these percentile equivalents that aren't always appropriate. Thus, to effectively communicate test results, the norm frame of reference should be established. For example: "From a national sample, 60 out of 100 high school seniors who attended college scored lower than you did, while 40 out of 100 scored higher."

Standard Scores

Normalized standard scores used in tests and inventories are based on standard deviation units in a normal distribution. Figure 3-1 shows the percentage of scores within each standard deviation unit and standard scores used by selected standardized tests. The first, the standard T score, has a range of 20 to 80, extending 3 standard deviations above the mean and 3 standard deviations below the mean. For all practical purposes, the entire range of scores of 99.72% of the cases will fall within +3 and −3 standard deviations. The middle 68% of the scores are within +1 and −1 standard deviations.

Approximately 95% of scores will fall between ±1.96 standard deviation units. A T score of slightly less than 60 is in the top 20% for a given test. Such points of reference make the standard score a valuable tool for interpreting assessment results. For example, a meaningful interpretation can be made of a score that is 1.5 standard deviations from the mean when normalized standard scores and their relationship to standard deviations are understood. Thus, the relative position of the standard score under the normal distribution provides a discernible point of reference for that score's variation from the average.

A frame of reference can easily be established for standardized tests by thinking of their scores in the same way. For example, a GATB score of 120 is 1 standard deviation from the mean, or at the 84th percentile. Likewise, 1 standard deviation below the mean (16th percentile) is equal to a GATB score of 80. The middle 68% of the scores are between the standard scores 80 and 120. A meaningful interpretation can thus be given to any standard score when the mean and standard deviation are known.

A *stanine* is a standard score on a scale with nine approximately equal units. The mean stanine is 5, and the standard deviation is 2. The advantage of the stanine is that scores are presented as a range rather than as points on a scale, as shown in Figure 3-3. In a normal distribution, the lower level, 1, represents the bottom 4% of the cases; stanine 5 represents the middle 20%; and stanine 9, the highest level, represents the top 4%. Thinking of a range rather than a point for score interpretation is more descriptive and deters emphasizing small differences. To be of practical significance, the difference between stanine scores must be 2 or more.

Stanine scores may also be thought of in broader categories, as Figure 3-3 illustrates. For example, stanine scores 1, 2, and 3 are considered below average; stanine scores 4, 5, and 6 are considered average; and stanines 7, 8, and 9 are above average. Cumulative percentile points (Figure 3-3) provide further possibilities for interpreting stanines as lower quarter, middle half, and upper quarter.

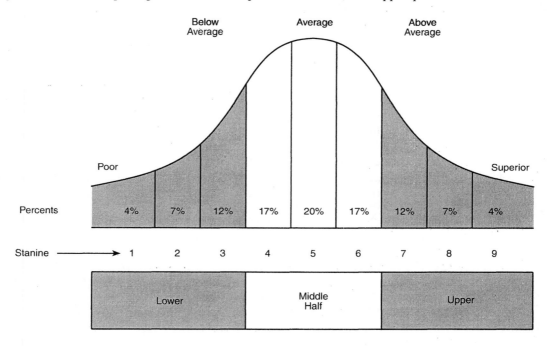

Figure 3-3

Grade Equivalents

Because of the familiarity of grade placement and its frame of reference, grade equivalents are often used to interpret achievement test scores. Norms for grade equivalents are derived from average raw scores of students in each grade level. These equivalents are expressed by a number representing grade level and the ten months of the school year, September through June. For example, 10.0 represents the beginning of the tenth grade in September; 10.5 represents average performance in February of that academic year.

Because of the idea of placement within a grade, misinterpretation of grade equivalents can occur. For example, a score of 8.5 on a science test for a student currently in the sixth grade should not be interpreted to mean the student has mastered the science courses taught in the seventh grade and the first half of the eighth grade and can now be placed in the second half of the eighth-grade science class. No doubt, the student has performed admirably on the science test, but grade equivalent scores are not to be regarded as performance standards. In this example, the student's raw score is close to the median or mean raw score made by students in the middle of the 8th grade. Although the student might have performed very well on the lower primary form of this achievement test, there were no 8th grade level items on the test given to 6th graders (Drummond, 2004). Also, grade equivalents are not to be considered comparable for all scales. For example, in the fifth grade, growth in learning a particular subject such as mathematics will be much greater than it will be in the ninth grade.

Criterion-Referenced Measures

In criterion-referenced measures, an individual's score is interpreted by its relative position within the distribution of scores obtained by the standardization sample or other groups of special interest. In other words, the interpretation of criterion-referenced test scores is based on how well the individual's performance matches a set of standards or external criteria judged by the test user to be suitable for the individual's grade level. The focus is on levels of performance within a limited range of specific skills or content. For example, criterion-referenced scores provide an index of how well an individual has mastered arithmetic computations or certain reading skills. In criterion-referenced tests, specific information is provided as to what the individual is capable of doing: for example, "The subject was able to subtract numbers with decimals" or "The subject used the correct verb form in a sentence." Scales from a criterion-referenced test are used to determine an individual level of performance with reference to a specified content criterion.

Accuracy of Measurement

This section presents several concepts regarding the accuracy of measurements that should also aid the counselor in transforming assessment results into meaningful interpretations. First, to understand the relative position of a score, the counselor must be aware of inherent error, which is specific for particular tests. Second, significant differences that may exist among subtests on any one test greatly affect the interpretation that may be given to the test results as a whole. Finally, inaccuracy in interpreting assessment results for educational and vocational planning can be reduced by constructing locally based expectancy tables. These concepts and their application to test interpretation are discussed and illustrated in the paragraphs that follow.

Standard Error of Measurement (SEM)

A score on a test should not be considered an exact point without any error. It is important to always keep in mind that the score a person obtains on a given inventory on a given day is not likely to be their true score, but that some "inherent error" exists. It is much more accurate to think of test scores as estimates of true scores. Thus, an individual's performance on a test can best be thought of as falling within a range or a band rather than as a point on a scale. The SEM is an estimate of the amount of error in a particular test score; it is often provided in the test manual. (If it is not in the manual, you can calculate the SEM by multiplying the standard deviation times the square root of 1 minus the reliability coefficient). By using SEMs, we are able to increase our confidence in interpreting scores as we use the SEM to construct "confidence bands" around a person's observed score. This enables us to say, "While your score was 85 today, we are 95% confident that your true score lies between 75 and 90."

You can calculate for any percent of confidence, however, it is easier to use the percentages represented on the normal curve at +/- 1, +/-2 or +/- 3 standard deviations (see Figure 3-1). To determine where someone's true score lies 68% of the time, you would calculate the SEM for +/- 1 standard deviation. To do this, you would multiply the standard deviation by 1 (because you want to know where the true score lies 68%, or +/- 1 SD of the time) and then add and subtract that number to the observed score to get a range. However, being able to predict 68% of the time isn't that impressive. So, you decide that you want to be able to predict 95% of the time (which is +/- 2 standard deviations), you would take that standard deviation and multiply it by 2 (for 2 standard deviations) and then add/subtract that number to the mean to obtain your range. You would follow the same procedures to obtain the confidence bands for 99%.

The traditional approach to using the SEM is illustrated by the following example. An individual receives a score of 105 (observed score) on a test that has a reported SEM of 5. We now want to obtain an estimate of the person's true score. Because of errors of measurement, observed scores are assumed to be normally distributed around the true score. Hence we can refer to standard deviation units to give us the limits of observed scores. In this example, the SEM is used as a standard deviation (SD). Therefore, 105 ±1 SD (5) = 100–110. Over all individuals, according to the normal distribution, true scores lie within this band 68% of the time. With an SD of 2, however, 105 ±2 SD (10) = 95–115. Over all individuals, true scores lie within this band 95% of the time. Therefore, the probability is high that the true score for the student in the example is between 95 and 115, and the probability is somewhat lower that the true score is between 100 and 110. What you can observe from this, is that as our confidence increases (we can say we are 95% certain where a true score lies), the range becomes larger, and thus our statement may lose some of its power. How powerful is it to say that you are 99% confident that a person's age lies between 0 and 100? Obviously, the standard deviation has a large impact on how wide the confidence bands will be. So, you need to determine the best balance between the observed score, standard deviation and confidence bands for each client and test.

Standard Error of Differences (SED) Between Two Subsets

In career counseling, it is often necessary to be certain when differences in subtest scores are significant. The differences between scores can be ascertained by computing the SED. The following example illustrates this method.

A multi-aptitude test battery reports T scores (mean = 50 and standard deviation = 10) for interpretation of subtest scores. On the abstract reasoning subtest scale, a reliability coefficient of .89 is reported. Another scale has a reported reliability coefficient of .95. To find the SED between the two tests, use the following formula:

$$SED = \sqrt{2 - r1 - r2}$$
$$SED = 10\sqrt{2 - .89 - .95}$$
$$SED = 4$$

WHERE r1 = reliability of subtest1; r2 = reliability of subtest 2

To determine whether the difference between the individual's scores on the test is a real difference rather than simply chance, the SED is multiplied by 1.96. Because ±1.96 standard deviation units on the normal distribution will include 95% of the cases, scores within that range will occur by chance only 5% of the time. In this case, the result is obtained by multiplying 4 by 1.96, which is 7.84, or approximately 8 points. Thus, we can interpret a difference of 8 points or more between the two subtests in our example as being meaningful.

Consider the Self-Directed Search (SDS) that has a SED of 8. The SED is important, because it helps you interpret the scores. If a person's Realistic score is 40 and their Social score is 35, you know that there isn't any significant difference between those two scores. So, in interpreting the results, you'd know that the two scores are interchangeable, and when looking up occupations by codes, the person should look up RS jobs as well as SR jobs. If, on the other hand, the R score was 40 and the next highest code was S, with a score of 20, that's over 3 SEDs away. Then you know that the person should only look at "R" jobs, not SR jobs. (The person should consider all combinations, as long as the R is first, so RSE, RIC, RAE, RCI, RES, etc.).

Expectancy Tables

In educational planning, a counselor often has to advise a student of chances of success in a particular college or university. An expectancy table constructed from the records of previous graduates and their performance at the university being considered provides relevant information. In Table 3-1 (see next page), a sample expectancy table has been constructed from the first-semester grade point averages and ACT composite scores.

The numbers that are not in parentheses are the numbers of students whose grade point averages are in the designated range. For example, two students whose ACT composite scores were in the range 26–28 earned grade point averages between 1.50 and 1.99. Seven students in this same ACT score range earned grade point averages between 2.00 and 2.49. The numbers in the parentheses are the cumulative percents of individuals within a particular ACT score range whose earned grades are in the corresponding grade point average cell or higher. For example, 88% of the individuals whose ACT composite scores were in the 20–22 range earned grade point averages between 1.50 and 1.99 or higher. Likewise, 92% of the individuals whose ACT composite scores were in the 11–13 range earned first-semester grade point averages of .50-.99 or higher.

To demonstrate the chances of success at the university being considered, the ACT composite score provides an index of academic success. For example, 81 out of 100 individuals whose ACT composite scores were 23–25 made a 2.00 grade point average or higher. The chances that individuals with the same ACT scores would make a 2.50 or higher grade point average are 48 out of 100.

Table 3-1	Sample Expectancy Table						

American College Text (ACT) Composite Scores	First Semester Grade Point Averages						
	0.00-0.49	0.50-0.99	1.00-1.49	1.50-1.99	2.00-2.49	2.50-2.99	3.00-3.49	3.50-3.99
32-35						(100) 1	(67) 1	(33) 1
29-31					(100) 1	(91) 2	(73) 4	(36) 4
26-28				(100) 2	(89) 7	(50) 4	(28) 3	(11) 2
23-25				(100) 5	(81) 9	(48) 6	(26) 6	(4) 1
20-22			(100) 6	(88) 13	(61) 15	(31) 12	(6) 3	
17-19		(100) 5	(92) 6	(83) 24	(46) 22	(12) 5	(5) 3	
14-16		(100) 5	(86) 9	(62) 13	(27) 8	(5) 2		
11-13	(100) 2	(92) 5	(72) 8	(40) 62	(16) 3	(4) 1		
8-10	(100) 2	(85) 4	(54) 5	(15) 2				
5-7	(100) 1							

Correlations

Understanding how factors are related help a counselor make appropriate interpretations and interventions. In measurement, we use the term "correlation" to describe relationships among constructs and scales. Correlations can be positive (when one factor is present, it's likely that another is present), negative (when one factor is present it's likely that the other factor is not), strong or weak, significant or insignificant. Correlations range from -1 to +1. A zero correlation would mean that there is no relationship between the two variables. A 1 (either positive or negative) means that there is a perfect relationship. If it's +1, the two variables are always present together, and if -1, they are never present together. Obviously, most correlations fall somewhere between +/- 1. The actual number is also important. A .23 correlation is much weaker than a .94 correlation. Correlations are generally reported with the symbol r.

Why is this useful? If a counselor administers a decision-making inventory, and the client's scores indicate a high level of indecision, the counselor might want to know what other issues might be affecting the career indecision. Through research, the counselor might discover that anxiety is the number one correlate of career indecision, but depression is a low correlate. So, instead of asking the client questions about depression, the counselor might ask about stress/anxiety instead and might incorporate stress management techniques, or introduce cognitive reframing exercises. It's important to know that correlations describe a relationship, but do not identify which variable is causing the other.

A final consideration when looking at correlations: you will often see a "p-value" behind the correlation. For example, $r = .43$, $p < .05$. The p-value is the amount of likely error in the correlation. Anything below .05 is usually considered statistically significant, meaning the relationship is interpretable and the error is low. If $p = .05$ or is higher, then the relationship does not mean much, statistically speaking. However, it is important data. Why? Because it's just as important to know what is related to a factor as it is to know what is not related.

Summary

In this chapter, we have discussed several methods used to interpret assessment results. These methods illustrate how assessment results can be transformed into meaningful information on characteristics and traits—information that can be used in career counseling. The concepts of measurement accuracy further illustrate how tests must be interpreted to enhance the usefulness of information provided in career counseling.

Questions and Exercises

1. From Figure 3-1, what are the approximate percentile equivalents for the following standard scores? GATB: 140, 61, 85; ACT: 15, 23, 36.

2. From Figure 3-1, what is the closest standard deviation to a standard score of 108 for a test that has a mean of 100 and a standard deviation of 10?

3. Why is it important to identify the norm reference group when using percentile equivalents to interpret assessment results? Illustrate your answer with an example.

4. What are the advantages of stanine scores over percentiles and grade equivalents?

5. Use the sample expectancy table (Table 3-1) to answer the following questions.

    a. What would be the chances of Bob's making a 2.00 grade point average or better with an ACT score of 30?

    b. What would be Joan's chances for a 2.00 grade point average or higher with an ACT score of 16?

    c. What advice would you offer to Bob and Joan?

6. If a person receives a 63 on the GATB, what would their score be in terms of percentiles? (Don't estimate, calculate)

7. If a person receives a 90 on the GATB, what would their scores be in terms of percentiles? (Don't estimate, calculate)

8. If a person received a 12 on the ACT, what would their score be in terms of percentiles? (Don't estimate, calculate)

9. If a person received a 428 on the College Entrance Exam, what would their score be in terms of percentiles? (Don't estimate, calculate – in this case, you might not want to start by figuring out the 1% increase, but start at the midpoint or a higher percentage).

10. If a person's raw score was 7 on the Decisiveness scale of the Career Decision Profile (see Chapter 9), and the mean is 12 and the S.D. is 3, where does this person's true score lie 68%, 95% and 99% of the time?

11. If a person's sten score on the 16PF (see Chapter 7) for Factors A, C and I are 2, 3 and 4 (with a mean of 5.5 and S.D. of .2), where does his/her true score lie 68%, 95% and 99% of the time, and which of the following occupations would you most highly recommend investigating, counselor, engineer or firefighter?

12. Do a literature search on a topic related to career testing or career counseling. For example, a search might include any combination of the following:

    • Anxiety, depression, perfectionism

    • Career choice, career satisfaction, undecided

    Using the article, look for a report of the correlations. Describe your findings to the class. An alternative activity might be to break into small groups and decide on a key construct for each group (career choice, career satisfaction, career decidedness, career change, career major, etc.) and have each member of the group research a correlate. Each group could then present their findings to the class.

4 Using Ability and Aptitude Tests

Ability measures have been associated with career counseling since the time of the early trait-and-factor approach to career guidance (Zunker, 2005). Simply stated, the trait-and-factor approach matched the individual's traits with the requirements of a specific occupation. The key assumption was that individuals have unique patterns of abilities or traits that can be objectively measured and that are correlated with the requirements of various types of jobs. Thus, appraising traits was the counselor's major task. Early vocational counseling programs advocated psychological testing in vocational counseling specifically to analyze an individual's potential in relation to requirements of training programs and occupations. The career counselor's major role was to help individuals assess their assets and liabilities through an evaluation of test results. These early approaches to career counseling inspired the study of job descriptions and job requirements in an attempt to predict success on the job from the measurement of job-related traits.

The attention to specific job requirements revealed the need for multi-trait measures. In particular, there was a need for a differential assessment of an individual's abilities. Multi-aptitude test batteries evolved to fill this need. Table 4-1 provides a comparison of aptitude scales covered by the most widely used multi-aptitude tests. The statistical technique of factor analysis provided the tools for measuring individual abilities and thus provided the foundation for multi-aptitude test batteries. The growth of career counseling and the need for selecting and classifying industrial and military personnel increased the demand for differential measures. The use of aptitude test results to select applicants for colleges and professional schools increased significantly with the growth in college enrollments after World War II. The armed forces have sponsored ongoing research programs to develop aptitude test batteries for their use. A number of multi-aptitude tests have also been developed for career counseling (Drummond, 2004; Whiston, 2000). The use of aptitude test results remains a prominent part of career counseling.

Table 4-1 Comparison of Multi-Aptitude Subscales

ASVAB	DAT	OASIS-III Aptitude Survey	MAB-II
General Science	Abstract Reasoning	General Ability	Information
Arithmetic Reasoning	Language Usage	Computation	Comprehension
Word Knowledge	Mechanical Reasoning	Vocabulary	Arithmetic
Paragraph Comprehension	Numerical Ability	Making Marks	Similarities
Mathematics Knowledge	Space Relations	Spatial Relations	Vocabulary
Electronics Information	Verbal Reasoning	Word Comparison	Digit Symbol
Auto and Shop Information			Picture Completion
Mechanical Comprehension			Spatial Picture Arrangement
			Object Assembly

In this chapter we concentrate on the use of aptitude tests for career development. We discuss two multi-aptitude batteries and give examples of their use. We also describe the limitations of multi-aptitude batteries. Finally, we provide a list of developmental strategies for aptitude test results.

Purpose of Aptitude Tests

An aptitude test is a measure of a specific skill or ability. There are two types of aptitude tests: multi-aptitude test batteries and single tests measuring specific aptitudes. Multi-aptitude test batteries contain measures of a wide range of aptitudes and combinations of aptitudes and provide valuable information that can be used in career decision making. Single aptitude tests are used when a specific aptitude needs to be measured, such as manual dexterity, clerical ability, artistic ability, or musical aptitude.

An aptitude is thought to be specified proficiency or the ability to acquire a certain proficiency (Drummond, 2004). It also may be defined as a tendency, capacity, or inclination to do a certain task. A common misconception is that aptitudes are inherited, unchangeable characteristics that need to be discovered and subsequently matched with certain job requirements. Such an assumption is misleading for the interpretation of aptitude test results (Drummond, 2004). Rather, aptitude should be viewed as the result of both heredity and environment; an individual is born with certain capacities that might or might not be nurtured by the environment. In essence then, aptitude tests reflect the interaction of heredity and environment and predict the capacity to learn.

Within this frame of reference, aptitude scores can provide a broad measure of an individual's experience and ability at the time of testing. For example, academic aptitude reflects the entire array of skills needed to meet the demands of an academic curriculum. Mechanical aptitude reflects all the skills needed to do mechanical work. Because aptitude scores are used to predict future performance in educational and vocational endeavors, they are a major element in career counseling. The probability of performing well on a job, in a training program, or in college is the kind of information the career counselor usually seeks. Matching the individual's abilities to job requirements has long been the subject of research by government, industry, and job-planning specialists.

One discussion among experts in the field concerns the difference between observed abilities and self-reported abilities. For example, Prediger (1995) cautions counselors to not automatically replace ability self-estimates with ability scores. Could there be a differentiation between what a person believes he or she can perform well, and how he or she actually performs? The question then becomes what are we measuring, actual aptitudes or an individual's confidence level with respect to certain aptitudes? Darcy and Tracey (2003) described self-efficacy as "an individual's estimate of his or her ability to successfully perform a particular behavior" (p. 221). The question of what is actually being measured speaks to the issue of inventory validity. Measures that require an individual to perform a task (such as geometry, typing, etc.) are likely to have greater validity, as compared with one that asks a person to rate his or her proficiency at the task. As we will discuss in the career development inventories chapter, beliefs a person has about his or her abilities, interests, problem-solving capability, and so forth are important to ascertain because they can strongly impact the way in which individuals complete inventories, see their options and make decisions.

Identifying Abilities by Holland's Types

In this section, abilities associated with Holland's types will be identified. Significant dialogue between client and counselor can be encouraged with examples of abilities that are type-related. Although each work environment requires specific tasks, the counselor can enhance an individual's career development by relating general abilities to work requirements. Discussion of abilities along with other data such as measured interests and personality traits should broaden the client's scope and focus in career decision making.

Counselors must recognize that many of the abilities measured by current standardized tests are not job specific; that is, the requirements of jobs vary from one work environment to another. Although there are similarities in job duties and responsibilities within a particular occupation, there are also distinct differences in the requisite skills necessary for appropriate performance. For example, an accountant in one firm might be required only to manage data, whereas an accountant in another firm might have to manage employees as well.

Table 4-2	**Abilities According to Holland Type**
Realistic	• Jobs associated with this type relate to things rather than to people and often involve hands-on activities. • Realistic occupations are likely to be blue-collar jobs requiring physical, mechanical, and spatial abilities. • White-collar realistic jobs include engineering and navigation.
Investigative	• This type encompasses the scientific professions, therefore requiring the highest educational level and highest level of intelligence of the Holland types (Gottfredson, 1980). • Intellectual skills such as verbal and nonverbal reasoning are important for success in occupations associated with this type.
Artistic	• This type includes several dimensions of abilities. • For example, it is generally agreed that creative ability depends on the specific type of creative work. Musical talent is quite diverse in abilities—consider the vocalist, the conductor, and the composer. However, some tests are designed to measure specific areas of musical talent. • Because predictive studies of artistic talents are not promising (Lowman, 1991), available screening tests should be followed by further evaluation by specialists in the diverse occupations associated with this type.
Social	• Different occupations require different patterns of social and interpersonal skills. • For example, machine operators need social skills to establish rapport with coworkers and supervisors, whereas a receptionist in the same plant requires interpersonal skills to deal with customers and strangers. • As with other types in the Holland system, identified social abilities present rich sources of information to be used in career decision making. • The counselor is in a good position to evaluate a client's social abilities that might be applicable to a specific occupation, especially when standardized tests offer little help in measuring social skills.
Enterprising	• This type is associated with managing others and with leadership skills. • Researchers such as Klemp and McClelland (1986) have identified such generic enterprising competencies as good planning skills, synthetic thinking, and the ability to conceptualize information and procedures. • Although some of these abilities may be measured by standardized instruments, the skilled interviewer helps identify these abilities in discussions of work and leisure activities. • People who have been leaders within their social organizations, team projects, and so on, are likely to have enterprising skills.
Conventional	• This type is primarily associated with clerical and numerical duties and the ability to understand and manipulate data. • Lowman (1991) has suggested that specific conventional abilities include perceptual speed and accuracy, perceptual speed of figure identification, and numerical computational ability. • In the higher-level jobs, such as accountant, general intelligence and reasoning ability are important.

The first step in career decision making can be started by recognizing identified abilities that are associated with occupations within the Holland types. Counselors need to point out to the client that identified abilities may be related to a number of careers and types, making it necessary to gather more information for specific job requirements. In addition, it should be noted that although an individual might have an aptitude, he or she might not have an accompanying interest in the same area. These contradictions should be explored during the session, and the counselor can help the client in examining other avenues in which that aptitude might be expressed.

Another helpful outcome of identifying a client's aptitudes is that these skills can then be incorporated into the career counseling process. For example, a person with strong conventional skills can begin to feel in control of the career exploration process as she or he organizes and summarizes the information gathered about self and occupations. An artistic person might find a creative way to pull together the information in a way that would express his or her knowledge about self or could be encouraged to implore this ability in identifying unusual ways to learn about careers. In addition, a counselor can incorporate words associated with each type when discussing career plans. For example, if working with an investigative type, the counselor might use words such as "exploring all your options," "examining the possibilities on your printout" or "I wonder what you'll discover about yourself."

Differential Aptitude Test (DAT)

The DAT is one of the better-known and most widely researched aptitude tests on the market. Form C consists of two levels. Level 1 is appropriate for students in grades 7 through 9, and Level 2 is appropriate for students in grades 10 through 12 and adults. The DAT includes verbal reasoning, numerical reasoning, abstract reasoning, perceptual speed and accuracy (two parts), mechanical reasoning, space relations, and spelling and language usage. In addition, a scholastic aptitude score can be calculated by summing the verbal reasoning and the numerical reasoning scales. The DAT is an 8 test battery, available in English and Spanish, and takes about three hours to complete.

Separate sex norms were derived from a stratified random sample of more than 60,000 students. The major purpose for separate sex norms was to allow comparisons between the sexes when significant differences occurred. An impressive amount of validity data correlates test scores with a variety of course grades and achievement test scores. And, although sufficient evidence indicates that the DAT is a good predictor of high school and college grades, there are limited data concerning the ability of the test to predict vocational success. Consistently high reliability coefficients are reported by sex and grade level. Long-term consistency is supported by various studies, including a follow-up of 1700 high school students four years after graduation and a seven-year follow-up of a smaller sample. Cronbach (1984) suggests that differential ability patterns are fairly well stabilized by mid-adolescence.

The DAT has been paired with the Career Interest Inventory (CII) to provide a more balanced assessment of two important aspects of career decision making: a person's aptitudes and interests. The combination of these two instruments provides a more complete profile of a client. The main purpose of the DAT/CII is to stimulate career exploration for students, including those who are interested in attending college, non-college-bound students, at-risk students, and adults. The developers state that one way the DAT/CII helps at-risk students is by showing the link between schoolwork and occupations. In addition to using the CII, the developers suggest using the Guide to Careers Portfolios: Student Workbook (Willson & Stone, 1994) as a tool to help students with the career planning process.

The CII provides measures of the following occupational groups: Social Service, Clerical Services, Health Services, Agriculture, Customer Services, Fine Arts, Mathematics and Science, Building Trades, Educational Services, Legal Services, Transportation, Sales, Management, Benchwork, and Machine Operation. Although the CII is not timed, on average it takes about 30 minutes to complete. Scores for the DAT are reported in percentile ranks, stanines, scaled scores, and normal curve equivalents for both sexes. CII results are reported by occupational-group consistency index and raw scores. Scoring is available via machine or by hand scoring.

The norm group for the CII was based on 192,000 students from 520 school districts in grades 7 through 12. The norm group for the DAT with the CII was based on 2000 adults from 43 programs (vocational technical, prison, community college, and adult basic educational programs) in 17 states. Internal consistency scores for the occupational groups ranged from .82 to .94. KR-20's, which provide conservative estimates of reliability or consistency, were used to determine test-retest reliabilities, which ranged from .80 to .90. The manual presents several examples of concurrent validity, with the DAT being compared with various achievement tests, although Willson and Stone (1994) state that reliability and validity information was inadequately provided. For further reviews of the DAT and CII, refer to Bennet, Seashore and Wesman (2002), Wang (1993), Stone (1993), Hambleton (1985), Pennock-Roman (1988), and Sander (1985). An international comparison between high school American and Netherlands students demonstrated that the subtests of the DAT equally measured their cognitive abilities with the exception of mechanical knowledge (Te Nijenhuis, Evers & Mur, 2000).

Interpreting the DAT

The DAT provides individual reports for interpretation. One type is a computer-produced profile, shown in Figure 4-1; the other, shown in Figure 4-2, is a hand-plotted profile. Both are interpreted in the same manner. Willson and Stone (1994) suggest that counselors should be familiar with a client's needs and purposes for taking the DAT/CII before interpreting the results, and counselors must be sensitive to how a client might interpret and integrate "low" scores. The percentiles show high, average, and low ranges, and the bar graph represents the range of percentiles (in which the individual's true score is said to be). The first step in interpreting the DAT is to observe whether the ends of bars overlap. There is a significant difference between any two that do not overlap. Two bars having an overlap of more than one-half their

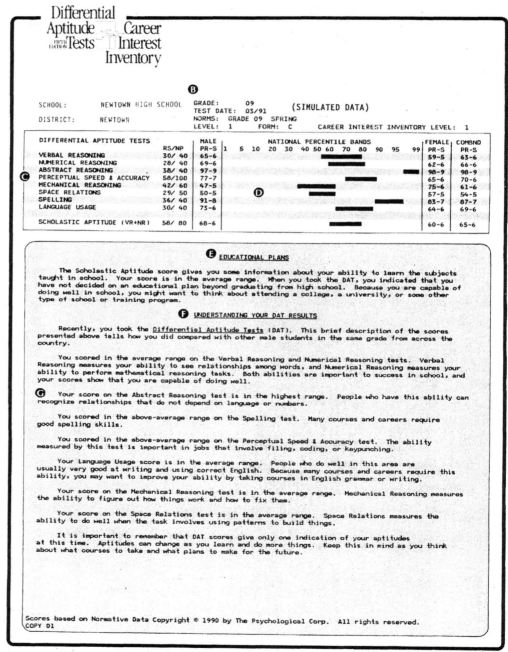

Figure 4-1   From the Counselor's Manual of the Differential Aptitude Tests - Fifth Edition with Career Interest Inventory. Copyright © 1990 by Harcourt Assessment, Inc. Reproduced by permission. All rights reserved. "Differential Aptitude Tests – Fifth Edition" and "DAT-5" are trademarks of Harcourt Assessment, registered in the United States of America and/or other jurisdictions.

length are not significantly different. If the overlap is less than half their length, a difference should be considered as probable and should be specifically determined by retesting.

The combination of verbal reasoning and numerical ability is a good index of scholastic aptitude. The verbal reasoning score is highly correlated with grades in a number of academic courses, especially English courses. The numerical ability score is highly correlated with grades in mathematics courses. Extensive research has been done with other combinations of DAT scores for predicting success in academic subjects and vocational courses (Linn, 1982; Pennock-Roman, 1988).

The DAT manual provides extensive information concerning individual DAT scores and predictors of course grades. Using this information, the counselor can ascertain which aptitudes are required for

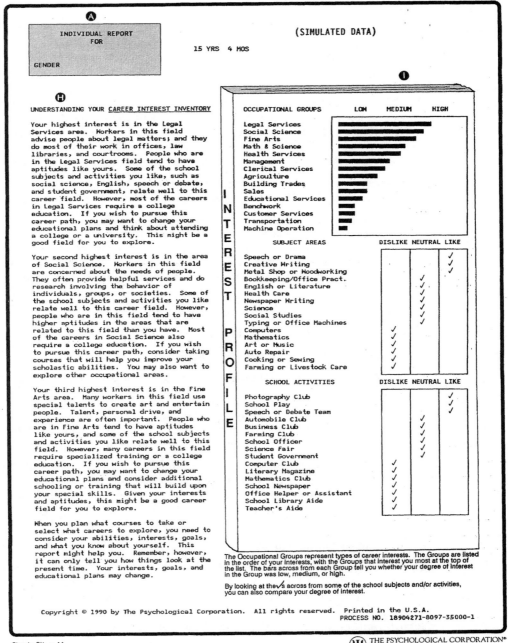

Figure 4-2   From the Counselor's Manual of the Career Interest Inventory. Copyright © 1990 by Harcourt Assessment, Inc. Reproduced by permission. All rights reserved. "Differential Aptitude Tests – Fifth Edition" and "DAT-5" are trademarks of Harcourt Assessment, registered in the United States of America and/or other jurisdictions.

certain courses and which aptitudes are useful in certain occupations. However, Willson and Stone (1994) caution against using the DAT as a predictor of academic or occupational success, and instead focus on its utility for clarifying of interests. In addition, a regression equation for predicting College Entrance Examination Board Scholastic Aptitude Test scores from a combination of DAT scores is provided for counseling individuals considering college. These interpretive materials provide excellent guidelines for using the results of the test. A number of reviews of the DAT have been published, including Willson and Stone (1994), Linn (1982), Anastasi (1988), and Pennock-Roman (1988).

Figure 4-2 shows a sample profile of a CII. A person's preferences for occupational groups are presented, in order of highest interest to lowest. Also reported are subject areas and school activities of interest, again in order of highest preference to lowest.

Case of a Male High School Student Interested in Legal Services

Adam, a high school freshman, came to the counseling center to see if a career in the field of law matched his skills. Although he was not an honors student, he excelled in courses such as creative writing and speech. The counselor and Adam decided that it would be worthwhile for Adam to take tests that would provide specific information about his skills and interests. They selected the DAT/CII primarily because the DAT provides an index of scholastic aptitude and measures of specific skills, and the CII would provide preferences for occupational groups, subject areas, and school activities.

The results of the DAT and CII are shown in Figures 4-1 and 4-2. In discussing the results with the counselor, Adam expressed pleasure with his scores on abstract reasoning and spelling but concern about his average scores on verbal reasoning, numerical reasoning, and language usage range.

ADAM: How am I ever going to get into college with average scores in English and math? And if I'm only average in the way I use language, does that mean that I won't make a good lawyer?

COUNSELOR: The skills that you mentioned are important in applying to college and in many professions such as law. Although they are important, they present only one part of the puzzle. Colleges and employers look for many things when considering applicants, such as GPA, work and volunteer experience, and letters of recommendation. With regards to your performance in these areas, you still have three more years to strengthen your skills. Can you think of some ways to do that?

ADAM: Well, I guess I could get a tutor, or study harder.

COUNSELOR: True. What else could you do?

ADAM: I could take some extra classes, or harder ones, to make myself stronger.

COUNSELOR: Now you've got the idea. Let's take a look at your CII report. What do you think that's telling us?

ADAM: Well, legal services is definitely my top interest, and it says here that some of these courses I'm good at, as well as some of my activities, are related to that field. It also says that I need a college degree to get a job. How hard will it be for me to get into college?

COUNSELOR: You have a lot of time between now and graduation to create and implement a strategy that will make going to college a more probable occurrence for you. It is very possible that you could go to several colleges with your current scores. However, if you know that college is a long-term goal for you or that law is the field in which you want to work, it is in your best interest to start working toward reaching your goals now.

ADAM: Yeah, that makes a lot of sense.

The counselor and Adam then worked together to create a general four-year plan. The plan listed educational goals as well as career goals, steps, and an estimated time line for completion. In this case, the DAT/CII helped confirm Adam's areas of strength, as well as highlight areas in which he had room to improve. Because he took the DAT/CII in his freshman year, he had plenty of time to take steps toward strengthening himself academically and vocationally.

Armed Services Vocational Aptitude Battery (ASVAB)

The ASVAB was originally developed to replace the separate army, navy, and air force classification batteries for selecting and classifying personnel and was first available to schools through the U.S. Department of Defense in 1968. This battery is designed primarily for high school seniors. The armed services have developed cooperative programs with school systems for administering this battery and furnish test results at no cost. The ASVAB takes about 2 hours and 24 minutes to complete. Exploring Careers: The ASVAB Career Exploration Guide (U.S. Department of Defense, 2002) is a supplement that

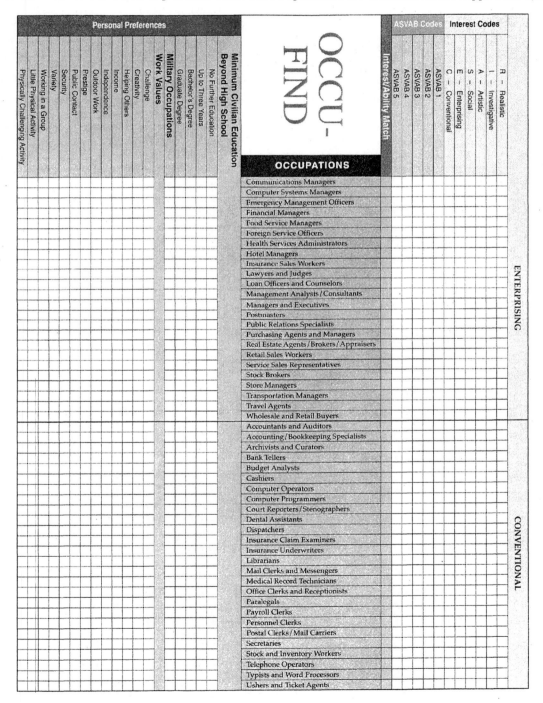

Figure 4-3   From Exploring Careers: The ASVAB Career Exploration Guide. U.S. Government Printing Office, 2003. Reprinted with permission.

enables students to become more actively involved in understanding their ASVAB scores and determining their next steps. By reading through the guide and completing the Interest-Finder (U.S. Department of Defense, 1995), students are able to identify their values, interests, skills, and educational goals, as well as identify features they want most in an occupation. In addition, students, parents and counselors can go to www.asvabprogram.com for additional information. Also included in the ASVAB program are three planners, entitled "My Educational and Career Plans," a "Coursework Planner" and a college major finder.

The OCCU-FIND (see Figure 4-3), organized by Holland types, allows students to see occupations that relate to their interests. In addition, they can see how important each skill set is to that occupation, the types of employers for that occupation (military, government or private sector), the military score for that occupation and page numbers in Military Careers or the Occupational Outlook Handbook specific to that occupation. The online OCCU-FIND includes about half of the occupations in O*NET and direct links to the online versions of Military Careers or the Occupational Outlook Handbook specific to the occupation of interest.

The ASVAB is a battery of tests that measure multiple aptitudes and allows comparison of the student's aptitudes with other students nationally. The Interest-Finder consists of 240 items and is based on Holland's theory of career development, including the RIASEC classification of personality and environments. A student would enter their scores on a gender specific percentile table to compare their scores to the norm group. The personal preference exercises are designed to help students identify their work values and their intentions for further training. In addition to the workbook, a recruiter's guide, technical manual, counselor manual, educator/counselor guide, student/parent guide, and a guide to military occupations and career paths entitled Military Careers are provided.

The ASVAB form 23/24 takes about three hours to complete and consists of eight tests (see Table 4-1). These tests combine to yield three career exploration scales: verbal, math, and science & technical skills. According to the manual, the verbal scale measures language and reading skills by combining Word Knowledge and Paragraph Comprehension tests. The math scale measures mathematical skills by combining the Mathematics Knowledge and Arithmetic Reasoning tests. The science and technical skills scale measures skills in those areas resulting from the General Science, Electronics Information and Mechanical Comprehension tests. Students' scores on the Career Exploration scales link with the KSA (Knowledge, Skills and Abilities) outlined by the U.S. Department of Labor's Occupational Information Network or O*NET (www.onetcenter.org). The Military Careers score combines the scores of the Verbal, Math, Mechanical Comprehension, and Electronics Information scores to estimate a student's potential for qualifying for enlisted occupations. For students interested in a military career, this score can be used with Military Careers, which describes 140 enlisted and officer careers. The final score is the Military Entrance Score, which determines if a student has met the standard for the entrance requirements for the military.

According to the developers, a person's ASVAB codes are a measure of his or her general levels of developed abilities. An aptitude can be defined as a person's current level of ability and his or her potential to gain relevant knowledge. Results are presented in percentiles, and a comparison is made across genders. Scores are reported in "bands," to account for potential testing error. Additional technical information and studies are provided in the Technical Manual for the ASVAB 18/19 Career Exploration Program (U.S. Department of Defense, 1994). Because the ASVAB has been so widely used (by 1.3 million students each year), it has been closely scrutinized. The early editions were greatly criticized by Cronbach (1979) and Weiss (1978). Cronbach suggested that the subtest scores were too unreliable to be used separately and that the use of the test in general should be limited. Weiss argued that the reliabilities of subtest scores were low primarily because the subtests were too short. Other reviews are more positive for both the test battery's psychometric characteristics and its interpretative materials (Hanser & Grafton, 1983). The use of the ASVAB as a recruitment tool for the armed forces has been substantiated as well. In their 1998 study, researchers (Laurence, Walls, Barnes, & Dela Rosa) found that 16 to 25% of those who enlisted in the armed services came from involvement in the ASVAB tests.

In 1994, Elmore and Bradley (1994) raised a concern about using the ASVAB Career Exploration Program with black and Hispanic students: A review showed that 80% of Hispanics and 86% of blacks were assigned a primary code of 4 or 5 as compared with non-Hispanic and non-black students. The potential problem in these cases is that without counselor support or intervention, such clients might investigate only occupations at those lower levels. The ASVAB manual, in contrast, cites several studies that indicate no difference by sex or race. For example, in a comparison of the aptitude factor structures of 9173 black, white, and Hispanic young men and women, no significant ethnic or sex differences were found (Ree & Carretta, 1995). Counselors should, however, use caution when using the ASVAB Career Exploration Program with black and Hispanic clients until more evidence has been collected.

Norms for the ASVAB were based on men and women ranging in age from 16 to 23 who were in 10th, 11th, or 12th grade, and they were selected by the National Opinion Research Center. The counselor's manual shows that the norm groups reflected the national population as indicated by the 1979 U.S. Bureau of Census. The sample was approximately equal for men and women from urban and rural areas. They used an over-sampling technique to ensure that there was an adequate representation of Blacks, Hispanics and economically disadvantaged. Finally, they weighted the sample so that it would exactly reflect the distribution of the national population. There were approximately 3,878 sophomores, 1,300 juniors and 1,200 seniors. The ASVAB has been shown to increase career exploration knowledge and reduce career indecision with a nationally represented group of 255 high school students versus 422 control group students (Baker, 2002).

Reliabilities are reported in terms of KR-20's and alternative forms. For the academic, mathematic, and verbal scales, the reliabilities range from .92 to .96. For the subtests, reliabilities ranged from .71 to .91. With regards to construct validity, the academic ability composite correlated with the California Achievement Test at .90, and at .85 with the DAT. The manual also reports other studies that showed a .83 correlation between the academic ability composite and the GATB, and .85 with a literacy measure from the Adult Basic Learning Examination. The ASVAB also has reported success in predicting entry-level success in various occupations, including electrical mechanical equipment repair occupations (.36 to .74), communication occupations (.36 to .52), data processing occupations (.39 to .77), and clerical and supply occupations (.53 to .73). The manual also describes results of several civilian validity studies of the ASVAB. Rogers (2002) noted that there was disagreement among reviewers about the predictive validity of the ASVAB to these civilian occupations. With respect to the Interest-Finder, a recent study (Wall & Baker, 1997) compared it with the Strong Interest Inventory and found that it yielded a six-figure composition (similar to the Holland hexagon). In addition, the Interest-Finder predicted high school courses and certain career choices for high school students. The Interest Finder was also found to be

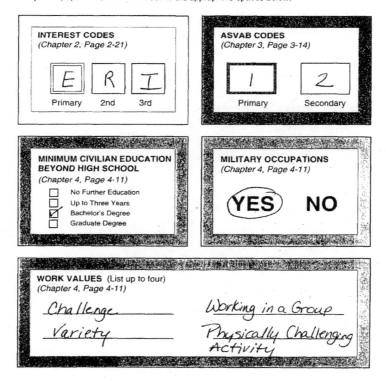

Figure 4-4   From ASVAB, 2005. Reprinted with permission.

correlated with the Strong Interest Inventory, which is evidence of its validity. For a detailed description of validity studies, see Armed Services Vocational Battery (ASVAB): Integrative Review of Validity Studies (Welsh, Kucinkas, & Curran, 1990). Rogers (2002) also provides an extensive review of the ASVAB.

Case of a High School Student Interested in the Armed Services

Corrina resided in a small rural community; the nearest city was 50 miles away. She had considered a career in the army and took the ASVAB during her junior year in high school. Later, she decided she didn't want to leave home and changed her plans. Her results are in Figure 4-4 (see previous page).

When she was a senior, however, Corrina reported to the counselor that she was reconsidering the armed services because of a lack of jobs in her community and the nearby city. Because an army recruiter was not available in the community, the counselor had been provided with ASVAB materials for counseling purposes. The counselor explained each of the scores in the following manner: "Your score on

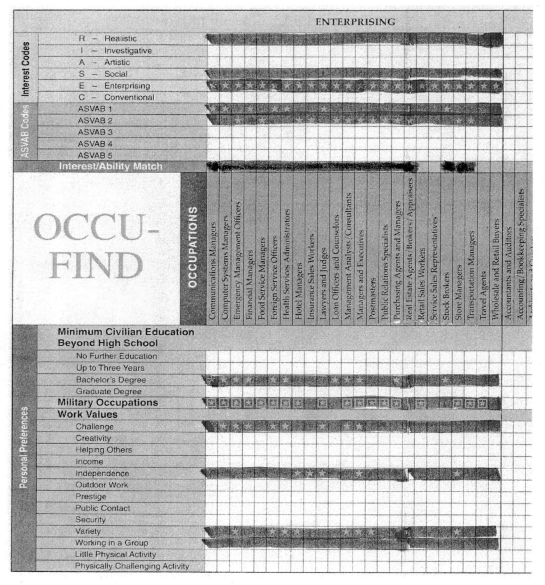

Figure 4-5   From Exploring Careers: The ASVAB Career Exploration Guide. U.S. Government Printing Office, 2003. Reprinted with permission.

the verbal composite is at the 67th percentile. This means that 67 students out of 100 in the eleventh grade scored lower than you did, while 33 out of 100 scored higher than you did. The band on the profile indicates the range of your score. In other words, your true composite score for verbal is somewhere within this range. The verbal composite is a measure of your vocabulary, understanding of scientific principles, and ability to understand written materials."

The counselor provided Corrina with a copy of the OCCU-FIND and told her to fill in her interest codes, ASVAB codes, and military careers scores (see Figure 4-5). From her use with the Interest-Finder, her primary code was Enterprising and her secondary code was Realistic. Her top two values were security and working in a group.

The OCCU-FIND allowed Corrina to identify those occupations that best matched her primary interests, ASVAB codes, and type of occupations preferred (military, government or private sector). After completing the OCCU-FIND, Corrina decided she would like to consider the occupations involving arbitrating and mediating. She read through various descriptions of occupations found in the online OCCU-FIND, and made plans to visit an army recruiter for more information about her career plans.

In Corrina's case, the ASVAB results were used to stimulate career exploration. This information encouraged Corrina to relate her skills and interests to job opportunities in the armed services.

Multidimensional Aptitude Battery II

The Multidimensional Aptitude Battery II (Jackson, 1998) is a level C instrument that measures both aptitudes and intelligence. In addition to the total score, there are 2 main scales with ten subscales. The Verbal Scale includes scores for Information, Comprehension, Arithmetic, Similarities, Vocabulary, and the Total or Full Scale IQ. The Performance Scale includes Digit Symbol, Picture Completion, Spatial, Picture Arrangement, Object Assembly, and the Total. The test is individually, group or computer-administered, available in three languages (English, French and Spanish), and takes about 100 minutes to complete.

Table 4-3	Correlations between MAB-II and WAIS		
		MAB-II	
		Verbal	Performance	Total
WAIS	Verbal	0.94		
	Performance		0.79	
	Total			0.91

Norming for the MAB-II included a complex approach of nine groups ranging in age and equally representative in gender in the United States and Canada. In addition, the groups were racially diverse, consisting of 200 people (the two oldest groups had 100 people each), and an equal distribution of managerial/professional/specialty occupations and technical/sales/service and labor occupations.

The reliability of the MAB-II is impressive. Internal consistency estimates for the subscales ranged from .70 for Arithmetic to .96 for the Spatial subscale, with coefficients for the full scales ranging from .96 to .98. Retest reliability has been reported at .97. The MAB-II also appears to have strong validity, with the following correlations with the Wechsler Assessment of Intelligence Scales (WAIS):

While the validity and reliability is strong, counselors should consider that the lowest intelligence score available on the MAB-II is 70. Thus, clients that are likely to be borderline in intelligence (between 65 and 80) should not take the MAB-II.

Using the MAB-II in Counseling

Bonnie has been talking with a counselor at the local college. She's been considering going back to school, but is concerned about how smart the "kids" are nowadays, and whether or not she can compete. She also wants to identify where her academic strengths might be so that she can narrow down the list of major options. She completed the MAB-II on computer and returned for an interpretation of her results.

COUNSELOR: So, Bonnie, what do you expect the results to be?

BONNIE: I'm hoping that I'm at least close to average.

COUNSELOR: What would that mean to you?

BONNIE: That I have what it takes mentally to achieve in college.

COUNSELOR: What else do you think it takes to achieve?

BONNIE: Determination, a support system, and a willingness to make sacrifices.

COUNSELOR: So being successful in college is dependent upon other factors than just being "smart enough." Well, let's see how you performed.

The counselor gave Bonnie a copy of her test results.

COUNSELOR: Well, as you can see on the front page here, your scores ranged from low average to superior on the MAB-II scales. What do you make of that?

BONNIE: That I got my wish. I can't believe that I did so well in math. I didn't expect that. What does information mean? That I'm "in the know?"

COUNSELOR: Well, to some degree, yes. Your verbal scale is higher than your performance scale – but both are still above average. Pages 4 and 5 consist of the scale descriptions. Take a minute to look over those. What do those scales suggest to you about your strengths?

BONNIE: I guess math really might be an option for me. I'm really floored by that! I don't know why I didn't do better on the picture arrangement, but I'm not one who really pays a lot of attention to details.

COUNSELOR: So, perhaps, given your scores in the math scales, you'd like to consider careers in that field?

BONNIE: I suppose I should. I'd also like to look into major and career fields that match my information scores – I wonder about journalism.

The counselor gave Bonnie an outside assignment of brainstorming career options that would match her areas of strength for discussion at the next session. In this situation, the MAB-II gave Bonnie the information she needed to see that she did have the cognitive ability required to be successful in school, and served as a springboard for discussion for career/major fields.

Multi-aptitude Tests: Limitations and Suggestions for Use

Although multi-aptitude tests provide differential measures of ability, expectations for the predictive value of the results may be too high. The scores from multi-aptitude test batteries should not be expected to pinpoint careers. The tests cannot answer specific questions such as "Will I be a good architect?" or "Will I be a good mechanical engineer?" or "Will I be a good surgical nurse?" Only partial answers to these questions can be expected. For example, a space-relation score on an aptitude battery should provide an index of the individual's ability to visualize the effect of three-dimensional movement, which is one of the aptitudes required of architects. However, many other factors, not all of which can be measured by a multi-aptitude battery, need to be considered by the prospective architect. It is therefore important to determine the individual's objectives before testing is accomplished.

"Should I consider being a mechanic?" "Do I have the aptitude to do clerical work?" "Is my finger dexterity good enough to consider assembly work?" Reasonable answers to these questions can be obtained from the results of aptitude tests. More important, however, a meaningful career search may begin once test results are evaluated. The results of multi-aptitude test batteries provide valuable suggestions and clues to be considered along with other information in career decision making.

Many of the following suggestions for fostering the career development of students and adults can be modified and used interchangeably to meet the needs of both groups. These suggestions should not be considered exhaustive of all possibilities of using assessment results to enhance career development; rather, they should be viewed as examples from which exercises can be developed to meet local needs and needs of other groups.

For Schools:

- Provide a list of reading-level appropriate words that represent various abilities and aptitudes for elementary students. Provide written directions that tie into the teacher's curriculum and goals. For example, following 3 step directions might be a goal for a kindergarten or first grade class. Consider how the following directions meets that goal: "Put your name on the paper, circle all the words that best describe you and put an x on the words that do not describe you at all."

- Create a crossword puzzle using a puzzle maker at a site such as discoveryschool.com, using definitions of traits as the descriptors.

- Use appropriate magazines to allow students to create a collage of what they are good at doing.

- Ask students to write a short paragraph on the subject of their personal strengths and weaknesses. Ask students to explain how they can improve their weaknesses.

- Increase awareness of occupations that are related to specific skills by dividing students into teams and giving each team the task to fill in a concept wheel specific to one trait. For example, a team might have "organization" written in a circle in the middle of their worksheet, and their task would be to draw lines coming out of that circle and adding a related occupation at the end of each of the lines.

- Divide students into groups and ask them to identify occupations that match their measured ability scores. Share their findings.

- Conduct a contest to determine who can find the most occupations that match ability subtest scores.

- Play "My Strengths" by having students make a list of the courses and hobbies in which they do best.

- After reviewing ability test results, have them determine whether there is a good match.

- Ask students to share "These Are My Skills," in which selected ability scores are used as a basis for describing their skills. Match the skills with occupations.

- Construct a job box or a service file that has pictures of various occupations. Ask students to match and identify job skills with their ability test results.

- Construct various displays that contain listings of occupations under categories such as verbal aptitude, numerical aptitude, spelling, and mechanical reasoning. Ask students to go to the display that contains occupations that match their test results. Find one or more and discuss.

- Ask students to read a vocational biography of someone in an occupation selected on the basis of ability test results.

- Using an ability test profile, ask students to make a list of several occupations to be considered for further evaluation.

- Ask students to construct resumés that outline their measured abilities.

- Distribute job notices from local newspapers. Have students choose three occupations and then classify each of the jobs into a primary Holland type. Then, have students identify the abilities that the employers are looking for. Create a table (on the blackboard) that has each Holland type as a header. As the counselor calls out each Holland type, have students who had an occupation classified as that type report the job skills required. After all the types have been addressed, have the class note themes, such as which type had the most skills, was there overlap of skills within each type (do they see "S" type skills in an occupation that is mostly "R"), was there overlap across types (did "C" type work show up across all the RIASEC categories) and what do these themes suggest about the world of work and how they should prepare for it?

For Adults:

- Ask adults to compare requirements of occupations with their ability test score results. Share with others.

- In groups, discuss skills needed for certain occupations. Use test results as examples.

- Ask adults to discuss individual strengths and weaknesses. Use test results as examples.

- Ask adults to develop personal profiles of developed abilities.

- Ask adults to discuss the relevance of identified abilities in the career decision-making process.

- Ask adults to share how abilities were developed from previous work and leisure experiences.

- Ask adults to share identified abilities that can be linked to emerging and changing occupational requirements.

- Have adults compare their aptitude test scores with those of other results, such as, an interest inventory or values card sort.

- Ask adults to discuss the relevance of developing abilities in learning over the life span. Use current test results as examples.

Other Aptitude Tests

In addition to the multi-aptitude batteries discussed in this chapter, a number of other batteries are on the market. Here are some examples:

- **Ball Aptitude Battery.** The BAB consists of two levels for grades 9 through 12 and adults. Subtests include Analytical Reasoning, Associative Memory, Auditory Memory Span, Clerical, Idea Generation, Inductive Reasoning, Numerical Computation, Numerical Reasoning, Paper Folding, Vocabulary Word Association and Writing Speed. Three reports are available including a basic profile report, a narrative report, and a pattern indicator.

- **Career Ability Placement Survey.** This test is used to measure abilities of entry requirements for jobs compiled by the authors in 14 occupational clusters. It can be self-scored or machine scored for junior high school, senior high school, college, and adult populations. The eight 1-page tests are timed for five minutes each, and scores are reported in percentiles, stanines and stanine ranges. National normative data provide comparisons of scores for mechanical reasoning, spatial relations, verbal reasoning, numerical ability, language usage, word knowledge, perceptual speed and accuracy, and manual speed and dexterity.

- **Flanagan Aptitude Classification Test.** This test consists of 16 separate tests: inspection, coding, memory, precision, assembly, scales, coordination, judgment/comprehension, arithmetic, patterns, components, tables, mechanics, expression, reasoning, and ingenuity. Each test measures behaviors considered critical to job performance. Selected groups of tests may be administered. The entire battery takes several hours. This test is designed primarily for use with high school students and adults.

- **Inventory of Work-Relevant Abilities (IWRA).** The IWRA is a self-scoring measure of 15 work-relevant abilities. These specific 15 abilities were identified through a study by Abe and Holland (1965), who reported that many of these abilities were not being assessed by other instruments. As a person scores his or her self-estimate, he or she also transfers that estimate to the job cluster columns, which are the RIASEC classifications. In the end, the individual has a scaled score for each of the Holland types. The scaled scores for the Holland types are then compared to obtain the top three types. The person's three-letter code is used to identify relevant World of Work map regions.

- **Kuder Skills Assessment.** The Kuder Skills Assessment provides a self-estimate of abilities, resulting in ratings in the following areas: Outdoor/Mechanical, Science/Technical, Sales/Management, Arts/Communication, Business Operations and Social/Personal Services. The skills assessment filters into the Kuder Career System, and clusters are linked into daily updated articles (online at www.kuder.com), as well as occupations in the online Occupational Outlook Handbook, the Kuder College Majors chart and college searches.

- MicroSkills IV. MicroSkills IV is a program that was designed to help people identify their skills and determine how the skills can be transferred to various occupations. The program consists of several options, including an activity requiring the person to prioritize 35 skills cards (from 72) into three categories based on how satisfying the skills are (very, moderately, and somewhat), comparing the person's skills with those most used in an occupation of interest, evaluating skills used in the past and/or future to generate an occupational list, and comparing those with skills most used in a specific occupation. The list of rated occupations is presented in chart format that demonstrates the relationship between the skills selected by the client and the occupational ratings. Clients can enter in five past jobs and these will be compared with other occupations and skills in those occupations evaluated. There is also an option that allows conversion for ASVAB, Career Occupational

Preference System Interest Inventory (COPS), Career Assessment Inventory (CAI), and the Strong Interest Inventory into related lists of skills and occupations.

- **Modern Occupational Skills Test.** The MOST is an aptitude test from London designed to assess applicant's skills for office, sales and managerial work. The MOST includes nine areas of assessment with three increasingly difficult levels. Level 1 includes Verbal Checking, Numerical Checking and Filing; Level 2 includes Numerical Awareness, Spelling & Grammar and Word Meanings; and Level 3 includes Numerical Estimation, Technical Checking and Decision Making.

- **OASIS-III Aptitude Survey.** The OASIS-III Aptitude Survey is a self or group administered inventory that was developed to assist students in grades 8 through 12 and adults in making career decisions. Specifically, the results provide information about relative strengths through two subtests, an aptitude survey and an interest survey. The OASIS-3 Aptitude Survey consists of the following subtests: General Ability, Verbal Aptitude, Numerical Aptitude, Spatial Aptitude, Perceptual Aptitude and Manual Dexterity. The inventory takes about 30-45 minutes to complete and may be hand or machine scored. Validity coefficients ranged from .6 to .8 when compared to General Aptitude Battery subtests of similar nature. Median alpha reliabilities were reported as ranging from .70 to .91. Blackwell and Lutyhe (2003) reviewed the OASIS 3 and stated that the instrument was both time and cost effective in helping career-undecided students in assessing their aptitudes and interests.

- **ONET Ability Profiler.** A paper and pencil inventory for individuals age 16 and older that measures the following abilities: verbal ability, arithmetic reasoning, computation, spatial ability, form perception, clerical perception, motor coordination, finger dexterity and manual dexterity. Available at http://www.onetcenter.org/AP.html.

- **Wiesen Test of Mechanical Aptitude.** This test is an example of a single aptitude test, focusing on mechanical aptitude of individuals 18 years and older. Its format is paper and pencil, and it takes about 30 minutes to complete. The developers state that the design of the WTMA has resulted in minimal gender and ethnic bias on the measure, and that individuals do not need to have previous experience in a shop class to understand the test. The multiple-choice questions include drawings of basic mechanical concepts.

Summary

Early trait-and-factor approaches to career counseling used ability measures. Multi-aptitude batteries evolved from a growing interest in intra-individual measurement. Ability measures can be used to stimulate discussion of personal characteristics and traits relevant for career decision making. An aptitude is a specific proficiency or an ability to acquire a certain proficiency. The aptitude tests discussed in this chapter measure a variety of skills and abilities.

Questions and Exercises

1. Define aptitude and illustrate how aptitude scores are used in career counseling.

2. What are the major differences between the DAT and the MAB-II? Give an example of a case and specify why you would choose one of these tests over the other to assess the individual's abilities.

3. Is it important for aptitude tests to provide separate sex norms? Why or why not?

4. Why are aptitude test scores generally better predictors of high school and college grades than of occupational success?

5. How would you prepare high school students to interpret the results of the ASVAB? Develop a list of major points you would cover for a presentation to a group or to an individual, parents, teachers and students. (The website for ASVAB has fact sheets for parents and students that might provide a great springboard).

6. A person has taken the Self-Directed Search and has a very strong Realistic code. Would you adjust the way that you normally counsel to be more congruent with this client's type? If so, what changes would you make? If not, explain why not.

7. How would you counsel an individual who claimed that she was not interested in the occupations suggested as a result of her aptitude test?

8. A 16-year-old student is struggling with post-graduation plans. He is currently in ROTC, and although he enjoys the discipline and the group's activities, he is not certain that he wants to pursue a military career. He has taken the ASVAB, and his workbook summary sheet is presented in Figure 4-4. In addition, the first page of the OCCU-FIND is also shown in Figure 4-3. How would you summarize this student's results, and how would you proceed?

9. Given the following MicroSkills IV profile (Figure 4-6), how would you interpret this person's scores? What other information would you like to have? What possible recommendations might you make? What would be your next step?

10. Amber, a ninth grade student has told you that she is interested in several careers, including counselor, nurse, dental hygienist, and physical therapist, but isn't sure she'd be "good" at any of those careers. Based on her student profile of the OASIS-3 (Figure 4-7 a, b and c), how would you advise her?

11. Demitri wants to explore career fields in which he is likely to be most successful. His results of the Kuder Skills Assessment are in Figure 4-8. What observations can you make about his profile, and what occupations might be related? What might some next steps be for Demitri?

12. Review the profile in Figure 4-9 of the CAPS. The abbreviations can be interpreted as MR = Mechanical Reasoning; SR = Spatial Relations; VR = Verbal Reasoning; NA = Numerical Ability; LU = Language Usage; WK = Word Knowledge; PSA = Perceptual Speed and Accuracy; and MSD = Manual Speed and Dexterity. How would you characterize this student's strengths and weaknesses? What recommendations might you make to this student? In what kind of career activities might this person excel? How might this person present in counseling? What changes might you make in your counseling approach with this individual?

MicroSkills IV Fall 1999 Release
Friday, August 18, 2000 - 12:23 PM

For: Robert
Page 1 of 4

Ratings Based Upon Past Jobs and Future Skills

Summary of Robert's Transferable Skills

These are the skills you selected as important to you in a future job:

Very Satisfying Skills

Number	Skill
07	Integrity
39	Writing
44	Visualizing
56	Planning
66	Directing Others

Somewhat Satisfying Skills

Number	Skill
02	Dependability
12	Emotional Control
18	Attending to Details
19	Following Procedures
23	Finger Dexterity
24	Manual Dexterity
33	Calculating
36	Budgeting
40	Editing
45	Drawing
51	Using Facts
52	Using Experience
58	Synthesizing
59	Serving
60	Treating
61	Tact
62	Cooperating
64	Advising
67	Initiating
72	Performing

Moderately Satisfying Skills

Number	Skill
01	Efficiency
03	Flexibility
41	Questioning
43	Conveying Emotions
46	Designing
54	Investigating
57	Analyzing
63	Understanding
65	Decision Making
71	Training

Holland Personality Type:

One way of grouping occupations is to use the Holland Personality Types. The skills you selected have been compared to the six Holland Personality Types. The ratings range from 0 to 100.

Your highest rating is in Social. This probably means you prefer to work with people, solving problems by discussing them and working together.

Type	Rate	Type	Rate
Realistic	9	Social	41
Investigative	24	Enterprising	26
Artistic	40	Conventional	18

Figure 4-6a   From Eureka Microskills. Reproduced with permission of publisher, EUREKA, CCIS.

MicroSkills IV Fall 1999 Release
Friday, August 18, 2000 - 12:23 PM

Ratings Based Upon Past Jobs and Future Skills

Past Job Skills - Detail

These are the past jobs selected as being most enjoyable for Robert.

    Job 1: Animal Caretakers and Keepers
    Job 2: General Office Clerks
    Job 3: Home Health Aides
    Job 4: Martial Arts Fighters (R)
    Job 5: Waiters and Waitresses

The following is a summary of 72 skills and their relative importance in your past jobs.

Skills	Job #:1	2	3	4	5	Skills	Job #:1	2	3	4	5
01 Efficiency	-	S	S	-	M	37 Numerical Reasoning	-	-	-	-	-
02 Dependability	S	S	S	-	V	38 Reading	-	S	S	S	S
03 Flexibility	V	M	V	V	-	39 Writing	-	S	S	-	S
04 Tenacity	S	-	-	S	-	40 Editing	-	-	-	-	-
05 Drive	-	-	S	V	-	41 Questioning	-	S	M	-	-
06 Conformity	-	M	-	-	S	42 Explaining	S	-	S	S	M
07 Integrity	-	S	S	-	S	43 Conveying Emotions	-	-	-	M	-
08 Tolerating Discomfort	V	-	-	S	M	44 Visualizing	M	-	-	M	S
09 Tolerating Repetition	-	S	-	-	V	45 Drawing	-	-	-	-	-
10 Responding to Pressure	S	M	-	M	M	46 Designing	-	-	-	-	-
11 Responding to Feedback	-	S	M	S	S	47 Sound Discrimination	S	M	-	M	S
12 Emotional Control	-	-	S	S	M	48 Color Discrimination	S	S	-	M	-
13 Handling Emergencies	S	-	V	-	-	49 Shape Discrimination	M	M	-	M	S
14 Risk Taking	S	-	-	S	S	50 Depth Perception	S	S	-	S	-
15 Caution	S	S	S	-	-	51 Using Facts	M	S	M	S	-
16 Precision	M	V	S	M	-	52 Using Experience	V	S	M	V	M
17 Alertness	S	S	M	-	S	53 Aesthetic Judgement	-	-	-	V	-
18 Attending to Details	-	M	S	M	S	54 Investigating	S	-	-	-	-
19 Following Procedures	M	V	V	S	S	55 Structuring	-	S	M	S	-
20 Verifying	S	V	-	-	S	56 Planning	M	S	-	S	-
21 Record Keeping	S	V	M	-	S	57 Analyzing	S	-	-	S	-
22 Sorting	-	M	-	-	-	58 Synthesizing	-	-	-	-	-
23 Finger Dexterity	S	M	-	S	S	59 Serving	S	V	V	-	V
24 Manual Dexterity	M	S	S	M	M	60 Treating	-	-	S	-	-
25 Motor Coordination	M	-	M	M	M	61 Tact	-	-	S	S	V
26 Rapid Reaction	S	M	-	S	M	62 Cooperating	S	S	S	S	S
27 Stamina	V	-	-	S	V	63 Understanding	-	-	M	-	-
28 Strength	V	-	V	-	S	64 Advising	-	-	S	-	S
29 Operating	M	M	S	-	-	65 Decision Making	-	-	-	S	-
30 Assembling	-	-	-	-	-	66 Directing Others	S	-	-	S	-
31 Adjusting	-	-	-	-	-	67 Initiating	-	-	-	-	-
32 Counting	-	S	-	-	S	68 Persuading	-	-	M	-	M
33 Calculating	M	S	-	-	S	69 Confronting	-	-	S	-	-
34 Measuring	-	-	S	-	-	70 Negotiating	-	-	-	-	-
35 Estimating	-	-	-	-	-	71 Training	-	-	S	-	-
36 Budgeting	-	-	-	-	-	72 Performing	-	-	-	V	-

Figure 4-6b   From Eureka Microskills. Reproduced with permission of publisher, EUREKA, CCIS.

MicroSkills IV Fall 1999 Release
Friday, August 18, 2000 - 12:23 PM

For: Robert
Page 3 of 4

Ratings Based Upon Past Jobs and Future Skills

Past Job Skills - Composites

These are the past jobs selected as being most enjoyable for Robert.

Job 1: Animal Caretakers and Keepers
Job 2: General Office Clerks
Job 3: Home Health Aides
Job 4: Martial Arts Fighters (R)
Job 5: Waiters and Waitresses

The following is a combined list of the skills that were used most often in the jobs you enjoyed in the past.

Very Satisfying Skills

Number	Skill
03	Flexibility
16	Precision
19	Following Procedures
52	Using Experience
59	Serving

Moderately Satisfying Skills

Number	Skill
08	Tolerating Discomfort
10	Responding to Pressure
21	Record Keeping
24	Manual Dexterity
25	Motor Coordination
26	Rapid Reaction
27	Stamina
28	Strength
49	Shape Discrimination
51	Using Facts

Somewhat Satisfying Skills

Number	Skill
02	Dependability
05	Drive
09	Tolerating Repetition
11	Responding to Feedback
12	Emotional Control
13	Handling Emergencies
17	Alertness
18	Attending to Details
20	Verifying
23	Finger Dexterity
29	Operating
33	Calculating
38	Reading
42	Explaining
44	Visualizing
47	Sound Discrimination
55	Structuring
56	Planning
61	Tact
62	Cooperating

Figure 4-6c From Eureka Microskills. Reproduced with permission of publisher, EUREKA, CCIS.

Ratings Based Upon Past Jobs and Future Skills

Relative Occupational Ratings

Occupational Ratings can go from 0 to 100. The higher the rating, the better the match between a composite of your past job skills plus the skills you would like to use in the future and the skills needed for an occupation. The highest rated occupations are listed. A score of 30 or higher is a close match. These occupations should be well matched to both your past and desired future skills.

Animal Health Technicians	36
Glaziers	36
Floor Covering Installers	36
Licensed Vocational Nurses	35
Recreation Program Directors	35
Parapsychologists (R)	34
School Psychologists (R)	34
Adult Education Teachers (R)	34
Lecturers	34
Driving Instructors (R)	34
Computer Software Training Specialists (R)	34
Casino Dealers (R)	34
Lifeguards (R)	34
Records Managers (R)	34
Employee Development Specialists (R)	34
Farm Labor Contractors	34
Psychiatric Social Workers (R)	34
Houseparents (R)	34
Genetic Counselors (R)	34
Electricians	33
Clothes Designers	33
Nursing Assistants	33
Home Health Aides	33
Bilingual School Teachers	33
Education Program Specialists	33
Sheet Metal Workers	33
Handcrafters	32
Railroad Engineers	31
Dietitians and Nutritionists	31
Millwrights	31
Crime Laboratory Technicians	31
Grounds Managers (R)	30
Beekeepers (R)	30
Ranchers	30
Dairy Workers (R)	30

Figure 4-6d   From Eureka Microskills. Reproduced with permission of publisher, EUREKA, CCIS.

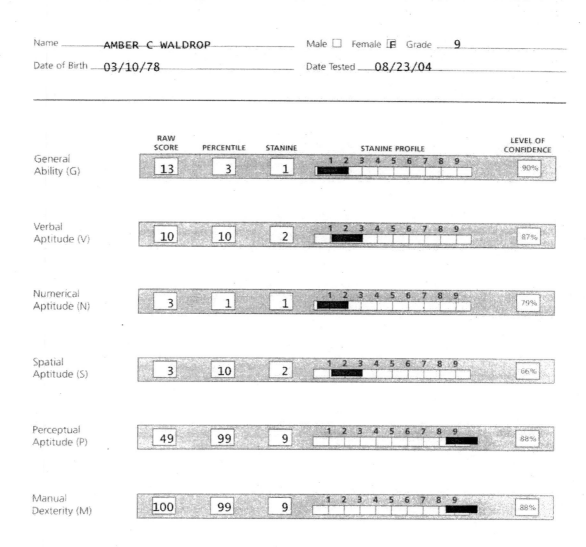

PRO-ED, 8700 Shoal Creek Blvd., Austin, TX 78757-6897
800/897-3202, Fax 800/397-7633, www.proedinc.com

Figure 4-7a   From The Occupational Aptitude Survey and Interest Schedule, Third Edition. Copyright © 2002 by R.M. Parker. Reproduced by permission of the publisher, PRO-ED.

Interpreting Your
Aptitude Survey Scores

The *Occupational Aptitude Survey and Interest Schedule–Third Edition* (OASIS–3) was developed to assist individuals in vocational exploration and career development. Two scores, percentile and stanine scores, are important in understanding your profile results.

The percentile and stanine scores on your profile compare your interests to a national sample of students. The percentile scores show the percentage of people scoring lower than you. If, for example, you score at the 90th percentile on the General Ability (G) scale, you score higher than 90% of the people in the national norm group on that scale. If you receive a score at the 10th percentile on Perceptual Aptitude (P), you score higher than 10% of the norm group.

The stanine, which ranges from 1 to 9, is an equal-interval score used in plotting your profile. Because all test scores have some error, it is important to know what confidence you can have that the test scores are accurate. The probability values shown for each of the six scales at the right of the profile show how much confidence you can have in your plotted stanine scores. For example, you can have 90% confidence that your G score is within ±1 stanine of the plotted score. This is the confidence you can have that, if you took the Aptitude Survey again, your score would not change by more than ±1 stanine, assuming your real abilities remained the same. Also, you can have at least 90% confidence that any scores that differ by 2 stanines are truly different. For instance, if your Verbal Aptitude (V) stanine is 9 and your Numerical Aptitude (N) stanine is 7, you can have 90% confidence that they are in fact different. A difference that large is not likely due to error of measurement.

Here are descriptions of the 6 scores that will help you understand what your profile means.

General Ability (G). The ability to learn and achieve in training or academic situations. People who get high scores "catch on" quickly in new situations, and are proficient in making judgments and in grasping underlying principles and solving problems. This factor is measured by the Vocabulary subtest plus the Computation subtest scores.

Verbal Aptitude (V). The ability to understand and use words effectively, to comprehend verbal concepts and language, and to express ideas clearly in words. People who score highly generally do well in school, particularly in subjects where verbal concepts are important. This factor is measured by the Vocabulary subtest.

Numerical Aptitude (N). The ability to do arithmetic and other numerical computations quickly and accurately. People who score highly on N may do well in such school subjects as math and physics. This factor is measured by the Computation subtest.

Spatial Aptitude (S). The ability to visualize two-dimensional objects in three-dimensional space, and to mentally manipulate objects through different spatial orientations. People who get high scores have the aptitude to perform well in school subjects and work involving drafting, art, architecture, clothes designing, and similar tasks. This factor is measured by the Spatial Relations subtest.

Perceptual Aptitude (P). The ability to compare and discriminate words, numbers, symbols, or other graphic material to see if slight differences exist between them. People who score highly in this area should do well in proofreading, copyediting, and nonverbal tasks that require attention to detail and rapid visual discriminations. This factor is measured by the Word Comparison subtest.

Manual Dexterity (M). The ability to coordinate eye and hand movements and perform manual tasks rapidly and accurately. High scores indicate the ability to manipulate tools and objects with speed and precision. This factor is measured by the Making Marks subtest.

Please use this information to learn more about yourself and about different occupations. Best wishes in finding a satisfying career!

Figure 4-7b   From The Occupational Aptitude Survey and Interest Schedule, Third Edition. Copyright © 2002 by R.M. Parker. Reproduced by permission of the publisher, PRO-ED.

Provided by:
National Career Assessment Services, Inc.
www.kuder.com

Congratulations **Demitri F.**! You have completed the Kuder® Skills Assessment. Your report will help you understand your skill level in several career clusters and guide you through another phase of the Career Exploration Process. Follow the steps and be sure to read all the information. You may want to review this report with your family, friends or a career counselor. As you proceed with your career exploration think of it as a journey, with each part an integral step towards your destination.

Step I. Review Your Skills Profile

Most occupations or jobs can be grouped into one of six areas. We call these areas Kuder® Career Clusters. Your skills profile is shown below. It should help you develop a clearer picture of the skills you possess related to hundreds of different occupations. Keep your top two or three highest skill areas (as indicated by Kuder® Career Clusters) in mind as you think about your future career plans, and save them in your Kuder® Electronic Career Portfolio under "Career Exploration and Favorite Sites". A description of each cluster is available by clicking on the name of the cluster in the chart below.

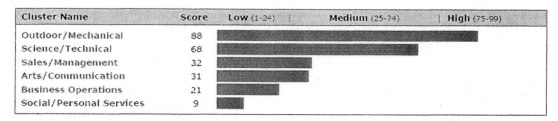

Cluster Name	Score	Low (1-24)	Medium (25-74)	High (75-99)
Outdoor/Mechanical	88			
Science/Technical	68			
Sales/Management	32			
Arts/Communication	31			
Business Operations	21			
Social/Personal Services	9			

Demitri, your scores are shown in percentiles, based on a combined norm group of males and females. For example, your score of **88** on the Outdoor/Mechanical cluster means that you scored higher than **88** percent of the norm group on skills related to Outdoor/Mechanical occupations.

THE IMPORTANT INFORMATION IS THE RANK ORDER OF THE CLUSTERS, NOT THE EXACT SCORES. You should think of your results in terms of , "I have the most skills in the Outdoor/Mechanical cluster, next most in the Science/Technical cluster, and so on.

Figure 4-8   From Kuder Skills Assessment. Reprinted with permission of National Career Assessment Services, Inc. All rights reserved.

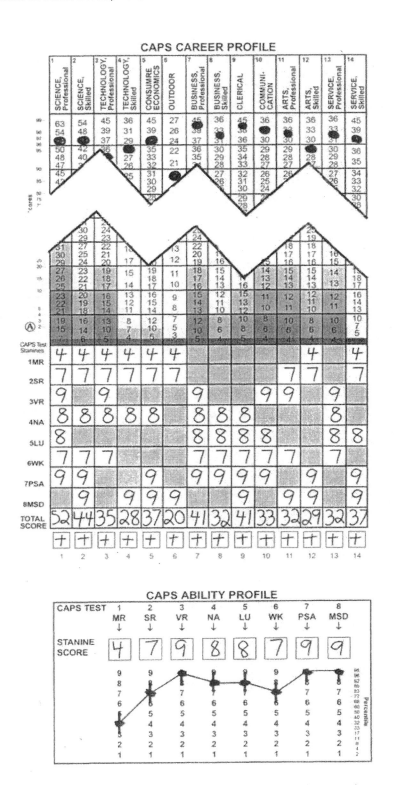

Figure 4-9 CAPS Ability Profile. Reproduced with permission of the publisher, EdITS.

5 Using Achievement Tests

The career counselor has to be concerned with each client's academic achievement. Levels of competence in reading, language usage, and mathematics may be the key to rejection or consideration of certain educational and vocational plans. In fact, most career planning in one way or another is related to academic proficiency. The decision to obtain education and training beyond high school is often based directly on developed abilities as measured by achievement tests. Many vocations that do not require college training do require that the individual be able to read, do arithmetic, and write. In fact, workers' survival in the 21st century will depend largely on their levels of training. The client's level of basic skills determines future training and career-planning opportunities.

Outcomes of achievement tests have been related to students' academic grades (Cooper, Lindsay, Nye, & Greathouse, 1998). Thus, achievement tests provide results that can be linked to most occupational requirements, not to mention that achievement tests can identify potential areas needing remediation (such as vocabulary), which might impact a person's job search (resumé, cover letter and interviewing capabilities). As always, counselors should review normative data and research on specific achievement tests when using or interpreting for diverse clients.

Career counselors should understand the difference between achievement tests and aptitude tests. Both measure learning experience. However, achievement tests measure learning of relatively restricted items and in limited content areas—that is, learning related to an academic setting. In a review of the literature, Petrill and Wilkerson (2000) report that achievement test results are affected by genetics and environmental influences. Aptitude tests measure specific skills, abilities, or achievement learned from a variety of experiences. Some professional test users argue, however, that there is actually little difference between what achievement tests and aptitude tests measure.

The Impact of Beliefs on Achievement Scores

In the previous chapter, we raised the question of how one's measured aptitudes can differ from their perception of their abilities, and we suggested that one's beliefs might affect a person's self-estimates of abilities. This has also been a concern of researchers interested in the use of achievement tests. For example, one researcher (Abu-Hilal, 2000) found that attitudes toward testing and academic aspirations significantly influenced the standardized achievement scores of high school seniors. Another study examined how beliefs impacted math achievement test scores for men and women revealed that women scored worse on math tests they thought would indicate whether or not they were especially weak in math. For the test that women believed would indicate whether or not they were especially strong in math, the women scored better, whereas the men scored worse (Brown & Josephs, 1999). Low self-concept has also been found to correlate with lower scores on 9 to 11 year olds' standardized achievement scores on math, reading, and spelling (Hay, Ashman, & Van Kraayenoord, 1998). Other researchers have reported similar findings (Bouffard, Markovitz, Vezeau, Boisvert, & Dumas, 1998; Marsh & Yeung, 1998; Rangappa, 1994).

As counselors using achievement test scores, it is necessary for us to evaluate the degree to which negative beliefs about self may have affected the student's achievement scores. Betz (1994; 1997) identified this as a crucial issue for women's career development. If girls embrace the idea that they are inferior in math and science, they will opt out of those classes—classes that would eventually lead to jobs in traditionally higher paying fields such as medicine and engineering. Betz pointed out that currently women make up 45% of the work force, yet only 16% of scientists and engineers. As discussed earlier, relying on the results of any one test as the sole basis for career decision making would be unwise. Instead, the counselor should employ various tools in assisting with a person's career decision and always be listening for and challenging negative self-talk that might be hindering the client's performance and subsequent options.

In this chapter, we first review and discuss one survey battery and give an example of the use of the survey battery in career counseling. We then review an achievement test designed to measure basic skills in arithmetic, reading, and spelling and give an example of its use. Next, a case example illustrates the use of achievement test results for self-concept development. This is followed by another case example that illustrates the use of achievement test results to develop self-efficacy. Finally, more strategies for the developmental use of achievement tests are listed.

Types of Achievement Tests

Numerous achievement tests are on the market today. They are usually either general survey batteries covering several subject areas or single-subject tests. They can be criterion-referenced or norm-referenced or both. Achievement tests are usually identified by grade level. It is important to establish the specific purpose for giving an achievement test to decide what type to use. The general survey battery should be chosen when comparisons of achievement in different content areas are needed. The survey battery provides a relatively limited sampling of each content area but, as the name implies, covers a broad spectrum of content areas. More items and more aspects of the subject are usually covered in a single-subject test than in a survey battery. The single-subject test should be chosen when a precise and thorough evaluation of achievement in one subject is needed.

Table 5-1	Survey vs. Single-Subject		
		Survey Battery	Single-Subject Test
Wanting to assess one area in depth			X
Wanting to assess a number of areas briefly and efficiently		X	

In educational planning, it is often desirable to choose a single-subject test when detailed information about a person's capabilities in that particular subject is necessary. The saving in testing time is also a major consideration in the decision to use a single-subject test. Both types of tests can be used as diagnostic instruments when measurement of specific skills or abilities and proficiencies can be related to occupational requirements. Detection of a specific deficiency is also valuable for referral to remedial programs.

Stanford Achievement Test (STAT)

The 10th edition of the Stanford Achievement Test (STAT) is a good example of a survey battery. This test was first published more than 50 years ago and has undergone numerous revisions. The test may be hand scored or computer scored. The publisher provides a comprehensive, computerized reporting service to assist local administrators with instructional planning and reporting to the public. The purpose is to inform about what students know and are able to do. The test is un-timed, although timing guidelines are included.

The first high school battery of the STAT was published in 1965. Developers of this test thoroughly reviewed textbooks and many different curriculum patterns. Items were edited by individuals from various minority groups and were evaluated in trial programs involving 61,000 students in 1445 classrooms in 47 different school systems. Frequent revisions of the test have been made to stay abreast of changing curriculum patterns. Several guides designed to aid in the interpretation of results enhance the general use of the test. Because of the high level of the skills assessed, this test is particularly useful for helping individuals make plans for college. Reviews by Drummond (2004), Brown (1993), and Stoker (1993) provide additional information for evaluating the development and use of this instrument.

A study of the eighth version of the STAT and gender differences (among 7th to 12th graders) in scores revealed only minimal differences (Slate, Jones, Sloas, & Blake, 1998). Reliability established by split-half estimates for each subtest range from .87 to .95. Reliability estimates based on KR-20 range from .86 to .94. Content validity is well documented by a thorough explanation of the evaluation and editing process for test items. Construct validity is based on correlations with prior editions of the test, internal consistency of items, and evidence of the decreasing difficulty of items with progress in school.

Interpreting the Stanford Achievement Test

Figure 5-1 illustrates how stanine scores and percentile equivalents are to be interpreted; their position under the normal distribution is a good frame of reference. The tenth edition of the Stanford Achievement Test Score Report presents raw and scaled scores, national and local percentiles, grade equivalents, and national grade percentile bands for each subtest and total score. A multiple-score report such as this one lends itself to meaningful interpretations for career counseling because the combination of scores displayed provides the counselor and the client with an overview of achievement by subject. Particular attention should be given to the scaled scores, which provide an index for comparing growth from one grade level to another.

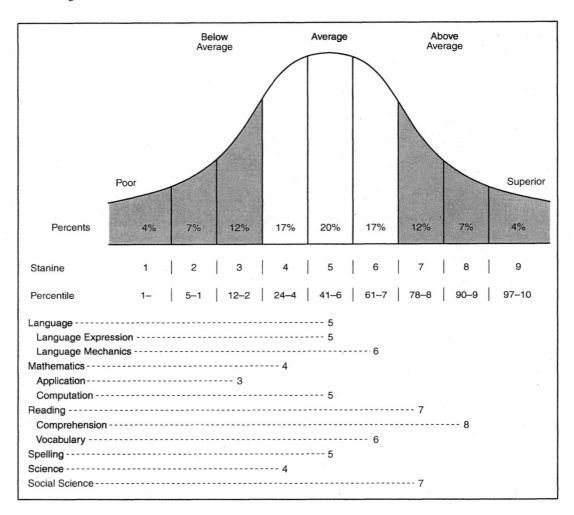

Figure 5-1

Table 5-2 contains fictitious scores for illustrating how raw scores are converted to scaled scores on a math computation test. By using such a table, you can compare performance in grade 9, for example, with the score in math computation in grade 12. However, the table should not be used to compare performance in one subject with performance in another. The advantage of scaled scores is that they provide equal units on a continuous scale for making comparisons.

Table 5-2	Interpreting Scaled Scores for Any Achievement Test

Number Right (Raw Score)	Reading Comprehension Scaled Score	Reading Number Right (Raw Score)	Reading Comprehension Scaled Score	Number Right (Raw Score)	Comprehension Scaled Score
40	284	26	258	13	226
39	284	25	257	12	221
38	283	24	255	11	216
37	282	23	254	10	214
36	280	22	251	9	210
35	279	21	249	8	205
34	276	20	248	7	201
33	275	19	245	6	195
32	274	18	242	5	193
31	273	17	238	4	188
30	269	16	237	3	184
29	268	15	231	2	181
28	262	14	228	1	178
27	261				

Case of a High School Student Referred to a Counselor Because of Poor Grades

Li, a junior in high school, was referred to the career counselor by his English teacher, who reported that Li was a poor student in English and, even with tutoring, had difficulty maintaining the level of performance necessary to pass the course. Earned course grades and comments from previous teachers reflected the same concerns. The teacher reported that Li's parents were insisting that he attends college, and Li was trying to meet their expectations of him. According to the teacher, Li was making a maximum effort but was having little success.

The counselor reviewed the results of an achievement test survey battery that had been administered during the current semester. A summary of Li's scores is shown in Table 5-3. The counselor concluded that the reported weaknesses in language usage were certainly verified by Li's recent achievement test results. The counselor found that previous test data for Li followed the same pattern —a weakness in language skills and average or better performance in mathematical computation.

Table 5-3	Achievement Test Survey Battery Results for Li

Test	National Percentile Equivalent	National Stanine
Reading comprehension	17	3
Vocabulary	20	3
Math reasoning	38	4
Math computation	57	5
Language usage		
Spelling	09	2
Grammar	11	3
Social science	19	3
Science	32	4

Li spoke softly and volunteered little information. He seemed proud of but also somewhat threatened by the fact that his two older brothers were attending college. He reported that his father owned and operated a manufacturing firm. Both his parents were college graduates.

When the counselor asked Li about his plans for the future, he answered with a well-rehearsed "I want to be an accountant." The counselor acknowledged Li's response positively and explored in more detail Li's interest in the field of business. During the course of the conversation, it became apparent that Li possessed little knowledge about the work activities of an accountant. To Li, the job was the same as bookkeeping. However, the counselor had established rapport with Li and had been able to get him to project into the future and to talk about what he perceived as a good job.

Before the next counseling session, the counselor consulted Li's math teacher: "Li has good computational skills and really tries hard; he certainly is not my top student in mathematics, but he does well in applications." This information confirmed the results of the previous test data and of the recently administered achievement test. The counselor was encouraged, for now he could include some positive facts when giving Li the test results.

At the next session, after a brief period of small talk designed to reinforce the rapport already established, the counselor suggested that they discuss the achievement test results. "Your score is at the 17th percentile on reading comprehension. This means that 17 out of 100 11th graders nationally scored lower than you while 83 out of 100 11th graders scored higher." The counselor explained the other scores in the same manner and then discussed groups of scores.

Li was particularly sensitive to his low scores in language usage. He commented that he had always had problems with English courses. The counselor asked that he explain how this problem could affect his plans for educational training and a career. Li acknowledged that he would have problems in college; his brothers had told him the English courses were difficult.

The counselor sensed that it was the right time to introduce encouraging information and an alternative potential career goal: "The field of business is broad and has many opportunities for you, particularly with your good math skills. We can explore some careers that require math skills, but that do not necessarily require a college degree. A couple of occupations that I can think of offhand are bookkeeping and bank teller." Li was delighted with this information and in subsequent counseling sessions made reports on several careers he had researched in the career resource center. He seemed most interested in bookkeeping.

In a meeting with the counselor, Li's parents expressed their appreciation for Li's enthusiasm and interest in career exploration. They said they had hoped that Li could attend college as his brothers had, but they recently came to the realization that Li was not as academically inclined. They now planned to encourage and support Li's interest in alternative careers.

In this case, the achievement test results were linked easily to educational planning and occupational information. Li and his parents recognized that his weak English skills would make it difficult for him to be a successful college student but that his relatively higher skills in mathematics opened other occupational opportunities.

Wide Range Achievement Test–Revision 3 (WRAT3)

The WRAT3, first standardized in 1936, revised in 1984, and revised again in 1993, is an example of an abbreviated achievement test measuring arithmetic, reading, and spelling. The arithmetic section can be given in approximately ten minutes and consists of counting, reading number symbols, and oral and written computation. The spelling section includes writing one's name, writing letters, and writing words from dictation. The reading section focuses on recognizing and naming letters and pronouncing printed words. The test can be given in a relatively short time when the arithmetic and spelling sections are given in a group setting. Whereas the 1984 version divided each subtest into two levels, the 1993 version reverted to only one level to make scoring easier on the recommendation of many users. There are two alternative test forms available, as well as a profile/analysis form to compare and combine the results from the two separate forms.

The norms for the WRAT3 involved more than 5000 people in a national stratified sample. The sample was stratified to reflect 1990 U.S. census data. Relative to technical information, the manual reports that the item separation indices for each of the nine tests were 1.00, which is the highest score possible. Item separation indices indicate how well the items define the variable being measured.

Median test coefficient alphas for the nine WRAT3 tests ranged from .85 to .95 and from .92 to .95 for the three combined tests. Test-retest reliabilities were reported as ranging from .91 to .98. The manual does not state the time interval between testings, but it does provide extensive information about how content and construct validity was achieved. The authors make statements about construct validity, but there are no studies cited to support those assertions.

Interpreting the WRAT3

The results are reported in percentiles, grade equivalents, stanines, standard scores, T scores, and scaled scores by age groups. The normative tables have a wide range; they are grouped by age from 5 years to 55–64 years. The standard scores have a mean of 100 and a standard deviation of 15.

The chief advantage of the WRAT3 is that it can be given in a relatively short time and can be used as a screening instrument for educational planning. It is particularly useful for testing individuals whose educational achievement is low; it gives an estimate of their developed abilities that can be used for vocational placement. Several case studies are reported in the manual to illustrate the use of the WRAT3.

The first page of the Profile/Analysis form (see Figure 5-2) displays a normal curve with several scales underneath, which allows the counselor to quickly see a graphical representation of how a person performed on the various scales. The second and third pages of the form show item maps for each of the academic variables, which are depicted as measures of the basic skills. An individual's level or progress can be plotted using these item maps, which allow a person to see the type and difficulty level of the items that are accomplished at an individual's particular skill level.

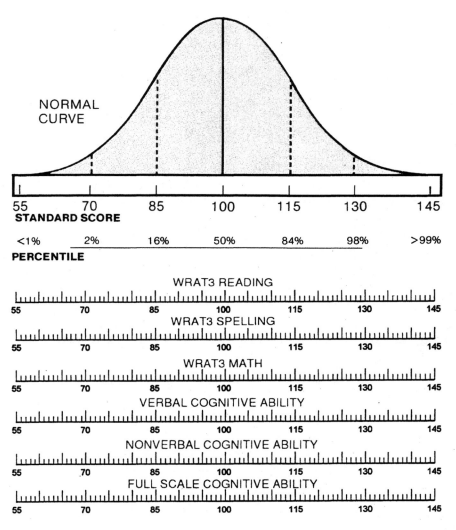

Figure 5-2   WRAT3 Profile Form. Copyright © 1993 by Wide Range, Inc. Reproduced with permission.

Case of a School Dropout Interested in Changing Jobs

Diana, 24 years old, dropped out of school when she was in the seventh grade. She had worked at a number of odd jobs but mainly as a nurse's aide and came to the career-counseling center to find out what the requirements were for licensed vocational nurse (LVN). After reviewing the requirements, she asked the counselor whether there was some way of determining how she would do in LVN training and in classes that prepare individuals to obtain a high school equivalency diploma. The counselor suggested that she take an achievement test to get a rough estimate of her educational level in arithmetic, reading, and spelling. The WRAT3 was selected because it specifically measures basic achievement in those areas and can be quickly administered and scored.

The results of the WRAT3 for Diana are listed in Table 5-4. The counselor recognized Diana's disappointment with her performance. However, the counselor pointed out that a high school diploma was not a prerequisite for entering the local LVN training program. In discussing why she wanted to be a LVN, Diana expressed a sincere desire to help people.

Table 5-4	WRAT3 Results for Diana		
Test	Stanine	Percentile	Standard Score
Arithmetic	3	12	82
Reading	2	09	80
Spelling	2	08	79

Before Diana returned for her next appointment, the counselor reviewed the items Diana had missed on the test. It was obvious that Diana's spelling skills were poor, but an item analysis of the arithmetic test revealed that she made a number of careless mistakes. A review of the reading test revealed that Diana's word attack skills were poor, probably because she had not been exposed to many of the words she missed.

At the next counseling session, the counselor reviewed her item analysis of Diana's test results by pointing out careless mistakes and a lack of self-confidence in attempting words on the oral reading test. Diana appreciated being given concrete examples of her mistakes; she realized that she might do better with greater exposure to academic materials. In subsequent meetings, Diana agreed to enter a remedial program sponsored by the high school learning assistance center. When Diana was asked about the decision, she stated, "I've always been afraid of tests. Now—could you believe it?—the test scores helped me see the light!" Diana's career exploration was enhanced in a number of ways by the test. First, she was encouraged to upgrade her vocational skills by further academic training. Second, she gained self-confidence by diagnosing the mistakes on her test. By encouraging her to upgrade her skills through educational programs, the counselor helped make other work opportunities available to Diana.

Using Achievement Test Results for Self-Concept and Self-Efficacy Development

The last two case studies in this chapter do not have specifically named achievement tests. The focus in these two cases is on how the results of achievement test scores are used for career development. Career counselors will find that numerous achievement tests on the market will meet individual and group needs.

As mentioned earlier in this chapter, self-concept and self-efficacy development are emerging topics of importance in career counseling today. Counseling programs designed to address these two topics are not limited to achievement test results; on the contrary, counseling programs may be developed from a variety and combination of assessment results.

The Case of the Client with Limited Educational and Vocational Experience

Rita was referred to the career counselor by a local social service agency. She had been deserted by her husband after ten years of marriage and left with three children. She had little work experience. Her school grades were poor, and she had dropped out of school while in the seventh grade to get married.

The counselor was not surprised to find that Rita was depressed. It became quite clear during the intake interview that Rita had developed a very poor self-concept; she was especially critical of her academic basic skills. She simply felt that she had little or nothing to offer an employer.

Although the counselor recognized that there might be many reasons for Rita's poor self-concept, an outstanding problem was her inability to identify functional skills and abilities that could be used to establish career goals. The counselor noticed that Rita was able to express herself fairly well and used proper grammar. Perhaps, he thought, Rita may have more ability than she realized. Her alertness gave at least some positive clues that she could, under the right circumstances, improve her basic skills.

As the interview continued, the counselor realized that he must build counseling strategies that focus on building a more positive self-concept. He reasoned that Rita's poor self-concept might make it very difficult for her to build enough self-confidence to aggressively pursue a training program or seek employment. It became clear that many hard recent personal experiences would make it difficult for Rita to project into the work world in a positive manner. Furthermore, she had experienced social forces that were major determinants of poor self-concept formation. As Rita saw it, an active life role in society was at this point an unattainable goal.

The Counseling Plan for Rita

The major focus of the counseling plan was the development of skills that could be used for employment to help meet the needs of her family. The first step would include developing a more positive self-concept through skill assessment and development. The counselor would emphasize positive aspects of measured skills and establish goals to improve them. Rita's strengths and weaknesses both would be approached in a positive manner; that is, strengths would be identified with required skills in occupations and weaknesses would be used as starting points for improving skills. Following is a summary of the counseling plan:

1. Suggest an assessment instrument designed for adults that evaluates basic skills in language usage, mathematics, reading, and writing.

2. Criterion-referenced scores would be used. Link the needs for basic skills to employment.

3. Use the results of assessment to determine a training program.

4. Ask Rita to describe a plan of action for improving basic educational skills.

5. Direct Rita to identify and appreciate personal interests and skills.

6. Assist Rita to clarify career and life goals based on an understanding of self.

7. Ask Rita to describe the relationships between personal behavior and self-concept.

8. Be prepared to offer other counseling needs.

In this case, the importance of self-concept formation was stressed, and the counselor decided that a direct link to employment was the best approach to use. Adults often react favorably to counseling programs that are clearly delineated and demonstrate how counseling goals are related to future employment. For Rita, it seemed particularly important to design a counseling program that provided a means of personal improvement to restore the self-confidence she was lacking. Like all clients, Rita must be able to project her self-concept into a work role.

The Case of the Girl Who Had Difficulty with Math

When Evita reported to the counseling center, she was confused about why she had been referred by her teacher. "So I have trouble with math like all other girls; so what?" she thought. "It doesn't make sense that because I can't get the problems in class, I'm sent to a counselor," she confided to a friend.

Although Evita's teacher had carefully explained that she believed Evita's poor performance in math was symptomatic of an underlying problem, Evita refused to accept that explanation. Realizing Evita's reluctance to visit the counseling center, Evita's teacher had a conference with a counselor.

Evita's teacher explained the problem as she saw it: "I have been trying to figure out why Evita's grades have been significantly dropping this year. She seemed to be an outstanding student, but when she started this last math course it seems that all of her grades dropped. I am not aware of personal or family problems, but this girl needs your help!" Evita had never been a problem student, and, as instructed, she reported to the counselor's office. The counselor immediately tried to comfort Evita by telling her that teachers often sent students to see her. After a briefing of the services offered at the counseling center and small talk design to establish rapport, Evita became more comfortable and begin to express herself.

During the course of several counseling sessions, the counselor made note of the number of times that Evita mentioned "girls are just not good in math." However, this feeling of lack of confidence in math seemed more pervasive. Evita begin to express doubts about her ability in other subjects and skills as well. The counselor remembered the teacher's remark that Evita's grades had been dropping in all subjects. The counselor scanned the results of several achievement tests over the past three years. A clear pattern of low achievement in all subjects was obvious from Evita's recent records. Yet, in further probes of Evita's activities during this time period, there was no evidence of any significant event that could be responsible for home or personal problems. There was also no evidence of substance abuse or poor health.

The counselor had established an excellent counseling relationship with Evita but had difficulty in finding underlying problems that could be contributing factors to a significant change in academic achievement. The counselor began to research specific problems in women's career development and found that self-efficacy was a significant problem for many women. For instance, Betz (1992) defines career self-efficacy as "the possibility that low expectations of efficacy with respect to some aspect of career behavior may serve as a detriment to optimal career choice and the development of the individual" (p. 24). Furthermore, self-efficacy deficits may lead to procrastination in or avoidance of making a career decision.

The counselor believed that she had found Evita's underlying problem, but she was wisely cautious. In counseling sessions, she carefully led to the subject of career choice and found that Evita was quite undecided about the future, which she expressed with overtones of lack of confidence and confusion about what the future might hold in store for her. It seemed clear that Evita had poor planning skills and had given little thought to career decision-making. In fact, she seemed to want to avoid these subjects as though she was not ready to tackle them.

Before talking to Evita's teacher and developing any counseling strategies, the counselor decided to wait for the next administration of achievement tests, which were to begin in a few days. When the results came in indicating another significant drop in achievement for Evita, the counselor developed a counseling plan.

Counseling Plan for Evita

The major thrust of this plan would be to increase Evita's expectations of efficacy by the following methods:

1. Provide opportunities for performing successfully, especially in math.

2. Select positive role models for visits and discussions.

3. Provide ways to deal with stress and anxiety.

4. Provide support and encouragement from significant others.

5. Discuss the problems of self-efficacy, especially as they affect women and their career development.

6. Discuss the impact of negative thinking on feelings and behavior, and introduce cognitive reframing exercises.

7. Develop a personal agency perspective that suggests that all individuals be responsible for their career development (Zunker, 2002).

In this case, achievement test results played an important role in providing objective data that ultimately led to the development of a counseling plan. The counselor and the teacher collaborated to help a very confused student regain momentum for completing course work in a timely manner. Evita discovered that what she told herself about herself greatly affected her behavior. She learned that when you expect positive results through self-evaluation, your performance usually improves.

▌ Suggestions for Career Development

Many of the following suggestions for fostering the career development of students and adults can be modified and used interchangeably to meet the needs of both groups. These suggestions should not be considered an exhaustive means of using assessment results to enhance career development; rather, they are examples from which exercises can be developed to meet local needs and needs of other groups.

For Schools:

- Ask students to identify personal strengths and weaknesses as measured by achievement test results. Using this information, identify related work tasks for selected occupations or career clusters. Ask students to identify relationships between ability and achievement.

- Ask students to develop a plan for improving their academic skills.

- Form discussion groups for the purpose of linking basic skills to occupations.

- Ask students to identify and compare levels of achievement to selected occupations. Ask students to discuss the relationships between student roles and work roles.

- Ask students to relate academic skills to interests and values.

- Ask students to identify basic skills used in selected occupations in the community and compare them with their own.

- Ask students to discuss the relationship of academic achievement and self-concept development.

- Ask students to discuss how one's self-talk impacts how he or she would describe their abilities and academic skills.

For Adults:

- Form groups and ask adults to discuss and identify the relationship of obsolescence to achievement results.

- Ask adults to identify the changes in training requirements for selected occupations. Match their achievement results with some new or different occupations.

- Ask adults to identify the necessity of acquiring basic skills for many occupations. Have them make a list of occupations with matching basic skills. Then compare achievement test results with requirements of selected occupations.

- Ask adults to identify and discuss the limitations of advancement in many occupations because of poor basic skill achievement. Using assessment results, have them develop plans for improving basic skills.

- Ask adults to discuss the necessity of training for making career transitions. Relate achievement to training requirements.

- Using achievement test results, have them develop educational plans to meet requirements of selected jobs.

- Have adults develop a positive view of self by assessing strengths, and potentials, from achievement test results.

- Ask students to compare self-rated achievement results with the results of a standardized test and share their conclusions.

Other Achievement Tests

Because many published achievement tests are currently available, the following list is far from complete. The following seven examples of various achievement tests include four survey batteries and three diagnostic tests.

- **Basic Achievement Skills Inventory (BASI).** A comprehensive achievement test for ages 8 to 80 that consists of 6 timed subtests, including Vocabulary, Spelling, Language Mechanics, Reading Comprehension, Math Computation and Math Application. The BASI was normed on a sample matching 2000 U.S. Census data and can be group or self-administered.

- **Basic Achievement Skills Individual Screener (BASIS).** This test is to be used for grade 1 through post-high school. It contains three subtests: Reading, Spelling, and Mathematics, with an optional writing exercise. BASIS is criterion and norm referenced. It is designed to help individuals (exceptional and special populations) formulate educational plans. It takes one hour to administer.

- **Iowa Test of Basic Skills.** This survey battery tests five major areas: vocabulary, reading comprehension, language skills, work-study skills (reading graphs and maps and using reference material), and mathematics. Some item overlap exists across grades. Scores are provided as grade equivalents and grade percentile norms.

- **Kaufman Test of Educational Achievement, Second Edition.** The KTEA-II is an individually administered battery that includes 5 composites (Reading, Math, Written Language, Oral Language and Comprehensive Achievement) and one Reading-related subtest that consists of six areas. The Comprehensive Form can be used on ages 4.6 through 25, and the Brief Form can be used on ages 4.6 through 90+. Scores are presented via standard scores, with a mean of 100 and a standard deviation of 15, age and grade equivalents, percentile ranks, stanines and normal curve equivalents.

- **Peabody Individual Achievement Test-Revised-Normative Update (PIAT-R/NU).** This test provides grade equivalents, age percentile ranks, and standard scores by age or grade for reading comprehension, reading recognition, written expression, mathematics, spelling, and general knowledge (science, social studies, fine arts, and sports). The PIAT is designed to be used with individuals from age 5 to adulthood. It takes 30 to 50 minutes to administer.

- **Stanford Diagnostic Mathematics Test-4th Edition.** A group-administered test, this test measures knowledge in basic concepts of math that are critical to future success in math, and also problem-solving strategies. The test has six levels, ranging from grades 1.5 to 13.0 and ranging in total time from 145 to 155 minutes.

- **TerraNova-Second Edition (TerraNova CAT).** An achievement test series used in public and private schools and provides results on Reading, Language, Mathematics, Science and Social Studies. Five performance levels are identified – Advanced, Proficient, Nearing Proficiency, Progressing and Step 1/Starting Out. Item content was developed after consultation with national, state and local standards.

- **Woodcock Johnson III.** The complete battery consists of achievement tests and tests of cognitive abilities. There are co-normed tests of general intellectual ability, specific cognitive abilities, scholastic aptitude, oral language and academic achievement.

Summary

Academic achievement is a primary consideration in educational and vocational planning. For educational planning, there is a direct relationship, and almost all jobs are linked to achievement of basic skills. Compared with aptitude tests, achievement tests measure much narrower content areas and more limited learning experiences. Aptitude tests measure broader areas of abilities and experiences. There are two types of achievement tests: general survey batteries and single-subject tests. Achievement test results are reported as norm-referenced scores, criterion-referenced scores, or both. Counselors should be aware of the potential of self-concept to affect an individual's performance on an achievement test.

Questions and Exercises

1. Explain the difference between achievement and aptitude tests. Illustrate your explanation with an example of a case in which you would use one or the other kind of test.

2. What is the difference between a norm-referenced and a criterion-referenced test? What circumstances would indicate when to use one or the other?

3. Describe cases in which you would use a general survey battery, a single-subject test, and a diagnostic test.

4. Give an example of how you would interpret a scaled score to an individual, and then illustrate how you would interpret a scaled score to a high school class.

5. Would you choose a norm-referenced or a criterion-referenced achievement test for a 54-year-old black mother of four who has never worked outside the home? Why?

6. A teacher has referred a third grade student, Ken Jones, to you for help with career decision making. The Individual Profile Report of the Terra Nova (a standardized achievement test) and basic

interpretation are presented in Figure 5-3a and b. Notice that there are four main content areas: reading/language arts, mathematics, science and social studies. How might his scores be related to his career interests and abilities? What are his apparent strengths and weaknesses? What type of interventions (career and other) might you make with this student? If you could rewrite or add portions to the interpretation, what changes might you make? How might a parent feel in receiving this information? Knowing that this information will be sent home, design an introductory sheet to aid parents in the interpretation. What other interventions might you do, pre- and post-testing, to prepare student and parents for the results?

7. A fifth-grade teacher has asked you to work with a group of students on career development who scored similarly (within 3 points of each other on each subscale) on the Woodcock Johnson III. A profile from one of the students is included in Figure 5-4. Based on this profile, what would you hypothesize the group's strengths and weaknesses to be? How might you tailor a group career counseling experience?

8. Kieta, a 2nd grade (8 year, 7 month) student, has completed the PIAT. Her mother wants to talk with you about her adjustment to the second grade. In her previous school, her grades were on a "C" or average level. Her results are presented in Figure 5-5a and b. Summarize her strengths and areas for improvement. If she was seeing you in a career-counseling group, how might you vary your interventions, activities or information, based on these results? What type of interpretations and suggestions can you make, based on her results?

9. Nick is a seventh grade student who recently completed the BASI. His results are presented in Figure 5-6a and b. How would you interpret his results to him, and to his parents? How would you interpret each of the following: confidence interval, percentile rank, performance, grade and age equivalents. Write up a brief summary of his results addressing these key factors.

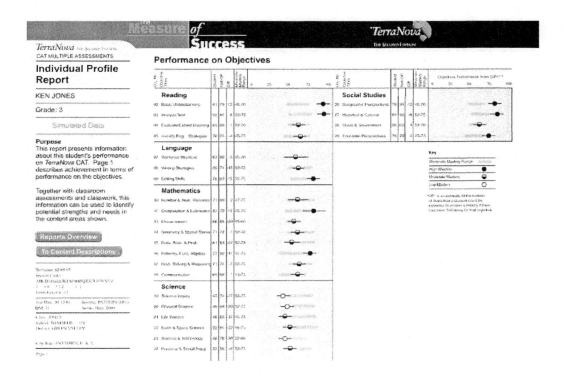

Figure 5-3a   TerraNova © 2000. Reproduced with permission of The McGraw-Hill Companies, Inc.

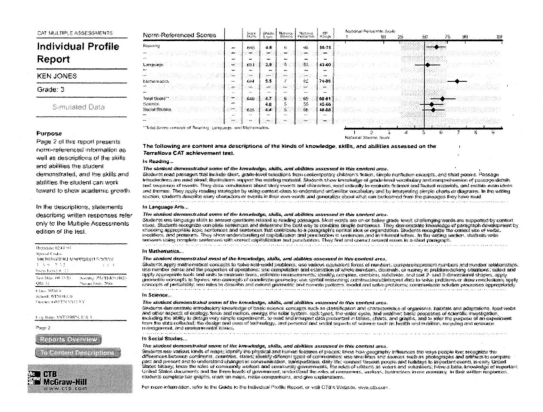

Figure 5-3b TerraNova © 2000. Reproduced with permission of The McGraw-Hill Companies, Inc.

Summary and Score Report - COMPUSCORE VERSION 1.1b   Page 4
T1.1B, Chris
September 14, 2000

| DISCREPANCIES | STANDARD SCORES | | | DISCREPANCY | | Significant at |
	Actual	Predicted	Difference	PR	SD	+ or - 1.50 SD (SEE)
Intra-Individual						
COMP-KNOWLEDGE (Gc)	122	96	+26	99.6	+2.62	Yes
L-T RETRIEVAL (Glr)	77	100	-23	5	-1.62	Yes
VIS-SPATIAL THINK (Gv)	120	98	+22	94	+1.53	Yes
AUDITORY PROCESS (Ga)	79	100	-21	7	-1.50	Yes
FLUID REASONING (Gf)	105	98	+7	72	+0.59	No
PROCESS SPEED (Gs)	104	98	+6	65	+0.40	No
SHORT-TERM MEM (Gsm)	68	100	-32	1	-2.38	Yes
PHONEMIC AWARE	71	100	-29	2	-2.09	Yes
WORKING MEMORY	76	100	-24	2	-1.97	Yes
BASIC READING SKILLS	74	100	-26	0.3	-2.74	Yes
READING COMP	94	98	-4	33	-0.45	No
MATH CALC SKILLS	107	98	+9	77	+0.73	No
MATH REASONING	117	97	+20	97	+1.94	Yes
BASIC WRITING SKILLS	74	100	-26	1	-2.41	Yes
WRITTEN EXPRESSION	92	99	-7	30	-0.53	No
ORAL EXPRESSION	112	98	+14	89	+1.20	No
LISTENING COMP	102	98	+4	65	+0.39	No
ACADEMIC KNOWLEDGE	125	97	+28	99.6	+2.65	Yes

| DISCREPANCIES | STANDARD SCORES | | | DISCREPANCY | | Significant at |
	Actual	Predicted	Difference	PR	SD	+ or - 1.50 SD (SEE)
*Intellectual Ability/Achievement Discrepancies**						
BROAD READING	79	99	-20	3	-1.89	Yes
BASIC READING SKILLS	74	99	-25	1	-2.20	Yes
READING COMP	94	99	-5	31	-0.50	No
BROAD MATH	115	99	+16	93	+1.44	No
MATH CALC SKILLS	107	99	+8	73	+0.61	No
MATH REASONING	117	99	+18	96	+1.71	Yes
BROAD WRITTEN LANG	79	99	-20	3	-1.82	Yes
BASIC WRITING SKILLS	74	99	-25	1	-2.26	Yes
WRITTEN EXPRESSION	92	99	-7	27	-0.60	No
ORAL LANGUAGE (Ext)	108	99	+9	77	+0.73	No
ORAL EXPRESSION	112	99	+13	86	+1.09	No
LISTENING COMP	102	99	+3	60	+0.25	No
ACADEMIC KNOWLEDGE	125	99	+26	99	+2.48	Yes

*These discrepancies based on GIA (Ext) with ACH Broad, Basic, and Applied clusters.

Figure 5-4

```
04/05/2001    Peabody Individual Achievement Test - Revised/NU

Examinee: Obatu, Kieta                 Sex: Female
School/Agency: North Community School  Grade: 2
Teacher/Counselor: Karla Liebowitz     Examiner: Emilio Juarez
                                  Reasons for testing
Test Date:  01/04/2001         -----------------------------------------------
Birth Date: 05/19/1992         Experiencing difficulties in reading
Age: 8-7
```

```
                              SCORE SUMMARY
================================================================================
Standard scores were derived from Age norm tables.
--------------------------------------------------------------------------------
Subtest or        68%         Raw    Grade   Age    Standard  %ile
Composite      Conf. Level    Score  Equiv.  Equiv.  Score    Rank   NCE
--------------------------------------------------------------------------------
General        +1.00 SEM       33            7-9      90       25     36
Information    Obtained Score  30     2.0    7-5      86       18     30
Subtest        -1.00 SEM       27            7-1      82       12     25

Reading        +1.00 SEM       25            7-2      82       12     25
Recognition    Obtained Score  23     1.5    6-11     80        9     22
Subtest        -1.00 SEM       21            6-8      78        7     19

Reading        +1.00 SEM       23            6-10     81       10     23
Comprehension  Obtained Score  20     1.2    6-7      77        6     18
Subtest        -1.00 SEM       17            6-4      73        4     12
--------------------------------------------------------------------------------
               +1.00 SEM       47            6-11     79        8     21
TOTAL          Obtained Score  43     1.3    6-9      77        6     18
READING        -1.00 SEM       39            6-6      75        5     15
--------------------------------------------------------------------------------
               +1.00 SEM       31            8-5      99       47     49
Mathematics    Obtained Score  29     2.6    8-1      95       37     43
Subtest        -1.00 SEM       27            7-10     91       27     37

               +1.00 SEM       24            6-7      80        9     22
Spelling       Obtained Score  22     1.0    6-5      77        6     18
Subtest        -1.00 SEM       20            6-2      74        4     13
--------------------------------------------------------------------------------
               +1.00 SEM      130            7-1      79        8     21
TOTAL          Obtained Score 124     1.5    7-0      77        6     18
TEST           -1.00 SEM      118            6-11     75        5     15
================================================================================
Written Expression II (Prompt A)
  Raw Score = 17  Developmental Scaled Score = 2  Grade-based Stanine = 2
--------------------------------------------------------------------------------
WRITTEN LANGUAGE         Scaled Score Sum = 2 + 2 = 4
   Age Standard Score = 74 +/- 4  %ile Rank = 4  %ile Range = 2 - 7
========================== APTITUDE ACHIEVEMENT ================================
Aptitude Test: K-ABC MPC
Aptitude Standard Score: 94          Aptitude Ach. Correlation: .65

Expected TOTAL READING Standard Score: 96
Standard Score Discrepancy: 19       Frequency of Occurrence: 5%

COPYRIGHT 1998, AMERICAN GUIDANCE SERVICE, INC., CIRCLE PINES, MN 55014-1796
```

Figure 5-5a   Peabody Individual Achievement Test (PIAT), Revised/NU. Reprinted by permission of American Guidance Services, Inc.

```
04/05/2001      Peabody Individual Achievement Test - Revised/NU        Page 2

EXAMINEE:Obatu, Kieta

                       DEVELOPMENTAL SCORE PROFILES
                          68% Confidence Level

                          Age Equivalent Profile
          Age           !
Equivalent Range! 4    5    6    7    8    9   10   11   12   13   14   15   16   17   18   19
================!-+---+---+---+---+---+---+---+---+---+---+---+---+---+---+---+
General Info.   !               ****
   7-1 to 7-9   !                    A
----------------!-+---+---+---+---+---+---+---+---+---+---+---+---+---+---+---+
Reading Recog.  !          ·  ***
   6-8 to 7-2   !                    A
----------------!-+---+---+---+---+---+---+---+---+---+---+---+---+---+---+---+
Reading Comp.   !          ***
   6-4 to 6-10  !                    A
================!-+---+---+---+---+---+---+---+---+---+---+---+---+---+---+---+
TOTAL READING   !           **
   6-6 to 6-11  !                    A
================!-+---+---+---+---+---+---+---+---+---+---+---+---+---+---+---+
Mathematics     !               ***
   7-10 to 8-5  !                    A
----------------!-+---+---+---+---+---+---+---+---+---+---+---+---+---+---+---+
Spelling        !        ***
   6-2 to 6-7   !                    A
----------------!-+---+---+---+---+---+---+---+---+---+---+---+---+---+---+---+
TOTAL TEST      !           **
   6-11 to 7-1  !                    A
================!-+---+---+---+---+---+---+---+---+---+---+---+---+---+---+---+
```

Figure 5-5b   Peabody Individual Achievement Test (PIAT), Revised/NU. Reprinted by permission of American Guidance Services, Inc.

BASI™

Basic Achievement Skills Inventory

Student Summary Report: BASI Level 3
Achilles N. Bardos, PhD

Student:	Sample, Nick A.
Student ID:	000000052
Birth Date:	07/23/1989
Grade:	7

Teacher:	Teacher, Karen A.
Class/Group:	12334
School:	Edwood Public
District Code:	12345

Timed:	Yes
ESL Student:	No
Accommodations:	No
Test Date:	04/10/2003
Report Date:	07/20/2004
Form:	B
Norms:	Spring / 7th Grade

Nick's BASI results are presented in the tables on this page. For example, he received a standard score (SS) of 88 in the Reading Total area. *Standard scores* compare Nick's performance with that of other 7th grade students in a national sample. *Confidence intervals* indicate the range of standard scores that is likely to include Nick's true score. *Percentile (%ile) scores* indicate what percentage of the norm group Nick scored as well as or better than. For example, Nick's percentile score in the Reading Total area indicates that his score was equal to or higher than the scores of 21% of 7th grade students in a national sample. *Grade-equivalent (GE)* and *age-equivalent (AE)* scores are also presented for the subtests.

The tables below present Nick's results for the various achievement areas included in each of the six BASI subtests. The results shown are percentage correct (PC) and a rating of his performance relative to that of other examinees. These results identify the areas in which he excels and those in which he might need help. They can also help track Nick's progress if he takes the BASI test again.

Composite or Subtest	SS	Confidence Interval	%ile	GE	AE	Performance
Reading Total	88	82-96	21			Below Average
Vocabulary	88	80-99	21	<3.0	<8-0	Below Average
Reading Comprehension	88	81-97	21	<3.0	<8-0	Average
Written Language Total	93	85-102	32			Average
Spelling	96	85-108	39	6.2	11-3	Below Average
Language Mechanics	95	86-104	36	4.2	8-9	Average
Math Total	89	80-100	23			Below Average
Math Computation	91	80-105	27	5.1	10-6	Average
Math Application	88	78-103	22	4.0	9-3	Average

SS = Standard Score (mean = 100, SD = 15)   %ile = Percentile Rank   GE = Grade Equivalent   AE = Age Equivalent   PC = Percentage Correct

Achievement Area	PC	Performance
Vocabulary	**35**	**Below Average**
Meaning, context, idioms	14	Below Average
Similar words, synonyms, antonyms	38	Average
Prefixes, suffixes, roots	50	Average
Verbal analogies	38	Average
Reading Comprehension	**40**	**Below Average**
Plot, main idea, topic sentence	40	Average
INFERENTIAL COMPREHENSION	39	Average
Theme, plot elements	38	Below Average
Cause, effect	0.0	Below Average
Compare, contrast	100	Average
Inferences, conclusions	67	Average
Purpose, technique, tone	50	Average
Fact, opinion, persuasion, bias	38	Average
Figurative language	0.0	Below Average
Setting	0.0	Below Average

Achievement Area	PC	Performance
Spelling	**63**	**Average**
Prefixes and suffixes	78	Average
Commonly misspelled words	50	Average
Spelling rules	50	Below Average
Language Mechanics	**50**	**Average**
Internal punctuation	27	Average
GRAMMAR	**59**	**Average**
Nouns, pronouns, articles	60	Average
Subject/verb agreement	64	Average
Adjectives, adverbs	67	Average
Double negatives	40	Below Average

Achievement Area	PC	Performance
Math Computation	**40**	**Average**
Whole numbers	40	Average
Fractions	33	Average
Decimals, order of operations, percents	50	Average
Integers, absolute value	43	Average
Algebra	33	Average
Math Application	**33**	**Below Average**
Whole numbers, money	43	Average
Fractions, proportions	0.0	Below Average
Decimals, percents	57	Average
Geometry	67	Average
Algebra	25	Below Average
Statistics, probability	40	Average
Measurement	0.0	Below Average

Figure 5-6a   BASI (Basic Achievement Skills Inventory) Copyright © 2004 NCS Pearson, Inc. Reproduced with permission of Pearson Assessments.

BASI ™

Basic Achievement Skills Inventory

Parent's Summary Report: BASI Level 3
Achilles N. Bardos, PhD

Student:	Sample, Nick A.
Student ID:	000000052
Birth Date:	07/23/1989
Grade:	7

Teacher:	Teacher, Karen A.
Class/Group:	12334
School:	Edlwood Public
District Code:	12345

Timed:	Yes
ESL Student:	No
Accommodations:	No
Test Date:	04/10/2003
Report Date:	07/20/2004
Form:	B
Norms:	Spring / 7th Grade

National Percentile

Composite or Subtest	Performance	10 25 50 75 99
Reading Total	Below Average	21
Vocabulary	Below Average	21
Reading Comprehension	Below Average	21
Written Language Total	Average	32
Spelling	Average	39
Language Mechanics	Average	36
Math Total	Below Average	23
Math Computation	Average	27
Math Application	Below Average	22

To the parent or guardian of Nick A. Sample:

Nick took the Basic Achievement Skills Inventory (BASI™) on April 10, 2003. His performance is summarized in the table at the left.

Nick's performance in the Reading Total area was in the Below Average range compared to the performance of a national sample of 7th grade students. His percentile score indicates that his Reading Total score was equal to or higher than that of 21% of the students in the national comparison group. The Reading Total area includes the Vocabulary and Reading Comprehension subtests. The Vocabulary subtest has questions that involve recognizing the meaning of words in isolation and in sentences, identifying synonyms and antonyms, and analyzing verbal analogies. The Reading Comprehension subtest has questions involving literal comprehension (for example, identifying details and facts in a passage) and inferential comprehension (for example, determining cause and effect relationships, making inferences, and drawing conclusions based on the information in a passage). Nick's Vocabulary score was in the Below Average range, and his Reading Comprehension score was in the Below Average range.

Nick's performance in the Written Language Total area was in the Average range compared to the performance of a national sample of 7th grade students. His percentile score indicates that his Written Language Total score was equal to or higher than that of 32% of the students in the national comparison group. The Written Language Total area includes the Spelling and Language Mechanics subtests. The Spelling subtest has questions that involve identifying correctly spelled and misspelled words. It also includes sight words, commonly misspelled words, and words with affixes. The Language Mechanics subtest has questions that involve recognizing and correctly using nouns, verbs, adjectives, and adverbs and following grammar and syntax rules. Nick's Spelling score was in the Average range, and his Language Mechanics score was in the Average range.

Nick's performance in the Math Total area was in the Below Average range compared to the performance of a national sample of 7th grade students. His percentile score indicates that his Math Total score was equal to or higher than 23% of the students in the national comparison group. The Math Total area includes the Math Computation and Math Application subtests. The Math Computation subtest has questions that involve applying the four basic arithmetic operations to whole numbers, fractions, and decimals, and simplifying numerical expressions and algebraic equations. The Math Application subtest has questions that involve solving word problems using the four basic arithmetic operations, reading and interpreting data presented in graphs and tables, measuring shapes, utilizing knowledge of geometry and algebra, and demonstrating knowledge of measurement principles as they relate to length, weight, perimeter, and money. Nick's Math Computation score was in the Average range, and his Math Application score was in the Below Average range.

If you need help interpreting these scores, please talk to Nick's teacher.

Comments:

_____

_____

_____

_____

_____

_____

_____

Figure 5-6b   BASI (Basic Achievement Skills Inventory) Copyright © 2004 NCS Pearson, Inc. Reproduced with permission of Pearson Assessments.

6 Using Interest Inventories

In one way or another, almost everyone has been involved in the exploration of interests to decide which activities to pursue in leisure, in a career, or in both. To help in this exploration, interest inventories have long been associated with career guidance. Strong (1943) pioneered the development of interest inventories by introducing innovative principles for measuring interests. He gathered data concerning individuals' likes and dislikes for a variety of activities, objects, and types of persons commonly encountered. He found that individuals in different occupations have common patterns of interests that differentiate them from individuals in other occupations. In this way, the results of interest inventories provide the opportunity for individuals to compare their interests with those of individuals in specific occupational groups. In addition, Fouad (1999) states that regardless of which specific measure is used, interest inventories appear to be generalizable across time. Finally, Holland, Powell, and Fritzsche's (1994) typology provides a system for matching interests with one or more of six types that have been discussed in the preceding chapters and will be more fully discussed in this chapter.

Because sex bias in interest assessment has received considerable attention, we present a summary of this issue at the beginning of the chapter. This summary is followed by a discussion of two widely used interest inventories: the Strong Interest Inventory and the Kuder Occupational Interest Survey. Other inventories reviewed are the Self-Directed Search (Holland, 1994b), the Harrington/O'Shea System for Career Decision-Making (Harrington & O'Shea, 2000), and the Campbell Interest and Skill Survey (Campbell, 1992). We provide several examples of the use of interest inventories.

Sex Bias and Sex Fairness in Interest Assessment

Since the mid-1970s, a considerable body of literature has been published on issues of gender bias and unfairness of career interest measurement. A major issue has been the limited career options available for women forecasted by the results of interest measures. In the meantime, the American Psychological Association (APA) has addressed sex bias in its publication of ethical principals (APA, 1992a). This prestigious national association focused on "individual and role differences" in mental health practices—more specifically in this context, "role differences" associated with gender. Much earlier, in the 1970s, the National Institute of Education (NIE) voiced its concern about sex bias found in interest inventories; this group argued that occupational options are limited primarily because of gender (Diamond, 1975). Thus, the concern for sex bias has been pervasive in the mental health professions and continues to be the focus for career service providers when they use interest inventory results. See Betz (1993) and Walsh and Betz (1995) for a more extensive discussion of this concern.

As the debate about sex bias in interest inventories continues to evolve, the issues have remained basically the same. First, do men and women have different interests? Two recent studies seem to suggest that they do. One study, using surveys from approximately 16,500 people and focusing on the Strong Interest Inventory, found sex-related differences on 28 occupational titles (Aros, Henly, & Curtis, 1998). Another study focusing on the results of the Self-Directed Search found sex differences when the first letter of a person's code was either "R" or "S" (Farmer, Rotella, Anderson, & Wardrop, 1998). The gender differences dropped out, however, when these two letters were the second letter of the code. In addition, those researchers found that men were more likely than women were to be in higher prestige jobs. Other researchers (Day & Rounds, 1997) reviewed women and men's patterns on the General Occupational Themes of the 1994 Strong interest inventory and concluded that "the sexes differ in how they perceive the world of work" (p. 216). In their research on sex typing and differential item functioning, Aros, Henly, and Curtis (1998) concluded that sextype is a factor in vocational preference, finding differences in both vocational preferences and measured interests according to sex. However, the researchers quickly add that sex-typing alone can not account for the difference in how women and men respond to items, stating that perhaps the items do not have equal indicators of the underlying dimensions of interest for women and men.

Others agree that men and women *still differ* in the way they endorse interest inventory items (Fouad & Spreda, 1995; Hansen, Collins, Swanson, & Fouad, 1993; Harmon & Meara, 1994). For instance, women are influenced to endorse items according to their socialization—that is, by what is considered appropriately feminine, such as nurturance, caring, warmth, and expression of emotion —the results of which may reinforce traditional occupations for women (Betz, 1994). In addition to socialization concerns, Betz (2000) raises the issue of the impact of differential histories on interest inventory outcomes. If women have been exposed to only traditional types of activities for women, how will they respond to traditionally male items presented on an inventory? Thus, interest inventory results might not reflect actual differences between men and women for occupational groups or specific occupations (Fouad & Spreda, 1995). Therefore, specific items on interest inventories require careful scrutiny to determine if they appropriately represent interests of both genders.

Second, are interest inventories constructed with the assumption that work is dichotomized into "man's work" and "woman's work"—or, in the language of measurements, is there content bias? For instance, terms that encourage role stereotyping, such as salesman or policeman, should be omitted (Hackett & Lonborg, 1993). As Betz (1992) points out, the main problem of sex restrictiveness in interest inventory results is that different score patterns for men and women encourage gender-stereotypic occupations.

Other psychometric qualities, such as the internal structure of inventories, can be another source of bias. For example, one specific source of bias may be found in the conversion of raw scores into norms that are used in profile interpretation (Hackett & Lonborg, 1994). In recent years, publishers have restructured and revised their inventories to lessen this problem. However, although improvements have been made in the psychometric quality of tests, this does not automatically translate into using the results of the instruments in a fair manner.

A related issue is whether to use raw, same-sex, or sex-balanced inventory scores. According to Holland, Fritzsche, and Powell (1994), the role of interest inventories is to provide a reflection of the current interests men and women have, and when standardized scores are used, the interests become modified and reality becomes obscured. Spokane and Holland (1995) obviously endorse raw scores as the most effective method of interpreting the results of interest inventories. Fouad and Spreda (1995) and Prediger and Swaney (1995) argue that, although raw scores might reflect reality, they might also endorse occupational segregation or sex-restrictive options for women. The argument boils down to the suggestion that raw scores should be used because they accurately reflect vocational aspirations of men and women that differ because of their life histories; Fouad and Spreda (1995) and Betz (1992) suggest that other methods should be used to increase the range of options for women.

Yet another issue involves the norm reference groups used for interpreting completed interest inventories. More explicitly, the prevailing question is whether sex bias in interest inventories can be most effectively overcome through the use of separate norms (reference groups by gender, often referred to as same-sex norms) or combined-gender norms (reference groups combining males and females).

Same-sex norms have the advantage of having one's score compared with patterns of interest of others who have similar gender-type socialization experiences. For instance, a woman can view her scores in reference to both male and female samples. Also, same-sex norms provide more options for exploration of interests (Hansen, 1990). Separate sex norms for men and women have been developed for the Strong Interest Inventory (SII) and the Kuder Occupational Interest Survey (KOIS). Apparently, both inventories plan to expand the number of feminine occupational scales as more data become available about women in different occupational roles.

According to Prediger and Swaney (1995), one way of reducing sex bias in interest inventories is by using sex-balanced scales found in the UNIACT, an interest inventory published by the American College Testing Company. This instrument was designed to measure basic interests common to occupations while "minimizing the effects of sex-role connotations" (Prediger & Swaney, 1995, p. 432). The construction of this inventory included the introduction of items that were considered typical of male and female role socialization; items that produced an appreciable difference in response by gender were eliminated. The rationale is that sex-balanced items will elicit similar responses from men and women, thereby eliminating different sets of scales. Prediger and Swaney (1995) argue that different sets of occupational scales for men and women perpetuate sex-role stereotyping because such tests inherently suggest that some work is typically male-oriented and other work is typically female-oriented.

What we have here is a difficult decision for the career counselor as to which inventory is most appropriate for specific clients. Perhaps a compromise is the best solution. Betz (1993) suggests that the counselor use both a same-sex norm inventory and a sex-balanced inventory. The basis for this recommendation is that both sets of norms will likely provide more options for career exploration. In addition, Hackett and Lonborg (1994) recommend using less structured assessments, such as card sorts and lifelines that will be more likely to engage the client in active discussion. Betz (2000) also recommends using an exploratory (versus confirmatory) approach with women, stating that the exploratory approach (viewing options as opportunities) is less constrictive than the confirmatory approach, which may lead to only examining traditionally female occupations. Again, a balance may be the best solution. Certainly, expanding career options for both men and women would be recommended.

At the same time, to completely ignore the validity and reliability of well-researched interest inventories that might confirm a client's interests (even interests that are traditional) seems imprudent. A counselor should take into consideration his or her own views on traditional careers for males or females, and be cognizant of whether or not he or she is forcing those views onto a client.

Racial and Cultural Bias of Interest Inventories

In addition to concerns of gender bias, counselors should be concerned with racial and cultural bias, not only with interest inventories, but with all inventories. In general, Holland's RIASEC model has proven to be valid for several American ethnic groups (Tak, 2004).Fouad and Mohler (2004) found minimal differences for congruence and differentiation among 5 racially diverse groups on Holland themes and specifically the SII. When Betz and Gwilliam (2002) compared self-efficacy to the RIASEC themes between European American and African American college students, they found very few racial differences.

As mentioned in chapter 1, a counselor should consider the culture from which a client comes and compare that to the normative data before administering any inventory. Considerations should include the amount of likely exposure by the client to the activities/interests being presented, and whether the occupational database of the inventory is similar to the occupational realities within the client's world.

Stability of Interests

In her chapter entitled "Stability and Change in Vocational Interests," Jane Swanson (1999) summarizes 5 themes that can be drawn from the review of 30 studies focusing on the stability of vocational interests. First, she states that the results of almost every study indicate that interests are incredibly stable over long periods of time, regardless of the types of measures used to identify interests, statistical measures given, or types of people tested. At the same time, however, she notes that for some people, interests do change dramatically over time and that this observation merits additional investigation to determine the causes for this. Third, interest stability appears to increase with age and higher differentiation and consistency as defined by John Holland's theory, while instability seems to be related to career decision making difficulty. Fourth, attempts to predict who will have stable interest scores have not yielded consistent information. Fifth, it appears that after a certain age, interests tend to stay the same, although they may become further clarified.

Finally, Swanson raises some interesting questions to ponder with respect to interest stability. She first asks, "How much stability is desirable?" This question requires some thoughtful reflection. Certainly, it would be premature to expect a first grader to have interests that have stabilized. Indeed, it might be premature to expect the same from a sophomore in college who had not engaged in many activities. Isn't it possible that someone who presents very stable interests is stating that because she or he wants to avoid the unpleasant feeling of being undecided or admitting that she or he might not know her or himself completely? Certainly, as a person begins to commit to a career, whether through a career path or training, some stability of interests is required. How unnerving it would be to commit oneself to a career of medicine, only to decide, one year later, that anthropology is the field that holds her interest.

Interpreting Interest Inventories

Each individual interest inventory comes with a manual that has suggested steps for successful interpretation. There are hundreds of interest inventories, however, and countless more are emerging as the Internet provides new avenues for aspiring test writers. It appears, however, that there should be some standard approach to interpreting interest inventories, regardless of which inventory is presented.

Zytowski (1999) identified five general principles that a counselor should follow when providing an interpretation of interest inventories. First, the counselor should prepare for the session. Specifically, counselors should know what the test results are, terms associated with the theory and report, and how that person's scores relate back to the normative group; have an understanding of all special scales, and be able to explain the test results in understandable terms. In addition, the counselor should take the time to review current research on correlations made about scales. For example, if a client has a very low flat profile, the counselor should be aware that one of the possible reasons for this is depression and should ask questions during the session to ascertain if depression is occurring. In addition, in this case, before the interpretive session, the counselor should know related symptoms of depression and recommended treatments.

Second, Zytowski (1999) recommends actively involving the clients in the results. Imagine sitting with a counselor who provides you with an excellent lecture of the background of the interest inventory you just took, how to go about interpreting each of the scales, the theory behind each scale, what each scale is related to, and so on. Although the information might be helpful, the likelihood is boredom after the first couple of minutes. Zytowski suggests helping clients view the occupations as tentative hypotheses that should be examined alongside of previous experience. Two questions he suggests include these: "What kinds of things like this have you done in the past?" or "How does this fit with what your friends say about you?" (p. 282).

Third, Zytowski reiterates the need for counselors to use "simple, empathetic communication" (p. 282), whether verbally or through the use of graphs, checkmarks, other graphics or body language.

Fourth, just as we recommended in Chapter 2, clients should be asked to restate their results using their own words. One purpose is to make sure that the client is not holding onto myths, such as "It says I should be . . ." Zytowski identifies a second purpose: that of translating the information received from the inventory into the person's developing self-concept. He suggests a role-play in which the client is asked to call a parent or friend and share his or her interest results. The fifth strategy involves using the inventory as a springboard to continuing career development. Some strategies might include narrowing the occupational list, action planning, examining the positives and negatives, shadowing, or reading career information. An additional strategy that we've found helpful is to have the client go back through his or her list of occupational alternatives and give reasons for crossing off items from the list. The counselor should keep a running list of the reasons. A second list can be created of the reasons a client gives for finding other occupations appealing. A third list can be made as the client discusses occupations that she or he is somewhat conflicted about considering. In discussing the occupations, what are the positives and the drawbacks of each one? If the client had to make a choice today to keep that occupation on the list or to drop it, which would be the choice and why? (This activity can help confirm and expand the client's understanding of his or her knowledge about self, as well as identify where potential conflicts of interests and values might lie).

Examples of Interests by Holland's Types

In this section, Holland's types will be further elaborated with emphasis on occupations associated with each type. In earlier discussions, general areas of interests were covered with some examples of specific occupations. More information about matching occupations with combinations of codes is given in the *Dictionary of Holland Occupational Codes* (Gottfredson & Holland, 1989). Other helpful references are Hansen (1985), Levin (1991), and Brew (1987).

Following are the six Holland's types as they relate to interests (following page):

		Table 6-1	Descriptors of Holland Types and Interests	

Type	Interests	Activities/Hobbies	Work Environments	Occupations
Realistic	Realistic people are interested in action-type occupations such as building, mechanics, machine operator, and repair.	Typical hobbies are fishing, camping, and working on cars.	They tend to like the outdoors and prefer to work in rural areas.	Some realistic occupations include carpenter, rancher, engineer, forester, veterinarian, and welder.
Investigative	People with high scores in investigative abilities have a strong interest in science. They like abstract tasks and solving problems while working independently.	Such activities as collecting data, conducting research, and organizing material for analysis appeal to investigative people.	They tend to prefer work environments that are in an office setting, such as laboratories.	Some investigative occupations include biologist, mathematician, psychologist, pharmacist, and dental hygienist.
Artistic	The artistic person values the aesthetics in life and is dedicated to self-expression.	Typical work activities are writing, composing, and designing while working independently.	Work environments include museums, theaters, galleries, and concert halls.	Examples of artistic occupations include artist, music teacher, photographer, and interior designer.
Social	Social people enjoy working with people and are concerned about the welfare of others.	Typical activities are informing, teaching, coaching, and leading discussions.	Work environments include social service agencies, religious establishments, mental health clinics, personnel offices, and medical facilities.	Examples of social occupations include teacher, guidance counselor, playground director, social worker, and juvenile probation officer.
Enterprising	Enterprising people tend to be ambitious and competitive and to seek leadership positions.	Typical activities include selling, managing, giving speeches, and leading groups of people.	Work environments include marketing agencies, investment banking firms, retail and wholesale firms, and small, independently owned businesses.	Examples of occupations include corporation executive, sales manager, elected public official, computer salesperson, and stockbroker.
Conventional	Being precise and accurate while attending to detail in well-defined activities are typical traits of conventional people.	Activities included in this type are keeping records, scheduling, and maintaining adopted procedures of an organization.	Preferred work environments include large corporations, business offices, and accounting firms.	Examples of occupations include bookkeeper, accountant, secretary, keypunch operator, cashier, and banker.

Interpreting Flat and Elevated Profiles

One problem that causes confusion for clients and counselors are flat or elevated profiles. Flat, or depressed, profiles consist of scores around the average range with little differences among scores. In contrast, elevated profiles have a large number of scores that are considered to be high in interest levels. These types of profiles can be used productively, as discussed by Hansen (1985).

Flat, depressed profiles may indicate one of the following:

1. *A narrow interest range and an individual with highly defined interests.* A profile with a narrow interest range will more than likely show high scores in one or two interest areas. Such an individual may be completely satisfied with an occupation and may have achieved significant positive feedback.

2. *A client with very little knowledge about the world of work and the workplace.* Such an individual may be reluctant to respond aggressively to questions about the work world.

3. *Mood swings.* An individual may be unwilling to differentiate among offered choices just because he or she is having a "bad" day.

4. *Indecisiveness.* An individual who is unwilling to make a commitment or a change could indicate a lack of readiness to respond to an interest inventory.

5. An unwillingness to work.

Flat, elevated profiles may indicate the following:

1. *Individuals who are reluctant to say "dislike" or "indifferent" to items.* Some may feel such responses would type them as negative individuals, and so their results show a high percentage of "like" items.

2. *A wide diversity of interests.* Focusing on only a few interests may be difficult for these individuals. Some researchers have demonstrated a link between elevated profiles on the Self-Directed Search and openness to experience, extraversion, and lower depressive personality (Fuller, Holland, & Johnston, 1999).

3. *Clients who are multi-potential or gifted in many areas.* Most people enjoy doing things they are good at. For clients who are good at many things, they may honestly endorse the majority of inventory items, resulting in an elevated, but flat profile. Negative thinking might need to be addressed, especially if the person is feeling pressured by others to choose. For example, a gifted client may receive much positive feedback from teachers in different fields (science, math, English, history) and parents, and may fear disappointing any of them.

4. *Clients with a great deal of experience.* Sometimes experience can help strengthen a person's view of what they truly like and truly dislike. At the same time, it can add complexity to the overall picture. If a client has worked in a variety of areas and developed skills in those areas, their inventory results may resemble those of the multi-potential or gifted client. We have found that in addition to examining current interests, including an exploration of work and life values with this type of client to provide useful information and direction.

5. *Client who have an inflated view of self.* Occasionally, a client may have some narcissistic tendencies, and test results, such as an elevated flat profile may be evidence of this. (This can be confirmed if the client asks for more and more tests, with a "tell me more about me" attitude).A counselor may decide to investigate whether a personality disorder is present, or may decide to point out during the interpretation that no one is equally good at every option or equally interested in all options, and that the task is to figure out which are the main interests and skills that the person would like to use on the job.

Knowledge of some of the reasons and causes for flat or elevated interest profiles prepares the counselor for suggesting intervention strategies. Although profiles of this type may seem to provide little in the way of counseling opportunities, this information can be of significant assistance in career planning.

Strong Interest Inventory® (Strong instrument)

The Strong instrument replaced the well-known Strong-Campbell Interest Inventory. The Strong instrument was based on research by E. K. Strong (1943) that covered several decades of compiling empirical information. He made no assumptions concerning the specific interest patterns of workers in the occupational groups he researched. Strong postulated that an individual who has interests that are similar to those of persons working in a given occupation is more likely to find satisfaction in that particular occupation than is a person who does not have common interests with those workers.

The current Strong instrument (1994) contains 317 items that measure a respondent's interests in 8 different areas, including occupations, school subjects, activities, leisure activities, types of people (whom the client would prefer working with every day), preference between two activities, personal characteristics, and preference in the world of work. It typically takes about 45 minutes to take the Strong instrument; the reading level is ninth grade. The appropriate age range is 14 years through adulthood. The Strong instrument has been translated for administration in Spanish, French, and Hebrew, in addition to several other languages.

The current version includes the Skills Confidence Inventory (SCI) (Betz, Borgen, & Harmon, 1996), which assesses an individual's degree of confidence in performing activities related to the six Holland themes. Confidence is reported on a scale from very little confidence to very high. When the Strong instrument and SCI are used in conjunction together, the counselor can explore discrepancies between interests and confidence, remembering that low confidence does not equate low ability – other issues like poor self-esteem might be influencing those scores.

Researchers (Betz, Schifano, & Kaplan, 1999; Tuel & Betz, 1998) report that the SCI has strong construct validity, test-retest reliability (Parsons & Betz, 1998), and tests show minimal self-efficacy differences with respect to gender (Betz, Borgen, Kaplan, & Harmon, 1998). In addition, Donnay and Borgen (1999) used the Strong instrument and SCI with 1105 workers from 21 different occupational groups. From their study, Donnay and Borgen concluded that confidence is a construct that is closely related to interests but still distinct in its own right; the SCI is a valid measure of tenured and satisfied workers; and the SCI has merit as a useful career inventory.

The Strong instrument report yields four categories:

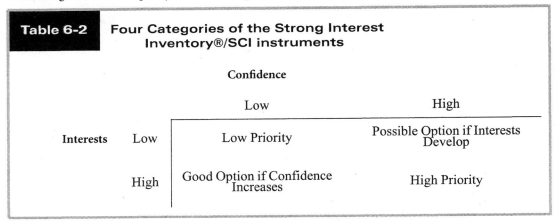

| Table 6-2 | **Four Categories of the Strong Interest Inventory®/SCI instruments** |

		Confidence	
		Low	High
Interests	Low	Low Priority	Possible Option if Interests Develop
	High	Good Option if Confidence Increases	High Priority

For example, consider the difference in this person's scores on confidence and interest in the artistic realm. Even though this person might feel confident in his or her ability to be artistic, this is not a major interest at this time. One possible intervention would be to examine other interests that are higher, and them brainstorm how the person's creative talent could be combined with that particular interest. If the bars were reversed, and the person's confidence was significantly less than his or her interest level, counseling might focus on ways to increase confidence, or perhaps identifying and challenging impeding thoughts. Chartrand, Borgen, Betz and Donnay (2002) suggest that recommending classes or workshops that instruction at the basic level would be a step toward building confidence. Other suggestions they made were observation in person or watching a video, talking with others in the field, relaxation or systematic desensitization, or pep talks from important people in the client's life.

Both paper and pencil and computer-administered forms are available, with users having similar reactions to both types (Hansen, Neuman, Haverkamp and Lubinski, 1997). In that research, however, it was found that those who used the computerized version often reported that it was easier to use. The Strong instrument has been as well researched as other inventories authored by Strong instrument. Subscales of the Strong instrument have been shown to predict first year grade point average for 677 college freshmen (Kahn, Nauta, Gailbreath, Tipps & Chartrand, 2002).

The stability of the Strong instrument is well documented, and reliability and validity studies suggest that the Strong instrument is well suited for career development counseling. Some concerns have been raised about how cultural groups may endorse items on the Strong instrument. Fouad and Walker (2005) found that culturally diverse groups endorsed some item sets of the Strong instrument that were likely measuring a secondary trait as well as the main trait expressed by the GOTs. Other concerns have been expressed about the high level of education reflected in the culturally diverse participants in the normative sample. The following reviews have been made of the previously published Strong-Campbell Interest Inventory: Crites (1978), Dolliver (1978), Johnson (1978), Lunneborg (1978), Anastasi (1988), and Aiken (1988). Donnay (1997) provides a review of the history of the development of the Strong instrument. Vacc and Newsome (2002) provided a thorough review of the Strong Interest Inventory® /SCI instruments.

The strength of the Strong instrument is the variety of data generated on the interpretive report. These data are useful in counseling and provide information that is usually not found on interest inventory profiles. The addition of the SCI allows counselors to examine how a client's specific self-talk might be impacting his or her options. Other possible profiles include the Strong Interest Inventory® instrument and the Myers Briggs Type Indicator ® instrument (Strong instrument/MBTI® instrument) in the Entrepreneur Report.

The Strong Interest Inventory®/MBTI® instruments provide a narrative report of the interaction between the person's main Holland type and his or her MBTI® instrument type, describing how the two interact at work, with work style, learning environment, leadership and risk taking/adventure. The report generates occupations for exploration and provides suggestions for career exploration. The report does not include the SCI, nor the gender comparisons of occupations but does integrate the Strong instrument and MBTI® instrument nicely, instead of merely tacking the results of the MBTI® instrument to the back of the Strong instrument. For example, the report points out potential discrepancies between interests and personality, such as an Enterprising personality with an Introverted personality preference.

Some research has found a relationship between MBTI® instrument scales and the Personal Style scales of the Strong instrument (Buboltz, Johnson, Nichols, Miller, & Thomas, 2000). Other researchers (Katz, Joiner, & Seaman, 1999) found that students who used the Strong instrument and MBTI® instrument together had more movement in their career goals than those who used either one alone. Additional research is needed on the validity of this pairing. Regardless of what it is paired with, the Strong instrument has a well-documented history, which increases confidence in using this instrument.

Interpreting the Strong Interest Inventory®

The Strong instrument manual (Harmon et al., 1994) has a chapter outlining general interpretation strategies when using the Strong instrument. In addition to specifying steps directly associated with interpretation, the authors provide a 12-step career counseling process to show how a counselor might integrate the Strong instrument.

The first page of the Strong instrument profile is called the "Snapshot," which summarizes the client's highest scores on the General Occupational Themes (GOTs), the Basic Interest Scales (BISs), and the Occupational Scales (OSs). As the name suggests, the purpose of the snapshot is to provide a quick overview of the client's results. The profile reports GOT and BIS scores in three ways: standard scores (mean of 50, standard deviation of 10), interpretive comments, and interpretive bars. The interpretive bars are useful to examine when scale scores differed for the men and women sample. According to Hansen (2000), when this occurs, the most valid and reliable scale is the one that is similar to the client's sex. When interpreting the GOTs, the counselor should focus on the client's general interests and then use that information as a bridge to the world of work. Because the GOTs are reported in terms of Holland codes, they should be interpreted in the context of that theory.

Hansen (2000) also suggests that once the client understands the difference in the six Holland types, the counselor should ask where and how the client expresses those interests in his or her life, including work, leisure, relationships, and so on. In addition, Hansen recommends an integration process by which clients compare what they already knew about their interests (from past experiences, how they spend their time, etc.) and the inventory results.

Generally, a client's highest BISs will fall within one or two of the RIASEC areas. The purpose of the BISs is to further clarify a person's interest within the GOTs. For example, a person may have a main GOT theme of Social and have a high interest in teaching but a low interest in medical services. The BISs serve another purpose as well: They help expand the client's understanding of the world of work via this "branching effect." A study on the ability of the BISs to predict major choice demonstrated that the BISs have impressive power when added to the six GOTs in predicting 22 of 24 majors of the 17,074 in the norm group (Ralston, Borgen, Rottinghaus, & Donnay, 2004). The information provided by the GOTs and BISs is useful in exploring a person's general interests, but also serve as an easy springboard into discussion of nonvocational interests, such as leisure activities and living environments (Hansen, 2000).

The next step is to examine the client's occupational scales in search of interest patterns or scores that show a degree of likeness between the client and individuals who are in particular occupations. According to Hansen (2000), these scales are the most useful in predicting future occupational choices. The rationale behind the OSs is the comparison of how similar an individual's interests are to the interests of others in specific occupations. The mean standard score of each occupation is 50. The interpretive comments range from similar to mid-range to dissimilar interests (with a negative score indicating strong dissimilarity). Hansen (2000) recommends that the counselor and client collaborate to identify common interests among the similar occupations.

Following these steps, the goal is to combine these three major scales to come up with an overall code. The manual provides information about how to do this, as well as what to do with "inconsistent" codes, when the codes for the three different scales are very different. The next step is to use the overall code to generate occupations that were not suggested by the Strong instrument. One way to do this is to use the *Dictionary of Holland Occupational Codes* (Gottfredson & Holland, 1989) or the *Occupations Finder* (Holland, 1994a).

Also a part of the Strong instrument, is the Personal Style Scales, which consist of the Work Style Scale, the Learning Environment Scale, the Leadership Style Scale, and the Risk Taking/Adventure Scale. A person who gains a high score on the Work Style scale prefers working with people to working with data, ideas, or things. The Learning Environment scale identifies the setting in which a person prefers to learn. Some clients may jump to the conclusion that a low score on this scale means that they are poor learners, when what it does suggest is that they are likely to be more interested in hands-on, practical, and applied knowledge. The counselor should make sure to fully describe what this and every scale is measuring. The Leadership Scale measures the preference of individuals to either work by themselves (lower scores) or managing the work of others (higher scores). This preference has also been related to Introversion and Extraversion preferences (Harmon et al., 1994). The Risk Taking/Adventure Scale separates those who prefer to have a high degree of adventure in their lives (high scores) from those who prefer consistency and lower degrees of risk (low scores).

According to Hansen (2000), men and younger people (Hansen, 1990) tend to score higher on this scale than women and adults. Some ways to use this information in counseling include helping a client understand how their style affects his or her career decision-making process, identifying training alternatives that are appropriate to the client's learning style, and exploring the degree to which the client is willing to take risks in choosing or changing careers.

Other information provided on the report includes the Total Responses, Infrequent Responses and Like Preferences (LP), Indifferent Preferences (IP), and Dislike Preferences) DP Indexes. The Total Responses Index shows how many of the 317 items the client responded to. Although it would take many omissions to affect the total profile scores, an alert to the counselor is printed if the client omits more than 17 items.

The Infrequent Responses Index is an indicator of profile validity (Hansen, 2000). The Index was created by including items for which less than 6% of males and females in the General Reference Sample gave a like response. If a client checked "like" to one of those items, it is scored as an infrequent response (because most people do not like that activity). According to Hansen (2000), the possible range of scores on this index for women is +5 to −7 and +7 to −8 for men. A negative score should signal the counselor to the possibility of an invalid profile. Hansen (2000) suggests that if this occurs, the best strategy is to talk with the client, to ensure that the directions were understood, to ascertain the client's attitude toward taking the inventory, and whether or not he or she was completely honest in responding to the items (was the client trying to come out a certain way?).

If the client indicates that he or she understood the directions, responded honestly, and had a positive attitude toward taking the Strong instrument (the client was not taking it to please someone else, for example), then the counselor should proceed with the interpretation. The LP, IP, and DP Indexes provide the percentages for which a person indicated like, indifferent and dislike on the inventory. According to Hansen (2000), most people average 32% (with a standard deviation of 12%) across all indexes. She also states that elevated and depressed profiles can be identified by either a 65% or higher response rate (for elevated) or 10% or lower response rate (for depressed). In addition, very high scores on the IP Index suggest indecisiveness. For flat profiles, Hansen recommends looking at the profile as a whole; if a consistent pattern of interests exist, the counselor should continue the interpretation. However, if the results appear random, then the counselor should use caution in interpreting or discontinue the interpretation.

Technical Information of the Strong Interest Inventory®

The Personal Style Scales consist of four subscales. According to a review of the 1994 properties, Donnay and Borgen (1996) report the following for the internal consistencies (Cronbach's alpha) and test-retest reliabilities for the four subscales:

Table 6-3	Internal Consistency Coefficients and Test-Retest of Strong Interest Inventory® Subscales	
	Internal Consistency	**Test-Retest**
Work Style	.91	.86–.91
Learning Environment	.86	.83–.91
Leadership Style	.86	.81–.88
Risk Taking/Adventure	.78	.85–.89

The alpha reliabilities for the GOTs ranged from .90 (social) to .94 (artistic), and test-retest reliabilities (3–6 months) ranged from .84 for enterprising to .92 for realistic. The alpha reliabilities for the BISs ranged from .74 (agriculture) to .92 (mechanical activities), and test-retest reliabilities ranged from .80 (culinary arts and teaching) to .94 (athletics). For a complete review of the validity, structure, and content of the Strong instrument (1994 version), see Donnay and Borgen (1996). For the SCI, internal consistency estimates ranged from .84 (Enterprising) to .88 (Realisic), with retest reliabilities after 3 weeks ranging from .83 (Realistic) to .87 on the Social scale (Betz, et al., 1996).

Additional research has examined how individuals from major racial groups differed on type assignment. Davison Aviles and Spokane (1999) found no significant differences by racial group (African American, Hispanic, White and Spanish primary language sixth to eighth grade students) on any of the Holland types, with one exception. Hispanic students scored higher on the Conventional scale than did White students. In addition, a more recent study (Lattimore & Borgen, 1999) found that the GOT patterns for college-educated satisfied workers to be very similar across African- American, Asian American, Caucasian-American, Hispanic-American, and Native American groups, with "no negative effects on occupational outcomes" for any of those groups.

Case of a College Freshman Undecided About a Career

This case study uses the sample report that is included in the Strong instrument manual. Robyn, a second-semester freshman in college, told the career counselor that she needed help in determining her interests. She added that none of the college courses she had taken so far had stimulated her to consider a specific career. As a result, she felt as though she were drifting. Her father, successful in business, was putting pressure on Robyn to make up her mind. Robyn appeared to be serious about wanting to determine her interests for career considerations.

COUNSELOR: We will gladly administer and interpret an interest inventory for you. However, I want you to understand that the results of the inventory may not pinpoint a career for you to consider.

ROBYN: Oh! I thought it would tell me what I should do for the rest of my life.

COUNSELOR: Many students share your belief. They have high expectations of interest inventories and are disappointed when they get their results. Realistically, we can expect to find some occupations for you to explore further or an occupational group you may wish to investigate. I should add that we also often find that a student will simply have his or her interests confirmed by a test.

ROBYN: Okay, that's fair enough. I need some information to help me get started toward making a career decision.

The counselor continued with an explanation of the career decision-making process. After she was satisfied that Robyn understood that interest inventory results are to be used with other factors in career exploration, the counselor discussed the selection of an interest inventory: "The Strong instrument provides a comparison of your responses to responses of individuals in a number of career fields. With these results you can determine how similar your interests are to those of individuals who have made a commitment to a specific career. You will also be able to identify some of your general occupational interests and some of your basic interests." The counselor and Robyn selected the Strong instrument because it includes many careers that require a college degree and suggests many occupational groups for further exploration.

The counselor began the interpretation session with a review of the career decision process. She then presented Robyn with the profile of the results. The counselor briefly reviewed the snapshot summary and then went on to explain the general occupational themes designated by certain letters: "The first is the R theme, which stands for realistic. Individuals who have high scores on this theme generally prefer to work with objects, machines, or tools. Examples are those in the skilled trades such as plumbers, electricians, and machine operators. Other examples are photographers and draftsmen. You have an average score for this theme." The counselor continued to explain each theme in a similar manner.

The counselor directed Robyn's attention to the summary code of her three highest general occupational themes. The counselor emphasized the importance of considering combinations of interests rather than considering just one high-interest area. In Robyn's case, the ACS summary code suggested an interest in occupations that involve art, writing, processing data, and instructing. The counselor suggested that consideration be given to different combinations of the summary code: CAS, SAC, and so on.

The counselor then went to the next part of the report and explained that the basic interest scales are also grouped according to one of the six themes. Robyn's highest scores were noted, and specific occupational scales were discussed. Finally, the counselor pointed out occupational scales with scores from 45 to 55. Several of the occupations seemed to interest Robyn. Finally, they reviewed the Personal Style Scales and discussed the implications of each in making decisions in general as well as career decisions.

The counselor suggested that they review the results of the Strong instrument by having Robyn summarize what she learned about herself: "I seem to be interested in artistic kinds of work. At least this was my highest general occupational theme. I also have an interest in conventional activities and socially related activities. I guess I like working with people to some extent, particularly influencing or persuading them. Specific occupations that interest me are librarian and legal work. I would like to explore those occupations in more depth." The counselor was satisfied with this summary, as Robyn was able to link the inventory results with potential career fields. The counselor encouraged Robyn to refer to the interest inventory results for other options if she was not satisfied with her career search.

Kuder Occupational Interest Survey (KOIS)

Kuder (1963) identified clusters of interests by administering questionnaires listing various activities to individuals employed in different occupational areas. Items that were highly correlated with one another were grouped together in descriptive scales. Groups of items that had lower correlations with one another were formed into nine clusters and designated as broad areas of interest. In this system, a specific occupational interest is determined by common factors or traits found within a broad area.

Kuder developed four inventories, as shown in Table 6-4. The two that are currently available are the Kuder General Interest Survey Form E and the KOIS Form DD. The most recent inventory, the KOIS, is described here to provide an example of the use of the inventories for career counseling. The format of the inventories requires that the individual respond to triads of items by indicating the most-liked and least-liked activity. The following scales are used in the Kuder surveys: outdoor, mechanical, computation, scientific, persuasive, artistic, literary, musical, social services, and clerical. These subtests make up the Vocational Interest Estimates on the KOIS. The KOIS also includes Occupational Scales and College Major Scales, and a list of specific occupations correlated with each scale is provided. None of the inventories has a time limit, but each can usually be taken in 30 to 40 minutes. The KOIS requires computer scoring.

Table 6-4	FOUR KUDER INVENTORIES		
Preference Schedule or Interest Survey	Form	Target Population	Scoring
Kuder Preference Record-Vocational*	CP and CM	High school students and adults	CP-Hand Scored CM-Machine Scored
Kuder Preference Record-Personal*	AH	High school students and adults	Hand scored
Kuder General Interest Survey	E	Junior/senior high school students	Hand scored
Kuder Occupational Interest Survey	DD	Students in grades 9-12, college students and adults	Computer Scored

The KOIS was designed to help measure a person's occupational and major field of study interests. It consists of 109 occupational scales, 40 college major scales, and 8 experimental scales. Individuals are instructed to mark the most- and least-preferred activity for each of 100 triads of activities. The authors use activities instead of occupational titles to avoid any preconceptions or faulty stereotypes about specific occupations. The results of the KOIS yield high, average, and low scores of vocational interest, which are shown in percentiles for both men and women.

Samples of the Vocational Interest Estimates, Occupations Ranking, and College Majors Ranking are shown in Table 6-5. The first box reports vocational interest estimates in percentiles, with scores compared with females and with males in rank order. Likewise, the second box reports occupational groups that are most similar and next most similar to the survey taker's interests. Comparisons of scores with other occupational groups are also presented. The third box includes correlations with the survey taker's interests and college major groups, by male and female. The numbers in the second and third box are neither percentiles nor standard scores but are lambda coefficients, and they come from the criterion group proportion that has the same response patterns as the person completing the KOIS. The authors state that these rankings serve to identify those occupations or majors that are most likely going to satisfy the individual in the real world. In terms of interest stability, Zytowski and England (1995) found that a

---

Table 6-5	**KOIS SAMPLE SCALES**

Sample Vocational Interest Estimates

Compared with men			Compared with women		
High			High		
	Musical	92		Musical	94
	Literary	83		Literary	79
Average			Average		
	Outdoor	65		Outdoor	72
	Scientific	60		Scientific	67
	Computational	40		Computational	49
Low			Low		
	Clerical	23		Clerical	19
	Social Service	8		Social Service	19
	Mechanical	4		Mechanical	2
	Artistic	1		Artistic	1

Sample KOIS Occupations Ratings

Compared with men		Compared with women	
Statistician	0.48	Engineer	0.43
Mathematician	0.46	Journalist	0.43
Bookstore Manager	0.46	Accountant, Certified Public	0.41
Librarian	0.45	Computer Programmer	0.41
Journalist	0.44	Lawyer	0.4
Printer	0.44	Dietician	0.39
Chemist	0.44	Nutritionist	0.38
Computer Programmer	0.43	Psychologist	0.38
Radio Station Manager	0.42	Bookstore Manager	0.37
		Pharmacist	0.37
		Librarian	0.37

Sample KOIS College Majors Ranking

The following college major groups have interest patterns most similar to yours:

Compared with men		Compared with women	
Music & Music Education	0.38	Mathematics	0.33
Mathematics	0.37	Engineering	0.31
Economics	0.37	Home Economics Education	0.3
Business Administration	0.36	History	0.29
Engineering	0.35	Music & Music Education	0.29
Physical Science	0.35	Political Science	0.29
History	0.34	English	0.28
Agriculture	0.33	Business Administration	0.28
Forestry	0.33	Foreign Language	0.27
Foreign Language	0.32		
English	0.32		
Political Science	0.32		

combination of a high occupational score and a low women-in-general or men-in-general score most predictive.

At the bottom of the report form (Figure 6-1), the verification (V) scale is used to determine whether the individual is sincere or capable of responding to the survey. A V score of 44 or less challenges the validity of the scale scores. Questionable survey results may be caused by carelessness, faking, or poor reading ability. If the V score is below 44, the counselor should make a determination of the cause before continuing the interpretation. (Specific instructions for determining the cause of low scores are provided in the test manual.)

The relationship of the individual's responses to the response patterns of a given occupational group is determined by a special correlation technique. More than three-fourths of the individuals in the 30 occupational groups compiled by Kuder scored .45 or higher on the items for their groups. Thus, a score of .45 or more indicates an occupational scale that should be considered in a career search. A word of

---

Kuder Occupational Interest Survey Report Form

Name _____   Sex FEMALE   Date 12/20/95
Numeric Grid No. _____   SRA No. _____

1. Dependability: How much confidence can you place in your results? In scoring your responses several checks were made on your answer patterns to be sure that you understood the directions and that your results were complete and dependable. According to these:

YOUR RESULTS APPEAR TO BE DEPENDABLE.

2. Vocational Interest Estimates: Vocational interests can be divided into different types and the level of your attraction to each type can be measured. You may feel that you know what interests you have already — what you may not know is how strong they are compared with other people's interests. This section shows the relative rank of your preferences for ten different kinds of vocational activities. Each is explained on the back of this report form. Your preferences in these activities, as compared with other people's interests, are as follows:

Compared with men		Compared with women	
HIGH		HIGH	
ARTISTIC	92	LITERARY	86
LITERARY	89	ARTISTIC	82
AVERAGE		AVERAGE	
SCIENTIFIC	49	SCIENTIFIC	58
CLERICAL	44	CLERICAL	36
SOCIAL SERVICE	28	PERSUASIVE	27
LOW		LOW	
PERSUASIVE	19	OUTDOOR	18
OUTDOOR	17	MUSICAL	11
MUSICAL	09	COMPUTATIONAL	11
COMPUTATIONAL	06	MECHANICAL	10
MECHANICAL	02	SOCIAL SERVICE	09

3. Occupations: The KOIS has been given to groups of persons who are experienced and satisfied in many different occupations. Their patterns of interests have been compared with yours and placed in order of their similarity with you. The following occupational groups have interest patterns most similar to yours:

Compared with men — MOST SIMILAR:
LIBRARIAN .61
BOOKSTORE MGR .58
INTERIOR DECOR .57
ELEM SCH TEACHER .57
NURSE .55
THESE ARE NEXT MOST SIMILAR:
MINISTER .53
AUDIOL/SP PATHOL .52
FILM/TV PROD/DIR .51

Compared with women — MOST SIMILAR:
BOOKSTORE MGR .71
LIBRARIAN .68
ELEM SCH TEACHER .66
THESE ARE NEXT MOST SIMILAR:
PHYSICIAN .64
DENTIST .63
FLORIST .63
SECRETARY .63
PHARMACIST .62

Compared with men — MOST SIMILAR, CONT.:
PHYSICIAN .51
MATHEMATICIAN .50
ARCHITECT .50
THE REST ARE LISTED IN ORDER OF SIMILARITY:
JOURNALIST .48
SOCIAL WORKER .48
X-RAY TECHNICIAN .48
PHYS THERAPIST .47
DENTIST .47
LAWYER .47
COUNSELOR, HS .47
CHEMIST .46
STATISTICIAN .46
PHARMACIST .46
SCIENCE TCHR, HS .45
OPTOMETRIST .45
PHOTOGRAPHER .45
PSYCHOLOGIST .45
COMPUTER PRGRMR .44
PRINTER .43
MATH TCHR, HS .43
PODIATRIST .43
POSTAL CLERK .42
TRAVEL AGENT .42
SCHOOL SUPT .42
FLORIST .41
PLANT NURSRY WKR .41
METEOROLOGIST .40
PAINTER, HOUSE .39
BUYER .39
TV REPAIRER .39
REAL ESTATE AGT .39
PERSONNEL MGR .39
CLOTHIER, RETAIL .38
VETERINARIAN .38
BOOKKEEPER .38
RADIO STATION MGR .37
FORESTER .37
BANKER .36
POLICE OFFICER .36
ENGINEER .36
TRUCK DRIVER .35
BRICKLAYER .35
PHARMACEUT SALES .34
EXTENSION AGENT .34
SUPERVSR, INDUST .34
AUTO SALESPERSON .34
WELDER .33
ELECTRICIAN .33
INSURANCE AGENT .32
MACHINIST .31
BLDG CONTRACTOR .31
ACCT, CERT PUB .31

Compared with women — MOST SIMILAR, CONT.:
AUDIOL/SP PATHOL .62
NURSE .62
SOCIAL WORKER .62
JOURNALIST .61
PHYS THERAPIST .61
DENTAL ASSISTANT .61
COL STU PERS WKR .61
OCCUPA THERAPIST .61
THE REST ARE LISTED IN ORDER OF SIMILARITY:
X-RAY TECHNICIAN .61
COUNSELOR, HS .60
PSYCHOLOGIST .59
INTERIOR DECOR .59
BEAUTICIAN .59
POLICE OFFICER .59
LAWYER .58
MINISTER .58
OFFICE CLERK .58
VETERINARIAN .58
PERSONNEL MGR .58
EXTENSION AGENT .57
SCIENCE TCHR, HS .57
MATH TEACHER, HS .57
BANKER .57
COMPUTER PRGRMR .56
BOOKKEEPER .56
NUTRITIONIST .56
RELIGIOUS ED DIR .56
DIETITIAN .55
BANK CLERK .55
INSURANCE AGENT .55
ACCT, CERT PUB .54
FILM/TV PROD/DIR .53
ARCHITECT .51
REAL ESTATE AGT .51
DEPT STORE-SALES .51
SERV ACAD CADET .49
FORESTRY .45

Compared with men — REST, CONT.:
CARPENTER .31
FARMER .31
PLUMBER .31
AUTO MECHANIC .30
PLUMBING CONTRAC .30

4. College Majors: Just as for occupations, the KOIS has been given to many persons in different college majors. The following college major groups have interest patterns most similar to yours:

Compared with men:
FOREIGN LANGUAGE .62
HISTORY .54
ENGLISH .53
THESE ARE NEXT MOST SIMILAR:
ART & ART EDUC .52
MUSIC & MUSIC ED .51
ART & MUSIC EDUC .50

Compared with women:
FOREIGN LANGUAGE .66
HISTORY .64
ENGLISH .64
ELEMENTARY EDUC .63
THE REST ARE LISTED IN ORDER OF SIMILARITY:
SOCIOLOGY .48
HOME ECON EDUC .44
POLITICAL SCI .43
DRAMA .42
SOCIOLOGY .41
PHYSICAL EDUC .41
PSYCHOLOGY .41
PHYSICAL SCIENCE .41
MATHEMATICS .40
NURSING .59
PSYCHOLOGY .59
MUSIC & MUSIC ED .59
ELEMENTARY EDUC .59
BIOLOGICAL SCI .58
HEALTH PROFESS .58
MATHEMATICS .58
ARCHITECTURE .57
ECONOMICS .33
ANIMAL SCIENCE .31
AGRICULTURE .31
ENGINEERING .31
BUSINESS ADMIN .28

Experimental Scales.

V-SCORE 56

	S	M	D
	.41	.46	.61

	M	W	MO
MBI	.71	.18	.69
F	.15		
D	.45		

7-3891

Figure 6-1 From the Kuder Occupational Interest Survey, Form DD, 1995, 1993, 1979, 1974, 1970, 1966, G. Frederick Kuder. Reprinted with permission of National Career Assessment Services, Inc. All rights reserved.

caution: Some high school students may score low on the occupational scales because of their lack of experience in and awareness of the world of work. Conversely, because of their current academic experiences, some high school students may score high on college major scales.

Occasionally, the majority of coefficients on a profile score below .31. These low scores may be a consequence of immaturity and a lack of experience and may thus indicate interests have not been crystallized. Low scorers may also have misunderstood the directions or may simply have marked responses in a careless, random manner. At any rate, if only a few coefficients reach .32–.39, caution should be used in interpreting the scores (Kuder, 1979).

Females, especially, should consider scores on opposite-sex scales when same-sex norm scales are not available. Significantly high scores reported for females on male norms indicate possible areas to consider in the career search. Broad patterns should also be considered because many individuals have not crystallized their interests.

A survey taker's report, primarily in narrative form, explains interest areas with a profile showing ten interest scales by percentiles and by low, average, or high. Then, occupational groups that are most similar and next most similar to the individual's interest patterns are presented with a narrative explanation of how the individual may use the results. Finally, college major scales are presented with an explanation of options to follow in the career decision-making process. In the final part of the report, several sources of more information on careers and specific occupations are provided.

The norm group for the KOIS vocational interest estimates included 1583 males and 1631 females from high schools, colleges, and private agency users. The norm group for the Occupational Scales consisted of groups of 200 or more males or females above the age of 25, who reported that they had been employed in their occupations for at least three years and were satisfied with their occupational choice. The College Major Scales norm groups consisted of 200 or more male or female juniors and seniors in colleges and universities.

Two types of reliability are reported in the KOIS manual. Test-retest reliabilities (two-week interval) for students in grade 12 and in college had stable coefficients, in that the median coefficient was .90. Other test-retest studies involving male high school seniors and female college seniors yielded coefficients in the .90s. One long-term study (approximately three years) of engineering students yielded a test-retest coefficient of .89. Concurrent validity was established by studying errors of classification of six validation groups. The findings suggested that the KOIS is able to discriminate among various criterion groups (Walsh, 1972). More data is needed on the predictive validity of this instrument.

The KOIS interpretive material is straightforward and easily used. The separation of occupational scales and college major scales adds to the flexibility and usefulness of this inventory. The KOIS has been reviewed by Brown (1982), Anastasi (1988), Aiken (1988), Herr (1989), and Tenopyr (1989). The Kuder General Interest Survey, Form E (KGIS-E) has been reviewed by Pope (2002).

Most recently, a computerized and online version (http://www.kuder.com/kuderonline) of Kuder's clusters has emerged, entitled *Kuder Career Search* (KCS). The KCS includes an activity preference inventory, a Person-Match scoring system, and a selection pool of individuals who are happily employed in an occupation that matches the interests of the client. The KCS is probably one of the best examples to date of a reliable, well-validated interest assessment that is fully integrated with the Internet (Ihle-Helledy, Zytowski, & Fouad, 2004). Internal consistencies were reported by these researchers as ranging from .65 to .86, with an average of .76 (See Table 6-6) and test-retest reliabilities after 14 days ranged from .72 -.92, with an average of .86.

Table 6-6	Alpha coefficients for the KCS
Art	0.86
Communications	0.77
Computations	0.72
Human Services	0.86
Mechanical	0.83
Music	0.72
Nature	0.65
Office Detail	0.71
Sales/management	0.71
Science/technical	0.77

Kelly (2002) determined that the KCS had concurrent validity when compared with the Self-Directed Search, Strong Interest Inventory. An impressive innovation with the KCS is that when an individual completes the KCS, their results are compared with norm group individuals who had a similar KCS response pattern (as opposed to comparing the results with people within a specific occupation). Both the computer and online versions have hotlinks from each job sketch to the online Occupational Outlook Handbook, each career cluster has a corresponding newsgroup on the internet (at the Kuder.com Web site), as well as counselor tips and other features currently in development.

The vocational interest estimates have been renamed "activity preferences," to be inclusive of non-vocational interests. These are shown in a percentile chart are reported and are similar to the KOIS scales, with some modifications: computations, art, human services, office detail, sales/management, nature, science/technical, communications, music, mechanical. When they are listed in standard order, they approximate the Holland hexagon. Scores above 90 are considered very high, between 75 and 90 are high, between 10 and 25 are low, and less than 10 are very low.

IV. PRESENTING YOUR

Person Match™!

You are a person, not a job title. Yet, when it comes to choosing careers, people tend to only think in terms of job titles or job descriptions, not the individuals behind them. That's why the Kuder Career Search developed Person Match™.

Person Match™ compares your interests with over 1500 real people in satisfying careers. On the following pages are the job sketches of the 5 individuals from the Kuder Career Search™ reference group whose activity preferences most resemble your own. They have all been fortunate to get into occupations they like – that are satisfying to them in significant ways. By reading about their jobs, you may explore possibilities for your own career.

Read the job sketches. Note from the sketches how the persons describe their work and the way they got into their present occupations; note whether they are working at a job they truly love, at two jobs or at a job that supports their interest in some activity that is really satisfying to them but doesn't pay, like community theater or volunteer work.

Can you find a theme or several themes common among them? Perhaps it will be a career field, like financial services. Or, it may be a characteristic common to most of them, like being your own boss or working at any level to be a part of an industry that excites you.

Carefully reading and acting on this information is a vital step in your journey toward a satisfying career. Use it well.

ACCOUNTING CLERK (330)

Although my educational background, which includes a Bachelor of Arts in psychology degree, does not correspond with my employment, I am fairly satisfied with my job in general accounting and am now planning to continue my education in business. I plan to earn a bachelor's degree in accounting and possibly to become a certified public accountant.

As the general accounting clerk in a small office, I handle the various accounting functions for the company. My regular duties include: handling accounts payable, receivables, payroll once a week, journal entries, and phone calls with vendors and/or customers to discuss account problems.

I like the kind of work I do, and the people I work with. I find job satisfaction in the challenge of my work, in problem-solving, and in the socialization within the workplace.

PHYSICIAN (279)

I have now worked as a physician for 9 years after completing my internship and other doctorate degree work. I like taking care of the sick, but find that the long hours and pressure of work being in private practice have become somewhat frustrating. If there are no emergencies, I work at the hospital from 8 a.m. to 12 noon and then at the office from 1 to 6 p.m.. At night I make house calls. Of course, emergencies can occur any hour of the day or night, so it is basically a 24 hour a day job. There is also the pressure of malpractice suits which has me somewhat dissatisfied. I am seriously thinking about using my educational background and experience in the medical field to go into teaching medicine and/or missionary work.

As well as the medical education necessary for entering this profession, I consider patience to be the most important attribute you can have to perform well.

I like the people I work with and the kind of work I do. My main satisfaction as a physician comes from patient gratitude.

Figure 6-2 From the Kuder Occupational Interest Survey, Form DD, 1995, 1993, 1979, 1974, 1970, 1966, G. Frederick Kuder. Reprinted with permission of National Career Assessment Services, Inc. All rights reserved.

The next part of the report compares the client's activity preferences occupational profiles of six clusters, and presents the clusters in order of similarity to the client's activity preference profile. The occupation chart is the next section of the report and provides a list of occupations by each cluster area and separated by educational level required. A unique aspect that the Kuder Career Search offers is the "Person Match Sketches." In this section, the computer provides a short (3 to 4 paragraphs) job report from 5 people whose activity preferences are most similar to the client's (Figure 6-2). An interesting note is that the Kuder Career Clusters actually mediate between the activity preferences and the Person-Matches (personal communication with Dr. Donald Zytowski, July 27, 2000). The people from whom these reports were taken reported being in satisfying careers and actually number more than 1500. They were drawn from the Kuder Career Search criterion reference group. The items from each of the scales have been modified, either by lengthening or by adding updated content to them for the purpose of improving reliability. The database of all the Person Matches is available in CD form or in the book *Kuder Book of People Who Like Their Work* (Hornaday & Gibson, 1995). The final two sections of the report include a list of 20 other person matches (without the job reports), and suggestions on how to continue career exploration. The purpose of the KCS, according to Zytowski (personal communication, July 27, 2000), differs from that of the KOIS in that it is meant to aid people in the career exploration process, whereas the KOIS is useful for those who want to confirm a tentative career choice.

Case of a High School Senior Rebelling Against Parental Expectations

Ann, a high school senior, had been the topic of conversation during many coffee breaks in the teachers' lounge at City High School. The teachers' major concern was her complete lack of interest in academic courses, although Ann's parents were well educated and were prominent members of the art and music groups in the city. Ann's grades reflected her lack of interest, and she had successfully resisted receiving any counseling assistance. Her parents finally convinced her to see the school counselor.

As expected, Ann approached the counselor in a casual manner and quickly admitted that the visit was her parents' idea. The counselor spent several sessions with Ann attempting to get her to respond positively. Ann showed enthusiasm only when the counselor brought up the subject of future plans. The counselor decided that she might be able to win Ann's confidence through career exploration.

Ann had taken the KOIS during her junior year, and a review of the results revealed that only a few of the coefficients reached .36 and .39. The counselor remembered that the manual mentioned that such scores should be used with caution. However, she decided to discuss the results with Ann. Ann said, "I didn't care about that test. What's the use of taking an interest inventory when you don't have many choices in the first place?" When asked to explain her remarks, Ann indicated that she had marked the inventory haphazardly without even reading some of the options. When the counselor asked her to explain her statements about not having many choices, Ann was rather hesitant. After a brief pause, she responded, "Nobody cares or understands, so why bother?" Ann eventually revealed that she felt hemmed in and unable to identify with her parents' expectations. She expressed a negative view of their lifestyle and emphasized that she wanted something different. She felt her parents were un-accepting of her needs and interests. Ann summed up her feelings: "So what's the use of saying what I want?" In the sessions that followed, the counselor encouraged Ann to express her interests and individuality.

Nevertheless, Ann remained confused about a career. She finally agreed to retake the KOIS but with a changed attitude and a different approach to responding to the choices. When the counselor received the results of the KOIS, she began by noting the V score. Because that score was well above .44, the scores were considered valid. Next, she reviewed Ann's high scores. Ann seemed eager to discuss the results when she arrived for the next counseling session. The counselor cautioned Ann that these scores would not solve all her problems but would provide vital information that could be used for career exploration. The counselor then explained the scores, and Ann pointed out those above .45. The counselor explained that Ann's musical preferences showed that 94% of women her age expressed less preference for musical abilities than she did. Regarding occupations and majors, Ann stated that engineering was a career that she had occasionally thought about from time to time. Although Ann seemed interested in the results of the KOIS, this was the first time she had given serious thought to exploring a career on her own, and she needed reinforcement from the counselor. She expressed an interest in working with people in some capacity but also recognized that her knowledge of careers and working environments was extremely limited. She agreed to become a part of a career decision-making group, which she entered armed with several occupational considerations provided by the KOIS. The counselor was pleased with Ann's progress, particularly in expressing her individual needs and interests.

Self-Directed Search (SDS)

The SDS is based on Holland's (1997) theory of career development. His theory consists of four main assumptions, with the main goal being the achievement of a "fit" between a person and his or her environment. An environment can be any arena in which a person finds himself or herself. Job titles, work place, majors or fields of study, and leisure activities are all examples of environments.

Table 6-7	Assumptions of Holland's RIASEC Theory
Assumption 1:	Personality can be classified into six distinct "types": Realistic, Investigative, Artistic, Social, Enterprising, and Conventional. Each personality is a combination, to some degree, of the six types.
Assumption 2:	There are six types of environments that share the same characteristics as the six personality types.
Assumption 3:	People are most satisfied in their environment when their three-letter personality code, derived from their interests and skills, matches that of the environment in which they are engaging.
Assumption 4:	Certain predictions can be made about the outcome of a certain personality combining with a certain environment.

In taking the paper or computer version of the SDS, individuals begin by making a list of occupational aspirations and then indicating likes or dislikes for certain activities. Next, individuals indicate activities that they can perform well or competently and identify occupations that appeal to or interest them. Finally, individuals evaluate themselves on 12 different traits based on previous experience.

Individuals calculate their scores according to easily understood directions and subsequently record the three highest scores in order. The three highest scores are determined by adding scores of responses to most-liked activities, activities done most competently, interest in occupations, and self-estimates of traits. These scores are organized to reveal a three-letter summary code representing the personality styles in Holland's typology—realistic, investigative, artistic, social, enterprising, and conventional. The person then refers to *The Occupations Finder* (Holland, 1994a) to identify occupations that match his or her exact code and combinations of that code (see Figure 6-3).

As an instrument, the SDS can be self-administered, self-scored, and self-interpreted. The SDS is available in several versions: Form R (for high school, college, adult), Form E (for those with limited education or reading skills, which is also available with an audiotape administration), Form CP (for professionals and adults in transition), and Career Explorer (for junior high students). The SDS comes in both paper and computer versions. The computer version allows for both administration of the inventory and inputting of scores (from the paper version) and produces an interpretive report and professional summary. A new online version is available at cost from the Psychological Assessment Resources Web site: http://www.parinc.com. There are currently some drawbacks to the online version. First, individuals cannot enter their aspirations, and therefore the counselor has to manually identify the client's aspiration summary code for comparison with the obtained code. Second, the professional summary is not generated, nor is the final page of the paper version that provides a breakdown of scores for each section (which would allow for comparison of interests and skills). Third, there is no way to generate a new list of occupations (for example, if the client reads through the types and believes she is really an IRS, rather than an IRC) without having to retake and pay for the inventory. Fourth, unlike the computerized version of the SDS, the online version does not include the My Vocational Situation, which can be very useful for counselors. The online version does reconfigure uncommon types to allow for only the first two letters, so a client will not end up with a type that has no matching occupations. Another caution for using online assessments in general is that there is no guarantee that the hardware won't "crash" in the middle (or at the end) of an administration, which can be extremely frustrating for clients.

The interpretive report is eight to ten pages long and provides the clients with information about Holland's theory, a basic interpretation of the results, and a list of occupations, fields of study, and leisure activities that might aid in career decision making. DOT *(Dictionary of Occupational Titles)* (U.S.

Portions of The Occupations Finder

Enterprising Occupations

Code	DOT	ED
ESI		
Attorney, Tax	(110.117-038)	6
Library Consultant	(100.117-014)	6
Music Therapist	(076.1127-014)	6
Budget Officer	(161.117-010)	5
Computer Operations Supervisor	(213.132-010)	5
Estate Planner	(186-117-038)	5
Executive Director, Red Cross	(187.117-038)	5
Flight Operations Manager	(184.117-038)	5
ESA		
Judge	(111.107-010)	6
Lawyer	(110.107-010)	6
Placement Director	(166.167-014)	6
Politician	(————————-)	6
Producer, Motion Pictures	(187.167-174)	6
Social Welfare Administrator	(195.117-010)	6
Advertising Agency Manager	(164.117-014)	5
Artist's Manager	(191.117-010)	5
ESC		
Director of Institutional Research	(090.167-018)	6
Outpatient Services Director	(187.117-058)	6
Administrative Assistant	(169.167-010)	5
Animal Shelter Manager	(187.167-218)	5
Business Manager	(191.117-018)	5
Circulation Manager	(163.167-014)	5
Credit and Collection Manager	(169.167-086)	5
Dietary Manager	(187.167-206)	5
ECR		
Executive Housekeeper	(187.167-046)	5
Incinerator Plant Supervisor	(955.131-010)	4
Mapping Supervisor	(018.167-030)	4
Supervisor (Protective Devices)	(692.137-014)	4
Test-Desk Supervisor	(822.131-030)	4
Furniture Assembly Supervisor	(763.134-014)	3

Rearrange your code letters in all possible ways.

Figure 6-3   Portion of the Occupations Finder adapted and reproduced by special permission of the Publisher, Psychological Assessment Resources, Inc., 16204 North Florida Avenue, Lutz, FL 33549, from the Self-Directed Search Form R The Occupations Finder by John L. Holland, Ph.D., Copyright 1970, 1972, 1977, 1985, 1989, 1990, 1993, 1994, 1996, 2000 by PAR, Inc. Further reproduction is prohibited without permission from PAR, Inc.

Department of Labor, 1991) and EOF *(Educational Opportunities Finder)* numbers are provided for each field of study listed. *The Occupations Finder* (Holland, 1994a), a workbook that accompanies the SDS, provides a listing of more than 1300 occupations by all codes and lists the DOT number and education development level for each occupation. In addition to the interpretive report, a professional summary report is available for counselors.

The purpose of this report is to highlight the client's results and to identify potential problem areas.

By examining a person's summary codes for each section (activities, competencies, self-ratings and so on) a counselor can point out discrepancies between the scores. (This page is also available in the paper and pencil version). For example, a person's Summary Code might be SCE, but when the counselor reviews the professional summary, she notices that the person scored himself very high in conventional activities on the competency and self-ratings sections and very low on the activities and occupations sections. Upon inquiry, the counselor learns that this client was a secretary for many years, thus acquiring many "conventional" skills. This type of information is critical to have when interpreting a person's SDS results.

Other information included in the professional summary of SDS is degree of congruence, summary code of a person's aspirations, coherence of aspirations, consistency, differentiation, and a list of the person's aspirations. If the person has taken My Vocational Situation (Holland, Daiger, & Power, 1980) on computer, his or her vocational identity and occupational information needs and barriers will also be listed, as well as critical items, which are those items on the vocational identity scale that the person responded to with "True."

Congruence has to do with how well a person's summary code matches his or her environment. In other words, how do a person's current interests compare with the occupations being considered? Another assumption of Holland's theory is that the agreement between a person and an environment can be estimated through a hexagonal model. A distinct difference between these two codes might indicate a need for further information about the occupational aspirations, a need for more experience within related fields (a counselor should examine the three skill sections and look for lower scores), or further exploration regarding the attractiveness of those occupations. A counselor could also examine the degree of congruence between a person's summary code and current occupation. A high degree of difference might help explain lack of satisfaction in the current situation.

By examining the *aspirations* listed and seeing the amount of *coherence* among those aspirations, a counselor can gain a picture of how stable a person's ideas are relative to occupational options. A person who has listed occupational aspirations that don't have a lot in common with each other might need special assistance, including information about these specific occupations, a schema for organizing the world of work, or more information about self, self-concept, and self-efficacy.

Another assumption is that the degree of *consistency* between views of self and work environments can be determined through the hexagonal model. Consistency has to do with how close the letters of the summary code are to each other. Codes that are closer together have more in common, whereas codes that lie opposite on the hexagon have much less in common. Therefore, a person whose code comprises opposite types (such as Social-Realistic) is expressing very distinct descriptions of self. By exploring the professional summary, a counselor can identify whether this report is the result of a difference in background, such as the previous example of a person with a large amount of clerical experience versus actual interests, or if the summary code is a true reflection of the person's interests. Someone whose first two codes are opposites might have to look at satisfying one of those types through leisure or volunteer activities.

The amount of *differentiation* between codes provides a counselor with a clearer picture of a person's code. This assumption suggests that the amount of differentiation in a person's code affects any prediction a counselor might make from a person's code. A "true" code would be one where the first letter is separated by 8 points from the next letter. A person whose scores are well differentiated has identifiable interests that are unlikely to shift drastically, whereas a person whose letters are less differentiated might be less clear as to what area truly interests him or her. Someone who has a high, undifferentiated code is indicating a lot of interests and skills in several areas. This type of person might be multi-potential or even indecisive. A person with low, undifferentiated scores might need more experiences in different environments to more clearly identify skills and interests, or might be experiencing a lot of negative self-talk that causes a negative self-rating. Thus, differentiation is an important factor to investigate when interpreting a client's code. If the top three codes are close together, then the person is more likely to find satisfying occupations when looking under various combinations of his or her initial code. On the other hand, a person who is highly differentiated will be more likely to be interested in those occupations that have the same primary code (first letter).

Using the SDS in Counseling

One of the main purposes of the SDS is to help clients expand their occupational, educational, and leisure options. Clients who are using the paper version are instructed to find the occupations related to their summary code. If, for example, an individual's summary code is RSC, the occupations listed under this code are primary occupations for further exploration. In the Holland system, the more dominant the primary modal personal style, the greater the likelihood of satisfaction in the corresponding work environment (Holland, 1992). To investigate other career possibilities, the individual is required to list related summary codes. In the preceding example, different combinations of the summary code RSC should be explored: SRC, SCR, CRS, CSR, and RCS. In the computer version, the primary occupations and occupations related to various code combinations are provided for the client.

Table 6-8	Holland's Personality Codes

Personality Types and Salient Characteristics

	Realistic	Investigative	Artistic	Social	Enterprising	Conventional
Traits Self-Rating	Hardheaded Mechanical Scientific Quiet Reserved Unassuming Highly Trained Low Self- understanding	Analytical Intellectual Curious Mechanical Scholarly Scientific Broad Interests Precise Thorough	Aloof Artistic Broad Interests Careless Disorderly Dreamy Idealistic Imaginative Intellectual Introspective Not Conforming Original Radical Rebellious Sensitive Sophisticated Unconventional Unusual Verbal Witty Complicated Power-seeking	Capable Enthusiastic Friendly Good Leader Kind Persuasive Not Scientific Sincere Trusting Understanding Receptive Sociable Warm	Aggressive Dominant Enterprising Extroverted Good Leader Not Quiet Not Scientific Persuasive Pleasure-seeking Popular Practical-minded Shrewd Sociable Speculative Striving Versatile Confident Energetic	Content Not Artistic Not Idealistic Normal Practical-minded Shrewd Speculative Conforming Conventional Not Original Rebellious Neat
Stereotypes of Types	Skilled Mechanically Inclined Trained Builders Practical Well Paid	Scientific Intelligent Studious Scholarly Brilliant Inventive Introverted Respected	Creative Imaginative Talented Expressive Sensitive Interesting Unconventional Temperamental	Important Influential Helpful Devoted Patient Understanding Friendly	Ambitious Aggressive Leaders Shrewd Busy Responsible Status Seeking Dynamic	Precise Mathematical Methodical Meticulous Unimaginative Invaluable Dull

Inventory and
Scales
	Mechanical
	Dogmatic
		Open
		Academic Type
		Analytical
		Curious
		Mechanical
		Scholarly
		Scientific
		Broad Interests
			Open
			Nonconforming
			Feminine
			Introverted
			Original
			Expressive
			Nonconformist
			  Type
				Extroverted
				Sociable
				Enthusiastic
				Liking to Help
				  Others
				Feminine
				Dependent
				Understanding
				  of Others
				Cooperative
				Interest in
				  Religion
				Collegiate Type
					Extroverted
					Sociable
					Dominant
					Enthusiastic
					Adventurous
					Dependent
					  (Group)
					Leadership
					Sociability
					Self-Confidence
					  (Social)
					Popularity
					Collegiate Type
						Conservative
						Dogmatic
						Vocational Type

Values	Institutional
	  Restraint
	Christian
	Conservative
	Docility
	
	Freedom
	True
	  Friendship (–)
	
	Ambitious
	Self-controlled
	Forgiving (–)
		Self-
		  Determination
		Theoretical
		Adolescent
		  Revolt
		
		Wisdom
		Family
		  Security (–)
		True
		  Friendship (–)
		
		Intellectual
		Logical
		Ambitious
		Cheerful (–)
			Self-Expression
			
			World of Beauty
			Equality
			
			Imaginative
			Courageous
			Obedient (–)
			Capable (–)
			Responsible (–)
			Clean (–)
			Logical (–)
				Service to Others
				Social
				Friendly Interest
				
				Equality
				Mature Love (–)
				Exciting Life (–)
				
				Helpful
				Forgiving
				Capable (–)
				Logical (–)
				Intellectual (–)
					Control of
					  Others
					Economic/
					  Political
					Dominant/
					  Striving
					
					Freedom
					World of
					  Beauty (–)
					
					Ambitious
					Forgiving (–)
					Helpful (–)
						Institutional
						  Restraint
						Christian
						Conservative
						Economic/
						  Political
						Docility
						Comfortable Life
						Self-Respect (–)
						World of
						  Beauty (–)
						True
						  Friendship
						Ambitious
						Polite
						Obedient
						Imaginative (–)
						Forgiving (–)

Table 6-8	Holland's Personality Codes (cont.)

Personality Types and Salient Characteristics

	Realistic	Investigative	Artistic	Social	Enterprising	Conventional
Life Goals	Inventing Apparatus or Equipment Becoming Outstanding Athlete	Inventing Valuable Product Theoretical Contribution to Science Technical Contribution to Science	Becoming Famous in Performing Arts Publishing Stories Original Painting Instrumental Musician or Singer Musical Composition Played or Published	Helping Others in Difficulty Making Sacrifices for Others Competent Teacher or Therapist Being Religious Person Being Good Parent Leader in Church Contributing to Human Welfare	Being Well Dressed Being Community Leader Influential in Public Affairs Expert in Finance and Commerce	Expert in Finance and Commerce Producing a Lot of work
Aptitudes and Competencies	Intelligence	Musical Talent Mechanical Comprehension Arithmetic Ability	Interpersonal (Seashore) Art Judgment (Meier) Spatial Visual (MPFB)	Leaderless Problem Solving Assessment	Clerical Group Discussion	Aptitudes (Minn. Clerical)
	Technical Competencies Mechanical Ability	Scientific Competencies Math Ability Research Ability Scientific Ability	Art Competencies Foreign Language Competencies Artistic Ability	Social and Educational Competencies Leadership and Sales Competencies Interpersonal Competency	Leadership and Sales Competencies Social and Educational Competencies Business and Clerical Competencies Interpersonal Competency	Business and Clerical Competencies Clerical Ability
Greatest Ability Lies in Area of	Mechanics	Science	Arts	Human Relations	Leadership	Business
Identifications	Thomas Edison Admiral Byrd	Madame Curie Charles Darwin	T.S. Eliot Pablo Picasso	Jane Addams Albert Schweitzer	Henry Ford Andrew Carnegie	Bernard Baruch John D. Rockefeller

Holland Codes adapted and reproduced by special permission of the Publisher, Psychological Assessment Resources, Inc., 16204 North Florida Avenue, Lutz, FL 33549, from the Self-Directed Search Professional User's Guide by John L. Holland, Ph.D., Amy B. Powell, Ph.D. and Barbara A. Fritzsche, Ph.D., Copyright 1985, 1987, 1994, 1997 by PAR, Inc. Further reproduction is prohibited without permission from PAR, Inc.

Once a person has obtained either a list of potential occupations or a printout, the counselor may want to have the client reduce the list by crossing off "unacceptable" options. An important step in this process would be to ask the client to verbalize why each choice is unacceptable. By doing this, certain avoidance themes might start to emerge, which could be further processed in counseling. A counselor may also want to show the client descriptions of the six types and ask whether he or she agrees with the personality code determined by the inventory. If there is a discrepancy, the counselor may want to examine the difference between the person's interests and competencies, as well as the degree of differentiation.

It may also be helpful to ask clients what they think of their list. Where does it fit? Does it make sense? Were there any surprises? Were there any occupations the client was hoping to see on the list that didn't make it? It should be noted that just because a client thinks the results are invalid, doesn't mean that they actually are. The counselor might look at individual items with the client to show how the client's responses yielded the results.

A counselor might also want to spend time on the aspirations or expressed interests section of the SDS. The clients could describe what is attractive about each of these fields, as well as what might be keeping them from pursuing each further. This information is useful as it reveals not only interests, but work preferences and sometimes work values. In addition, the counselor can look for congruence between the client's summary aspiration codes and summary code on the inventory.

In addition to helping a client learn about his or her RIASEC code and seeing accompanying options, knowing a person's Holland code can provide information about how the counselor might best work with that client. For example, a conventional type might be more apt to appreciate and follow a detailed action plan, whereas an artistic type might find a detailed plan to be uncreative and claustrophobic. A social or enterprising type might be more interested in talking through the career planning process, whereas an investigative or realistic type might want to spend the majority of the time trying out the job activities on the computer or with the career resource books. It might also be helpful for the client to see how the Holland codes relate to other factors, such as values, life goals, aptitudes/competencies, traits, stereotypes of the specific types, major abilities, and famous figures associated with the various types (see Table 6-8).

Technical Aspects of the SDS

The 1994 version of the SDS included expanded norm groups for both the SDS codes and scales. The norm sample for the 1994 assessment booklet was composed of 2602 students and working adults. The sample included 1600 females and 1002 males, who ranged in age from 17 to 65 years (mean = 23.5), with 75% Caucasian, 8% African American, 7% Hispanic, 4% Asian Americans, 1% Native Americans, and 5% from other ethnic backgrounds.

Internal consistency was calculated by KR-20 and yielded coefficients ranging from .67 to .94 from samples of 2000 to 6000 college freshmen. Of that group, coefficients for men ranged from .63 to .88 and for women, from .53 to .85. Test-retest reliabilities (three- to four-week intervals) for high school students yielded a median coefficient of .81 for boys and median coefficient of .83 for girls. A sample of 65 college freshmen yielded test-retest reliability coefficients ranging from .60 to .84 over a seven- to ten-month interval. There appears to be sufficient evidence of content validity from item content. A number of studies supporting the predictive validity of the SDS have been compiled and are reported in the SDS manual (Holland, 1994b). Dumenci's (1995) results of a study of 800 students provide support for the convergent and discriminant validity of the SDS. A more recent by Helwig and Myrin (1997) examined the occurrence and stability of Holland codes in a three-generation family and found a high degree of stability of the codes. Others (Einarsdottir, Rounds, AEgisdotter & Gerstein, 2002) found that for Icelandic and American samples, both the Self-Directed Search and the RIASEC model provided a good fit for both groups.

Holland (1997) and Gottfredson (2002) suggested that the self-estimates and self-ratings of the SDS can be viewed as self-beliefs (Holland) or measures of self-efficacy (Gottfredson) related to the specific types. Two researches (Lindley & Borgen, 2002) sought to investigate how self-efficacy plays itself out with Gottfredson's suggestion for men and women. They found the following significant correlations for men: Investigative ($r = .40$), Enterprising ($r = .34$) and Conventional ($r = .43$). Women's self-efficacy scores were significantly and positively correlated to all of the RIASEC summary scales, ranging from $r = .17$ (Artistic) to $r = .34$ (Enterprising). This differs from an earlier report by Betz and Klein (1996) which found men's general self-efficacy to be significantly related to all Holland summary scores, and women's related only to Investigative, Social, Enterprising and Conventional. Regardless of the differences, one fact is evident – generalized self-efficacy is related to the RIASEC types.

The SDS is designed to furnish the individual with a model of systematic career exploration. Although the SDS can be self-interpreted, the individual should be stimulated to seek further career guidance. Many individuals will want to clarify their interests with a counselor who can provide additional information for career decision-making. The SDS provides results that can be easily incorporated into group and individual career counseling programs.

One of the major criticisms of the SDS centers on a need for monitoring the self-scoring of the instrument. Also, individuals often need assistance in using The Occupations Finder (Holland, 1994a). Finally, more data are needed, and should be reported in the manual, on the use of the SDS for women, minority groups, and adults. Extensive reviews of the SDS include those by Anastasi (1988), Aiken (1988), Ciechalski (2002), Dumenci (1995), Manuelle-Adkins (1989), and McKee and Levinson (1990).

A helpful book for those who consistently use (or plan to use) the SDS is The Self-Directed Search and Related Holland Materials: A Practitioner's Guide by Reardon and Lenz (1998). Holland is to be commended for encouraging people to consider their careers by using a straightforward format. Other benefits of Holland's theory and subsequent inventories include simplicity of theory, easy-to-understand vocabulary, organizational framework, face validity, and the translation to practice from theory (Rayman and Atanasoff, 1999). Spokane and Catalano (2000) cite additional benefits as low cost of the SDS, the self-administration, and the numerous continuing studies that focus on its usefulness. The popularity of the SDS demonstrates the need for this type of format. His theoretical approach to personality development as a primary consideration in career decision-making has greatly influenced methods for presenting results on a number of widely used interest inventories.

Case of a Group Program in a Community College

A community college counseling center regularly offered seminars in career exploration, and a major component of the program involved interest identification. In one all-male group, the SDS was administered with the counselor monitoring the scoring.

After each student had recorded his own SDS code, the counselor explained Holland's six modal personal styles and their corresponding codes, then grouped students according to their personal styles. Using The Occupations Finder, each group was assigned the responsibility of writing and presenting at the next session a description of its primary modal personal style and of one or more specific occupations that matched this style.

In the next counseling session, the counselor explained how to use The Occupations Finder for locating specific occupations by summary codes. The counselor noted that DOT codes as well as educational levels were listed for each of the summary codes. When the counselor was sure that everyone understood how to use the booklet, he made this assignment: "Each of you is to use the career resource center library and write a description of two more occupations under your summary code using our career planning notes to record your comments. Bring these completed forms with you to our next session." During the next group meeting, the counselor encouraged members to relate problems encountered with locating careers according to their summary codes and to ask questions concerning their career exploration. Each member was encouraged to investigate other combinations of his SDS code.

For example, the counselor suggested that the individual who made the report on drafting (RIE) should investigate occupations under IRE, IER, and other combinations. Each member was requested to share his career planning notes with other members in his group. All group members were invited for individual counseling sessions and were encouraged to evaluate other occupations they were considering, including the educational/training requirements and potential for employment.

Career Decision Making-Revised (CDM-R): The Harrington-O'Shea Decision Making System

The CDM-R (Harrington & O'Shea, 2000) can also be self-administered and self-interpreted. This system has been constructed on Holland's (1992) theory of career development framework. Five of Holland's six occupational types have been given different names in CDM: Realistic has been changed to crafts, investigative has been changed to scientific, artistic has been changed to the arts, social remains as is, enterprising has been changed to business, and conventional has been changed to office operations (Harrington & O'Shea, 1992). Care was taken to make all items in the system applicable to both men and women; the results are reported independently of sex. There are two levels of the CDM: Level 1 is less complex, consisting of a 96-item interest inventory, and designed for younger students (7th to 10th grade) and for people who have difficulty reading. Level 2 is for mature students (11th and 12th grade) and adults, consisting of 120 gender neutral items. Both are also available in Spanish. Level 1 takes about 20 minutes to complete; Level 2 takes about 45 minutes.

The format for Level 2 requires that individuals choose their top two preferences of career clusters, followed by their two favorite school subject areas and their preferred training or education option for the future. Then they complete a 120-item interest inventory. Results can either be hand scored by the client (or counselor) or machine scored. The results (raw scores) are then transferred to the interpretive folder, which includes a summary profile, a career clusters chart, a guide to majors and training programs based on major interests, and tips for continuing career exploration. Figure 6-4 shows a completed summary profile for Level 2. The CDM appears to be a comprehensive system, integrating many of the key elements necessary for making successful career decisions. The CDM 2000 incorporates the interest inventories used in the CDM.

Interpretation

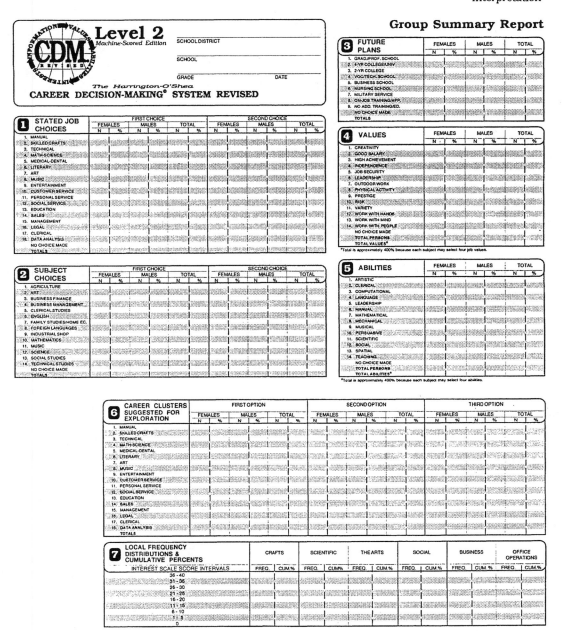

The 1993 CDM-R manual provides a variety of case studies, covering congruent profiles, need for exploration, possible sex stereotyping, profiles that are lacking in consistency, unrealistic career goals, vocational confusion, need for compromise, and low scale scores. In addition, the manual describes a Group Summary Report (see Figure 6-5), which is compiled by the machine-scored CDM-R. This option compiles CDM-R results for groups and is useful for curriculum planners by summarizing career goals, interests, and subject choices. Sex and percentage breakdowns accompany each scale.

Internal consistencies for Level 1 (N = 965) ranged from .88 to .93, with a median alpha of .90. Level 2 (N = 996) alphas ranged from .92 to .95, with a median alpha of .93. Test-retest data is provided for both

CAREER CLUSTERS	TYPICAL JOBS	SCHOOL SUBJECTS	WORK VALUES	ABILITIES
SCIENTIFIC — ☐ Math-Science	**Computers:** Computer Programmer G-030-C; Computer Scientist F-020-C; Computer Security Specialist L-031-C; Database Administrator E-039-C; Network Administrator E-061-C; Network Analyst E-031-C; Software Engineer F-030-C; Systems Analyst E-039-C; Web Site Developer E-032-032-C; Webmaster E-030-032-C — **Design:** Architect F-001-C; Landscape Architect G-001-C — **Engineering:** Aerospace Engineer F-002-C; Chemical Engineer G-008-C; Civil Engineer F-005-C; Computer Engineer E-078-C; Electrical and Electronics Engineer E-003-C; Mechanical Engineer G-002-C — Metallurgical, Ceramic and Materials Engineer F-006-C; Mining Engineer P-010-C; Nuclear Engineer F-003-C; Petroleum Engineer F-019-C — **Laboratory Technology:** Medical Lab Technologist F-078-C; Pharmacist F-074-C — **Life Sciences:** Agricultural Scientist F-040-C; Biologist F-041-C; Environmental Scientist NA-029-C — Forester G-040-C; Pharmacologist F-041-C; Soil Conservationist C-040-C — **Mathematics:** Actuary F-026-C; Mathematician F-078-C; Statistician G-020-C — **Physical Sciences:** Chemist C-072-C; Geologist C-030-C; Meteorologist F-055-C — Oceanographer F-024-C; Physicist/Astronomer P-021, 011-C — **Other:** Economist F-060-C; Engineering Science Computer Systems Manager G-002-019-C; Experimental Psychologist F-045-C; Market Research Analyst G-050-C; Math-Science Teacher G-091-C; Operations Research Analyst G-020-C; Urban and Regional Planner F-018-C	Agriculture; Art; English; Finance; Math; Science; Technology	Creativity; Good Salary; High Achievement; Independence; Job Security; Leadership; Outdoor Work; Prestige; Variety; Work with Hands; Work with Mind	Artistic; Computational; Language; Leadership; Manual; Mathematical; Mechanical; Scientific; Spatial; Teaching — Social; Spatial
SCIENTIFIC — ☐ Medical-Dental	**Dentistry:** Dentist F-072-C; Orthodontist F-072-C — Chiropractor G-074-C; Dietician/Nutritionist G-077-C; Optometrist G-079-C; Physical Therapist E-076-C; Speech Pathologist E-076-C — **Health Specialties:** Audiologist E-076-C — **Medicine:** Anesthesiologist F-070-C; Cardiologist G-070-C; General Practitioner G-070-C; Neurologist F-070-C — Obstetrician F-070-C; Orthopedist F-070-C; Pathologist F-070-C; Pediatrician G-070-C — Psychiatrist F-070-C; Radiologist F-070-C; Surgeon F-070-C; **Veterinary Medicine** Veterinarian G-073-C	Agriculture; English; Math; Science	Creativity; Good Salary; High Achievement; Independence; Job Security; Leadership; Prestige; Variety; Work with Hands; Work with Mind	Language; Leadership; Manual; Mathematical; Mechanical; Scientific
BUSINESS — ☐ Sales	**Purchasing:** Buyer F-162-C; Purchasing Agent F-162-C — **Sales:** Automobile Sales G-273-A; Counter/Rental Clerk G-295-A; Dispensing Optician G-299-A; Employment Interviewer G-165-A; Financial Planner F-250-C — Kind Raiser G-293-A; Insurance Sales F-250-A; Manufacturer's Representative G-278-A; Real Estate Sales G-250-A; Retail Sales Worker G-290-279-A — Route Sales Driver E-592-A; Stock and Bond Sales F-250-C; Travel Agent G-252-A; Wholesale Sales Representative G-260-279-T — **Technical Sales:** Computer and Business Services Sales Representative E-253-C; Sales Engineer G-002-015-C. Note: These are sales agents for many other goods and services.	English; Management; Math; Finance — For Sales Engineers: Science; Technology	Creativity; Good Salary; High Achievement; Independence; Leadership; Variety; Work with Mind; Work with People	Clerical; Computational; Language; Leadership; Mathematical; Persuasive — Scientific; Social
BUSINESS — ☐ Management	**Administration:** Administrative Service Manager P-169-A; Legislative Assistant NA-169-A; Office Manager F-169-T; Bank Manager E-186-C; Business Executive P-189-C; Government Administrator P-188-A — **Management:** Auto Service Station Manager F-185-A; Chef G-313-T; Construction Superintendent G-182-A; Farm Manager P-180-T; Food Service Manager G-187-A — Human Resources Manager F-166-C; Sales/Marketing Manager F-163-A — Funeral Director E-187-T; Health Care Manager G-187-T; Hotel/Motel Manager G-187-A; Production Manager P-183-A; Property/Real Estate Manager G-186-C; Restaurant Manager G-187-A — Retail Store Supervisor F-185-A — **Planning:** Contractor G-182-A; Industrial Engineer G-012-C; Management Consultant P-189-C	Agriculture; Finance; English; Languages; Management; Math; Science; Social Science	Creativity; Good Salary; High Achievement; Independence; Leadership; Prestige; Variety; Work with Mind; Outdoor Work; Work with People	Computational; Language; Leadership; Mathematical; Persuasive; Scientific — Social
BUSINESS — ☐ Legal	**Contracts and Claims:** Claims Adjuster G-241-A; Tax Examiner G-119-T — **Safety/Law Enforcement:** Building Inspector G-168-T; Customs Inspector F-168-A; FBI Agent P-375-C; Fire Chief P-373-A — **Law:** Judge P-111-C; Lawyer P-110-C; Paralegal Assistant F-119-T — Food and Drug Inspector F-168-T; Industrial Hygienist NA-079-C; Police Chief P-375-A; Private Detective F-378-A; Social Agent P-375-C	English; Finance; Management; Math; Science; Social Science	Creativity; Good Salary; High Achievement; Independence; Job Security; Leadership; Prestige; Role; Variety; Work with Mind; Work with People	Computational; Language; Leadership; Persuasive; Scientific — Social

Figure 6-5 CDM Group Summary. From the Harrington-O'Shea Career Decision-Making ® System Revised (CDM 2000): Career Clusters Chart, scientific and business sections, by Thomas F. Harrington and Arthur O'Shea © 2000. Published by American Guidance Service, Inc. 4201 Woodland Road, Circle Pines, MN 55014-1796. Reproduced with permission of the publisher. All rights reserved. www.agsnet.com

groups and is divided by female and male over a two-week and five-month period. The following table summarizes this data:

Table 6-9	Internal Consistency Coefficients for CDM			
High School	**2 wks (range)**	**2 wks (median)**	**5 mos (range)**	**5 mos (median)**
Female	.78–.90	.85	.67–.86	.81
Male	.76–.88	.80	.69–.87	.77
College	**2 wks (range)**	**2 wks (median)**	**5 mos (range)**	**5 mos (median)**
Female	.78–.88	.86	.50–.85	.75
Male	.76–.93	.91	.68–.86	.82

The authors have accumulated impressive evidence of construct and concurrent validity primarily by comparing the CDM-R scales with corresponding SII and SDS scales. Predictive validity is addressed for earlier versions. For example, in an 11-year longitudinal study, CDM results and choice of college major during the freshman year were compared, with the results indicating that 76% had graduated with a major that was congruent with their freshman CDM scores. Although this is an impressive finding, the manual does not provide any predictive information for the 1992 version. For further evaluation of this instrument, refer to the reviews by Campbell and Raiff (2002), Droege (1984), Vansickle (1994), and Willis (1982).

The CDM-R provides a comprehensive model for career decision making. It can best be used for those in junior high school and older subjects (including adults). Minority group norms are available, and the authors claim the test has no sex bias. Although scores can be self-interpreted, the authors recommend seeing a professional for continuation of career planning. Again, the major purpose of the CDM-R is to provide data that will encourage self-exploration in the career decision process.

Case of Using the CDM-R 2000 in Counseling

Leesa, a ninth-grade student was very impressed by a recent career speaker that the counseling center brought to school. What really appealed to her was not the field that the speaker came from, but the advice she gave on identifying, preparing for and following one's own dream. Leesa said that she wanted to start now, to figure out a general career direction, so that she could plan her summers and even the clubs she would join to help her develop in that area. Her CDM-R 2000 profile is presented in Figure 6-3. After reviewing the summary profile with Leesa, the counselor asked Leesa to work on the Career Clusters Chart for homework. When Leesa returned for her follow-up session, she described the activity to the counselor.

LEESA: Well, here's what I've narrowed it down to: scientific or business fields.

COUNSELOR: That's interesting—it kind of goes along with what you've been considering all along. But even though you've narrowed it down in terms of general fields, there are quite a lot of possibilities within each of those areas.

LEESA: Don't I know it? I was hoping that this was going to get easier, as I got closer to figuring out which area I wanted to go into. But, instead, it seems to be getting more confusing.

COUNSELOR: It can be overwhelming to see so many options. Let's look at the fields you've chosen. What commonalities did you see between those two fields?

LEESA: Agriculture! I really never considered that before. That just doesn't seem like me, raising fish and all.

COUNSELOR: Now, hold on . . . remember our deal? We're not going to cross off any alternatives until you know enough about them. I bet you'd be surprised to see a lot of interesting jobs within the field of agriculture, that don't involve fish.

LEESA: OK, you're right. I don't want to close off any options just yet. OK, besides agriculture, they both involve math, English, and science, and I'm pretty good at those classes. They share similar values, such as Creativity, High Achievement and Good Salary. Outdoor work is also pretty common, but I don't know if I'd want to be outdoors a lot, especially if the weather was bad.

COUNSELOR: So maybe that would be something to check out in your volunteer work.

CAMPBELL INTEREST AND SKILL SURVEY INDIVIDUAL PROFILE REPORT

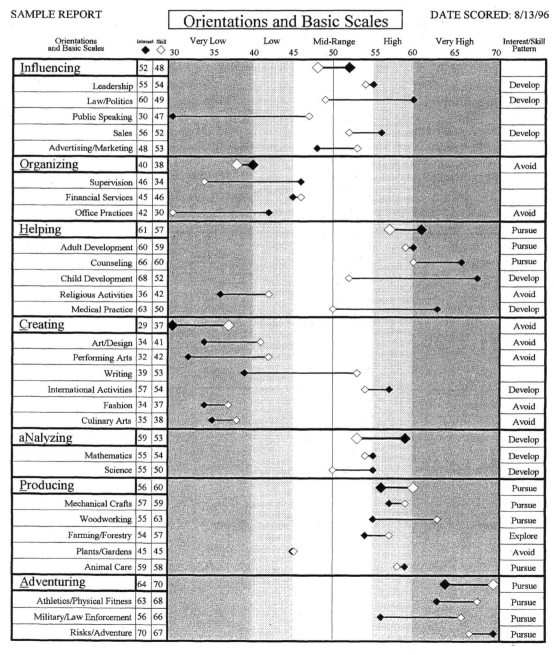

Figure 6-6

LEESA: That's a good point. These areas also have leadership abilities in common. I guess I should make an effort to be a leader, maybe even a president of a club.

COUNSELOR: So, you've got some short-term goals: Join a club or two in one of these areas, making a good effort to be a leader, and find a summer job or volunteer work that requires outdoor work. What else makes sense to you?

LEESA: I think I want to give myself a goal of reading about each of these fields, maybe one every 2 weeks. Then I can start identifying occupations that seem to match me on interests, values and skills, and narrow the list as I find those that don't. Maybe we could work together to create some type of a chart?

COUNSELOR: I think that's a great idea. You're probably going to need to balance all that head knowledge you'll be getting from the reading with real life experiences.

LEESA: Yeah. Can you help me meet some people in the fields I decide on?

COUNSELOR: I'd be happy to do it. Why don't we first start with making your chart, and then you get back to me, say, in a month, and tell me what you're leaning towards?

LEESA: Sounds great to me!

The counselor and Leesa proceeded to make a chart of the general fields she was interested in. Then they identified potential occupations that came to mind. Across the top of the page, Leesa identified her most important interests, values, and skills. The counselor pointed Leesa to some general books on careers in science and business, from which Leesa was able to expand her list. During the weeks that followed, Leesa was able to narrow her list from her reading. As an experience in leadership development, the counselor asked Leesa to take the initiative in inviting a medical technologist to speak to interested students. Leesa had to locate a speaker, generate interest among students, schedule a room, and introduce the speaker. In this example, Leesa was able to work closely with the counselor to create opportunities to further clarify her interests, test her abilities, and examine her options. The CDM served as a stepping stone from which Leesa was able to create her own organizational chart for career development.

Campbell Interest and Skill Survey (CISS)

The CISS is described by its developers (Campbell, Hyne, & Nilsen, 1992) as a "survey of self-reported interests and skills" (p. 1), the main purpose of which is to help clients determine how their occupational interests and skills mesh in the world of work, thus enabling better choices. The CISS, which is available in both English and Spanish, also provides parallel scales that provide an estimate of clients' confidence in their ability to perform various occupational tasks. It consists of 200 interest items and 120 skill items, and clients respond to the items on a 6-point response scale. The CISS, which takes about 35 minutes to complete, uses gender-neutral norms and provides combined gender scales to allow for the broadest interpretation of scores.

The CISS evolved from a long history of quality instruments, starting with the Strong Vocational Interest Blank. For a review of the history of the development of the CISS, the reader is referred to Campbell (2002). The current version is said to be built on a new model for classifying major occupational orientations. The seven orientation scales include Influencing, Organizing, Helping, Creating, Analyzing, Producing, and Adventuring. As is easily seen, the scales are very similar to Holland's general occupational themes, with a couple of additions.

The report summary contains information in three types of scales: 7 Orientation Scales; 29 Basic Scales, such as law-politics, counseling, and mathematics, which are categorized within the 7 Orientation Scales; and 60 Occupational Scales, such as attorney, which are also within the Orientation Scales. There are also 2 extra scales: The Academic Focus Scale is designed to help clients estimate how comfortable and successful they will be in a formal educational setting. The Extraversion Scale is designed to show the amount and intensity of interpersonal interactions the individual is likely to seek out daily. The report provides a description of each measure and a numerical and geographical representation of scores and interpretive comments to help clients better understand the results. Scores used in the reports are standardized, reported as T-scores with a mean of 50 and a standard deviation of 10. Reports are generated either by computer software, online or via a mail-in service. In addition to the report, the CISS Interest/Skill Pattern Worksheet encourages further planning.

Norms for the Orientation and Basic Scales consisted of 1790 women and 3435 men representing 65 different occupations. Given that item responses were found to differ for women and men (e.g, women choosing more artistic activities as opposed to mechanical), unisex norms were developed by separating separate raw score means by gender and then giving each gender equal weighting. Reliabilities of the CISS appear adequate. For the interest and skill scales of the Orientation Scales, the median alpha coefficient was .87, and the median alpha for the 29 Basic Scales was .86. Median test-retest coefficients at a three-month interval included interest and skill scales of the Orientation Scales, .87 and .81; Basic Scales, .83; and Occupational Scales, .87 (interests) and .79 (skills).

Sullivan and Hansen (2004) found the constructive validity of the interest scales of the CISS to be strong when compared with the Strong Interest Inventory. With respect to predictive validity, Hansen and Neuman (1999) found that the CISS interest component had good to excellent predictive validity for student choice of college major. When comparing the CISS and the Strong Interest Inventory, these researchers found a similar concurrent validity for the interest component and a lower validity for the skills component of the CISS. For a thorough review of the CISS, see Boggs (2002) and Fuqua and Newman (1994b).

Using the CISS in Counseling

Figure 6-6 provides a look at a sample Orientations and Basic Scales sheet, which occupies one page of the 11-page report profile. As the sheet demonstrates, interests are represented by a black diamond, and skills are represented by a clear diamond. With these two dimensions, four possibilities can occur:

Table 6-10	CISS Analysis			
			Interests	
			High	Low
Skills		High	Pursue	Explore
		Low	Develop	Avoid

This sample profile contains a wealth of information. In one page, it combines a ranking of a person's self-reported interests and skills and helps frame this information in a way that is easy to comprehend for both the client and the counselor. The use of the grid provides a game plan for what is to occur next in counseling. The client might choose to pursue occupations by gaining more information about them, doing informational interviews, researching on the Internet or shadowing. A client who is really "set" on one career but doesn't have the skills for it may be encouraged to "develop" in that area.

The game plan would then be to identify ways for the client to gain the knowledge and/or skills necessary, either through volunteering, taking a course or workshop, or working. A client who has occupations listed in the "explore" category might represent someone who prematurely eliminates options because he or she generalizes one activity they don't "like" to an entire occupational field. Occupations listed in this category suggest that there may be ways of using those skills that they like in an interesting way. For the "Avoid" category, a client and counselor could choose to just ignore those occupations or traits, but we have found that it helps clarify their knowledge about themselves by exploring the themes involved with occupations listed in that category.

 CISS*(CAMPBELL" INTEREST AND SKILL SURVEY)

Basic Scales

The following profile takes you one layer deeper into the basic scales under each Orientation. Basic Scales reflect types of work and activities within each Orientation.

	Standard Scores		Basic Scales	Interest/ Skill Pattern
	I	S	Very Low 30 · 35 — Low 40 · 45 — Mid-Range 50 · 55 — High 60 · 65 — Very High 70	
Influencing	74	73		Pursue
Leadership	67	69		Pursue
Law/Politics	71	74		Pursue
Public Speaking	66	68		Pursue
Sales	79	69		Pursue
Advertising/Marketing	70	71		Pursue
Organizing	78	76		Pursue
Supervision	78	67		Pursue
Financial Services	78	76		Pursue
Office Practices	84	70		Pursue
Helping	76	78		Pursue
Adult Development	69	69		Pursue
Counseling	69	69		Pursue
Child Development	73	72		Pursue
Religious Activities	71	74		Pursue
Medical Practice	77	77		Pursue
Creating	72	81		Pursue
Art/Design	68	75		Pursue
Performing Arts	70	79		Pursue
Writing	67	68		Pursue
International Activities	65	73		Pursue
Fashion	80	77		Pursue
Culinary Arts	70	70		Pursue
aNalyzing	75	77		Pursue
Mathematics	72	75		Pursue
Science	74	74		Pursue
Producing	77	80		Pursue
Mechanical Crafts	78	77		Pursue
Woodworking	68	72		Pursue
Farming/Forestry	73	77		Pursue
Plants/Gardens	68	75		Pursue
Animal Care	74	76		Pursue
Adventuring	76	78		Pursue
Athletics/Physical Fitness	71	73		Pursue
Military/Law Enforcement	77	74		Pursue
Risks/Adventure	71	72		Pursue
			Very Low — Low — Mid-Range — High — Very High	

Scores: I (▬) = Interests; S (▬) = Skills

Figure 6-7

Suggestions for Career Development

Many of the following suggestions for fostering the career development of students and adults can be modified and used interchangeably to meet the needs of both groups. These suggestions should not be considered all the possibilities for using assessment results to enhance career development; rather, they are examples from which exercises can be developed to meet local needs and needs of other groups.

For Schools:

- Ask students to identify interests as components of personal uniqueness. Share the results with others.
- Ask students to use interest results to match their personal goals and needs. Summarize in a paragraph, verbally or artistically.
- Ask students to identify and compare interest results with selected occupations. Share in groups.
- Ask students to compare interest results with achievement scores. Discuss results.
- Ask students to compare interest results with aptitude scores. Write about findings, or create a chart or graph that demonstrates the comparison.
- Ask students to link interests to a variety of occupations. Share in group discussions.
- Ask students to develop a list of on-site community visits from their interest inventory results. Share their findings.
- Ask students to relate how different interests among individuals must be respected to maintain positive peer relationships.
- Ask students to discuss how interests influence career behavior patterns.
- Ask students to link occupational interests to academic interests.
- Ask students to interview someone they know about his or her interests and how that person meets those interests (through work, leisure, etc.). Share results in class.

For Adults:

- Ask adults to give examples of how interest inventory results can verify and reinforce self-concepts.
- Ask adults to give examples of how interests can influence adjustments, adaptations, and socialization in work environments.
- Ask adults to discuss how interests influence career and life goals.
- Ask adults to discuss how interests are related to learning and leisure.
- Ask adults to discuss how some interests have remained the same over the life span and others have changed.
- Ask adults to discuss how interests influence relationships with peer affiliates in the work place.
- Ask adults to discuss how interests have influenced career decision –making. Use current inventory results as an example.

Other Interest Inventories

The following are examples of other interest inventories currently being used. This list is far from complete, as a considerable number of interest inventories are currently published. Some measure general interests, whereas others measure interests in specific occupational fields.

California Occupational Preference Survey. The target population for this inventory is middle school, high school, and college students and adults. Reported scores are raw scores and percentiles for science, consumer economics, outdoor, business, clerical communications, arts, service, and technology. Scoring can be done on site or by computer.

- Career Assessment Inventory. This inventory (paper-and-pencil or online administration) can be administered in 45 minutes. It is for individuals 15 years and older. Four types of scales are provided. One is a general occupational theme scale based on Holland's RIASEC model, providing a measure of an individual's orientation to work. Basic interest scales provide measures of interest and their relationship to specific careers. Occupational scales compare a person's interests to those of people who have been happily employed in an occupation for several years. Non-occupational scales are also provided. There are currently two versions: The enhanced version focuses on careers requiring various amounts of postsecondary education, and the vocational version focuses on careers requiring two years or less of postsecondary of training. This inventory is designed to be used primarily with individuals who are not planning to go to college.

- Career Directions Inventory. The CDI is a machine-scorable inventory for high school and college students. 100 triads of job-related activities are presented for which the client selects the most and least preferred. The report provides a "sex-fair" profile of 15 basic interest scales, including: Administration, Art, Assertive, Clerical, Food Service, Industrial Arts, Health Service, Outdoors, Personal Service, Persuasive, Sales, Science & Technology, Systematic, Teaching/Social Service and Writing.

- Career Exploration Inventory-Second Edition (CEI). This inventory allows clients to reflect on past, present, and future activities that they might enjoy doing. The CEI is designed to integrate work, learning, and leisure. Test results link to GOE codes for use with high school and adult populations.

- Career Targets. Career Targets is an interest inventory housed within a planning guide for middle school students reading on a 6th grade level that includes an aspirations section, information/exercises on career clusters, knowledge-building games such as matching occupational titles to a 1-line job description skills activities, understanding and responding to want ads, a next steps page, and other relevant activities meant to expand thinking about potential career options.

- COIN Clue. Designed for elementary students reading at a third grade level, COIN Clue is a self-administered and self-scored booklet (available in English and Spanish) that helps students connect what they currently do and enjoy doing at school, home and for leisure, to the world of work. In addition to many fill in the blank self-reflection exercises, there are word finds of occupations in a certain career field, matching games (between job titles and descriptions), poster finds, and many other activities.

- Guide for Occupational Exploration Inventory-II (GOE-II). This relatively brief interest inventory examines seven sources of career interest: leisure activities, home activities, education & school subjects, training, work settings, work experience, and overall interest. The person is asked to rate his or her interest level (1 = low or no interest, 2 = some interest, 3 = high interest) on each of these sources against the 12 GOE interest areas (artistic, scientific, plants and animals, protective, mechanical, industrial, business detail, selling, accommodating, humanitarian, leading and influencing, and physical performing). Scores can range from 7 to 21, with those of 14 or higher indicating higher than average interest. Also included is an extensive occupational information chart, which outlines the 12 interest areas and subgroups, representative job titles, and related leisure and home activities.

- Interest Determination, Exploration, and Assessment System (IDEAS). This 128-item (drawn from the Career Assessment Inventory–Enhanced), paper-and-pencil inventory is designed to introduce the concept of career exploration to students and adults. It is appropriate for students 13 years and older and adults who are beginning the career exploration process, but it can also be used with special education students and students who are at risk.

- Jackson Vocational Interest Survey. This inventory is designed to assist high school and college students and adults with educational and career planning. Scores are reported by raw score, standard scores, and percentiles by 34 basic interest scales and 10 general occupational themes. This inventory also compares the individual's score to college and university student groups by 13 major areas such as engineering, education, and liberal arts. The inventory can be hand or machine scored, and a computerized extended report is available.

- Korean Strong Interest Inventory (K-SII). The K-SII is a translated and adapted version of the Strong Interest Inventory. Simply translating an inventory into another language does not ensure automatic generalizabilty to another country or culture. Along with the translation, items on the Strong that were not appropriate for Korean culture, such as "Latin language" or "football" were replaced with more culturally relevant but also similar terms, such as "Chinese letter" and "soccer." Tak (2004) provides a validation study of the K-SII with 4,619 college students from 33 universities and 2 colleges.

- Occupational Aptitude Survey and Interest Schedule–3 (OASIS-3). This instrument is designed to measure 12 interests areas: Artistic, Scientific, Nature, Protective, Mechanical, Industrial, Business Detail, Selling, Accommodating, Humanitarian, Leading-Influencing, and Physical Performing. The survey is untimed, but most students finish the inventory in 30 minutes. Norms for junior and senior high school students are available by male and female and combined sex. Scores expressed in percentiles and stanines can be used for vocational exploration and career development.

- ONET Career Interests Inventory. Based on the O*NET Interest Profiler (http://www.onetcenter.org/IP.html), this inventory includes 180 activities that a client rates as either liking, disliking or unsure and resulting in the RIASEC types. The inside of the inventory includes job titles related to each type and divided by "zones" – ranging from zone 1 (little or no preparation needed) to zone 5 (extensive preparation needed).

- Vocational Preference Inventory (VPI). A measure of vocational interests, the VPI summarizes people's interests in terms of Holland codes by assessing their preferences for or against 160 occupations. It takes about 15 to 30 minutes, and only one minute to hand score. The VPI consists of 11 scales: Realistic, Investigative, Art, Social, Enterprising, Conventional, Self-Control, Status, Masculinity/Femininity, Influence, and Acquiescence. The VPI scales have an average internal consistency of .88.

Summary

Interest inventories have a long association with career counseling. Strong and Kuder were pioneers in the interest measurement field. Holland's RIASEC theory of careers has greatly influenced the presentation of many of the current interest inventories. The NIE guidelines on sex bias (Diamond, 1975) and possibly feminist critique (Lewin & Wild, 1991) have led to some reduction in sex biases on interest inventories. However, we need to continuously reevaluate our approach to interest measurement.

Questions and Exercises

1. In what instances would you choose the Strong Interest Inventory® over the KOIS? Give reasons for your choice.

2. How would you explain to a high school senior that measurements of interests do not necessarily indicate how successful one will be in an occupation?

3. A college student states that he knows what his interests are but can't decide on a major. How would you justify suggesting that he take an interest inventory?

4. How would you interpret an interest inventory profile that has no scores in the above average category? What would you recommend to the individual who took the inventory?

5. Defend or criticize the following statements: Interests are permanent over the life span. An individual will have the same interests in 2020 as in 1987.

6. What are the benefits and drawbacks of online interest inventories, such as the Kuder Career Search, or the online version of the Self-Directed Search? How could you integrate such a tool into your counseling? How could you minimize the negatives?

7. Carole, who wants to return to the workforce after her children have started school, tells you the occupations she is currently considering include office manager, teacher, and nurse. She'd like to take an interest inventory to help her find out which might be the best fit for her. Do you have an initial

reaction to Carole's aspirations? How would you balance what you would actually say to Carole with what your initial reaction was? Which interest inventory would you recommend, and why? How would you help Carole expand her options without directly or indirectly negating the validity of her first choices?

8. John Switch, a 33-year-old male, has taken the Strong Interest Inventory® in hopes of learning more about possible career options. His profile is presented in Figures 6-8a and b. How would you interpret his profile? What interventions might you suggest? How do his interest and confidence levels differ? What impact might that have on his options? Which occupations look the most promising? The least? How would you interpret his personal style scales? From the information given in this report, how do you think John is in interpersonal relationships, on the job, in a job search?

GENERAL OCCUPATIONAL THEMES

SECTION 1

The General Occupational Themes (GOTs) measure six broad interest patterns that can be used to describe your work personality. Most people's interests are reflected by two or three Themes, combined to form a cluster of interests. Work activities, potential skills, and values can also be classified into these six Themes. This provides a direct link between your interests and the career and education possibilities likely to be most meaningful to you.

Your *standard scores* are based on the average scores of a combined group of working adults. However, because research shows that men and women tend to respond differently in these areas, your *interest levels* (Very Little, Little, Moderate, High, Very High) were determined by comparing your scores against the average scores for your gender.

THEME DESCRIPTIONS

THEME	CODE	INTERESTS	WORK ACTIVITIES	POTENTIAL SKILLS	VALUES
Realistic	R	Machines, computer networks, athletics, working outdoors	Operating equipment, using tools, building, repairing, providing security	Mechanical ingenuity and dexterity, physical coordination	Tradition, practicality, common sense
Conventional	C	Organization, data management, accounting, investing, information systems	Setting up procedures and systems, organizing, keeping records, developing computer applications	Ability to work with numbers, data analysis, finances, attention to detail	Accuracy, stability, efficiency
Investigative	I	Science, medicine, mathematics, research	Performing lab work, solving abstract problems, conducting research	Mathematical ability, researching, writing, analyzing	Independence, curiosity, learning
Enterprising	E	Business, politics, leadership, entrepreneurship	Selling, managing, persuading, marketing	Verbal ability, ability to motivate and direct others	Risk taking, status, competition, influence
Artistic	A	Self-expression, art appreciation, communication, culture	Composing music, performing, writing, creating visual art	Creativity, musical ability, artistic expression	Beauty, originality, independence, imagination
Social	S	People, teamwork, helping, community service	Teaching, caring for people, counseling, training employees	People skills, verbal ability, listening, showing understanding	Cooperation, generosity, service to others

YOUR HIGHEST THEMES	YOUR THEME CODE
Realistic, Conventional, Investigative	**RCI**

THEME	CODE	STANDARD SCORE & INTEREST LEVEL	STD SCORE
Realistic	R	HIGH	63
Conventional	C	HIGH	59
Investigative	I	HIGH	59
Enterprising	E	MODERATE	47
Artistic	A	LITTLE	39
Social	S	VERY LITTLE	35

The charts above display your GOT results in descending order, from your highest to least level of interest. Referring to the Theme Descriptions provided, determine how well your results fit for you. Do your highest Themes ring true? Look at your next highest level of interest and ask yourself the same question. You may wish to highlight the Theme descriptions on this page that seem to fit you best.

Figure 6-8a

What are his strengths and weaknesses? How do you interpret his confidence scales? What type of interventions might foster a greater deal of confidence?

9. Consider the profiles of the Self-Directed Search and accompanying case information in Figures 6.8 a through e. In each of these scenarios, how might the client present in counseling? What affective and behavioral characteristics might also be present? What other concerns (in addition to career) might need to be addressed? Using the Occupations Finder or other appropriate tools, identify potential occupations or majors that might be appropriate for each client to consider. How would your counseling approach differ with each case?

10. Jamal has come to you at the end of his junior year requesting help in deciding what he wants to do after graduation. He is an avid car lover, and knows the stats of all the current and classic vehicles. In

LEVELS OF SKILLS CONFIDENCE BY THEME

Your *Skills Confidence Inventory* results describe how you perceive your own capabilities in performing activities related to the same six broad areas represented by the General Occupational Themes. Keep in mind that these results may not reflect your actual abilities; the results reflect how you rate yourself. Your own rating may influence what kinds of activities you try or avoid and may determine what occupations or educational programs you consider as possibilities for exploration.

Your confidence in each of the six areas is shown below in rank order. Your Skills Confidence Theme code summarizes the areas in which you feel most confident performing particular activities. Your Skills Confidence Theme code is RCS.

THEME	CODE	CONFIDENCE SCORE & LEVEL (1 2 3 4 5)	SCORE (1–5)	TYPICAL SKILL AREAS
Realistic	R	VERY HIGH	4.9	Outdoor work, construction, repair
Conventional	C	VERY HIGH	4.7	Finance, computers, organization
Social	S	HIGH	3.8	Education, counseling, social service
Investigative	I	MODERATE	3.2	Research, math, science
Artistic	A	MODERATE	3.1	Creative expression, music, design
Enterprising	E	MODERATE	2.9	Sales, speaking, management

COMPARISON OF LEVELS OF SKILLS CONFIDENCE AND INTEREST

The chart below compares your skills confidence levels with your interest levels as measured by the *Strong*. Your Skills Confidence Theme code is RCS. Your *Strong* Theme code is RCI. Use this comparison to help you select Themes you'd like to explore further to find satisfying career, educational, and leisure options. Also, refer to Understanding Your Results on the *Skills Confidence Inventory* available from your career professional for more information.

THEME	CODE	Less → More (FURTHER EXPLORATION if highest level of confidence is moderate / FURTHER EXPLORATION)	PRIORITIES FOR CAREER EXPLORATION
Realistic	R	CONFIDENCE / INTEREST	High priority
Conventional	C	CONFIDENCE / INTEREST	High priority
Social	S	CONFIDENCE / INTEREST	Possible option if interests develop; needs careful consideration
Investigative	I	CONFIDENCE / INTEREST	Good option if confidence in skills can be increased
Artistic	A	CONFIDENCE / INTEREST	Low priority
Enterprising	E	CONFIDENCE / INTEREST	Good option if confidence in skills can be increased

Total responses out of 60: 60

Figure 6-8b Modified and reproduced by special permission of the Publisher, CPP, Inc., Mountain View, CA 94043 from the Strong Interest Inventory® Instrument. © 1933, 1938, 1945, 1946, 1966, 1968, 1974, 1981, 1985, 1994, by CPP, Inc. Further reproduction is prohibited without the Publisher's written consent. Strong Interest Inventory is registered trademark of CPP, Inc.

addition to knowing the technical information, he enjoys working on cars in his spare time, and learning about the new computers that make them run. He has taken the Kuder Career Search and has come to you for help in interpreting the results and determining his next steps. His Activity Preference Profile is shown in Figures 6-10 a – c. How would you summarize Jamal's interests, and what recommendations would you make for next steps?

11. The Kuder Career Search compares an individual's results to people in the norm group who had similar response patterns on the KCS. Is this preferred over comparing the individual to people in similar occupations, or gender/racially similar groups? Why or why not? What are the benefits/drawbacks of this approach?

12. A 38-year-old client has taken the CEI. His results are presented in Figures 6-11. What type of summary statements might you make about his interests? What might you do to examine the link between his leisure and learning activities and work? The author of the CEI, John Liptak, also has a chart that encourages individuals to list items for the past 5 to 10 years, the present and the future with respect to work, leisure, and learning activities. What might be some benefits of this approach?

13. Refer back to the CISS results presented in Figure 6-7. How would you interpret this profile? What type of suggestions would you make to this person with respect to the four-factor model of CISS?

14. What observations can you make about the JVIS profile in Figure 6-12, a-c. What careers might you recommend, and which should this client avoid? Can you make some assumptions about how this client might present in counseling or in a job interview? How does the information provided in the JVIS compare to that of other interest inventories?

15. A student is trying to identify her interests. The results of her COPS inventory are presented in Figure 6-13. Given that summer is quickly approaching, she wants to make the best use of her time and spend it getting some experience. What types of experiences would be most beneficial for this student to explore? What is your role as a counselor in helping her create those experiences? On what criteria should she evaluate the experience?

16. Based on the CAI report in Figure 6-14, which of the RIASEC categories should this client further investigate? What type of interventions (hands-on approaches, CACG, research, talking to a counselor, etc.) might this client prefer over others? What inferences can you make when you compare this client's profile to scores of the opposite sex?

17. Create a brief scenario and sample questions (e.g., general themes, potential interventions, suggested occupations, etc.) around the GOE Interest Inventory-II Profile shown in Figure 6-15. Exchange your scenario with a partner and answer your questions. Then compare your answers – how are they similar? How are they different?

18. A student has told you that he is considering several careers and is having trouble narrowing them down. His OASIS-Interest inventory results are in Figure 6-16 a and b. What hypotheses do you have, based on his results? Are any specific fields indicated? How will you help him narrow down his options?

Self-Directed Search Profiles
SDS Case 1

	R	I	A	S	E	C
Activities	10	9	10	10	10	10
Competencies	9	10	10	8	10	10
Occupations	9	8	7	9	7	10
Self-Estimates	7	7	7	6	5	6
	7	7	6	5	7	6
Summary Scores	42	41	40	38	39	42

Figure 6-9a

SDS cases. Adapted and reproduced by special permission of the Publisher, Psychological Assessment Resources, Inc., 16204 North Florida Avenue, Lutz, FL 33549, from the Self-Directed Search Professional User's Guide by John L. Holland, Ph.D., Amy B. Powell, Ph.D. and Barbara A. Fritzsche, Ph.D., Copyright 1985, 1987, 1994, 1997 by PAR, Inc. Further reproduction is prohibited without permission from PAR, Inc.

Joanne is a junior in the gifted program at her high school. She is active in many school and community clubs, including student government, computer club, young artisans, peer mediator group, math drill team, and the archery club. She is well-liked and performs well in all of her classes. Her involvement in the clubs plus her demanding course-load prohibit her from having at job at this time. She comes to you because she is having a hard time deciding which major to write down on the college applications she is completing. Her results from the Self-Directed Search are presented above. How would you interpret these results? What questions might you have for Joanne? What recommendations would you make for helping her?

SDS Case 2

	R	I	A	S	E	C
Activities	3	2	1	1	2	3
Competencies	1	1	2	1	0	2
Occupations	1	3	4	3	2	1
Self-Estimates	2	4	3	2	1	2
	2	2	1	3	2	1
Summary Scores	9	12	11	10	5	9

Figure 6-9b

SDS cases. Adapted and reproduced by special permission of the Publisher, Psychological Assessment Resources, Inc., 16204 North Florida Avenue, Lutz, FL 33549, from the Self-Directed Search Professional User's Guide by John L. Holland, Ph.D., Amy B. Powell, Ph.D. and Barbara A. Fritzsche, Ph.D., Copyright 1985, 1987, 1994, 1997 by PAR, Inc. Further reproduction is prohibited without permission from PAR, Inc.

Richard has come to you by the strong urging of his spouse that he find a job. He has been unemployed since he was let go from a large corporation that had given many lay-offs. "I just didn't expect that I would be one of the first to be fired. I mean, I showed up everyday, worked hard, and was a strong team player. I thought I was doing well." He goes on to tell you that he and his wife are struggling financially and are expecting their second child in the next month. She will take maternity leave for 6 weeks, but prefers to work part time while the child is young. The severance pay from Richard's job helps, but will be discontinued next month. He has brought in his Self-Directed Search, which he completed as part of the outplacement services offered by the company. "This is supposed to tell me what else I'd be good at, but to be honest, I don't even feel up to looking at other options. That job was my dream job. I'll never find anything like that again." How would you proceed with Richard? What does his profile suggest? What counseling interventions might you make?

SDS Case 3

	R	I	A	S	E	C
Activities	9	4	2	12	5	2
Competencies	8	2	3	9	4	3
Occupations	9	3	4	9	2	1
Self-Estimates	7	3	2	7	5	5
	6	2	1	6	2	2
Summary Scores	39	14	12	43	18	12

Figure 6-9c SDS cases. Adapted and reproduced by special permission of the Publisher, Psychological Assessment Resources, Inc., 16204 North Florida Avenue, Lutz, FL 33549, from the Self-Directed Search Professional User's Guide by John L. Holland, Ph.D., Amy B. Powell, Ph.D. and Barbara A. Fritzsche, Ph.D., Copyright 1985, 1987, 1994, 1997 by PAR, Inc. Further reproduction is prohibited without permission from PAR, Inc.

Pat has been seeing you in counseling for relationship concerns. During the last session, however, Pat reports feeling dissatisfied at work. The two of you decide that taking the Self-Directed Search might yield some insights into Pat's interests and show the degree of fit between Pat's interests and current position. Pat's results are presented above. Pat is currently working as a lab technician. "While I enjoy the 'hands-on' part of my job, I feel so isolated most of the time. I'd really like to do more team work. The job itself is pretty nice, and I like the hours. Do you think I ought to quit my job?" What do you make of Pat's profile? How congruent are Pat's interests to the job? What interventions might you make? What types of other occupations might Pat want to investigate? Should Pat stay or leave the current position?

SDS Case 4

	R	I	A	S	E	C
Activities	3	8	9	8	6	1
Competencies	9	2	2	3	4	12
Occupations	3	7	0	9	5	1
Self-Estimates	6	1	9	2	3	7
	6	2	2	1	3	7
Summary Scores	27	20	23	23	21	28

Figure 6-9d SDS cases. Adapted and reproduced by special permission of the Publisher, Psychological Assessment Resources, Inc., 16204 North Florida Avenue, Lutz, FL 33549, from the Self-Directed Search Professional User's Guide by John L. Holland, Ph.D., Amy B. Powell, Ph.D. and Barbara A. Fritzsche, Ph.D., Copyright 1985, 1987, 1994, 1997 by PAR, Inc. Further reproduction is prohibited without permission from PAR, Inc.

Suzanne is a recently divorced single mother of two grade-school children. While she was married, she kept the books for her husband's business. Now she is finding herself out of work and needing a job that will pay more money and offer better benefits. Her ex-husband is on-time and diligent about child-support payments, but she wants to feel less dependent on his money and more independent. Now that the kids are in school all day, she feels ready to pursue a career but is unsure how to start. She is open to going back to school, and has done research to find out about scholarships and financial aid. She has taken the Self-Directed Search and is waiting for you as her counselor to provide her with an interpretation of the results and to identify some follow-up steps. What type of observations can you make about Suzanne's profile (you might have to look into the subscales, in addition to the total score). What statements might you make about differentiation and consistency? What recommendations or "next steps" might you recommend?

SDS Case 5

	R	I	A	S	E	C
Activities	0	12	6	12	6	11
Competencies	1	8	10	10	4	9
Occupations	0	12	4	11	3	4
Self-Estimates	3	7	4	7	2	2
	1	1	6	1	4	6
Summary Scores	10	35	39	52	15	29

Figure 6-9e   SDS cases. Adapted and reproduced by special permission of the Publisher, Psychological Assessment Resources, Inc., 16204 North Florida Avenue, Lutz, FL 33549, from the Self-Directed Search Professional User's Guide by John L. Holland, Ph.D., Amy B. Powell, Ph.D. and Barbara A. Fritzsche, Ph.D., Copyright 1985, 1987, 1994, 1997 by PAR, Inc. Further reproduction is prohibited without permission from PAR, Inc.

Jeremy completed the Self-Directed Search as part of a small group (about 8) that was focusing on career exploration. The group consisted of teenagers who were at-risk for dropping out of high school. Jeremy stated that he wanted to be a police detective or be in the Navy Seals and that he had "contacts" that could help him get into those jobs. "I don't want to do any of those soft jobs that work with people," he said. However, you noticed that he did not write those occupational aspirations down on the aspiration portion of the SDS, even when you asked "Didn't you say you were thinking about becoming a police detective or Navy Seal? Why don't you write down those two options here?" Jeremy was the first one finished with the SDS, taking about 5 minutes to get through it. When asked if he needed help scoring it, he said, "No." After the group was dismissed, you took time to look over each person's aspirations and double-check the addition on their hand-written profiles. You noticed that Jeremy still had not filled in the aspirations section, and that there were some incorrect additions with his final profile. What observations might you make about Jeremy, how he approached the SDS, and the results? How might you proceed with him?

Provided by:
National Career Assessment Services, Inc.
www.kuder.com

Congratulations **Demtri F.**! You join more than 100 million people who have taken a Kuder® Interest Assessment. By reviewing your results and following the steps within the report you will learn how to begin your career exploration process. As you move through the report be sure to read all the information and answer the questions. We suggest that you review this report with family, friends, or a career counselor.

Step I. Review Your Kuder® Career Clusters Ranking

Occupations or jobs can be grouped into one of six areas. We call these areas career clusters. Your interests have been scientifically compared to a large group of occupational profiles and the results are presented below in rank order from best to least fit. Demtri, focus your attention on your top two clusters. Click on them to read their descriptions. As you read each description think about how similar the job activities are to what you might enjoy doing. But remember, life experiences influence your interests and career choices, and they may change over time. Adults today report having seven or more jobs in a life time, but usually the jobs remain in one or two clusters. This is why identifying your top two clusters is so important. Remember there are many different types of jobs in each of the clusters. In a moment you will be able to read about the jobs some people have who happen to have very similar interests to yours.

To help you keep track of your top clusters, click on the ☆ to place them in your Kuder® Electronic Career Portfolio under "My Favorites".

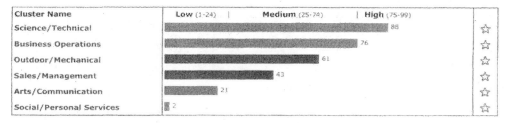

Cluster Name	Low (1-24)	Medium (25-74)	High (75-99)	
Science/Technical			88	☆
Business Operations			76	☆
Outdoor/Mechanical		61		☆
Sales/Management		43		☆
Arts/Communication	21			☆
Social/Personal Services	2			☆

Step II. Meet People With Interests Like Yours

When it comes to choosing careers, people tend to only think in terms of job titles, not the individuals behind them. In fact, most career assessments match you to job titles or occupations only. But, you are not a job title or occupation. We know that people who have similar interests find happiness and success in a wide range of careers. That's why we developed Person Match. Person Match compares your results with nearly 2000 people in satisfying careers. They represent over 90% of the occupations available in the United States today. They come from all walks of life and all regions of the United States. Your Person Match results are presented below. These are people who have interests most like yours. They all have found satisfying careers, and you can learn about them by reading their job sketches. Click on the person you would like to meet. Why? Because you might discover someone with interests like yours in a career you never thought of, or you might find someone doing exactly what you want to do. Either way it is a great way to explore. Even though their occupations may differ, they all have interests very much like you!

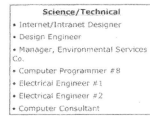

Science/Technical
- Internet/Intranet Designer
- Design Engineer
- Manager, Environmental Services Co.
- Computer Programmer #8
- Electrical Engineer #1
- Electrical Engineer #2
- Computer Consultant

Business Operations
- Supervisor, Food Lab.
- Deputy Clerk, U.S. Court
- Controller (CPA)
- Accountant/Craft Shop Owner
- Accounting Clerk
- Office Manager #1
- Registered Sales Assistant

Figure 6-10   From the Kuder Occupational Interest Survey, online assessment, 2000, G. Frederick Kuder. Reprinted with permission of National Career Assessment Services, Inc. All rights reserved.

STEP 4

The CEI *Interest Profile*

Notice that the totals you completed in Step 3 are numbered 1 through 15. These totals indicate your level of interest in each of 15 clusters of related activities. The higher your total, the higher your interest in that cluster. The 15 clusters are listed next to each total.

The profile below allows you to transfer your total score for each interest cluster and arrange them in graphic form. The sample entry in the orange box below shows you how one person marked a total score of 13. In a similar way, transfer your scores from the totals in Step 3 and mark the appropriate location for each total score on the profile below. The result will allow you to compare your scores in the various interest clusters more easily.

When you have completed the profile, open the *CEI* and continue with Step 5.

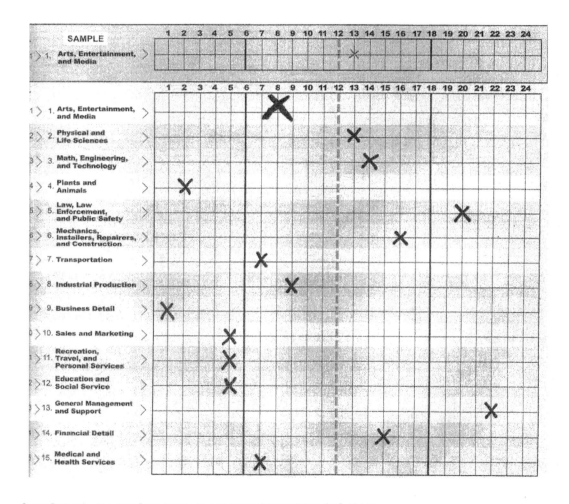

Figure 6-11   Career Exploration Inventory. Reproduced with permission of the publisher, Jist Publishing.

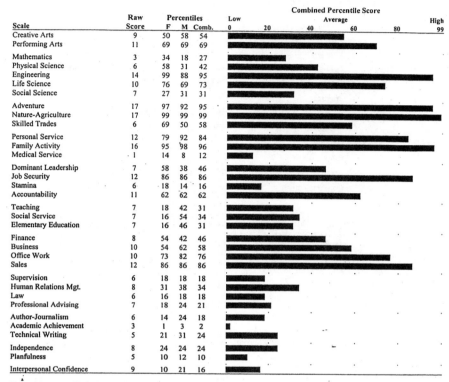

	JVIS Basic Interest Profile

The profile below shows your scores on the 34 JVIS Basic Interest scales. A high score indicates that you show a preference for working in settings involving the activities described by the scale name. A low score indicates that you would prefer not to work in such settings and would probably find such work unsatisfying.

	Raw	Percentiles			Combined Percentile Score
Scale	Score	F	M	Comb.	Low 0 — 20 — Average 40 — 60 — 80 — High 99
Creative Arts	9	50	58	54	
Performing Arts	11	69	69	69	
Mathematics	3	34	18	27	
Physical Science	6	58	31	42	
Engineering	14	99	88	95	
Life Science	10	76	69	73	
Social Science	7	27	31	31	
Adventure	17	97	92	95	
Nature-Agriculture	17	99	99	99	
Skilled Trades	6	69	50	58	
Personal Service	12	79	92	84	
Family Activity	16	95	98	96	
Medical Service	1	14	8	12	
Dominant Leadership	7	58	38	46	
Job Security	12	86	86	86	
Stamina	6	18	14	16	
Accountability	11	62	62	62	
Teaching	7	18	42	31	
Social Service	7	16	54	34	
Elementary Education	7	16	46	31	
Finance	8	54	42	46	
Business	10	54	62	58	
Office Work	10	73	82	76	
Sales	12	86	86	86	
Supervision	6	18	18	18	
Human Relations Mgt.	8	31	38	34	
Law	6	16	18	18	
Professional Advising	7	18	24	21	
Author-Journalism	6	14	24	18	
Academic Achievement	3	1	3	2	
Technical Writing	5	21	31	24	
Independence	8	24	24	24	
Planfulness	5	10	12	10	
Interpersonal Confidence	9	10	21	16	

Each of the names in the **Scale** column represents an area of interest. The column labelled **Raw Score** lists the number of activities you preferred in each area. The three **Percentile** columns show how your raw scores compare to those of the females, males, as well as the combined females and males, in a large group of students and young adults. Each percentile score is the percentage of people that received a raw score equal to or less than yours. The bars at the right illustrate the scores in the **Combined Percentile** column. Use the longer bars to identify your areas of greatest interest. Short bars show you the areas in which you are not interested. Bars that end in the middle indicate that your interest in that area is about average.

Figure 6-12a Jackson Vocational Interest Survey. Reproduced with permission of the publisher, Sigma Assessment Systems, Inc.

General Occupational Themes

Studies with the JVIS have revealed 10 general patterns of interest. These patterns reflect general orientations to the world of work, rather than specific interests in particular areas. Your scores on these 10 General Occupational Themes are plotted below.

			Female Percentile Score					
	Percentiles		Low			Average		High
Theme	Male	Female	0	20	40	60	80	99
Expressive	58	50						
Logical	46	79						
Inquiring	27	31						
Practical	95	95						
Assertive	16	18 .						
Socialized	34	38						
Helping	46	12 ,						
Conventional	66	62						
Enterprising	34	31						
Communicative	8	4						

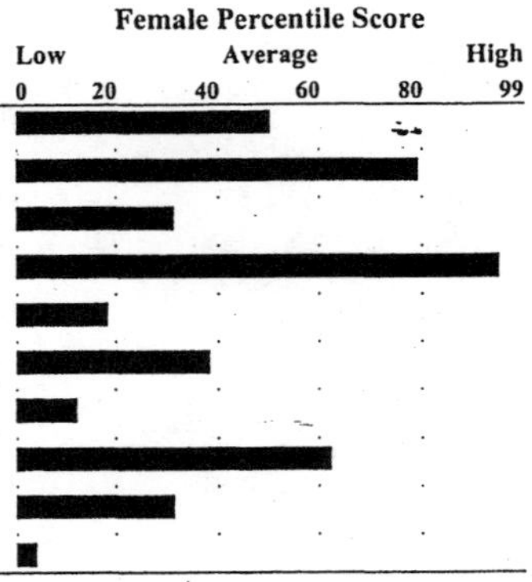

Descriptions of each of the themes in the **Theme** column can be found below. The two **Percentile** columns compare your General Occupational Theme scores to the females, and then the males, in a large group of students and young adults. Each percentile score is the percentage of people that received a score equal to or less than yours. The bars at the right illustrate how your General Occupational Theme scores compare to people of your own sex.

Figure 6-12b Jackson Vocational Interest Survey. Reproduced with permission of the publisher, Sigma Assessment Systems, Inc.

Similarity to Job Groups

Ranked below is the similarity of your JVIS Basic Interest profile to the interests of people working in 32 job groups. A positive score indicates that your profile shows some degree of similarity to those already in the job cluster, while a negative score indicates dissimilarity.

Score	Similarity	Job Group
+0.70	Very Similar	Construction/Skilled Trades
+0.65	Very Similar	Agriculturalists
+0.58	Similar	Machining/Mechanical and Related Occupations
+0.50	Similar	Occupations in Life Sciences
+0.46	Similar	Engineering and Technical Support Workers
+0.39	Moderately Similar	Protective Services Occupations
+0.36	Moderately Similar	Medical Diagnosis and Treatment Occupations
+0.36	Moderately Similar	Occupations in Computer Science
+0.35	Moderately Similar	Health Service Workers
+0.35	Moderately Similar	Occupations in Fine Art
+0.30	Moderately Similar	Sport and Recreation Occupations
+0.29	Moderately Similar	Occupations in the Physical Sciences
+0.29	Moderately Similar	Occupations in Commercial Art
+0.19	Neutral	Mathematical and Related Occupations
+0.15	Neutral	Service Occupations
+0.08	Neutral	Assembly Occupations-Instruments & Small Products
0.00	Neutral	Occupations in Music
-0.01	Neutral	Occupations in Entertainment
-0.15	Neutral	Occupations in Merchandising
-0.19	Neutral	Clerical Services
-0.20	Neutral	Sales Occupations
-0.22	Neutral	Occupations in Accounting, Banking and Finance
-0.38	Dissimilar	Occupations in Writing
-0.39	Dissimilar	Personnel/Human Management
-0.40	Dissimilar	Occupations in Pre-school and Elementary Teaching
-0.45	Dissimilar	Teaching and Related Occupations
-0.50	Dissimilar	Occupations in Law and Politics
-0.51	Dissimilar	Administrative and Related Occupations
-0.60	Very Dissimilar	Occupations in Religion
-0.63	Very Dissimilar	Counsellors/Student Personnel Workers
-0.66	Very Dissimilar	Occupations in Social Science
-0.71	Very Dissimilar	Occupations in Social Welfare

Descriptions, sample job titles and suggested readings for each of your three highest ranked job groups are presented on the next six pages. Remember, the ranking of these job groups reflects the similarity of your JVIS Basic Interest profile to those of people employed in these areas. The ranking is not a reflection of your ability to perform any required duties or to benefit from training in these areas. You may find this information useful in planning your education and your career. Your counsellor or adviser can be of help to you in this process.

In the descriptions that follow, *National Occupational Classification* (NOC) codes are listed along with sample job titles. Use these codes to locate additional information in the *NOC Occupational Descriptions* volume. There, you will find information about the sample job titles, as well as related job titles bearing the same, or a similar, NOC code. You will find that the skill type, major, minor and unit group numbers identified in this report will aid in locating occupations about which you will wish to learn more. The *NOC Occupational Descriptions* volume may be found at your local library, your counsellor's office, or at the Internet site http://cnp2001noc.worklogic.com. Additional information can be found in the suggested readings listed along with each of your top three job groups.

Figure 6-12c Jackson Vocational Interest Survey. Reproduced with permission of the publisher, Sigma Assessment Systems, Inc.

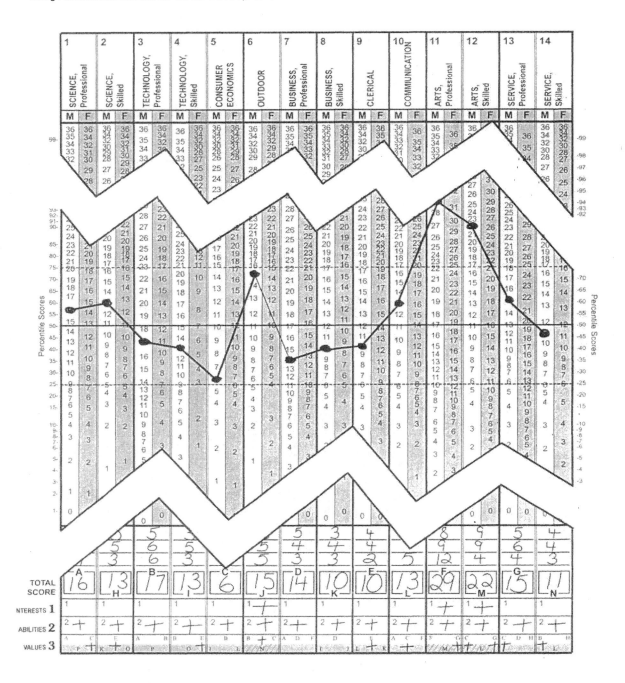

Figure 6-13   COPS reproduced with permission of the publisher, EDITS.

Career Assessment Inventory™ - Enhanced Version
ID 101010101

Profile Report
Page 2

GENERAL THEME SCALES

Scale	Std. Score	Very Low	(35)	Low	(43)	Average	(57)	High	(65)	Very High	Average Opp. Sex
R Realistic	45					★					41-55
I Investigative	54					★					42-56
A Artistic	48				★						46-59
S Social	51					★					44-57
E Enterprising	44				★						42-56
C Conventional	43				★						43-57

Your scores indicate that you should also investigate the additional occupations listed at the end of this report.

BASIC INTEREST AREA SCALES

Basic Interest Area	Std. Score	Very Low	(35)	Low	(43)	Average	(57)	High	(65)	Very High	Average Opp. Sex
Realistic Theme											
Mechanical/Fixing	49					★					41-54
Electronics	46				★						41-53
Carpentry	53					★					42-56
Manual/Skilled Trades	39			★							41-53
Protective Service	53					★					41-53
Athletics/Sports	44			★							41-54
Nature/Outdoors	41			★							42-56
Animal Service	62								★		44-57
Investigative Theme											
Mathematics	43				★						42-56
Sci. Research/Dvlpmt	55					★					42-56
Medical Science	68									★	44-58
Artistic Theme											
Writing	46				★						44-58
Creative Arts	49					★					47-59
Performing/Entertaining	47				★						44-56
Social Theme											
Community Service	52					★					44-57
Educating	55					★					43-57
Medical Service	65									▼	44-58
Religious Activities	36			★							44-56
Enterprising Theme											
Public Speaking	45				★						42-56
Law/Politics	47				★						42-56
Mgmt/Supervision	48				★						42-56
Sales	44			★							41-56
Conventional Theme											
Office Practices	50					★					43-58
Clerical/Clerking	38			★							44-57
Food Service	53					★					46-58

Figure 6-14 Career Assessment Inventory. Reproduced with permission of Pearson Assessments.

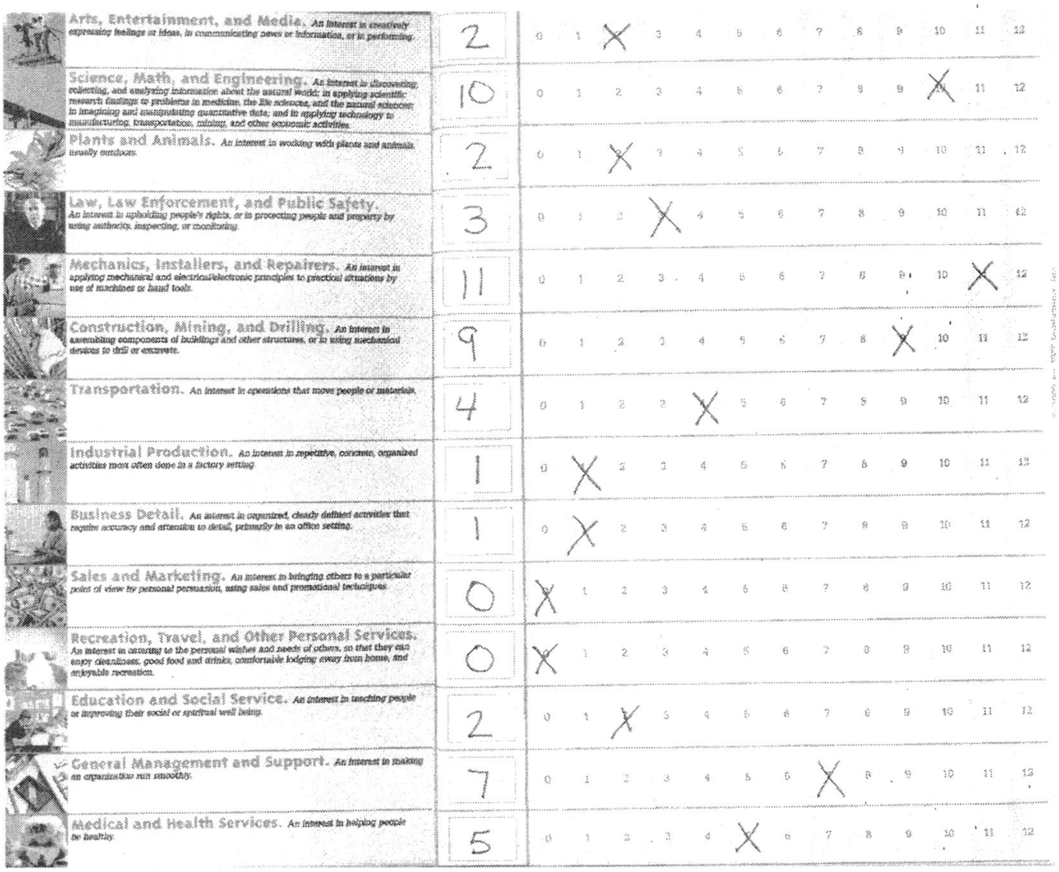

Arts, Entertainment, and Media. An interest in creatively expressing feelings or ideas, in communicating news or information, or in performing. — **2** — X at 2

Science, Math, and Engineering. An interest in discovering, collecting, and analyzing information about the natural world; in applying scientific research findings to problems in medicine, the life sciences, and the natural sciences; in imagining and manipulating quantitative data; and in applying technology to manufacturing, transportation, mining, and other economic activities. — **10** — X at 10

Plants and Animals. An interest in working with plants and animals, usually outdoors. — **2** — X at 2

Law, Law Enforcement, and Public Safety. An interest in upholding people's rights, or in protecting people and property by using authority, inspecting, or monitoring. — **3** — X at 3

Mechanics, Installers, and Repairers. An interest in applying mechanical and electrical/electronic principles to practical situations by use of machines or hand tools. — **11** — X at 11

Construction, Mining, and Drilling. An interest in assembling components of buildings and other structures, or in using mechanical devices to drill or excavate. — **9** — X at 9

Transportation. An interest in operations that move people or materials. — **4** — X at 4

Industrial Production. An interest in repetitive, concrete, organized activities most often done in a factory setting. — **1** — X at 1

Business Detail. An interest in organized, clearly defined activities that require accuracy and attention to detail, primarily in an office setting. — **1** — X at 1

Sales and Marketing. An interest in bringing others to a particular point of view by personal persuasion, using sales and promotional techniques. — **0** — X at 0

Recreation, Travel, and Other Personal Services. An interest in catering to the personal wishes and needs of others, so that they can enjoy cleanliness, good food and drinks, comfortable lodging away from home, and enjoyable recreation. — **0** — X at 0

Education and Social Service. An interest in teaching people or improving their social or spiritual well being. — **2** — X at 2

General Management and Support. An interest in making an organization run smoothly. — **7** — X at 7

Medical and Health Services. An interest in helping people be healthy. — **5** — X at 5

Figure 6-15   GOE-II reproduced by permission of the publisher, JIST Publishing.

Interest Schedule Profile

Name .... DARCI E MUNDFROM .... Male ☑M Female ☐ Grade ....1....

Date of Birth ..... 08/06/91 .... Date Tested .... 08/23/04 ....

SCALE	RAW SCORE	PERCENTILE	STANINE	STANINE PROFILE	LEVEL OF CONFIDENCE
Artistic	21	60	6	1 2 3 4 5 6 7 8 9	97%
Scientific	20	75	6	1 2 3 4 5 6 7 8 9	88%
Nature	21	67	6	1 2 3 4 5 6 7 8 9	97%
Protective	27	85	7	1 2 3 4 5 6 7 8 9	92%
Mechanical	20	75	6	1 2 3 4 5 6 7 8 9	93%
Industrial	21	90	8	1 2 3 4 5 6 7 8 9	88%
Business Detail	22	75	6	1 2 3 4 5 6 7 8 9	93%
Selling	21	80	7	1 2 3 4 5 6 7 8 9	88%
Accommodating	20	80	7	1 2 3 4 5 6 7 8 9	84%
Humanitarian	25	85	7	1 2 3 4 5 6 7 8 9	87%
Leading-Influencing	23	80	7	1 2 3 4 5 6 7 8 9	81%
Physical Performing	20	60	6	1 2 3 4 5 6 7 8 9	88%

PRO-ED, 8700 Shoal Creek Blvd   Austin, TX 78757-6897
800/897-3202, Fax 800/397-7633 www.proedinc.com

Figure 6-16a OASIS-3 Aptitude Survey, Third Edition Humanitarian Worksheet © 2002 by R. M. Parker. Used with permission of the publisher, PRO-ED.

Interpreting Your
Interest Schedule Scores

The *Occupational Aptitude Survey and Interest Schedule–Third Edition* (OASIS-3) was developed to assist individuals in vocational exploration and career development. Two scores, percentile and stanine scores, are important in understanding your profile results.

The percentile and stanine scores on your profile compare your interests to a national sample of students. The percentile scores show the percentage of people scoring lower than you. If, for example, you score at the 90th percentile on the Artistic scale, you score higher than 90% of the people in the national norm group on that scale. If you receive a score at the 10th percentile on Industrial, you score higher than 10% of the norm group. If you are in 8th through 12th grade, percentile scores are shown that compare your scores (a) to those of your own gender for scales where males (M) and females (F) score differently (MEC, BUS, ACC, HUM, & PHY) or (b) to a total (T) normative group of males and females combined for scales where there are no gender differences (ART, SCI, NAT, PRO, IND, SEL, & LEA). If you are an adult in postsecondary education, percentile scores are shown that compare your scores to the total normative group of males and females combined. In this adult group there are no differences between male and female scores.

The stanine is an equal-interval score used in plotting your profile. Because all inventory scores have some error, it is important to know what confidence you can have that the inventory scores are accurate. The probability values shown for each of the 12 scales at the right of the profile show how much confidence you can have in your scores. For example, you can have 87% confidence that your Artistic score is within ±1 stanine of the plotted score. This is the confidence you can have that, if you took the Interest Schedule again, your score would not change by more than ±1 stanine, assuming your real interests remained the same. Also, you can have at least 95% confidence that any scores that differ by 2 stanines are truly different. For instance, if your Artistic stanine is 9 and your Scientific stanine is 7, you can have 95% confidence that they are in fact different. The difference is not due to error of measurement.

Here are descriptions of the 12 scores that will help you understand what your profile means.

1. Artistic (ART). This scale measures your interest in the creative expression of ideas and feelings. This interest may be satisfied by a variety of activities including writing or editing; performing in music, drama, or dance; painting or sculpture; or modeling clothes.

2. Scientific (SCI). A high score in this area indicates an interest in doing scientific research and developing theories and scientific applications. This interest may be satisfied by working with scientific equipment in a laboratory; by exploring new medical treatments to improve the health of humans and animals; by developing new knowledge in mathematics or physics, or by discovering new facts about the earth and universe.

3. Nature (NAT). This scale measures your interest in working with plants and animals in an outdoor setting. You may satisfy this interest by working in farming, forestry, and fishing. You may enjoy physical work outdoors or may enjoy managing a farm or related businesses and services.

4. Protective (PRO). High scores in this area suggest an interest in using legal authority to protect both people and property. People with high scores may enjoy work in law enforcement or fire fighting, or in leadership and management positions in protective service organizations.

5. Mechanical (MEC). A high score on this scale indicates an interest in applying mechanical principles to practical situations involving the use of tools and machines. Jobs that satisfy this interest include engineering and related technical-scientific work, operating and maintaining mechanical equipment in a factory or laboratory, operating land or water vehicles, flying airplanes, or building and repairing things on a large or small scale.

6. Industrial (IND). This scale measures your interest in repetitive, regular work activities in a factory setting. Jobs that satisfy this interest include inspecting, sorting, and weighing manufactured goods. Machine setup and operation or supervision of other workers might also be enjoyed.

7. Business Detail (BUS). A high score in this area suggests that you may enjoy office work. This interest may be satisfied by work as an office manager, bookkeeper, receptionist, secretary, or by a variety of related jobs.

8. Selling (SEL). High scores on this scale indicate an interest in providing information about a product and persuading others of its value and desirability. Jobs that satisfy this interest involve selling products or services in stores, offices, or customers' homes.

9. Accommodating (ACC). This scale measures your interest in providing services for the convenience and comfort of others. Hospitality services in airplanes, restaurants, and hotels, or hair and beauty care are examples of work that may satisfy this interest.

10. Humanitarian (HUM). A high score on this scale indicates an interest in helping people with problems of a physical, social, emotional, or religious nature. A job in counseling, nursing, physical therapy, or rehabilitation may satisfy an interest in this area.

11. Leading-Influencing (LEA). This scale measures your interest in leading and influencing others by using verbal and numerical abilities. Jobs that may satisfy this interest include jobs in administration, finance, law, education, social research, or public relations.

12. Physical Performing (PHY). High scores in this area show an interest in performing physical activities before an audience. A job in professional sports as a player or official, or performing physical feats such as acrobatics, may satisfy this interest.

Please use this information to learn more about yourself and about different occupations. Best wishes in finding a satisfying career!

Figure 6-16b　OASIS-3 Aptitude Survey, Third Edition Humanitarian Worksheet © 2002 by R. M. Parker. Used with permission of the publisher, PRO-ED.

7 Using Personality Inventories

Counselors turn to personality inventories to measure individual differences in social traits, motivational drives and needs, attitudes, and adjustment—vital information in the career exploration process. A number of career theorists have stressed the importance of considering personality factors and characteristics in career guidance. Super (1990) emphasizes the importance of self-concept in career counseling, Holland (1997) relates modal personal style to work environments, and Dawis (1996) suggests that personality style determines how one interacts within an environment. Prediger (1995), when reviewing trait-and-factor theory, observes that clients should evaluate occupations from a broad perspective—that is, by giving consideration to a broad range of human traits.

An earlier review by Lowman (1991) focuses specifically on the use of personality inventories for the clinical practice of career assessment. Although there appears to be an increased interest in the use of personality inventories for career counseling, they have not been extensively used for several reasons: (1) Because personality inventories were originally developed primarily to measure psychopathology, their use for career assessment has been limited. Although efforts were made to relate personality measures to career-fit projections, the results have not been impressive (Lowman, 1991). (2) More personality measures are needed that are specifically designed to evaluate those personality traits that are relevant to success in certain careers. At this time, only one study has examined the relationship between personality and career success. These researchers (Judge, Higgins, Thoresen & Barrick, 1999) examined the relationship between the "Big Five" personality factors as measured by the NEO Personality Inventory–Revised (PI-R) and career success, defined as intrinsic (job satisfaction) or extrinsic (income and occupational status). These researchers found that intrinsic and extrinsic career success was predicted by higher levels of conscientiousness, general mental ability predicted extrinsic career success, and a negative relationship existed between neuroticism and external career success.

More research is definitely needed to establish relationships between occupational fit and personality variables and between abilities and interests and personality variables. On a positive note, Table 7-1 outlines research focusing on the relationship between personality and career related issues. Although the list is impressive, most of the topics have only one or two studies associated with them, which translates into a great need for more research in this area, and which means that the outcomes of these studies should be viewed as preliminary data.

In the meantime, personality measures should be used as a means of evaluating support for or opposition to a career under consideration. For example, an individual may find support for a sales career from a high score on a personality trait that is related to interpersonal skills. Nevertheless, the score alone should not be viewed as a predictor of success or failure in a sales career but, rather, should be compared with other data, including abilities and interests.

Like interest inventories, personality measures provide topics for stimulating dialogue. Through discussion, the individual confirms or disagrees with the results and comes to understand the relationship of personality characteristics to career decisions. Tokar, Fischer, and Subich (1998) provide an excellent review on the use of personality inventories and career counseling with its related issues (career choice, career change, satisfaction and organizational outcomes such as job performance).

In this chapter, four personality inventories are used as examples to illustrate how these measures can be used in career development counseling. Keep in mind that these inventories provide opportunities for clients to experience a view of self as they discuss relevant issues about themselves and others in the search for an appropriate work environment. In addition, this chapter includes exercises for career development and a list of several personality inventories.

<table>
<tr><td colspan="2">**Table 7-1**   Specific Career Issues and Related Research Studies Focusing on the Relationship Between Personality and Career-Related Issues</td></tr>
</table>

Aptitudes	Carson, Stalikas, & Bizot, 1997
Career choice	Katz, Joiner, & Seaman, 1999; Krug, 1995; Paige, 2000; Stilwell, Wallick, Thal, & Burleson, 2000
Career decidedness	Lounsbury, Tatum, Chambers, Owens, & Gibson, 1999; Neuman, Gray, & Fuqua, 1999
Career Holland type	Blake & Sackett, 1999
Career self-efficacy	Tuel & Betz, 1998
Career maturity	Lundberg, Osborne, & Minor, 1997
Career obstacles	Healy & Woodward, 1998
Career orientation	Pulkkinen, Ohranen, & Tolvanen, 1999; Randolph & Wood, 1998
Career stability	Pulkkinen et al., 1999
Career transitions	Heppner, Fuller, & Multon, 1998
Career type and colleague type preference	Wampold, Mondin, & Ahn, 1999
Elevated interest profiles	Fuller, Holland & Johnston, 1999
Job satisfaction	Krug, 1995

Sixteen Personality Factor Questionnaire (16PF, Fifth Edition)

The first form of the 16PF was published in 1949 (Cattell, Eber, & Tatsuoka, 1970). There are now several forms for measuring the same 16 personality dimensions in individuals 16 years and older. Four forms (A, B, C, D) have an adult vocabulary level; three forms (E, F and the 16PF Select) are for low-literacy groups.

The current version available is the 5th edition and is considered to be a broad measure of normal adult personality. The 16PF consists of 185 items (3 choice response format), takes as long as 50 minutes to complete by hand (as long as 35 minutes by computer), has a reading level of fifth grade, has 16 primary scales (made up of 10–15 items each), 5 global factors, and 3 additional scales. The 16PF can be hand scored, mailed in, or computer scored.

The 16 primary personality characteristics, or factors, are source traits or combinations of traits considered to be components of an individual's personality. Items in the test were selected because they correlated highly with a particular factor, but a given item may also correlate with other factors. Thus, a combination of items measures each distinct factor, but parts of that factor may be correlated with parts of other distinct factors. Understanding this principle aids in interpreting this instrument. In addition to the 16 primary factors (seen in Figure 7-1, following page), are 5 global factors, which are presented in Table 7-2, as well as an Impression Management index (measuring social desirability responses) and Acquiescence and Infrequency indices.

The first 10 traits in the 16PF are designated by letters A–M, used for identifying these personality factors within a universal standard system. This alphabetical identification system is widely used by professional psychologists when referring to personality factors. In the fifth edition, the letter codes remain, but are accompanied by labels, such as warmth. In communicating the meaning of the personality factors to the general public, more descriptive terms are used. The factors Q1 through Q4 have been given these labels because they are unique to the 16PF.

Attention should be directed to factor B, which is considered an intelligence scale. This scale has been designed to give equal weight to fluid and crystallized ability factors and to provide a dimension of general ability. This scale should be supplemented with other intelligence tests when providing career counseling for occupations requiring high-ability levels.

Interpreting the 16PF

The following 16PF personality factors make up the profile and are reported by the use of stens: warmth, reasoning, emotional stability, dominance, liveliness, rule-consciousness, social boldness, sensitivity,

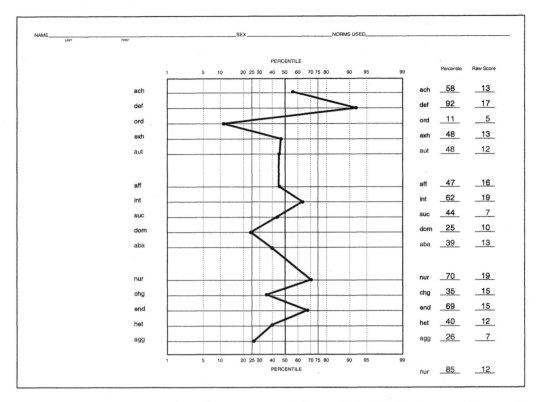

NAME _____ LAST _____ FIRST _____   SEX _____   NORMS USED _____

Figure 7-1

vigilance, abstractedness, privateness, apprehension, openness to change, self-reliance, perfectionism, and tension. A bipolar description is provided for each source trait to make the interpretation of scores meaningful. Because the scales are bipolar, both high and low scores have meaning. The authors caution against interpreting low scores as "bad" or "weaknesses"; the scores are merely indicators of personality.

The right side of the "pole" is the plus side; the left side of the pole is the minus side. The authors suggest that, because of the short nature of many of the scales, individuals' results should be interpreted as an estimate of their true score, rather than as their actual true score. When a person completes the 16PF, his or her raw scores are then converted into sten (standardized) scores, based on a 10-point scale, with a mean of 5.5 and a standard deviation of .2. Most people are expected to score in the middle. Scores of 4 and 7 are called "low-average" and "high-average," respectively, because they are on the line between average and distinctive or extreme scores. Scores between 4 and 7 are in the average range, and scores below 4 and above 7 are in the low and high ranges, respectively. The manual provides a series of suggested steps for interpreting a person's scales.

Table 7-2   **Global Factor Scale Description**

Factor		Left Meaning	Right Meaning
EX	Extraversion	Introverted, Socially Inhibited	Extraverted, Socially Participating
AX	Anxiety	Low Anxiety, Unperturbed	High Anxiety, Perturb-able
TM	Tough-Mindedness	Receptive, Open-Minded, Intuitive	Tough-Minded, Resolute, Un-empathic
IN	Independence	Accommodating, Agreeable, Selfless	Independent, Persuasive, Willful

A major part of the research on the 16PF in the 1970s was devoted to identifying vocational personality patterns and occupational fitness projections. However, the current version of the 16PF does not include extensive vocational information, nor does it provide a list of potential occupations. What is included in the report is a breakdown of the Holland themes (see Figure 7-2).Individuals interested in the occupational links of the 16PF should refer to the Personal Career Development Profile described later in this chapter.

Cattell Comprehensive Personality Interpretation

Randy P. Sample
December 03, 1998

16PF Primary Scores

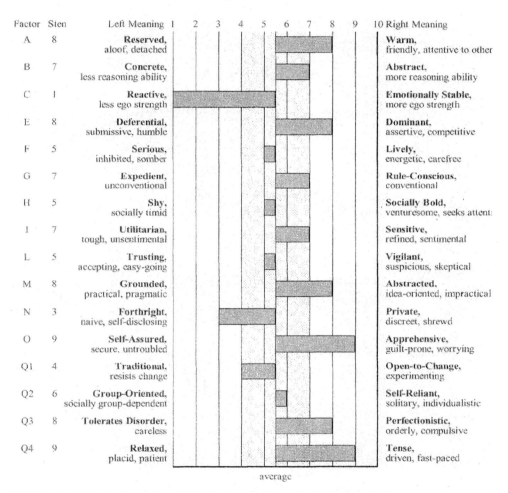

Factor	Sten	Left Meaning	1	2	3	4	5	6	7	8	9	10	Right Meaning
A	8	Reserved, aloof, detached											Warm, friendly, attentive to other
B	7	Concrete, less reasoning ability											Abstract, more reasoning ability
C	1	Reactive, less ego strength											Emotionally Stable, more ego strength
E	8	Deferential, submissive, humble											Dominant, assertive, competitive
F	5	Serious, inhibited, somber											Lively, energetic, carefree
G	7	Expedient, unconventional											Rule-Conscious, conventional
H	5	Shy, socially timid											Socially Bold, venturesome, seeks attent:
I	7	Utilitarian, tough, unsentimental											Sensitive, refined, sentimental
L	5	Trusting, accepting, easy-going											Vigilant, suspicious, skeptical
M	8	Grounded, practical, pragmatic											Abstracted, idea-oriented, impractical
N	3	Forthright, naive, self-disclosing											Private, discreet, shrewd
O	9	Self-Assured, secure, untroubled											Apprehensive, guilt-prone, worrying
Q1	4	Traditional, resists change											Open-to-Change, experimenting
Q2	6	Group-Oriented, socially group-dependent											Self-Reliant, solitary, individualistic
Q3	8	Tolerates Disorder, careless											Perfectionistic, orderly, compulsive
Q4	9	Relaxed, placid, patient											Tense, driven, fast-paced

average

The publication of the 16PF generated considerable controversy, especially about Cattell's claim that the instrument measures source traits of normal personality functioning (Bloxom, 1978). Specifically, Cattell's use of factor analysis as a method of discovering the causal traits that lead to comprehensive descriptions of personality has been challenged (Walsh, 1978). According to Anastasi (1988), factor analysis should be used for grouping test items and then matching these against empirical criteria in validity studies. Cronbach (1984) complains that there is no consistency in classifying and defining psychological traits. Cattell provides 16 personality factors, but other theorists have combined or have extended the list of these personality dimensions. The current developers of the 16PF have a link on their Web site that answers the question "Does the 16PF measure the Big Five?" The developers answer affirmatively and provide a comparison of collapsed Cattell factors to the Big Five and the NEO PI-R (see Table 7-3).

Table 7-3	Comparison of the "Big Five" Personality Factors		
Cattell's Big Five		Goldberg's Big Five	Costa & McCrae's First Factor Model
Introversion/Extraversion		Surgency	Extraversion
Low Anxiety/High Anxiety		Emotional Stability	Neuroticism
Tough Mindedness/Receptivity		Intellect	Openness
Independence/Accommodation		Agreeablenes	Agreeableness
Low Self-Control/High Self-Control		Conscientiousness	Conscientiousness

Furthermore, Cattell suggests that personality inventories like the 16PF are not built around a definite theory. It appears that we can best use the 16PF results for promoting discussion in career counseling. Extensive reviews of this instrument are provided by Schuerger (2000), Harrell (1992), Aiken (1988), Kaplan and Saccuzzo (1993), and Olson and Matlock (1994).

Schuerger (2000) presents five specific strategies for interpreting the 16PF. First, the counselor should "consider the context of the assessment" (p. 100). This would include the purpose for testing, who will use the information, and demographic information about the client. Second, he suggests reviewing the answer sheet for missing items, overly neat marks, and any patterns. The third step is to review the validity scales. Fourth, he suggests reviewing the scores and score combinations in a specific order: "global scores and patterns of globals; any inconsistencies of primary factor scores within the globals; very high or very low primary scores; patterns of primary factor scores" (p. 100). Fifth, he recommends then taking the information gained from the 16PF and applying it to the original questions that prompted its use.

Psychometric properties have improved in the latest edition of the 16PF. Test-retest reliabilities (two-week interval) of the 16PF average about .80 and .70 for a two-month interval. Internal consistency reliabilities range from .65 to .85, with an average of .74. The norms were based on an age range from 15 to 92. The norms were based on a stratified random sampling using U.S. Census figures (1990) according to gender, race, age, and educational variables. The norm sample consisted of a total of 4449 individuals.

The basic interpretive report is similar to the narrative report of the fourth edition of the 16PF. It begins with a table of the response style indices, gives a graphical representation of the individual's scores on the global factors and 16 specific factors scores. What it does *not* include is a brief description of what the graphs mean, or what the client's highest or lowest scores mean. The scores that are more than one standard deviation from the mean are highlighted, which suggests that these are the significant ones to consider. A brief interpretation of what high, average and low scores mean would be helpful, especially if the client might take a copy of the report home. This is followed by a breakdown of how the individual's scores on the sixteen factors fed into each of the five global factors, and an interpretation for the individual is included for each of the five factors. Next, information is displayed about how the client's scores relate to self-esteem and adjustment, social skills, and leadership and creativity. Finally, a summarization of predicted vocational activities, or Holland types and related general occupational fields (such as art and music) are presented. A scores-only report option is available as well.

As mentioned earlier, the vocational section of this edition of the 16PF is still under construction. Currently, no list or descriptions of occupations are provided with the profile. A vocational activities section still exists and is based on Holland's typology and the RIASEC themes (see Figure 7-3). The Basic Interpretive Report provides a predicted sten for each of Holland's six general occupational themes. A narrative description is given in the report for any sten above an 8. If the client has no stens above an 8, then his or her two or three (if the stens are tied) highest stens are discussed. Using Holland's model as a foundation, a client's scores are discussed in terms of compatibility of highest themes. The themes are described on the basis of (1) typical SDS item endorsement, (2) related 16PF personality factors that are related to the six types, and (3) occupations for which high scorers indicate definite preferences on the SDS.

Several studies have explored how personality factors as measured by the 16PF relate to occupational fields and educational pursuits. Blackman (2003) compared pilot applicants/incumbents' scores on the 16PF to those of the general population. She found that the pilot group scored significantly higher on intelligence, emotional stability and maturity, with significant differences noted on most of the other personality scales as well. She suggested that this distinct pilot profile may be due to the high-risk nature of job. In a study of sign language interpreters, Seal (2004) found that abstract reasoning was extremely high for 18 of the 28 interpreters. Noel, Michaels and Levas (2003) found that the 16PF was able to distinguish undergraduate business students by major (accounting, management information systems and marketing). In a study of online versus traditional learners, MacGregor (2002) found that the online learners rated themselves as more introverted, serious, and shy, as well as less independent, and more tough minded. What these studies show are that certain 16PF profiles may exist for occupational groups and specific types of students/learners.

Personal Career Development Profile (PCDP) and PC\DP Plus

The Personal Career Development Profile (PCDP), developed by Walter (1984), is a computer interpretation of the 16PF designed specifically for career guidance. The most recent version is the 1998 edition, to correlate with the fifth edition of the 16PF. The format is narrative and graphical in style and non-technical in nature. The PCD Profile includes the following: problem-solving patterns; patterns for coping with stressful conditions; patterns of interpersonal interaction, organizational role, and work setting; patterns for career activity interests, and personal career lifestyle effectiveness considerations.

In addition, the PCDP provides several graphical representations of occupational interest patterns (which include the same categories as the Campbell Interest and Skill Survey: Influencing, Organizing, Creating, Helping, Analyzing, Producing and Venturing), broad patterns (emotional adjustment, creative potential, effective leadership, elected leadership, leadership preference, structured situation pattern, formal academic interest, work pattern preference, learning situation preference, and risk-taking/adventure interest), leadership/subordinate role patterns, career activity themes, career field interest scores, and occupational interest patterns. The PCDP is appropriate for individuals aged 16 years and older. One strength of the PCDP is that it not only helps individuals identify their interests but also provides that information in the form of a profile that includes observations about their choices/preferences, emphasizes their personal strengths, and helps them look for deeper meanings regarding their personalities.

The personal career lifestyle effectiveness considerations provide constructive feedback about how this person's personality might cause problems on the job and interpersonally. The person is encouraged to "be aware of and work consciously to guard against the impact of" various tendencies, such as "the tendency to make spur-of-the-moment decisions" or "doing or saying things that others may view or interpret as being unnecessarily direct." The 16PF profile of the PCDP is in the same layout as the basic 16PF interpretive report and needs to have some brief explanations added to make it more user-friendly.

Two career-related report versions are available: the regular PCDP and the PCDP Plus. The PCDP Plus includes the regular PCDP (which also includes the 16PF profile) plus an additional seven pages that focus on helping clients review their profiles and develop action plans. The PCDP Plus suggests three steps, including reading the report and underlining the statements that best describe self, circling the statements that surprise or concern or areas that could be improved, and completing the plus exercises. The exercises ask the client to respond in writing to questions about problem-solving patterns, patterns for coping with stressful conditions, patterns for interpersonal interaction, organizational and work-setting patterns, work-related experience, and career activity interests. The exercises end with a section on work-related, educational, and career goals; needs for improved personal effectiveness; and action plans for goal attainment.

The PCD Profile report is comprehensive; as many as 50 specific occupations are compared with each individual's 16PF scores. In addition, profile similarities are provided for occupational groups. The report is designed to be easily interpreted by professionals and by most individuals who complete the questionnaire. The PCDP and PCDP Plus provide a balance of mental health and career information for the counselor and the client to work with. As career counseling educators, we consistently emphasize how career issues and mental health issues are intrinsically linked to each other. These profiles provide a great example of that natural relationship.

Case of a Mid-Career Change

Mr. Sample reported to a community college counseling center for pre-enrollment counseling concerning a major and a career choice. He was 34 years old, was married, had two children, and had spent ten years in the navy as a yeoman. His duties as a yeoman included doing clerical work and handling the payroll. Mr. Sample said that he did not reenlist in the navy because he wanted to spend time with his family. He was now seeking training for a job that would provide his family with a comfortable living. He expressed interest in a variety of business careers such as clerical work, banking, and computer programming. He had saved enough money to see him through a couple of years of training.

Mr. Sample had graduated from high school with average grades. His extracurricular activities had included collecting stamps and building boat models. Mr. Sample's interests were fairly well determined, and the skills he had developed in the navy could be applied to the careers under consideration. The counselor thought that an informal skills identification survey and a personality inventory would be useful to stimulate further career exploration. Mr. Sample and the counselor chose 16PF and the PCD Profile because of their non-technical format and the career profiles they yield.

Mr. Sample's profile is shown in Figure 7-3, a–g. The counselor asked Mr. Sample to read the profile carefully before discussing it. After they discussed each of the profile patterns, the counselor asked Mr. Sample to summarize what he had learned about himself.

16PF® Fifth Edition
Personal Career Development Profile

Name: John Sample
Date: August 21, 2000

This report describes Mr. Sample's typical personal lifestyle patterns. The narrative in his report is based on his scores from the 16PF Fifth Edition Questionnaire and additional predictive research.

The PCDP is founded on 35 years of research and consulting experience of organizational and management professionals. This experience revealed that people who are effectively directing the course and growth of their careers reflect personal strenghts anchored to five important areas of behavior covered in this report:

- Problem-Solving Resources
- Patterns for Coping with Stressful Conditions
- Interpersonal Interaction Styles
- Organizational Role and Work-Setting Preferences
- Career Activity Interests

The purpose of this report is to help Mr. Sample broaden his understanding of himself and to plan well for his future. Although successful people possess personal strengths inherent to these behavioral patterns, no lifestyle can be classified as "the best way of doing things." Various styles may aid in one's efforts to be successful, happy, and productive.

A helpful understanding of Mr. Sample's reported personal strengths should also take into account other significant information about him, such as his work and leisure experiences, education and skills. So, if Mr. Sample wants to benefit fully from this report, he should discuss his profile with a skilled career counselor or trained professional. **Of utmost importance, though, this report should be treated confidentially and responsibly.**

Figure 7-3a

COUNSELOR: Do you feel that your past working experience has helped you in dealing with stressful conditions?

MR. SAMPLE: Well, yes, I believe that had I taken this test sometime earlier, like in my early twenties, it probably would have had different results. I think that the experiences I've had have certainly helped me to put things in perspective.

COUNSELOR: You have had to make some important decisions in the past, and you seem to be well satisfied with those decisions. You seem to have decided now that you want to be with your family,

---

Personal Career Development Profile

NAME: John Sample
DATE: August 21, 2000

PROBLEM-SOLVING RESOURCES

This section describes Mr. Sample's unique problem-solving resources: What are his overall strengths for solving most problems? How does he usually approach resolving problems which confront him?

Mr. Sample functions quite comfortably with problems and situations that involve abstract reasoning and conceptual thinking. He is very alert mentally. He can see quickly how ideas fit together and is likely to be a fast learner. Mr. Sample appears to be quite able to learn well from his experiences. He can usually be counted on to use his experience to advantage in solving most problems.

He tends to believe that when difficulties are faced they normally get resolved, but that it's quite helpful when he has the advice of others. However, when necessary, Mr. Sample is able to work creatively, to get beyond what is normally viewed as customary or accepted, and to come up with new ideas and ways for approaching problems in efforts to resolve them.

PATTERNS FOR COPING WITH STRESSFUL CONDITIONS

The personal patterns Mr. Sample presently reflects in efforts to cope with stress and pressure in life are described in this section: Depending on the situation, how does he tend to react to emotionally charged events? What is he likely to do when faced with conflict or opposition on the part of others?

For the most part, Mr. Sample seems to be well-adjusted. He does not usually show signs of tension and worry. He usually strives to take most situations in stride and to manage them in a balanced and adaptive way. He rarely allows his emotional reactions to get in the way of what he does or tries to do in situations and relationships. He seems to be quite casual in the way he reacts to some circumstances and situations. However, when situations call for a good deal of self-control, he may tend to follow his own urges and feelings, rather than consciously restraining himself in what he does. He seems to be quite self-assured. He seems to experience a rather strong sense of adequacy about his ability to handle most situations. He appears, too, to have little need to explain his actions to himself or to other people. At the present time, he presents himself as a person who is relaxed and composed. He does not seem to be worried or frustrated. As a result, he probably does not really wish to change himself in any major way. He may come across to some people, though, as being too complacent and self-accepting. Generally, when Mr. Sample is faced with conflict or disagreement from others, he likes to look at all the facts and then usually tries to work out the best solution possible to the problem.

INTERPERSONAL INTERACTION STYLES

This section covers Mr. Sample's styles for relating and communicating with others: How does Mr. Sample usually react in dealing with others? What are his major sources of gratification and satisfaction when building relationships with others?

On the whole, Mr. Sample tends to give about equal amounts of time and attention to the relationship between himself and others. But, he also tends to value some alone time on occasion.

- 2 -

Personal Career Development Profile   NAME: John Sample
                                                       DATE: August 21, 2000

Although Mr. Sample may become somewhat concerned when he finds himself in situations that require a lot of personal contact with others, he usually tries to look on the bright side of things. As a consequence, he is able to recover from his concerns with a fairly positive outlook on his part. He usually feels best about what he does when he is being really helpful to others in some way. He seems to have concern for people who may need assistance and support from him. He likes to put forth a feeling of warmth when interacting with others. Mr. Sample is generally quite at ease when approaching and talking with people in most social gatherings. Mr. Sample is usually quite forward when meeting and talking with others. Mr. Sample may sometimes want to get others to do something so much that he may try too hard, and as a result, he could run the risk of coming across as overly pushy and demanding in such instances.

Mr. Sample is normally inclined to state his desires and opinions clearly and quite forcefully. He likes to have things his way most of the time and prefers freedom from other people's influence. Although Mr. Sample usually likes to be free from other people's influence, he can usually adjust his manner, and can be thoughtful of most people's concerns or needs when it is important to do so. He tends to feel closest to people who are competitive and who understand the importance of being in firm control of their lives and what they do to reach their goals. Sometimes, Mr. Sample may be in such a hurry to get things done that he may forget how others may be affected by his actions and how others may feel about matters that are important to them. He appears to like having other people around him focus their attention on whatever he is talking about or doing. Even so, Mr. Sample appears to want to be cheerful and active in his dealings with most people. He also usually tries his best to be as lively as possible in most social situations. Nevertheless, Mr. Sample may be quite personally guarded when relating to some people. For the most part, he tries to be accepting of people since he tends to be trusting and accepting of himself and what he does in life. Mr. Sample tends to gain his greatest satisfaction in life from being involved in activities that have chances for personal achievement while competing with others. When things are going well between himself and others, he likes to have influence over other people as he faces and meets difficult challenges.

ORGANIZATIONAL ROLE AND WORK-SETTING PREFERENCES

This section describes Mr. Sample's unique style for fulfilling leadership/subordinate roles in organizational settings and his work-setting preferences: What leadership style does he call upon when working with others? Hoe do others react to him? In what type of organizational setting and environment does he feel most comfortable and productive?

Mr. Sample tends to be seen as a leader by most people. He usually responds well when requested to take on a leadership role with them. He likes to be in charge of activities, especially with a group of friends or co-workers. He usually feels comfortable in situations that require him to provide direction over others. He enjoys taking charge and initiating action to get things accomplished. His group members, too, are likely to respond favorably to his leadership patterns. If he were to take on a leadership role, he would probably strive to administer duties by focusing attention on the conditions that foster or hinder performance of subordinates rather than on personnel problems. Being solution-seeking, he would strive to remove personality and power struggles from the work situation. Mr. Sample generally prefers to build feelings of mutual respect and interdependence among people. He likes to share with others whatever power may be necessary to accomplish the work at hand. He appears to value objective working relationships between superiors and subordinates. Mr. Sample appears to want to be a source of objective criticism and feedback to others. He also likes to be part of work settings where responsibility,

- 3 -

Personal Career Development Profile   NAME: John Sample
                                                        DATE: August 21, 2000

power and accountability are shared with others. He is overly careful, at times, about keeping personal matters private.

Mr. Sample generally feels at his best doing things that require dependability and rather precise attention to what is done. He likes to work within a rather structured framework where what is expected and how it will be done are fairly well spelled out. He is likely to enjoy the day-to-day operational details involved in running various aspects of a business endeavor.

CAREER ACTIVITY INTERESTS

Career activity interests are an important part of Mr. Sample's personal strengths and his general personality orientation. The purpose of this section is to provide information which may either support his present career choices or assist him to explore, consider and plan for another career/avocational direction.

The career activity interests presented in this section, however, should not be treated as recommended career/avocational choices. Some may not appeal to him. Others may not relate well to his training, experience or expressed interest. Since these interest patterns are derived from one set of test scores and specific predictive research, a careful analysis by him and a trained professional may bring to mind other alternatives that may lead to even more appealing and meaningful life planning.

Career/Avocational Activity Interests

Mr. Sample's personal lifestyle patterns suggest he is similar to persons who are likely to enjoy activity interests that entail:

- **Influencing:** Convincing, directing or persuading others to attain organizational goals and/or economic gain -- activity characteristic of persons who find satisfaction working on the sales, marketing, and management aspects of business, or in the professions of consulting, law and politics. They usually enjoy having the opportunity to exercise control over matters important to them, like to have some degree of influence over people, and to work in situations where they can make decisions and persuade others to their viewpoints in efforts to get things accomplished.

- **Organizing:** Initiating procedures, managing projects and directly supervising the work of others -- activity characteristic of that performed by people who enjoy working in situations whereby they can handle the details of organizational productivity, data systems, and accuracy of information processing. They usually find satisfaction solving day-to-day problems to bring orderliness to situations, planning budgets and cash flow, and handling investments.

Career Field and Occupational Interests

The career fields and occupations presented in this section are those found to be related to Mr. Sample's broad activity interests. Again, these interest patterns are derived from test scores and predictive research. Consequently, they should not be treated as recommended career choices. Some may not appeal to him. Others may not relate well to his training, experience or expressed interests. Counseling with a trained professional, therefore, may bring to light even

- 4 -

and that decision has prompted you to consider a career that keeps you at home. The patterns of interpersonal interaction suggest that you are focusing your thoughts primarily on inner feelings and your own personal situations and have made your decisions based primarily on them.

MR. SAMPLE: Well, yes, I think that I have always felt confident in myself, and I have usually made decisions based on that confidence. In other words, I have felt fairly self-reliant and like to control working situations by doing the work myself.

COUNSELOR: Well, how would these feelings affect your performance in managerial or leadership positions?

MR. SAMPLE: Yes, I've thought about that. I may have some problems in expecting too much of others; I sort of experienced that in the navy. However, my superior in the navy was able to depend on me, and I feel that I followed through on most assignments fairly well. But not being able to delegate work could be a problem for me as a manager.

The counselor and Mr. Sample continued their discussions concerning interpersonal relationships and problem-solving patterns. Whenever applicable, the counselor related work environments to personality characteristics. In the final phase of the counseling session, career development was discussed.

MR. SAMPLE: I see they have recommended a number of career considerations. However, I think I can eliminate some of those right off. For example, I don't believe I am interested in computer

Personal Career Development Profile

NAME: John Sample
DATE: August 21, 2000

more choices for consideration and meaningful life planning.

Career fields directly related to Mr. Sample's unique activity interests are:

- Advertising/Marketing, Sales, Management, Law/Politics, Public Speaking, Supervision.

In addition, Mr. Sample's personal lifestyle patterns suggest he is also similar to persons who express interest for the following career field(s):

- Counseling, Teaching, Athletics.

Occupations directly related to Mr. Sample's unique activity interests are:

- Corporate Trainer, Financial Planner, Hotel Manager, Human Resources Director, Marketing Director, Realtor, School Administrator, Manufacturer's Representative, Retail Store Manager, Public Relations Director, Elected Public Official, Insurance Agent, Advertising Executive, CEO/President, Bank Manager, Attorney, School Superintendent, Media Executive, Investment Manager, Buyer, Credit Manager, Hospital Administrator.

In addition, Mr. Sample's personal lifestyle patterns suggest he is also similar to persons who express interest for the following occupation(s):

- Community Service Director, Social Science Teacher, Police Officer, High School Counselor, Guidance Counselor, Military Officer.

In summary, the career field and occupational information presented above is based on an analysis of Mr. Sample's general personality patterns. **So, the career information provided is not meant to be exhaustive, nor is it meant to suggest career choices for which he may have proven abilities, skills, interests, or experience and training.** Within the broad world of work, there are many, many more career fields and occupations which could be identified and considered by him. Rather, the career information provided herein is limited by the research basic to this report.

Figure 7-3e Copyright © 1995-1998 and 2000 by Verne Walter Associates, Inc., Vista, CA and The Institute for Personality and Ability Testing, Inc., Champaign, Illinois, USA. Reproduced by special permission of the publisher.

programming, actuarial services, or a retail store career. I think I lean more toward working with people in some capacity.

COUNSELOR: Good! You've been able to eliminate some of the possibilities. I noticed in your patterns for career activity interests that you are a "people person" and prefer to be involved with people with some sort of relationship, like solving problems with them or encouraging relationships between people.

Personal Career Development Profile

NAME: John Sample
DATE: August 21, 2000

PERSONAL CAREER LIFESTYLE EFFECTIVENESS CONSIDERATIONS

The final section of Mr. Sample's report covers a summary of his broad personal patterns: What are the characteristics of Mr. Sample's basic lifestyle patterns? To which of his behavioral patterns could he give most attention in efforts to achieve greater interpersonal and work-related performance effectiveness?

Mr. Sample's lifestyle is typical of people who value independence and self-directedness. He generally prefers to have control over his personal and work-related situations coupled with a tendency to be actively and forcefully self-determined in his thinking and actions. He likes to be in charge of projects, and to accomplish things by being as solution-seeking as possible and to work in a business-like manner. He seldom needs to be shielded from the truth so that subordinates are able to communicate easily and directly with him. Mr. Sample might very well feel most comfortable and able to experience the greatest degree of satisfaction if he is involved in work that must be carried out in an organized and orderly setting.

Mr. Sample would most likely function with greater personal effectiveness, both on-the-job and in other personal-career situations, if he would try to be aware of and work consciously to guard against the impact of:

- his tendency to sometimes overlook the need to give enough thought to himself or to take enough time for quiet, deep thinking about things that are important to him;
- the tendency to make spur-of-the-moment decisions, rather than giving enough thoughtful consideration of future consequences of such actions;
- the tendency to take unnecessary risks, especially when a more cautious approach could be taken to what is being done;
- tendencies to become overly impatient when confronted with what he may view as possible roadblocks to doing things valued by him as being important;
- being overly confident about his ability to handle most any problem or situation that comes up, when more accurate thinking and more realistic planning may be required to accomplish what he most desires to do;
- taking on assignments in such an expedient way that he could overlook critically important details that require thoughtful deliberation and planning;
- seeking too much attention from others in his relationships with them;
- a tendency to expect others to accept his ideas about how best to solve problems needing to be resolved;
- doing or saying things that others may view or interpret as being unnecessarily direct;
- being in such a hurry to get things done that he does not see how others may be affected by his approach;
- tendencies to be less prepared and organized than he could strive to be because he may not be aware of his need to build more effective work habits than he seems to have at this time;
- urges to change from one career field or job to another, or to not stay with one organization long enough to feel as if he belongs there;

and in addition,

- taking on activities or assignments that involve ordinary, routine tasks without much creative thought or tasks that may not fully challenge Mr. Sample's intelligence or curiosity.

Figure 7-3f Copyright © 1995-1998 and 2000 by Verne Walter Associates, Inc., Vista, CA and The Institute for Personality and Ability Testing, Inc., Champaign, Illinois, USA. Reproduced by special permission of the publisher.

MR. SAMPLE: I understand that personnel work is a very good field, and I believe that I may be interested in pursuing this as a possible career. I'm not quite sure what area of personnel work I would like to get into, but I would definitely like to look into this as a possible career field.

COUNSELOR: Very well. We have some information in our career resource center on this topic, and I can also recommend some people for you to see. What about other considerations? Perhaps you should look at two or three fields at this time.

Personal Career Development Profile   NAME: John Sample
Career Interest Scores   DATE: August 21, 2000

OCCUPATIONAL INTEREST SCORES - Page 3 of 3

Mr. Sample's 16PF results were used to predict the **Occupational Interest Scores** presented on this page. These occupational interest scores reflect only a similarity in personality to persons who express interest for these occupations. **These scores are intended for personal career development purposes only and are inappropriate for making personnel selection decisions.** Scores **DO NOT PREDICT** ability or suitability for performance of job duties.

ANALYZING INTEREST

	Female	Male	Combined
Biologist	4.5	3.3	*
Chemist	4.8	3.9	2.1
Computer Programmer	4.7	3.9	2.5
Dentist	6.0	4.5	*
Geographer	4.9	4.3	*
Geologist	5.8	6.3	*
Mathematician	5.3	3.4	*
Math/Science Teacher	*	*	2.4
Medical Researcher	*	*	2.3
Physician	5.4	6.1	1.0
Physicist	4.7	3.7	*
Statistician	*	*	3.5
Systems Analyst	*	*	4.2
Veterinarian	3.2	4.0	1.0

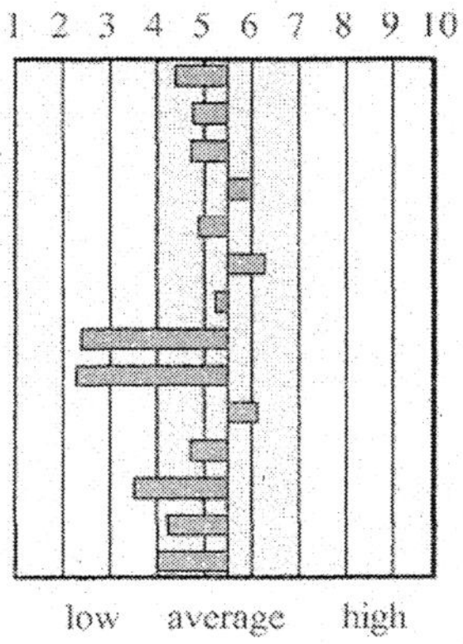

PRODUCING INTEREST

	Female	Male	Combined
Agribusiness Manager	*	5.5	2.5
Airline Mechanic	*	*	4.2
Auto Mechanic	4.9	4.0	*
Carpenter	4.5	3.5	2.5
Electrician	5.3	5.0	3.6
Engineer	5.0	4.8	*
Farmer	2.9	4.7	*
Forester	4.7	4.0	*
Landscape Architect	*	*	4.3
Test Pilot	*	*	4.3

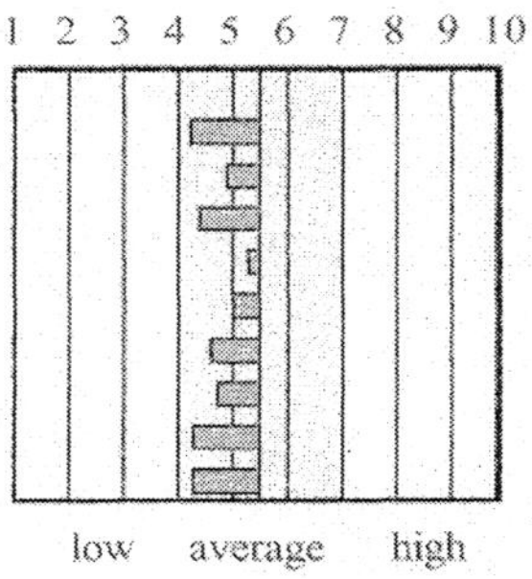

VENTURING INTEREST

	Female	Male	Combined
Athletic Coach	*	*	3.5
Athletic Trainer	7.0	7.2	3.7
Emergency Medical Technician	5.6	5.8	1.3
Fitness Instructor	*	*	3.5
Military Enlisted Personnel	3.9	4.3	*
Military Officer	7.4	7.2	7.6
Police Officer	8.2	6.5	4.9
Ski Instructor	*	*	1.7

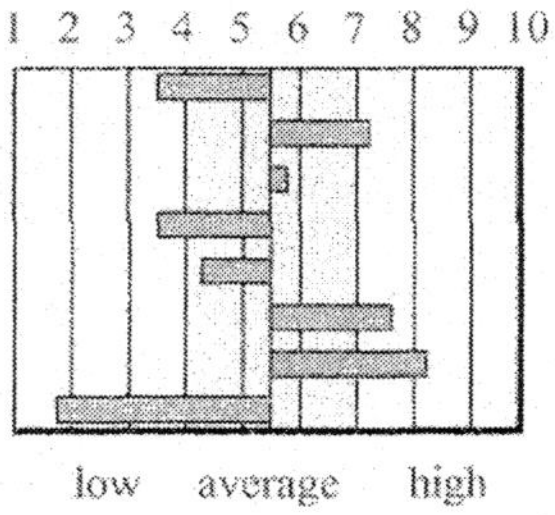

* Indicates no solid predictive data to predict meaningful scores. The Female/Male and Combined-Sex labels refer to the gender on which the scores are computed. Female/Male and Combined-Sex Score research is explained in the PCDP manual.

Figure 7-3g

MR. SAMPLE: I agree. I want to take a look at what might be available in different branches of personnel work, but I'm not sure what kind of industry I would like to work in.

The counselor and Mr. Sample continued to discuss possible career considerations using the list of careers provided on the computer printout as a stimulus. Mr. Sample was able to expand this list and thus consider a number of different options.

Myers-Briggs Type Indicator® (MBTI®) Instrument

The MBTI® instrument is a measure of psychological types described by C. G. Jung (1971), who suggested that the basic differences in behavior are the way individuals prefer to use their perception and judgment in organizing information and making decisions. According to Jung, people differ in interests, values, motivation, and skills through individualized judgments that have been formed by numerous perceptions of events and experiences. This instrument is designed to measure perception, judgments, and attitudes used by different types of people. Unlike many other personality instruments, the MBTI® instrument is a measure of normal personality traits. The two-choice format of the 93 items requires individuals to choose between items that measure:

EXTRAVERSION	E	vs.	I	INTROVERSION
SENSING	S	vs.	N	INTUITION
THINKING	T	vs.	F	FEELING
JUDGING	J	vs.	P	PERCEIVING

These four preference dimensions serve to identify how a person energizes (E vs. I), perceives information (S vs. N), makes decisions (T vs. F) and demonstrates his or her lifestyle (J vs. P). Responses to items are rated according to a prediction ratio, and the total rated scores provide an index to the respondent's preferences. For example, higher total points for E compared with I would translate into an individual having a preference for Extraversion rather than Introversion. Numbers are also assigned to preferences to indicate the strengths of the preference. A low score can indicate that there is no or little difference between preferences. See Table 7-4 (next page) for a summary of the four preference dimensions.

The issues of reliability and validity are complex with this inventory. The problem has to do with violations of a key MBTI® Instrument assumption, that the outcome of the MBTI® Instrument is types, not a continuous score. A criticism of many reliability and validity analyses for the MBTI® Instrument centers on the use of the type scores as continuous variables, instead of predicting consistency of types (Fleenor, 2001; Mastrangelo, 2001). According to Mastrangelo, one study found that the internal consistency estimates for single scales ranged from .83-.97 for a four week interval. However, the consistency for all four scores occurred in 65% of 424 respondents after four weeks, and 35% having consistency with three types. He suggests that this finding is somewhat troubling given the emphasis on the interactions among the four preferences as opposed to the specific four preferences. He goes on to state that the four preference interaction only predicted 3 of 73 dependent variables, as opposed to the individual preferences predicting 16-36. Carpraro and Carpraro (2002) confirmed strong retest reliability estimates and internal consistency for the MBTI ® Instrument in their meta-analytic analyses across several studies. At this time, it appears that there is more support for the reliability/validity of the individual preferences than for the overall synergistic type.

According to Jungian theory of psychological types, each type has gifts and strengths as well as potential for vulnerability. The differences between types provide clues for developmental activities as well as being indicators of preferences for career direction. The manual recommends that counselors become familiar with Jung's theory before using this instrument.

Healy and Woodward (1998) investigated the relationships among MBTI® Instrument scores and career obstacles. They found that high JP scores for women related to lack of resolve in the decision-making process and internal psychological obstruction relative to choosing a career. For men, higher TF scores correlated with more obstruction by external demands. In addition, men with either high ST or high NF scores also scored high on being more reluctant to change, while high NT men were most likely to have an obstacle of insufficient networks. Although this preliminary research and link between personality and career obstacles is interesting, the researchers strongly suggest not relying solely on the MBTI® Instrument scores to predict obstacles, but to use the MBTI® Instrument in conjunction with other information.

Table 7-4   Summary of the Different MBTI® Preference Dimensions

---

EXTRAVERSION

Description: like to focus on the outer world of people and activity. They direct their energy and attention outward and receive energy from interacting with people and from taking action.

Characteristics:
- Attuned to external environment
- Prefer to communicate by talking
- Work out ideas by talking them through
- Learn best through doing or discussing
- Have broad interests
- Sociable and expressive
- Readily take initiative in work and relationship

INTROVERSION

Description: like to focus on their own inner world of ideas and experiences. They direct their energy and attention inward and receive energy from reflecting on their thoughts, memories, and feelings.

Characteristics:
- Drawn to their inner world
- Prefer to communicate in writing
- Work out ideas by reflecting on them
- Learn best by reflection, mental "practice"
- Focus in depth on their interests
- Private and contained
- Take initiative when the situation or issue is very important to them

SENSING TYPES

Description: like to take in information that is real and tangible—what is actually happening. They are observant about the specifics of what is going on around them and are especially attuned to practical realities.

Characteristics:
- Oriented to present realities
- Factual and concrete
- Focus on what is real and actual
- Observe and remember specifics
- Build carefully and thoroughly toward conclusions
- Understand ideas and theories through practical applications
- Trust experience

INTUITIVE TYPES

Description: like to take in information by seeing the big picture, focusing on the relationships and connections between facts. They want to grasp patterns and are especially attuned to seeing new possibilities.

Characteristics:
- Oriented to future possibilities
- Imaginative and verbally creative
- Focus on the patterns and meanings in data
- Remember specifics when they relate to a pattern
- Move quickly to conclusions, follow hunches
- Want to clarify ideas and theories before putting them into practice
- Trust inspiration

THINKING TYPES

Description: like to look at the logical consequences of a choice or action. They want to mentally remove themselves from the situation to examine the pros and cons objectively. They are energized by critiquing and analyzing to identify what's wrong with something so they can solve the problem. Their goal is to find a standard or principle that will apply in all similar situations.

Characteristics:
- Analytical
- Use cause-and-effect reasoning
- Solve problems with logic
- Strive for an objective standard of truth
- Reasonable
- Can be "tough-minded"
- Fair—want everyone treated equally

FEELING TYPES

Description: like to consider what is important to them and to others involved. They mentally place themselves into the situation to identify with everyone so they can make decisions based on their values about honoring people. They are energized by appreciating and supporting others and look for qualities to praise. Their goal is to create harmony and treat each person as a unique individual.

Characteristics:
- Empathetic
- Guided by personal values
- Assess impacts of decisions on people
- Strive for harmony and positive interactions
- Compassionate
- May appear "tenderhearted"
- Fair—want everyone treated as an individual

JUDGING TYPES

Description: like to live in a planned, orderly way, seeking to regulate and manage their lives. They want to make decisions, come to closure, and move on. Their lives tend to be structured and organized, and they like to have things settled. Sticking to a plan and schedule is very important to them, and they are energized by getting things done.

Characteristics:
- Scheduled
- Organize their lives
- Systematic
- Methodical
- Make short- and long-term plans
- Like to have things decided
- Try to avoid last-minute stresses

PERCEIVING TYPES

Description: like to live in a flexible, spontaneous way, seeking to experience and understand life, rather than control it. Detailed plans and final decisions feel confining to them; they prefer to stay open to new information and last-minute options. They are energized by their resourcefulness in adapting to the demands of the moment.

Characteristics:
- Spontaneous
- Flexible
- Casual
- Open-ended
- Adapt, change course
- Like things loose and open to change
- Feel energized by last-minute pressures

The MBTI® Instrument is more appropriate for high school students and adults, with a reading level estimated to be at the seventh to eighth grade level. Form M contains 93 items, Form Q contains 144 items, and Form J contains 290 items. The MBTI® Instrument has been used in a variety of settings, including businesses, counseling, education, conflict resolution, team building, and management development. Although the inventory takes about 30 minutes to complete, there are no time limits and scoring can be done by stencil or by computer.

Table 7-5 Characteristics Associated with Each MBTI® Type

	ISTJ	ISFJ	INFJ	INTJ
Introverts	Quiet, serious, earn success by thoroughness and dependability. Practical, matter-of-fact, realistic, and responsible. Decide logically what should be done and work toward it steadily, regardless of distractions. Take pleasure in making everything orderly and organized—their work, their home, their life. Value traditions and loyalty.	Quiet, friendly, responsible, and conscientious. Committed and steady in meeting their obligations. Thorough, painstaking, and accurate. Loyal, considerate, notice and remember specifics about people who are important to them, concerned with how others feel. Strive to create an orderly and harmonious environment at work and at home.	Seek meaning and connection in ideas, relationships, and material possessions. Want to understand what motivates people and are insightful about others. Conscientious and committed to their firm values. Develop a clear vision about how best to serve the common good. Organized and decisive in implementing their vision.	Have original minds and great drive for implementing their ideas and achieving their goals. Quickly see patterns in external events and develop long-range explanatory perspectives. When committed, organize a job and carry it through. Skeptical and independent, have high standards of competence and performance— for themselves and others.
	ISTP	**ISFP**	**INFP**	**INTP**
	Tolerant and flexible, quiet observers until a problem appears, then act quickly to find workable solutions. Analyze what makes things work and readily get through large amounts of data to isolate the core of practical problems. Interested in cause and effect, organize facts using logical principles, value efficiency.	Quiet, friendly, sensitive, and kind. Enjoy the present moment, what's going on around them. Like to have their own space and to work within their own time frame. Loyal and committed to their values and to people who are important to them. Dislike disagreements and conflicts, do not force their opinions or values on others.	Idealistic, loyal to their values and to people who are important to them. Want an external life that is congruent with their values. Curious, quick to see possibilities, can be catalysts for implementing ideas. Seek to understand people and to help them fulfill their potential. Adaptable, flexible, and accepting unless a value is threatened.	Seek to develop logical explanations for everything that interests them. Theoretical and abstract, interested more in ideas than in social interaction. Quiet, contained, flexible, and adaptable. Have unusual ability to focus in depth to solve problems in their area of interest. Skeptical, sometimes critical, always analytical.
	ESTP	**ESFP**	**ENFP**	**ENTP**
Extraverts	Flexible and tolerant, they take a pragmatic approach focused on immediate results. Theories and conceptual explanations bore them—they want to act energetically to solve the problem. Focus on the here-and-now, spontaneous, enjoy each moment that they can be active with others. Enjoy material comforts and style. Learn best through doing.	Outgoing, friendly, and accepting. Exuberant lovers of life, people, and material comforts. Enjoy working with others to make things happen. Bring common sense and a realistic approach to their work, and make work fun. Flexible and spontaneous, adapt readily to new people and environments. Learn best by trying a new skill with other people.	Warmly enthusiastic and imaginative. See life as full of possibilities. Make connections between events and information very quickly, and confidently proceed based on the patterns they see. Want a lot of affirmation from others, and readily give appreciation and support. Spontaneous and flexible, often rely on their ability to improvise and their verbal fluency.	Quick, ingenious, stimulating, alert, and outspoken. Resourceful in solving new and challenging problems. Adept at generating conceptual possibilities and then analyzing them strategically. Good at reading other people. Bored by routine, will seldom do the same thing the same way, apt to turn to one new interest after another.
	ESTJ	**ESFJ**	**ENFJ**	**ENTJ**
	Practical, realistic, matter-of-fact. Decisive, quickly move to implement decisions. Organize projects and people to get things done, focus on getting results in the most efficient way possible. Take care of routine details. Have a clear set of logical standards, systematically follow them and want others to also. Forceful in implementing their plans.	Warmhearted, conscientious, and cooperative. Want harmony in their environment, work with determination to establish it. Like to work with others to complete tasks accurately and on time. Loyal, follow through even in small matters. Notice what others need in their day-by-day lives and try to provide it. Want to be appreciated for who they are and for what they contribute.	Warm, empathetic, responsive, and responsible. Highly attuned to the emotions, needs, and motivations of others. Find potential in everyone, want to help others fulfill their potential. May act as catalysts for individual and group growth. Loyal, responsive to praise and criticism. Sociable, facilitate others in a group, and provide inspiring leadership.	Frank, decisive, assume leadership readily. Quickly see illogical and inefficient procedures and policies, develop and implement comprehensive systems to solve organizational problems. Enjoy long-term planning and goal setting. Usually well informed, well read, enjoy expanding their knowledge and passing it on to others. Forceful in presenting their ideas

Interpreting the MBTI® Instrument

The manual contains a description of 16 possible psychological types (see Table 7-5 on previous page) the counselor may use for interpretive purposes. Table 7-5 also provides a list of descriptors commonly associated with each one of the preference dimensions. The profile presents brief descriptions of psychological types and combinations of types according to four preference classifications. Preferences are classified as very clear, clear, moderate, and light. A popular use of the MBTI® Instrument has been within the field of career counseling. Because it has an extensive database, a Career Report is available to show clients the 50 most and 25 least popular occupations for a person with a particular code. An appendix in the manual contains tables of occupations empirically attractive to psychological types.

The use of the MBTI® Instrument in career counseling is not without controversy, however. According to Carlson, Stalikas and Bizot (1997), the MBTI® Instrument has yielded satisfactory split-half and test-retest reliabilities and favorable validity coefficients. In general, Carlson recommends using the MBTI® Instrument for career counseling. Healy (2002), however, suggests that many of the stated purposes for use of the MBTI® Instrument have not been researched, and should thus be viewed as hypotheses. He states that this is especially true if "the MBTI[® Instrument] is to be substituted for other measures for purposes such as selecting college majors or occupations or improving communication" (p. 365-366).

Two studies have reported on the relationship of MBTI® Instrument type to career choice. The first (Stilwell, Wallack, Thal, & Burleson, 2000) focused on those in a medical career and found that type among physicians has remained steady since the 1950s, with the main change being a movement towards the more judgmental factor. The second study (Paige, 2000) reported that the following codes made up 68% of those employed as dental hygienists: ESTJ, ISTJ, ESFJ, ISFJ. One researcher (Cummings, 1995) recommended that the MBTI® Instrument be re-normed for each continuum by age, after finding significant age group effects on each dimension of the MBTI® Instrument. Healy (1989) has suggested that the MBTI® Instrument be considered experimental and not be routinely used in career counseling.

McCaulley (1990) has suggested that the MBTI® Instrument is a measure of preferences and not of abilities and accomplishments; therefore, counselors should consider it as a form of hypothesis testing. More specifically, the MBTI® Instrument provides a measure for understanding perceptual and cognitive styles. Sharf (1992) points out that combined norms of men and women are used, whereas separate norms by sex would be more helpful.

Before using the MBTI® Instrument, counselors are encouraged to read both pro (Carlson, 1989) and con (Healy, 1989) articles as well as reviews (Fleenor, 2001; Mastrangelo, 2001; Thompson & Ackerman, 1994). Counselors are also encouraged to recognize the complex nature of interpreting the MBTI® Instrument. Additional research on the predictive validity of the MBTI® Instrument with career choice, career satisfaction and other career variables is imperative.

Case of a Confused Adult Concerning a Future Work Role

Chuck had considered going for counseling for several months before making an appointment. "Why am I having difficulty holding on to a job?" he mused. "I can't seem to be satisfied with anything anymore — my whole life seems to be a waste of time. Maybe, just maybe, a counselor can help me." With much ambivalence, Chuck reported for his first counseling session. After appropriate introductions and small talk, the counselor began:

COUNSELOR: Chuck, I noticed on your request form that you want to discuss your future. Could you be more specific?

CHUCK: Huh—well—yes—I've had problems settling down and finding something I like to do.

COUNSELOR: You've not been able to find a satisfactory job.

CHUCK: Yes— but it's more than that—I don't know how to say it, but I feel different than other people I've worked with. I don't seem to fit in, and I'm not sure what I do that irritates others.

As the conversation continued, Chuck stated that he had had numerous jobs but soon became bored with them and either was fired or quit. He made reference to a lack of interest in work.

CHUCK: It's more than just identifying interests—I don't understand myself and how and why I think the way I do. I seem to be out of sync with other people.

The counselor made note of Chuck's desire for identifying interests and later in the conversation made the following comment:

COUNSELOR: Chuck, earlier you mentioned identifying interests—would you like to take an interest inventory questionnaire?

CHUCK: Not now, but maybe later. I'm more interested in knowing what kind of person I am—like maybe my personality.

As the conversation continued, it became apparent that Chuck would benefit from an inventory that would provide insights into his perception of the world around him. The counselor suggested an inventory that might help clarify perceptions of self and provide him with a better understanding of his judgments concerning the behavior and actions of peer affiliates in the workplace. For this purpose the counselor chose the MBTI® Instrument.

The results of the MBTI® Instrument indicated that Chuck's preference scores were INTJ, as described here:

> Usually have original minds and a great drive for their own ideas and purposes, in fields that appeal to them, they have a fine power to organize a job and carry it through with or without help. Skeptical, critical, independent, determined, sometimes stubborn. Must learn to yield less important points in order to win the most important. Live their outer life more with thinking, inner more with intuition. (Myers & McCaulley, 1985, p. 21)

After the counselor explained how to interpret the report form, Chuck read the description of his reported type.

CHUCK: One thing is for sure—I prefer Introversion and I like to think things over a long time—sometimes too much because I never get anywhere.

COUNSELOR: Do you agree with the description of your identified type?

CHUCK: Some of it, I guess, but one point is really true; I'm stubborn and I like to come out on top.

Chuck continued to reflect on the results of the inventory, and the counselor encouraged him to express his thoughts fully concerning his self-evaluations. This instrument helped establish rapport between Chuck and the counselor, and after several more counseling sessions a career decision-making model was introduced to Chuck to provide direction for career exploration.

The results of the MBTI® Instrument reinforced Chuck's strengths and pointed out some areas for improvement. Chuck was now better prepared to further evaluate his interests, experiences, and other factors in pursuit of the career decision.

The list of occupations attractive to his preference scores provided in the MBTI® Instrument manual were discussed and put aside for future reference. Chuck and the counselor decided that he was now ready to explore interests, values, and aptitudes in more depth before developing a list of specific occupations to explore. In this case, the MBTI® Instrument was used to provide a basis for discussing perceptions of peer affiliates in the workplace.

NEO 4

The NEO 4 (Costa & McCrae, 1998) is a personality inventory that measures four key constructs that include several subscales (See Table 7-6 on next page).

The NEO 4 is a shortened version of the NEO-PIR, and focuses on positive traits. The NEO 4 is applicable for individuals or in a group setting where career counseling, employee training and learning about self is the focus.

The instrument examines different styles of an individual's personality, including interests, interactions, activity attitudes learning and character styles that are organized by a circle graph. A graph comprised of concentric circles and then divided into quadrants and t-scores (with the center equaling a "T" of 50) exists for each of the styles, and respondents can plot their results onto each graph. The NEO 4 consists of 192 continuous (i.e., not dichotomous) items and takes about 25 minutes to complete the entire inventory.

There are two forms of the NEO PI-R. Form S is appropriate for both college-aged people and adults and is designed for self-reports. Form R was designed for observer reports and is meant to supplement self-reports. An optional one-page summary sheet (see Figure 7-5) provides clients with a description of what their profiles mean. The NEO 4 is appropriate for individuals who are 17 or older.

One criticism of the NEO 4 is that no additional standardization efforts were reported. The authors suggest that because it is the same inventory as the NEO-PIR, the normative information applies.

Table 7-6	NEO Factors and Subscales

Extraversion	• Warmth
	• Gregariousness
	• Assertiveness
	• Activity
	• Excitement-Seeking
	• Positive Emotions
	• Total
Openness to Experience	• Fantasy
	• Aesthetics
	• Feelings
	• Actions
	• Ideas
	• Values
	• Total
Agreeableness	• Trust
	• Straightforwardness
	• Altruism
	• Compliance
	• Modesty
	• Tender-Mindedness
	• Total
Conscientiousness	• Competence
	• Order
	• Dutifulness
	• Achievement Striving
	• Self-Discipline
	• Deliberation
	• Total

However, in this newest version, the neuroticism scale is no longer reported, and there are fewer items on the inventory, and thus the NEO 4 is a different test. Additional research needs to be conducted to validate this version of the NEO.

The concentric circles graphs are used to help interpret individual's scores on each of the domains. T scores between 45 and 55 are found in the inner-most circle, between 35 and 65 are found in the middle circle and beyond 35 and 65 are found in the outer area. Among the information provided is the T score (related to the appropriate norm group) for the client's scale scores. The further away the t score is from 50, the more distinct the characteristic is, and the more an accurate interpretation can be made.

Visually speaking, this would apply to intersecting scores that are plotted closer to a line drawn in the middle of a quadrant and that also are in the outer circle.

Given that no additional statistics were included in the manual for the NEO 4, the following is provided as a look at what was found for the previous version, the NEO-PIR. The 1995 U.S. Census projections were used to create a norm base reflecting sex, age, and race distributions. Internal consistency coefficients for both forms have been reported at .86 to .95 for domain scales, and from .56 to .90 for facet scales. Kurtz, Lee and Sherker (1999) reported that the NEO PI-R had good to adequate internal consistency and stability. With regards to test-retest reliability, a six-year longitudinal study of the neuroticism, openness, and Extraversion scales showed stability coefficients ranging from .63 to .79. For earlier reviews of the NEO PI, see Leong and Dollinger (1991) and Ben-Porath and Waller (1992). Leong and Dollinger (1991) summarize their impression of the NEO PI by stating that "the NEO PI must be regarded as one of the best state-of-the-art tests available for the general and systematic assessment of normal personality" (p. 536). For a more extensive review of the NEO 4, see Bahns (2001) and Henington (2001).

Using the NEO 4 in Career Counseling

The developers suggest several ways to use the NEO 4 in counseling. For use in career counseling, they provide some general ideas about how the scales might relate. For instance, the NEO results should not replace the results of traditional career inventories but should *confirm* or *clarify* career inventory scores.

The relationships between main traits and an individual's career-seeking behaviors, may be anticipated. For example, "open" people might be open to exploring a wide range of career opportunities to the point of being indecisive, whereas closed individuals might be reluctant to expand their options. Extroverted individuals might be more likely to enjoy "enterprising" careers such as sales, politics, and so on, whereas an introverted person might be more interested in "investigative" careers such as science or research. Some research has been conducted on the relationship between elevated profiles on the Self-Directed Search and the NEO PI-R scales. Fuller, Holland, and Johnston (1999) found that those with elevated profiles were likely to score higher on openness and extraversion and lower on depressive features. A meta-analytic study (Larson, Rottinghaus, & Borgen, 2002) also showed overlap, with the strongest relationships between the following pairs: Artistic and Openness, Enterprising and Extraversion, Social and Extraversion, Investigative and Openness, and Social and Agreeableness scales.

Research on the NEO-PIR are worth mentioning. Research with the Conscientiousness scale has yielded some interesting results. There is a correlation between the Conscientiousness scale and the Military Leadership scale (Gough & Heilbrun, 1983). Also, scores on the Conscientiousness scale were found to consistently predict job performance ratings (Barrick & Mount, 1991). Although the developers do not link scores on the Neuroticism scale with career interests, they do suggest that someone with a high neuroticism score will probably be unsatisfied in all the careers he or she is considering. Another interesting finding came from a research question investigating the relationship between personality and career transitions (Heppner, Fuller, & Multon, 1998). The researchers found that four of the five factors predicted self-efficacy. The developers discuss several options for interpreting profiles, including noting a few traits, comparing spouse ratings (from Form R), and examining facet scales across domains.

California Psychological Inventory 434™ (CPI™ 434) Inventory

The CPI™ 434 Inventory was designed to measure common characteristics of "normal" individuals above age 13, is written on an 8th grade reading level and is designed for use in career counseling as well as human resources. The publisher cites uses of recruitment and development of successful employees, leadership preparation, enhancing organizational relationships and teamwork. The inventory comprises 3 Vector Scales, 20 Folk scales, and 13 Special Purpose scales as shown in Table 7-7. Results for most of these scales are presented in a CPI™ 434 Inventory report, though just the first 7 Special Purpose scales (Managerial Potential through to Tough Mindedness) are actually computed. The CPI™ 434 Inventory attempts to describe an individual as if they were being described by objective and knowledgeable others.

The CPI™ 434 takes about 50 minutes to complete, can be individually or group-administered (by a professional with C-level qualifications) and can yield three different reports. The CPI™ 434 Inventory Profile provides a five page snapshot. Separate charts comparing the individual's scores to same-gender and total male/female scores are included. Raw and standard scores are also included. The CPI™ 434 Inventory Narrative Report provides a comprehensive interpretation of the individual's scores, including predictive statements about behavior. The CPI™ 434 Inventory Configural Analysis Report includes information from the Narrative Report but also reports on analyses of scale combinations, including "empirical" and "speculative" sections. These results can be blended in with other pertinent information to predict and describe likely employment fit, leadership abilities, achievement motivation and other characteristics.

The norm groups include 3000 male and 3000 female high school (50% of the normative group), college, and adult individuals (thus, care should be taken when using with individuals prior to high school level) and several representatives from special populations. Sixteen of the 20 folk scales and 9 of the specialty scales' internal consistency estimates ranged from were at or above .7. Internal consistency estimates for the 3 vector scales ranged from .77-.88. Retest reliabilities were reported for 1, 5 and 25 year retests, with the highest seen for the first year scores, ranging from .6 to .8.

The construct validity of the CPI™ 434 Inventory has been well explored, and tends to have moderate to strong correlations with instruments measuring similar constructs, ranging from .4 to .8 for the Folk and Vector scales (Atkinson, 2003). The 431 page manual includes new norms for 52 samples of males and 42 samples of females, including graduate students in various fields, college majors, members of different occupations, and so on.

Table 7-7	Scales of the California Psychological 434 (CPI™ 434) ™ Inventory		

Folk Scales	Special Purpose Scales	Vector Scales
Dominance (Do)	Managerial Potential	v. 1 Internality-Externality
Capacity for Status (Cs)	Work Orientation	v. 2 Norm Questioning – Norm Favoring
Sociability (Sy)	Creative Temperament	v. 3 Self-Realization
Social Presence (Sp)	Leadership	
Self-Acceptance (Sa)	Amicability	
Independence (In)	Law Enforcement Orientation	
Empathy (Em)	Tough-Mindedness	
Responsibility (Re)	Baucom Scale for Masculinity	
Socialization (So)	Baucom Scale for Femininity	
Self-Control (Sc)	Leventhal Scale for Anxiety	
Good Impression (Gi)	Wink-Gough Scale for Narcissism	
Communality (Cm)	Dicken Scale for Social Desirability	
Well-Being (Wb)	Dicken Scale for Aquiescence	
Tolerance (To)		
Achievement via Conformance (Ac)		
Achievement via Independence (Ai)		
Intellectual Efficiency (Ie)		
Psychological-Mindedness (Py)		
Flexibility (Fx)		
Femininity-Masculinity (Fm)		

Savickas, Briddick and Watkins (2002) examined the relationship between personality type (as measured by the CPI™ 434 Inventory) and career maturity. They found that Alphas had the highest level of career maturity, Betas demonstrated better developed decisional and information competencies than Alphas, and were the highest on informational competence. Deltas showed the lowest degree of career maturity, and Gammas being more divided in their responses. They did note that external Gammas displayed "more mature attitudes toward planning" (p. 39). They also found that the four types were similar in career development competence and level of realization supports, suggesting that individuals in each type can "develop the competencies needed to realize their potential at work and in relationships" (p. 38). For in-depth reviews of the CPI™ 434, see Atkinson (2003) and Hattrup (2003).

Using the CPI™ 434 Inventory in Career Counseling

The CPI™ 434 Inventory provides a wealth of information for discussion with the client. In general, higher scores on each of the scales, and a higher scores overall suggest greater levels of interpersonal functioning. The Profile Report is divided into four sections. Part I describes the reliability/validity of the individual's protocol, including the number of items left blank. If the protocol is deemed unreliable, the counselor should not proceed with an interpretation, but should seek to understand the reasons for this. For example, were there too many missed items, inconsistency in responses due to boredom or lack of understanding or motivation, or did the client present themselves in an overly favorable light?

Part II describes the Classification Type and Level for the individual. A graph visually indicates which quadrant the client fits into, based on the interaction of vectors 1 and 2 scores. There are four classification types or lifestyles/ways of living, represented by 4 quadrants, including Alpha, Beta, Gamma and Delta types.

Table 7-8 (next page) describes the four quadrants, based on descriptions provided by Savickas et al. (2002, pp. 27-28). Vector three is divided into effectiveness levels ranging from 1 to 7, with scores on the higher end being most favorable in self-actualization of a person's type, and scores on the lower end representing feelings of inadequacy and dissatisfaction within a person's type.

Table 7-8	Interactions of CPI™ 434 Inventory Vectors		

		Vector 2: Orientation to Social Norms	
		Low (norm-questioning, rule-doubting)	**High** (norm-accepting, rule-favoring)
Vector 1: Orientation to People (moving toward or away from people)	**Low** (participative, involved and extraversive orientation)	**Gammas:** Externally oriented, extraverted, and involved. Questions or doubts norms. Skeptical of legitimacy of authority. Innovative.	**Alphas:** Externally oriented, extraverted, and involved. Outgoing, readily accept social norms, focus on constructive and appropriate behavior
	High (internal, detached, introversive)	**Deltas:** Internally oriented, introverted, and detached. Questions and doubts norms. Seen as artistic or intellectual due to creativity and imagination. Disagree with conventional behavior.	**Betas:** Internally oriented, introverted, and detached. Comfortable with norms, but more private and reflective than Alphas. Show conventional behavior.

It is recommended that the results and descriptions of the CPI™ 434 Inventory be combined with other information about the individual, such as information from interest inventories, work samples and structured interviews. Another recommendation is to tell clients that the CPI™ 434 both describes characteristics specific to the individual as well as comparing those results to larger groups of similar individuals (such as managers and executives).

Part III includes an analysis of the individual's scores on the 20 folk concept scales. Two different graphs are included that allow the client to see his/her scores as compared to same sex gender and both genders. The information is divided into 4 classes. Class 1 is comprised of the first seven scales (shown in Figure 7-4a), and represents interpersonal style and how the client interacts with others. Class 2 is comprised of the next seven scales, and represents the degree to which an individual endorses and internalizes normative conventions. Class 3 is comprised of the next 3 scales, and reflects cognitive/intellectual functioning and need for achievement. Class 4 is comprised of the last 3 scales and reflects broad styles of thinking or behavior and serve to add an enhancement of scores on the previous scales.

In Part IV, seven of the special purpose scales are described and presented in conjunction with gender specific and both gender standardized scores. Higher scores are reflective of greater levels of the variable. For example, a standard score of 85 on Work Orientation reflects that the person is well above average on that scale, and is seen by others as reliable and conscientious with respect to work.

Case of a High School Teacher Contemplating a Career Change

Marc has been teaching high school for several years. While he enjoys his work, and values the interaction he has with his students, the desire to make a better income has become more salient to him. He has been contemplating moving into administration within the school system, but is not sure that he has the personality for management. He has been consulting with the school counselor on the issue, and completed the CPI™ 434 Inventory to assess his personality. Figure 7-4a and b (next page) includes portions of his initial CPI™ 434 inventory report.

Counselor: Hi, Marc. I have the results of the CPI™ 434 Inventory that you completed last time.

Marc: Great! I'm looking forward to seeing what it has to say about me.

Counselor: It is interesting how your answers to questions can result in consistent themes about your personality. As I looked over your results, though, I have some concerns about some of the scores. Do you see this Gi score? It is above 70, which suggests that you may have answered the questions in a way to make yourself be seen in a good light.

Marc: What do you mean?

Counselor: Most of us want to make good impressions on others. Is it possible that you were trying to make a good impression on me?

Marc: I guess I was nervous that the results might not come out right if I didn't exaggerate just a little.

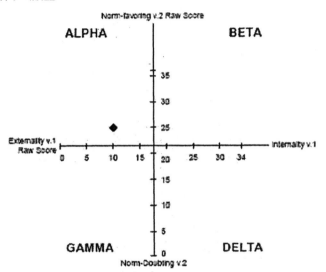

ALPHA 7 MALE   1/15/04

The scores on v.1 and v.2 obtained by JOHN SAMPLE place him in the Alpha quadrant, as shown above. The following brief description of the Alpha type gives some of the important implications of this classification.

The Alpha type or lifestyle is defined by below average scores on vector 1, and above average scores on vector 2. Alphas, therefore, tend to be involved, participative, entrepreneurial, and rule-favoring. At their best, they can be charismatic leaders and instigators of constructive social action. At their worst (low scores on v.3), they are rigid in their beliefs, intolerant of those who think differently, authoritarian and punitive, and seemingly incapable of introspection or candid self-evaluation.

In regard to ego integration as indicated by the v.3 scale score, JOHN SAMPLE is at level 7, suggesting an unusually favorable realization of the potentialities of his type. For persons at this level, one can expect exceptional initiative, self-confidence, constructive ambition and decision-making skills, plus a talent for leadership.

Figure 7-4a

Counselor: That's certainly understandable, but the problem is that we can't place much confidence in the results. Let me ask you, would you be willing to complete the inventory again, but this time give yourself permission to answer the questions as honestly as possible – knowing that you could fake out the test, but that you are choosing to be as transparent as possible so that the results will better reflect your personality?

Marc: Yes, I think that would be a good idea.

Marc retook the CPI 434 (tm) Inventory, and this time, though the scores were still very close to the threshold for being called fake good, the report was found to be valid

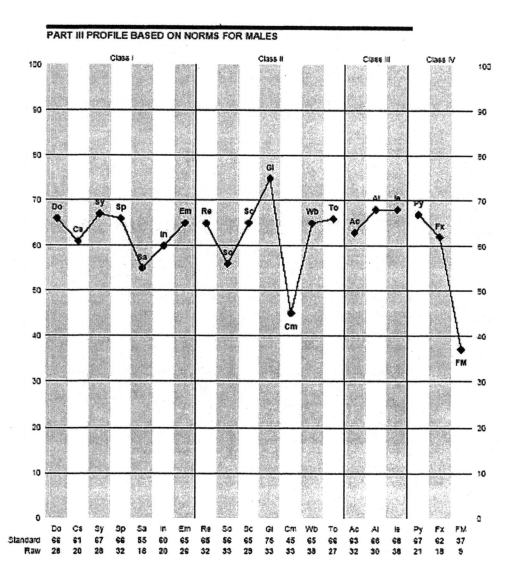

Figure 7-4b

Counselor: Marc, can you tell me how you approached the CPI™ 434 Inventory differently this time around?

Marc: Yes. Even though I was tempted to answer in a certain way – when I knew I "should" be more this way than that, I went ahead and answered as honestly as I could.

Counselor: I can see that.s that we can have more confidence in these results. You've had a chance to look over your report. Your scores were very high on leadership and management as indicated in your Leadership and Managerial Potential scales. What are your initial reactions?

Marc: I guess I'm excited. I thought that I had some leadership qualities, but I didn't realize they were very high. It's good to hear that I'm heading in the right direction, I suppose. I wasn't sure what the lower score on Cm meant. Can you help me with that?

Counselor: Sure. I have a brief description of each of those scales to help you better understand the results. Let's walk through each part of the report. In Part 1, you see that the report is reliable. That's important – if it was unreliable, we wouldn't be able to proceed because we couldn't have confidence in the results. In Part 2, you see that your scores classify you as an "Alpha" type. I have a highlighter here – why don't you look through that description and highlight the parts that seem to really reflect your personality?

Marc: OK. I guess I am pretty entrepreneurial and I generally follow the rules. And, I guess my wife would tell you that I can be stubborn at times, too. I'd like to think I have a "talent for leadership" – but I guess only time will tell.

Counselor: Let's think about that – I'm sure you can think of some times when you shown some "talented leadership."

Marc: Well, sometimes it is difficult to lead high school students into a deeper reflection of World History, so I guess it takes a certain degree of talent to lead them there. I also enjoy leading our Boy Scouts troop, too.

Counselor: All right! So, maybe you don't have to wait and see if you have that potential – you have some examples right now. As you can see, you scored at a level 7 on vector 3, which means that you feel comfortable and satisfied with your personality type. In Part 3, you see the detail of personality indicators. There's one graph that shows your scores in comparison to other males, and a second graph that illustrates how your scores compare to both males and females. You can see that you are above average on all of the scales, with the exception of Communality and Femininity/Masculinity as indicated by the Cm and F/M scales.

Marc: Yeah – what does that mean?

Counselor: Generally, the scores closer to the heavy line in the graph are more like those of the general population. For example, if you scored a 90 on the Do or Dominance scale, that would mean that you are probably very aggressive and bossy, while a 10 on that scale would suggest that you get stepped on a lot because you let people dominate you. It's probably better to be closer to the average.

Here's a highlighter. Why don't you read through the description of the scales and highlight the characteristics that you think are most like you?

After doing this, the counselor asks:

What themes did you note?

Marc: Being responsible and reliable seems to come up a lot. I set goals, follow the rules and am a good guy. Also, that I'm open and positive. I guess you could say I "play well with others."

Counselor: I think you are correct in noticing those. Let's take a look at another score. See, your score on the Gi or Good Impression scale is 75. This is one of the scales that alerted me to the idea that you were over-self representing. Even though you retook the inventory, your results here are still quite high. It suggests that you tried really hard to make yourself look as good as possible, probably exaggerating to achieve that, and that you are quite concerned about the reactions of others. Are there times that you use manipulation to get your way?

Marc: That's what it suggests? Yes, I've always been "seen" as a rock, the one people run to. I can't be seen as weak, I have to put up a good front. As for manipulation, yes, sometimes I resort to that, but only if it seems like the only way to make things happen.

Counselor: Well, we can spend some more time talking about how that approach is working for you, and how it may adversely affect your managerial and leadership qualities that we briefly mentioned earlier. But for right now, let's go on with the report…What did you think about the descriptions I gave you for the Communality (Cm) and Femininity/Masculinity (F/M) scales?

Marc: I don't think I'm that much of a non-conformist, and I guess, yes, I'm not one to sit back and daydream. I'm a doer. I don't like that it said that I'm not creative, though.

Counselor: Ok, Yes, you can see that while the Cm score dipped below the average, it is still close to that line — so you are "within normal limits for the general population" on that one. And your action-oriented, task/goal-oriented approach is suggested by your lower F/M results.

Let's go on to Part 4. In this section, you see a report of some special scales. Not all of them apply to you, but there are a few of interest. 50 is still our midpoint for comparison. As you can see, you have several above 50. On the back of the handout I gave you is a description of the scales in this part of the report. What do you think about your results?

Marc: I guess it's saying that I've got what it takes to be a good leader.

Counselor: Yes, you do have some qualities that are useful for managers and leaders, being decisive and confident. Can you think of some times when those characteristics might not be as positive?

Marc: Sure. I've been told that sometimes I'm bossy and insensitive. I guess at times, I'm overly direct.

Counselor: So, there are two sides to the coin. When you take those strong leadership qualities to the extreme, your efforts at being an effective leader can be thwarted.

Marc: Yeah, I see that. It's something I need to be aware of.

After finishing the review of the CPI™ 434 report, the counselor and Marc began to discuss other ways of exploring whether or not moving into administration was a good decision at this time. In this case, the CPI™ instrument provided Marc with an organization of his personality strengths, highlighted some potential areas of weakness and confirmed his current career aspiration.

Edwards Personal Preference Schedule (EPPS).

The EPPS measures 15 personality variables based on Murray's (1938) manifest needs. The inventory is untimed, can be taken in approximately 40 minutes, and can be hand or computer scored. As individuals select these statements, they are indicating needs as measured by this instrument. Thus, someone choosing statements associated with the achievement variable may have a strong need to be successful, to be a recognized authority, to solve difficult problems. Likewise, someone choosing statements associated with the succorance variable might have a strong need to have others provide help and to seek encouragement from others.

The following 15 personality variables are measured by the EPPS (Edwards, 1959/1985): *Achievement* —a need to accomplish tasks well; *Deference* —a need to conform to customs and defer to others; *Order* —a need to plan well and be organized; Exhibition—a need to be the center of attention in a group; *Autonomy* —a need to be free of responsibilities and obligations; *Affiliation* —a need to form strong friendships and attachments; *Intraception* —a need to analyze behaviors and feelings of others; *Succorance* —a need to receive support and attention from others; *Dominance* —a need to be a leader and influence others; *Abasement* —a need to accept blame for problems and confess errors to others; *Nurturance* —a need to be of assistance to others; *Change* —a need for variety and novel experiences; *Endurance* —a need to follow through on tasks and complete assignments; *Heterosexuality* —a need to be associated with and attractive to members of the opposite sex; *Aggression* —a need to express one's opinion and be critical of others.

Split-half reliabilities for the 15 scales of this inventory range from .60 to .87; test-retest reliabilities (one-week interval) range from .74 to .88. Few validity data are reported in the manual. Independent validation studies have yielded inconclusive results (Anastasi, 1988). According to Anastasi (1988), the

EPPS needs "(a) revision to eliminate certain technical weaknesses particularly with regard to item form and score interpretation, and (b) properly conducted validation studies" (p. 546). For further evaluation of this instrument, see reviews by Cronbach (1984), Anastasi (1988), Cooper (1990), and Kaplan and Saccuzzo (1993).

Some international researchers have explored how the constructs of the EPPS correlated with factors such as gender, age, mental health status and coping style. In their study of Japanese Open University students, Takigasaki and Fujimura (2004) found that women were more likely to rate Deference and Endurance higher. In addition, age was positively correlated with Order and negatively correlated with Heterosexuality. Wang, Ye and Tao (2002) compared results of the EPPS, Symptom Checklist-90 (a mental health inventory), and the Coping Style Questionnaire for Chinese college students. Positive correlations were found between the Mature Coping Style and the following EPPS factors: Achievement, Domination, Affinity and Expression; while negative correlations were found between Immature Coping Style and Orderliness, Autonomy, Support and Persistency. For the SCL-90, 4 factors were positively related, including Obedience, Humble, Heterosexuality, and Aggression, while 6 factors were negatively correlated, including Achievement, Orderliness, Autonomy, Affinity, Domination, and Support.

Suggestions for Career Development

Many of the following suggestions for fostering the career development of students and adults can be modified and used interchangeably to meet the needs of both groups. These suggestions do not exhaust all possibilities for using assessment results to enhance career development but, rather, provide examples from which exercises can be developed to meet local needs and needs of other groups.

For Schools:

Using identified personality traits, ask students to write a composition describing themselves.

Ask students to develop an ideal work environment that matches their personality characteristics and traits.

Ask students to develop a list of occupations that match their personal characteristics and traits.

Ask students to identify and discuss personal uniqueness by comparing personality characteristics and traits with abilities, achievements, and interests.

Ask students to share, describe, and discuss how differences among people can influence lifestyle and work-related goals.

Ask students to form groups according to personal characteristics and traits and to share future goals.

Ask students to write a short paragraph identifying what they consider to be personal characteristics and traits of someone in a chosen occupation. Have them compare and contrast these with their personal traits and characteristics.

Have students role-play "Who Am I?" based on personal characteristics and traits.

Using personality results, ask students to project their future lifestyle in five or ten years.

For Adults:

Ask adults to describe how their personal characteristics and traits influenced their career development.

Ask adults to describe how their personal characteristics and traits influenced perceptions of their work role.

Ask adults to share how their personal characteristics and traits influenced lifestyle preferences.

Ask adults to describe the match or lack of match between their personal characteristics and traits and past work environments and peer affiliates.

Ask adults to describe how their and their spouse's personality characteristics and traits influenced perceptions of dual career roles.

Ask adults to share and discuss how their personal characteristics and traits can influence their interactions with supervisors and peer affiliates in the workplace.

Ask adults to identify personal characteristics and traits that have contributed to their desire for a career change.

Ask adults to discuss and identify how their personal characteristics and traits could influence choices in the career decision-making process.

Other Personality Inventories

In addition to the personality inventories discussed in this chapter, the reader may find the following inventories useful in career counseling. The evaluation of the normative sample and the description of the scales will help determine their usefulness.

- **Adolescent Personality Questionnaire.** Designed for ages 11-22, this self-report personality inventory measures personal style or normal personality, problem-solving abilities and preferred work activities. An optional "Life's Difficulties" section addresses problematic issues for this age group, allowing them indicate which specific ones are areas of concern.

- **Adult Personality Inventory.** This is a computer-scored and interpreted self-report questionnaire for ages 16 and above, examining factors such as personality, interpersonal style, and career lifestyle preferences. It includes 21 scales, 4 validity scales, pattern codes and item responses.

- **Children's Personality Questionnaire.** This instrument is designed to measure 14 primary traits of children. Broad trait patterns are determined by combinations of primary scales. Scores are presented by percentile and standard scores. Separate and combined sex tables are available.

- **Coopersmith Self-Esteem Inventory.** This inventory is designed to measure attitudes toward self and social, academic, and personal contexts. The scales are reported to be significantly related to academic achievement and personal satisfaction in school and adult life. One form is designed for children ages 8–15, and the adult form is designed for ages 16 and above.

- **Early School Personality Questionnaire.** This instrument is designed to measure personality characteristics of children ages 6 to 8. Questions are read aloud to students by teachers or can be administered by an audiocassette tape. This questionnaire is untimed, and scores are presented in 13 primary personality dimensions similar to the 16PF. Separate and combined-sex tables are available.

- **Gordon Personal Profile—Inventory.** The newest version contains both the Gordon Personal Profile, which measures four aspects of personality: ascendancy, responsibility, emotional stability, and sociability, and the Gordon Personal Inventory, which measures cautiousness, original thinking, personal relations, and vigor. This inventory contains a forced-choice format in which respondents react to alternatives by indicating which choice is most like themselves and which is least like themselves. Percentile ranks for high school, college, and certain occupational groups are provided.

- **Guilford-Zimmerman Temperament Survey.** This self-report survey is a measure of the following traits: general activity, restraint, ascendance, sociability, emotional stability, objectivity, friendliness, thoughtfulness, personal relations, and masculinity. Norms were derived from high school, college, and adult samples in several occupations. Single scores and total profiles may be used to determine personality traits to be considered in career decision making.

- **PeopleMapper.** A brief assessment from the UK of how people are most likely to behave in work situations. Eleven work-related dimensions are assessed: Change Oriented, Risk Taking, Competitive, Socially Confident, Work Oriented, Stamina, Perfectionist, Time Managed, Outgoing, Warm, and Worrying. A summary report provides information on five key areas: impact at work, motivation and energy, approach to work, interaction with others and coping with pressure.

- **Self-Description Inventory.** This instrument seems to have a promising future for measuring self-concepts in grades 2 to 6. At the present time, norms are based on responses from students in New South Wales, Australia. Items require responses to simple declarative sentences on a five-point scale in which the individual indicates false, mostly false, sometimes false/sometimes true, true, or mostly true. Results present nonacademic self-concepts (physical abilities, physical appearance, peer relations, and parent relations), and academic concepts are derived from responses to such simple declarative sentences as "I'm good at mathematics." Finally, a general self-concept is derived from a combination of the nonacademic and academic scores.

- **Vocational Implications of Personality and VIP Jr.** A personality inventory that has 85 questions or 65 questions for the junior level. It is computer-administered inventory, available in English and Spanish. The report includes a personality classification, descriptions of learning style, decision making style, and operational style. A personality graph shows how a client's type relates to other types. Finally, a list of careers organized by GOE interest clusters relevant to the client's personality type is represented.

- **Work Adjustment Inventory (WAI).** The WAI is an 80-item temperament measure, appropriate for clients ages 12-22, that relates to work activities, work environments, other employees and other aspects of work. It consists of six scales, including Activity (high scores showing importance of work to self), Empathy (high scores reflecting higher levels of empathy), Sociability (high scores indicating a greater deal of preferring to interact with others), Assertiveness (higher scores indicating higher assertiveness), Adaptability (higher scores indicated higher ability to adapt, higher levels of energy and being ready to face challenges) and Emotionality (high scores may be indicative of either being overly critical or a great amount of concern about how others are evaluating self). The WAI Quotient compares the person's overall score to the score of the normative sample (Mean = 100, SD = 15).

Summary

Several career theorists have stressed the consideration of individual characteristics and traits in career exploration. Personality measures provide individuals with the opportunity to examine their views of themselves. Computer-generated narrative reports may provide the impetus needed for improving the quality and increasing the quantity of personality measures used in career counseling. The computer-generated interpretive reports described in this chapter provide examples of the potential use of personality inventories.

Questions and Exercises

1. How would you explain the suggestion that personality measures act as mirrors to help individuals examine their views of themselves? What are the implications for career counseling?

2. Give an example of a counseling case in which you would recommend using a personality inventory.

3. A faculty member has recommended using a personality inventory as a predictive instrument for academic success. What would you reply?

4. Explain how you would establish the need for a personality inventory during a counseling interview.

5. What would your strategy be for interpreting personality inventory results that conflict with an individual's career goals?

6. Given the NEO Style graph in Figure 7-5, what interpretations can you make? Would this person be excited or frustrated in a career counseling group? How might she be in a job interview? What observations can you make? What is the significance of her score being closer to the center (as opposed to the edge)?

7. Given the PCDP profile in Figure 7-6, a–f, describe this individual's main personality characteristics. How might these characteristics help and hinder this person on the job or in a job search? How might these characteristics impact the way in which this person goes about making the current career decision or views of career counseling? What occupations are suggested?

8. The MBTI® Instrument is often given to work teams as a way to improve communications. Figure 7-7 the comparison of an individual's type with the type of the rest of the workers in his area. Based on

the results, how well do you think the person fits in with the organizational climate at work? Where might they work together well, and in what types of situations might there be confusion?

9. Review the results of one or more personality inventories you have taken. If they were taken several years ago, do you think the results may have changed? What are the implications of your scores with respect to your career choice, interactions with others, strengths, and areas for growth?

10. How might you link personality inventory results with the results from interest or aptitude inventories?

11. Jean Paul, a seventh grade student, has been told that he needs to make some decisions regarding his high school courses. He has been actively involved in many clubs at school, ranging from chess club, the debate team, baseball, the art club and student government. "I just like a lot of things – I don't want to give up any of these." Instead of giving an interest inventory, which will most likely yield what he already knows, that he "likes a lot of things," the decision is made to give the VIP Jr. Using the sample profile in Figure 7-8a-c, what conclusions can you draw his personality and wide interests? What types of career interventions would Jean probably prefer over others? Knowing some personality traits, which one might present as strengths in career counseling, and which might present as weaknesses? What information does the graph provide? What about the occupational lists?

12. What are your thoughts about personality testing and children? Given the results of the Children's Personality Questionnaire in Figure 7-9, how would you predict that he would make a career choice? What interventions would he respond most positively/negatively to? How would he best learn about careers? What type of careers might be suggested that would fit his emerging personality?

13. John is trying to decide what to do after high school. He's not sure if he wants to go straight to a 4 year college, a 2 year college, or take some time to work and figure out what he wants to do. His profile of the Adolescent Personality Questionnaire is presented in Figure 7-10a-c. What observations can you make about his personality? What might be contributing to his indecision? Based on his personality, what type of interventions are suggested? Part of his report includes suggestions for the counselor. How useful do you find this information?

14. Grace, a senior in high school, has completed the Work Adjustment Inventory in hopes that the results will help her decide on a career path. She is currently considering law (others are suggesting that this is a prestigious career path), and admits that she feels some pressure to head in that direction. She has a 3.4 grade point average. She says she doesn't have a lot of friends, and describes herself as being more "quiet." What other inferences can you make, based on her WAI profile (see Figure 7-11). How well does law fit with her personality? Are there certain law specialties that fit better than others? Considering that she will be attending college in less than a year, what interventions might you approach with her to better prepare her for this transition? What other careers might be a better fit?

15. Consider Jane's MBTI® Instrument profile in Figure 7-12. What general observations can you make about her personality? Strengths? Weaknesses? Which career counseling interventions might work best with Jane if she was seeking to make a career choice, or engage in the job search process? What type of work activities might Jane enjoy more than others, based on her personality profile?

Style of Interests

Vertical Axis: Extraversion (= 43 *T*)

Horizontal Axis: Openness (= 56 *T*)

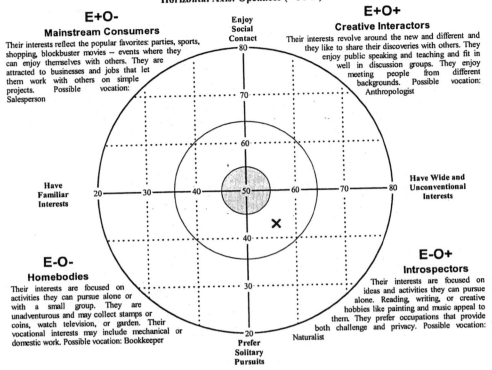

E+O-

Mainstream Consumers

Their interests reflect the popular favorites: parties, sports, shopping, blockbuster movies — events where they can enjoy themselves with others. They are attracted to businesses and jobs that let them work with others on simple projects. Possible vocation: Salesperson

E+O+

Creative Interactors

Their interests revolve around the new and different and they like to share their discoveries with others. They enjoy public speaking and teaching and fit in well in discussion groups. They enjoy meeting people from different backgrounds. Possible vocation: Anthropologist

Enjoy Social Contact

Have Familiar Interests

Have Wide and Unconventional Interests

E-O-

Homebodies

Their interests are focused on activities they can pursue alone or with a small group. They are unadventurous and may collect stamps or coins, watch television, or garden. Their vocational interests may include mechanical or domestic work. Possible vocation: Bookkeeper

E-O+

Introspectors

Their interests are focused on ideas and activities they can pursue alone. Reading, writing, or creative hobbies like painting and music appeal to them. They prefer occupations that provide both challenge and privacy. Possible vocation: Naturalist

Prefer Solitary Pursuits

Figure 7-5 NEO Style Graph. Adapted and reproduced by special permission of the Publisher, Psychological Assessment Resources, Inc., 16204 North Florida Avenue, Lutz, Florida 33549, from the NEO Personality Inventory-Revised by Paul Costa and Robert McCrae, Copyright 1978, 1985, 1989, 1991, 1992 by PAR, Inc. Further reproduction is prohibited without permission from PAR, Inc.

16PF® Fifth Edition
Personal Career Development Profile

Score Summary Pages

Name: John Sample
Date: August 21, 2000

The score pages that follow are intended for qualified professionals. The 16PF Fifth Edition scores and patterns relative to Mr. Sample's report include:

- Global Factor Patterns
- 16PF Primary Factor Profile
- Response Style Indices
- Broad Patterns
- Leadership/Subordinate Role Patterns
- Career Interest Scores
- Career Activity and Career Field Interest Scores
- Occupational Interest Scores
- Item Responses

Professional users of this report should consult the PCDP Manual for explanations of the scores reported here. The PCDP Manual presents useful information for consulting with clients about the 16PF Fifth Edition and the PCDP Report. The Manual also provides references to available 16PF Fifth Edition resource books. These resources should be consulted when further understanding of the personality scale scores is required.

The information in these pages is confidential and should be treated responsibly.

Figure 7-6a

Personal Career Development Profile
Score Summary/16PF Scores

NAME: John Sample
DATE: August 21, 2000

GLOBAL FACTOR PATTERNS

Factor	Sten	Left Meaning	1 2 3 4 5 6 7 8 9 10	Right Meaning
EX	6.3	Introverted		Extraverted
AX	2.5	Low Anxiety		High Anxiety
TM	5.4	Receptive		Tough-Minded
IN	8.3	Accommodating		Independent
SC	3.4	Unrestrained		Self-Controlled

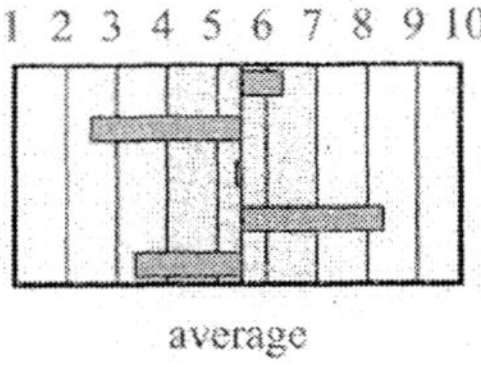

average

16PF PRIMARY FACTOR PROFILE

Factor	Sten	Left Meaning	1 2 3 4 5 6 7 8 9 10	Right Meaning
A	8	Reserved, Impersonal		Warm, Attentive to Others
B	9	Concrete Thinking		Conceptual Thinking
C	8	Emotionally Changeable		Emotionally Stable
E	10	Deferential, Cooperative		Dominant, Assertive
F	7	Serious, Restrained		Lively, Spontaneous
G	4	Non-Conforming, Expedient		Rule-Conscious, Dutiful
H	8	Shy, Timid		Socially Bold
I	5	Unsentimental		Sensitive, Sentimental
L	3	Accepting, Trusting		Vigilant, Suspicious
M	6	Practical, Grounded		Abstracted, Imaginative
N	8	Forthright, Genuine		Private, Discreet
O	4	Self-Assured, Unworried		Apprehensive, Worried
Q1	5	Traditional		Open to Change
Q2	6	Affiliative		Self-Reliant, Individualistic
Q3	3	Tolerant of Disorder		Perfectionistic
Q4	4	Composed, Relaxed		Tense, Driven

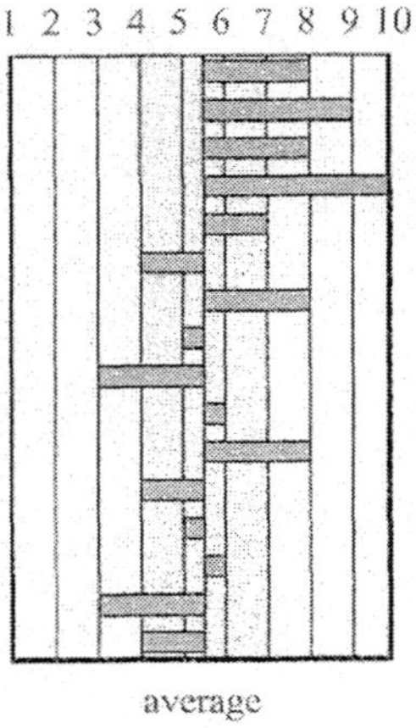

average

RESPONSE STYLE INDICES

	Raw Score	
Impression Management	10	within expected range
Infrequency	1	within expected range
Acquiescence	48	within expected range

All response style indices are within expected ranges.

Figure 7-6b

BROAD PATTERNS

The Broad Patterns reported in this section are predicted from 16PF Fifth Edition scores. The PCDP Manual provides a full explanation of these patterns.

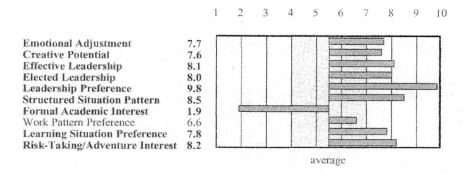

Emotional Adjustment	7.7
Creative Potential	7.6
Effective Leadership	8.1
Elected Leadership	8.0
Leadership Preference	9.8
Structured Situation Pattern	8.5
Formal Academic Interest	1.9
Work Pattern Preference	6.6
Learning Situation Preference	7.8
Risk-Taking/Adventure Interest	8.2

average

LEADERSHIP/SUBORDINATE ROLE PATTERNS

The Leadership/Subordinate Role Patterns reported in this section are predicted from 16PF Fifth Edition scores. The PCDP Manual explains the research projects involved, and provides a full explanation of these projected, research-based patterns and scores.

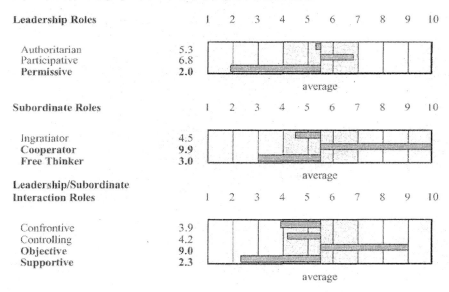

Leadership Roles

Authoritarian	5.3
Participative	6.8
Permissive	2.0

average

Subordinate Roles

Ingratiator	4.5
Cooperator	9.9
Free Thinker	3.0

average

Leadership/Subordinate Interaction Roles

Confrontive	3.9
Controlling	4.2
Objective	9.0
Supportive	2.3

average

Figure 7-6c   Copyright © 1995-1998 and 2000 by Verne Walter Associates, Inc., Vista, CA and The Institute for Personality and Ability Testing, Inc., Champaign, Illinois, USA. Reproduced by special permission of the publisher.

Personal Career Development Profile
Career Interest Scores

NAME: John Sample
DATE: August 21, 2000

CAREER INTEREST SCORES

The Career Interest Scores reported on this and the next three pages use 16PF Fifth Edition personality scores to predict these well-known and researched career activity, career field and occupational interest scores. As such, all predicted interest scores only reflect the similarity of one's personality patterns to persons who actually express interest for them. The research projects basic to these predicted Career Interest Scores are explained in the PCDP Manual.

Career Interest Scores should be reviewed for explorative counsel to help Mr. Sample learn whether he actually has interests related to his predicted scores. **These scores DO NOT PREDICT his ability, experience or suitability for making career choices. These scores are also inappropriate for making personnel selection decisions or for predicting performance on any job duties.**

CAREER ACTIVITY and CAREER FIELD INTEREST SCORES

Career Activity Interest Scores reflect the broad areas of career interests found throughout the world of work. **Career Field Scores** reflect interests in broad categories of work fields which are subscales of the Career Activity Interests. Again, Mr. Sample's 16PF personality scores were used to predict his similarity to persons who express interest for them.

Influencing Interest	10.0
Advertising/Marketing	10.0
Law/Politics	9.7
Management	9.8
Public Speaking	9.7
Sales	10.0

Helping Interest	7.0
Child Development	6.3
Counseling	9.0
Religious Activities	4.7
Social Service	6.1
Teaching	8.8

Organizing Interest	7.8
Office Practices	6.0
Supervision	8.6

Analyzing Interest	3.7
Data Management	5.3
Mathematics	4.1
Science	3.8

Creating Interest	5.3
Art	4.4
Arts/Design	6.7
Fashion	6.3
Music/Dramatics	5.0
Performing Arts	7.3
Writing	5.6

Producing Interest	3.9
Agriculture	3.8
Mechanical Activities	4.9
Mechanical Crafts	5.3
Woodworking	6.9

Venturing Interest	6.5
Athletics	8.1
Military/Law Enforcement	7.4

*NOTE: Scores range from 1 through 10. Scores of 8-10 are considered very high. Scores of 1-3 are considered very low. Scores of 4-7 are average.

Figure 7-6d Copyright © 1995-1998 and 2000 by Verne Walter Associates, Inc., Vista, CA and The Institute for Personality and Ability Testing, Inc., Champaign, Illinois, USA. Reproduced by special permission of the publisher.

Personal Career Development Profile
Career Interest Scores

NAME: John Sample
DATE: August 21, 2000

OCCUPATIONAL INTEREST SCORES - Page 1 of 3

Mr. Sample's 16PF results were used to predict the **Occupational Interest Scores** presented on this page. These occupational interest scores reflect only a similarity in personality to persons who express interest for these occupations. **These scores are intended for personal career development purposes only and are inappropriate for making personnel selection decisions.** Scores **DO NOT PREDICT** ability or suitability for performance of job duties.

INFLUENCING INTEREST

	Female	Male	Combined
Advertising Executive	7.6	6.4	**9.2**
Attorney	8.4	8.5	**8.8**
Buyer	6.6	**7.9**	*
CEO/President	*	*	**9.2**
Corporate Trainer	8.5	9.5	**10.0**
Elected Public Official	8.8	**9.3**	*
Financial Planner	*	*	**10.0**
Hotel Manager	*	*	**10.0**
Human Resources Director	9.4	9.8	**10.0**
Investment Manager	**8.1**	7.2	*
Manufacturer's Representative	*	*	**9.8**
Marketing Director	9.0	8.6	**10.0**
Media Executive	*	*	**8.5**
Public Relations Director	7.9	7.2	**9.4**
Realtor	9.1	9.3	**10.0**

1 2 3 4 5 6 7 8 9 10

low   average   high

ORGANIZING INTEREST

	Female	Male	Combined
Accountant/CPA	5.7	**7.1**	5.4
Actuary	4.8	**5.5**	*
Bank Manager	3.1	6.6	**8.9**
Bookkeeper	4.3	5.5	**6.2**
Business Education Teacher	4.9	**5.5**	*
Credit Manager	4.6	**7.8**	*
Hospital Administrator	*	*	**7.6**
Insurance Agent	*	*	**9.3**
Medical Records Technician	2.6	*	*
Nursing Administrator	*	*	**6.0**
Nursing Home Administrator	6.3	7.3	*
Paralegal	**5.4**	*	*
Restaurant Manager	*	*	**5.0**
Retail Store Manager	*	*	**9.5**
School Administrator	9.9	9.5	*
School Superintendent	*	*	**8.7**
Secretary	*	*	**4.4**

1 2 3 4 5 6 7 8 9 10

low   average   high

* Indicates no solid predictive data to predict meaningful scores. The Female/Male and Combined-Sex labels refer to the gender on which the scores are computed. Female/Male and Combined-Sex Score research is explained in the PCDP manual.

Figure 7-6e   Copyright © 1995-1998 and 2000 by Verne Walter Associates, Inc., Vista, CA and The Institute for Personality and Ability Testing, Inc., Champaign, Illinois, USA. Reproduced by special permission of the publisher.

Personal Career Development Profile
Career Interest Scores

NAME: John Sample
DATE: August 21, 2000

OCCUPATIONAL INTEREST SCORES - Page 2 of 3

Mr. Sample's 16PF results were used to predict the **Occupational Interest Scores** presented on this page. These occupational interest scores reflect only a similarity in personality to persons who express interest for these occupations. **These scores are intended for personal career development purposes only and are inappropriate for making personnel selection decisions.** Scores **DO NOT PREDICT** ability or suitability for performance of job duties.

CREATING INTEREST

	Female	Male	Combined	1 2 3 4 5 6 7 8 9 10
Architect	5.4	3.7	4.5	
Art Teacher	4.4	5.0	*	
Artist, Commercial	5.3	5.4	3.1	
Artist, Fine	4.9	4.3	*	
Broadcaster	6.8	7.2	*	
English Teacher	6.8	5.8	*	
Fashion Designer	*	*	6.5	
Interior Decorator	5.2	4.7	*	
Liberal Arts Professor	*	*	3.8	
Librarian	5.1	4.7	4.9	
Medical Illustrator	4.6	3.8	*	
Musician	4.5	4.3	4.3	
Photographer	5.1	4.6	*	
Psychologist	7.2	6.4	3.8	
Reporter	6.8	6.0	*	
Sociologist	7.0	6.3	*	
Teacher, K-12	*	*	2.4	
Technical Writer	4.8	4.1	*	
Translator/Interpreter	5.0	3.9	7.0	
Writer/Editor	*	*	5.6	

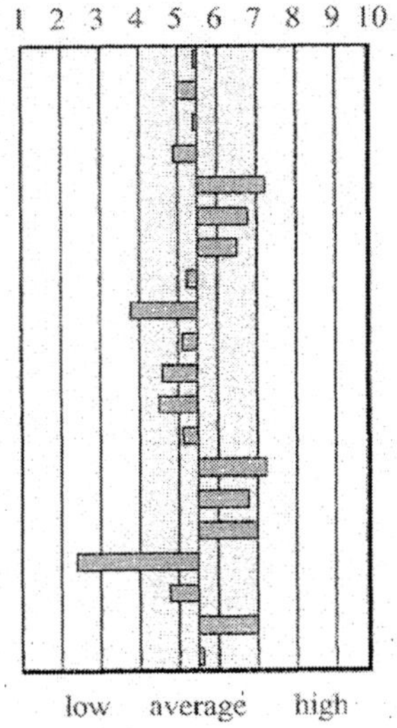

low   average   high

HELPING INTEREST

	Female	Male	Combined	1 2 3 4 5 6 7 8 9 10
Child Care Worker	4.5	*	4.1	
Community Service Director	8.4	8.5	*	
Elementary School Teacher	4.1	*	*	
Foreign Language Teacher	5.1	4.4	*	
Guidance Counselor	*	*	7.6	
High School Counselor	8.1	7.4	*	
Minister	7.1	7.1	*	
Nurse, LPN	2.5	3.1	*	
Occupational Therapist	3.9	5.1	*	
Religious Leader	*	*	3.2	
Social Science Teacher	8.3	8.5	*	
Social Worker	6.6	6.1	5.0	
Special Education Teacher	4.8	5.4	*	
Speech Pathologist	5.4	6.4	*	

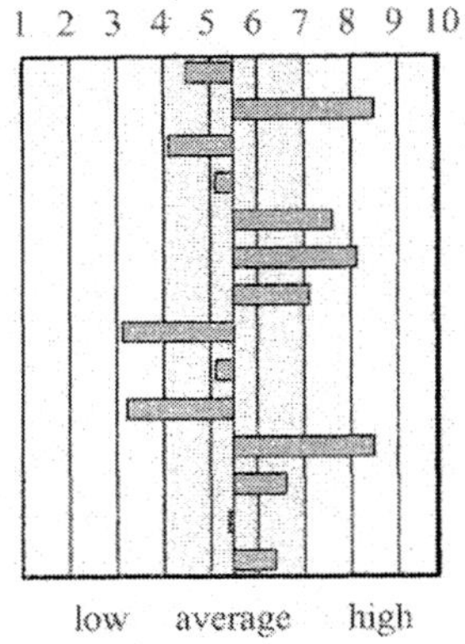

low   average   high

* Indicates no solid predictive data to predict meaningful scores. The Female/Male and Combined-Sex labels refer to the gender on which the scores are computed. Female/Male and Combined-Sex Score research is explained in the PCDP manual.

Figure 7-6f

TEAM TYPE

The type table below shows the types as reported by the members of your team.

ISTJ	ISFJ	INFJ	INTJ
ISTP	ISFP	INFP 1	INTP
ESTP	ESFP	ENFP 1	ENTP
ESTJ 1	ESFJ 1	ENFJ	ENTJ

**NUMBER OF PEOPLE
ON YOUR TEAM WITH
EACH PREFERENCE**

Extraversion	3
Introversion	1
Sensing	2
Intuition	2
Thinking	1
Feeling	3
Judging	2
Perceiving	2

YOUR TEAM TYPE IS ESFJ

Your team type is derived by counting the number of team members with each preference. On your team, however, there are an equal number of people with a preference for Sensing and Intuition and for Judging and Perceiving. Observation of other teams with a similar balance suggests that your team may behave *as if* the team type were ESFJ.

You indicated that *your* type is ESTJ.

Figure 7-7   Modified and reproduced by special permission of the Publisher, CPP, Inc., Mountain View, CA 94043 from Myers-Briggs Type Indicator® Form-M by Katherine C. Briggs, Isabel Briggs Myers. Copyright 1998 by Peter B. Myers and Katharine D. Myers. All rights reserved. Further reproduction is prohibited without the Publisher's written consent. Myers-Briggs Type Indicator, MBTI, Myers-Briggs, and Introduction to Type are trademarks or registered trademarks of the Myers-Briggs Type Indicator Trust in the United States and other countries.

Your V.I.P. Profile Summary

You are what VIP calls an "Enthusiast". An "Enthusiast" relates well to other people. You make things happen. "Enthusiasts" are sometimes referred to as "Producers". That is, you get things started and get excitedly involved. "Enthusiasts" are interested in a variety of school subjects and are always coming up with new ways and ideas to get things done. You like learning about yourself and your world around you. People like being with you because you are warm and understanding, and always willing to help someone. You as an "Enthusiast" are a natural leader.

When planning for a career, you might want to think about jobs that let you use your creative skills, like the arts, communication or any of the human service areas. You might consider a career that lets you work with people rather than competing with people.

You are outwardly centered which means you are keenly aware of what is going on around you and what is happening to others. You like being with people and people like being with you.

You, the "Enthusiast", learn things primarily holistically. That is you learn the concept about something then you learn the important details at a later time. This personality function enables you to have lots of interests and an awareness about many subjects. You also learn some things incrementally which means step-by-step. This method helps you learn complicated tasks in an orderly way. The fact that you learn comfortably in each way is an asset. Problems may arise when you are not aware of when you use each type. Try to balance yourself and learn when to concentrate on details and when to just get the concept.

You are decision dependent. When you make an important decision, you automatically consider other people's feelings, views and opinions. You also make sure your decision is based on what is best for everyone and everything. This is an important personality function because this helps make you kind. However, learn to determine which decisions need other's considerations and views and which ones you need to make on your own, then make them.

You are open in your operational style. That is when you start something you are flexible in how to do it. When some other activity comes along you do not get upset at having to change or start over. You are open to change and can adapt well to any situation. Openness is an excellent personality trait, because you are easy going and you base your activities on what is important at the time. Openness does have its drawbacks. There are times when it is important that a job or assignment be completed as soon as possible without delay. Try to determine when these situations are and get started and finish it.

Figure 7-8a   VIPJR. Reproduced with permission of the publisher, Talent Assessment, Inc.

V.I.P. Personality Graph

This VIP graph can help you understand your personality and how it relates to other personality types. Your personality type is outlined in stars. The personality most like you is called your kindred soul and is outlined with the letter "k". Your kindred soul makes decisions and learns just like you, but their inward centeredness (introvert) or outward centeredness (extrovert) is different. The personality type most opposite of you is outlined with the letter "o". This personality type functions or learns and makes decisions in a style different than you. Your opposite is also different than you in centeredness.

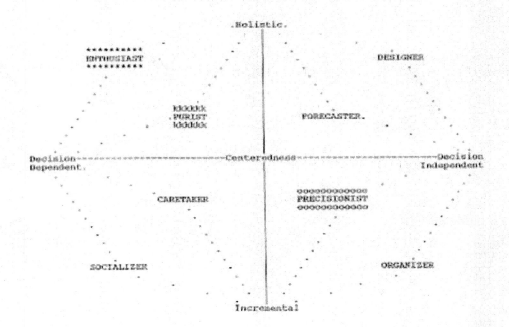

Figure 7-8b   VIPJR. Reproduced with permission of the publisher, Talent Assessment, Inc.

Here is a list of suggested GOE Interest Clusters an "Enthusiast" might wish to explore for possible careers.

Artistic (PIC cluster 5)

01.01	Literary Arts
01.02	Visual Arts
01.03	Performing Arts: Drama
01.04	Performing Arts: Music
01.05	Performing Arts: Dance
01.07	Elemental Arts
01.08	Modeling

Scientific (PIC clusters 1, 8, 9, 10, 11)

02.03	Medical Sciences

Plants and Animals (PIC cluster 1)

03.02	General Supervision: Plants and Animals
03.02-04	Services
03.03	Animal Training and Service
03.03-01	Animal Training
03.03-02	Animal Service

Mechanical (PIC cluster 1, 2, 3, 4, 5, 7, 8, 9, 11, 15, 16, 17)

05.01	Engineering
05.01-01	Research
05.01-02	Environmental Protection
05.01-03	Systems Design
05.01-05	Sales Engineering
05.01-07	Design
05.03	Engineering Technology

Selling (PIC cluster 3)

08.01	Sales Technology
08.02	General Sales
08.03	Vending

Accommodating (PIC clusters 3, 9, 12, 14)

09.01	Hospitality Services

Humanitarian (PIC clusters 10, 14)

10.01	Social Services
10.01-01	Religious
10.01-02	Counseling and Social Work
10.02	Nursing, Therapy and Specialized Teaching Services

Leading-Influencing (PIC clusters 2, 3, 4, 5, 6, 13, 14)

11.02	Educational and Library Services
11.02-01	Teaching and Instructing, General
11.02-04	Library Services
11.03	Social Research
11.03-01	Psychological
11.03-02	Sociological
11.03-03	Historical
11.03-04	Occupational
11.03-05	Economic
11.04	Law
11.04-01	Justice Administration
11.04-02	Legal Practice
11.04-03	Abstracting, Document Preparation
11.05	Business Administration
11.07	Services Administration
11.07-01	Social Services
11.08	Communications
11.08-01	Editing
11.08-02	Writing
11.08-03	Writing and Broadcasting
11.08-04	Translating and Interpreting

Figure 7-8c   VIPJR. Reproduced with permission of the publisher, Talent Assessment, Inc.

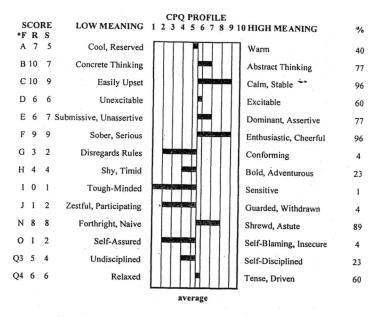

CPQ PROFILE

SCORE *F R S	LOW MEANING	1 2 3 4 5 6 7 8 9 10	HIGH MEANING	%
A 7 5	Cool, Reserved		Warm	40
B 10 7	Concrete Thinking		Abstract Thinking	77
C 10 9	Easily Upset		Calm, Stable	96
D 6 6	Unexcitable		Excitable	60
E 6 7	Submissive, Unassertive		Dominant, Assertive	77
F 9 9	Sober, Serious		Enthusiastic, Cheerful	96
G 3 2	Disregards Rules		Conforming	4
H 4 4	Shy, Timid		Bold, Adventurous	23
I 0 1	Tough-Minded		Sensitive	1
J 1 2	Zestful, Participating		Guarded, Withdrawn	4
N 8 8	Forthright, Naive		Shrewd, Astute	89
O 1 2	Self-Assured		Self-Blaming, Insecure	4
Q3 5 4	Undisciplined		Self-Disciplined	23
Q4 6 6	Relaxed		Tense, Driven	60

average

* "F" designates the factor scale, "R" designates the Raw score for each factor and "S" designates the Sten score for each factor.

PRIMARY PERSONALITY CHARACTERISTICS OF SIGNIFICANCE

He approaches problems with calm emotional stability and realism.

His style of expression is often lively, optimistic, and enthusiastic.

His regard for strict rules and respect for fine moral obligations is low.

As a person, he is realistic, tough-minded, and unsentimental.

At school and elsewhere, he is a solid member of a group, zestfully playing his part and sharing the experiences of his group.

In his dealings with others, he is shrewd and polished and is insightful regarding his own behavior and that of others.

He usually feels secure and self-assured and under no need for any self-justification.

BROAD INFLUENCE PATTERNS

The personality orientation is neither extraverted nor introverted. His attention is balanced equally between the outer environment and inner thoughts and feelings.

His approach to tasks and problems places equal emphasis upon getting things done and upon emotional relationships.

His life style is balanced between need to control the environment and willingness to adapt to what is available.

At the present time, his general level of anxiety is no higher nor lower than what would be expected.

His general capacity to work creatively, to transcend custom, and to generate new ideas is extremely low.

The probability that he will effectively accept a role of central authority in any group situation is average.

Figure 7-9

APQ Guidance Report   John M. Gideon
Personality Profile   January 18, 2002

```
┌─────────────────────────────────────────────────────────────────────┐
│                          Testing Indices                              │
│                                                                       │
│   Index                  Raw Score    Percentile                      │
│   Impression Management      1           25%        within expected range │
│   Central Responses         10           ---        within expected range │
│   Missing Responses          0           ---        within expected range │
└─────────────────────────────────────────────────────────────────────┘
```

PERSONALITY PROFILE

The scores below are presented as "stens", which have a mean of 5.5 and a standard deviation of 2.0. Scores of 5 and 6 are average. A score of 7 is high average and 4 is low average. Scores of 8, 9, and 10 are high; scores of 1, 2, and 3 are low. Extreme scores (9, 10, 1, 2) may be considered a "statement" about self.

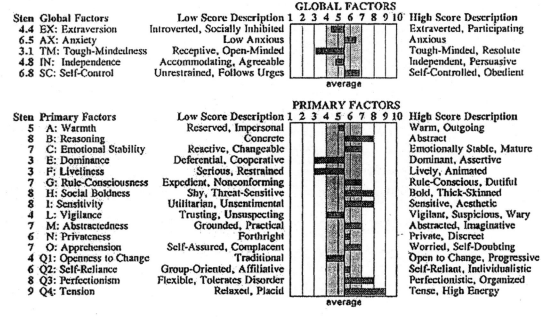

GLOBAL FACTORS

Sten	Global Factors	Low Score Description	1 2 3 4 5 6 7 8 9 10	High Score Description
4.4	EX: Extraversion	Introverted, Socially Inhibited		Extraverted, Participating
6.5	AX: Anxiety	Low Anxious		Anxious
3.1	TM: Tough-Mindedness	Receptive, Open-Minded		Tough-Minded, Resolute
4.8	IN: Independence	Accommodating, Agreeable		Independent, Persuasive
6.8	SC: Self-Control	Unrestrained, Follows Urges		Self-Controlled, Obedient

average

PRIMARY FACTORS

Sten	Primary Factors	Low Score Description	1 2 3 4 5 6 7 8 9 10	High Score Description
5	A: Warmth	Reserved, Impersonal		Warm, Outgoing
8	B: Reasoning	Concrete		Abstract
7	C: Emotional Stability	Reactive, Changeable		Emotionally Stable, Mature
3	E: Dominance	Deferential, Cooperative		Dominant, Assertive
3	F: Liveliness	Serious, Restrained		Lively, Animated
7	G: Rule-Consciousness	Expedient, Nonconforming		Rule-Conscious, Dutiful
8	H: Social Boldness	Shy, Threat-Sensitive		Bold, Thick-Skinned
8	I: Sensitivity	Utilitarian, Unsentimental		Sensitive, Aesthetic
4	L: Vigilance	Trusting, Unsuspecting		Vigilant, Suspicious, Wary
7	M: Abstractedness	Grounded, Practical		Abstracted, Imaginative
6	N: Privateness	Forthright		Private, Discreet
7	O: Apprehension	Self-Assured, Complacent		Worried, Self-Doubting
4	Q1: Openness to Change	Traditional		Open to Change, Progressive
6	Q2: Self-Reliance	Group-Oriented, Affiliative		Self-Reliant, Individualistic
8	Q3: Perfectionism	Flexible, Tolerates Disorder		Perfectionistic, Organized
9	Q4: Tension	Relaxed, Placid		Tense, High Energy

average

WORK ACTIVITY PREFERENCES

Holland Type Themes: (5 is highest; 0 is lowest)	Manual	Scientific	Artistic	Helping	Sales/Managerial	Procedural
	4	5	3	2	1	0

Figure 7-10a

APQ Guidance Report   John M. Gideon
Inferences   January 18, 2002

INFERENCES ABOUT INTERACTING WITH Mr. Gideon

The prior pages of this report have presented results of the assessment descriptively. In contrast, this material is inferential, some of it highly so. Where possible, the degree of certainty has been indicated. The emphasis here is on the interactions between adolescent and counselor, adolescent and teacher, and perhaps adolescent and parent. This material is not meant for distribution to Mr. Gideon, but is for professional use only.

Drive to Get Help and Comfort Level in Talking to a Helper

Based on Mr. Gideon's degree of psychological discomfort, strength of motive for getting help should be medium because Anxiety is in the mid-range.

In terms of Mr. Gideon's accessibility in counseling and similar social interactions:

-- he is not likely to have trouble with general conversation because Warmth (Factor A) and Social Boldness (Factor H) are at least average.

-- he is likely to feel relatively comfortable revealing personal matters because Privateness (Factor N) is in the average range.

Key Motive Patterns, Suggestions for Counselors, Teachers, Parents

In terms of primary motive pattern, Mr. Gideon seems to be artistic, oriented to beauty and creativity. Persons with this motive can tolerate ambiguity, are imaginative, and do not care about practical issues or rules and orderliness. If they are in the visual arts, such persons occasionally have trouble understanding verbal or quantitative thinking. They may think in images, and if so, it will take extra effort to understand them.

In terms of secondary motive pattern, Mr. Gideon seems to be orderly, oriented to procedures and rules. Persons high on this motive like predictable tasks and value rules for their own sake. They may have trouble with abstractions or ambiguous situations, and prefer procedures and an organized approach. Such persons will tend to go along with the advice of an expert or authority figure, and they will expect that figure to act the part, in dress, in demeanor, and/or in authoritative stance.

These two motives may conflict, he may sometimes be pulled to creativity and sometimes to orderliness.

Other Considerations for Interaction with Mr. Gideon:

Because Reasoning (Factor B) is high, Mr. Gideon will learn quickly and is likely to be able to apply reasoning to solve problems in life. Such persons may prefer principles to procedures, and they like appeals to their powers of reasoning.

Figure 7-10b

APQ Guidance Report
Inferences (continued)

John M. Gideon
January 18, 2002

INFERENCES ABOUT PARTICULAR AREAS OF CONCERN FOR Mr. Gideon

Unlike earlier pages of this report, the following material is inferential, some of it highly so. Where possible, the degree of certainty has been indicated. The emphasis here is on application areas: probable success in school and learning styles, career choice, and problems of adjustment. This material is not meant for distribution to Mr. Gideon, but is for professional use only.

School Concerns: School Achievement

Based on appropriate personality and ability factors, Mr. Gideon's predicted grade point average (GPA) is 3.6, on a 4-point scale with A = 4, B = 3, and so on. If Mr. Gideon is experiencing difficulty in school, the following points may be relevant:

General ability is not likely to be the source of problems, because the Reasoning (Factor B) score is 8 on a 10-point scale. This conclusion should be verified, if possible, by results from another standard measure of academic potential.

Mr. Gideon's score on Rule-Consciousness (Factor G), a personal characteristic that is known to be related to school success, was in the middle range. It is not likely that this characteristic is contributing to problems he may be having in school.

On Perfectionism (Factor Q3), a measure of Mr. Gideon's organization and attention to detail, he had a score of 8 on a 10-point scale. If he is having school problems, they are probably not related to any deficit in organizational skill or attitude.

School Concerns: Learning Style

People learn in various ways, with favorite learning styles differing by cognitive preference and also by personality and interests. This section presents some ideas about what kind of learning environment will best suit Mr. Gideon.

Mr. Gideon's style is similar to those who prefer intellectual activities, problem-solving, and causal explanations; who can tolerate ambiguity and thrive on deciphering and solving puzzles. They are comfortable in school and like teachers who are intellectual and challenging.

Career Concerns: Finding a Job that Fits

Sometimes a person is working, doing a good job, and is still not comfortable with the job or even the career. It is commonly found that workers are more comfortable when their personalities match the work to be done. The approach here is to present a few broad areas in which Mr. Gideon is likely to share interests and personality characteristics with typical workers. Mr. Gideon's highest two or three Holland-like variables are printed below. If he did not answer all the questions, a caution is presented to that effect. The younger the client, the more likely it is that these suggestions need to be presented tentatively.

Scientific Type. Mr. Gideon is intellectual, interested in ideas, science and math, figuring things out, and causal explanations. Typical occupations would be scientist, computer analyst, or medical doctor. The results from Reasoning (Factor B) are consistent with the Scientific Type.

Figure 7-10c

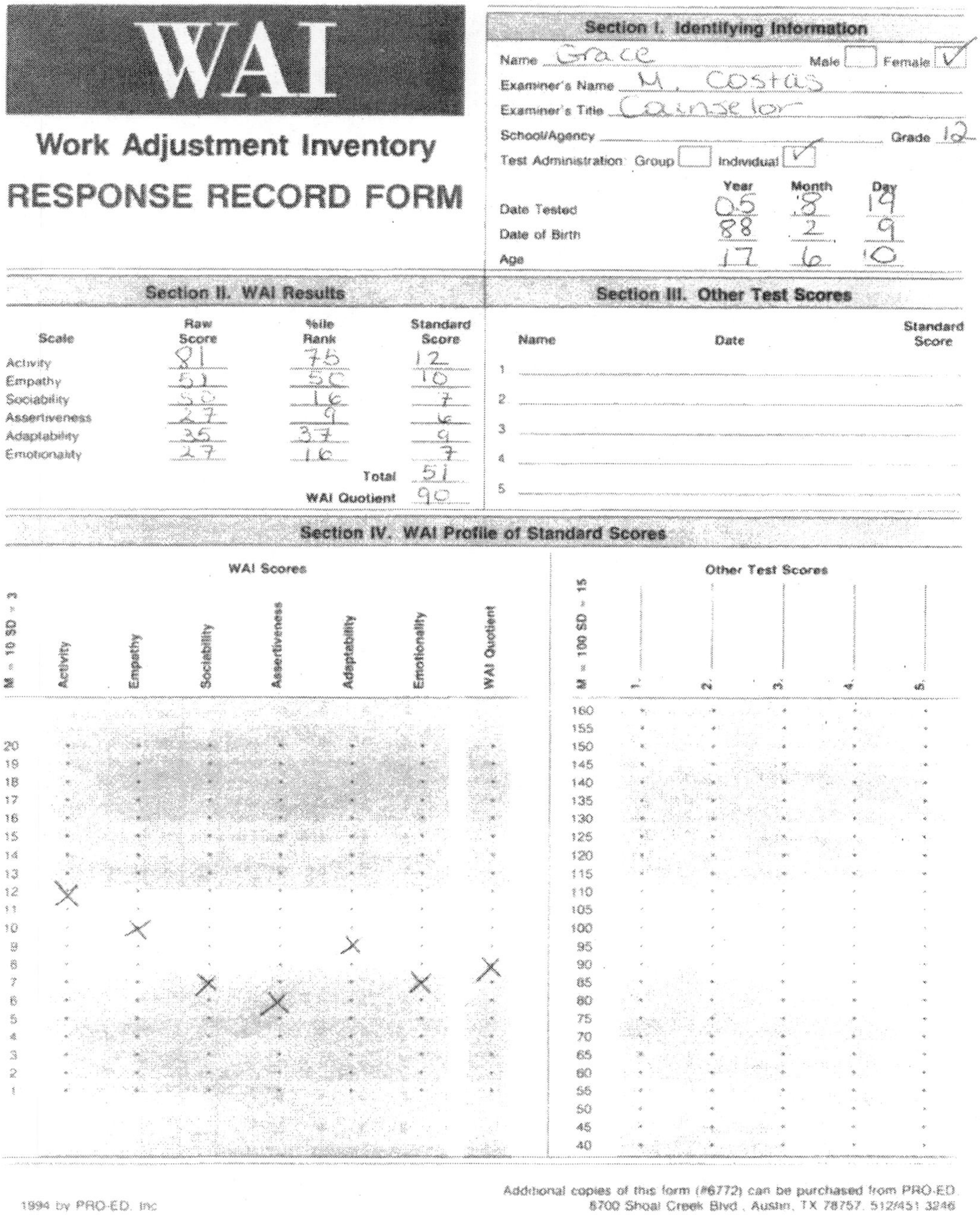

WAI

Work Adjustment Inventory

RESPONSE RECORD FORM

Section I. Identifying Information

Name Grace Male [ ] Female [✓]
Examiner's Name M. Costas
Examiner's Title Counselor
School/Agency ______ Grade 12
Test Administration: Group [ ] Individual [✓]

	Year	Month	Day
Date Tested	05	8	19
Date of Birth	88	2	9
Age	17	6	10

Section II. WAI Results

Scale	Raw Score	%ile Rank	Standard Score
Activity	81	75	12
Empathy	51	50	10
Sociability	50	16	7
Assertiveness	27	9	6
Adaptability	35	37	9
Emotionality	27	16	7
		Total	51
		WAI Quotient	90

Section III. Other Test Scores

	Name	Date	Standard Score
1			
2			
3			
4			
5			

Section IV. WAI Profile of Standard Scores

WAI Scores: M = 10 SD = 3; Activity, Empathy, Sociability, Assertiveness, Adaptability, Emotionality, WAI Quotient

Other Test Scores: M = 100 SD = 15; 1., 2., 3., 4., 5.

1994 by PRO-ED, Inc.

Additional copies of this form (#6772) can be purchased from PRO-ED
8700 Shoal Creek Blvd., Austin, TX 78757. 512/451-3246

Figure 7-11 Work Adjustment Inventory. Copyright © 1994. Reproduced by permission of the publisher, PRO-ED.

Myers-Briggs Type Indicator®
Career Report

Summary of Your MBTI® Results

Your responses on the MBTI instrument indicate that your reported type is: ENFP

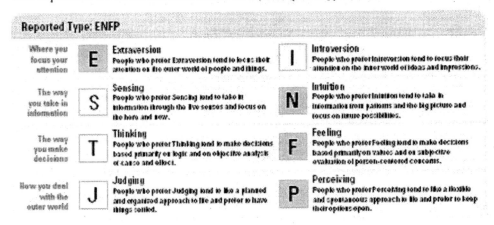

Your responses on the MBTI assessment not only indicate your preferences; they also indicate the relative *clarity* of your preferences—that is, how clear you were in expressing your preference for a particular pole over its opposite. This is known as the *preference clarity index*, or pci. The bar graph below charts your pci results. Note that a longer bar suggests you are quite sure about your preference, while a shorter bar suggests you are less sure about that preference.

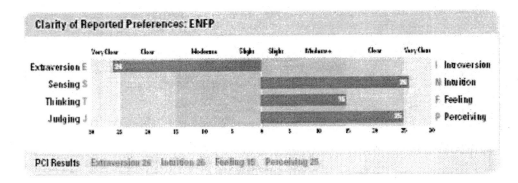

---

8 Using Value Inventories

Increasing awareness of the relationship between individual values and career selection and satisfaction has focused attention on the measurement of values and how this information can be used in career development counseling. For instance, clarification of values has come to be identified as one of the relevant components of career decision-making (Drummond, 2000).

The usefulness of value assessment in career counseling was underscored by Gordon (1975) in the 1970s and more recently by Brown (1996; 2002). Because some current career development theories support the proposition that all life roles are to be considered in the developmental process, there has been a renewed interest in value clarification. Career-related values can differ according to culture and gender. In one study, Feather (1998) compared the values of Canadian, Australian, and American students and found that the Canadian students scored lower on the affiliative contentment values, whereas Australian students rated pro-social values more highly and conformity lower.

American students scored higher on achievement, competency, and conformity values. Niles and Goodnough (1996) identified several themes with respect to the use of values inventories: Values should be considered in the context of life development and culture and career counselors should encourage the discussion of career values as a way to enhance personal development. Both sets of researchers found sex differences in value preferences.

Value assessment overlaps the measures of interest and personality. For example, Herringer (1998) surveyed 65 undergraduate students with the Rokeach Values Survey and Golberg's Five Factor Model of Personality. Herringer found the values of conformity, self-direction, maturity, and altruism to be related to the personality variable of openness. Security, achievement, maturity, and altruism were related to conscientiousness, while achievement and altruism were related to agreeableness, and conformity was related to neuroticism. The choice among the different inventories in career counseling depends on the purpose for using the results. For example, confusion and conflicts in values concerning religion, work, politics, and friends might best be resolved by discussing the results of a value inventory; the results are directly related to the purpose of testing. A counselor may choose a value inventory because he or she plans an exercise in value clarification. Another counselor may determine that value preferences are more easily related to considerations of career exploration than are measured traits from personality and interest inventories. Thus, the choice between a value, personality, or interest inventory should be primarily determined by the client's needs and the objectives of counseling.

Defining values is a complex task. Because value judgments are an integral part of an individual's priorities and worldviews, most definitions are general in nature. Brown (1996), drawing from the early work of Rokeach (1973), has built a value-based holistic model for career development using the following definition of values: "Values are beliefs that have cognitive, affective, and behavioral components" (p. 339). According to Brown (1996), the cognitive aspect of values consists of desired outcomes and the means by which one achieves these outcomes. The affective components of values are the positive and negative emotions one experiences as one interacts with the environment.

Some beliefs are more strongly held than others. The behavioral components of values include the goal-directed actions individuals take to satisfy their values. Using this frame of reference, values are the most important components that influence human functioning. For example, the development of standards from which individuals judge their own behavior and the behavior of others are the major focus of many counseling programs.

In this chapter, an inventory that measures needs and values is discussed. In addition, a general values inventory is reviewed, followed by a review of a measure of temperament dimensions of personality and values as related to work rewards. Finally, a measure of values that are often associated with life roles is discussed, followed by suggestions for career development and other values inventories.

An observation of research activity reveals that not much has been reported during the past five years relative to career-values assessment or specific inventories, nor have new values inventories been created.

In our experience, discussion of a client's career-related values has been an integral and valuable part of the career counseling process. We hope that a resurgence of interest in these and new values assessment will appear in the near future.

Minnesota Importance Questionnaire (MIQ)

This questionnaire is designed to measure vocational needs that are considered to be important aspects of work personality. The MIQ consists of statements that represent 20 psychological needs. Each need is related to one of 6 work-related values. Values are defined as "standards of importance" for a person (Rounds, Henly, Dawis, & Lofquist, 1981, p. 4). The instrument was based on the philosophy that a person's needs affect his or her choices of work environments, and the degree to which those needs are being met will directly affect a person's satisfaction in that environment.

Currently there are two forms of the MIQ, both of which are self-administered. The ranked form requires that the individual prioritize preferences concerning an ideal job, whereas the paired form requires that the individual choose between paired statements, which results in 190 paired comparisons. Clients are instructed to choose the statement that is more important to them when thinking about an ideal job. The number of times a statement is chosen over other statements will reflect the client's needs, and the client's values can be determined by examining how the needs cluster together. The developers suggest that the paired form may be preferred for use with individual clients, specifically for those clients who might find it easier to focus on pairs of needs at a time.

With the ranked form, clients are given 21 statements, which are presented in 21 blocks, each block consisting of 5 statements. Clients are told to think of their ideal jobs, then to rank-order the statements in each set with respect to that job. The ranked form takes about 15 minutes to complete, and the paired form takes about 30 to 40 minutes. In both forms, the MIQ assesses the importance of 6 values associated with 20 work needs, shown in Figure 8-1 (next page) as a part of a sample report form. For example, the value "achievement" has two associated work needs: ability utilization and achievement.

Examples of statements found in the questionnaire are also presented. The sample report also presents scores that range from 0.0 to –1 for values and work needs as unimportant, and from 0.0 to +3 for those measured as important. There are normative data for different age groups (18–70) and by sexes. Kapes, Mastie, and Whitfield (1994) report that "occupational correspondence scores are based on occupational reinforcer ratings from employers and supervisors in 185 occupations representative of the world of work" (p. 220). With respect to norm groups, Brooke and Ciechalski (1994) reported, "The MIQ does not use norm groups; rather each individual's profile is determined by his/her response to the questions" (p. 223).

In addition to estimating a person's needs and values, the MIQ presents information on estimates of a reinforcer that exists in 185 occupations. The occupations chosen are representative of many career fields. According to the developer, job satisfaction can be predicted by the relationship between a person's needs and estimation of occupational reinforcers, or occupational reinforcer patterns (ORPs). The purpose of an ORP is to identify and describe the reinforcers that are available in a work environment to satisfy an employee's needs and values. According to the manual, job satisfaction and dissatisfaction can be predicted by the degree to which a person's needs and values correspond or fail to correspond to ORPs. ORP information is presented on the individual occupations as well as occupational clusters (formed from occupations with similar ORPs). In addition, *DOT* codes are listed for each ORP.

Results present an individual's relative position on six values (achievement, comfort, status, altruism, safety, and autonomy) and component needs that define each value. A client's specific needs, or "preferences for reinforcers," can be seen by examining the scale values, where higher values indicate a stronger preference. In addition to identifying the client's preferences or reinforcers, a counselor can also help the client identify his or her values, which can be interpreted by where the score falls. A value with a score above zero indicates that it is important to the person whereas a value with a score below zero indicates less importance. According to Brooke and Ciechalski (1994), it is important to take an ipsative approach when scoring the MIQ because two profiles that appear exactly the same could actually indicate differing levels of needs for each person. The ipsative approach is a manner of interpreting profiles in a personalized way to each client. The actual scores are not the priority with this approach but, rather, what the scores mean to the client is.

Through factor analysis, the need scales have been reduced to six underlying dimensions or values as follows: (1) *achievement* (ability utilization, achievement); (2) *comfort* (activity, independence, variety, compensation, security, working conditions); (3) *status* (advancement, recognition, authority, social status); (4) *altruism* (co-workers, social service, moral values); (5) *safety* (company policies and practices, supervision-human relations, supervision-technical); and (6) *autonomy* (creativity, responsibility) (Rounds et al., 1981).

Because of the emphasis placed on these values for career counseling, they are further clarified as follows:

1. *Achievement*: This value is associated with work environments that provide opportunities for individuals to use their abilities to the fullest and experience a sense of achievement. For example, a brick mason is able to build a wall using a design pattern he or she has mastered.

2. *Comfort*: The important reinforcers for this value include experiencing a variety of tasks associated with a job, having the opportunity to take independent actions in a pleasing work environment, receiving adequate compensation, and feeling secure.

3. *Status*: How one is perceived by others and preferably recognized as an authority are important components of this value. Social status and opportunities for advancement in the workplace are high priorities.

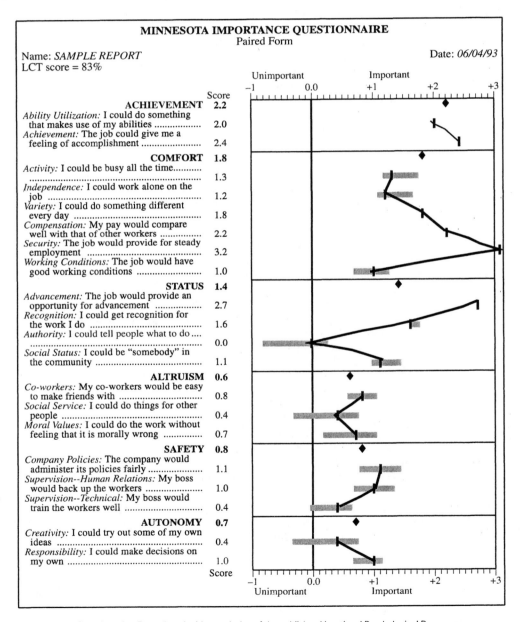

Figure 8-1   Minnesota Importance Questionnaire. Reproduced with permission of the publisher, Vocational Psychological Resources.

4. *Altruism*: The needs associated with this value are doing work that is considered morally correct and being identified with social service in a work environment that has compatible peer affiliates.

5. *Safety*: Orderliness, structure, and predictability in the workplace are needs associated with this value. Other factors are clear-cut company policies and practices, particularly those involving safety issues and lines of authority.

6. *Autonomy*: This value is associated with a work environment that provides ample opportunities for creative expression and assuming responsibility for one's actions.

According to Brooke and Ciechalski (1994), reliability coefficients for the MIQ ranged between .30 and .95, with the majority being between .75 and .81, and MIQ scores were "relatively stable" when examined about a year later. Benson (1985) suggests that the technical aspects of the MIQ are acceptable but that further research is needed to validate the benefits of the use of ORPs in the interpretation process. Benson also believes that the technical manual should be updated with more thorough information concerning reliability and validity studies and, more important, that the MIQ should be clearly tied to a specific theoretical orientation. For additional reviews of the MIQ, see Lachar (1992) and Layton (1992).

Interpreting the MIQ

A sample MIQ report form is shown in Figure 8-2. The individual's responses on the MIQ are compared with ORPs for 90 representative occupations. A summary of the concept of ORPs is presented here. For more in-depth information, refer to Lofquist and Dawis (1984).

To achieve consonance or agreement between individual and work environment, the individual must successfully meet the requirements of the job, and the work environment must fulfill the requirements of the individual. Stability on the job, which can lead to tenure, is a function of correspondence between the individual and the work environment. The process of achieving and maintaining correspondence with a work environment is referred to as work adjustment.

Four key points of the theory of work adjustment and person-environment correspondence theory can be summarized from Dawis and Lofquist (1984) and more recently by Dawis (2002):

work personality and work environment should be amenable;

individual needs are most important in determining an individual's fit into the work environment;

individual needs and the reinforcer system that characterizes the work setting are important aspects of stability and tenure; and

job placement is best accomplished through a match of worker traits with the requirements of a work environment.

Dawis and Lofquist (1984) have identified ORPs found in the work environment as being vital to an individual's work adjustment. They have evaluated work settings to derive potential reinforcers of individual behavior. In the career counseling process, individual needs are matched with occupational reinforcers to determine an individual's fit into a work environment. Some examples of occupational reinforcers are achievement, advancement, authority, co-workers, activity, security, social service, social status, and variety. ORPs and occupational ability patterns are given for 1700 careers in the *Minnesota Occupational Classification System* (Rounds et al., 1981).

The strength or the importance of a need on the MIQ is indicated by a C index, as shown in Figure 8-2. If the C value is greater than .49, then that occupation is considered satisfying or of value to the client. A C index between .10 and .49 indicates likely job satisfaction, and a C index less than .10 indicates no job satisfaction. The sample report form in Figure 8-2 indicates that the scores predict "Satisfied" for several of the representative occupations, including the following: electronics mechanic, elevator repairer, office-machine servicer, and statistical-machine servicer. When interpreting the results of the MIQ, the counselor should remember that job satisfaction is an important predictor of job tenure and so should recognize the factors associated with job satisfaction. Individual needs and values are significant components of job satisfaction (Dawis, 1996). These factors should be delineated in career counseling programs designed to enhance work adjustment.

Case of a Client Beginning a Career Search

The results of the MIQ are rich sources of information to stimulate dialogue in the career counseling process. The results may be used with individuals or in groups discussing work adjustment patterns. For the individual who is beginning a career search, value systems can be the topic of interesting dialogue. For example:

SETH (CLIENT): I have heard about values, but this is the first time I have discussed them with anyone. I agree they ought to be considered important.

COUNSELOR: The results of the MIQ indicate that you place a high value on autonomy and achievement. Let's take a look at some of the occupations that match up with these values.

As the counselor and Seth discussed specific occupations, the counselor was also interested in having the client gain a thorough knowledge of the autonomy and achievement values.

COUNSELOR: Let's return to the two values mentioned earlier. What do autonomy and achievement as values mean to you?

SETH: You said that achievement means that I like to experience the opportunity to do well on a job.

MIQ correspondence report. Figure 8-2

COUNSELOR: Yes, that is an important part of that value. But how will you know if that is possible in some of the occupations we discussed?

SETH: Hey, man, that's right! Whew! That is a good question.

The counselor then explained ORPs and how they can be identified in some occupations. The salient psychological needs manifested in work environments are powerful counseling tools that can help individuals identify the potential for job satisfaction. In this case, the MIQ is used with measures of aptitude in the matching process. In helping individuals delineate their need and value systems, counselors can use instruments such as the MIQ. However, the ORPs may become more elusive with predicted changes in job requirements.

Case of a Client Considering a Career Change

Work adjustment counseling is another area where the MIQ can be of great assistance. For example:

MEG (CLIENT): I told you that I don't know why I hate my work. Oh, I have some ideas and we discussed them but I can't put my finger on it.

COUNSELOR: Well, let's take a look at the results of the MIQ you took the other day.

The counselor pointed out that one of the highest index scores related to the altruism value. The counselor gave a brief explanation of the value and asked Meg to respond to the results in terms of what this might have to do with her work problem.

MEG: You know that I don't have much education, and some of these terms are new to me. But as I figure it, I don't fit into this job I just took.

COUNSELOR: That's good, Meg. Now tell me more about not "fitting in." Meg went on to state that she felt uncomfortable around her co-workers and in fact felt rejected by them probably because she did not like their approach to the work. She felt strongly that her coworkers made little effort to do a good job.

Although Meg had recognized her displeasure with the work environment, she was not quite able to specify problems with any feeling of certainty and might have continued indefinitely in an unhappy situation. The dialogue between counselor and client about the results of the MIQ helped Meg verbalize her problems and clarify, to some extent, her needs in a work situation. Meg decided to consider jobs that would provide reinforcers for her needs and match her level of skills.

In these two counseling cases, values became the central point of discussion that led to better understanding of values taken from the MIQ and of how these values affect job satisfaction and adjustment. Job satisfaction is a significant variable in determining productivity, job involvement, and career tenure. Career counselors should use occupational information to assist clients in matching needs, interests, and abilities with patterns and levels of different reinforcers in the work environment.

For example, the reinforcer of achievement is related to experiences of accomplishment in the workplace. Social service is related to the opportunities that a work situation offers for performing tasks that will help others. The developer of the MIQ will continue to develop ORPs, especially as work environments change in nature and content.

Survey of Interpersonal Values (SIV)

The SIV measures six ways in which an individual could want to relate to other people. These interpersonal values are broadly associated with an individual's personal, social, marital, and occupational adjustment. Gordon (1967, p. 1) defines the values measured by this instrument as follows: support—being treated with understanding; conformity—doing what is socially correct; recognition—being looked up to and admired; independence—having the right to do whatever one wants to do; benevolence—doing things for other people; leadership—being in charge of other people.

The inventory can be administered in 15 minutes. It consists of sets of three statements from which the individual must choose the most important and the least important. Three different value dimensions are represented in each triad. For example:

To have a meal at noon.
To get a good night's sleep.
To get plenty of fresh air.1

KR-20 reliability estimates range from .71 to .86. Test-retest correlations for an interval of 15 weeks range from .65 to .76. Black (1978) considers these reliabilities adequate, whereas LaVoie (1978) believes they are not high enough for individual interpretations. Predictive validity is based primarily on studies demonstrating significant differences between groups of workers, such as managers and subordinates, in a variety of settings. Validity is also demonstrated by correlations between the SIV and other inventories, such as the Study of Values and the Edwards Personal Preference Schedule. The SIV has been reviewed by Mueller (1985).

Interpreting the SIV

The SIV scores are interpreted by percentile equivalents with norms available for both male and female groups. The following groups constituted the normative samples: ninth-grade vocational students, high school students, vocational junior college students, college students, and adults.

Minority groups are included in all norm groups. Percentile equivalents are grouped into five levels: very high—94th to 99th percentile; high—70th to 93rd percentile; average—32nd to 69th percentile; low—8th to 31st percentile; very low—1st to 7th percentile. In addition to percentile equivalents, means and standard deviation by sex are provided for each of the six values for the normative groups and for additional samples including foreign students.

The SIV is recommended for use in vocational guidance, where values can be related to occupations under consideration, and in personal counseling, where identified values can provide stimulus for discussion.

Despite these recommendations, relatively little information are available concerning the use of SIV results in career counseling. In a separate publication, profiles are presented for various classes of occupations with recommendations for individual counseling. These profiles are based on seven typological clusters developed from factor analysis: bureaucratic managerial (values controlling others in structured and regulated ways), influential indifferent (values controlling and influencing others with little concern for them), independent assertive (values personal freedom), bureaucratic subordinate (values conformity), welfare of others (values helping others), reciprocal support (values having warm, reciprocal relationships with others), and institutional service (values being of service to others).

Using these clusters, a series of profiles for a variety of occupations are given. For example, managerial and supervisory personnel generally value bureaucratic management and devalue reciprocal support. Retail clerks are generally service-oriented and are concerned with the welfare of others. Other occupations are reported in a similar fashion. One hopes that additional occupational groups will be described in the SIV manual in the future.

The use of the SIV would be greatly enhanced if the author would provide illustrations of its use in the manual. A detailed explanation of the interpretation of the scales would also increase the utility of this inventory. In addition, a clarification of the meaning and significance of high and low scores is lacking. The SIV seems appropriate for use with individuals and groups, particularly for helping individuals toward self-discovery in the career decision-making process. The results can also be used for improving interpersonal relationships generally and specifically within the work environment.

Case of an Older Woman Searching for a Career for the First Time

Ms. Lunt was considering a career for the first time in her life. She had recently been granted a divorce after a bitter legal battle with her husband. She told the counselor that her divorce presented her with the challenge of reevaluating her total lifestyle. She emphasized that a part of this reevaluation involved clarifying her values and establishing goals. The counselor suggested a values inventory, and the SIV was selected because of its indication of interpersonal values.

The SIV results suggested that Ms. Lunt highly valued support, conformity, and benevolence. The counselor asked Ms. Lunt to express the meaning of these values in relation to her recent divorce and need to rely on herself for support. Ms. Lunt immediately recognized that her strong need for support might be overemphasized at this point in her life. However, Ms. Lunt concluded that this value was probably long-standing and should be considered in her career plans.

The counselor suggested that Ms. Lunt consider a work environment that would be congruent with her value system—environments where she would be treated with understanding and kindness, where social conformity would be valued, and where she would be able to help others. Ms. Lunt decided that even though support was her highest measured value, she was more interested in a career that would provide her with the opportunity to help others. Ms. Lunt then evaluated careers in social service.

The SIV results provided the stimulus for relating Ms. Lunt's interpersonal values to a variety of occupations. Ms. Lunt was able to find several occupations in the social service group that would allow her to help others and to conform to social norms.

Suggestions for Career Development

Many of the following suggestions for fostering the career development of students and adults can be modified and used interchangeably to meet the needs of both groups. These suggestions for using assessment results to enhance career development are examples from which exercises can be developed to meet local needs and needs of other groups.

For Schools:

- Using the subtests from selected values inventories, ask students to identify occupations that they believe would meet the needs of individuals who have these values. Compare theirs with each group.

- Using an identified value and its definition, have students develop a list of work environments and occupations that might satisfy the selected value. Compare the results with their scores and discuss.

- Have students interview workers and compare their values with their own. Share results.

- Ask students to compare the results of a work values inventory with their interests and abilities. Develop a selected list of occupations that meet requirements of all variables.

- Form discussion groups of students who have the opposite or the same values.

- Have students discuss how values can influence people's likes and dislikes of certain occupations. Use identified values or examples.

- Have students compare their work values with their parents' occupations. Share their conclusions in groups.

For Adults:

- Ask adults to identify relevant values that have contributed to their desires for career change.

- Ask adults to identify and describe values that influenced their initial career choice. Contrast and compare these values with current values.

- Ask adults to share and describe how their values have influenced their search for meaning in life. Use currently held values as examples.

- Ask adults to describe how their values are integrated into lifestyle preferences. Discuss major decisions.

- Ask adults to describe and identify how their values have developed. Relate relevant experiences.

- Ask adults to identify and share the importance of identifying values in career decision making. Give examples.

- Ask adults to describe how the purposes behind one's actions are influenced by value orientation. Use currently held values as examples.

- Ask adults to describe how values determine a person's interests in social groups. Compare social groups in different work settings with their values.

- Ask adults to compare their work values with work environments.

- Ask adults to identify and discuss how their values determine work ethics, orientation, and adjustment.

- Ask adults to describe and discuss how their values have the potential for fulfilling their needs and desires. Give examples.

- Ask adults to describe how values in general and specific work values influence career choices. Give examples of each.

Other Value Inventories

The following value inventories should be evaluated for their use in career counseling. These instruments may stimulate discussions of values and their relationship to career decision-making.

- **Career Orientation Placement and Evaluation Survey.** This instrument, for junior high through community college, presents results for seven work values on a bipolar scale as follows: investigative versus accepting, practical versus carefree, leadership versus supportive, orderliness versus flexibility, recognition versus privacy, aesthetic versus realistic, and social versus reserved.

- **Survey of Personal Values.** The SPV is a self-scored inventory that measures 6 values that impact how clients cope, with results suggesting how a person might approach a job. The 6 values include personal mindedness, achievement, variety, decisiveness, orderliness and goal orientation. This inventory is appropriate for high school and above.

- **Rokeach Values Survey.** Each part of this two-part instrument contains an alphabetical list of 18 values defined by short phrases. Individuals are required to rank-order the two lists. Part 1 consists of "terminal" values: freedom, happiness, national security, true friendship, and so forth. Part 2 contains "instrumental" values: ambition, cheerfulness, courage, obedience, and so forth. This instrument has been used with individuals ranging in age from 11 through adulthood. It is recommended as a general measure of values.

- **Salient Beliefs Review.** The purpose of this inventory is to compare personal beliefs about life and work with those of the specific work place of a client. Specific dimensions include change, balance, energy, community, calling, harmony and unity. Clients rate themselves and their place of employment in four key areas: personal beliefs, organizational policies, personal behaviors, and organizational practices. A client can compare how personal beliefs and personal actions overlap, and how organizational beliefs compare to the organizational practices (i.e., do their actions reflect their beliefs). Figure ?? shows four charts offer a visual of how personal beliefs interact with organizational beliefs and polices, and how personal actions interact with those two variables. A "zone of opportunity" is demonstrated when there is a gap between the scores, and presents a possible place for changes to be made.

- **Super's Work Values Inventory-Revised.** A 15-minute inventory in which 12 work values are defined and then ranked. The values include Creativity, Independence, Income, Achievement, Work Environment, Mental Challenge, Supervision, Lifestyle, Prestige, Variety, Co-Workers and Security. Occupations are listed by educational level within clusters and linked to the Occupational Outlook Handbook.

- **The Values Scale.** This instrument, a research edition in developmental stage, is a measure of intrinsic and extrinsic life-career values. Examples of its 20 scales are: ability utilization, economic rewards, lifestyle, personal development, and cultural identity. This instrument has the potential of becoming a very valuable career development counseling tool.

- **Values Arrangement List.** A seven-page inventory that helps individuals prioritize 21 life values such as achievement, happiness, love, and wisdom and 21 operational values such as accountability, courage, and tolerance. Also available are the Val-Cards (a card sort) and VAL-OR for organizations.

- **Work Orientation and Values Survey.** The WOVS provides a ranking of 32 values-related items. Scores translate into 8 main values, including: Earnings and Benefits, Working Conditions, Time Orientation, Task Orientation, Mission Orientation, Managing Others, Co-Worker Relations, and Supervisor Relations. Additional activities encourage further exploration of these values.

Summary

In this chapter, the relationship between individual values and career selection and satisfaction has been stressed. Because values tend to remain fairly stable over the life span, general values and work values need to be considered in career counseling. The value assessment instruments discussed in this chapter measure value constructs involved in an individual's relationship with other people, associated with everyday living, inherent in personality types, and associated with the satisfactions men and women seek in their work.

Questions and Exercises

1. What are the similarities and differences between personality and value inventories? How do these similarities and differences affect their use in career counseling?

2. An individual indicates a high priority for financial independence but also aspires to a relatively low-paying job. What would be your strategy in counseling this person?

3. What are the arguments for and against using a value inventory as a selection instrument for job placement?

4. How would you justify the use of value inventories for individuals who indicate an interest in social service occupations?

5. What are the distinctions between work values and general values? How can both be used in career counseling?

6. Given the COPES profile shown in Figure 8-3, how would you summarize this person's values? How might they interact with potential career choices of accountant, teacher, engineer or counselor? What might a next step be?

7. How have your values changed since high school? Do you notice any trends? In reviewing the six needs identified by the MIQ, how would you rank your most and least important values? How have your values affected the career choices you've considered and committed to, or jobs that you have taken?

8. A current emphasis in the field of counseling and also specifically in career counseling is the role of spirituality in people's lives. Classifying spirituality as a value, how has your spirituality (or the spirituality of others) affected your career choices?

9. Consider that you are a counselor in the Human Resources office in a corporation, and you are working with a department to improve morale. The entire department completed the SBR. Figure 8-4 represents one person's profile, although when you calculate the means for the organizational policies and practices, you find that the scores indicated by this individual are representative of others' responses from the department (not including the department managers – whose averages on those two variables are consistently around 4.5). What interpretations might you make from this profile? What interventions might you suggest/make? What would your next steps be?

10. Consider the WOVS profile in Figure 8-5. Which values are most pertinent? Least pertinent? How do you think these values are expressed in the work place? What questions or follow up activities would you suggest to delve deeper into the results for the client?

11. Given the profile of Super's Work Values Inventory-R (Figure 8-6), what interpretations might you make? What type of interventions might this person prefer? What type of careers might fit? What if you combined the results of this inventory with the Kuder Skills Assessment results in Chapter 4? How would your interpretation differ?

Minnesota Importance Questionnaire

Correspondence report for *SAMPLE REPORT*   *06/04/93*

The MIQ profile is compared with Occupational Reinforcer Patterns (ORPs) for 90 representative occupations. Correspondence is indicated by the C index. A prediction of *Satisfied (S)* results from C values greater than .49, *Likely Satisfied (L)* for C values between .10 and .49, and *Not Satisfied (N)* for C values less than .10. Occupations are clustered by similarity of Occupational Reinforcer Patterns.

	C Index	Pred. Sat.		C Index	Pred. Sat.
CLUSTER A (ACH-AUT-Alt)	.17	L	**CLUSTER B (ACN-Com)**	.36	L
Architect	.11	L	Bricklayer	.29	L
Dentist	.11	L	Carpenter	.44	L
Family Practitioner (M.D.)	.27	L	Cement Mason	-.03	N
Interior Designer/Decorator	.24	L	Elevator Repairer	.74	S
Lawyer	.27	L	Heavy Equipment Operator	.37	L
Minister	.11	L	Landscape Gardener	.07	N
Nurse, Occupational Health	.06	N	Lather	.11	L
Occupational Therapist	.15	L	Millwright	.29	L
Optometrist	.33	L	Painter/Paperhanger	.41	L
Psychologist, Counseling	.08	N	Patternmaker, Metal	.43	L
Recreation Leader	.02	N	*Pipefitter*	.58	S
Speech Pathologist	.11	L	Plasterer	.07	N
Teacher, Elementary School	.20	L	Plumber	.40	L
Teacher, Secondary School	.25	L	Roofer	.01	L
Vocational Evaluator	.06	N	*Salesperson, Automobile*	.51	S
CLUSTER C (ACH-Aut-Com)	.48	L	**CLUSTER D (ACH-STA-Com)**	.64	S
Alteration Tailor	.46	L	*Accountant, Certified Public*	.51	S
Automobile Mechanic	.43	L	*Airplane Co-Pilot, Commercial*	.60	S
Barber	.31	L	*Cook (Hotel-Restaurant)*	.57	S
Beauty Operator	.23	L	Department Head, Supermarket	.42	L
Caseworker	.31	L	Drafter, Architectural	.48	L
Claim Adjuster	.47	L	*Electrician*	.66	S
Commercial Artist, Illustrator	.51	S	Engineer, Civil	.35	L
Electronics Mechanic	.57	S	Engineer, Time Study	.29	L
Locksmith	.45	L	*Farm-Equipment Mechanic I*	.73	S
Maintenance Repairer, Factory	.49	L	*Line-Installer-Repairer (Telephone)*	.50	S
Mechanical-Engineering Technician	.28	L	*Machinist*	.67	S
Office-Machine Servicer	.69	S	*Programmer (Business, Engineering Science)*	.55	S
Photoengraver (Stripper)	.54	S	*Sheet Metal Worker*	.63	S
Sales Agent, Real Estate	.18	L	*Statistical-Machine Servicer*	.72	S
Salesperson, General Hardware	.35	L	*Writer, Technical Publication*	.55	S
CLUSTER E (COM)	.47	L	**CLUSTER F (Alt-Com)**	.33	L
Assembler, Production	.35	L	Airplane Flight Attendant	.09	N
Baker	.56	S	Clerk, General Office, Civil Service	.32	L
Bookbinder	.58	S	Dietitian	.21	L
Bookkeeper I	.55	S	Fire Fighter	.33	L
Bus Driver	.23	L	Librarian	.21	L
Key-Punch Operator	.49	L	Medical Technologist	.39	L
Meat Cutter	.49	L	Nurse, Professional	.13	L
Post Office Clerk	.43	L	Orderly	-.01	N
Production Helper (Food)	.47	L	Physical Therapist	.24	L
Punch-Press Operator	.44	L	Police Officer	.23	L
Sales, General (Department Store)	.33	L	Receptionist, Civil Service	.27	L
Sewing-Machine Operator, Automatic	.29	L	Secretary (General Office)	.30	L
Solderer (Production Line)	.45	L	Taxi Driver	-.02	N
Telephone Operator	.42	L	Telephone Installer	.44	L
Teller (Banking)	.38	L	Waiter-Waitress	.26	L

Figure 8-2   Minnesota Importance Questionnaire. Reproduced with permission of the publisher, Vocational Psychological Resources.

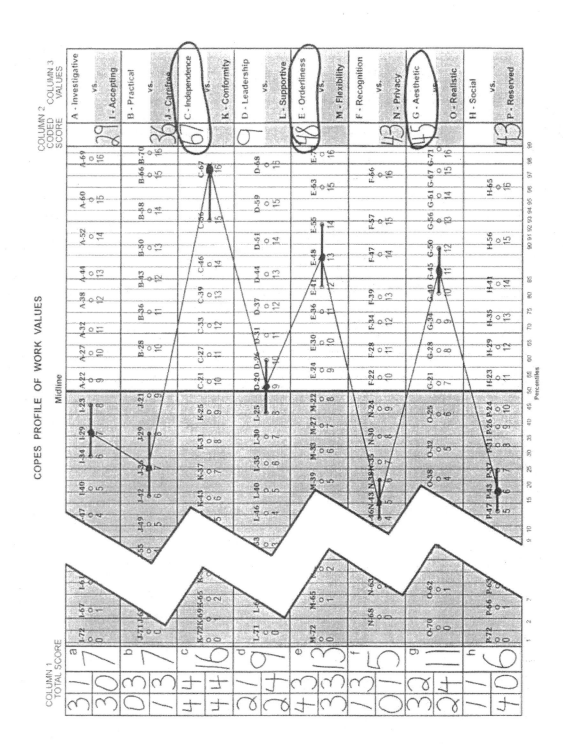

Figure 8-3   COPES. Reproduced with permission of the publisher, EDITS.

Chart 3 — Mark your Personal Beliefs scores with an **X** and circle your Organizational Policies scores with an **O**.

		Personal Beliefs vs Organizational Policies					
X	**O**			Scores			Dimension
1	15	5	X	3	2	(1)	Change
2	16	X	4	3	2	(1)	Balance
3	17	X	4	3	2	(1)	Energy
4	18	5	X	3	(2)	1	Community
5	19	X	4	3	2	(1)	Calling
6	20	X	4	3	2	(1)	Harmony
7	21	5	4	(X)	2	1	Unity

Chart 4 — Mark your Personal Beliefs scores with an **X** and circle your Organizational Practices scores with an **O**.

		Personal Beliefs vs Organizational Practices					
X	**O**			Scores			Dimension
1	22	5	X	(3)	2	1	Change
2	23	X	4	3	2	(1)	Balance
3	24	X	4	3	2	(1)	Energy
4	25	5	X	3	(2)	1	Community
5	26	X	4	3	2	(1)	Calling
6	27	X	4	3	2	(1)	Harmony
7	28	5	4	(3)	2	1	Unity

Chart 5 — Mark your Personal Behaviors scores with an **X** and circle your Organizational Policies scores with an **O**.

		Personal Behaviors vs Organizational Policies					
X	**O**			Scores			Dimension
8	15	5	X	3	2	(1)	Change
9	16	5	X	3	2	(1)	Balance
10	17	X	4	3	2	(1)	Energy
11	18	5	4	X	(2)	1	Community
12	19	X	4	3	2	(1)	Calling
13	20	X	4	3	2	(1)	Harmony
14	21	X	4	(3)	2	1	Unity

Chart 6 — Mark your Personal Behaviors scores with an **X** and circle your Organizational Practices scores with an **O**.

		Personal Behaviors vs Organizational Practices					
X	**O**			Scores			Dimension
8	22	5	X	(3)	2	1	Change
9	23	5	X	3	2	(1)	Balance
10	24	X	4	3	2	1	Energy
11	25	5	4	X	(2)	1	Community
12	26	5	4	3	2	1	Calling
13	27	X	4	3	2	(1)	Harmony
14	28	5	4	3	2	1	Unity

Figure 8-4   Salient Beliefs-Revised. Reproduced with permission of the publisher, JIST Publishing.

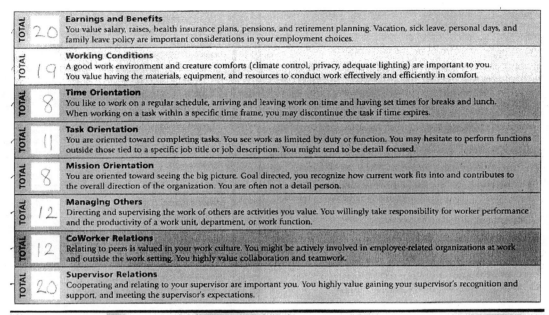

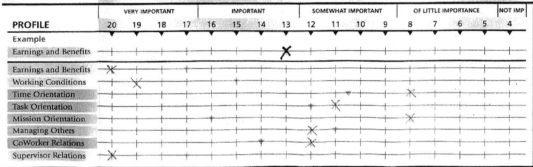

Figure 8-5   WOVS. Reproduced with permission of the publisher, JIST Publishing.

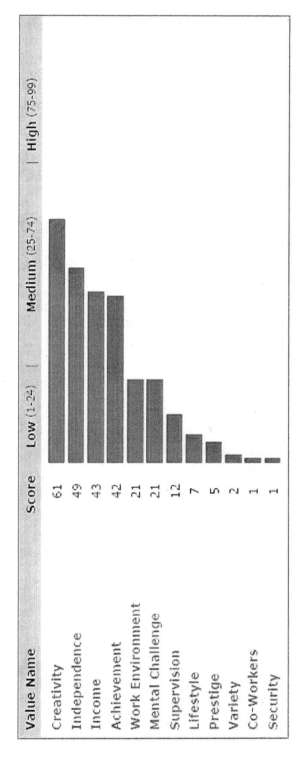

Figure 8-6 Super's Work Values Inventory - Revised. Reprinted with permission of National Career Assessment Services, Inc. All rights reserved.

9 Using Career Development Inventories

Perhaps the greatest area of growth in the field of career assessment has been in the area of career development inventories. These inventories are designed to measure different aspects of career development that could interfere with an individual's progress toward career maturity. For instance, a career beliefs inventory measures faulty beliefs that interfere with decision making, and another inventory measures certainty and indecision. Other concepts measured by contemporary career development inventories include career maturity, levels of dysfunctional thinking, anxiety, self-esteem/efficacy, and cognitive clarity. In addition, the inventories may focus on career decision-making.

According to Savickas (2000), the assessment of career decision making focuses on the process of making a career choice, whereas other inventories such as interest and aptitude assessments (and the subsequent matching to occupations) address the content involved in making a career choice. The inventories in this chapter measure different aspects of career development or career maturity that are relevant in career development counseling. Essentially, because career maturity inventories were developed from a developmental theoretical perspective, they are designed to measure developmental stages or tasks on a continuum. The degree of an individual's career maturity is determined by the individual's location on the developmental continuum. Six dimensions of career maturity developed by Super (1990) are the following:

1. an attitudinal dimension determining whether the individual is concerned with making a vocational choice;

2. a competence dimension concerning specificity of career information and planning skills;

3. a dimension providing an index of an individual's consistency of preferences;

4. a dimension of self-concept development;

5. a dimension indicating an individual's independence in making decisions about work; and

6. a dimension concerning the individual's ability to make realistic preferences consistent with personal goals. Individuals who score high on all dimensions are considered vocationally mature (Savickas 2000).

How individuals go about making career decisions and how decided they are is the focus of several inventories, including the Career Development Inventory, Career Decision Scale, My Vocational Situation, and the Career Decision Profile. Research (Barnes & Herr, 1998) has shown that career interventions such as an interest inventory, individual counseling, computer-assisted career guidance system, or teaching decision making strategies (Mau, 1999) can improve career certainty and identity.

How one's beliefs affect career decision making and choices has received much attention in the past few years. From the perspective that self-esteem and self-efficacy has as its basis self-talk (from a cognitive point of view), these factors also comprise beliefs about self. We've talked in previous chapters about the impact that self-talk can have on self-estimates of interests, achievement, and aptitudes. The Career Thoughts Inventory, Career Beliefs Inventory, Career Decision-Making Self- Efficacy Scale, and many others are designed to identify negative beliefs that might affect the way one views self and occupational options and engages in career decision making. Recently, researchers have shown that lower levels of career decision-making self-efficacy are related to higher levels of career indecision (Bergeron & Romano, 1994; Betz & Luzzo, 1996; Betz & Voyten, 1997; Taylor & Popma, 1990; Wulff & Steitz, 1999). One study has also shown that those with greater levels of meta-cognitive activities such as controlling and monitoring self-talk had higher levels of career decidedness (Symes & Stewart, 1999). In this chapter, we review several inventories related to career maturity, career development, vocational identity and barriers to these factors.

Career Maturity Inventory (CMI)

The CMI (Crites & Savickas, 1995b) was designed to measure the attitudes and skills a person has for making a career decision. In other words, the CMI measures how "ready" a client is for making a career decision. The CMI is complemented by the Career Developer (CDR), which was designed to help people acquire the attitudes and competencies that they were lacking. For example, the first item on the Attitudes Section is "Everyone seems to tell me something different; as a result I don't know what kind of work to choose." In the CDR, underneath this statement is the explanation of a more career mature response: "The more career mature response to this statement is DISAGREE. You should choose an occupation which you think you might like and in which you think you can find success." The CMI consists of 50 statements: 25 for the Attitude scale, and 25 for the Competence test, and is currently available for counselors at http://www.vocopher.com.

The Attitude scale measures a person's attitudes and feelings about making a career choice and entering the work force. The Competence test measures a person's knowledge about occupations, and the decisions that are involved in making a career choice. The total of both scores measures a person's level of career maturity. The CDI takes about 45 minutes to complete and uses an "agree/disagree" response system.

According to Crites and Savickas (1996), the CDR was developed to "teach" the CMI. They reported research findings that indicated that when people were shown the reason that a certain response was either mature or immature, their post-CMI scores improved *and* they made career choices that were more consistent with their interests and aptitudes. The 1978 version for both the Attitude scale and Competence test consisted of five subscales for each.

In an effort to improve reliability, the subscales were dropped in the 1995 version but are still represented on the CMI by five questions per subscale. The items for the 1995 Attitude scale were selected from the 1978 Attitude scale, and the developers report that the validity and reliability therefore remain unchanged. For the 1995 Competence test, new items were written to more accurately reflect the model of career maturity described by Crites (1978), and the response format was changed from multiple choice to agree/disagree. In addition, items were balanced with respect to gender and ethnic groups. The developers concede that although the construct validity has been well established for the 1978 version, more empirical evidence is needed to prove the construct validity of the newest version.

Interpreting the CMI

The degree of career maturity may be determined by evaluating responses to the inventory and each scale score report. This information can be used for counseling purposes. For example, if a review of the responses on the Attitude scale indicates that an individual lacks independence in career decision making, counseling programs designed to encourage independent thought and recognition of personal assets should be considered. Likewise, a finding of a lack of occupational information (Competence Scale 2) or of poor planning skills (Competence Scale 4) suggests specific counseling procedures. Having a more positive attributional style has been associated with higher levels of career maturity (Powell & Luzzo, 1998).

Patterns on the CMI profile also provide relevant information for evaluating career maturity and deciding on counseling approaches. For example, an individual's results may be relatively high on the Attitude scale but low on the Competence scale for looking ahead. In this case, the individual may be ready to make a career decision, but does not have the planning skills necessary to follow through.

Individual responses may also be evaluated for counseling considerations. For example, individuals who have difficulty in assessing their assets and liabilities might profit from counseling sessions in which they can clarify their characteristics and traits. The CMI can be administered to a wide range of individuals, which increases its usefulness. The items have been drawn primarily from actual counseling cases. The author acknowledges that longitudinal research is needed to provide further measures of career development aspects. For in-depth reviews, refer to Healy (1994), Katz (1982), Frary (1984) and McDivitt (2002).

Case of a Prevocational Training Program

A prevocational training program was designed for adults residing in small towns and rural areas within a 50-mile radius of a university in south central Texas. The major purpose of the program was to assist disadvantaged adults in preparing for employment. The instructor was interested in knowing which components of the program were most effective in improving perceptions of and dispositions toward the world of work and in improving knowledge of occupations and planning skills. The 1978 version of the CMI was selected as an evaluation tool because it could answer these questions. Garcia, Zunker, and Nolan (1980) report that pretest and posttest scores on the CMI showed changes in a positive direction on the Attitude scale. Specifically, the results suggested significant improvement in the graduates' orientation toward work and perception of the world of work. However, the Competence test revealed that the classes were not having a significant effect on the class members' planning skills.

This information made the instructor aware of program deficiencies and suggested ways to improve certain parts of the program. Learning experiences designed to enhance knowledge of occupational and career decision-making skills were added to the program. For example, time was devoted to research in the university career development resource center, and information was given to individual clients concerning jobs in general and in the community. This case illustrates how a career maturity inventory may be used in evaluating program effectiveness and in identifying parts of programs that are in need of improvement.

Career Thoughts Inventory (CTI)

The CTI (Sampson, Peterson, Lenz, Reardon, & Saunders, 1996) was designed to measure the degree of a person's dysfunctional thinking and how that can affect the career decision-making process. The CTI consists of 48 items and 3 scales: Decision-Making Confusion, Commitment Anxiety, and External Conflict. The CTI total score indicates a person's overall dysfunctional thinking. It can be used for high school, college, and adult clients. The reading level is sixth grade, and it takes about 7 to 15 minutes to complete.

A workbook developed by the same authors helps clients learn about how negative thoughts affect the career decision-making process, learn how to identify which areas might need further attention, and learn how to challenge and then alter negative thoughts to more realistic ones. The CTI manual briefly describes the cognitive information processing theory (Peterson, Sampson, & Reardon, 1991; Peterson, Sampson, Reardon, and Lenz, 2002) from which this instrument was developed.

Using the CTI in Counseling

The CTI test booklet was designed as a carbonless form. This allows for ease of scoring, in that after a client completes the CTI, the counselor can remove the top sheet and easily add up the scores for the total and the scales. The total and scaled scores are then transferred to the profile sheet (located on the back of the instrument), where the raw scores are listed in conjunction with T scores and percentiles. Separate profiles (including T scores and percentiles) are presented for high school, college, and adult clients.

The CTI total scores have demonstrated a negative correlation with vocational identity, career certainty, and knowledge about occupations and training, which means that the higher the CTI score, the lower the scores on these other factors. In addition, the CTI total score was positively correlated with indecision, neuroticism, and vulnerability; a person with high CTI scores is more likely to have high scores on those particular factors. The manual provides more information on career and personality factors that are related to the CTI total and scale scores. The design and psychometric properties of the CTI are described in an article by the creators of the inventory (Sampson, Peterson, Lenz, Reardon & Saunders, 1998).

Several studies have recently focused on the CTI and related mental health and career issues. Railey and Peterson (2000) found that those in a repeat offender group (versus a first time offender or probation group) had significantly higher scores on the Commitment Anxiety scale. Dysfunctional career thoughts have been shown to be a strong predictor of indecision, and are also related to depressive thinking (Saunders, Peterson, Sampson, & Reardon, 2000). Higher CTI scores appear to affect some Holland types more than others (Wright, Reardon, Peterson, & Osborn, 2000).

The authors suggest the following four-step process for using the CTI in counseling:

1. Choose two or three items that were endorsed as "strongly agree" or "agree."

2. Ask the client to talk about his or her feelings and thoughts about each item.

3. Using the CTI Workbook, discuss the process of reframing negative thoughts.

4. Taking the items identified in Step 1, have the client practice reframing the statements. Consider assigning homework that focuses on reframing other highly rated statements.

The manual identifies four levels of intervention, based on the client's total score. Level 1 requires the least intensive intervention, and Level 4 requires the most intensive intervention. Suggested interventions for each level are provided in the manual.

The norms for the CTI include 571 adults, 595 college students, and 396 high school students. Information on client norms (N = 376) is also provided. Test-retest reliabilities for the CTI total after a four-week period were reported as .86 (college students) and .69 (high school). Test-retest reliabilities for the other scales ranged from .74 to .82 for college students, and from .52 to .72 for high school students. Internal consistency coefficients for the CTI total score ranged from .93 to .97, with the following ranges for the other scales: Decision-Making Confusion, .90 to .94; Commitment Anxiety, .79 to .91; and External Conflict, .74 to .81. The manual provides sufficient information on content, construct, convergent, and criterion-related validity, indicating that the CTI is a valid instrument for measuring dysfunctional thinking.

Case of the Diving Board Syndrome

Keith, a college junior, came to the career center to discuss his career plans with a counselor. When the counselor asked Keith what career options he was considering, he stated film directing. After a pause, he also stated that he was interested in real estate, advertising, and possibly management and that teaching was always an option. Then he commented that he had read that management information systems were a hot field for the future, and he wanted to learn more about that subject. When asked about his first choice, he stated that being a film director was a dream, but so few people are successful at it, and he wasn't sure it was the best choice for him anyway.

Based on his comments, which clearly indicated career decision-making problems, the counselor suggested that he complete an inventory that would help clarify his needs. Keith agreed. His CTI profile is presented in Figure 9-1. After Keith completed the CTI, the counselor then provided further clarification

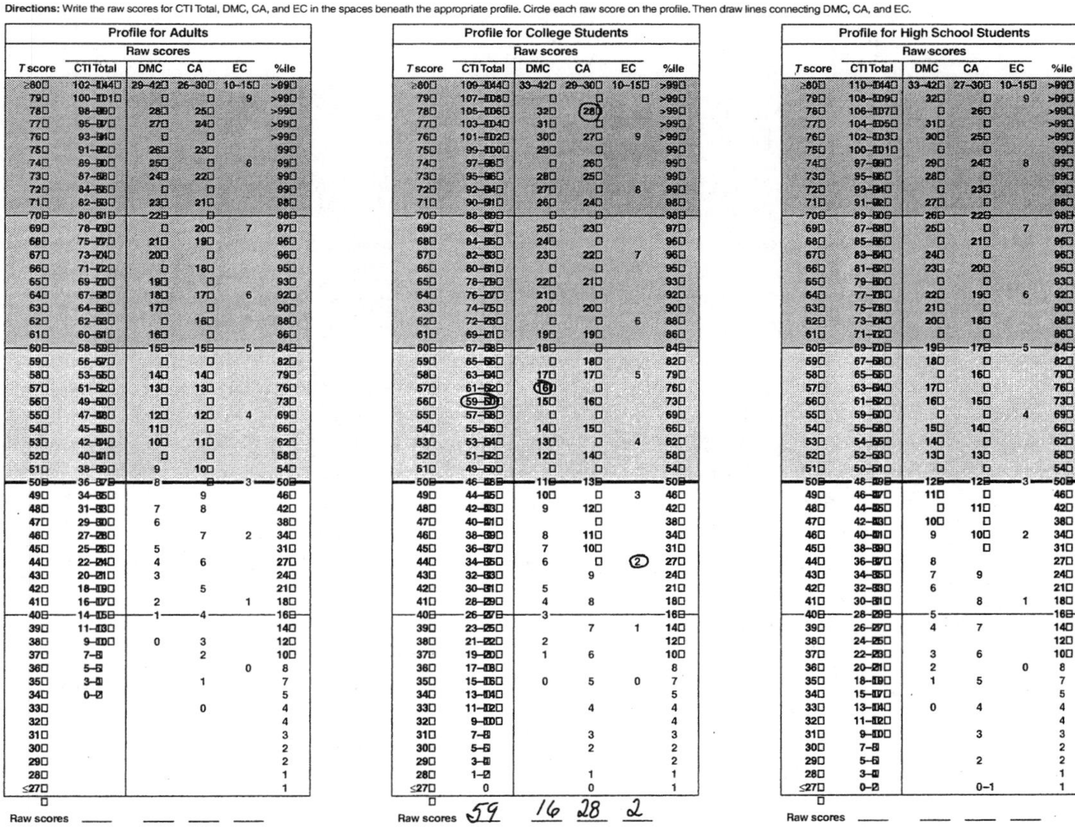

Directions: Write the raw scores for CTI Total, DMC, CA, and EC in the spaces beneath the appropriate profile. Circle each raw score on the profile. Then draw lines connecting DMC, CA, and EC.

Profile for Adults						Profile for College Students						Profile for High School Students					
	Raw scores						Raw scores						Raw scores				
T score	CTI Total	DMC	CA	EC	%ile	T score	CTI Total	DMC	CA	EC	%ile	T score	CTI Total	DMC	CA	EC	%ile

Raw scores (College Students): **59   16   28   2**

Figure 9-1 Career Thoughts Inventory. Adapted and reproduced by special permission of the Publisher, Psychological Assessment Resources, Inc., 16204 North Florida Avenue, Lutz, Florida 33549, from the Career Thoughts Inventory by Sampson, Reardon, Lenz, Peterson and Saunders, Copyright 1994, 1996 by PAR, Inc. Further reproduction is prohibited without permission from PAR, Inc.

about the purpose of the inventory: to identify thoughts that get in the way of making effective career decisions. Then counselor provided a brief description of the meaning of each scale.

The counselor stated that Keith's high score on the Commitment Anxiety scale suggests that he seemed to be having difficulty committing to a career option and that he might have some anxiety about what would happen when he made the decision. The counselor asked how much research Keith had done on his first option, film director. Keith pulled out a notebook that had articles, names of contacts, job task descriptions, and job outlook information on the field of film.

COUNSELOR: You have an impressive amount of information on the field of film. Based on what you know about yourself and what you know about this option, do you think this is a good choice for you?

KEITH: It sounds like it involves a lot of things I enjoy doing and that I'm good at, but still, I just don't know . . .

COUNSELOR: It's almost like getting to the edge of a diving board. You look at the water in the pool, but something inside, perhaps fear, is keeping you from diving in.

KEITH: What if I go for it, major in film, do all the right things, and I still fail?

COUNSELOR: What do you think is keeping you from committing to this option?

KEITH: I guess I'm afraid. I just want to know that I'll have a job, you know. I'd hate to go through all this education to end up living with Mom and Dad again.

Keith and the counselor continued to discuss Keith's fear of failure and began working on reframing the negative thoughts that were disempowering him. In addition, they started working on a plan to help him gain experience and skills in the film industry.

In this case, the CTI was used as a screening tool to identify the client's needs for support and assistance in the process of decision making. Second, the CTI identified problems that needed attention and specific intervention. Finally, the CTI workbook offered activities to help clarify the client's thought process when making a career decision.

Career Beliefs Inventory (CBI)

The CBI was designed as a counseling tool to help clients identify faulty beliefs that interfere with career decision making and subsequent career development. A fundamental idea of the CBI is that people make assumptions, and often overgeneralizations, based on a small number of actual experiences. These assumptions, or beliefs, directly affect how people make decisions and act on those decisions. People can act in ways that make sense to them, based on their own experience, but they might actually be acting in ways that hinder the accomplishment of a desired goal.

The CBI consists of 96 items and is answered by using a five-point rating scale from strongly agree to strongly disagree. The results are reported by 25 scales, representing themes that are important in decision making, and an index to estimate response accuracy. The 25 scales are organized under five headings as follows: "My Current Career Situation," "What Seems Necessary for My Happiness," "Factors That Influence My Decisions," "Changes I Am Willing to Make," and "Effort I Am Willing to Initiate."

Each of the 25 scales provides a description of the meaning of a low score, the meaning of a high score, and an exploration of why it can be useful to explore low scores. This information can be very helpful when counselors initiate discussions with clients. For example, under factors that influence decisions and the Control scale, it is suggested that the counselor find out who is exerting the most influence on the client in the decision-making process, how, and why. All suggestions that are given as a result of low scores provide examples for developing intervention strategies.

The instrument is un-timed and is recommended for eighth-graders through adults. The manual suggests that the CBI might be especially helpful for individuals who are planning a future career, choosing a major, making a career transition, planning a recovery from being laid off, expanding career aspirations, reacting to feelings of job burnout, or planning retirement years. The directions are very clear and easily followed. Scoring is available in hand-scoring format or mail-in format to Palo Alto, California, or Washington, D.C., although there are no instructions for hand scoring provided in the manual. Another criticism of the manual is that there are no guidelines for determining what scores should be considered highly dysfunctional versus scores that are moderately and minimally dysfunctional (Wall,

1994). In addition to the CBI, *Exploring Your Career Beliefs* is a workbook that provides activities to promote further exploration of career beliefs and integration of SII or MBTI results.

Interpreting the CBI

The results may be interpreted to groups or individually, and the following six-step model is recommended for interpretation:

1. Listen to the client's concerns and communicate your understanding of the client's situation.

2. Use the results to identify possible categories of beliefs and explore how they might be blocking progress. Low scores are the best indicators of problems.

3. Use probing procedures to tease out specific beliefs.

4. Have clients elaborate on identified beliefs, especially what would be required to disconfirm them.

5. If an identified belief is most important to a client, elicit steps to test the accuracy of the belief.

6. Have clients plan actions to take if beliefs are found to be inaccurate.

Case studies are given as examples of how the results can be used most effectively. Also included in the manual is the rationale for the CBI. Before using this instrument, counselors should become familiar with Krumboltz's social learning theory of career decision making (Mitchell & Krumboltz, 1990). Wall (1994) suggests that an excellent use of the CBI is using specific items as stimuli for discussion within the interview with the client. Fuqua and Newman (1994a) note that once faulty beliefs are identified, counseling can be tailored to address specific client needs. Krumboltz and Vosvick (1996) caution counselors to remember that the beliefs outlined on the CBI are not necessarily right or wrong beliefs, and that the client must make the decision whether or not a certain belief is helping or hindering.

The norms for this instrument were developed from 7500 people in the United States and Australia. Percentile ranks and standard scores are given for employed and unemployed adults, male and female employed adults, full-time adult students, undergraduate college students, high school students, and junior high school students. Test-retest reliabilities are provided for high school and college students and range from .27 to mid .70s, with a median of .60. The low test-retest reliability may be because many of the scales have only two items.

Alpha reliability coefficients are given for all groups in the norm sample and have approximately the same ranges as the test-retest reliabilities. There is some concern about the internal consistency reliabilities of several of the scales, and some researchers (Fuqua & Newman, 1994a) suggest reorganizing the scales via factor analysis as a way of improving validity and reliability. Other researchers (Walsh, Thompson, & Kapes, 1997) also point out through their research that even though career clusters can be reproduced through factor analysis, these clusters do not match the scale clusters that are included in the CBI reports. Although several validity studies were conducted between scales and satisfaction ratings and between other inventories such as the Strong Interest Inventory, the Self-Directed Search, and the Myers-Briggs Type Indicator, the manual points out that there is no single meaningful criterion against which one can validate career beliefs. In summary, this instrument was developed for providing information about career beliefs that can be used in career counseling but not as the basis for selection or classification. For full reviews of the CBI, see Wall (1994) and the *Journal of Counseling and Development* (1994, vol. 72, No. 3), which features a special issue on the CBI.

Case of the Reluctant Decision Maker

Bev was accompanied to a community counseling center by a friend who was also a client for career counseling. Bev needed a great deal of support and encouragement before she agreed to make an appointment. Bev quit high school when she was in the tenth grade to work in a fast-food establishment. She recently completed a high school equivalency course and received a diploma. Now 22, she continues to live with her parents. Her father is a factory worker, her mother is a homemaker, and she has four siblings. She asked for help to find a better job.

The counselor discovered that Bev had taken part in a career counseling program while in the high school equivalency program.

BEV: Yes, I took several tests before I finished my training.

COUNSELOR: Do you recall the kind of tests?

BEV: One was for interests and the other one was an aptitude test.

COUNSELOR: Good! What did you decide after going over the results?

BEV: Well, I decided to think about two or three different jobs, but I didn't get anywhere.

COUNSELOR: Explain more fully.

BEV: I thought the counselor there was supposed to tell me more about what I should do and what I'm qualified for.

As Bev and the counselor continued their discussion, it became apparent that she had some faulty beliefs about career decision making. She evidently thought that someone would decide for her or provide a recipe for choosing a job with little effort on her part. In addition, the counselor suspected that there were some underlying reasons Bev was not taking appropriate actions to solve her problems, but this would have to be confirmed by additional data and observation.

BEV: I just was not able to decide, and I really needed more help.

COUNSELOR: Could you tell me more about the help you needed?

BEV: I don't know—I just couldn't see myself in those jobs. I thought there would be steps you take to find out. I just don't know about all those jobs. My family makes fun of me when I talk about more school.

COUNSELOR: Tell me more about your family.

BEV: They all have low-paying, labor-type jobs and think that I should be like them—just get by and shift from one job to another. Some of the time I think they are right—maybe I'm not cut out to do any other kind of work.

After further discussion, the counselor confirmed some faulty beliefs that might be preventing Bev's progress in the decision-making process. The counselor based such opinions on the following observations that appeared to form a pattern of thinking and viewing the world that could inhibit Bev's career development:

- Apparent anxiety about career planning
- Lack of flexibility in decision making
- Lack of willingness to consider new occupations
- Self-observation generalizations blocking her efforts to make a decision
- Faulty beliefs about career decision making and occupational environments
- Lack of family support

COUNSELOR: Bev, we can help you make a career decision, but first we both should learn more about your career beliefs. Would you be interested in taking an inventory test that would help us understand more about your beliefs and your assumptions about careers.

BEV: Sure, I guess so, but I don't understand how it would help.

COUNSELOR: Let me explain how we will use the results. We can find out about some of the factors that influence your decisions, what may be necessary to make you feel happy about your future, and the changes you are willing to make. Discussing these subjects should help in clarifying your role and my role in the career decision-making process.

The results of the CBI indicated low scores on several scales, especially on acceptance of uncertainty and on openness. Low scores on these scales indicate that excessive anxiety leads to viewing career decision making as overwhelming, and her scores suggested that Bev had fears about the reactions of others. After the counselor explained the inventory, the following exchange took place:

COUNSELOR: Bev, could you tell me the reasons you are uncertain about your career plans?

BEV: Nobody in my family has ever had much schooling. I guess it's not in me to go for more education or training.

COUNSELOR: So you believe that you cannot be successful in higher education because your family has not.

BEV: Yes, I suppose that's true.

COUNSELOR: Could you tell me why you feel this way?

BEV: They don't think I can do it.

COUNSELOR: How did you do in the courses for the high school equivalency?

BEV: I made good grades—above C in every course and I got two A's.

COUNSELOR: What does this tell you about your ability to do academic work?

BEV: OK, I was successful here, but that doesn't mean I could do the same in college.

COUNSELOR: You are right. There are no guarantees, but we have known for a long time that past academic performance is a good indicator of future performance in school.

BEV: But my brother and mom keep telling me we aren't the kind to go to college.

COUNSELOR: If I provide you with some information about your chances of making a C or better in community college, would you be willing to talk with your family about the options you are considering for the future?

After receiving agreement from Bev to talk with her parents about further education and her desire to change jobs, the counselor planned to have Bev discuss the reasons her parents felt the way that they did and the effect this had on her thinking about her future plans. The counselor hoped to lead Bev into recognizing that faulty beliefs about her own future were affecting her ability to make decisions in her own best interests.

Each of the scales that Bev scored low on were discussed in a similar manner—that is, faulty beliefs were identified and discussed, followed by specific plans of action that she would take if the belief proved to be inaccurate.

In this case, the CBI provided the stimulus for discussing relevant problems that inhibited a client from making choices in her best interests. Bev's counselor will need to spend considerable time in attempting to change faulty beliefs that have been ingrained through socialization for a considerable period of time. Bev must actively participate in this process to deal appropriately with questions of changes.

Career Development Inventory (CDI)

The CDI is available for two groups: CDI-S is for middle school and high school students, and CDICU is for college and university students. Form IV of the CDI consists of two parts. The first part measures two attitudinal aspects of career development (planfulness and exploration) and two cognitive aspects (career decision making and career and occupational information). The first part, entitled "Career Orientation", comprises four scales: Career Planning, Career Exploration, Decision-Making, and World of Work, each consisting of 20 items. The second part, entitled "Knowledge of Preferred Occupation" consists of 40 items. A client answers the questions with respect to one occupational group that he or she selects from a list of 20 on the back of the answer sheet. The questions in this section address type of work performed and characteristics of workers in that field, such as interests and values. The first part can be administered in 40 minutes and the second part in 20 minutes. Separate sex norms are provided for grades 9 through 12. According to Savickas (2000), the inventory must be computer scored. The manual indicates that the four basic scales of the CDI are at a suitable reading level for grades 8 through 12, but the Knowledge of Preferred Occupational Group scale could be difficult for students in grade 9 and below.

Attitudinal aspects of career development are measured by two scales: (1) the planfulness scale measures how much time the individual has devoted to planning career-related activities, such as courses in school; and (2) an exploration scale indicates whether the individual has used educational and occupational information resources. Cognitive aspects of career development are also measured by two scales: (1) the career decision-making scale measures knowledge of the principles of career decision making; and (2) the career and occupational information scale is a measure of the individual's knowledge of and perspectives on the world of work.

The second part of the inventory consists of a single test, Knowledge of Preferred Occupational Group. First, the individual selects a preferred occupational group from 20 families of related occupations. Second, the individual selects the most appropriate level of education or training, duties, personal characteristics required for entry and getting established, and rewards and satisfactions, for the preferred occupational group.

Three other scales are formed by combining the four basic scales. Career Planning and Career Exploration combine to make the Career Development–Attitudes (CDA) scale. Decision-Making and World of Work scales are combined to create the Career Development–Knowledge and Skills scale (CDK). The third scale is a composite of the four basic scales and provides an indicator of a client's level of career maturity, called the Career Orientation Total.

Interpreting the CDI

The CDI yields two different kinds of data useful for counseling purposes. First, a composite score provides a multidimensional measure of vocational maturity. This score is useful as a single measure of vocational maturity, although the authors make it clear that not all dimensions of vocational maturity are measured. Second, five trait scores indicate specific strengths and weaknesses and provide an evaluation of the individual's readiness to make career decisions. (Strengths are identified as being above the 75th percentile; weaknesses as below the 25th). These scores are useful for determining whether further developmental experience is necessary to increase readiness for decision-making.

With respect to interpretation, Savickas (2000) suggests beginning with the examination of client scale scores to identify strengths and weaknesses. The next step would be to examine the client's score on the Career Planning scale. A lower score would suggest a lack of planning, an unawareness of this need to plan, or a low value on work salience. Following this, the counselor would examine the Career Exploration score, which measures the willingness of an individual to use and evaluate sources of information about careers, with lower scores being indicative of a person who does not see this as a priority. The next scale to examine would be the World of Work Information score. Low scores on this scale suggest a need for career information, including types of potential careers. Next, the counselor would examine the Decision-Making scale score. Clients with low scores on this scale would in essence be stating that they are not sure how to go about making a career choice. If this is the case, the counselor should focus on decision-making strategies.

The CDI is useful as a diagnostic measure because it indicates an individual's readiness to make educational and occupational choices. The results provide an index of attitudes toward career planning, knowledge of occupations, and skills necessary for career decision-making. Curriculum and guidance programs may also be evaluated using the CDI for their effectiveness in supporting attitudes and in teaching skills necessary in the career decision-making process. Earlier forms of this instrument have been reviewed by Bingham (1978), Ricks (1978), and Hilton (1982). For more recent reviews, see Savickas (2000), Savickas and Hartung (1996), Pinkney and Bozik (1994), Locke (1988), Hansen (1985), and Johnson (1985).

Norms for the CDI-S were based on a national sample of students (N = 5039) in grades 9 through 12. Norms for the CDI-CU were based on 1345 undergraduate students. The manual suggests developing

Table 9-1	Internal consistencies of the Career Development Inventory
Career Planning scale	.89
Career Exploration scale	.78
World of Work	.85
Decision-Making	.67
Knowledge of Preferred Occupational Group scale	.60
Career Development-Attitudes	.84
Career Development-Knowledge and Skills	.86
Career Orientation Total	.85

local norms, which Pinkney and Bozik (1994) endorse as a good idea, especially if the typical clients seen in a particular setting are not represented by the norms reported in the manual. No data are provided on minority groups, and the authors suggest that care be taken when using the CDI with minority clients or disadvantaged students because results may indicate that they are less mature than they actually are. In fact, one study (Lundburg, Osborne, & Miner, 1997) found significant differences in scores on the CDI between Mexican-American and Anglo-American adolescents. Internal consistencies on the four basic scales are included in Table 9-1.

Pinkney and Bozik (1994) suggest that counselors be cautious when using the Decision-Making scale and the Knowledge of Preferred Occupational Group scale with clients because the scores are calculated on opinion responses rather than on behavior or knowledge. The manual includes adequate information about content and construct validity.

Case of Using CDI Questions in Group Counseling

The high school career counselor and one of the teachers reviewed the results of the CDI that had recently been administered to junior and seniors in their school. Their major goal was to establish programs for students based on needs indicated by the CDI results. Typical of the programs was the one developed for students with particularly poor scores on the planning section of the inventory. The students volunteered for participation in the program.

Both the teacher and the counselor were concerned with the students' lack of knowledge of working environments and their naive and nonchalant attitudes concerning the world of work. The teacher and counselor wanted to provide a program that would help these students take a realistic approach to career planning and that would reach all these students in a short period of time. The strategy was to use selected items from the CDI section measuring planfulness to stimulate group discussion.

Several specific tasks were identified as the major objectives: clarify career planning attitudes, evaluate time spent thinking about and planning careers, identify courses associated with potential career plans, increase awareness of relevant activities associated with career planning, and clarify reasons for considering work environments in relation to careers. The following dialogue illustrates how the strategy of using CDI questions was employed to meet the specific objectives.

COUNSELOR: The major goal of this counseling session is to encourage each of you to devote more time to career planning. We will begin our session by discussing some of the questions in the CDI. Each of you has an inventory booklet for this purpose. (The counselor continued by presenting sample questions that she had previously identified. One of the questions dealt with the purpose of learning about actual working conditions of jobs being considered.)

JAN: If you don't know anything about a job, how can you be expected to choose it?

ROBERTO: Yeah, you have to know what the requirements are to make a decision about it.

JAMAL: You should also know where you will be working—I mean, what places and how.

ROSA: I remember that my brother told me he never would have taken the job he has if he had known more about it. He gets all dirty, and the other guys talk rough and threaten him. He is trapped in that job, and he can hardly wait to find another job.

COUNSELOR: Very good! You have illustrated why it is important to thoroughly investigate the requirements of occupations you may be considering and the kind of people you will be associating with in those occupations. Now, let's look at another question. Jan, what was your answer for Question 1: "Taking classes that will help me decide what line of work to go into when I leave school or college"?

JAN: I'm not sure, but I believe I answered, "Not given any thought to doing this." [Pause] I really haven't thought about it much. I guess I'm just enjoying myself now and not considering the future.

BERTHA: I heard that more and more women are going to have to work to support their families, so I believe we have to plan for jobs in the future like the boys do.

ROSA: I agree. The sooner we get started thinking about the jobs, the better prepared we will be.

JAMAL: We guys had better get started, too!

The counselor provided the opportunity for each member of the group to respond to other key questions from the CDI. After the implications of the questions were discussed, the counselor reiterated the need to think about and plan various career-related activities. This case illustrates the use of inventory questions to create discussion topics related to identified goals and specific tasks.

Career Decision Scale (CDS)

The CDS (Osipow, Carney, Winer, Yanico, & Koeschier, 1987) was designed to measure career indecision, identify career decision-making difficulties, and act as a follow-up procedure to evaluate the effectiveness of a career intervention. The CDS was based on the idea that "a finite number of relatively discrete problems" (Osipow, 1980, 1987, p. 4) keep people from being able to make or commit to a career decision. According to Osipow and Winer (1996), it was hoped that the CDS would point clients to issues that they should explore when trying to understand their career indecision.

The CDS consists of 19 items, comprises two scales—Certainty and Indecision—and takes about 15 minutes to complete. Clients respond to the items in a Likert-scale four-point manner, ranging from 1 = "not at all like me" to 4 = "like me." Item 19 is an open-ended item that allows clients to add any additional information they think would be helpful. The Certainty Scale score is calculated by adding the ratings for the first two items (ranging from 2 to 8), whereas the Indecision Scale score is calculated by adding the ratings for items 3 through 18 (ranging from 16 to 64). Scale scores that are at or below the 15th percentile are considered significant, as are indecision scores that are at or above the 85th percentile.

Counselors should generally expect the Certainty scale and Indecision Scale scores to be in the opposite direction. If they are either both high, or both low, the counselor should consider whether the protocol is valid. Savickas (2000) states that from his experience, a profile with two low scores usually indicates someone who is undecided, but comfortable about the indecision, and those with two high scores are typically those that make strong commitments to several options over a short period of time. A profile that indicates high certainty and low indecision suggests that the person might not need in-depth assistance at this point with making a decision. For those people whose scores are in the middle (between the 16th and 84th percentiles), the counselor should talk with the clients more about their purposes for seeking career counseling and their specific career needs. When a person's scores indicate low certainty and high indecision, targeted interventions with more counselor support may be warranted, whereas a person with high certainty and low indecision will most likely need less help in the career decision-making process. Being able to identify those clients who need less support enables a center to provide its most costly commodity—individual counseling—to those who need it most.

The authors caution clinicians to remember that indecision is not always a negative indicator and may even be appropriate, depending on the client's developmental level. Savickas (2000) suggests examining the discrepancy between ratings on major choice certainty versus career choice certainty. If the major choice certainty score is higher by 2 or 3 points, Savickas recommends examining whether the client has a plan ("I'm going to major in communications"), but not a clear goal ("but I have no idea what I'll do after I graduate"). The opposite would be true for someone with higher career certainty than major choice certainty; that person has a goal ("I want to be a manager"), but no plan ("Which major would best prepare me for that?"). In either case, Savickas suggests talking with the client about how he or she made that first decision and trying to identify the factors that affect the decision. For example, was the choice of major to please someone else, or was the career choice a completely informed one?

The norm groups for the CDS consisted of high school and college students. The Indecision scale was also normed on adults who were seeking to continue their education and on women who were returning to college. Test-retest reliabilities for total CDS scores (Osipow, Carney, & Barak, 1976) ranged from .82 to .90 for college students in psychology courses, and were approximately .70 for another group of college students at the end of six weeks (Slaney, Palko-Nonemaker, & Alexander, 1981). Item correlations for the Certainty and Indecision scales range from .34 to .82, with the majority of correlations falling between .60 and .80. According to Harmon (1994), the evidence for the validity of the CDS is "impressive." There has been much argument over whether subscales exist for the CDS, and various empirical studies have come up with different answers. More extensive reviews of the CDS, which also summarize the subscale arguments, have been provided by Savickas (2000), Harmon (1994), Allis (1984), Herman (1985), Slaney (1985), and Osipow and Winer (1996).

Case of a Confused Community College Student

Sari, a second-year student at a community college, met with a counselor for the purpose of deciding on a career. Sari told the counselor that she planned to apply to several universities.

SARI: I discovered that the universities I planned to attend require that you identify a major, and I haven't done that yet. I'm just not sure.

COUNSELOR: You have come to the right place! We should be able to help you make a decision. To start the process, perhaps you can identify options you have considered.

Sari was able to identify business, education, and English as possible majors. As they continued their discussion about Sari's future plans, the counselor introduced the possibility of taking an inventory to help in the career decision process. She then informed Sari of the purpose of the CDS, and Sari agreed that the results should help her decide, or at least provide some directions for her future plans.

The counselor was not surprised with the CDS results of a low certainty score and a high indecision score. To help Sari identify reasons for a high indecision score, the counselor suggested they discuss items on the indecision scale that was marked "exactly like me." After a thorough discussion of each identified item, the counselor asked Sari to summarize her needs that had emerged from their discussion. Sari identified two needs, "more information about specific careers and to learn more about my abilities." The counselor agreed and added two more—self-confidence and approval of her choice from others.

In this case, the CDS served as a springboard for identifying which interventions might be helpful (occupational information and self-assessment), as well as an indicator for what issues might be interfering with Sari's ability to make a successful decision. Although a lack of information about her personality and career options can be easily remedied, the issues of self-confidence and a need for external approval will need to be discussed further in counseling and revisited throughout Sari's decision-making process to ascertain their separate and combined impact.

My Vocational Situation (MVS)

MVS (Holland, Daiger, & Power, 1980) is intended to measure the degree to which three factors— lack of vocational identity, lack of information or training, and barriers—might be affecting a person's ability to make an effective career decision. The Vocational Identity scale consists of 18 true/false items, such as "I don't know what my major strengths and weaknesses are." The "falses" are scored to produce a maximum score of 18. The higher the score is, the higher the level or the clearer the sense of a person's identity will be (Holland, Johnston, & Asama, 1993). According to Holland (1992, p. 28), the Vocational Identity scale "measures the clarity of a person's vocational goals and self-perceptions." This definition was further described by Holland, Johnston, and Asama (1993) as being "the possession of a clear and stable picture of one's goals, interests, and talents," which should "lead to relatively untroubled decision-making and confidence in one's ability to make good decisions in the face of some inevitable environmental ambiguities" (p. 1).

A strong (high) vocational identity is demonstrated by an ability to narrow the options one is considering to a reasonable number and having confidence in one's ability to make career decisions (Leung, Conoley, Scheel, & Sonnenberg, 1992). Conversely, Leung and colleagues (1992) define a poor vocational identity as an inability to narrow multiple, often unrelated options to a reasonable number, accompanied by a lack of confidence in one's ability to make career decisions. In a study that examined correlates of vocational identity for gifted juniors in high school (from China), Leung (1998) found that those who had tentative college majors and career choices had higher levels of vocational identity, compared with those who did not. In addition, higher levels of vocational identity were related to congruence of the students' Holland types to majors, but not to careers.

Vocational identity has been found to be related to a variety of other career factors. Super, Thompson, Lindeman, Jordaan, and Myers (1981) found vocational identity to be related to vocational maturity for both males ($r = .63$) and females ($r = .67$). High vocational identity has also been associated with a higher sense of well-being (Henkels, Spokane, & Hoffman, 1981). Costa and McCrae (1985) found a relationship between five NEO Personal Inventory scales and identity, with higher scores reflecting extroversion, conscientiousness, and non-neuroticism. Lucas (1999) identified the needs of adult career changers as identified by the MVS as needs for career information, lack of clarity about self and options, and worries about self-confidence, independence, and assertiveness. In their review of recent research on the MVS, Holland, Johnston, and Asama (1993) summarized that "other personality scales or inventories . . . imply that high scorers possess ego identity, hope, are tolerant of ambiguity, are inner-directed, value using special abilities, being creative and original, and wanting to exercise leadership" (p. 5).

Reliability estimates for the MVS were reported at .89 for the Vocational Identity scale (Holland, Daiger, & Power, 1980). Test-retest reliability was found to be at .75 for intervals ranging from one to three months and .64 at three to five months (Lucas, Gysbers, Buescher, & Heppner, 1988). For construct validity, Monahan (1987) found that high levels of decidedness, as measured by the Occupational Alternatives Question (OAQ) are related to high levels of vocational identity.

The concurrent validity between vocational identity items and career indecision items on the Career Decision scale (Osipow, Winer, & Koschier, 1976) was found to be –.73 (Williams-Phillips, 1983).

Using the MVS in Counseling

According to Westbrook (1983) and Leung and colleagues (1992), the MVS can help a counselor quickly differentiate clients according to their level of needs. In addition, a client's score can be useful in designing and implementing individualized treatment interventions. For example, when a client has a low score on the Vocational Identity scale (VI), this client might not be able to limit career options, and periodic support throughout the career decision process may be necessary. In addition, the informational items may identify the exact type of information clients are lacking for making a decision, and they can pinpoint issues that might need further exploration in counseling.

In addition to the overall score, responses to individual items can be probed to gain more information concerning the client's experience in making a career decision. For instance, the item "I am unsure of myself in many areas of life" suggests a rich source of information for counseling intervention programs.

The Case of the Test That Should Tell All

Miguel, a college freshman, walked into the career center and asked if he "could take those tests that tell you what you can do for a job." The student helper, without cracking a smile, suggested that he might want to talk to a counselor. Miguel reluctantly agreed to see a counselor.

After some small talk to establish rapport, the counselor outlined the services and purpose of the career center. Miguel reacted favorably and agreed to commit the necessary time for career exploration. Eventually, the counselor and Miguel agreed that the MVS could be helpful in making a career decision.

The results of the MVS were as the counselor suspected: Miguel had a relatively low score in vocational identity. In the next counseling session, the counselor focused on some of Miguel's responses to the Vocational Identity scale, such as "I don't know what my major strengths and weaknesses are." She then had Miguel describe himself to her as a worker, student, friend, and son. She jotted down the adjectives he provided. Later she asked him to describe what other activities he was involved in at the university. After he described his activities, the counselor asked how he thought his fraternity brothers, soccer teammates, and coach would describe him. She also had Miguel state how his sister might describe him. Again, she jotted down the adjectives.

In this case, the counselor used the list of adjectives to point out strengths and possible weaknesses from Miguel's self-perspective—how he felt others might describe him. The MVS Vocational Identity scale served as a stimulus for self-evaluation and exploring the many facets of self that need to be evaluated in the career decision process. As Miguel progressed through his career search, he, like many others, recognized that the answers to a career decision take time and commitment.

Career Decision Profile (CDP)

The CDP (Jones, 1986) is an inventory composed of 16 questions with three scales, including a Decidedness scale (how clearly clients view their vocational plan), and a Comfort scale (how certain a client is of career choice). Both of these scales consist of two questions each, and have a response range from 1 (strongly disagree) to 8 (strongly agree), which means each scale score (Decidedness and Comfort) can range from 2 to 16. These first two scales can then yield four possible subtypes: decided-comfortable, decided-uncomfortable, undecided-comfortable and undecided-comfortable.

Some empirical support for these subtypes has been found (Lucas & Wanberg, 1995). The third scale is composed of four sections designed to help clients focus on career decisions and are labeled (1) Self-Clarity, (2) Knowledge about Occupations and Training, (3) Decisiveness, and (4) Career Choice Importance. Each of these scales has three items ranging from 1 (strongly disagree) to 8 (strongly agree), which means each scale score can range from 3 to 24. Each of these scores is subtracted from 27 (to correct for negatives). Therefore, lower scores indicate greater needs in that area. A publication entitled *The Career Decision Profile: Interpretation Tool* is used to help clients understand the meaning of their scores. One suggestion from this publication is that any scores that are below 10 are significant and should be explored further. According to Jones and Lohmann (1998), the CDP can be used for the following reasons: examining a client's career indecision, screening for readiness, determining what level of career services are appropriate, and for evaluating the outcomes of counseling.

The construction and validation of the CDP are discussed in an article by Jones (1989), in which he reports retest reliabilities of the CDP scales ranging from .71 to .80 for a three-week period. Retest reliability for the Decidedness scale was .66 at three weeks, and the alpha coefficient was .85. In addition, there was a significant relationship between the Decidedness scale and a measure of career salience (r = .39, p < .0001). Retest reliability for the Comfort scale was .76 for three weeks, with an alpha coefficient of .82. The Comfort scale was found to be correlated with a measure of decidedness (r = .65, p < .0001) and with career indecision (r = −.31, p < .001). Internal reliabilities of the CDP scales ranged from .73 to .85.

Some interesting relationships among CDP scales and other measures were also reported in this article (Jones, 1989). First, Self-Clarity had a significant relationship with trait anxiety (r = −.37, p < .0001) and a significant relationship (r = .36, p < .001) with identity achievement status. Second, Knowledge about Occupations and Training had no significant relationship with anxiety or identity, but was related to career salience (r = .29, p < .001). Third, the Decisiveness scale was found to have a negative correlation (r = −.35, p < .001) with trait anxiety, and Career Choice Importance was related to career salience (r = .45, p < .0001).

Case of "I've got to choose by Thursday"

Rebeccah came into the career counseling center during the last week of classes to choose a major. The counselor asked her what prompted her to come in at this time.

REBECCAH: I'm going home on Thursday and my parents are going to bug me all through the vacation if I don't have a plan.

COUNSELOR: Well, what do you think? Do you feel that you need to have a plan?

REBECCAH: They're probably right. I really don't have a clue as to what I want to go into, and I guess I might as well get started now.

After the counselor explained the instrument, Rebeccah agreed to take the CDP. Her scores were as follows: Decidedness = 2, Comfort = 8, Self-Clarity = 3, Knowledge about Occupations and Training = 3, Decisiveness = 16, and Career Choice Importance = 11. Rebeccah's scores indicated ambiguity on the comfort scale, and her responses within the Career Choice Importance section indicated that she felt a need to make a choice now, but that her future career was only somewhat important to her at this time and that she didn't have any strong interests in any occupational field. The counselor decided to ask Rebeccah about her desire and readiness to make a choice at this time.

COUNSELOR: Rebeccah, how do you feel about being undecided?

REBECCAH: I need to decide, I guess. Then I could start taking classes toward my major. I just need to have something in mind to tell my parents when I go home. I guess I can always change my mind later.

COUNSELOR: Sounds like it might be more important to your parents that you make a decision now, than it is for you.

REBECCAH: I know that I need to choose something, but I feel like I've still got some time to check things out.

COUNSELOR: Deciding when is the right time to choose is up to you. If you decide to take more time, are there things you could be doing to help you learn more about yourself, programs of study, and the variety of occupations that are out there?

Rebeccah and the counselor established a time line and made a goal for choosing a major by the end of the next semester. In addition, because the CDP highlighted Rebeccah's need for self-clarity and knowledge about occupations and training, they brainstormed possible activities that Rebeccah could do during the semester to enhance both of those areas and help her toward her goal of making a decision. Rebeccah also decided to show her plan to her parents, believing that they would be satisfied in seeing that she was "working on it."

Career Factors Inventory (CFI)

The CFI was developed by Chartrand, Robbins, and Morrill (1989) to provide a measure of self-identified difficulties that people experience when making career decisions. It is appropriate for high school students and beyond, and may help those considering a career change or a first career or unemployed persons seeking a job. The self-scorable CFI consists of 21 questions that are supposed to measure emotional and informational needs associated with making a career decision. It consists of two major scales, "Lack of Information or Self-Knowledge", which breaks into two subscales (Need for Career Information and Need for Self-Knowledge) and "Difficulty in Making Decisions", which also divides into two subscales (Career Choice Anxiety and Generalized Indecisiveness).

Lewis and Savickas (1995) reported that the results of their research substantiated the claims for construct and concurrent validity of the CFI. For a thorough explanation on the development and potential uses of the CFI, see Chartrand and Nutter (1996).

Career Decision Self-Efficacy Scale (CDSE Scale)

The CDSE was created by Taylor and Betz (1983) to evaluate the degree of confidence a person voices in making career decisions. The 50 item CDSE Scale was developed from the Social Constructivist Career Theory. The CDSE Scale also includes questions that reflect the degree of confidence a person has in performing specific tasks that are associated with making career decisions.

Career decision-making self-efficacy has been found to be related to level of career decidedness (Bergeron & Romano, 1994; Betz & Luzzo, 1996). In fact, two studies found that career beliefs as measured by the CDSE Scale were the best predictor of career indecision (Betz & Voyten, 1997; Luzzo, 1995). The results of the CDSE Scale can be used to create interventions designed to increase clients' levels of self-efficacy as it pertains to career decision-making. Another researcher (Gianakos, 1999) examined how people might perform if compared on their career decision-making patterns. She found that people whose careers could be classified as stable or multiple-trial had greater career decision-making self-efficacy, compared with those who had a conventional or unstable pattern.

The strengths of this instrument include its basis on theory, whereas the main weakness is that all of the validity and reliability studies were conducted on college students (Luzzo, 1996). A briefer version of the original CDSE Scale has also been found to be similar psychometrically and comparably valid (Betz, Klein, & Taylor, 1997; Peterson & delMas, 1998), which contradicts an earlier study (Robbins, 1985) that suggested the validity of the CDSE Scale was weak.

Other Measures of Career Development for Future Use

The following inventories reflect the variety of career development issues discussed in this chapter, including decision-making, self-efficacy, and indecision.

- Adult Career Concerns Inventory (ACCI). This instrument assesses an individual's career state and vocational maturity. This inventory, a research edition in developmental stage, is a measure of Super's (1990) hierarchy of life stages: exploration (crystallization, specification and implementation), establishment (stabilizing, consolidating, advancing) maintenance (holding, updating, innovating), and disengagement (decelerating, retirement planning, retirement living). One research study identified three potential patterns of career exploration: those who were maintaining a current position, those who were recycling through a current position, and those who were moving into a new position (Niles, Anderson, Hartung, & Staton, 1999). For a review of the development of the ACCI, see Cairo, Kritis, and Myers (1996).

- Career Attitudes and Strategies Inventory (CASI). This inventory is designed to measure a variety of attitudes, experiences, and obstacles that affect adults' careers. There are nine scales of work adaptation as follows: Job Satisfaction, Work Involvement, Skill Development, Dominant Style, Career Worries, Interpersonal Abuse, Family Commitment, Risk-Taking Style, and Geographical Barriers. Counselors use this instrument to help predict whether a client is more likely to continue in a certain work environment or seek to change jobs. In addition, the client's profile can be used to identify obstacles that are hindering career development. For a review of the CASI, see Gottfredson (1996).

- **Career Development Inventory – College and High School Editions.** According to the manual, the purpose of the CDI is to help individuals evaluate how well they are "constructing" their career path. It consists of the following scales: Career Planning (CP) – knowledge of personal career plans; Career Exploration (CE) – using good and poor sources of information; Decision Making (DM) – ability to apply knowledge to decision making; World of Work Information (WW) – a test of career awareness and occupational knowledge; Career Development – Attitudes (CDA) – combines the CP and CE scales; Career Development – Knowledge and Skills (CDK) – combines the DM and WW scales; Career Orientation Total (COT) – combines CP, CD, DM, and WW and serves as a measure of 4 aspects of career maturity. Scores between the 40th and 60th percentiles suggest that the client's scores are similar to others in his or her grade level. Lower scores indicate deficits; higher scores indicate awareness and appropriateness of choices.

- **Career Decision-Making Difficulties Questionnaire (CDDQ).** This inventory was designed to help indecisive individuals and their counselors better understand the specific difficulties clients are facing in making a career decision. Based on a taxonomy of decision-making difficulties, the CDDQ is structured with 10 different decision-making categories. Undecided students have been shown to have higher scores on the CDDQ, indicating decision-making difficulties, Career Decision Scale scores, and lower career decision-making self-efficacy scores (Osipow & Gati, 1998). Reliability and validity of the CDDQ have been supported (Lancaster, Rudolph, Perkins, & Patten, 1999).

- **Coping with Career Indecision (CCI).** The CCI is a career indecision instrument that focuses on how people cope with career indecision and identifies four types of undecided students: low agency/high distress, high agency/high distress, low agency/low distress, and high agency/low distress (Larson & Majors, 1998). In addition, a factor analysis yielded four content areas, including subjective career distress and obstacles, active problem solving, academic self-efficacy, and career myths (Larson, Toulouse, Ghumba, Fitzpatrick, & Heppner, 1994). Those researchers also found that those with higher scores on this inventory also had lower vocational identity, less career certainty, more career indecision, and more ineffective problem-solving appraisal.

- **Decisional Process Inventory (DPI).** This 70-item inventory is based on the Gestalt theoretical principle of homeostasis and attempts to measure how decided individuals are relative to a career choice. Content and criterion-related validity of the inventory has been found (Hartung, 1995). A revised version of the DPI has also found reliable and valid (Hartung & Marco, 1998).

Summary

The concept of career development has evolved from developmental approaches to career guidance and career education programs. Several emerging career development inventories reflect a more inclusive approach to career development counseling. Inventories now include such factors as dysfunctional thinking, anxiety, and cognitive clarity. The current emphasis on assessing a person's level of career development includes examining potential and real obstacles or barriers that might hinder the career decision-making process and exploring the person's level of career maturity. Inventories provide a rich source of information from which counselors may build group and individual counseling programs.

Questions and Exercises

1. What are career development inventories designed to measure?

2. Defend or criticize the following statement: Level of career development is easily measured. Defend your position with illustrations.

3. At what stage in the educational process can career development inventory results be used in career counseling programs? Illustrate with three examples.

4. How might you justify the use of a career development inventory to evaluate career education programs? Career counseling interventions?

5. What are the advantages of using questions taken directly from a career development inventory to stimulate group discussion? Are there any concerns about reliability/validity of this issue that a counselor should consider?

6. How do career beliefs, career self-efficacy, or career thinking affect a person's decision-making ability?

7. Think of three creative ways to help clients reframe their negative career thoughts.

8. How might someone's culture or gender affect how that person scores on a career development inventory?

9. Interview a counselor who uses one of the career development inventories reviewed in this chapter. What instrument does this counselor use? Why? How does he or she determine when it's appropriate, introduce it, score it, and go about interpreting it?

10. A sixth-grade girl wants to get started on planning her career. She's made statements like "I'm ready to get this all figured out" and "I want to have this decided by the end of the week." Before giving her an interest assessment, you decide to administer the CMI. Her answer sheet is shown in Figure 9-2. Her total score for career maturity was 33. Her score on the Attitudes scale was 13, which is at the 68th percentile in the manual. Her score on the Competence scale was 20, which is at the 99th percentile in the manual. How do you interpret these results? Would you feel confident in moving on to an interest survey, or are there other activities or interventions you would do first?

11. Given the CDP profile shown in Figure 9-3, how decided and comfortable would you say Sarah is with her career choice at this time? What do her subscale scores suggest? Which of the four groups (as described in the CDP section) is Sarah likely to fall into? What are the implications of that? What type of interventions or next steps might you recommend?

12. A client's CDS scores include Certainty = 2 and Indecision = 76. How would you interpret this person's scores? What does it say about his or her level of indecision and certainty? What next steps might you recommend?

13. How would your counseling approach differ with a person who had a 2 on the vocational identity scale of the MVS versus one who had a 6, versus one who had a 14?

14. A 16-year-old female has taken the CDSE. Each total subscale ranges from 0 to 45 points, with zero being no confidence, and 45 being complete confidence. Her scores include:

	Client Score	Mean	Standard Deviation
Self-Appraisal	38	36.5	6.5
Occupational Information	24	36.7	7.1
Goal Selection	20	35.6	8.2
Planning	17	35.4	8.2
Problem Solving	4	34	6.9
TOTAL	103	178.2	31.6

How would you interpret these results? What direct and indirect interventions might you employ?

15. A client has taken the CTI as part of a screening inventory. His raw score results include Total = 78, DMC = 22, CA = 16, and EC = 5. How would you interpret these results (use Figure 9-1 as a guide) if the client were a high school student? A college student? An adult? How would your interventions vary at each stage?

16. The CASI profile of a mid-career changer is presented in Figure 9-4. What do this person's scores suggest to you? What are the most pertinent issues this person is facing? Looking over the career obstacles list, what type of interventions would you provide? Are there any career obstacles (whether or not they are checked) that you would want to refer to another counselor with specialties different from yours?

17. Take some time and research the tenets of Super's theory of career maturity. After exploring the different tenets, consider the ACCI profile in Figure 9-5. What might be the concerns of this 50-year old female? What would the next steps be?

18. Given the CDI profile in Figure 9-6, how would you summarize this high school student's career decision plans thus far? What interventions might you use? What recommendations might you make?

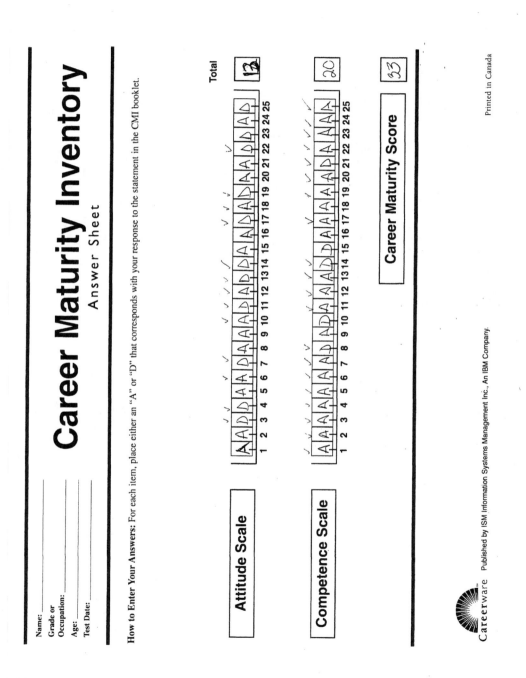

Figure 9-2   Career Maturity Inventory. CMI copyright by Vocopher 2005, reproduced by permission of Vocopher.com

Summarizing Your Answers

Step 1
Go to page 1. Add your ratings for the two statements under "Decidedness,"
and write the sum in its box below:
Do the same thing for "Comfort."

Decidedness   Comfort

Step 2
For pages 2 and 3, add your ratings for each of the sections and write their sum
in the box below. Then subtract these sums from 27. Write the answer for each in
the shaded box.

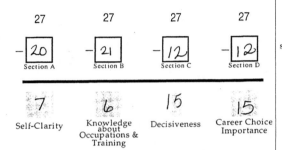

Put sum of each
section in box and
subtract from 27

Answer after
subtracting

4

Figure 9-3   Career Decision Profile: Reproduced by permission of the author, Lawrence K. Jones.

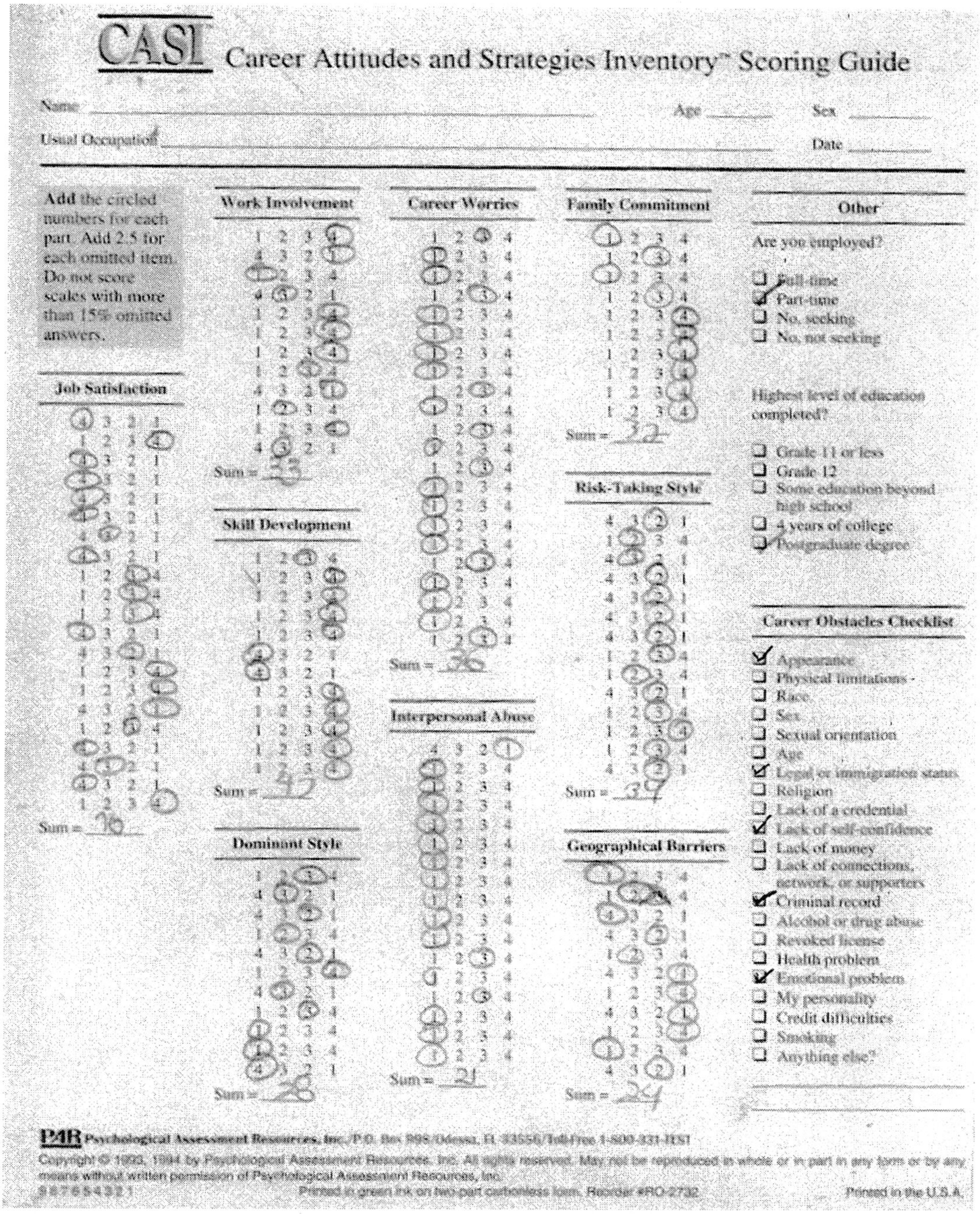

CASI Career Attitudes and Strategies Inventory™ Scoring Guide

Name ______ Age ______ Sex ______

Usual Occupation ______ Date ______

Add the circled numbers for each part. Add 2.5 for each omitted item. Do not score scales with more than 15% omitted answers.

Job Satisfaction — Sum = 70

Work Involvement — Sum = 33

Skill Development — Sum = 47

Dominant Style — Sum = 28

Career Worries — Sum = 36

Interpersonal Abuse — Sum = 21

Family Commitment — Sum = 32

Risk-Taking Style — Sum = 37

Geographical Barriers — Sum = 24

Other

Are you employed?

- ☐ Full-time
- ☑ Part-time
- ☐ No, seeking
- ☐ No, not seeking

Highest level of education completed?

- ☐ Grade 11 or less
- ☐ Grade 12
- ☐ Some education beyond high school
- ☐ 4 years of college
- ☑ Postgraduate degree

Career Obstacles Checklist

- ☑ Appearance
- ☐ Physical limitations
- ☐ Race
- ☐ Sex
- ☐ Sexual orientation
- ☐ Age
- ☑ Legal or immigration status
- ☐ Religion
- ☐ Lack of a credential
- ☑ Lack of self-confidence
- ☐ Lack of money
- ☐ Lack of connections, network, or supporters
- ☑ Criminal record
- ☐ Alcohol or drug abuse
- ☐ Revoked license
- ☐ Health problem
- ☑ Emotional problem
- ☐ My personality
- ☐ Credit difficulties
- ☐ Smoking
- ☐ Anything else?

PAR Psychological Assessment Resources, Inc./P.O. Box 998/Odessa, FL 33556/Toll-Free 1-800-331-TEST

9 8 7 6 5 4 3 2 1 Printed in green ink on two-part carbonless form. Reorder #RO-2732 Printed in the U.S.A.

Figure 9-4 CASI. Adapted and reproduced by special permission of the Publisher, Psychological Assessment Resources, Inc., 16204 N. Florida Avenue, Lutz, Florida 33549, from the Career Attitudes and Strategies Inventory by J. L. Holland and G. D. Gottfredson, Copyright 1993, 1994 by PAR, Inc. Further reproduction is prohibited without permission from PAR, Inc.

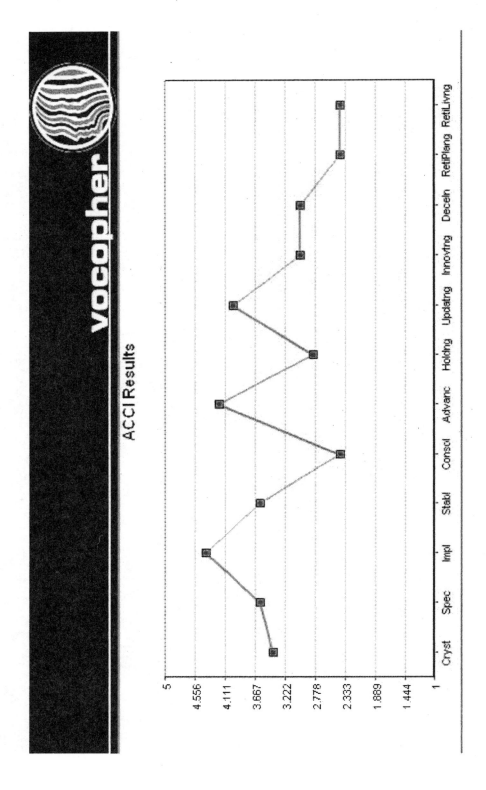

Figure 9-5   Adult Career Concerns Inventory. ACCI copyright by Vocopher 2005, reproduced by permission of Vocopher.com.

The Career Development Inventory

Congratulations, you have completed the High School Career Development Inventory. Your results can be seen below.

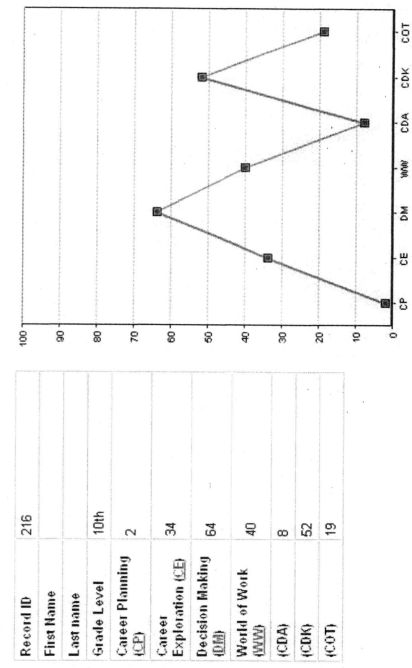

Record ID	216
First Name	
Last name	
Grade Level	10th
Career Planning (CP)	2
Career Exploration (CE)	34
Decision Making (DM)	64
World of Work (WW)	40
(CDA)	8
(CDK)	52
(COT)	19

Figure 9-6   Career Development Inventory: High School. CDI copyright by Vocopher 2005, reproduced by permission of Vocopher.com

10 Using Card Sorts in Career Counseling

Having clients identify occupational likes and dislikes does not always require a paper and pencil. The hands-on approach of sorting cards into different piles offers a nice alternative to traditional testing approaches. Given that clients might prefer not to engage in "testing" (Galassi, Crace, Martin, James & Wallace, 1992), the card sort might be a more innocuous way to help clients organize their thoughts about interests, skills, values, occupations or other issues.

One major advantage of card sorts is that students have often been stimulated to openly express and evaluate their preferences when sorting and during the discussion of results. A second advantage is that the nature of the card sort places the client in control of organizing his or her own world of work (Hartung, 1999). In this chapter, we will explore the use of card sorts and present a variety of card sorts that are designed for specific purposes.

Card Sorts

Card sorts are typically not seen or interpreted as standardized instruments but are more often pictures that are symbolic of a client's thought process and, more specifically, about perceptions of careers and work. Although not many researchers have investigated the use and effectiveness of card sorts, Slaney and MacKinnon-Slaney (1990) report from their review of existing literature that card sorts are "as successful . . . in predicting the career choices of clients, reducing their career undecidedness, demonstrating changes in their career choices, and increasing satisfaction with their career choices" as currently available standardized instruments are.

Goldman (1983) describes the process of sorting the cards as a type of projective activity, in which one projects a subjective sense when evaluating an occupation in terms of personal values, goals, interests, abilities, and so on. Thus, although the cards to be sorted remain the same for each client, the meaning each client attributes to the cards can be vastly different. Goldman suggests that the accuracy of a client's interpretation of what is presented on a card is not the most important measure; rather, the client's interests, values, and skills that are exposed by the stimuli are significant for the counseling process. Indeed, the phenomenological context of card sorting provides a unique opportunity for exchange that is not always evidenced with by reviewing standardized testing results (Hartung, 1999).

Types of Card Sorts

The cards that are used for sorting can be any shape, size or color. Most cards that are produced are similar to playing cards in shape. Usually, a word representing an occupation, interest, hobby/leisure activity, value, skills, etc., is typed on one side of the card. The back of the card may have a description of the occupation or word. Other information might include Holland type, salary, or training required. The following are representations of cards created by counseling students and reprinted with their permission.

Traditional Cards:

Figure 10-1a Sample student card sorts. Reproduced by permission of the authors.

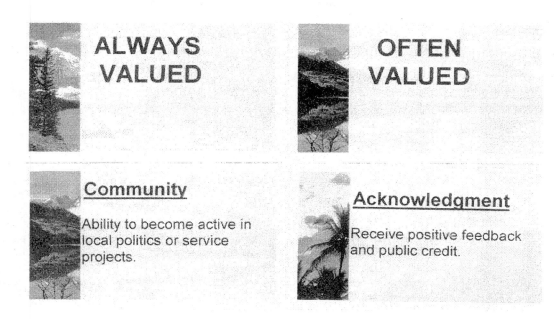

Figure 10-1b   Sample student card sorts. Reproduced by permission of the authors.

Figure 10-1c   Sample student card sorts. Reproduced by permission of the authors.

Task Approach Behaviors

How people approach the task of sorting cards also provides important clinical information (Goldman, 1983). Are they impulsive, quickly sorting the cards into piles, or are they slow and more deliberate about the process? How organized are the piles (do you see hints of perfectionism or obsessive-ness?) Do they seem hesitant or seem to need confirmation that "they are doing it right," and what kind of questions does their behavior raise for the counselor? Do they ask a lot of questions or make responses that indicate that they need more information about the world of work? All these "task approach" factors may be important to consider when working with a client.

Advantages of Card Sorts

Several researchers have commented about the advantages of using card sorts. One is that the client immediately sees the results. You do not have to wait for a computer or some other external source to take the client's information and produce a list (Crouteau & Slaney, 1994). Instead, clients see and understand that their "results" are the outcome of decisions they have made. According to Slaney and MacKinnon-Slaney (1990), the client is the primary agent in the intervention and is actively engaged in producing, monitoring, and evaluating the results.

Another advantage of the card sort is that "it interweaves assessment with counseling in a continuous process" (Goldman, 1995, p. 385). The counselor can help the client "dig deeper" (p. 385), to gain more of an understanding of why he or she placed the occupations in a certain way. A variety of issues can then be explored, including the client's interests, values, skills, goals, inhibitions, occupational stereotypes, and life experiences. In this sense, collaboration between the client and counselor is enhanced.

Observing the manner in which a client sorts the cards has been mentioned previously as an advantage. In addition, because of the projective nature of the task, card sorts can be used with a variety of clients, without the need to discriminate among different languages, ethnicities, genders, ages, or mental abilities (Goldman, 1995). Also, when a counselor is present during the process, the use of an assessment intervention as a dynamic part of counseling becomes more evident.

Flexibility of the card sort approach and the ability to use card sorts with a variety of clients in diverse settings are two additional advantages. In addition, administrative costs are fairly inexpensive, and the procedures are easy to follow. Using card sorts in conjunction with other standardized assessments can enhance the career counseling process by providing subjective information that complements and serves as a framework for the objective results.

Another advantage is the freedom that comes with the actual card-sorting task. Counselors can instruct clients to sort the cards in a variety of manners. Slaney and MacKinnon-Slaney (1990) offer several suggestions for sorting. For example, clients could sort the cards by different time periods, to show how they would have sorted them five or ten years ago compared with how they would sort them now. A

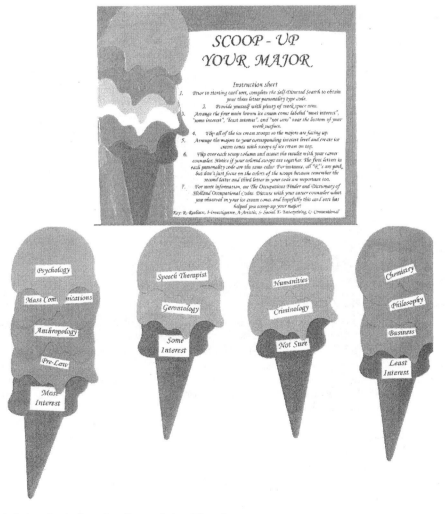

Figure 10-1d   Sample student card sorts. Reproduced by permission of the authors.

second alternative is sorting the cards with relation to feelings, to contrast the results of the sort when clients are feeling optimistic versus pessimistic.

If the clients report some pressure from important others regarding their decisions, the clients can be instructed to sort and label the cards from their own perspective first, and then to repeat the task but imagine doing it from the important other's perspective. People with disabilities might sort the cards as if they had no disability, and women might sort the cards from a man's perspective to reveal potential thoughts that are limiting current options.

Clients Who Might Benefit from Card Sorts

Slaney (Slaney & MacKinnon-Slaney, 1990), in describing his Vocational Card Sort, identified the following clients for whom the card sort experience would be an "appropriate career intervention":

1. Undecided clients, especially those who have not developed a strong sense of their vocational identity and who have not experienced nor explored the occupational possibilities within the world of work.

2. Older clients, who can draw upon their previous work and life experiences.

3. Female clients, who might have stereotypical thoughts about occupations and therefore limit their opportunities.

4. Clients with "psychopathology" or limits in mental abilities (however, Slaney cautions that the counselor must make a clinical judgment regarding the level of impairment or comprehension).

5. Younger clients who are trying to assess their interests, values, skills, and so on.

6. "Intellectually oriented clients who like to control their own decision-making" (p. 341).

7. Those clients whose "inventoried interests" differ from their "expressed interests" (p. 341).

Sorting Alone or with the Counselor Present

Card sorts can be administered with or without the counselor being present. Both approaches have advantages and disadvantages. Working alone can foster a sense of independence and reinforce the idea that the client has "the capacity to find the answer to [his or her] own career problems" (Slaney & MacKinnon-Slaney, 1990, p. 349). A second advantage is that a counselor may have more time to attend to other tasks, including seeing other clients, while a client is working on the card sort. Without the presence of a counselor, however, it is difficult to ascertain the degree to which a client energetically investigates his or her reasons behind the choices of card placement.

There are several advantages to using card sorts with the counselor present. In addition to many advantages listed earlier, the counselor and the client can become co-facilitators during the process, with both sharing the problem-solving responsibilities (Slaney & MacKinnon-Slaney, 1990). When present, the counselor can alert the client to "here and now issues of decision-making style, as well as historical and future concerns" (Slaney & MacKinnon-Slaney, 1990, p. 366). Pinkney (1985) suggests that two main purposes of a counselor being present during the task are to help clients clarify reasons behind their choices, including why they chose to accept some occupations and reject others, and to provide support for clients during the process.

Slaney and MacKinnon-Slaney (1990) also reported clients' tendency to give simple answers in response to questions asking why an occupation was placed in a certain category. A trained counselor would be able to help the client explore for deeper issues. We have found that counselors can listen for clues to assist clients to explore, and then confront, any negative self-talk that clients might be imposing on themselves.

Sorting Procedures

The basic instructions for an occupational card sort are as follows. Clients are first instructed to sort the cards into three piles under the headings "Would Not Choose," "Would Choose," and "No Opinion." Clients are then instructed to re-sort the cards in each of the three categories to form subgroups within those categories. The subgroups are based on the client's reasoning. For example, clients would take the occupations in the "Would Not Choose" category and identify why they rejected each occupation that was placed in that category. During the process, common themes for rejecting may begin to emerge, and these then form the basis for the subgroups.

The final step involves the counselor asking the client about the themes and the client's reasoning. Tyler (1961) stated, "I ask him to tell me what it is that each of his groups represents. I record on the data sheet the label or explanation he gives for each and the number of the items he classifies together under this heading" (p. 196). The counselor would continue to ask questions to further clarify the client's view of himself or herself in the world of work. Tyler's final step includes asking the client to identify subgroups (from the positive and negative group) that are most important to the client.

Pinkney (1985) suggests that the use of a card sort is especially helpful when a client has obtained a flat profile on an interest inventory. By exploring the client's reasons for grouping cards in a certain way, a counselor can gain information about the client's thoughts and beliefs that might have led to a flat profile. Pinkney states that clients with a flat profile are unlikely to have more than one occupational theme in the "Would Choose" pile because of the small number of occupations in that category. We have found, however, that a person with an elevated flat profile is likely to have several cards, and thus several themes, in the "Would Choose" file. A counselor should show extra support during "theme analysis" with these clients in case the card sort is showing a too-narrow or even frivolous approach to career choice.

Pinkney (1985) labels the type of themes identified for the "Would Not Choose" pile as "avoidance themes," stating that clients are often more comfortable describing avoidance themes and "often seem well-prepared to defend such themes" (p. 337). Slaney, Moran, and Wade (1994) state that in the process of labeling "negative" subgroups, clients' confidence in their ability to make logical, successful choices is reaffirmed. According to Pinkney (1985), the focus of the discussion of avoidance themes is "to explore the issue of over-generalization" (p. 337). He states that having a desire to avoid certain activities is appropriate, but that clients with flat profiles "seem to carry on avoidance to an extreme with little exploration" (p. 337). A counselor's role in this situation is to help the client see how avoiding affects the career development process, including limiting options.

The Peterson and Lenz Approach

Peterson and Lenz (1992) encourage clients to approach the card-sorting task in a different manner. After giving the client 36 occupational cards (from the Occ-U-Sort; Jones, 1980), the client is asked to sort the cards into "groups of related occupations" (p. 1). While the client is sorting, the counselor focuses on how the client makes sense of the somewhat ambiguous directions. Was the client's approach methodical, or did it appear to be unorganized? How is the way in which the client sorts the cards similar to the way the client makes decisions? Also, what emotions are expressed during the task?

Once the cards are sorted, the client is asked "to arrange the piles in some relation to each other, and then to label each pile" (p. 1). The counselor then draws a "map," or a representation of how the cards are arranged, on a piece of paper and writes down the occupational titles in each pile and the label the client gave each pile. The counselor should also be aware of the total number of piles.

According to Peterson and Lenz (1992), the median is between five and seven piles, which they state is a picture of occupational maturity. A person with less than five piles might need more specific information on the world of work, whereas a person with more than seven might need help integrating the pieces of knowledge he or she has.

The next step—asking clients about which pile they identify with the most and least and how those two piles are different—allows the counselor to gain an understanding of how clients view themselves and the world of work. Peterson and Lenz (1992) recommend that the way to get the most out of this step is to listen carefully to the words the person is using when contrasting the two piles. Listening to "sort talk" is one of the counselor's most important roles. Sort talk also comes into play in the next step, where the client is asked to point out where different family members would fit. A counselor should listen for information about important people in the client's life, as well as any family rules about career decisions. In addition, the counselor can help the client identify gender patterns—for example, that all the women in the client's life are found in a certain pile—and discuss how these patterns relate to the client's current options and decision-making process. Figure 10-1 shows what a completed map might look like.

Using the Card Sort Results to Draw a Cognitive Map

One unique idea is to use the card sort as a "mapping task" (Peterson, 1998), which enables the counselor to understand how a client perceives and produces occupational knowledge. The steps are virtually the same ones outlined by Peterson and Lenz (1992) but with some modifications.

Specifically, Peterson (1998) modified the task by adding a seventh step, in which the client is asked to recall the process that was used when the cards were initially sorted. The other modification occurs after the client identifies which piles are most and least like himself or herself. Peterson suggests asking the client to describe each occupation in the pile that was identified as most similar.

Self-Guided Booklet

Lawrence K. Jones, Ph.D.

Would you like to be a lawyer or a casket maker? A doctor? A dinkey operator or a pickle pumper? Although some of these are better known than others, all are real occupations.

There are more than 20,000 occupations to choose from. With so many options, you may need help in making a wise choice. *Occ-U-Sort* is designed to help you do that. The heart of the *Occ-U-Sort* system is a set of cards. Each card has the name of an occupation on the front (along with some numbers and letter codes) and a description of that occupation on the back. An example of one of the cards is shown below. Further explanations of the numbers and letter codes will be given as you work through this booklet.

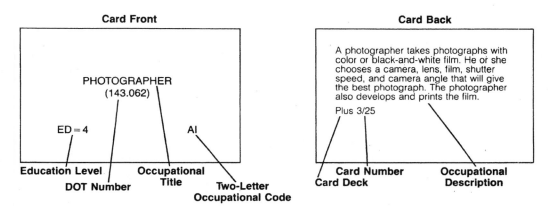

Card Front

PHOTOGRAPHER
(143.062)

ED = 4   AI

Education Level
DOT Number   Occupational
                    Title
                 Two-Letter
                 Occupational Code

Card Back

A photographer takes photographs with color or black-and-white film. He or she chooses a camera, lens, film, shutter speed, and camera angle that will give the best photograph. The photographer also develops and prints the film.

Plus 3/25

Card Number
Card Deck   Occupational
                   Description

You will sort the *Occ-U-Sort* cards and use the information printed on them to learn more about yourself and your career possibilities.

Use a pencil to complete the seven steps on the following pages. Since you are doing this for yourself, spelling and penmanship are not major concerns. The most important thing is that *you* can read what you write.

Turn the page and begin.

Figure 10-2   Reproduced by permission of the author, Lawrence K. Jones.

Similar to other card sorts, but emphasized more heavily in this approach, the client's verbalizations during the sorting are seen as critical pieces of information because they provide a "semantic network of their world of work" (Peterson, 1998, p. 3). In addition to client verbalizations, Peterson stated that in his experience, the manner in which a person approaches the task (linear versus circular) provides him with an initial picture of how this person goes about the decision-making process, particular personality traits this person is likely to have, and what type of interventions might be more successful.

For example, linear problem solvers tend to be logical and methodical in their approaches and might prefer detailed, individual plans of action in which recommended steps are written and prioritized. A circular problem solver, most evident from the way the person places all the cards on the table first and then begins to see and create emerging patterns, might reject the predictability and seemingly inflexible (uncreative) boundaries a written plan may impose. Instead, this person might opt for more creative, spontaneous interventions.

In this task, 36 of the Occ-U-Sort cards (Jones, 1980) were chosen because of the equal number of occupations represented across the Holland codes. According to Peterson (1998), the main purpose of the task is not to expand occupational alternatives but, rather, to "assess cognitive process and structure" (p. 4). In other words, the focus is on how the client proceeds through the task and imposes structure on the ambiguous situation at hand. Therefore, and because of the time involved with having clients verbalize every thought, only 36 cards were used.

In using this method, Peterson examined how an expert (counselor) and a novice (high school age client) would approach and complete the task. He found a significant difference between the two, in that the expert was found to "produce more thought units, more meta-cognitions, more justifications, greater propensity to voluntarily label the piles, greater frequency of attempts, less placing (set aside) and fewer preverbal utterances," which Peterson says are "indications of higher levels of complexity, differentiation and integration of cognitive structure and cognitive skill in executing the task" (p. 11). In addition, he noted that the expert's map showed a higher degree of abstract thinking and integration of occupations (from knowledge, personal experience, and so on). One reason Peterson suggests for this difference in performance is that the novice's attention is focused on doing the task "right" and perhaps on learning about new occupations, which leaves little room in his or her mind for higher-order thinking.

Peterson's findings have important implications for career counselors and the interventions they choose for their clients. People who show a strong approach and understanding of who they are and how they presently fit into the world of work would be better able to successfully use a computer-assisted career guidance (CACG) system, whereas people who are lacking in self-knowledge or knowledge about the world of work expect that the CACG will find a "magic answer." Peterson suggests that such people would likely benefit from experiential opportunities in which they can learn about themselves and about occupational fields of interest. Another application of his findings is that, by paying attention to client verbalizations, the counselor can identify areas that need to be discussed more thoroughly, such as negative self-concept, parental conflict, or lack of self-confidence as a good problem solver.

In addition to occupational card sorts, a variety of other card sorts are available that have been developed to explore values, skills, and majors. Because the availability of research on the use and effectiveness of card sorts is limited, most of the card sorts reviewed have not been researched adequately. The categories of card sorts reviewed include occupational, values, skills, and majors.

Occ-U-Sort

The Occ-U-Sort developed by Jones (1980) is one of the most researched card sorts (Jones, 1983; Jones & DeVault, 1979; Kapes, Mastie, & Whitfield, 1994; Slaney & MacKinnon-Slaney, 1990). Although it is no longer being produced, the basis and general steps serve as a good foundation for all other card sorts and may prove useful to counselors who are creating their own card sorts. Occ-U-Sort contains 60 cards for each of three different groups of users: eighth-graders, high school students, and adults. This instrument is designed primarily to encourage career exploration by stimulating thinking about motives for making occupational choices.

The front side of each card contains an occupational title, *DOT* number, general educational level, and a two-letter Holland occupational code. The backside gives the occupational description along with card identification material (see Figure 10-3).

According to Jones (1980, 1983), the Occ-U-Sort has several goals. These include helping clients to:

SUMMARY SHEET OF PRIORITIZED VALUES

Copy the headings of your values cards onto this form as you have listed and prioritized
them. This will provide you a stable record and ready reference sheet of your choices.

ALWAYS VALUED	OFTEN VALUED	SOMETIMES VALUED	SELDOM VALUED	NEVER VALUED
Work on Frontiers of knowledge	Location	High Earnings Anticipated	Power and Authority	Work under Pressure
Creativity	Security	Profit, Gain	Supervision	Stability
Independence	Advancement	Affiliation	Competition	Physical Challenge
Time Freedom	Help Society	Community	Adventure	
Exercise Competence	Moral Fulfillment	Artistic Creativity	Fast Pace	
Influence Others	Knowledge	Aesthetics	Precision Work	
Help Others	Challenging Problems	Change and Variety		
Recognition	Make Decisions	Excitement		
	Creative Expression	Job Tranquility		
	Intellectual Status			
	Status			
	Work Alone			
	Public Contact			
	Friendships			
	Work with Others			

Figure 10-3   Adapted from Richard L. Knowdell, Career Values Workbook (CareerTrainer, 2005). Used with permission.

1. think about their motives and perceptions of self;

2. better clarify their needs and job requirements;

3. expand their awareness of attractive options;

4. explore nontraditional careers; and

5. identify characteristics that are important to them as they choose a career.

Slaney and MacKinnon-Slaney (1990) provide an extensive review of critiques of the Occ-U-Sort.

After a brief introduction to the card sort materials, each client is instructed to sort the cards into three piles: "might choose," "would not choose," and "uncertain." The "would not choose" cards are then re-sorted into smaller piles according to the person's reasons for rejecting them. Likewise, the "might choose" cards are re-sorted, but this time according to why they have been identified as possibilities for future occupational choice. Jones (1980) has identified this particular step as an exercise in values clarification.

Next, the client is directed to one or more guide booklets as needed. For instance, a Self-Guided Booklet, shown in Figure 10-2, may be used to assist clients toward the next steps in the process of career exploration. Another self-help device, a record sheet, assists clients in organizing their card choices according to "would not choose" or "might choose." On this form, clients are directed to record why certain occupations are appropriate and to develop a list of occupations by preference. Finally, clients are to record Holland Occupational Codes for several chosen occupations, identify related occupations, and read a brief description of all Holland codes. On a list of "things to think about," clients are to consider educational levels required by chosen occupations, health and physical limitations, and how chosen occupations would affect their lifestyles. Throughout this entire process, clients are encouraged to verbalize their thoughts and questions.

The Occ-U-Sort has received some criticism regarding some claims in its technical manual (see Kapes, Mastie, & Whitfield, 1994; Slaney & MacKinnon-Slaney, 1990). In two different studies (Jones & DeVault, 1979; Jones, 1983), however, no significant differences were found between students who used the Self-Directed Search and those who used the Occ-U-Sort. One distinct advantage suggested by the author is the sex-fairness of this approach in career decision making.

Case of a College Sophomore Trying to Choose a Major

A 20-year-old sophomore named Jorge came to the career counseling office for the stated purpose of choosing a major. Jorge's beginning statements suggested his almost urgent concern for finding a job after graduation, especially since he had practically no idea how to choose a career. During the dialogue, the counselor offered Jorge several options, including the process of focusing on possible careers first, followed by identifying potential majors that could be used for career development.

Conversely, another option offered was to focus on potential majors first, followed by careers related to majors. After some discussion, Jorge decided that he wanted to focus on careers first. To gain an understanding of how much Jorge knew about various careers, the counselor asked Jorge to write down as many occupations as he could. When Jorge had finished, the counselor counted the occupations on the list. There were 17, many of which did not appeal to Jorge. The counselor introduced the Occ-U-Sort as an activity that would help increase the number of career options Jorge was considering and show some other factors that were important to Jorge in choosing an occupation.

Jorge sorted the cards into three piles, and then re-sorted the cards in the "would not choose" pile according to his reasons for rejecting them. Four main themes were found: (1) too boring (when further explored, the reason was repetitive tasks); (2) too much education required; (3) not enough money (Jorge wanted a $28,000 starting salary—a statement that reflected a lack of occupational knowledge and that would need to be discussed further); and (4) blue-collar work (Jorge wanted a position that his parents would call "respectable"; might tie in to the pay reason as well).

Jorge then re-sorted the "might choose" pile according to his reasons for choosing them. Three main reasons were identified: (1) good starting salary; (2) exciting (various tasks, unpredictable schedule); and (3) prestige associated with the job. When he prioritized these piles, Jorge's first choice was excitement (variety) of work tasks, followed by good starting salary and then prestige.

The counselor used the record sheet to estimate the overall Holland Code of Jorge's "might choose" pile and then showed Jorge how to identify occupations that were similar to the occupations in that pile. At that point, Jorge decided that the next step would be to learn more about specific occupations. The counselor helped Jorge locate information on the occupations he was interested in and suggested that, while learning about the occupations, Jorge pay careful attention to those factors he had identified as important, in addition to seeing what majors were typically associated with the occupation in question. Through his experience with the Occ-U-Sort, Jorge was able to identify potentially satisfying occupations, clarify what was important to him in choosing a career, and learn different ways for classifying occupations. In addition, two issues emerged that would be important to discuss with his counselor: a misconception about starting salaries and the impact of parental influence on his current thinking. Overall, the Occ-U-Sort proved to be a helpful step in Jorge's process of learning more about himself and the world of work.

The Career Values Card Sort Planning Kit

The Career Values Card Sort Planning Kit (Knowdell, 1995a) allows users to clarify their values by sorting 41 cards into one of five categories. Each card identifies a value and briefly describes the value. The five categories are labeled: "Always Valued," "Often Valued," "Sometimes Valued," "Seldom Valued," and "Never Valued." Clients are instructed to place the five categories in a row, making five columns, and then to sort the value cards into the appropriate column. Clients are further instructed to have no more than eight values in the "Always Valued" column. After the cards are sorted, clients are told to prioritize the cards within each column, and then copy the results onto a summary sheet (see Figure 10-4).

Following this step, clients are given a Career Values Worksheet, which begins with a place for writing out the type of career decision they are trying to make. The next section encourages clients to write down their eight most important values and describe how they apply to that decision. The third section provides a place to list potential conflicts and a place to brainstorm how those conflicts might be resolved. The final section encourages clients to express what they have learned and to identify the next step.

Using the Career Values Card Sort in Counseling

Claire, a 30-year-old woman, came to the career center "seeking a career change." In the intake interview, Claire indicated that she had spent several years in a sales job that had provided good financial returns but caused her to be away from her family a considerable amount of time. As Claire put it, "I want to focus more on balancing family and career." Furthermore, she informed the counselor that she was ready to start having children and to devote her work outside the home to "something new and different." As Claire reasoned, the time had arrived for a change.

As the intake interview continued, Claire made statements that indicated that she was not completely sure about her value orientation. For instance, she stated, "I think I have my priorities in order, but I am not sure—I think I am right to change positions now, but there are times when I regret losing the contacts I made in sales work." After the intake interview was completed, the counselor suggested that a measure and discussion of career values could be productive for answering some of her basic questions about the future.

Claire strongly agreed and liked the idea of a card sort. The Career Values Card Sort was suggested because of its focus on career values orientation. After the purpose of the instrument was explained, Claire chose to begin as soon as possible. The counselor gave Claire the Career Values Card Sort and

MOTIVATED SKILLS MATRIX

	HIGHLY PROFICIENT	COMPETENT	LITTLE OR NO SKILL
TOTALLY DELIGHT IN USING	Teach, Train Motivate Counsel	Plan, Organize Act as Liaison	Visualize
ENJOY USING VERY MUCH	Make Arrangements Expedite Make Decisions Perceive Intuitively Sell Stage Shows Design	Synthesize Initiate Change Interview for Info Host or Hostess Portray Images Entertain, Perform	
LIKE USING	Deal with Feelings Generate Ideas	Observe Write Implement Classify Treat, Nurse	Plant, Cultivate Monitor Estimate
PREFER NOT TO USE	Evaluate Negotiate	Supervise Prepare Food Carpentry Skills Proofread, Edit	Mechanical Skills Transport Test
STRONGLY DISLIKE USING	Read for Information Analyze Mediate	Tend Animals Maintain Records Count Budget	Skilled Crafts Compose Music Physical Agility

Figure 10-4   Adapted from Richard L. Knowdell, Motivated Skills Workbook (CareerTrainer, 2005). Used with permission.

explained that an important first step is to identify what factors are important to her when considering career options. Claire sorted and prioritized the cards. After completing the remaining instructions, the counselor helped her process the results.

COUNSELOR: Claire, tell me what you learned about your values.

CLAIRE: Well, there are a lot of things that are important to me—things I didn't even realize. There are also things that don't appeal to me at all. I guess my highest values right now are time, freedom, security, and working with others.

COUNSELOR: How are those values different from the ones you had, say, five or ten years ago?

CLAIRE: I guess these values were always here but were not the priority at the time. Let's see . . . five or ten years ago, my main values would have been status, fast pace, and advancement. I guess those are still important to me (pointing to the "Often Valued" pile), but they are not priorities right now.

COUNSELOR: So, what you need in a job has changed. How will this affect the careers you are currently considering?

CLAIRE: I'll need to find out whether or not those careers will meet my values—what's important to me and my family right now.

As the dialogue continued, the counselor decided to discuss the degree to which Claire's husband's values matched her own and how their likes and dislikes might affect her decision. The counselor also focused on conflicting values such as high salary versus working predictable hours. Finally, the counselor let Claire decide if she wanted further self-exploration or to go on with the identification of specific occupations or career fields. Claire opted for further self-exploration, for, as she put it, "Now that I have started this process, I may as well get to the underlying reasons for change." In this case, a card sort encouraged self-exploration by introducing values that are very meaningful for inclusion in career exploration and lifestyle. Claire wisely decided that she needed more time to sort out a variety of considerations in making career and family changes that could affect her life for many years in the future.

Motivated Skills Card Sort Planning Kit

The Motivated Skills Card Sort contains 56 cards, including 48 skill cards and 8 category cards. According to Knowdell (1995b), there are six objectives for using the Motivated Skills Card Sort: to identify how proficient you are within a "broad range of transferable skill areas; to identify your level of motivation to use these skills; to identify skills you feel would be useful to develop or improve to make progress in your career; to identify skills you wish to emphasize and minimize using in future work assignments; to sketch a scenario of career satisfaction building upon your motivated skills and identify factors you will need to address in order to accomplish it; and to apply learning's from the MSCS to your career directions" (p. 5).

To use this card sort, the client deals the cards twice. The first time, the cards are placed in the following categories (placed in a column, forming five rows): "totally delight in using," "enjoy using very much," "like using," "prefer not to use," and "strongly dislike using." By sorting into these categories, a person identifies his or her level of motivation for each skill, that is, how much the person enjoys or does not enjoy using a particular skill. The client then places three other categories of cards into three columns. These categories include the following headings: Highly Proficient, Competent, and Little or No Skill. The cards in the "totally delight in using category" are then resorted relative to the three "proficiency" categories. The same procedure is followed with the remaining four rows.

The client is then instructed to re-sort the cards within each "cell," observing related skills and creating subgroups to reflect the similarities. A matrix sheet allows the client to record the results (see Figure 10-5 for a sample of a completed matrix), and the manual includes several worksheets to aid the client in interpreting the results. The manual also includes eight supplementary activities to help the career planner in the process. A copy of one of the supplementary activities, called "Skill Wheels" is shown in Figure 10-6. The purpose of the skill wheel is to broaden a person's ideas about how a particular skill can be used and be marketable in the working world. Although a skill in organizing closets and cabinets in a home might not seem very marketable, the person who came up with the organizing system for shoes, hangers, and so on made a handsome profit from that skill.

Supplementary Activity #6

Skill Wheels

Each of your key functional-transferable skills is like the hub of a wheel with spokes going out in a 360° circle representing the incredibly varied directions you can go in with that skill in the world of work.

With two of your strongest, most motivated skills, brainstorm ways of using them in the world of work, defining projects and settings that could become a job for you. Let your imagination run free in generating traditional and non-traditional money-making ideas that appeal to you. Fill in as many spokes of the wheel as you can.

Example:

Motivated Skill: *Organizing*

SKILL WHEEL

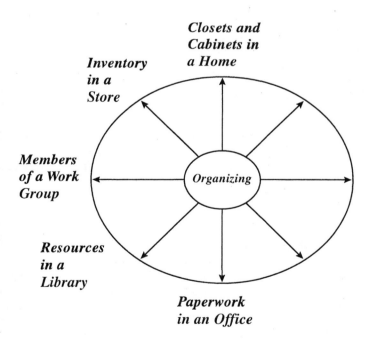

Figure 10-5   Adapted from Richard L. Knowdell, Motivated Skills Workbook (CareerTrainer, 2005). Used with permission.

Other Commercially Available Card Sorts

Although one advantage of card sorts is that counselors can create them with relative ease, several published versions are available, complete with supporting materials and activities.

Occupational Interests Card Sort Planning Kit (OICS). This card sort consists of 113 Occupational Interest Cards, each listing an occupational title. According to the manual, there are five objectives for using the card sort: "to define and cluster occupations holding high appeal for you; to identify characteristics shared in common by these occupations; to identify fields holding high appeal for you; to clarify degree of readiness, skills, and knowledges needed, and competency-building steps for entry into highly appealing occupations; and to apply learnings from the OICS to your career decisions" (p. 5).

O*NET Career Values Inventory. Based on the Work Importance Locator (http://www.onetcenter.org/WIL.html), this inventory includes 20 values cards that a client places in one of five columns, ranging from *Most Important* to *Least Important.* Scoring boxes yield scores for the RIASEC types. The inside of the inventory includes job titles related to each type and divided by "zones" – ranging from zone 1 (little or no preparation needed) to zone 5 (extensive preparation needed).

SkillScan. This card sort includes a set of 64 cards describing one of seven types of skills. The categories include communication, humanitarian, leadership/management, mental analytical, mental creative, creative expression, and physical. The cards are color coded according to category. The developers state that the goal of SkillScan is to help users gain an understanding of their specific skills and "general areas of strength" and to increase their awareness and understanding of how their transferable skills could be applied to a variety of work tasks.

Values Driven Work. The goal of the Values Driven Work card sort is to help clients identify and then align their values with their careers. Congruence between a person's values and his or her work leads to more satisfaction, whereas lack of congruence leads to less satisfaction and, often, more frustration. This card sort allows clients to examine values in four different areas: intrinsic values, work environment, work content, and work relationships.

VISTA Life/Career Cards. This card sort system consists of four packs of RIASEC-color coded cards, including Values, Interests, Skills and Traits. Clients sort one pack at a time into three piles. For example, if sorting the Skills cards, a client would sort the cards under one of these header cards: "Most Proficient," "Somewhat Proficient" and "Not Proficient". After sorting all the cards in one pack, the client would take the cards in the "Most" category and choose 10 that best describe him/her, and then organize them in the form of a pyramid (see Figure 10-7a) with the most important card on top and the least important four cards on the bottom. The client then transfers the name of the cards and the primary Holland RIASEC type from the cards to a worksheet (see Figure 10-7b). The client would repeat these steps for each pack, and then summarize their total Holland scores.

Vocational Exploration and Insight Kit (VEIK). The VEIK is a part of a complete career exploration system and includes 84 occupational titles to be sorted into three categories: "would not choose," "in question," and "might choose." VEIK combines a card sort, the Self-Directed Search, and an instructional booklet, including "Understanding Yourself and Your Career," the "Occupations Finder," "Action Plan Workbook," and a "Counselor's Guide." The cards were created to cover each of the six Holland types equally and to be attractive to people who are at or pursuing various levels of education. Half of the occupations require a college degree; the other half is equally divided between those requiring a high school diploma or less and those requiring a postgraduate degree. The occupations are the same ones that are included in the SDS and the VPI. The VEIK can take three or four hours to complete.

Summary

Card sorts have been a part of the career counselor's bag of interventions for decades. Although many of the original card sorts are no longer being published, card sorts are relatively easy and inexpensive to create and offer a number of possibilities for administration and interpretation. As one should with any instrument, the counselor should have a purpose in mind for using a card sort and a hypothesis about how the process and outcome might help the client in his or her career decision-making process.

Questions and Exercises

1. Think about the setting in which you would like to work. Create a card sort (and accompanying instructions or worksheet) that might help clients in your setting. Practice giving the card sort to a colleague. How would you interpret the process and outcome? What changes would you make, based on the practice session?

2. List at least three reasons why a client might be willing to try a card sort rather than a computer-assisted career guidance (CACG) system?

3. Create a table that compares the pros and cons for using card sorts.

4. How would you use a person's results on a values card sort with a printout of occupational titles he or she obtained after interacting with a CACG?

5. As technology advances, card sorts might become computerized. Describe the positives and negatives of this possibility.

6. What types of client might benefit from using a card sort? Discuss your opinions with a colleague. What types of clients might not find a card sort a useful intervention?

7. Review the client's values card sort results in Figure 10-4. How would you proceed with this client? (Assume she has just finished filling out this values card sort sheet, and says to you, "Well, here it is"). Roleplay with a colleague.

8. Is it possible to be in a job that violates important work values? Explain your answer. How might you counsel a person in that situation?

9. Review the list of skills in Figure 10-5, adding other skills that you think you possess and enjoy using. Choose one or two that you are good at and greatly enjoy using. Create a skill wheel as in Figure 10-5, brainstorming ways you might use that skill in work. When you've exhausted your list, ask a colleague to add to it.

10. Rachelle had been attending college for 2 years, and then decided to take some time off to figure out who she "really is" and what she "really wants" out of life and her career. She's been working a couple of jobs over the past year to save up money for when she returns to college. She feels like it's time to begin to "get serious" about her life and wants some help figuring out what she should do. After talking with her, you and she decide that a card sort activity might be appropriate. She started by completing the VISTA traits card sort. Her pyramid and corresponding worksheet are in Figure 10-6a and b. What are some preliminary observations that you can make about her personality? Can you identify some career fields she might lean towards? What is the danger of relying on the results of one sort (rather than the results of the four packs)? What might be some next steps or questions you might ask her, based on this preliminary profile?

11. Savannah has decided it is time to make a career change. She is sure of her interests and skills. She enjoys writing, creating, and leading - and also describes herself as organized but also a dreamer. She is currently an accountant in a state department. She reports feeling like she is just a number, and that she doesn't feel excited about what she does. There's been a lot of internal stress lately at the office, and she says her work is very repetitive with no real opportunities to "shine". She is considering several career options, including opening her own business, working with the elderly, and consulting. She's open to other ideas. Her results from the O*NET Career Values Inventory are presented in Figure 10-7. What do her results suggest? How do these compare to her aspirations? How would you proceed?

Figure 10-6a VISTA. Reproduced with permission of publisher, VISTA.

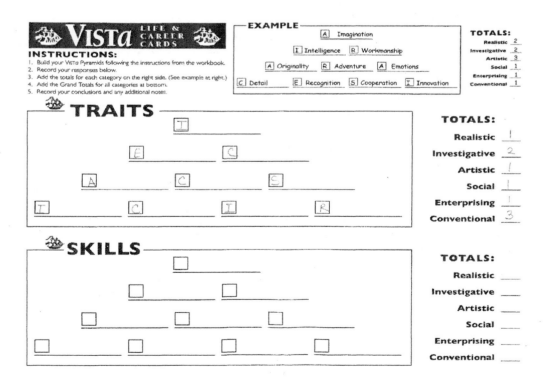

Figure 10-6b VISTA. Reproduced with permission of publisher, VISTA.

Value 1

Achievement

Total Score _____

If Achievement is your highest work value, look for jobs that let you use your best abilities. Look for work where you can see the results of your efforts. Explore jobs where you can get the feeling of accomplishment.

Job Titles with High Ratings for Achievement

Little or no preparation needed (job zone 1): Ambulance Drivers and Attendants, Except Emergency Medical Technicians; Etchers, Hand; Farmworkers, Farm and Ranch Animals; Forest and Conservation Workers; General Farmworkers; Home Health Aides; Models; Painting, Coating, and Decorating Workers; Printing Press Machine Operators and Tenders; Production Inspectors, Testers, Graders, Sorters, Samplers, Weighers; Semiconductor Processors; Truck Drivers, Light or Delivery Services.

Some preparation needed (job zone 2): Agricultural Equipment Operators; Automotive Specialty Technicians; Carpenter Assemblers and Repairers; Commercial Divers; Emergency Medical Technicians and Paramedics; Fabric and Apparel Patternmakers; Fire Inspectors; Floral Designers; Forest Fire Fighters; Forest Fire Inspectors and Prevention Specialists; Gem and Diamond Workers; Makeup Artists, Theatrical and Performance; Medical and Clinical Laboratory Technicians; Medical Appliance Technicians; Motorcycle Mechanics; Municipal Fire Fighters; Private Detectives and Investigators; Radio and Television Announcers; Sales Representatives, Agricultural; Sales Representatives, Electrical/Electronic; Sales Representatives, Wholesale and Mechanical Equipment and Supplies; Sales Representatives, Wholesale and

Sheriffs; Shoe and Leather Workers and Repairers; Singers; Tile and Marble Setters; Timing Device Assemblers, Adjusters and Calibrators; Transit and Railroad Police.

Medium preparation needed (job zone 3): Actors; Advertising Sales Agents; Aircraft Body and Bonded Structure Repairers; Athletes and Sports Competitors; Automotive Body and Related Repairers; Automotive Master Mechanics; Brickmasons and Blockmasons; Bus and Truck Mechanics and Diesel Engine Specialists; Cabinetmakers and Bench Carpenters; Caption Writers; Chemical Technicians; Civil Drafters; Compensation, Benefits, and Job Analysis Specialists; Electrical and Electronics Repairers, Commercial and Industrial Equipment; Electricians; Electronic Drafters; Engravers/Carvers; Environmental Compliance Inspectors; Farm Equipment Mechanics; Fashion Designers; First-Line Supervisors/Managers of Personal Service Workers; Highway Patrol Pilots; Industrial Engineering Technicians; Insurance Adjusters, Examiners, and Investigators; Insurance Sales Agents; Interpreters and Translators; Mapping Technicians; Merchandise Displayers and Window Trimmers; Motorboat Mechanics; Museum Technicians and Conservators; Orthotists and Prosthetists; Outdoor Power Equipment and Other Small Engine Mechanics; Photographers, Scientific; Photographic Retouchers and Restorers; Police Patrol Officers; Precision Etchers and Engravers, Hand or

---

WORK VALUES TO CAREERS CHART

Machine; Professional Photographers; Public Address System and Other Announcers; Radio Operators; Rail Car Repairers; Rough Carpenters; Sales Representatives, Chemical and Pharmaceutical; Silversmiths; Sketch Artists; Sound Engineering Technicians; Stone Cutters and Carvers; Stringed Instrument Repairers and Tuners; Umpires, Referees, and Other Sports Officials.

Considerable preparation needed (job zone 4): Adult Literacy, Remedial Education, and GED Teachers and Instructors; Advertising and Promotions Managers; Aerospace Engineering and Operations Technicians; Air Traffic Controllers; Aircraft Engine Specialists; Airframe-and-Power-Plant Mechanics; Airline Pilots, Copilots, and Flight Engineers; Architects, Except Landscape and Naval; Architectural Drafters; Art Directors; Atmospheric and Space Scientists; Audiologists; Boat Builders and Shipwrights; Broadcast News Analysts; Broadcast Technicians; Camera Operators, Television, Video, and Motion Picture; Cartographers and Photogrammetrists; Cartoonists; Chemists; Child Support, Missing Persons, and Unemployment Insurance Fraud Investigators; Child, Family, and School Social Workers; Civil Engineering Technicians; Civil Engineers; Commercial and Industrial Designers; Commercial Pilots; Compensation and Benefits Managers; Computer Hardware Engineers; Computer Programmers; Computer Software Engineers, Applications; Computer Software Engineers, Systems Software; Computer Support

Specialists; Construction Carpenters; Creative Writers; Criminal Investigators and Special Agents; Dancers; Dietitians and Nutritionists; Editors; Education Administrators, Elementary and Secondary School; Education Administrators, Preschool and Child Care Center/Program; Educational Psychologists; Educational, Vocational, and School Counselors; Electrical Drafters; Electrical Engineering Technicians; Electronics Engineering Technicians; Elementary School Teachers, Except Special Education; Epidemiologists; Exhibit Designers; Farm and Home Management Advisors; Financial Managers, Branch or Department; Fire Investigators; First-Line Supervisors/Managers of Police and Detectives; Forensic Science Technicians; Glass Blowers, Molders, Benders, and Finishers; Government Service Executives; Graphic Designers; Human Resources Managers; Interior Designers; Jewelers; Management Analysts; Market Research Analysts; Marketing Managers; Mathematical Technicians; Mechanical Drafters; Mechanical Engineering Technicians; Medical and Clinical Laboratory Technologists; Medical and Public Health Social Workers; Medical Scientists, Except Epidemiologists; Mental Health and Substance Abuse Social Workers; Mental Health Counselors; Middle School Teachers, Except Special and Vocational Education; Mobile Heavy Equipment Mechanics, Except Engines; Model Makers, Metal and Plastic; Model Makers, Wood; Municipal Fire Fighting and Prevention Supervisors; Music Arrangers and Orchestrators; Network Systems and Data Communications Analysts; Nuclear Medicine

Technologists; Occupational Therapists; Opticians, Dispensing; Optometrists; Painters and Illustrators; Patternmakers, Wood; Pewter Casters and Finishers; Pharmacists; Photoengravers; Physical Therapists; Physician Assistants; Pipe Fitters; Podiatrists; Poets and Lyricists; Police Detectives; Public Relations Specialists; Purchasing Agents, Except Wholesale, Retail, and Farm Products; Radiologic Technologists; Registered Nurses; Reporters and Correspondents; Secondary School Teachers, Except Special and Vocational Education; Self-Enrichment Education Teachers; Social and Community Service Managers; Special Education Teachers, Middle School; Special Education Teachers, Preschool, Kindergarten, and Elementary School; Special Education Teachers, Secondary School; Speech-Language Pathologists; Statisticians; Stonemasons; Substance Abuse and Behavioral Disorder Counselors; Surveyors; Training and Development Managers; Urban and Regional Planners; Vocational Education Teachers, Postsecondary; Vocational Education Teachers, Middle School; Vocational Education Teachers, Secondary School.

Extensive preparation needed (job zone 5): Aerospace Engineers; Agricultural Sciences Teachers, Postsecondary; Anesthesiologists; Anthropology and Archeology Teachers, Postsecondary; Archivists; Area, Ethnic, and Cultural Studies Teachers, Postsecondary; Art, Drama, and Music Teachers, Postsecondary; Athletic Trainers; Biological Science Teachers, Postsecondary;

Figure 10-7   ONET Values. Reproduced with permission of the publisher, JIST Publishing.

11 Computer-Assisted Career Guidance (CACG) and Online Assessments

In the last three decades, the use of CACG assessment has steadily increased. One of the primary reasons for the growth of computer-based assessment is that results are immediately available to clients. Computer-based assessment programs also interpret results to clients in terms of occupational fit with lists of career options. However, some concerns about the validity of computer-based assessment instruments have been expressed by independent researchers (Sampson, 1994; Sampson & Pyle, 1983) and by professional organizations such as the American Counseling Association (1995) and the American Psychological Association (1985, 1986). With the explosion of Internet access, many so-called "tests" are readily available with just a click of a mouse. In this section, we will review some advantages and disadvantages of computer-based assessment processes, including online testing.

Sampson (1994) identified six different possible assessment processes associated with CACG:

1. Clients respond to an online instrument. This process increases validity of the instrument but also increases time clients must spend online.

2. Clients input scores from an instrument completed offline. The obvious advantage is that clients spend less time online. The distinct disadvantage is that clients might not be fully aware of how assessment results relate to occupations.

3. Clients have control of online self-assessment. Clients using this system can judge variables they consider important. However, considerable online use could be a disadvantage, in that extended use might be undesirable to clients, or might reinforce the false idea that the computer has all the answers.

4. A system-controlled online self-assessment is used. Simplifying assessment by reducing options is considered an advantage for some clients. The disadvantage is a significant reduction in the client's control of the system.

5. Pre-structured offline self-assessment is available. More students will have access to the system but could be overwhelmed by the comprehensive nature of some guidebooks used with this program.

6. The user has control of online sequencing of self-assessment, clarification, and reassessment. This system should improve the client's acceptance of using self-assessment, especially with clarification material available; however, more online time is needed for this process.

Other problems associated with CACG assessment include various forms of validity of instruments, scoring, search, and interpretive functions. Confidentiality, counselor resistance, and lack of training can also be problems (Carson & Cartwright, 1997). A recent study (Oliver & Zack, 1999) on Web-based career assessments found some discouraging results: moderate test interpretation of results to the user, limited confidentiality, low correlations with the NCDA guidelines for online career planning, limited information about the site developers and psychometric information.

Be aware that validity of CACG assessment systems should meet the same set of standards used for other psychometric measures. For instance, the validity of scoring standardized instruments includes the weighting of items into scales and assurance of error-free scoring. However, errors in these two processes are difficult to identify in computer-based assessment. Thus, career service providers might not be aware of potential errors and subsequent misleading results.

Finally, interpretive statements generated by computer-based testing systems should be carefully evaluated for their validity. One must ask for some evidence of proof that interpretative statements have been carefully evaluated and are indeed valid results that clients can fully understand and apply to their search process.

As computer-based assessment continues to grow, career service providers must insist that system developers and independent researchers meet the testing standards that have been clearly defined by the American Psychological Association. Evidence of valid testing standards should be clearly delineated in promotional materials as well as in professional manuals.

Goals of Computer-Assisted Career Guidance Systems

To understand the goals of CACGs, a general definition of the systems must be understood. Although not all CACG systems are alike in philosophy or features, the trend has been that systems are becoming more similar in features and associated costs (Sampson, 1994). Computer-assisted guidance (CAG) was defined by Katz (1984) as a system that enables users to enhance their understanding of self and to develop decision-making skills, which means that the system must provide information about the user as well as about the options. Harris-Bowlsbey (1990) further defined CACGS as "on-line systems whose purpose is to engage the user in interactive material that either teaches and monitors a career planning process, or at least provides data to be used by the individual in educational and vocational decision making" (p. 11). The main elements of all CACG systems have been identified as "the dissemination of occupational and educational information, generation of occupational alternatives, and self-assessment" (Sampson, Peterson, & Reardon, 1989, p. 144). For the purposes of understanding, CACGS are defined as

> systems of interrelated assessment, generation of alternatives, and information dissemination subsystems, often coupled with counseling interventions and various print and media-based support resources, that are used within an organization to assist individuals in making current career decisions, as well as improving their capacity to make effective career decisions in the future. (Sampson, 1994, p. 2)

Inherent in these definitions of CACGS are some of the goals of CACGS, as defined by software developers and career theorists. Identifying the goals of CACG systems serves two important functions: creating a criterion against which CACGS can be evaluated and providing a structure by which the appropriateness of a client's expectations can be measured. Appropriate system use was a concern raised by Katz (1984): As CACG systems grow in popularity as viable career planning interventions, more clients may seek to use them to address issues that are not appropriate for CACG use.

Several articles have identified potential goals for CACG systems (Crites, 1982; Harris-Bowlsbey, 1984; Katz, 1984; Lenz, Reardon, & Sampson, 1990; Peterson, Ryan-Jones, Sampson, Reardon, & Shahnasarian, 1994; Sampson, 1984; Sampson, Reardon, Lenz, Ryan-Jones, Peterson, & Levy, 1993). According to Sampson (1984), "the ultimate aim" of computer applications in counseling is to "assist clients in meeting their needs" (p. 187). In applying that same goal to CACGS, Peterson and colleagues (1994) state that "the goal of any CACG system intervention should be to assist individuals in developing career decision-making skills" (p. 191).

The five most commonly stated goals for CACGS seem to be the following:

Table 11-1	Goals for CACS
1. Enhancing client self-knowledge	(Crites, 1982; Harris-Bowlsbey, 1984; Katz, 1984; Lenz, Reardon, & Sampson, 1990; Sampson et al., 1993)
2. Providing information about options	(Cairo, 1983; Clyde, 1979; Harris, 1974; Hoppock, 1976; Parish, Rosenberg, & Wilkinson, 1979; Pitz & Harren, 1980; Super, 1983)
3. Increasing options to consider	(Fretz, 1981; Harris, 1974; Lenz, Reardon, & Sampson, 1990; Parish, Rosenberg, & Wilkinson, 1979; Pitz & Harren, 1980; Sampson & Peterson, 1984; Sampson, Peterson, & Reardon, 1989)
4. Improving decision-making skills or supporting the decision-making process	(Harris-Bowlsbey, 1990; Katz, 1984; Peterson et al., 1994; Reardon, Shahnasarian, Maddox, & Sampson, 1984; Sampson, et al., 1993; Sampson & Peterson, 1984; Sampson, Peterson, Lenz & Reardon, 1992; Zmud, Sampson, Reardon, Lenz, & Byrd, 1994)
5. Enhancing confidence/certainty	(Clyde, 1979; Harris, 1974; Parish, Rosenberg, & Wilkinson, 1979; Sampson, 1984)

Outcomes of Computer-Assisted Career Guidance Systems

Research exists to show that clients are different after having an interaction with a CACG. In his review of the literature, Sampson (1984) reported five main outcomes clients experienced as a result of using CACGS. These include having a positive reaction to using the system, expanding knowledge about self and the world of work, becoming more specific about work and educational plans, experiencing a greater confidence regarding one's ability to make career decisions, and increasing motivation to use other resources as part of career planning. Other studies investigating the outcomes of CACGS included topics such as effective CACG use as predicted by Holland types (Lenz, 1993); the impact of CACG use on vocational identity (Barnes & Herr, 1998; Sampson, Reardon, Shahnasarian, Peterson, Ryan-Jones, & Lenz, 1987) and decidedness (Sampson et al., 1987); the social influence of CACGS, in terms of expertness, attractiveness, and trustworthiness (Sampson et al., 1987); user evaluations on a CACGS capability to enhance self-analysis, synthesis of alternatives, and computer effect (Sampson et al., 1987); comparison of CACG rating to career counseling ratings (Sampson, Peterson, Reardon, Lenz, Shahnasarian, & Ryan-Jones, 1992); and overall satisfaction ratings (Zmud et al., 1994).

Lenz (1993) investigated the effective use of CACG systems as predicted by Holland's theory. She used a regression analysis to examine the relationship between clients' reactions (N = 206), using SIGI PLUS and specific client characteristics (gender, personality, level of vocational identity, career decidedness, and differentiation). The results indicated people with higher Social and Enterprising scores were more likely to rate the CACG lower on its ability to acquire self and occupational knowledge. In addition, none of the specific client characteristics (including My Vocational Situation [MVS] identity scale and the Occupational Alternatives Question [OAQ]) was a significant predictor of the "degree to which the system helped users identify career alternatives" (p. 251) or of Computer Effect (another subscale of the CACG evaluation form), which measured the "degree to which individuals found interacting with the computer rewarding" (p. 251).

Another study (Sampson, Shahnasarian, & Reardon, 1987) examined the relationship between using DISCOVER and using SIGI on several constructs, including occupational certainty, vocational identity, career exploration, and decision-making style of 109 college students. During the orientation meeting, all students completed the MVS (Holland, Daiger, & Power, 1980) and the OAQ (Slaney, 1980), in addition to other forms. Students were divided into three groups: DISCOVER, SIGI, and control. Following interaction with the systems, all three groups were re-administered the MVS and OAQ, among other instruments. No significant differences were found among the groups on any of the dependent measures at pre-, post-, or follow-up testing.

The second part of this technical report investigated user perceptions of CACG expertness, attractiveness, and trustworthiness (Sampson, Shahnasarian, & Reardon, 1987) for students using DISCOVER or SIGI and students in a control group. Both groups of students who used a CACG system rated the system significantly more positively (LSD = 4.88, p < .05) in attractiveness than did the control group. The researchers interpret this finding as a change in perception as a result of user interaction with a CACG.

User evaluations of system effectiveness have also been investigated (Peterson et al., 1994). One hundred twenty-six volunteer students from an introductory psychology class completed the Computer-Assisted Career Guidance Evaluation Form (CACG-EF) (Peterson, Ryan-Jones, Sampson, Reardon, & Shahnasarian, 1987) after being randomly assigned to one of three systems: DISCOVER, SIGI, or SIGI PLUS. The CACG-EF, a modified version of the *Counselor Rating Form* (Barak & LaCrosse, 1975), was developed to measure clients' perceptions of how effective a CACG had been in relation to three scales: Analysis, Synthesis, and Computer Effect. The Analysis scale consisted of items related to needs for occupational knowledge, knowledge of occupational rewards and demands, and clarifying self-knowledge. The Synthesis scale included items related to the attractiveness of CACG systems. In this study, the researchers found that most students rated the systems positively on all three dimensions.

Sampson et al. (1993) revealed that once adults interacted with a CACG system, their perceptions of the expertness of the system declined. In this same study, use of a CACG system (either DISCOVER or SIGI PLUS) resulted in positive gains in vocational identity. Subjects in the DISCOVER group or in the control group (who had unstructured use of print and AV materials) showed increases in their levels of decidedness.

Another study (Zmud et al., 1994) examined responses from 112 students who used a CACG system on four constructs: attitudes toward computers, user satisfaction with human-computer interface, satisfaction with computer use, and satisfaction with decision/task support. From analysis of the ratings, three factors emerged within "the attitude toward computers" construct: clients perceive computers to be enjoyable, non-threatening, and easy to use. Three factors also emerged from the satisfaction with the decision/task support construct: quality of occupational recommendations, provision of information on self, and provision of information of occupations.

How do clients rate CACGS in comparison with actual career counseling sessions? In one study (Sampson, Peterson, Lenz, & Reardon, 1992), students were divided into three groups: SIGI, DISCOVER, and a control group. All groups completed the Computer Rating Form (Peterson et al., 1987). When means of the Computer Rating Form for SIGI and DISCOVER were compared with the means of previous studies, which used the Counselor Rating Form in actual counseling sessions, researchers found that CACGS ratings and career counseling session ratings had similar means when examined on the expertness factor. CACGS received much lower ratings than did career counseling sessions on the attractiveness and trustworthiness dimensions. In addition, the control group means rated CACGS much lower on the three social influence variables, in comparison with counselors. This was especially true for the attractiveness factor.

Client Expectations about Computer-Assisted Career Guidance Systems

Clients do have certain expectations about CACGs (Osborn, Peterson, Sampson & Reardon, 2003). These expectations include increasing career options, enhanced self-knowledge and strengthened occupational knowledge. Krumboltz (1985) identified seven presuppositions or beliefs that can lead to the misuse of CACGS. Although Krumboltz addresses these presuppositions to counselors, some generalizability to clients can be seen as well. These presuppositions include:

1. The stated purposes for using a computer include all the real purposes.

2. Because it's high technology, the computer is better.

3. The computer knows best which occupations match client characteristics.

4. Certain occupations require special temperaments.

5. Questions about job preferences and personal characteristics can be answered yes or no.

6. Obtaining a satisfying entry-level job for a client is the important task in career counseling.

The computer can tell clients what they should do. (Krumboltz, 1985, pp. 166–169)
Others have raised concerns about expectations related to interest inventories. Brandel (1982) reports a frustration in working with clients on vocational inventories, when, after being told the purposes of such instruments, clients later say that the inventory told them "what they were good at" or "what they should be" (p. 225). Krumboltz (1985) suggests that computerized systems may substantiate faulty expectations that clients hold by promising too much in the way of linking personality traits with a list of occupations. Seeing the test as the "authority" that will provide answers to life's questions has been identified as another faulty cognition (Knefelkamp & Slepitza, 1976).

According to Sampson, Peterson, and Reardon (1989), it is the counselor's responsibility to determine how appropriate a CACG might be for a particular client. This type of prescreening involves two factors: the degree to which a client's needs are congruent with the goals of the system and "the emotional, physical, and cognitive capacity of the client to use the CACG system" (Sampson, Peterson, & Reardon, 1989, pp. 146–147). If the counselor determines that an interaction with a CACG is appropriate, Sampson, Peterson, and Reardon (1989) suggest addressing the following seven main areas with the client prior to system use:

1. The potential benefits and limitations of using a particular CACG system;

2. Common client misperceptions (meta-cognitions) that the computer will provide a "magical" answer or that the computer can be the sole information resource for decision-making;

3. The fact that prior experience with computers is not required for successful CACG system use;

4. The importance of a "playful" risk-taking attitude toward career exploration, for example, generating diverse lists of occupations;

5. The importance of obtaining printouts of key CACG system displays, such as self-assessment, generation of occupational alternatives, and so forth;

6.   Confidentiality and computer record-keeping procedures, if available; and

Review of any available written introductory materials of exercises for the CACG system (pp. 145–147). With several of CACG systems available, it is helpful for consumers to have a way to compare the differences in features and costs. The Center for the Study of Technology in Counseling and Career Development at Florida State University has created a report that compares several systems (17 in 1998) on both college/adult systems and junior high/middle school systems. Included in the tables are comparisons of system content, user-friendly features, support materials and services available from developers, and costs. Also included are bibliographies for each of the systems and information on specific areas related to CACGS, such as ethical issues, disability issues, and multicultural issues. Interested parties can review this information at http://www.career.fsu.edu/techcenter/, as well as the most recent review of CACGs by these researchers. Sampson, Reardon, Norris et al. (1996) suggest that the purpose of this document is to enable consumers, CACG developers, policy makers, and researchers to "make important decisions concerning such systems" (p. 1). One important goal is finding a system that best meets their clients' needs. For example, certain areas may have a higher number of people interested or employed in military occupations and, therefore, would need a system with military occupations.

Using CACG in Counseling

Most CACG systems have different modules or sections that a counselor can use. A counselor should be thoroughly familiar with the different aspects of a CACG, as with any other assessment, before "prescribing" it as an intervention. "In terms of promoting career exploration and decision-making, a good CACG system that is poorly used may be no more effective than a poorly designed system" (Sampson & Norris, 1995, p. 3). Some systems develop a recommended pathway for clients based on how they respond to some introductory questions, such as "I need to choose a major" or "I have an occupation in mind and want to see how to prepare for it." At other times, the counselor could to suggest specific modules that might be most appropriate for the client, given the client's career development needs. As with any assessment, there are key points at which a counselor may choose to intervene.

Sampson, Peterson, and Reardon (1989) suggest five potential counseling intervention points, including before, during (including three midpoint interventions), and after CACG system use. Interventions occurring prior to system use prepare the client for successful use with the initial modules or sections of a CACG. When the counselor describes the specific components of a particular CACG system, "the client is then potentially better prepared conceptually to use the system, and more confident that he or she is capable of successful system use" (Sampson, Peterson, & Reardon, 1989, p. 147). The purpose of an intervention between CACG appointments would be to provide the client with the opportunity to discuss his or her progress with the CACG. It also allows for readjustment of the original plan for using a CACG. Sampson and Johnson (1993) suggest intervening after the search feature, after the typical information and preparation module, and after the decision-making module. When a client has finished using the system, an intervention allows the client to integrate what he or she has learned, where he or she is in the career planning process, and how he or she wants to proceed. Within each intervention, one purpose is to identify and correct client misperceptions, whether by clarifying their expectations of what using the CACG will be like (addressed during orientation); identifying and correcting dysfunctional ideas that could affect the self-assessment, search, and decision-making aspects of a CACG (which would be addressed during the midpoint interventions) (Sampson & Johnson, 1993); or reassessing potentially dysfunctional thoughts, such as "The test told me to be . . ." during an exit interview.

Online Assessments

The topic of internet career assessment is similar to the topic of diversity. While the prevalence and importance of these topics might, at first glance, suggest a separate chapter, isolating these topics from other issues is, in a sense, unnatural. Diversity is a natural part of each person, and should be considered when talking about interests, aptitudes, values, etc. Many of the inventories reviewed and listed throughout this text are available online and the online sites housing the inventories include supplementary activities and information. A good example of this is the Kuder Career Survey (Chapter 6). Once a client has completed the inventory, they have access to the Kuder site (www.kuder.com), read daily articles and learn about people who are in careers of interest.

While this may be the case, counselors should be aware of the ethical issues surrounding Internet testing (see Chapter 15). For example, online translations of paper and pencil inventories need to be validated and tested for reliability. Also, given that the Internet knows no geographic boundaries, online tests are available internationally. However, the same validation and reliability issues apply for tests originating in one country that are used in another. Counselors should remember that educational systems, occupational structures and options that are available in America may not be available to clients in other countries. Use of these inventories in a culturally inappropriate way may raise false hopes and expectations, or increase career confusion.

SIGI PLUS

SIGI (VALPAR, 2004) is a comprehensive, interactive CACG designed to help individuals with the process of making a career decision. SP consists of eight modules, from which users can select those most appropriate to their decision. The eight sections are Self-Assessment, Search, Information, Skills, Preparing, Coping, Deciding, and Next Steps. Users can exit the system at any point and can choose to have their records remain in case they want to return later. An online version is also available for institutional intranet use. Counselors can customize the online version, putting in their own URLs, or can link to other faculty, employers, and college alumni networks. Figure 11-1a-c shows screen shots of the SIGI Values card game, Information topics and a compare feature of the Information module.

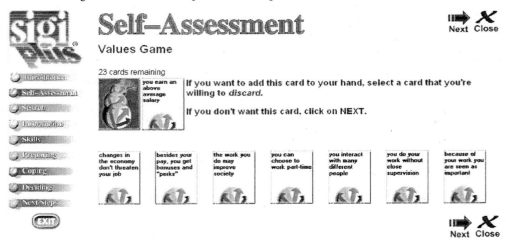

Figure 11-1a   SIGI Plus. Copyright © by Valpar International Corporation. Reprinted by permission.

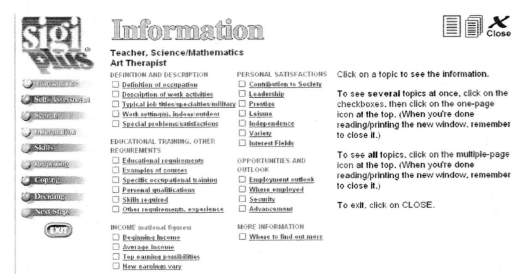

Figure 11-1b   SIGI Plus. Copyright © by Valpar International Corporation. Reprinted by permission.

Information

Teacher, Science/Mathematics	Art Therapist
Definition of occupation	
Instructs middle or junior high school students in physical and life sciences or mathematics. Instructs high school students in areas such as biology, chemistry, physics, earth and space sciences, algebra, geometry, trigonometry, calculus, discrete mathematics, probability, statistics and computer science. A few teach in elementary schools that have special, rather than regular classroom teachers for mathematics and/or science. For a video about Secondary School Teachers, see http://realvideo.acinet.org/ramgen/31308.rm. (If you encounter a technical problem, click Help or Introduction.)	Utilizes art media, creative art process and patient/client response to created art productions to treat and help rehabilitate individuals with mental, emotional, physical and developmental disorders. Determines and implements a client's therapeutic, school or mental health program. Helps clients communicate thoughts and feelings, resolve emotional conflicts, reduce anxiety, foster self-awareness, increase self-esteem, manage behavior and improve social skills. May work in individual, couple, family and/or group therapy formats. May work as primary therapist or as member of treatment team with psychiatrist, psychologist, social worker, medical doctor/nurse or educational personnel. May specialize in a particular setting, such as hospice and bereavement, or in one age/population group, such as geriatric or pediatric.
Variety	
A great amount	*A great amount*
Gradual change in students as they graduate or move out of town; differences in their backgrounds, interests and abilities. Problems vary every day. Scientific discoveries	Clients are of varying ages and come from wide variety of backgrounds; each has own set of problems and presents unique challenge. Therapist uses wide variety of

Figure 11-1c   SIGI Plus. Copyright © by Valpar International Corporation. Reprinted by permission.

The professional manual provides information about using SP with clients, interpreting SP printouts, and determining when certain modules of SP might be most helpful. Included is a training resource guide that contains several case studies, a bibliography of related research, and installation/operational information. A training video is also provided.

Case of an Occupation Explorer

Eugene wanted to see what occupations might be "good" for him. After talking with a counselor, Eugene agreed that SP might be a good place to start to help him organize information about himself and to generate some new options. Through Self-Assessment, Eugene learned that the values of security and independence were essential to him in his job. During Search, he identified occupations related to his major (English) and occupations that matched his two highest values (see Figure 11-2, next page). Once he had his list of occupations, he met with the counselor to discuss the options on his list. He went through his printout and crossed through the options that "just weren't him." The counselor asked him to go back through the ones he'd crossed out and discuss the reasons he crossed them off the list. The counselor wrote down the reasons and kept track of those that Eugene repeated.

The counselor then asked Eugene what he thought he needed to help him narrow down his options. Eugene stated that he needed to learn more about the occupations that were left on his list. He returned to SP and used the Information, Preparing, and Next Steps sections. At that point, he and the counselor created a plan of activities to help him decide among his options.

Eugene used information in the career center and narrowed his list to five options. At that point, he decided to meet with people who were involved in those five occupational fields to get a personal flavor of what each was like. The counselor encouraged Eugene to ask questions that were reflective of his values, such as, "It's important to me to have a great deal of variety on the job. How much variety do you have in your position?"

After the interviews, Eugene had narrowed his options to two and decided to revisit SP again. He used the Deciding section, which allowed him to weigh the pros and cons of each of his options. SP provided a framework for helping Eugene learn about himself, expand his career options, and focus on the occupations that most reflected his values.

Self-Assessment

Values

Here's how you weighted your Values. Later you can use your Important Values in

- **SEARCH**
- **INFORMATION**
- **DECIDING**

That's why you may want to **PRINT** this summary. **To** continue, click on **CLOSE.**

Values	Importance
Variety	E Essential
Independence	3 Very Important
Pleasant Co-Workers	3 Very Important
Leadership	3 Very Important
Fringe Benefits	3 Very Important
Contribution to Society	2 Desirable
Prestige	2 Desirable
Challenge	2 Desirable
Flexible Hours	2 Desirable
On-the-Job Learning	2 Desirable
Advancement	2 Desirable
Security	2 Desirable
Leisure	2 Desirable
High Income	2 Desirable
Easy Commute	1 Not Important
Staying Put	1 Not Important

Figure 11-2 SIGI Plus Values Listing. Copyright © by Valpar International Corporation. Reprinted by permission.

DISCOVER for Colleges and Adults

DISCOVER for Colleges and Adults (American College Testing Program, 2005) is a comprehensive CACG program designed to help individuals clarify their interests, abilities, experiences, and values and understand how they fit in the world of work. A sitemap of what DISCOVER offers is seen in Figure 11-3. Using DISCOVER has been shown to positively affect students' vocational identity (Barnes & Herr, 1998) and career maturity (Luzzo & Pierce, 1996).

Figure 11-3 DISCOVER Site Map. Copyright © 2005 by ACT, Inc. All rights reserved. Reproduced with permission.

Case of an Instructor Using DISCOVER in a Career Planning Course

As part of a career-planning course, students were instructed to complete the Career Journey Inventory in the *Career Planning Guidebook*. The lecture that followed focused on how jobs are organized in relation to the World-of-Work Map, explaining that by learning about their values, interests, skills, and other experiences, class members could see the "regions" that best "fit" them.

Class members were instructed to explore DISCOVER outside of class and to bring results of their inventories and occupational information printouts with them to the next meeting. Figure 11-4a and b include examples of the UNIACT Inventory and a portion of the information module.

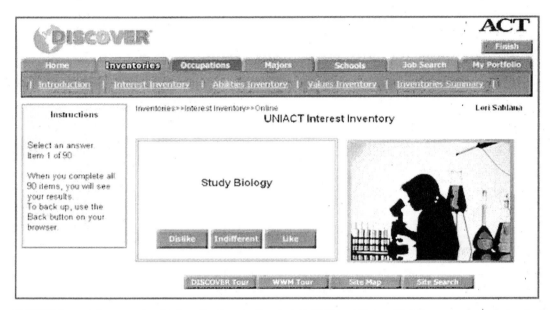

Figure 11-4a   DISCOVER Interest Assessment and Information Sample. Copyright © 2005 by ACT, Inc. All rights reserved. Reproduced with permission.

Figure 11-4b   DISCOVER Interest Assessment and Information Sample. Copyright © 2005 by ACT, Inc. All rights reserved. Reproduced with permission.

During class, the instructor divided the members into smaller groups and had them discuss where they were on the World-of-Work Map (see Figure 11-5) and what occupations they were currently considering. Before the next class, the instructor printed a batch report of users and tentative occupational choices to identify career areas that were of interest to most students. He then contacted several people in the fields of interest and invited them to come to class to discuss their work with interested students.

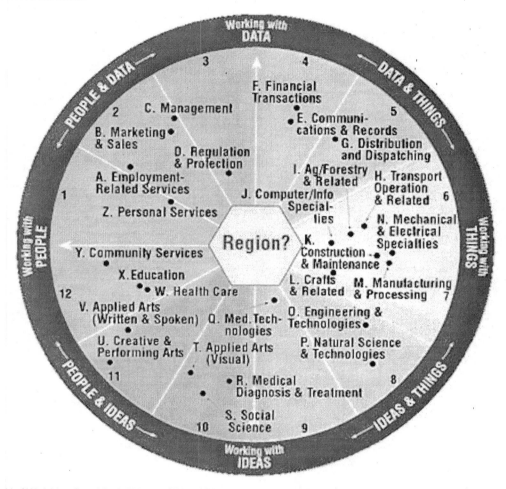

Figure 11-5 World-of-Work Map. Copyright © 2005 by ACT, Inc. All rights reserved. Reproduced with permission.

During the next several classes, students listened to and talked with the various representatives. Once these presentations were completed, the instructor had the students revisit DISCOVER and use Module Six to identify possible education and training paths to their careers of interest.

CHOICES

CHOICES (Bridges, 2005) is a CACG designed to help individuals explore occupational and educational options, divided into "work" and "learn" categories (see Figure 11-6, next page). The Interest Profile is set up in a "fun" format to which the person responds in one of five ways, ranging from "No Way" to "Love," while the Work Values Sorter is an online type of card sort (see Figure 11-7a and 11-7b, next page).

In addition to CHOICES and CHOICES CT, there is a middle school/junior high version called Career Futures and one of the first in elementary interest assessment and career guidance, "Paws in Jobland" (see Figure 11-8, next page). This elementary online career site has several "fun" interactive activities to enhance career exploration of elementary students.

A Client with Time Constraints

Myra, a 37-year-old architect has begun to consider a career change. "I like the creativity and seeing my ideas being transformed into reality, but I'm starting to grow tired of all the legal aspects that I have to work around, and the demands of customers. I'd like to find a job that would incorporate my creativity and something hands-on, but with less contact with people."

After talking with Myra, her counselor decided that taking an interest inventory might allow her to see where her interests cluster. "After we see where your main interests lie, we can then see what occupations use those interests. It would also be helpful for you to read about some of the occupations that emerge, as well as reorganizing your resumé and brushing up on interview skills."

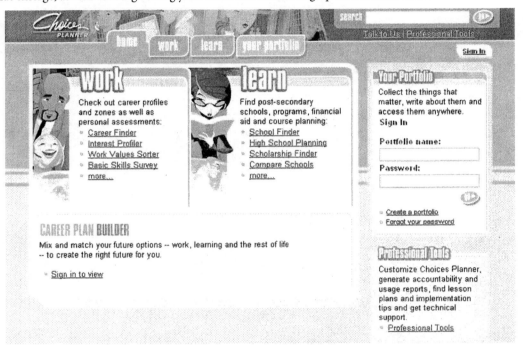

Figure 11-6   CHOICES Planner assessments main site. Reproduced with permission of the publisher, Bridges Transitions, Inc.

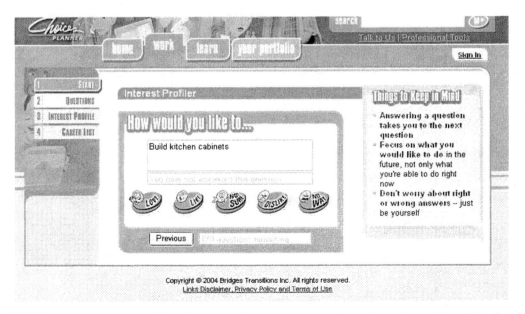

Figure 11-7a   CHOICES Interest Profiler Sample and Work Values Sorter Sample. Reproduced with permission of the publisher, Bridges Transitions, Inc.

"I think all of that's important, but it seems like it will take a lot of time—and that's one thing I don't have a lot of right now. I can barely find the time for my session with you, much less to be thumbing around on a computer or making appointments to talk with other people, unless they're willing to meet later at night or on the weekends." Myra seemed discouraged.

"I may have a solution that will help. We have a new program that allows our clients to take an interest inventory, ask career experts questions, and research occupations, either here in the office or at home. You can take the interest inventory at home and bring the results back for our next session. You can choose to go farther if you wish, but why don't we set taking the interest inventory as your goal to have completed by our next session."

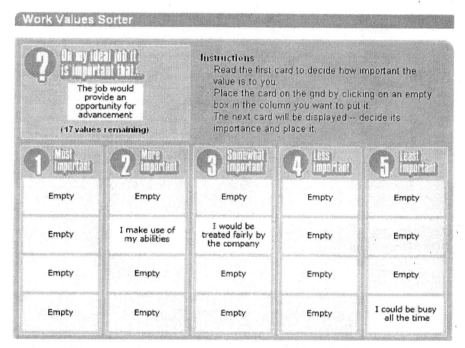

Figure 11-7b CHOICES Interest Profiler Sample and Work Values Sorter Sample. Reproduced with permission of the publisher, Bridges Transitions, Inc.

Figure 11-8 Paws in Jobland main site. Reproduced with permission of the publisher, Bridges Transitions, Inc.

The Career Key

The Career Key (Jones, 1990) is a career assessment tool with informational links provided as a public service free of charge on the Internet. After accessing the World Wide Web page, a person can take the Career Key inventory, learn about making career decisions, or identify jobs that link with assessment results. The questions on the inventory were developed to assess a person's resemblance to the six Holland types. The inventory consists of five checklists: 36 jobs (in which a person clicks on jobs that are appealing), interests, skills, how a person sees himself or herself, and values.

After the person completes the Career Key inventory, the computer scores the responses and creates a brief profile, indicating the scores (a three-letter code is not calculated). The person can then choose to see occupations that match his or her highest scored type. Occupations are classified by a method, developed by Jones (1980), that combines Holland's six types and the work groups of the *Guide for*

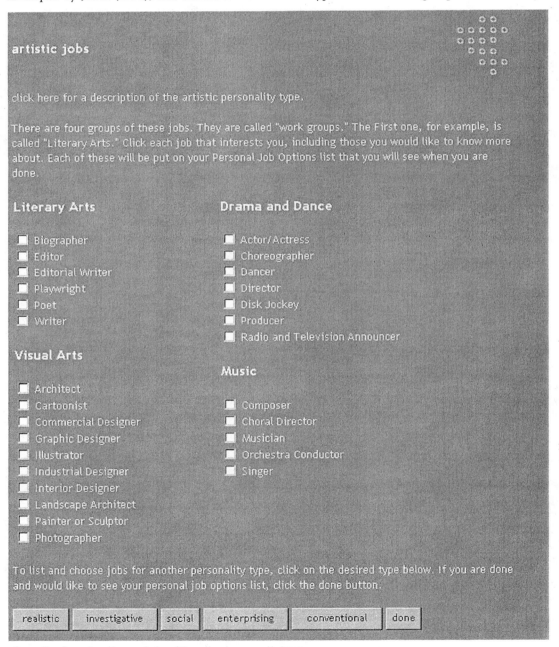

Figure 11-9   Career Key. Reproduced by permission of the author, Lawrence K. Jones.

Occupational Exploration. For example, Artistic occupations are divided into four GOE work groups: Literary Arts, Visual Arts, Drama and Dance, and Music (see Figure 11-9, which is taken from the part of the Career Key that was created to appeal to adults).

The person then clicks on occupations to consider for further exploration. A list of occupations can be compiled across the Holland types. Each occupation is linked to its particular page in the online *Occupational Outlook Handbook*, which allows users access to up-to-date information on jobs of interest. In addition, a person can save his or her document, and the hot-links are preserved.

Satisfactory validity and reliability, comparable to validity and reliability studies for the Self-Directed Search, were found for the original Career Key (Jones, 1990, 1993; Jones, Gorman, & Schroeder, 1989). According to Jones (1997), the major impetus for putting the Career Key on the Internet was to create a site that could be used by middle schoolers. Later, in 1999, the entire site was revised and now services middle school students through adults. In the most recent study (Jones, Sheffield, & Joyner, 2000) on the Career Key, researchers found that middle school students evaluated Career Key similarly to the Self-Directed Search Career Explorer and the Job-OE. In a similar study, Levinson, Zeman and Ohler (2002) compared the web-based version of Career Key with the SDS-Form R, and then took the Career Key 2 weeks later. They found retest reliability to range between .75 and .94, and validity coefficients at or above .65.

The availability of career inventories such as Career Key on the Internet is bound to increase. Although the validity of this instrument is satisfactory, there is no guarantee that every career inventory being placed on the Web will have adequate reliability and validity. This raises an ethical concern about people making career and life decisions based on the results of a report.

Professional counselors know to examine these issues before placing confidence in a test, but how often do clients ask for technical data about an instrument? A person using an inventory as a part of the counseling process has the benefit of a professional interpreting results and scales and can bring up issues not measured by the test. The Career Key contains a link to the developer's e-mail, which seems to be an ethically sound step. In addition, the site contains an online manual (reporting reliability and validity information), various educational modules, a decision-making guide and other helpful resources. Although the Career Key has an explicit statement about privacy and disclosure, many online, free career "tests" do not. This issue of confidentiality is yet another issue to consider; there is a potential for abuse anytime a user provides personal information on the Internet. These concerns and others will need to be addressed by professional organizations in the very near future.

Case of a Determined Middle-Schooler

A middle-schooler came into his counselor's office one day, asking for a career test. He wanted to see what occupations might fit his personality and to learn about those occupations. Unfortunately, the computers at the middle school did not have the memory needed to run career programs. The counselor suggested the student visit the local library, access the Career Key on the Internet, and then make an appointment with her to discuss the results. After the student returned from the library with his printouts, he made an appointment with the counselor.

COUNSELOR: Tell me about your experience at the library.

MATIAS: Well, the librarian showed me how to get on the Web, and from there, it was pretty easy. I took the Career Key and it showed me that my main group is Realistic.

COUNSELOR: What does that mean to you?

MATIAS: Well, it means that I like to do things with my hands, and I like to see things happen. It's neat, because that's what my dad and grandpa are into as well.

COUNSELOR: And what about the occupations it suggested?

MATIAS: They seemed OK. After I got my list, I picked some careers that really looked good to me, and when I clicked on them, it took me to another area that told all about them. It was really cool!

COUNSELOR: Well, where do you think you want to go from here?

MATIAS: Right now, I think I want to keep going with this hands-on stuff. I really like it, and I think I'm good at it, too. So, I guess for my elective, I'm going to look at either mechanics, shop, or maybe computers. I'm gonna talk with my Dad as well about maybe helping out in the shop, too.

In this case, the use of the Career Key helped Matias to learn about his personality, as well as occupations of interests, and to make some educational plans to further clarify that knowledge. Counselors who suggest an Internet tool should be familiar with it themselves and be willing to help the client interpret and use the results.

Other CACG Systems

In addition to the CACGs reviewed in the chapter, several other systems are described briefly in this section.

- **Career Explorer (CX online).** Created for middle-high school students, CX online includes a plethora of information, including over 900 career profiles, over 200 career videos (including Spanish videos), expert interviews, a college student diary, a portfolio system and varied articles.

- **Career Information System.** This system incorporates the IDEAS assessment, and also includes a Spanish occupation sort. Described are 367 occupational categories, with additional information provided on industries, self-employment, military, job search, researching employers. Several modules on education and training are included. Although this system has some Oregon-specific information, its usefulness extends to other states as well.

- COIN. This career guidance system provides a self-assessment and information on an impressive number of occupations. It is available for Windows, Macintosh, and DOS. A middle-school version, COIN JR., is also available, as are systems for earlier levels, including COIN CLIMB K-2, COIN CLIMB 3-5, and COIN CLUE 5-6.

- **Making Better Career Decisions (MBCD).** An Internet-based career planning system, available at http://web.mscc.huji.ac.il/es/cddq/mbcd-g-i.htm, created by Gati at the Hebrew University. The 90-minute assessment (called a "dialogue") results in a listing of potential occupations and majors for further exploration. Gati, Kleiman, Saka and Zakai (2003) reported that the MBCD increased decidedness for about half of 712 participants.

- O*NET Inventories. This website (http://www.onetcenter.org/tools.html) includes links to the following career exploration tools: O*NET Ability Profiler, Interest Profiler, Computerized Interest Profiler, Work Importance Locator and Work Importance Profiler.

- OSCAR. Short for "Orientation System for Careers", OSCAR (http://oscar.nie.edu.sg/) is an online interactive career system developed in Singapore with the purpose to encourage exploration versus prescribing a career. It renames Holland's Realistic, Artistic and Conventional types as "Practical," "Creative" and "Administrative" types. Within the information section, pictures of Singapore workers are included.

- Vocopher. A professional website for researchers and counselors, available at www.vocopher.com. The site currently houses several versions of the Career Development Inventory, the Adult Career Concerns Inventory and the Career Maturity inventory.

Summary

In this chapter, we explored the use of CACGS and Internet assessments as viable tools in counseling. CACGS allow individuals to quickly expand their career options by seeing what occupations "match" their values, interests, and skills. As with any psychometric instrument, a counselor should be familiar with the different components a CACG or Internet assessment offers and should take all associated assessments before asking a client to do the same. CACGS can hold immense amounts of data about occupations. The counselor must help clients make sense of the data and use the data in a way that helps them progress toward their career goals. Finally, the counselor should be knowledgeable of the ethical issues involved with CACG and Internet career testing.

Questions and Exercises

1. A woman trying to choose a career path comes to you with her printout of occupations. How do you proceed?

2. What are the pros and cons associated with having a client use a CACG or online assessment versus a traditional interest inventory?

3. What would you say to a person who came to your counseling office and said, "I heard there was a computer that will tell me what I should be?"

4. What type of client characteristics might suggest that a CACG is not an appropriate tool?

5. Suppose your organization is thinking about purchasing a new CACG. Create a plan for selecting, implementing and evaluating the new system.

6. A student has come to you for help in making a career choice. He is a member of the 4-H club, volunteers for a charity that builds homes for disadvantaged people, and enjoys drawing, especially during his business class. While working on Career Targets within COINJR, the counselor comes by and sees the screen in Figure 11-10. Based on the career clusters, how would you characterize this student's interests? What occupations might link with his interests? What advice might you give this student in narrowing down his options? What type of counseling interventions would you make with this student that would help him progress? What type of interventions would coincide with his interests? How would your counseling style change? What other information would you like to have about this student?

7. Given the Self-Assessment Values summary of SIGI PLUS shown in Figure 11-11, how would you proceed in advising/counseling Jason? What types of rewards are likely to motivate for him on the job?

8. Figure 11-12 holds the results of a student's Career Finder inventory. What observations can you make about this person, how she might be in counseling, and potential next steps?

9. A middle-school student's Career Key results are presented in Figure 11-13. What next steps might you suggest?

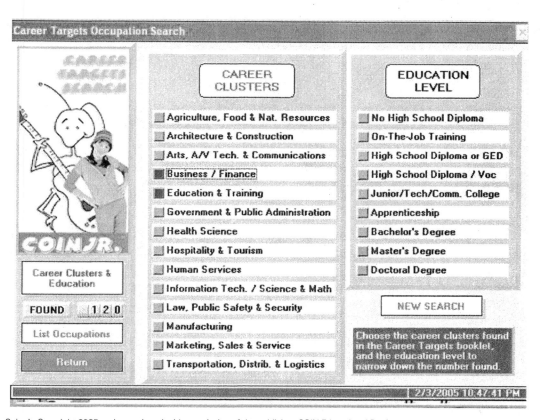

Figure 11-10   Coin Jr. Copyright 2005 and reproduced with permission of the publisher, COIN Educational Products.

Self-Assessment

Values

Here's how you weighted your Values. Later you can use your important Values in

- **SEARCH**
- **INFORMATION**
- **DECIDING**

That's why you may want to **PRINT** this summary. **To continue, click on CLOSE.**

Values	Importance
Variety	E Essential
Independence	3 Very Important
Pleasant Co-Workers	3 Very Important
Leadership	3 Very Important
Fringe Benefits	3 Very Important
Contribution to Society	2 Desirable
Prestige	2 Desirable
Challenge	2 Desirable
Flexible Hours	2 Desirable
On-the-Job Learning	2 Desirable
Advancement	2 Desirable
Security	2 Desirable
Leisure	2 Desirable
High Income	2 Desirable
Easy Commute	1 Not Important
Staying Put	1 Not Important

Figure 11-11   SIGI Plus Values. Copyright © by Valpar International Corporation. Reprinted by permission.

Results 1-20 of 486 Next > Career and description	Highest Level Basic Skills
<u>Aircraft Pilot</u> -- Flies airplanes and helicopters to carry out a wide variety of tasks, such as transporting passengers and cargo, dusting crops, spreading seed for reforestation, testing aircraft, tracking criminals, monitoring traffic, and rescuing and evacuating injured persons.	Active learning Active listening
<u>Anesthesiologist</u> -- Administers anesthetics during surgery or other medical procedures.	Active learning Active listening
<u>Artillery Officer ... (Military - Officer)</u> -- Directs artillery crew members as they position, maintain, and fire guns, cannons, howitzers, and rockets at enemy positions and aircraft.	Active learning Active listening
<u>Audiologist/Speech Pathologist</u> -- Examines and provides remedial services for persons with speech and hearing disorders.	Active learning Active listening
<u>Biomedical Equipment Repairer</u> -- Installs, tests, adjusts, and repairs electronic and electrical medical equipment, such as patient monitors, EKG equipment, x-ray units, defibrillators, anesthesia apparatus, and sterilizers, in hospitals or other health care facilities.	Active learning Active listening
<u>Cartographer</u> -- Collects and analyzes geographic data from geodetic surveys, aerial photographs, satellites images, and global positioning systems.	Active learning Active listening
<u>Chemical Equipment Operator</u> -- Operates equipment to control chemical changes or reactions in the processing of industrial or consumer products.	Active learning Active listening
<u>Civil Engineer</u> -- Performs engineering duties in planning, designing, and overseeing the construction and maintenance of structures and facilities such as roads, airports, bridges, dams, pipelines, power plants, and water and sewage systems.	Active learning Active listening
<u>Civil Engineering Technician</u> -- Applies theories and principles of civil engineering in planning, designing, and overseeing the construction and maintenance of structures and facilities, under the direction of engineering staff or physical scientists.	Active learning Active listening
<u>Commercial and Industrial Designer</u> -- Develops and designs manufactured products such as cars, home appliances, and children's toys.	Active learning Active listening
<u>Computer Security Specialist</u> -- Coordinates and implements security	Active learning

Figure 11-12 Career Finder. Reproduced with permission of the publisher, Bridges Transitions, Inc.

your personal job options list

the career key

enrico ,

Below you will find the six different personality types, your score for each type (if you took the test), and the list of related jobs that you chose for each type. To learn more about a job, simply click on the job title and you will be directed to a job description provided by the Occupational Outlook Handbook. You may print your results by choosing the print command from your browser's menu. When you are done viewing these results, please return to "your choices ..." to explore the rest of the Career Key website.

realistic = 7	investigative = 16	artistic = 9
Engineers	Chemist	Writers and editors,
Television-Radio Repairer	Oceanographers	including technical writers
Electrician	Space Scientist	Cartoonist
	Conservation Scientist	Dancer
	Audiologist	Singer
	Dentist	
	Pharmacist	
	Actuary	
	Computer Programmer	

social = 9	enterprising = 5	conventional = 2

Figure 11-13   Career Key. Reproduced by permission of the author, Lawrence K. Jones.

12 Using Assessment for People with Disabilities and the Academically Disadvantaged

Since the early 1970s, attention has been focused on rehabilitation services for people with physical and mental disabilities and on career counseling programs for people who are academically disadvantaged. Career assessment for people with disabilities first began within the field of vocational rehabilitation. The original purpose was to identify individuals who were eligible for state and federal rehabilitation services and to identify what specific services each individual needed to be successfully placed in a job (McCray, 1982). The major goal of these services and programs was and is to maximize each individual's potential for employment. F. R. Albritton (personal communication, October 29, 1996) cautions that a major criticism of special vocational assessments designed for people with disabilities has been that they tend to focus on a person's weaknesses, rather than on the person's strengths, whereas the reality is that people get hired because of their strengths, not their weaknesses. Therefore, when interpreting a client's profile to the client, a counselor should help the client focus on his or her strengths and how to enhance other skills. In support of this point of view, one study examined the top five jobs people with varying disabilities obtained and found a great deal of similarity, suggesting that the more important factor was functional ability, rather than type of disability (Walls & Fullmer, 1997). This might be true, but it might also suggest that the envelope needs to continue to be pushed on the types of jobs that are available and encouraged for people with disabilities (Sowers, Cotton, & Malloy, 1994).

As the national trend has been toward including those with disabilities in educational and work settings, vocational assessment of people with disabilities has become more prominent (Levinson, 1994). During the past ten years, two main public laws, the Carl D. Perkins Vocational Education Act (P.L. 98-524) and the Individuals with Disabilities Education Act (IDEA) (P.L. 94-142), were passed, requiring equal access to training and employment for people with disabilities and people who are disadvantaged. These and other legislation, including the American with Disabilities Act of 1990 (P.L. 101–336), have led to intense scrutiny of assessment methods and procedures.

Chartrand and Rose (1996) defined *at-risk* as "persons who, because of political, economic, social, and cultural conditions, have limited access to educational and occupational opportunities" (p. 341). Albritton (personal communication, October 17, 1996) defined *disadvantage* as any need that is not being met or any force (external or internal) that gets in the way of a person's reaching his or her career or educational goal(s). Often, people who are disadvantaged have problems in career development and finding work because of a "cycle of poverty and other social problems," such as discrimination (Chartrand & Rose, 1996, p. 342). In one study, Jones and Womble (1998) found that even though at-risk students had positive perceptions about school and careers, many believed their career options were limited because of gender or ethnicity. Hackett and Byars (1996) state that this might affect clients' beliefs about the likelihood that their efforts will be rewarded by society.

In this case, Chartrand and Rose (1996) suggest that "traditional interest exploration may be necessary but not sufficient" (p. 344). Instead, a counselor might have to explore clients' beliefs about the likelihood that society will let them achieve their goals. The diverse needs of people with disabilities and people who are disadvantaged might require specially designed assessment instruments to assist them in career planning.

How do the beliefs of rehabilitation personnel and employers compare regarding the barriers to employment that people with disabilities or disadvantages encounter? According to Fabian, Luecking, and Tilson (1995), there was some discrepancy between what rehabilitation personnel and employers identified as barriers. Many rehabilitation personnel identified factors associated with the economy, such as lack of jobs and poor economy, whereas many employers referred to lack of job training and information about people with disabilities. In a similar study (Michaels & Risucci, 1993) specifically focusing on people with traumatic brain injuries, rehabilitation personnel were more likely to cite functional limitations as the most problematic factor, whereas employers most often cited poor work performance. In addition, the rehabilitation counselors were more likely to rate accommodations as more problematic than did employers. These studies both serve as helpful reminders that helping professionals, whether school, mental health, career, or rehabilitation counselors, need to be aware of their own biases and be very careful not to assume that others hold the same opinion.

The challenge of meeting people's special needs is complicated by the fact that both people with disabilities and people who are disadvantaged have a variety of ethnic and racial backgrounds. It has been claimed that many tests are discriminatory because their norms are based on white, male, middle-class individuals and, therefore, do not account for the unique characteristics of other cultural and ethnic groups or the special needs of people with disabilities. In fact, a main criticism of career development research is the neglect of "empirical research" for those who are at-risk (Fitzgerald & Betz, 1994). The issue of test discrimination will no doubt affect the future research efforts of numerous individuals in the counseling profession.

Counselors can use several different ways to help a person with a disability explore career options and make career decisions. Figure 12-1 (next page) shows an early model of career intervention with populations who are disadvantaged. These interventions include interviews, observations, written tests, performance tests, work samples, and situational assessments (Levinson, 1994). Performance tests are "manipulative tests that minimize the use of language . . . usually designed to assess specific abilities related to the performance of a job" (Levinson, 1994, p. 95).

Work samples involve having an individual complete selected tasks that are required by a particular occupation, such as typing a letter or answering a phone (secretarial work sample) or changing a tire (automotive work sample). According to Levinson (1994), there are three general phases of work samples, beginning with demonstration, followed by training, and ending with performance of the tasks. Situational assessment techniques involve placing clients in either a real or a simulated work setting and then having them be evaluated by peers or supervisors via observation, interviews, and rating scales. The purpose of situational assessment techniques is to identify a person's interests and aptitudes and demonstrated work habits. They are best used in conjunction with formal assessments.

According to Albritton (personal communication, October 17, 1996), the current focus is on the transferability of skills for people in vocational rehabilitation, individuals with a developmental disability, or those classified as disadvantaged. Figure 12-2 (next page) shows a condensed version of the Transferability of Skills Matrix. The purpose of this type of worksheet is to gain information about the client's history and to make educated projections for future satisfying occupations. This profile is also used to determine how much money the individual was making before the disability and to project what the person would be making during the rest of his or her employed life. The Transferability of Skills Worksheet analyzes GED levels, aptitudes, physical demands, environmental conditions, temperaments, and GOE interests areas for a person's successful jobs and then summarizes the highest levels of performance and overall temperaments and interests. These data can be entered into one of several computer systems that will "dump" a list of occupational options that match the person's summarized strengths and preferences. For a more complete review of using transferable skills and abilities profiles, see Saxon and Spitznagel (1995).

Levinson (1994) describes a "comprehensive vocational assessment" as including psychological, social, educational-academic, physical-medical, and vocational functioning assessments. Table 12-1 (after next page) shows specific elements that could be measured within these assessments. Within the field of counseling, it is becoming more and more evident that career decisions do not occur in a box, isolated from all other areas of a person's life. If a person has just lost his or her job, one could expect there to be an impact on that person's psychological functioning (self-esteem, anger, depression), and perhaps an impact on the family as well. In addition, if that person was unable to find work for a while or had been a significant financial contributor to the family, other demands such as for rent, food, and transportation could become more pertinent. Take this same situation and apply it to a person who has just acquired a disability or who is disadvantaged, and the effects become more complex.

Career Research on Specific Disabilities

Learning disabilities are one of the most common disabilities reported on college campuses. Several different studies have been conducted on the influence of a learning disability on career-related factors.

In their study, Hitchings, Luzzo, Retish, Horvath, and Ristow (1998) found that students with learning disabilities had more difficulties compared with students with other disabilities when asked to describe how their disability affected their indecision. According to Adelman and Vogel (1990), the most common difficulty of 89 college-educated workers with learning disabilities was processing difficulties. Some examples were retention, time required to finish work, and number or letter reversals.

MODEL FOR VOCATIONAL EVALUATION
OF THE DISADVANTAGED

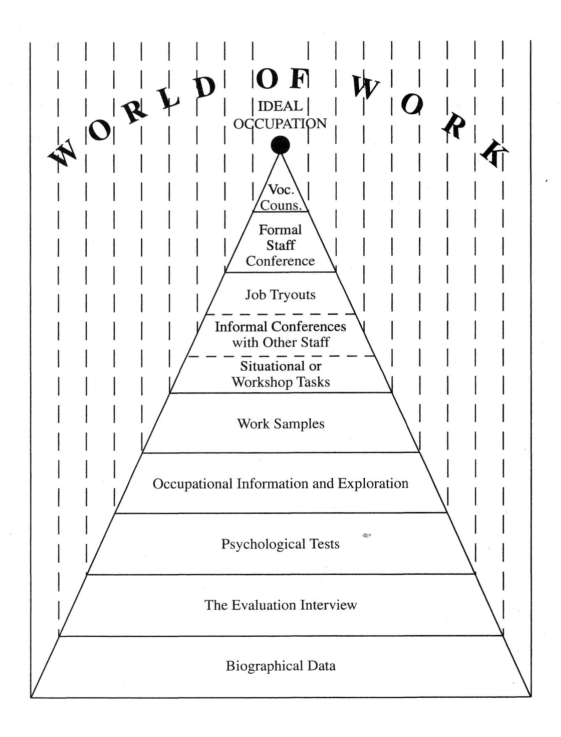

Figure 12-1 Model for Vocational Evaluation from Department of Health, Education, and Welfare, supported by research grant #12-p-55140/4-0Y, Julian Nadolsky, principal investigator.

Client's Name ______________________________

	D.O.T. Code #	D.O.T. TITLE		Code	Code	SVP Duration (1-9) D	GED (1 — 6) (Low) (High) Reasoning R	Math M	Language L	APTITUDES (low) 5 4 3 2 1 (high) Intelligence G	Verbal V	Numerical N	Spatial Perception S	Form Perception P	Clerical Perception Q	Motor Coordination K	Finger Dexterity F	Manual Dexterity M	Eye/Hand/Foot Coord. E	Color Discrimination C
WORK HISTORY			1																	
			2																	
			3																	
			4																	
			5																	
			6																	
			7																	
	Pre-Vocational Profile (Summary Of Job History)																			
	Worker Traits To Be Evaluated (check)																			
	Residual Functional Capacity (Transferability To Current Level Of Functioning)																			
	Consultants Reports & Vocational/Assessment Procedures Utilized (footnote)																			
JOB POSSIBILITIES			1																	
			2																	
			3																	
			4																	
			5																	
			6																	
			7																	
VOCATIONAL OUTCOME			1																	
			2																	
			3																	
			4																	
			5																	
			6																	
			7																	

FOOTNOTES on Consultant's Reports & Vocational/Assessment Procedures

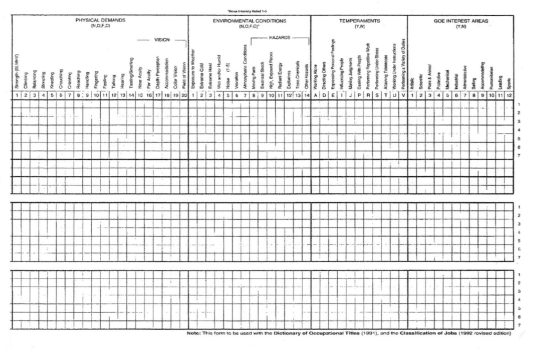

Figure 12-2a Transferability of Skills Matrix. Copyright © 1992 Elliott & Fitzpatrick, Inc. Reprinted by permission.

*Noise Intensity Rated 1-5

PHYSICAL DEMANDS (N,O,F,C)

	1 Strength (SLMHV)	2 Climbing	3 Balancing	4 Stooping	5 Kneeling	6 Crouching	7 Crawling	8 Reaching	9 Handling	10 Fingering	11 Feeling	12 Talking	13 Hearing	14 Tasting/Smelling	15 Near Acuity (VISION)	16 Far Acuity (VISION)	17 Depth Perception (VISION)	18 Accommodation (VISION)	19 Color Vision (VISION)	20 Field of Vision (VISION)
1																				
2																				
3																				
4																				
5																				
6																				
7																				
1																				
2																				
3																				
4																				
5																				
6																				
7																				
1																				
2																				
3																				
4																				
5																				
6																				
7																				

ENVIRONMENTAL CONDITIONS (N,O,F,C)*

	1 Exposure to Weather	2 Extreme Cold	3 Extreme Heat	4 Wet and/or Humid	5 Noise (1-5)	6 Vibration	7 Atmospheric Conditions	8 Moving Parts (HAZARDS)	9 Electrical Shock (HAZARDS)	10 High, Exposed Places (HAZARDS)	11 Radiant Energy (HAZARDS)	12 Explosives (HAZARDS)	13 Toxic Chemicals (HAZARDS)	14 Other Hazards (HAZARDS)
1														
2														
3														
4														
5														
6														
7														
1														
2														
3														
4														
5														
6														
7														
1														
2														
3														
4														
5														
6														
7														

TEMPERAMENTS (Y,N)

	A Working Alone	D Directing Others	E Expressing Personal Feelings	I Influencing People	J Making Judgments	P Dealing With People	R Performing Repetitive Work	S Performing Under Stress	T Attaining Tolerances	U Working Under Instructions	V Performing a Variety of Duties
1											
2											
3											
4											
5											
6											
7											
1											
2											
3											
4											
5											
6											
7											
1											
2											
3											
4											
5											
6											
7											

GOE INTEREST AREAS (Y,N)

	1 Artistic	2 Scientific	3 Plant & Animal	4 Protective	5 Mechanical	6 Industrial	7 Administrative	8 Selling	9 Accommodating	10 Humanitarian	11 Leading	12 Sports
1												
2												
3												
4												
5												
6												
7												
1												
2												
3												
4												
5												
6												
7												
1												
2												
3												
4												
5												
6												
7												

Note: This form to be used with the **Dictionary of Occupational Titles** (1991), and the **Classification of Jobs** (1992 revised edition)

Figure 12-2b Transferability of Skills Matrix. Copyright © 1992 Elliott & Fitzpatrick, Inc. Reprinted by permission.

<table>
<tr><td colspan="2">**Table 12-1**   **Elements for a Comprehensive Vocational Assessment**</td></tr>
</table>

Psychological Functioning	Vocational Functioning
• Intelligence/Cognitive Abilities	• Interests
• Needs	• Aptitude
• Values	• Career Maturity
• Temperament	• Work Habits
• Behavioral Tendencies	
	Physical Functioning
Educational/Academic Functioning	• Vision
• Language Skills	• Hearing
• Reading Skills	• Strengths
• Computational Skills	• Endurance
• General Knowledge	• Dexterity
	• Health
Social Functioning	
• Social/Interpersonal Skills	
• Independent Living Skills	
• Adaptive Behavior	

"Current vocational Assessment Models for Students with Disabilities" by E.M. Levinson, 1994, Journal of Counseling and Development, 73, pp. 94-101.

These individuals used the following strategies to help them complete their work: taking extra time to complete the work, asking for help, and taking extra care to monitor for errors. With respect to career maturity, Ohler, Levinson, and Barker (1996) found that there were different predictors for those with learning disabilities (versus those without), including the quantity of work experiences and the number of accommodations predicting high maturity. Rojewski (1996) found that when compared with students without learning disabilities, those with learning disabilities tended to aspire to lower-prestige careers (especially females), and were more likely to be indecisive. There is a noticeable lack of research on career-related factors and people with specific disabilities. There is also a relative lack of career inventories created for people with specific disabilities, such as visual disabilities. The SDS does have a Braille-version, but it is only one example.

Elements for a Comprehensive Vocational Assessment

People with disabilities might be able to use interest, personality, and values inventories that were normed on non-disabled individuals. On the other hand, as it would be presumptuous to automatically conclude that these instruments yield equivalent, non-discriminatory results for minorities, it would also be irresponsible to make the same assumption for people with disabilities. In addition, even within minority groups, several subgroups exist, such as Chicano and Latino within the Hispanic culture. We do not assume that all Hispanics have the same career values, goals, and decision-making styles. The same is true for people with disabilities. Instead of lumping every person with a disability into one general category, it might be useful to examine the unique experiences of specific disabilities on career-related issues. Gillies, Knight, and Baglioni (1998) found that people with visual impairments (versus those without) were less satisfied with their career development and training and support they had received. A 20-year study (Crewe, 2000) on the work outcomes of people with spinal cord impairments showed that 74% were working either full or part time, with the majority working full time. Crewe cited the following factors as contributing to the vocational success of this group: having early work experiences, comprehensive rehabilitation services, and holding a strong work ethic. People with disabilities might benefit from using the same assessments that people without disabilities use to identify interests, values, personality dimensions, or career decision-making difficulties.

For example, a comparison of Career Maturity Inventory scores between students with disabilities and those without a disability yielded no significant differences (Hitchings, Luzzo, Retish, Horvath, & Ristow, 1998). Similarly, Alston and Burkhead (1989) found that type of disability had no significant effect on career indecision. In another study on career maturity, Ohler, Levinson, and Barker (1996) found that there were no differences in career maturity for those with learning disabilities and those without. A third study found no differences between work salience for people with visual impairments and those without visual impairments (Gillies, Knight, & Baglioni, 1998). On the other hand, some studies have shown people with disabilities to have higher career indecision (Enright, 1996) and lower career decision-making self-efficacy (Luzzo, Hitchings, Retish, & Shoemaker, 1999; Mazurek & Shumaker, 1997). As a side note, Thompson and Dickey (1994) found that the following factors positively affected the self-perceptions of individuals with disabilities: being satisfied with college major, knowing what type of job to seek following graduation, having paid work experience, and having an acquired (versus congenital) disability.

The instruments we review in this chapter were designed specifically for those who are either academically disadvantaged or have a disability. In the first part of this chapter, examples of tests and inventories designed specifically for people who are academically disadvantaged are reviewed. In the second part, specially designed measuring instruments for people with disabilities are discussed.

Specifically, the chapter reviews two achievement tests and one interest inventory for people who are academically disadvantaged and for individuals who have disabilities. Also, a prevocational information battery that measures skills considered important for employability and one work sample test for use with people with disabilities is reviewed. Sample cases illustrate the use of assessment for these groups. The tests described in this chapter can be supplemented when appropriate with some of the inventories and tests discussed previously.

Adult Basic Learning Examination (ABLE)

ABLE was designed to measure the general educational level of adults who have not completed high school. It is used to determine achievement ranging from the primary grades to the 12th-grade level and can be used for educational planning or training for job placement. Three levels have been developed: level I (grades 1–4), level II (grades 5–8), and level III (grades 9–12). Two forms are available for each level. Levels I and II are not timed; level III is timed, but the time limits allow most individuals to complete the test. Currently counselors can administer ABLE to clients to help determine which level is appropriate. Split-half reliabilities are satisfactory; they tend to be in the .80s and .90s for each subtest. Correlations between ABLE and the Stanford Achievement Test subtests are primarily in the .70s.

ABLE measures achievement in vocabulary, reading comprehension, spelling, number operations, and problem solving. The test was not designed to be a diagnostic instrument in that the results do not reveal specific weaknesses in any of the areas tested. The test was constructed to cover typical adult problems, tasks, and activities; for example, newspaper articles are used in the reading section of the test. The authors report that the questions in the test help establish rapport between the individual and the counselor because they are common problems encountered by many adults.

Interpreting the ABLE

Although the norms are based on 4000 adults in various settings in 41 states, the authors of ABLE strongly suggest that, for meaningful interpretation, local normative samples be established whenever possible. This point is well founded; because of the great diversity in the adult population, normative samples for adults should be carefully scrutinized before making any significant career decisions based on test scores. Every effort should be made to find a norm population that closely matches the individual being tested in ethnic background, experience, and training.

Table 12-2 provides some descriptive information on adult samples; this information should be carefully considered for all achievement tests designed for adult use. The ABLE manual does an excellent job in describing the adult population used in the development of ABLE. In addition, each subgroup is clearly described—for example, the high school equivalency candidates in a particular section of a state. The descriptive information on sex, age, race, socioeconomic status, and educational background should allow a counselor to determine whether the local adult population matches the test sample closely enough to provide meaningful interpretations of the test results.

An important characteristic of ABLE test results is that they correspond to Stanford Achievement Test results—that is, scores from ABLE can be converted to Stanford Achievement Test score equivalents. With this conversion, the counselor has access to a vast amount of information on school achievement available from research conducted with the Stanford test.

ABLE is well constructed and meets its primary goal of measuring levels of achievement of adult groups. Reviews of ABLE are provided by Anastasi (1988), Fitzpatrick (1992), and Williams (1992, 1994). According to Williams (1994), ABLE scores can be used in a variety of ways in career counseling, including "assessing functional literacy, employability skills, and ability to profit from training" (p. 60).

Table 12-2	**Adult Samples for Achievement Tests**
Number of Cases:	Each subtest should have an adequate number of samples that match the group in characteristics to be tested.
Sex and Age:	Each subtest should contain balanced numbers from each sex. Age distributions by percentage of representation from age ranges should resemble the groups to be tested. For example, what percentage of the sample was in the 50-and-over range, and what was the median age range?
Race:	There should be an adequate number of ethnic groups represented in each subtest. The standard group should consist of the same ethnicities or races as the examinees.
Educational Level:	Determine the median grade level of the standard group. Each educational level should contain adequate samples of both sexes and ethnic groups.
Place of Residence:	The sample group should be representative of the persons with whom the examinees are compared. The backgrounds of the sample members should be consistent with potential users.
Socioeconomic Status:	Socioeconomic backgrounds should be consistent with potential users. Should one use assessment results whose scores were developed from a predominantly male urban, white middle class for a female who is an ethnic minority from a rural poor background?

In summary, seek the answers to the following questions:

Is the sample representative of my clients?

Does the sample include enough cases?

Does the sample group consist of the sort of person with whom my clients can be compared?

Is the sample appropriately subdivided?

Case of a School Dropout Seeking Work

Gus had a poor educational background. During Gus's school years, the truant officer was constantly after him. Gus disliked school so much that he ran away from home and worked for several years as an able seaman in the merchant marine. The counselor tried to make Gus feel comfortable when he reported for his first session. It was apparent that Gus felt out of place. Gus needed placement in a local job because he had the responsibility of taking care of his aging parents and maintaining their home. However, the counselor was concerned about Gus's educational background and decided that some measure of his academic abilities was necessary. The counselor planned to administer the ABLE to determine whether Gus had the educational background required for employment in a local firm. Because ABLE provides measures of spelling, reading, and numerical competence, the counselor had discovered that a total battery score provided a fairly reliable estimate of an individual's ability to perform in local industry. Fortunately, the counselor had collected data from and developed local norms based on individuals placed in this firm.

When Gus was first approached about the possibility of taking an achievement test, he was intimidated. The counselor explained that the test was designed to cover typical adult problems, tasks, and activities and was not like a test that a student would take in high school. She also added that the scores would help her determine whether Gus was capable of working at a local firm. Gus's anxiety was somewhat lowered by this explanation; he was particularly interested in placement in the local firm, for he had heard that working conditions were fairly good and the pay was reasonable.

Working there, he reasoned, would provide him with an outside income to maintain a home. The results of ABLE indicated that Gus's chances of success in the local firm were fairly good; he scored in the fifth stanine with the local norms developed by the counselor.

COUNSELOR: Your scores are in the average range compared with others from our community who has taken this test during the last eight years. This indicates to me that you have a fairly good chance of being successful in the local firm we have discussed. However, if you want to move up in the firm, you will need further training in the basics such as reading and arithmetic.

GUS: It has been a mighty long time since I have taken a test like this. I don't know what to say except that I was able to do a little studying on my own when I wasn't doing my chores, and I would like very much to improve my reading, spelling, and arithmetic skills.

The counselor explained to Gus that, even though the test was a fairly good indication of his ability to compete in the local firm, he would have to adjust to a working environment that was different from the one he was accustomed to. She explained that he now would be working with people whose values might be quite different from his. The counselor offered to help Gus adjust to the new working environment and to provide him with suggestions for upgrading his educational skills.

In this case, results from ABLE not only were used as a link to local employment but also provided a basis for discussing adjustments to a new working environment. In addition, the test results provided an opening for the counselor to discuss the importance of upgrading basic educational skills for occupational mobility.

Wide Range Interest-Opinion Test (WRIOT II)

The WRIOT (Jastak & Jastak, 1979) is a pictorial interest inventory developed for measuring interests and attitudes (motivators) of people who are academically disadvantaged and people with severe disabilities. The 450 pictures of people engaged in a variety of activities are presented in groups of 3 (150 combinations); the individual chooses the most liked and the least liked. The picture format of the WRIOT means that reading ability is not required. In fact, the manual reports that it has been used successfully with deaf and blind populations. The activities portrayed in the pictures come from a wide range of unskilled, technical, professional, and managerial occupations.

The WRIOT is un-timed and may be administered to groups or individually. The authors report that the time for individual administration is approximately 40 minutes, and for group administration, 50–60 minutes. Scoring is done either by hand or by computer. Split-half reliability coefficients by the Cureton formula (Guilford, 1954) for each scale in the 1979 edition range from .83 to .95 for males and from .82 to .95 for females. Validity was established by correlations between the WRIOT and the Geist Picture Interest Inventory. Most correlations are high and within satisfactory ranges. However, additional validity studies are needed for women, people who have mental retardation, and various ethnic groups.

Interpreting the WRIOT

The results are measurements of motivators (likes and dislikes), including both interests and attitudes. The results are organized into 18 interest clusters and 8 attitude clusters. The computer format, shown in Figure 12-3 (next page), shows a graphic representation of a person's strength of interest in each of the 18 clusters, as well as the 8 more general attitude clusters, and gives a level of self-projected ability, aspirations level, and social conformity. The manual provides a definition of each interest cluster with information on correlations with other clusters by sex and job title and lists of positive and negative items as related to the cluster. The 8 attitude clusters are similarly defined. Norms for all scales are available by sex and age (from age 5). Means and standard deviations by sex and age are also provided for each interest and attitude cluster.

The results are reported by standard score (mean = 50, S.D. = 10) for each cluster and attitude scale. The profile reports scores by five categories ranging from very low (20–31) to very high (69–80). Scores of 50 or more are considered positive interests and attitudes; below 50, negative. The authors suggest that the individual consider the entire profile of scores (both negative and positive measures) in career exploration.

The manual for the WRIOT has been well prepared in that each scale is clearly defined. Several case studies are provided in the manual as are as cluster descriptions that identify correlated job activities by sex. Additional information on using the test with people with mental retardation and individuals who have reading problems is needed because this instrument was designed especially for nonreaders. The difficulty in hand scoring the test will most likely make computer scoring mandatory for most users. This instrument has been reviewed by Zytowski (1978), Hsu (1985), Manuelle (1985), Organist (1985), and Thomas (1994). One of the main suggestions by Thomas (1994) is to update the pictures to represent more current job activities.

WRIOT2 Interest Clusters

The 16 scales in the Interest Cluster evaluate the needs, motives, and values that influence an occupational choice.

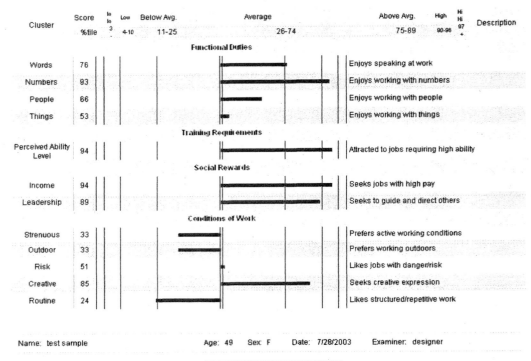

Name: test sample   Age: 49   Sex: F   Date: 7/28/2003   Examiner: designer

WRIOT2 Occupational Clusters

Scales in the Occupational Cluster show the extent of interest in 17 types of careers.

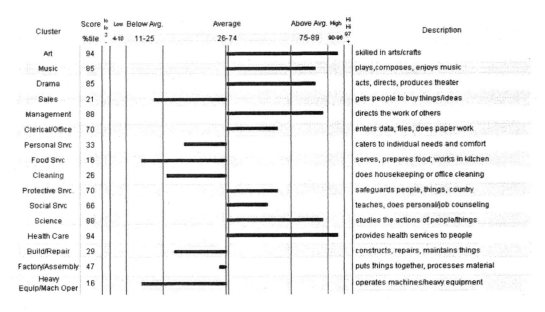

Figure 12-3a   WRIOT2 Computerized Scoring Report. Copyright 2003 by Wide Range, Inc. Reproduced with permission.

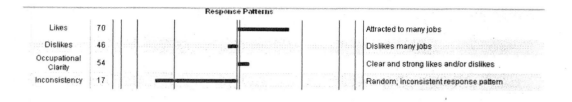

Response Patterns

Likes	70		Attracted to many jobs
Dislikes	46		Dislikes many jobs
Occupational Clarity	54		Clear and strong likes and/or dislikes
Inconsistency	17		Random, inconsistent response pattern

Holland Type Clusters

The Holland Type Cluster describes the performance according to six occupational themes.

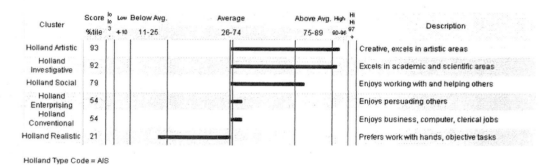

Cluster	Score %tile	lo lo 3	Low 4-10	Below Avg. 11-25	Average 26-74	Above Avg. 75-89	High 90-96	Hi Hi 97+	Description
Holland Artistic	93								Creative, excels in artistic areas
Holland Investigative	92								Excels in academic and scientific areas
Holland Social	79								Enjoys working with and helping others
Holland Enterprising	54								Enjoys persuading others
Holland Conventional	54								Enjoys business, computer, clerical jobs
Holland Realistic	21								Prefers work with hands, objective tasks

Holland Type Code = AIS

Comments

Top Occupational Interests:

HEALTH CARE - EXTENDED DESCRIPTION

Workers in this group are involved in the prevention, diagnosis, and treatment of diseases, disorders, or injuries. Most workers in this group deal with sick, injured, or disabled people. Medical doctors commonly specialize in specific kinds of illnesses, or special areas or organs of the body. Nurses and physical therapists care for and treat people and some are involved in health education and sickness prevention. Nurses aides, child- and adult-care workers assist professionals in treating the sick or injured. They care for the elderly, the very young, or the disabled. Frequently these workers help people do the things they cannot do for themselves. A wide variety of work environments is available to health care workers ranging from large city hospitals and clinics, schools, industrial plants, nursing homes, day care centers, and private homes. Women are over two times more likely than men to obtain high scores on the Health Care scale.

ART - EXTENDED DESCRIPTION

Workers in this group create original works of art or do commercial art work, using such techniques as drawing, painting, photographing, and sculpturing to express or interpret ideas or to illustrate various written materials. Some artists design products, settings, or graphics (such as advertisements or book covers), and oversee the work of other artists or craftsmen who produce or install them. Others teach art, or appraise or restore paintings and other fine art objects. Advertising agencies, printing and publishing firms, television and motion picture studios, and museums employ artists. They also work for manufacturers and in the retail and wholesale trade. Many are self-employed, operating their own commercial art studios or doing free-lance work. Women are over two and one-half times more likely than men to obtain high scores on the Art scale.

ART – CAREER FACTS

What kind of work would you do?

Your work activities would depend upon your specific job. For example, you might

— paint or sketch portraits, landscapes, and other subjects in oils, watercolors, or charcoals.

— design and supervise the construction of scenery for plays.

— plan the arrangement of advertising materials for a department store.

— draw accurate and precise pictures of diseased body organs to illustrate articles in medical journals.

Figure 12-3b WRIOT2 Computerized Scoring Report. Copyright 2003 by Wide Range, Inc. Reproduced with permission.

Case of a High School Student Lacking Basic Education Skills

Shortly after Arturo's arrival at Central High, his teacher referred him to the counselor's office for placement in a proper educational program. The teacher reported that Arturo had a low reading level and could not compete with the students in her class. She had talked briefly to Arturo about his background but did not have the time to investigate the reasons for his lack of educational achievement.

The counselor discovered that because Arturo's family had moved around a great deal in the last ten years, he had missed a significant amount of schooling. When the counselor mentioned tests, Arturo said that he had taken a series of tests at the school he had previously attended. The counselor called the school and asked for the test results.

The achievement test indicated that Arturo was performing very much below grade level in all areas. He was particularly low in language skills, with a third-grade reading level. The counselor discovered that Arturo's mother spoke only Spanish and his father knew little English. Arturo stated that he forgot the English he learned at school after spending a summer at home. Arturo explained that he had some interest in academic subjects but was more interested in finding a job because his family needed an additional source of income. However, Arturo was unable to specify a vocational choice.

The counselor selected the WRIOT as an instrument that might provide some stimulus for discussion of future occupations. Because this inventory measures interests by having the individual respond to activities portrayed in pictures, Arturo's poor reading ability did not handicap him. As expected, Arturo had little interest in academic subjects but did show a high interest in mechanics, machine operations, and outdoor activities. The counselor was pleased to see that Arturo scored on the positive side of the ambition scale, which supported his claim of wanting to improve his vocational skills and income. Arturo agreed with the high score on the sex stereotype scale in that he basically preferred work traditionally done by men. The results also indicated that Arturo was highly motivated by his likes versus his dislikes.

Arturo responded positively to the results and indicated that he felt that they were a fairly good measure of his interests. He added that he much preferred to work with his hands rather than reading or writing. The counselor turned to the mechanics scale description and reviewed some of the key positive items, as shown in Figure 12-4. The counselor noticed that the positively keyed items included upholstering, assembling, repairing, servicing, and construction work. The job titles for this scale include automobile mechanic, cabinet maker, carpenter, concrete layer, construction worker, draftsman, electrician, gas station attendant, television repairer, roofer, and machine assembler. The counselor pointed out to Arturo that he also had a high level of interest in machine operations and was interested primarily in outdoor work. Arturo stated that he liked working with machines and working outdoors, but he had never given a great deal of thought to specific jobs. The counselor presented some of the occupations from the list as a point of reference for discussion. Arturo obviously needed additional information about requirements, environments, and skills needed for career exploration. Specific occupations Arturo selected for further investigation included electrician's helper, auto mechanic, sheet metal worker, and machine operator.

The counselor pointed out that certain academic skills would be required in these jobs and that it would therefore be necessary for Arturo to apply himself in the academic area as well as in specific training programs. The counselor suggested that Arturo visit the vocational-technical training division of the school to learn about the jobs he had elected to explore.

The results of this interest test provided the opportunity for the counselor to help Arturo identify and clarify his interests through activities portrayed in pictures. His motivation for career exploration was also significantly increased by the discussion of the test results. In addition, the results were easily linked to occupational groups and to specific occupations. Finally, the counselor was able to emphasize academic requirements in addition to specific occupational requirements.

Transferability of Work Skills

According to F. R. Albritton (personal communication, October 29, 1996), an emphasis on the transfer of skills is the most current trend in the field of vocational rehabilitation and working with people with disabilities or people who are disadvantaged. Figure 12-5 shows a sample of a completed Transferability of Work Skills Worksheet. Evaluators can use this worksheet with clients to help determine what specific jobs clients might be good at and enjoy doing. The first step is to list as many as seven jobs in a client's history. These should be jobs the client was successful at, but not a two- or three-week experience that the person did not enjoy. After finding the *DOT* number for each, the evaluator can use *Classification of Jobs*

(Field & Field, 1992) or similar resources to find much of the other information needed to complete the form, such as aptitudes, physical demands, and environmental conditions. Temperaments and interest levels are recorded by self-report. The Pre-Vocational Profile provides a client's job history. Instead of totaling the numbers, the evaluator writes down the highest level the client achieved. For example, if a person had mostly 3s and 4s and one 2 on verbal aptitude, the evaluator would write down a "2" because the client was working at that level on a particular job.

F. R. Albritton (personal communication, October 29, 1996) cautions that a counselor or evaluator should not rely completely on a computer dump of codes for aptitudes, demands, and environmental conditions but, instead, should make sure that the suggested marks reflect the reality of the person's job. Job tasks are not stable across positions. The counselor should remember that the purpose of this profile is to provide as realistic a picture as possible of a person's past level of performance to predict what his or her future performance might have been without a disability and what his or her current level is at the time of testing.

Mechanics

O— Mechanics

Cluster Items
The following items are consistently liked by persons wishing to engage in **Manual Building** and **Repair** activities and are therefore positively correlated with this cluster.

Female	Key Positive Items	Male
2 A. upholster chair		2 A. upholster chair
6 C. put up steel girders		6 C. put up steel girders
20 C. repair telephone lines		20 C. repair telephone lines
41 B. repair TV sets		31 B. assemble machines
43 A. repair record players		41 B. repair TV sets
47 B. make cabinets		43 A. repair record players
48 B. cut out dress patterns		47 B. make cabinets
65 A. construct field fences		50 C. repair steeples
73 C. do masonry work		61 B. service cars
78 C. repair office machines		71 C. install traffic lights
82 C. build roofs		73 C. do masonry work
95 C. build bridges		78 C. repair office machines
106 C. do carpentry work		82 C. build roofs
110 C. pour concrete floors		95 C. build bridges
141 A. make candy		106 C. do carpentry work
		110 C. pour concrete floors
		139 B. install electric fixtures
		140 C. lay bricks

Female	Secondary Positive Items	Male
5 B. do plumbing work		5 B. do plumbing work
17 B. bake pastry		10 C. polish floors
32 C. repair appliances		29 B. work as ship steward-stewardess
37 C. skin dive		46 B. set type for print
61 B. service cars		48 B. cut out dress patterns
70 A. work on airplanes		49 C. sell hardware
71 C. install traffic lights		57 C. paint house
75 B. run steamroller		66 A. drive dump truck
84 B. wrap packages		67 C. spray trees
87 C. operate a bulldozer		74 B. run a mixing machine
91 C. trim hedges		84 B. wrap packages
101 C. check soil temperature		87 C. operate a bulldozer
128 A. saw lumber		91 B. operate cranes
142 C. repair shoes by machine		112 B. examine leaf etchings
149 A. do welding		122 A. operate street cleaner
		141 B. run duplicating machine
		142 C. repair shoes by machine
		145 C. operate power hammer

The following items are consistently disliked by persons wishing to engage in **Manual Building** and **Repair**. Their negative choices are positively correlated with this cluster.

Female	Key Negative Items	Male
2 C. sell appliances		5 C. broadcast the news
20 B. explain sales graph		20 B. explain sales graph
32 A. massage person's back		22 B. sell real estage
50 A. chauffeur		33 A. conduct orchestra
58 B. pitch baseballs		42 B. carry trays in restaurant
75 C. serve as congressperson		49 A. sell fire, burglary insurance
86 B. drill recruits		70 B. file archives, records
87 B. act as army general		71 A. work as bartender
88 C. work as receptionist		83 B. guide tours
89 B. attend executive meetings		85 B. collect coins
95 B. advise on bank loans		87 B. act as army general
114 C. prepare newspaper ads		107 C. speak at club
127 C. argue before jury		134 B. sell theater tickets
142 A. run city as mayor		141 C. sing in opera
149 B. sell stocks and bonds		142 A. run city as mayor
		149 B. sell stocks and bonds

Definition
Choices in this cluster express preferences for the designing, building, assembling, erecting, maintaining, and repairing of three-dimensional structures.

Significant Correlations with other clusters:
Females: Positive: art (A), machine operation (P), outdoor (Q)

Negative: literature (B), sales (E), management (F), office work (G), protective service (I), social service (J), social science (K), number (N)

Males: Positive: art (A), physical science (M), machine operation (P), risk (T)

Negative: literature (B), music (C), drama (D), sales (E), management (F), personal service (H), social service (J), social science (K), number (N)

Job Titles
Titles may recur in clusters positively correlated with this one.

airplane mechanic
automobile designer
automobile mechanic
automotive engineer
beekeeper
boiler inspector
boiler mechanic
bookbinder
bridge builder
building inspector
cabinet maker
camera repairperson
carpenter
civil engineer
combustion engineer
concrete layer
construction foreperson
construction inspector
construction worker
dental technician
die designer
die maker
draftsman, draftswoman
electrical engineer
electrician
electricians helper
factory foreperson
farm foreperson
fence builder
gas station attendant
gift wrapper

gunsmith
hardware salesperson
heating repairperson
house painter
industrial engineer
leaf examiner
machine assembler
manufacturing foreperson
masonry worker
mechanic
mechanical engineer
medical lab technician
office machine repairperson
pattern cutter
phonograph repairperson
plumber
radio operator
radio technician
recording engineer
refrigeration engineer
roofer
ship steward, stewardess
steel worker
telephone repairperson
television repairperson
toolroom manager
traffic light installer
typesetter
x-ray technician

Figure 12-4 WRIOT Computerized Scoring Report – Mechanics. Copyright 2003 by Wide Range, Inc. Reproduced with permission.

After the work history has been completed, the information can be fed into a computer to generate a list of potential jobs. The job possibility section is filled out after the client has had a chance to look at the suggested options. This narrowing of options should be done in cooperation with the client. When examining the job possibilities, both the counselor and client will be able to identify what strengths might be used on the job, as well as where the person might want to gain additional skills. The vocational outcome section is a record of employment the person received.

Transition to Work Inventory (TWI)

This inventory (Friedman, Cameron, & Fletcher, 1995) is designed to compare job-related activities with job-related abilities and to identify job accommodation needs for adolescents or adults with severe disabilities. The TWI consists of two scales: the Job Analysis scale summarizes working activities and conditions and their likeliness of occurrence for each position; the Worker Analysis scale summarizes the strengths and weaknesses for each worker and the likelihood of successful performance of each of the activities. A Profile Sheet combines both the scales to identify any discrepancies between the job demands and the worker's capabilities. Items with large discrepancies between the job and the worker pinpoint behaviors requiring accommodation or job redesign. Scores are linked to hundreds of successful interventions.

The TWI was developed for persons with severe disabilities, including moderate to severe mental retardation (MR), severe emotional disturbance, or behavioral disturbance such as autism and developmental disabilities. It should be administered on an individual basis. The Job Analysis scale takes about 35 minutes to complete, as does the Worker Analysis scale. Each scale consists of the same 81 items and is scored separately.

The TWI presents work activities and conditions that can cause problems requiring accommodation for people with severe disabilities. Each item represents critical incidents where performance breakdowns have occurred for individuals with similar disabilities. Many of the items represent social interaction activities; others cover motor, speech, and visual activities. The manual reports inter-rater and test-retest

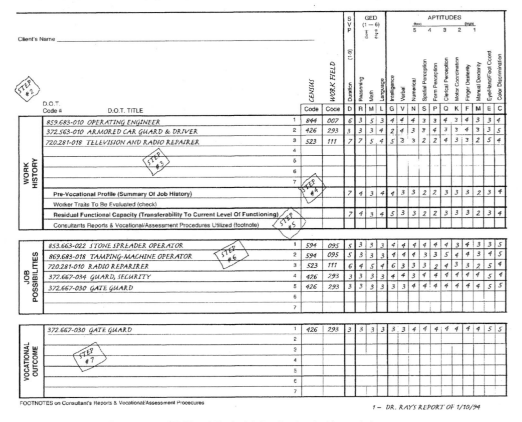

Figure 12-5a Completed Transferability. Copyright © 1992 Elliott & Fitzpatrick, Inc. Reprinted with permission.

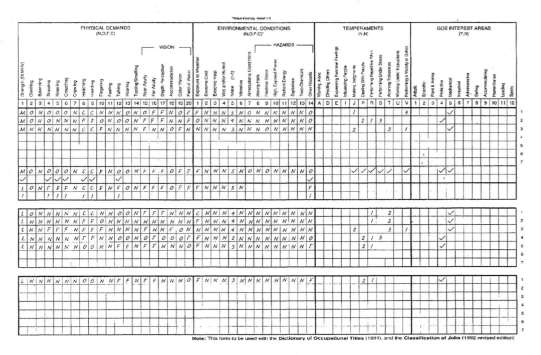

Figure 12-5b   Completed Transferability. Copyright © 1992 Elliott & Fitzpatrick, Inc. Reprinted with permission.

reliability, as well as criterion-related validity with workers with various serious disabilities. In addition, Fletcher, Friedman and Pasnak (1998) found the TWI to have good reliability and strong predictive validity.

Social and Prevocational Information Battery–Revised (SPIB-R)

The SPIB-R (Halpern, Raffeld, Irvin, & Link, 1986) was developed to measure life skills considered to be relevant to helping students and adults with mild mental retardation make the transition to community life. The entire test consists of 277 items, which are mostly true/false or can be answered by picture selection and are administered verbally, either individually or in a group setting. The SPIB-R consists of nine tests, including job search skills, job-related behavior, banking, budgeting, purchasing, home management, physical health care, hygiene and grooming, and functional signs. Each of the tests takes from 15 to 25 minutes to complete, about 3 hours total.

Technical data are reported for the earlier versions of the SPIB-R. Reliability estimates obtained by KR-20 for each subtest ranged from .65 to .82 with a median of .75. Test-retest reliabilities over two-week intervals are approximately the same. Meyers (1978) considers the validity acceptable because these scales provide more adequate information for placement and identification of needs than could generally be expected from subjective ratings and appraisals. Overton (1992) suggests that the norms under-represent minorities. The SPIB-R has been reviewed by Daniels (1985), Hegenauer and Brown (1990), Mealor (1991), and Tittle and Hecht (1994). Tittle and Hecht (1994) suggest that the interpretation of subtest scores should occur in the context of a person's background information and observations.

Interpreting the SPIB-R

Three norm-referenced groups are available for interpreting the results of the SPIB-R: junior high school students, senior high school students, and combinations of junior and senior high school students. The authors suggest a task-analysis method of evaluating specific competencies in each domain measured by the SPIB-R. For this evaluation method, each content area is divided into sub-content areas. For example, for job-related behavior, the sub-content areas are knowledge of role and duties of a supervisor, knowledge of appropriate communications, knowledge of what constitutes job completion, and recognition and knowledge of appropriate relations with fellow employees. Each sub-content area also provides the basis for developing instructional activities and for measuring the outcome of the instructional activities.

SPIB-R results give the career counselor some indication of the readiness of people with disabilities to enter the job market. In addition, the information obtained from this battery can be used to establish counseling programs that assist individuals in making an adequate adjustment to the work environment.

Case of a Group Program Based on SPIB-R Results

The teacher of EMR (educable mentally retarded) students made an appointment in early October to see the counselor. She informed the counselor that several of her students would be ready for placement at the end of the school year; however, the SPIB-R administered at the beginning of the fall term indicated that some students did not have appropriate job-related behaviors and job search skills. The teacher requested help from the counselor in developing modules that would simulate work environments to teach the students about supervisor-worker relationships, the importance of communication on the job, and factors affecting job performance.

Additional modules would be developed to teach students how to prepare resumés, how to conduct themselves in interviews, and how to increase their knowledge of sources of occupational information. The following outline is for the module designed to promote an understanding of supervisor-worker relationships.

Module I: To promote understanding of supervisor-worker relationships.
Objective: To understand the role of the supervisor.
Strategy: Worker-supervisor simulation.
Participants: Two students.
Materials: Eighteen pencils, six rubber bands.
Activity:
1. Worker is given order by supervisor to secure six pencils together with rubber bands.
2. Supervisor inspects work, makes suggestions, and gives constructive criticism, then changes the order to secure five pencils together.
3. Classmates, as observers, identify supervisor as boss and identify the supervisor's activities as praising, criticizing, suggesting, instructing, inspecting, and assigning duties.

In this case, the SPIB-R results identified the need for an educational program and provided the specific data for forming instructional units. A posttest provides data for evaluating the effectiveness of the program and for determining the need for additional programs.

Pictorial Inventory of Careers (PIC)

The Pictorial Inventory of Careers (Kosuth, 1992) was developed by Talent Assessment, Inc., as a measure of vocational interests that uses pictures instead of descriptive sentences. The PIC was created for people in middle and high school, adults, those with vocational disabilities, and those who are disadvantaged. A main purpose of this assessment is to help clients find potential career areas to explore and to target their training to help them reach their career goals. The PIC consists of 119 different scenes on videocassettes of various vocational-technical careers organized in 17 clusters. The PIC is different from other picture inventories in that the focus is on the work environment rather than on the worker. Specific vocational areas that the PIC assesses include agricultural, business–data processing, business–retailing/sales, business–secretarial, communications–arts/graphics, electrical/electronics, engineering technology, environmental services, food services, health services, protective services, science and laboratory, service–barber/cosmetology, service–personal, trade and industry–construction, trade and industry–mechanical, and trade and industry–metal trades.

The PIC has two program levels. Program 1 is for regular vocational students, and Program 2 was designed for students who are low-functioning or who have disabilities. The PIC is scored by computer and may be compiled in different formats. The standard report format includes information on job preferences, career areas, job titles to explore, and vocational programs to consider.

Technical Aspects of the PIC

A person's preferences, separate from their raw scores, are classified as negative (scores of 7–16), neutral (scores of 17–25), and positive (scores of 26–35). In a three-week test-retest study, there was a shift of one category (for example, from neutral to positive) 25% of the time, and a shift of two categories (for example, from positive to negative) less than 1% of the time. Reliability estimates of raw scores ranged from .61 for the food services cluster to .93 for the trade and industry–construction cluster.

To validate the PIC, the developers identified a sample population for each of the 17 career clusters, with the sample sizes ranging from 30 to 49. The samples were administered the PIC, and those scores were compared with scores of the "normal" population by use of a standard t-test formula. All t-scores for each cluster were found to be significant at the .01 level. Wircenski (1994) states that reliability and validity of the PIC are adequate. However, more research is necessary to verify the validity and reliability estimates.

A counselor using the PIC should focus on three main areas of the inventory: the person's stated interest preference, preference scores, and percentile ranks. The counselor can focus on the degree to which there is agreement among the person's interests in specific categories as well as in the clusters. According to Wircenski (1994), the PIC can be used within the counseling session and is especially helpful in formulating suggestions, identifying realistic expectations, understanding physical requirements, exploring employment opportunities, and serving as a springboard for further career-related discussion. One criticism of the PIC is that the occupations presented would require reading as a part of the job task

PIC DV2000 CAREER PREFERENCE PROFILE

This is a list in descending order of your preferences to the 17 career clusters in the PIC DV2000 Program. The top three (Five in the expanded Report) are highlighted and indicate your strongest choices.

The (+) indicates career areas that you felt positive about. The (-) indicates career areas that you felt negative about, and the (0) indicates career areas that you felt neither positive nor negative about.

PREF	CAREER AREA	SCORE	PCTILE
(+)	Service-Fire Science	35	98
(+)	Service-Barbering/Cosmetology	32	98
(+)	Food Services	28	95
(+)	Business-Data Processing	28	95
(+)	Electrical/Electronics	28	95
(+)	Health Services	26	85
(+)	Science and Laboratory	26	80
(0)	Communications/Art Graphics	25	80
(0)	Engineering Technology	24	75
(0)	Business-Secretarial	19	65
(-)	Criminal Justice	18	55
(-)	Agriculture/Environmental	15	30
(-)	Business-Retailing/Sales	10	05
(-)	Service - Personal	10	10
(-)	Trade & Industry - Construction	10	20
(-)	Trade & Industry - Mechanical	10	30
(-)	Trade & Industry - Metal Trades	10	35

Figure 12-6   Pictorial Inventory of Careers. Reproduced with permission of the publisher, Talent Assessment, Inc.

and therefore might not be realistic or appropriate (Parish & Lynch, 1988; Wircenski, 1994). For example, the description of food services includes measuring ingredients and following recipes. Another concern is the report itself. How does a person with limited vocabulary make sense of a printed report? Wircenski (1994) also suggested that many of the scenes appear to be outdated as evidenced by the type of automobiles, hairstyles, and clothing.

Case of a Relocated High School Graduate

Adriana, having just graduated from high school, wanted to learn more about career opportunities. She was originally from Miami, but her parents had recently moved to a small city for a job change. Fluent in Spanish, but limited in English, Adriana wanted to start working to save money for college. During an interview with a high school counselor, Adriana discovered that the available career tests were in English. Although she could have had a friend translate the statements and the results, Adriana asked if there was another way.

The counselor showed her the PIC, which requires no reading. Adriana was curious about this and decided to try it. Her results are shown in Figure 12-6 (previous page). The counselor worked with Adriana with the help of her friend who could translate to explain the results. Adriana seemed most interested in the electronics jobs. Adriana decided, with the counselor, that her next steps should include locating electricians in the city who also spoke Spanish and then trying to get some experience. In addition, the counselor gave her a list of colleges that offered scholarships for students with diverse backgrounds, including one for women entering nontraditional career fields. In this case, Adriana was able to use the PIC to help identify her interests and careers that might fit her current needs. The PIC results also served as a springboard for discussion of other activities that might help her find employment.

The Reading-Free Vocational Interest Inventory–2 (R-FVII: 2)

The R-FVII (Becker, 1988) is described by the manual as a "non-reading vocational preference test" for use with individuals with mental retardation or learning disabilities and with people who might otherwise be considered disadvantaged. Instead of verbal symbols or written statements, clients are presented with pictures of three different work activities at a time, from which they circle the one they prefer. The forced choice method results in a ranking within each of the triads. The pictures have been updated and have a more easily identifiable target figure. The inventory addresses 11 key interest areas, including automotive, building trades, clerical, animal care, food service, patient care, horticulture, housekeeping, personal service, laundry service, and materials handling. The R-FVII: 2 clusters include mechanical, outdoor, mechanical/outdoor, clerical/personal care, and food service/handling operations. Consisting of 55 triads of pictures, the R-FVII takes about 20 minutes to complete. Raw scores are transformed into standard scores to enable comparison with "normal" groups.

The individual profile sheet provides a snapshot view of a client's vocational preferences in relation to each other. Scores above the 75th percentile are described as significant and are said to indicate strong preferences. Scores below the 25th percentile are significant in that they reveal a client's lack of preference. Scores between the 25th and 75th percentile are in the average range, and the manual suggests that many of the interests within this area will gravitate toward one end or the other, given additional time and experience by the client.

Technical Aspects of the R-FVII

The developers followed a norming procedure similar to Kuder's by dividing the United States into regions and testing samples of educable individuals with mental retardation (MR) and learning disabilities (LD) in grades 7 through 12. The public school norms included 2132 males with MR, 2054 males with LD, 2163 females with MR, and 1967 females with LD from public schools in 30 states.

The sample of adults with MR consisted of 1121 males and 1106 females from 36 community-sheltered workshops and vocational training centers in 17 states. Although the manual does not define *disadvantaged*, the norm group for disadvantaged men consisted of 897, with 781 for the female norm group, taken from 24 various centers in 15 states. Test-retest reliabilities for a two-week period ranged between .70 and .80 for all groups. KR-20s were calculated to determine internal consistencies, which ranged from .61 to .94, with a median of .82. Concurrent validity was demonstrated when the R-FVII was compared with the Geist Picture Interest Inventory (Geist, 1964), and many significant correlations were found. The manual discusses in detail how other types of validity were examined. For other reviews, see Diamond (1982), Holden (1984), Domino (1988), Miller (1992), and Cantwell (1994).

Case of Using the R-FVII in a MR Classroom

In beginning a unit on career development, Mr. Carroll, a classroom teacher for a ninth-grade MR class, asked the counselor if there was a career test that his students could take to help them identify career options. The counselor talked with Mr. Carroll about the developmental level and other characteristics of the class and decided that a class administration of the R-FVII would be the most appropriate tool.

The counselor and the teacher discussed what activities might help the children prepare for the R-FVII and what follow-up activities might help them integrate what they learned. They decided that having the children cut pictures out of magazines and newspapers that showed people working would be a good show-and-tell project that would help them become familiar with different types of work.

Then the counselor would administer the inventories in class and explain the purpose of the R-FVII and how to complete it. The counselor then would train the teacher's aide on how to score the profiles and train the teacher on how to interpret them. After the R-FVII, the counselor, teacher, and aide prepared a one-page summary sheet for each student, including a list and description of his or her highest preferences and sample occupations. Students were told to star the occupations they were most interested in and were then shown various ways to get information about the occupations. Finally, they were assigned the task of making a presentation to the eighth-grade MR class on their favorite occupation and why.

Other Instruments for People with Disabilities and the Academically Disadvantaged

The diverse needs of people with disabilities and those who are educationally disadvantaged necessitate specially designed assessment instruments. The following are examples of the kinds of instruments that may serve some of the purposes of assessment for these groups of individuals.

Adaptive Behavior Scales. This instrument was designed to help identify a person's strengths and weaknesses in the following areas: independent functioning, numbers and time, social behavior, disturbing interpersonal behavior, economic activity, prevocational/vocational activity, trustworthiness, stereotyped and hyperactive behavior, language development, self-direction, self-abusive behavior, and responsibility. There are two versions: one for school (for ages 3 to adult) and one for residential and community members. The purpose of the school version is to help determine the presence of mental retardation or need for special education assistance. The purpose of the residential and community form is to evaluate the degree to which a person is able to adapt to life situations and then applying that information to education, training, and placement decisions.

Ashland Interest Assessment. This assessment includes 144 pairs of work-related activities and was developed for use with people with learning disabilities or developmental delays, brain injuries, limited English ability, limited education, chronic employment and similar conditions. The inventory consists of 12 scales, including: Arts and Crafts, Personal Service, Food Service, Clerical, Sales, General Service, Protective Service, Health Care, Mechanical, Construction, Plant or Animal Care and Transportation.

Barriers to Employment Success Inventory – Second Inventory. The purpose of the BESI is to identify barriers that might interfere with people getting and being successful on a job. It consists of 50 items, resulting in scores for five clusters, including *Personal, Physical and Psychological, Career Planning, Job Seeking Skills,* and *Education and Training.* A place for creating an action plan is included in the inventory.

Geist Picture Interest Inventory. A special edition of this interest inventory for Spanish-speaking and bilingual males uses pictures of occupational activities. The general interest areas are persuasive, clerical, mechanical, musical, scientific, outdoors, literary, computational, artistic, social service, dramatic, and personal service. There are separate forms for males and females, and it may be individually or group administered.

IDEAS. An inventory created as a self-exploration tool for students in middle-high school, and especially for special education and at-risk students. It consists of 16 basic scales organized by

Holland types. Specific scales include Realistic (Mechanical/Fixing, Protective Services, Nature/Outdoors), Investigative (Mathematics, Science, Medical), Artistic (Creative Arts, Writing), Social (Community Service, Educating, Child Care), Enterprising (Public Speaking, Business, Sales), and Conventional (Office Practices, Food Service).

Purdue Pegboard. The Purdue Pegboard was created to measure gross movement ability (capability to move hands, fingers, and arms) and fingertip dexterity (capability to control manipulative measurements of small objects). A client uses the pegboard, pegs, washers, and collars to complete a variety of tasks with the left hand, the right hand, and both hands together. Results can be scored in 10 minutes and can be compared with percentile scores for several different classifications, including assembly job applicants, production work job applicants, electronics production work applicants, and other populations with disabilities. Another useful outcome of the results is that it allows employers to find the best applicants for a job that requires manual dexterity.

Talent Assessment Program (TAP). The TAP consists of a battery of 10 hands-on tests, requiring no reading, with the purpose of clarifying functional aptitude for those in middle school or high school, adults, those with vocational disabilities, and those who are disadvantaged. TAP measures form perception, ability to follow patterns, retention of form and detail, fine discrimination, color discrimination, tactile discrimination, fine motor control, manual dexterity, quality performance, and the ability to use large tools.

Tests of Adult Basic Education (TABE). The four levels of this test are designed to identify the need for instruction/training in basic skills. The subtests are reading vocabulary, reading comprehension, arithmetic reasoning, and arithmetic fundamentals. The results can also be used to help choose community colleges, trade education, or government-funded basic skills programs. Work-related components address the Job Training Partnership Act, vocational tech, and school to work program requirements, and other results predict success on the General Educational Development (GED) tests. The TABE Work-Related Foundation Skills has four forms available: trade/technical, business/office, health and general. In addition, TABE Work-Related Problem Solving assesses basic problem solving skills in a work context.

Transition to Work Inventory. This is an 84-item inventory of non-work activities that was created for individuals who have little or no work experience, and/or limited education/training. Scores connect to the 14 GOE areas, and are then related (on the inside of the assessment) to job titles, self-employment options and related education and training possibilities. The publishers of TWI suggest that the TWI is useful for clients in "welfare to work programs," offenders who are transitioning back to civilian life and work, those transitioning from rehabilitation to work, and for people with little or no work experience, among others. A portion of the inventory booklet is dedicated to career journaling and career planning.

Vocational Decision-Making Interview (VDMI). The VDMI is a paper and pencil individually administered inventory of 54 questions with the purpose of creating a structured interview that will lead to a formal evaluation of a person's decision-making abilities and job readiness. The authors state that it is appropriate for high-risk populations including those in substance abuse programs. Each answer is scored "1" if it meets the scoring criteria outlined on the question and scoring sheet and "0" if it does not meet the criteria. An empty box next to the questions and scoring criteria allows for observational comments and notes. The VDMI addresses three key areas:

- Decision Making Readiness (how ready is a client to make a career decision as evidenced by their occupational knowledge and decision making skills).

- Employment Readiness (how motivated the client is to find a job, and are there external pressures affecting his/her decision-making ability).

- Self-Appraisal (how knowledgeable a person is of his/her own interests, skills, etc.).

Work Adjustment Inventory. This inventory is appropriate for clients' aged 12 to 22 who are starting to work. The WAI consists of six scales, including Activity, Empathy Sociability, Assertiveness, Adaptability and Emotionality. The WAI, written at a 3rd grade reading level, is useful for individual planning for at-risk students and students with disabilities.

Summary

Legislation that requires equal access to training and employment for people with disabilities and people who are disadvantaged has encouraged the development of specially designed assessment instruments. These instruments must meet the needs of individuals from many ethnic and racial backgrounds. In this chapter, the counselor has been encouraged to carefully evaluate the reference groups from which the assessment data have been derived. Norm groups should match the individuals being tested in cultural background and other characteristics. Once again, it should be noted that in many cases, using general population instruments, such as many of those reviewed in this book, might be appropriate with these populations. The counselor might have to make adjustments in the way a test is administered, and the counselor should review the literature on any instrument that has been used with a special population to acquaint himself or herself with the strengths, weaknesses, and so on of that particular instrument with that particular culture or group.

Questions and Exercises

1. Why is it important to have specially developed norm data for people with disabilities and those who are disadvantaged?

2. Explain how you would use aptitude test results for people with disabilities when special norms for people with disabilities are not available.

3. An individual states that he has been turned down for jobs because of his low educational achievement. He claims that he can read, spell, and do some arithmetic. He is now confused about what kind of job he wants. While considering other counseling needs, what kind of assessment instruments would you use?

4. Should pictorial interest inventories for nonreaders include activities that depict high-level jobs requiring college degrees? Explain your answer.

5. Explain how you could most effectively interpret test data to an individual with a disability who is applying for a job in a local industry. Under what conditions would the results be most meaningful?

6. A client with a severe visual impairment comes to you for career counseling. Her interest inventory results confirm the educational options she has been considering: medicine and engineering. She is particularly interested in becoming a physician. How would you advise this student? What potential barriers does she face? What type of accommodations might she need for success? How probable is success, or is that a question you can answer?

7. If you were a school counselor, how would you go about encouraging at-risk students to take career inventories seriously? Design a program that would be comprehensive in nature and include career testing as one component. What other components would you include? How difficult would a program like this be to implement in the schools?

8. Julie recently finished taking night classes to complete her GED and wants to enroll in a vocational-technical school. Because of her problems in high school and her learning disability, Julie is concerned about her ability to complete a degreed program in her desired field, computer technology. The program requires all its students to complete the TABE to identify academic strengths and weaknesses. Julie's profile is shown in Figure 12-7. How would you interpret these results to her?

9. Charles, a 20-year old, and his parents have asked you to do an evaluation of his abilities. Charles was injured in a car accident and has spent considerable time in rehabilitation. Charles and his parents want to have an accurate assessment of his abilities so he can begin career planning. Prior to his accident, he was considering a career as an automobile mechanic or an electrician. His TAP results are presented in Figure 12-8a-b. Interpret the percentiles. How realistic might his pre-injury aspirations be? What accommodations would be necessary? What other inventories might you want to administer?

10. Amber, a 22-year-old with cerebral palsy has just completed the PAES. Her results are shown in Figure 12-9a-d. How would you interpret her scores? Are there any that you would like further clarification on? What might be some next steps? What questions would make sense to ask Amber at

this point? How would those questions differ from those you would ask of a person with no disability? How might your role differ?

11. Emily, a senior at high school, is excited about finishing high school, but less enthusiastic about her career options after graduation. When asked about her work or volunteer experiences, she says she doesn't have any – she spent her free time studying and hanging out with friends, mostly at karaoke bars. She wasn't a member of any clubs or sports. She's open to attending a two-year college, but really wants to find a job. She's excited about an upcoming television talent show, and is hopeful that she'll be discovered there. Her interest profile of the TWI is shown in Figure 12-10. What observations can you make about her interests, and how would you proceed with the interpretation? Also, how might you integrate her results with other activities she can engage in before she graduates to help her make herself more marketable?

12. You have been seeing a client, Melanie, in a domestic abuse shelter. She has never worked outside the home. Having no means of support, and a great deal of self-doubt, she is struggling with finding a way to support herself. She has a bachelor's degree in history, but sees that as being useless. After agreeing with you that there are some things getting in the way of her getting out there (in the work world), she takes the BESI to see what those "things" might be. Her results are in Figure 12-11. What observations can you make about her profile? What interventions might you pursue? How does mental health counseling and career counseling overlap?

13. Noah has been seeing a counselor for 2 years to help him with his alcohol addiction. His addiction has impacted his ability to keep a job, and he has been fired on several occasions due to tardiness, absenteeism and falling asleep on the job. He's been sober for the past 2 months and says that he is ready to try to find work again. The counselor wants him to have a successful job search experience, but is concerned about his readiness, and thus administers the VDMI. Noah's results are in Figure 12-12. What general interpretations can you make about his results? How do these results compare to those in the norm group? How should Noah's counselor proceed? Is administering an interest, skill or personality inventory appropriate at this point? Is so, why? If not, why not – and what would you recommend instead?

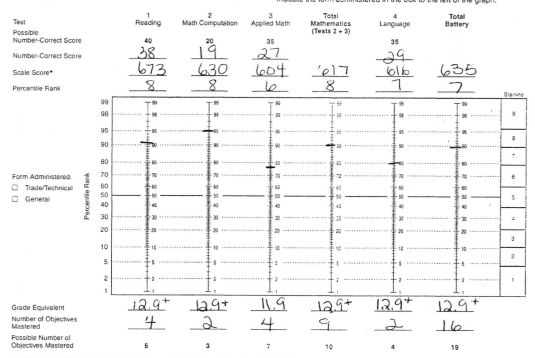

Tests of Adult Basic Education

TABE™

Individual Diagnostic Profile

Work-Related Foundation Skills

Trade/Technical Form and General Form Level D

Name __Julie Mann__

I.D. Number _____ Test Date __4 / 21 / 00__

Examiner/Teacher _____

School/Program _____ Test Form _____

DIRECTIONS

Identifying Data: Record the Examinee's Name, I.D. Number, Test Date, Examiner's Name, School or Program, and Test Form in the appropriate spaces.

Part 1 Summary of Scores and Percentile Rank Profile:

(1) In the profile section below, enter the number of correct responses for each test in the spaces labeled Number-Correct Score.

(2) Refer to the tables in the Norms Book to convert the number-correct scores to scale scores. A scale score for Total Mathematics is obtained by averaging the scale scores of the two math tests.

(3) Refer to the appropriate tables in the Norms Book to obtain other scores, such as percentile ranks and grade equivalents. Enter these scores in the appropriate spaces. The corresponding stanine for percentile rank may be determined by referring to the far right-hand column of the graph. The Number of Objectives Mastered may be summarized from the information in Part 2.

(4) On the graph, mark a short, heavy line across the vertical bar at the point that corresponds to the percentile rank for each test and total. The position of these lines on the profile gives a graphic representation of the examinee's relative achievement in the test content areas.

(5) To show examinee growth, you may want to administer another form of Work-Related Foundation Skills later, recording the results on this document. Indicate the form administered in the box to the left of the graph.

Test	1 Reading	2 Math Computation	3 Applied Math	Total Mathematics (Tests 2 + 3)	4 Language	Total Battery
Possible Number-Correct Score	40	20	35		35	
Number-Correct Score	38	19	27		29	
Scale Score*	673	630	604	'617	616	635
Percentile Rank	8	8	6	8	7	7

Form Administered:
☐ Trade/Technical
☐ General

	1 Reading	2 Math Computation	3 Applied Math	Total Mathematics	4 Language	Total Battery
Grade Equivalent	12.9+	12.9+	11.9	12.9+	12.9+	12.9+
Number of Objectives Mastered	4	2	4	9	2	16
Possible Number of Objectives Mastered	5	3	7	10	4	19

*Scale Score for Total Mathematics = Scale Scores for (Math Computation + Applied Math) ÷ 2
*Scale Score for Total Battery = Scale Scores for (Reading + Total Mathematics + Language) ÷ 3

Figure 12-7 Tests of Adult Basic Education. Copyright © 1995 Reprinted by permission of the McGraw-Hill Companies, Inc.

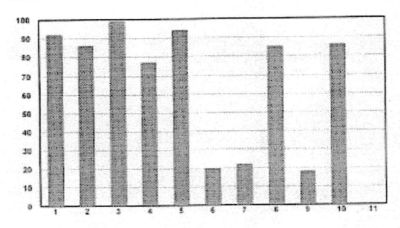

03/01/2001

Group# 1 Test Times and Percentiles for: John J. Sample

	TAP Test	Time (mins)	Percentile
1.	Structural and Mechanical Visualization:	8.7	92
2.	Discrimination by Size and Shape:	5.4	86
3.	Discrimination by Color:	1.9	99
4.	Discrimination by Touch:	3.2	77
5.	Fine Finger Dexterity:	7.8	94
6.	Gross Manual Dexterity:	6.5	20
7.	Fine Finger Dexterity with Tools:	9.3	22
8.	Gross Manual Dexterity with Tools:	7	85
9.	Visualization of Flow Patterns:	5.9	18
10.	Retention of Mechanical and Structural Detail:	8.2	86

Figure 12-8a   Talent Assessment Program. Reproduced with permission of the publisher, Talent Assessment, Inc.

Interpretation of Tests For: John J. Sample

TAP Test 1:

Your assessment scores indicate you have a strong aptitude in the area of visualization. Visualization can also be restated as form and spatial perception. Individuals with this strength usually find it easy to follow diagrams, charts and plans, and reproduce things with accuracy and ease. These individuals usually do well on jobs in any of the mechanical industrial, or building trades areas that require a high degree of visualization provided they are interested in and have acceptable aptitude levels in other job components.

TAP Test 2:

Your assessment scores indicate you have a high degree of fine discrimination of very similar objects. This is a much needed aptitude in many jobs, especially in electronics and the mechanical and industrial trade areas.

TAP Test 3:

Your assessment scores indicate you have a high degree of aptitude in discriminating very similar colors. Good color discrimination is an important attribute for doctors, dentists, artists, decorators, paper hangers, paint manufacturers, horticulturists, cosmetologists, safety engineers, automobile painters, farm industrial equipment painters, tile setters, textile manufacturers, stain glass workers, assemblers, electronic technicians, and laboratory technicians.

TAP Test 4:

Your assessment scores indicate you have a strong aptitude in the area of tactile discrimination. Jobs requiring this attribute are: needle trades, upholstering, plastic furniture finishing, auto body work, floor finishing, paper hanging, sandblasting, ceramics, jewelry making, as well as physical therapy and other health occupations. Good tactile discrimination is critical for dental hygienist, dental lab technicians, and other areas of the dentistry field.

TAP Test 5:

Your assessment scores indicate you have a strong aptitude in the area of fine finger dexterity. Many jobs require that an individual work extensively with their hands. Individuals having this strength should have no problem on jobs such as electronics, carburetor repair, small parts assembly, and jewelry making, provided they are interested and have acceptable aptitude levels in other job components. Your Assessment scores also show your ability to work continuously and diligently for a period of time without becoming frustrated with this type of work. High levels of this attribute lead into the field of dentistry, as well as computer programming and electronics assembly. This aptitude coupled with the ability to visualize three dimensional structures as found in Test #1 opens up many fields in the technical and high technical work areas.

TAP Test 8:

Your assessment scores indicate you have a strong aptitude in the area of gross manual dexterity. The ability to work with tools not only requires the use of one hand but also encompasses the use of the other hand in a bi-manual coordinated effort. This aptitude coupled with the aptitude found in manual dexterity (Test #6), visualization (Test #1), and small parts handling (Test #5) would enable individuals to seek many opportunities in the mechanical, industrial, and building trades areas provided they are interested and have acceptable aptitude levels in other job components.

TAP Test 10:

Your assessment scores indicate you have a strong aptitude for form and spatial retention. Test #1 indicates the aptitude for form and spatial perception which relates directly to following directions, charts and graphs. Test #10 indicates the aptitude for remembering the structural details performed on an original task. This aptitude is essential for those people in the investigative mechanics area such as diagnostic technicians who must assemble items without the use of a manual. A worker who is capable of remembering how to re-assemble a mechanical device or set forms for pouring concrete is certainly much more valuable than one who is completely dependent on directions and supervision.

Figure 12-8b Talent Assessment Program. Reproduced with permission of the publisher, Talent Assessment, Inc.

PAES - Practical Assessment Exploration System

Student: Example One   Grade: 9

School: Orange Park   Evaluator: Shelley McGann

Quality of Work Completed

TOTAL Number of Activities Attempted	137
TOTAL Number of Activities Completed Correctly	137
Number of Activities Expected to Complete	168
Amount of Production Standard Met	82%

Attendance

Hours Present for PAES	67

Aptitude Scores

	Aptitude	% of activities completed
Business/Marketing	52%	57%
Home Consumer Science	50%	46%
Industrial Technology	60%	71%
Manipulatory Processing & Production	70%	100%
Average Aptitude Score	64%	

Aptitude Scores above 60% are considered as semi-competitive or semi-independent level funtioning - possibly but not necessarily requiring support services to succeed in regular practical arts / vocational classes or entry-level employment.

Aptitude Scores between 30% and 60% are considered as needing additional job skills awareness and training experiences preparing the student for regular practical arts classes and/or employment.

Aptitude Scores below 30% are considered as needing very basic job skill awareness and training - possibly job coach - before being considered for community employment

Figure 12-9a   PAES. Reproduced with permission of the publisher, Talent Assessment, Inc.

PAES - Practical Assessment Exploration System

Interest Ratings

	High	Moderate	Low
Business/Marketing	47%	53%	0%
Home Consumer Science	56%	44%	0%
Industrial Technology	67%	27%	7%
Manipulatory Proc. & Prod.	2%	88%	10%

Amount of Evaluator Assistance Required

	Independent	Verbal	Gesture	Demonstration	Task Intervention
Business/Marketing	74%	15%	6%	3%	0%
Home Consumer Science	44%	36%	12%	8%	0%
Industrial Technology	50%	33%	13%	3%	0%
Manipulatory Proc. & Prod.	85%	6%	4%	4%	0%
Average	67%	20%	8%	4%	0%

Quality of Work Completed - First Trial Accuracy

	Correct	Few Errors	Many Errors	Needs Instruction
Business/Marketing	65%	35%	0%	0%
Home Consumer Science	76%	24%	0%	0%
Industrial Technology	77%	17%	7%	0%
Manipulatory Proc. & Prod.	79%	21%	0%	0%
Average	74%	24%	1%	0%

Figure 12-9b   PAES. Reproduced with permission of the publisher, Talent Assessment, Inc.

PAES - Practical Assessment Exploration System

Work Rate	Competitive Employment	Semi-Competitive Employment	Non-Productive
Business/Marketing	6%	68%	26%
Home Consumer Science	4%	56%	40%
Industrial Technology	37%	47%	17%
Manipulatory Proc. & Prod.	38%	50%	13%
Average	23%	55%	22%

Number of Trials to Complete Activity Totally Correct

	One Trial	Two Trials	Three Trials	More than Three Trials
Business/Marketing	65%	32%	3%	0%
Home Consumer Science	76%	20%	4%	0%
Industrial Technology	77%	23%	0%	0%
Manipulatory Proc. & Prod	77%	21%	2%	0%
Average	74%	24%	2%	0%

Figure 12-9c   PAES. Reproduced with permission of the publisher, Talent Assessment, Inc.

PAES - Practical Assessment Exploration System

Summary of Skills

First Column Ratings:

0 = student did not complete this activity
1 = Completed accurately on the FIRST TRIAL with NO ASSISTANCE
2 = Completed accurately with MINIMAL ASSISTANCE or FEW TRIALS
3 = Completed accurately with MUCH ASSISTANCE or MANY TRIALS

Second Column Ratings:

0 = student did not complete this activity
1 = High Interest
2 = Moderate Interest
3 = Low Interest

Industrial Technology

Assistance	Interest		
		Shop Measurement	
1	2	SM1	Whole Inch
1	2	SM2	1/2 Inch
3	3	SM3	1/4 Inch
2	3	SM4	1/8 Inch
0	0	SM5	1/16 Inch
0	0	SM6	All Above
		Screws & Nails	
2	2	SN1	Claw Hammer
1	2	SN2	Hammer, Awl, Screwdriver
1	2	SN3	Hammer, Awl, Screwdriver
0	0	SN4	Hammer, Awl, Screwdriver
0	0	SN5	Hammer, Hand Drill, Scrdrv
0	0	SN6	Small Parts w/Screwdriver
		Wood Project	
1	1	WP1	Saw, Square, Tape
2	1	WP2	Saw, Square, Tape
2	1	WP3	Brace & Wood Bit
2	1	WP4	Sandpaper
1	1	WP5	Hammer, Drill, Screwdriver
1	1	WP6	Wood Stain
		Electrical Project	
2	1	EP1	Wiring a Lamp Plug
1	1	EP2	Wiring a Lamp Socket
1	1	EP3	Wiring a Doorbell
0	0	EP4	Preparing Wire Ends
0	0	EP5	Wiring a Ceiling Light
0	0	EP6	Wiring Receptacle & Light Sw.

Assistance	Interest		
		Wrenches and Bolts	
2	2	WB1	Adjustable Wrenches
1	2	WB2	Ratchet Box & Open End Lg
1	2	WB3	Ratchet Box & Open End Sm
0	0	WB4	Allen Wrenches/Machine Bolts
0	0	WB5	Socket/Box End Wrenches
0	0	WB6	Various Wrenches w/Var Bolts
		Hand Saws	
2	1	SS1	Crosscut Saw & Tri-Square
2	1	SS2	Coping Saw & Tri-Square
2	1	SS3	Hacksaw & Tri-Square
1	1	SS4	Hacksaw on Conduit
1	1	SS5	Crosscut Saw Notch Block
1	1	SS6	Coping Saw to Cut Pattern
		Metal Project	
1	1	MP1	Ruler, Scribe, Tin Snips
2	1	MP2	Wooden Jig to Shape Metal
2	1	MP3	Metal Punch, Riveting Tool
2	1	MP4	Pipe Cutter on Pipe
2	1	MP5	Pipe Threader on Pipe
0	0	MP6	Pipe Reamer on Pipe

Figure 12-9d   PAES. Reproduced with permission of the publisher, Talent Assessment, Inc.

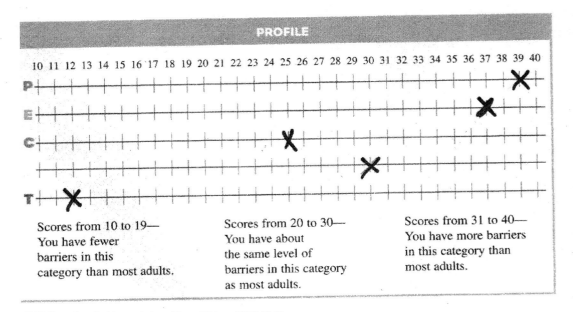

TWI Interest Profile

Occupational Clusters/Interest Groups	LOW	MEDIUM	HIGH
01. Arts, Entertainment, and Media	6 7 8 9 10 11 12 13	14 15 16 17 18 19 20 21 22	23 24 25 26 ⓐ27 28 29 30
02. Science, Math, and Engineering	6 7 8 9 10 11 12 ⑬ 14 15 16 17 18 19 20 21 22		23 24 25 26 27 28 29 30
03. Plants and Animals	6 7 ⑧ 9 10 11 12 13	14 15 16 17 18 19 20 21 22	23 24 25 26 27 28 29 30
04. Law, Law Enforcement, and Public Safety	⑥ 7 8 9 10 11 12 13	14 15 16 17 18 19 20 21 22	23 24 25 26 27 28 29 30
05. Mechanics, Installers, and Repairers	⑥ 7 8 9 10 11 12 13	14 15 16 17 18 19 20 21 22	23 24 25 26 27 28 29 30
06. Construction, Mining, and Drilling	6 7 8 ⑨ 10 11 12 13	14 15 16 17 18 19 20 21 22	23 24 25 26 27 28 29 30
07. Transportation	6 7 ⑧ 9 10 11 12 13	14 15 16 17 18 19 20 21 22	23 24 25 26 27 28 29 30
08. Industrial Production	6 7 8 9 10 11 12 13 ⑭ 15 16 17 18 19 20 21 22		23 24 25 26 27 28 29 30
09. Business Detail	6 7 8 9 10 11 12 13 14 ⑮ 16 17 18 19 20 21 22		23 24 25 26 27 28 29 30
10. Sales and Marketing	6 7 8 9 10 11 ⑫ 13	14 15 16 17 18 19 20 21 22	23 24 25 26 27 28 29 30
11. Recreation, Travel, and Other Personal Services	6 7 8 9 10 11 12 13	14 15 16 17 18 19 20 21 22	23 24 25 ⓐ26 27 28 29 30
12. Education and Social Service	6 7 8 9 10 11 12 13	14 15 16 17 18 19 20 21 22	23 ⓐ24 25 26 27 28 29 30
13. General Management and Support	6 7 8 9 10 11 12 13	14 15 16 17 18 19 20 21 22	23 24 25 26 27 ⓐ28 29 30
14. Medical and Health Services	6 7 8 9 10 11 12 13	14 15 16 17 18 ⑲ 20 21 22	23 24 25 26 27 28 29 30

Figure 12-10 Transition to Work Inventory. Reproduced with permission of the publisher, JIST Publishing.

PROFILE

10 11 12 13 14 15 16 17 18 19 20 21 22 23 24 25 26 27 28 29 30 31 32 33 34 35 36 37 38 39 40

P   ✗

E   ✗

C   ✗

                        ✗

T ✗

Scores from 10 to 19—
You have fewer
barriers in this
category than most adults.

Scores from 20 to 30—
You have about
the same level of
barriers in this category
as most adults.

Scores from 31 to 40—
You have more barriers
in this category than
most adults.

Figure 12-11 BESI. Reproduced with permission of the publisher, JIST Publishing.

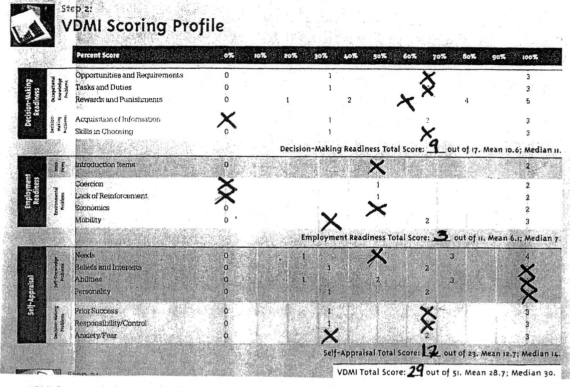

Figure 12-12 VDMI. Reproduced with permission of the publisher, JIST Publishing.

13 Using Non-standardized Self-Assessment Inventories

In recent years, career counseling programs have incorporated self-assessment techniques to identify individual characteristics and traits. Self-assessment inventories include a variety of self-scored questionnaires, checklists, and rating and ranking formats that evaluate specific characteristics for use in career counseling. For example, Bolles (2000) uses self-assessment of developed skills as a vital step in career decision making. Harrington and O'Shea (2000) recommend the use of self-estimates of ability in their system of career decision making. McKinlay (1990), who developed a questionnaire for identifying skills and interests, uses it to obtain appropriate career information from a computerized system. Goodman (1993) points out the value of non-standardized self-assessment for career counselors, but because of the preponderance of standardized tests, many counselors overlook non-standardized techniques.

Be aware that we are not attempting to undermine the use and value of standardized assessment devices; rather, we are suggesting that creative career counselors might find that the development of techniques that meet specific local goals are also valuable for clients. For instance, non-standardized instruments can be used to stimulate discussion of career options and supplement or raise questions about information obtained in other ways. Furthermore, non-standardized instruments can be used effectively with standardized inventories. Career decision-making is a process in which all aspects of individuals should receive consideration. When career counseling programs incorporate all relevant information, including non-standardized self-estimates, the chances of the career decision being dominated by any one source decreases.

In this chapter, examples of non-standardized approaches to self-assessment are presented. Some are illustrated with a brief case study, whereas others are simply described.

Work History via Resume Analysis

Resumes can be used as a career exploration tool. They provide a snapshot of a client's work experiences. In addition to noting general themes about job titles and places of employment, a counselor can help the client generate personal themes about values, interests and skills. One technique is to have the client outline in detail the job activities or duties for each paid and unpaid activity on the resume. The client can then place a checkmark or an asterisk by those activities he or she enjoyed doing, and an x by those activities he or she disliked immensely. Duties without a mark are considered neither really liked or disliked. After each job duty has been marked, a summary list of likes and dislikes could be created, and then prioritized.

COUNSELOR: Raphael, I see you brought your resume with you. That's great – I think it will help us gain a clearer picture of what you've done and help us figure out where you're headed.

RAPHAEL: Well, it forced me to put my resume in order and to update it some.

COUNSELOR: That's true. You know, many times you'll see resumes that begin with a summary of professional skills. Looking over the different tasks you've done, how would you describe your skills?

RAPHAEL: Well, I'm a good communicator, and a creative problem solver. I am resourceful, persistent and thorough.

COUNSELOR: Which of those do you think you thrive at?

RAPHAEL: Creative problem-solving. I always seem to come up with out-of-the box ideas that people really gravitate towards.

COUNSELOR: What I'd like you to do now is to look over your resume, and use this yellow highlighter to mark job tasks that you really enjoyed doing. When you're done, we'll use a blue highlighter to mark the job tasks you just detested – you may not have listed those on your resume, but you can write them back in.

RAPHAEL: Wow – I think I'm starting to see some themes here.

COUNSELOR: OK, tell me about it.

RAPHAEL: I really enjoyed being over short-term projects, where I was pretty independent to do my own thing. I didn't prefer the team approach where everyone's ideas had equal weight, because I enjoy bringing my own ideas to life.

COUNSELOR: I'd like you to go through each of your job listings one more time, and write down 1-2 word descriptors that immediately come to mind on how you feel about that job.

RAPHAEL: That's very telling. Those jobs, the ones where I lacked independence or creativity – the words that came to mind were "jail" and "stifled." The other jobs had descriptors of "fun," and "energetic".

COUNSELOR: You've just demonstrated why it's important to be doing work that you enjoy.

RAPHAEL: Yeah, I guess I have.

COUNSELOR: So, as we move on and begin to look at occupational alternatives, and as you interview and consider job offers, you should keep in mind what made you thrive at work, and what specific factors stifled your creativity at work.

In this example, the resume served as a career exploration tool in which Rafael began to see some patterns in his interests and skills, and solidified what he was looking to have – as well as looking to avoid – in a career.

Five Lives

One of the most helpful activities we have come across is called "Five Lives." This activity is perhaps most useful at the onset of career counseling, even before asking the typical questions of "What are you interested in" or "What are you good at"? The counselor simply asks the client "If you were able to live five completely different lives, what would they be?" A simple question, but the answers are often rich with meaning.

The question in itself is very important. One might say, "Well, I ask my clients what options they are considering at the time, and that's the same thing." Sort of. Although both questions ask the person to elaborate past one option, only the first question allows the person to temporarily dismiss real or perceived barriers and to entertain their realistic and idealistic aspirations. It is crucial to identify the "idealistic" or unrealistic aspirations. These dreams offer a window into what the person values. The Happenstance Approach holds that people's curiosity becomes blocked by asking too many "What" questions, such as "What are you good at" or "What do you want to do?" These questions tend to lead to pat answers and uncreative solutions. Once the person has identified five occupations (either writing them down or stating them), the counselor has many options from which to proceed. We usually find it helpful to be more open-ended, asking the client to tell me about each of the options, including what's attractive about each.

Other ideas include looking for positive themes or patterns (i.e., the client's interests, values, skills, and goals), asking how much the client knows about each occupation (to determine world of work knowledge), examining the degree of congruence between his or her self-knowledge and occupational aspirations, identifying real or perceived barriers ("What's keeping you from following each of these aspirations?"), and helping the client learn how to implement certain aspects of the aspirations into their life via leisure. Another possibility is linking the aspirations and the client's current occupation to Holland codes and examining them for congruence. By using this activity, the next steps seem to emerge naturally. What does the client need most at this point— assessment of interests, information about occupations, decision making strategies, or more discussion on barriers?

A main goal of this technique is to introduce the process of career counseling in a less formal and traditional manner, giving the client permission to dream about his or her potential, versus "getting down to business" and staying focused in reality. This is important because many clients will dismiss aspirations that are actually quite within the realm of possibilities. This happens because of real or perceived barriers, such as "I won't be able to provide for my family if I just quit my job and open my own business." The counselor's role is to then help the client entertain how the client can work around that barrier. By giving permission to be anything, with no reality pressures, the counselor allows for creative thinking and problem solving by the client to overcome the obstacles and actualize his or her dreams. Other goals include assessment of self and occupational knowledge, identification of barriers, identifying potential sex role stereotyping, assessment of client's confidence level, increasing motivation in the process, and determining the client's career counseling need(s) and appropriate next steps.

We have used this technique in individual counseling and classroom settings. The actual process of listing can take anywhere from 5 to 15 minutes, with the average time being around 8 minutes. In individual counseling, the follow-up continues with various questions as just described. In addition, we ask the client to find out the "Five Lives" of his or her parents, siblings, partner, and so forth. Often, some overlap exists, which contributes to the client's sense of connectedness to important others. In the classroom, we ask the class how they might follow up with this question. After brainstorming ideas, we have them pair up and ask the questions. This often takes 20 to 30 minutes to complete. Then we ask volunteers to share their observations with the class.

Example of Five Lives Activity

Heather came to a career counselor very frustrated with her inability to narrow down an occupational choice. "There are just so many options. I'm afraid I'll miss the best one for me. I mean, there are careers I think I'd enjoy, but how do I know if I'd enjoy that one the most?"

COUNSELOR: Let's go with that. If you could have five different lives to live, what would they be?

HEATHER: I only get to choose five? Well, I'll just go with what comes to mind. First, I'd be a rich, single woman. Second, I'd be the President of the United States. Third, I'd be an advertising executive. Fourth, I'd be a consultant. I guess my fifth life would be a private investigator.

COUNSELOR: Very interesting lives! Tell me more about the first one.

HEATHER: Well, if I could be rich and single, I'd be free to do what I wanted, and I wouldn't have anything keeping me from doing it. Shoot, I could make all of my career interests hobbies, and if I didn't like it, no big deal, I'd move on to the next one.

COUNSELOR: So, having freedom in making choices and permission to make mistakes without receiving a lot of punishment is something you dream about.

HEATHER: Well, I don't know if I dream about it or not, but it sure would make things easier if I didn't have to worry about failing.

COUNSELOR: Which brings us to life number 2. Seems like being the President would add a lot of pressure about failing.

HEATHER: Yeah, you'd end up failing somebody all the time. That's not why I chose that one. I liked the power, the definitiveness that goes with being President. When he signs a bill, it's law, and it takes a literal act of Congress to change it.

COUNSELOR: So, it'd be nice to be certain about what you're doing.

HEATHER: Yeah. But I guess, now that I think about it, that being the President wouldn't really make my top five lives. Knowing that my decisions affected others so much would be a terrible burden.

COUNSELOR: Which goes back to life number 1.

HEATHER: Yep. Rich and single. No dependents, no strings attached.

The counselor and Heather continued discussing her five lives. Through the conversation, Heather began to realize the amount of pressure she was putting on herself to find a perfect job and how she tended to obsess about the impact of her potential failures on others. An issue of wanting to be control emerged in her lives as well. Heather acknowledged that she was feeling completely out of control with this decision, and that she liked the confidence associated with people in those careers. In this example, the use of the Five Lives activity opened a discussion and allowed for insight into what was keeping Heather stuck.

Assessing Interests

Goodman (1993) presents an intriguing method of assessing interests adapted from Simon, Howe, and Kirschenbaum (1972). She suggests that activities she has devised stimulate students to want to know more about their interests. The following description of the exercise contains a brief case study. The clients are instructed to write down 20 things they like to do. They can list activities done at work; leisure activities, such as movies, parties, reading; or taking classes. She assigns the following codes to each interest listed.

1. Put a T next to each item on your list that you would enjoy more with more training.

2. Put an R next to each item on your list that involves risk—physical, emotional, or intellectual.

3. Put a PL beside those items that require planning.

4. Indicate with an A or a P or A/P whether you prefer to do the activity alone, with people, or both.

5. Next to each activity, put the date when you last engaged in it.

6. Star your five favorite activities. Discussion can ensue from any or all of these codings or from the list itself. The implications for career decision making are, hopefully, obvious, but perhaps a mini case study will make the point clearer.

Mellina, a 28-year-old student at a community college, comes to see you for help in career decision making. She will graduate with a liberal arts associate's degree in about six months and has no concrete plans. She supports herself by waitressing but does not wish to continue this work after she completes her degree. After listing her "20 things" and coding them, she finds that most of the items on her list involve being with people, involve some risk, and do not require more training to enjoy. She says she is absolutely tired of school and does not want any more training in anything! As you discuss the list further, you jointly discover that she likes activities that require planning; she is usually the person in her crowd who plans things. This role also often involves persuading other people to go along with her plans. This can be difficult on occasion, as her plans often involve risk, such as going on a mountain hiking trip without reservations at the endpoint.

Mellina is frustrated that she hasn't done very many of her favorite things in the last couple of years. That is one of the reasons she is anxious to be done with school. As you talk, it seems clear that she is willing to work in a setting where her salary depends on her own efforts (risk), and her interest in planning and persuading others leads you to think that sales might be an area for her to pursue. Your next steps then are to help her think about areas of sales and to gather information about the many varieties of sales jobs.

Ideal Day

A common technique that career counselors use as a non-standardized way of assessing a client's interests, values, and life roles is through their descriptions of an ideal day. The instructions, although simple, can vary according to counselor and client. The simplest instruction is to ask a client to either write or record his or her thoughts about an ideal workday, starting when she or he wakes up in the morning and ending when she or he goes to sleep that night. Another approach is to use guided imagery to "walk" the client through the ideal day. Some suggested guides might be "You're waking up. How do you wake up? Is there an alarm, or do you wake up naturally. Before you get out of bed, look around your room. What does it look like? Is anyone with you?" One problem with guiding them through the ideal day is that the counselor could spend too much time on one topic (of his or her interest), and might go too quickly past another topic (of particular interest to the client).

Sample Case of an Ideal Day

Jacques was more of an Artistic type: that was plain to see by the way he dressed, wore his hair, and communicated. He was very resistant to being categorized, and so wanted no part of traditional inventories. Still, he did want a clearer picture of his future. For an early activity, the counselor asked Jacques to create a collage that would be a picture of who he was. Jacques was very excited about this activity and created a 3-D design out of various objects. In the next session, he shared with his counselor meanings he attached to the sculpture. Based on his creative approach, the counselor decided to use the non-standardized approach of an ideal day.

COUNSELOR: Jacques, I think it might be useful to talk about your ideal day. I'm going to turn the lights down a little bit and have you relax. You're going to close your eyes and using your imagination, walk through that perfect workday somewhere in your future.

JACQUES: OK. Just don't let me fall asleep.

The counselor played some soft music in the background, dimmed the lights slightly and began with some general relaxation techniques, having him begin by tensing and then releasing muscles in his body, beginning in his feet and ending with his face. As Jacques relaxed, the counselor began, speaking softly and leaving pauses in between the directions and questions.

COUNSELOR: OK, Jacques. I want you to imagine that it's about seven months after you graduated. It's a regular workday for you. You've had a good night's sleep, and it's time to wake up. How do you wake up? Is there an alarm, or a partner? What time are you waking up? Before you get up, look around you. What does your room look like? What smells, sounds and colors are you aware of? Do you look different than you do now?

All right. You move through your place, getting dressed and eating breakfast. What clothes are you wearing as you prepare for work? What do the other rooms look like?

You're ready to go to work. Do you leave your place, or do you work at home? What happens next? Do you drive or walk to work? If you drive, what are you driving? How far is it to work? As you walk outside, take notice of your neighborhood, what it looks like.

You're at work now. Are you alone or with people? Do you have an office? What does it look like? It's time to start working. You're excited, because you are going to be doing your favorite thing. What type of work are you doing? Are you working by yourself or with a team? What are you feeling?

It's time to go home now. Take a look at your watch. What time is it? What are your plans after work?

You're headed home now, and the evening is yours. What will you be doing?

At last, it's time for bed. As you fall asleep, you reflect on what a good day it has been, and what made it such a good day.

The counselor pauses and waits for Jacques to open his eyes, which he does after several seconds.

JACQUES: That was something – I could really see some things very clearly, and others were kind of hazy. I really enjoyed looking at my surroundings along the way.

COUNELOR: Tell me about what you saw.

Jacques described his ideal day to the counselor. As they talked, they were able to reveal some values Jacques had that previously the counselor had not known, such as his need for independence. They went on to discuss what occupations might lead him to the dream living environment he hoped for.

Career Genogram

Another non-standardized assessment that is a useful tool is the career genogram. Genograms are used extensively in family counseling, with the purpose of obtaining a graphic picture of a person's heritage. With career counseling, the purpose is to gain a graphic picture of the client's career heritage. What have family members done in the past? What themes are evident among gender, other factors? The counselor would work with the client to create a genogram, in the same way a genogram is normally created (start with either self or relative, indicating marriages, children, divorces, etc.). What gives a genogram a career emphasis is going back through the genogram and identifying each person's career. Many other options exist. For example, it might be interesting to note highest level of education achieved, career paths each took, any dominant values, stress-related illnesses, and so forth. Using this tool can help the client see a connection between where he or she is relative to where his or her predecessors have been.

When introducing the career genogram, you should start with the client's primary relationship (partner/spouse), followed by children. Then the counselor would have the client start diagramming his family background, going back a generation at a time. Once the genogram has been completed, the client should go back and write in the careers/jobs, skills, talents and other relevant information for each person on the genogram. If the extended family is small, the client could also include close friends.

Some questions/activities might include:

- Writing down perceived work/education values for each person and then noting themes.

- Analyzing occupations for Holland type and then comparing to personal type.

- Have the client identify people on the genogram who are most like the client, and then ask how satisfied they are in their career, how they make career decisions, and what advice they would give to the client.

- Are there any pressures toward or away from certain careers?

- How do family members balance work and play?

Okiishi (1987) described use of career genograms as a career counseling tool.

Holland Party Game

A great career group or classroom guidance activity involves a non-standardized intervention with the six Holland types. Participants are given a basic, one sentence description of each of the Holland types. Before the session, the counselor has placed cards with the first letter of each type around the room. After reading through the types and selecting their top three choices, participants are asked to find their letter and stand there. What happens next is up to the counselor and client. It could be relatively non-structured, letting participants talk with others in their group before moving on to their second choices, or it could be more structured. One particularly interesting activity is to assign each group the task of organizing for a party. I have found, on a fairly consistent basis, that the "S" types typically don't get much planned, as they are having fun talking about the party, while the "A" types tend to focus on the party theme, and "E" types discuss who they can bring in to speak, and how they can get funding for the party. Regardless of the approach, the counselor can make notes of how many are in each group, and then use the class numbers as examples describing consistency and differentiation. The party game could be used with individuals as well as groups.

Checklists

A final type of non-standardized self-assessments includes checklists. These are often counselor homemade tools created out of necessity when funds are limited and a need exists. For example, a counselor might not be able to afford a values inventory, so he or she creates a list of values and has students prioritize their top and bottom five. This then serves as ground for discussion. Other checklists might include interests, skills, hobbies, career beliefs, career worries, coping strategies, or majors. The list could be exhaustive. The purpose for these checklists is not to achieve high reliability, but to provide the client and counselor with a springboard for discussion. Counselor can also use information to create self-assessment checklists. For example, if a counselor knows that a client is interested in a particular occupation, she can go to a reliable source, such as the Occupational Outlook Handbook and the ONET Center, and create a card sort or a checklist of each of those occupations and for carnival.

Summary

In this chapter, we have discussed some non-standardized self-assessment methods. Evidence indicates that self-estimates of ability are valid. Many self-assessment questionnaires and checklists have been developed to evaluate specific characteristics that are of interest in career counseling. The use of self-assessment is encouraged to lessen the chances that career decision making will be dominated by any one source. Non-standardized self-assessment devices have limitations but can help stimulate discussion and supply supplementary information for career exploration. For an additional discussion of non-standardized assessments, readers should refer to Zunker (2005).

Questions and Exercises

1. What are the major advantages of using self-assessment measures in career counseling?

2. What strategy would you use to introduce standardized measures of interests and values after using a non-standardized one?

3. Build a self-assessment instrument for measuring values of high school seniors. Explain how you would incorporate this instrument into a career counseling program.

4. Work through the non-standardized self-assessments discussed in this chapter, including five lives, ideal day, assessing interests, and creating your career genogram. What have you learned about yourself that you might not have learned with standardized assessments?

5. Experiment with the ideal day experience. Which approach is more effective, writing the ideal day down or describing it to a partner?

6. A client's five lives are given in the following list. What kind of interpretations can you make from her descriptions?

7. If I could be anything at all, I'd be a homemaker. I'd have lots of children, and a husband that had a good paying job. I'd write books on the side, but mostly I'd be at home, enjoying myself in my children and other hobbies. I'd learn to be a great chef, and actually try some of the recipes that I carefully copy down all the time and then shove into that little box.

8. I guess my second life stems from the first. I'd love to be a chef – a pastry chef. I'd like to own a comfy little shop where people come in and relax from the pressures of the outside world. They'd enjoy coffee and one of my pastries. We'd have good conversations and there would be a great deal of comfort in the routine.

9. I guess I've always thought about being a missionary, getting out there and working with those who don't have as much as I do. I guess that's about as adventurous as I get. It'd be cool to think that you were doing something that had God's stamp of approval on it.

10. I think I'd like to be a writer. Not a reporter, but a writer of what I want to say. Maybe children's books, maybe a novel.

11. Last one! I would love to be a singer. Well, I am a singer now, but just haven't been recognized by any one with connections. I guess I really wouldn't like all the touring and demands on my personal life. Maybe if I could just go record some songs and then hang out at home while my CDs sold millions. Yes, that'd be the life.

12. Find a career of interest either on the O*NET or the Occupational Outlook Handbook. Use the descriptors to create a checklist. Then take the checklist. What surprises or gaps were there if any? Use this information to develop a personal career plan for yourself.

14 Combining Assessment Results

In each preceding chapter, the discussion of assessment was necessarily limited to one type of inventory or test. We do not want to give the impression, however, that segregating individually measured characteristics and traits is good practice. On the contrary, career counselors should consider the totality of individual needs. Each measured characteristic provides a rich source of information for stimulating discussion about goals and for enhancing self-understanding. It is becoming more common for inventories to measure more than one factor. For example, clients can choose to take the Strong Interest Inventory along with the Myers Briggs Type Indicator, which yields a report of interests and personality. The Differential Aptitude Test is paired with the Career Interest inventory, and many of the computer-assisted career guidance programs include measures of values, interests and skills that culminate in an overall profile. The career counselor's aim is to encourage combining all of the available information in the career planning process.

In this chapter, a counseling case illustrates the use of a conceptual model for using assessment results in a university counseling center. In addition, the use of a combination of assessment results is illustrated by cases that use the results of several tests and inventories discussed in preceding chapters. Finally, the use of a computerized assessment program is illustrated.

Using a Model for Combining Assessment Results

In the following illustration of a conceptual model for using assessment results, both major and minor components of the model are identified to demonstrate a sequential order of events. Although this is a contrived situation, it closely resembles an actual counseling case at a university counseling center.

Marvin, a 20-year-old college sophomore, was referred to the counseling center by one of his instructors. He informed the receptionist that he needed help choosing a major. The receptionist assigned Masoud, a career counselor, to Marvin's case.

Step 1. Analyzing Needs

A. Establish the Counseling Relationship

COUNSELOR: Hi, Marvin. I'm Masoud. Come into my office and let's talk. I see that you were referred by Mr. Goss.

MARVIN: Yes, sir. He's my math instructor.

COUNSELOR: I know Mr. Goss well. He's a great professor, isn't he?

MARVIN: I really like him! I guess because he's so fair to everyone and he's real easy to talk to.

COUNSELOR: Right. Most students have told me that. Do you live in the city, Marvin?

MARVIN: No. I live out on Hunter Road.

COUNSELOR: That's a nice area. Now, let's see how we can help you. You mentioned to the receptionist you need help in choosing a major.

MARVIN: Yeah. I just can't decide. But, let me tell you the whole story. Do you have the time?

COUNSELOR: You bet. We'll take as much time as we need. Tell me, how do you go about making decisions?

Marvin informed the counselor that he was interested in forestry but wasn't able to attend a college that offered forestry as a major because he was financially unable to live away from home and felt he should not leave his aged parents. He was somewhat disappointed but seemed to accept the reality of the situation.

MARVIN: Well, I really look up to my big brother. If I'm leaning one way, and it's a real important decision, I always call him.

B. Accept and Adopt the Counselee's View

COUNSELOR: I understand your concern. That's not the ideal situation for you, perhaps, but let's follow up on your interest in forestry. Tell me something about that.

MARVIN: Well, I like to be outdoors—growing up in the woods and all—our house is right on a river, and I've fished and hunted all my life. I just like it outside. I probably couldn't make it being penned up in an office all day long.

COUNSELOR: Okay, you like the outdoors, and that's a good point we need to keep in mind when you are considering college majors or careers. What else can you tell me about forestry?

The counselor's question was an attempt to determine whether Marvin had investigated the nature or work involved in forestry. Also, the counselor wanted to measure the depth of Marvin's commitment to this kind of work.

MARVIN: Okay, see, I read up some on forestry in a career book and it sounded just like the kind of work I'd like. You know, watch the growth of trees and how they survive. And I also looked at some college catalogs to find out which ones offered it as a major. That's about when I realized I couldn't go with forestry because I just can't leave my parents now.

Following further discussion of forestry, the counselor was satisfied that Marvin was indeed committed. The counselor concluded that occupations related to forestry would be a good point for discussion in the future.

C. Establish Dimensions of Lifestyle

COUNSELOR: Earlier, you mentioned that you like to hunt and fish. What other leisure activities do you enjoy?

MARVIN: Oh, I collect rocks and I go horseback riding; plus I like to watch basketball, and I play a little tennis.

COUNSELOR: Do you belong to any clubs on campus?

MARVIN: Yes, I'm a member of the science club, and I've thought about joining a fraternity.

During these discussions, the counselor made occasional notes reflecting pertinent information about Marvin. Included in the notes are the following statements:

Expressed an interest in forestry
Likes the outdoors
Grew up in a country home
Has given considerable thought to a career
Commitment to outdoor work seems firm
Interested in science
Likes to be around animals
Collects rocks
Likes team sports
Some interests are fairly well crystallized
Is disappointed about inability to pursue forestry degree, but has accepted the situation fairly well

D. Specify Needs

COUNSELOR: Let's get back to your reason for coming here. You mentioned that you wanted help in choosing a major that is available at this university.
(Marvin nodded.)

COUNSELOR: Okay, one of the first things we can do is to further explore your interests. For example, you stated a strong need to work outdoors and a definite interest in forestry. Would you like to explore other interests and link them to possible major and career options?

MARVIN: Right. That's what I came here for. I'd like to take one of those interest tests.

COUNSELOR: I believe that would be a good first step, and we can arrange for you to take an interest inventory during your next appointment. But before we decide on a specific interest inventory, tell me how you are doing academically in college.

Marvin informed the counselor that he had maintained a high B average in all of his course work. He explained that he did best in math and science courses.

MARVIN: I've always liked math and science, and I make my best grades in these courses. So far, I have an A in biology, chemistry, and math.

The counselor decided that an aptitude or achievement test was not necessary at this time, since Marvin had established a good academic record. The counselor would review Marvin's transcript before the next appointment.

Step 2. Establishing the Purpose

COUNSELOR: Now, let's get back to the interest inventory. How do you think an interest inventory will help you in choosing a major?

MARVIN: Well, I hope it will give me some ideas about possible majors.

COUNSELOR: Right, it will. We usually expect that results will verify some previously expressed interests and will also introduce new possibilities to explore. How does this sound to you?

MARVIN: Let's go for it!

COUNSELOR: Great! Later we can decide if other testing is necessary. Now, let's check with the receptionist for a testing time.

Step 3. Determining the Instrument

When selecting an interest inventory for Marvin, the counselor reviewed the notations he had made earlier and, in fact, reconstructed the entire conversation with Marvin. He concluded that Marvin could benefit most from an interest inventory that provided occupational college major scales as presented by the Kuder Occupational Interest Survey (KOIS). His rationale was that Marvin had crystallized his interests fairly well at this point in his life and was more in need of specific information, such as college major scale scores, and less in need of information pertaining to broad areas of interest such as general occupational themes. The counselor decided that the KOIS would also be a good instrument to provide Marvin with specific college majors to consider in the career decision-making process. Scores on college majors and occupational scales can be compared on the Kuder Occupational Interest Survey report (see page ??).

Step 4. Using the Results

During the pre-interpretation phase, the counselor reviewed the profile scores from the interest inventory. He noticed that Marvin's highest occupational scale scores were for forestry worker, civil engineer, county agricultural agent, mathematician, and veterinarian. His highest college major scale scores were forestry, mathematics, biological science, civil engineering, animal husbandry, and physical science. These results seemed to verify Marvin's expressed interest in the outdoors, mathematics, and sciences.

In reviewing Marvin's transcript of earned college credits, the counselor found that Marvin's grade point average was a high B. Marvin had done extremely well in mathematics and science courses, earning grades of A's. His outstanding performance in mathematics and science courses linked well with his interest in mathematics, civil engineering, and biological and physical sciences.

Marvin reported promptly for the next counseling session. After asking Marvin what had transpired since their last meeting, the counselor presented the profile of interest scores.

COUNSELOR: As you recall, in our discussion of interest inventories, we agreed that we could get some suggestions for college majors from the results. I believe you will be pleased to find that there are a number of majors indicated for your consideration. But, remember, this information is only one factor we should consider in the career decision-making process.

MARVIN: Right.

The counselor then explained the occupational major scale scores follows: COUNSELOR: The asterisk by this list of college majors (pointing to the profile) indicates that your responses were very similar to responses of satisfied individuals who are majoring in these fields of study. Your highest scores in mathematics on the college major scales are typical of satisfied people who are majoring in mathematics. According to these results, a major in mathematics should be one of the majors for you to consider.

MARVIN: (Pause.) Yeah, I do like math, but I'm not really all that interested in being a mathematician. What do they do besides teach?

COUNSELOR: Good question. I think you will find our career library helpful in answering questions like this one. In fact, I think it would be a good idea for us to make a list of all the college majors and related careers you might want to explore further, as well as important questions that you have about them, like what exactly they do.

Marvin agreed that he would be interested in researching several majors suggested from the results of the interest inventory. The counselor also discussed how interests in certain college subjects could be related to the occupational scales on the interest inventory.

COUNSELOR: One of your highest interests on the occupational scales is civil engineering. Can you link high interests in college major scales to this occupation?

MARVIN: Oh, I see. Yeah, civil engineers have to be sharp in mathematics.

COUNSELOR: That's right. The point is, if you don't want to be a mathematician, you can link this interest and your proficiency in math to a number of occupations.

Using this procedure to discuss the results of the interest inventory, the counselor assisted Marvin in developing a list of majors and occupations he would research in the career library. It was agreed that Marvin was to do his research within a 30-day period. After three weeks, Marvin came in for an appointment.

COUNSELOR: Hi, Marvin. I've been wondering how you made out. I noticed you busy at work in the career library several times.

MARVIN: Yes, I went through quite a bit of material.

COUNSELOR: Before you tell me what you found, let's review the list of majors and occupations you were to research.

MARVIN: Okay, but I eliminated several right away.

As they looked over the previously prepared list of majors and occupations, Marvin also reviewed the notes he had made from his research.

MARVIN: I still would like to be a forester, but I found that civil engineering might be a good substitute.

COUNSELOR: Tell me more about how you came to that conclusion.

MARVIN: Well, as you know, I like the outdoors and I'm pretty good in math, and I read that civil engineers do spend a lot of time surveying in the open country. Also, our college offers a degree in civil engineering. This appeals to me. I think I might like a job like this, but I'm not completely sure.

COUNSELOR: Your conclusions sound logical. The civil engineer occupation does fit the pattern of your expressed interests that we reviewed from the interest inventory, and you have a good background in math and sciences. But, you still seem to have doubts.

MARVIN: Yeah, I'd like to know more about it.

COUNSELOR: Would you like to talk to someone who is a civil engineer?

MARVIN: Hey, that'd be great!

The counselor arranged for Marvin to visit a civil engineer assigned to the state highway department. Then the counselor and Marvin identified some private surveying companies in the phone book and after a few calls, found an engineer who was willing to meet. He also suggested that Marvin visit the chairman of the civil engineering department. Marvin opted to visit the practicing engineers first. In addition to discussing civil engineering, Marvin and the counselor explored several other career options. However, Marvin, preoccupied with visiting the civil engineers, gave little attention to other possible alternatives.

Two weeks later, Marvin was back for another counseling session after having visited the work sites of two civil engineers. Surprisingly, Marvin lacked his usual enthusiasm when he greeted the counselor.

COUNSELOR: It's good to see you again, Marvin. I hope you found the visits to the engineers to be informative.

MARVIN: It was okay, I guess.

COUNSELOR: You don't seem to be too excited about what you found.

MARVIN: No, I'm not. I don't really think now that I'd like being a civil engineer.

COUNSELOR: Would you mind sharing your observations with me?

MARVIN: Well, it turns out they have to be inside and do more office work than I had thought, looking up materials, reading land titles, and plotting grades. That part of it sure doesn't appeal to me. I just have this thing about working outdoors. Also, they don't make much money, either!

As Marvin and the counselor continued to discuss civil engineering and other occupations, it became clear to the counselor that Marvin was in need of further clarification of interests, values, and preferred lifestyles. The counselor shifted the discussion to analyzing needs.

COUNSELOR: Marvin, during this conversation there have been some key factors discussed that are most important for you to consider in planning for the future. For example, you found several work requirements in civil engineering that were not to your liking. You also brought up the fact that the pay scale of civil engineers does not meet your financial requirements. The point is that, on this visit, you learned a great deal about a particular occupation and some very important factors about yourself. Would you agree?

MARVIN: You're right. I had the wrong impression about civil engineering, and I guess it took a trip out there to make that clear. Besides, when I started researching in the career library, I realized that I hadn't thought about a lot of things concerning work.

COUNSELOR: We all learn through experience.

MARVIN: Yeah, I guess that's right, but now what?

COUNSELOR: You mentioned that you learned more about yourself when you made the on-site visitation. Could you explain more fully?

MARVIN: Oh, I guess I started thinking about a lot of things, like I know now that I want to make a lot of money, you know. I need to be able to afford to buy some land, and have a nice car and even a stable full of horses. I just didn't realize that this was all a part of what I was supposed to be deciding. I suddenly realized that the decisions I make right now will have a lot to do with all this stuff in the future like for the rest of my life, even. Whew, heavy stuff.

COUNSELOR: Perhaps I can help you clarify more of these important factors like the ones you mentioned.

MARVIN: Yep, that's what I need, all right. I'm just not ready to make that big a decision yet.

The counselor had returned to the first step in the model for using assessment results: analyzing needs. He was now ready to further specify needs, part of Step 1.

COUNSELOR: What we have been discussing are values. You have verified your interests and now we have shifted to considering a most important dimension—value clarification. For example, how strongly do you value a variety of tasks on a job, or prestige, independence, creativity, and a feeling of accomplishment?

MARVIN: (Pause.) I never even thought of those things before.

The counselor was now in the position to again establish the purpose of using assessment results.

COUNSELOR: Would you like to learn more about your values?

MARVIN: That sounds interesting.

COUNSELOR: We have found that value clarification is an important part of career decision making. Many individuals find that the discussion of values is an enlightening experience that helps clarify expectations of life and work. I believe that an inventory that measures satisfaction one seeks from work would be helpful to you.

Marvin agreed that value clarification would help him at this point in the decision process, and an appointment was made for administering a values inventory. In determining the instrument, the counselor decided using the values component in the self-assessment section of SIGI PLUS (VALPAR International, 2005) would be most helpful for Marvin, primarily because the focus of attention at this point was on values associated with work.

The values section measures several work values by having a person rank traits from essential to not desired for personal job satisfaction. The counselor's strategy was to link specific work values with college majors and occupational interest patterns as measured by the previously administered interest inventory. The counselor's rationale was that Marvin needed a values measure that could provide direct association with work to stimulate discussion about satisfactions derived from work.

When Marvin completed that section of SIGI PLUS, he gave a copy of the printout to the counselor, who then began preparation for using the results. The counselor made notes of the three highest values—leisure, security, and working in main field of interest—and the three lowest values—high income, prestige, and independence. Using these results, the counselor felt that he could stimulate discussion concerning work values and their relation to career choice.

When Marvin came to the next appointment, the counselor explained the purpose of the values exercise and began reviewing the printout.

COUNSELOR: Marvin, I'd like you to look at this and tell me your definition of each of these values.

Marvin spent considerable time looking over his printout and describing each value. When he finished, he had the following discussion with the counselor.

MARVIN: This is interesting. I'm surprised about some of the results, but yet when I think of what I really like and value, I guess I'm not all that surprised.

COUNSELOR: Could you be more specific?

MARVIN: Remember when I came back from the visit with the civil engineer, I said they didn't make enough money for me? Well, that's not really a big thing with me. I guess that I was just frustrated because civil engineers turned out to not be a good substitute for what I really want. Anyway, my low ranking of high income as a value is right, I think.

COUNSELOR: What about the other values?

MARVIN: Time for leisure and working in my field of interest are right on target.

COUNSELOR: Can you relate these values to college majors and occupations as measured by the interest inventory?

MARVIN: I guess you probably have opportunities for leisure in almost any occupation, so that's no big deal. As for working in my field of interest, forestry, that's *real* important to me—essential. Isn't there some way I could still go into forestry?

The depth of Marvin's commitment to forestry was again made very clear in this discussion and others that followed. Assessment of interest and work values stimulated Marvin to consider alternative college majors and occupations, but he also came to the conclusion that his dream of becoming a forester was an overwhelming desire for which there was no substitute.

Step 5. Making a Decision

Marvin decided to continue college on a part-time basis in order to find a job from which he could save the necessary funds to attend a university that offered forestry. Even though he was reluctant to leave his parents to attend college, they encouraged him to pursue his interest.

Case Summary

This case illustrates how assessment results can be used at various stages in the career decision-making process and, in particular, how they can encourage further exploration and clarification. In Marvin's case, assessment results were used when the need was established. An interest inventory focused attention on career alternatives that Marvin had not considered and reinforced his expressed interest in outdoor work. When Marvin and the counselor agreed that value clarification was an important dimension to consider in the career decision-making process, a values exercise was used. In each instance, the purpose of assessment results was clearly established. As Marvin experienced a greater sense of awareness, he was greatly assisted in the career decision-making process by the use of carefully selected assessment inventories.

Combining Separate Tests and Inventories

Inventories and computer-assisted career guidance systems are becoming more complex and including multiple measures of interests, skills, and so on, but another way to obtain results on the various components of career choice is to combine several tests and inventories. Let's look at four cases in which the results of more than one test or inventory are combined. The results of an interest inventory and a career development inventory were used to assist Janeesha in career planning. The results of the DAT, the KOIS, and the MIQ were combined to provide information designed to stimulate Ari's career exploration. For Kwok, achievement and aptitude test results were combined with the results of an interest inventory to enhance the self-awareness so vital to career decision making and educational planning. Computerized inventories measuring abilities, interests, and values were used to help Flo decide on a career direction.

Case of a High School Senior Lacking Career Orientation

Janeesha was both confused and infuriated by her poor scores on the Career Development Inventory (CDI)—specifically with her low scores on the decision-making scale. She thought she was as ready as anyone was to make a career decision. "What's all this nonsense about self-evaluation?" she asked herself as she waited outside the counselor's office. "After all, I have been in school almost 12 years, my grades are good, and I'm ready to go to college. Or am I ready to go to college? Maybe I should go to work? Oh well, I'm just like the rest of my classmates: I'll know what to do when I graduate."

The counselor sensed that Janeesha was upset. He realized that Janeesha had rarely received what she considered low scores on a test. She had been a model student throughout her school career. With emotional overtones, Janeesha immediately brought up the issue of low scores. The counselor acknowledged her concerns and suggested that they evaluate her scores by studying the content of the inventories.

The counselor explained that the CDI was different from tests on which one received grades; the CDI was used primarily as a counseling tool to help students develop skills for career planning and decision making. This information seemed to have little effect on Janeesha's emotional state. The counselor allowed considerable time for Janeesha to express her feeling of frustration. She eventually returned to the content of the inventories. As they discussed the profile, the counselor asked Janeesha if she would like to look at some of the item responses. They started with the results of the career-planning and decision-making scales.

JANEESHA: I missed quite a few of the questions dealing with understanding how to make career decisions. I don't know what that means.

COUNSELOR: Okay, let's look at some of the items.

Their review revealed that Janeesha had difficulty recognizing various aspects of work and working conditions. Although she was threatened by her answers on the items, she recognized the differences between her responses and those considered appropriate. As Janeesha became increasingly defensive, however, the counselor decided to set up another meeting to give himself time to plot strategy and create a more productive atmosphere.

Janeesha seemed relaxed at the beginning of the second conference. The counselor hoped that she would be able to accept suggestions for programs that could help her. He began by informing Janeesha that career decision making was a learned skill and that knowledge of working conditions came with experience.

While discussing the results of an interest inventory, Janeesha commented that she had low scores there, too. The counselor agreed that Janeesha had a flat profile, but again he emphasized that this was not a test used to give grades for high scores. In fact, the counselor commented that the results of the CDI and the interest inventory were somewhat similar because she had admitted to having little knowledge about the world of work and had narrow, well-defined interests. This, he stated, could be the main reason for the "low scores," or flat profile. Finally, he explained that she had difficulty responding to questions and choices on the interest inventory because of her lack of involvement in work activities; she simply had little knowledge of occupations and work environments.

The combined results of the interest inventory and the CDI pointed out problems Janeesha would have in career planning. As she recognized her lack of knowledge of occupations and lack of career decision-making skills, she became convinced that action was necessary. The counselor was now in a position to suggest methods to overcome her inexperience, including visits to workplaces. In this case, the results of two inventories provided both Janeesha and the counselor with specific information to be used in planning intervention strategies to overcome recognized deficits.

During the fall semester of his senior year in high school, Ari made an appointment to see the career counselor for help in planning his future. He informed the counselor that he thought about going to college "like everyone else," but he also thought about going to work after graduation. His parents were indifferent about his plans and left these decisions to him. After a rather lengthy conversation concerning Ari's likes, dislikes, and options, Ari agreed with the counselor that a battery of tests and inventories would help with decision making. Specifically, Ari was to take the Differential Aptitude Test (DAT) to help

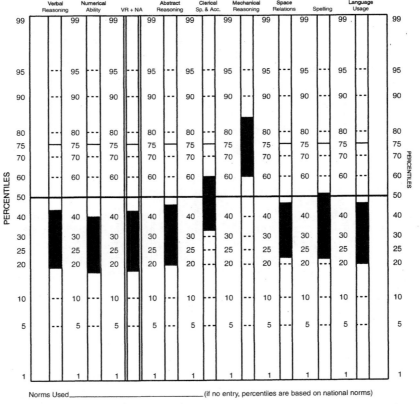

Norms Used_____ (if no entry, percentiles are based on national norms)

*F — first (fall) semester testing and percentiles; S — second (spring) semester testing and percentiles.

Figure 14-1   From Differential Aptitude Tests – Fifth Edition. Copyright © 1990 by Harcourt Assessment, Inc. Reproduced with permission. All rights reserved. "Differential Aptitude Tests – Fifth Edition" and "DAT-5" are trademarks of Harcourt Assessment, registered in the United States of America and/or other jurisdictions.

him understand his abilities and then relate these abilities to his interests as measured by the KOIS and his values as measured by the Minnesota Importance Questionnaire (MIQ).

As the counselor reviewed the results of the DAT, shown in Figure 14-1 (previous page), she questioned whether Ari currently possessed the aptitude necessary for college work. She was particularly concerned about the low scores in verbal reasoning and numerical ability, as these two scores provide a fairly reliable index for predicting academic success. She was aware that colleges vary in their requirements and did not want to eliminate this option, but at the same time, Ari's low scores had to be considered in their discussion. She also noticed that his highest score was in mechanical reasoning.

The results of the KOIS were valid (V score above .45). The highest occupational scores (males) were for engineer, mechanical engineer, industrial, and auto mechanic. Ari's highest college major scores (males) were for engineering, mechanical engineering, civil engineering, and physical education. The counselor wondered whether Ari's apparent interest in occupations that require a college degree reflected a current interest Ari had in attending college, rather than his true interests, especially given his low aptitude for college work.

On the MIQ, Ari's highest scores were in supervision–human relations (values a supportive supervisor), social status (values recognition in the community), and working conditions (values pleasant work environments). His lowest scores were in creativity (values ability to try out own ideas), responsibility (values being able to make own decisions), and independence (values working on his own). These results were of particular interest to the counselor because Ari placed a high value on the working environment but a low value on intellectual stimulation.

Ari seemed somewhat embarrassed by the DAT scores, but he stated that he did not consider himself a good student. The counselor then asked about his interest in attending college. Ari replied: "Well, all of my friends are going to college, and I figure that I ought to go, too. I got through high school somehow, and I ought to be able to make it in college." These remarks indicated that Ari did not know what college would be like. His reason for going to college reflected little knowledge of college requirements and a lackadaisical attitude toward exploring other options available to him.

When the counselor mentioned Ari's high score on mechanical reasoning, Ari expressed an interest in mechanics and other jobs such as television repair and electric engine repair. The counselor followed this expression of interest with a description of occupations in technical fields—auto mechanics and related trades. Her purpose was to introduce several career options Ari had not considered. The counselor then moved on to the results of the MIQ. A discussion of values as related to work environments held Ari's attention.

ARI: Yeah, I like to work around people who are friendly and visit a lot. The way I see my life is a job 8-to-5, five days a week, and a chance to go fishing and hunting.

COUNSELOR: Okay, now that you have come to that conclusion, we should examine other parts of the inventory. Your lowest score was in intellectual stimulation, which means that you do not place a high value on work that permits independent thinking.

ARI: I guess that's right. That doesn't interest me. I just want a job that's not too complicated. I don't care about being independent, and I'm not interested in artistic things.

The counselor then linked the results of the assessment instruments to occupational requirements. She suggested that Ari attempt to develop a list of occupations that would be related to his high mechanical reasoning score. Next, he was to relate these occupations to his interests and work values. The counselor helped Ari begin this assignment by suggesting several occupations to consider, including jobs that would require apprentice training and for which technical training courses were offered.

Ari reported for the next counseling session early. He seemed eager to get started.

ARI: "Do you think everybody should go to college? I've been thinking that maybe college isn't for me. This assignment you gave me helped me see that I'm actually more interested in jobs that require some education and training, but not necessarily a four-year program."

When the counselor asked Ari to explain how he arrived at this conclusion, Ari replied: "When we started talking about my values, I realized that I was thinking about college because most everyone else was. That isn't really me; besides, my grades and test scores are not very high."

The counselor and Ari continued their discussion and reached some tentative conclusions. Ari would not give up the idea of college completely, but he would explore other options also. He therefore looked into occupations that require college training as well as into technical occupations and trades.

In this case, the combined test results provided the stimulus for considering career options from several perspectives. Measuring aptitudes, interests, and work values provided Ari with information he had never considered for career exploration. The discussions of the results helped Ari relate his characteristics and traits to occupational and educational information. He was stimulated to explore several different options and gained an understanding of the complexities of the world of work.

Case of a High School Senior with a Poor Attitude Towards School

Being the last one to enter the classroom and the first one to leave typified Kwok's attitude toward school. Most teachers wondered why he bothered to stick around for his senior year. Perhaps it was the good time he was apparently having, or maybe it prevented him from having to go to work. The counselor had made numerous attempts for two years to get Kwok interested in coming in for counseling, but Kwok managed to evade the counselor's office. Thus, the counselor was quite surprised when Kwok's name appeared on the appointment list.

Kwok further amazed the counselor when he asked for help in planning what to do after high school. He informed the counselor that he began thinking about his future because of the results of a test he had taken. He explained that the entire class had been required to take several tests and that his teacher informed him that he had scored high on the aptitude test. The counselor and Kwok set up another meeting in a few days so that the counselor could gather the test data. In the meantime, the counselor suggested that Kwok take an interest inventory. The counselor was interested in maintaining Kwok's enthusiasm as well as in obtaining a measure of his interests.

The counselor discovered that Kwok did indeed do well on the DAT, which had been administered to all seniors. The counselor was surprised to find that his scores were above the 90th percentile for verbal reasoning and numerical ability. Abstract reasoning and mechanical reasoning also were significantly high (above the 75th percentile). The counselor wondered why Kwok let all this talent go to waste during his school career.

Achievement test scores reflected Kwok's poor academic performance. Most scores were below the 50th percentile (national group) with the exception of mathematics reasoning, which was at the 75th percentile. The counselor concluded that even Kwok's high aptitude could not make up for the academic work he had not done.

The Self-Directed Search (SDS) provided insights into Kwok's modal personal style; enterprising was his dominant personality type. An enterprising person, according to the SDS description, is adventurous, extroverted, and aggressive—a good description of Kwok. Although Kwok didn't use these characteristics in academic endeavors, he was considered a leader by his peer groups. His summary code, ECS (enterprising, conventional, social), suggested that he would prefer sales jobs such as insurance underwriter, real estate salesperson, and grain buyer (Holland, 1994a).

In the next session, Kwok told the counselor that he was planning to attend college and devote much more of his energy to college courses than he had to high school courses. The counselor took this opportunity to point out the discrepancies between Kwok's aptitude test scores and his grades and achievement test scores. He emphasized that Kwok had the potential for making much better grades than he had in the past. Kwok was quick to agree that he had goofed off and would have to pay the price now. The counselor suggested that Kwok enroll in a summer course sponsored by the community college learning resource center to upgrade his basic skills and improve his study habits.

Kwok was undecided about a career because he had given little thought to his future. The SDS results provided him with several specific occupations to consider.

KWOK: I think I would like sales work of some kind or to have my own business. Do you think I should study business?

COUNSELOR: That may be a good possibility. However, I think you should take the time to research what is offered in a typical school of business at a university. But first, let's consider what's involved in career decision making.

The counselor continued by emphasizing the importance of self-understanding in career planning. He discussed the significance of modal personal style, as identified by the SDS. Kwok recognized that the results of the aptitude and achievement measures also contributed to his self-understanding; they provided stimulus for further discussion. As a result, Kwok was challenged by the counselor to devote time to researching the world of work in relation to his personal characteristics. Kwok thanked the counselor for helping him establish some direction and set up several appointments to discuss and evaluate the careers he was exploring because of his personal characteristics.

Case of a Divorced Woman Searching for a Career Direction

Flo had been encouraged by her sister and friends to attend a job club at the nearby women's center. She experienced immediate support from the job club group and found that other divorced women with children were in the process of deciding future alternatives. Eventually, Flo was given an appointment with a volunteer counselor. She related information about her background to the counselor, who summarized it as follows:

Marital status: divorced for eight months after a 10-year marriage.

Children: four children, ages 9, 7, 4, and 2.

Financial situation: child support payments and state welfare assistance.

Work experience: had never worked outside the home.

Educational level: high school graduate—grades were above average in the A and B categories, and she was on the honor role several times.

Strongest and most interesting subjects: science courses such as chemistry and biology.

Living accommodations: renting an apartment owned by her sister who lives next to her. Good schools are nearby.

Occupations considered: none seriously because she was devoted to raising her children. In high school, she had considered being a nurse, medical doctor, or dentist. She expressed an interest in helping others and working with people, but at this point in her life, she did not have a career preference or direction.

The women's center was fortunate enough to have the computerized career guidance system for adults, DISCOVER (ACT, 2005). This computer-assisted career guidance program is designed to assist adults through a systematic career exploration and decision-making process. It contains large databases that provide up-to-date information about occupations and educational opportunities and contains inventories that measure interests, abilities, and work-related values.

Under the counselor's direction, Flo entered the DISCOVER system with the approach that she was completely undecided, eventually choosing to take the ability, interests, and value inventories. The counselor explained, "Each of these inventories will provide us with different snapshots of factors that are important to you, that you might want to consider. We'll also be able to see how all three of these fit into the whole picture. For example, you might have interests in the medical field, but not the skills. By taking all three inventories, we can see how your interests, values and skills overlap and how they differ.

Figure 14-3 shows Flo's results. The counselor began by asking Flo what she thought about the results.

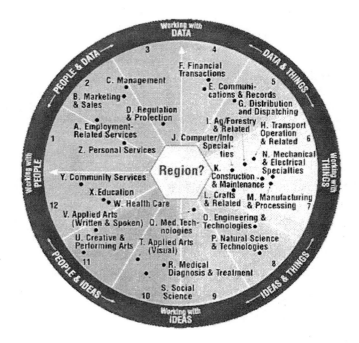

Figure 14-2   World-of-Work Map. Copyright 2000 by ACT. Inc. All rights reserved. Reproduced with permission.

FLO: Well, I guess that there weren't any fields that captured my interests, values and skills.

COUNSELOR: True – in the best-case scenario, you'd find several occupations that match all three of these areas. Remember, though, that not every occupation is listed here. Tell me what observations you can make about the other combinations or themes that you see.

FLO: I guess where I have interests and values, that's two out of three. I'd just have to focus on building my skills in that area. As for themes, I think it's interesting that it didn't come out that I was interested in medical treatment or medical technologies and yet I do have interests in health care.

COUNSELOR: What do you make of that?

FLO: That maybe there's a lot of different jobs within the medical field? I guess I need to learn more about that.

COUNSELOR: I think you're right. Occupational fields are complex. There may be certain jobs within the medical field that match your interests, values and skills, and others that do not match at all. Doing some research on occupations in health care and the medical field would make sense as a next step.

In the sessions that followed, Flo and the counselor discussed several occupational options from the list presented by the computer-assisted career guidance system. Other occupations were added for exploration purposes. Flo found more information from the computerized database concerning work tasks, employment outlook, income potential, and paths of training. She had verified and learned some new things about herself from the results of the inventories that she had completed. She kept these results in mind as she explored occupations, and she felt that the major benefit from talking with the counselor and using the computerized career guidance system was the fact that she was able to develop a frame of reference to use in career decision making. As she read job descriptions from the computer's file, she was able to evaluate each one from the vantage point of how she could accomplish the job training requirements and still care for her four children.

FLO: This has been a completely new experience for me. During my marriage I never considered working because my husband had a marvelous income and I was happy with raising a family. I'm excited about a future career role, but I still want and have the responsibility of raising my children.

COUNSELOR: It sounds like the next step would be for you to talk with some people in the field to find out how feasible it is to balance work and family in those occupations.

Flo eventually decided to choose dental assistant primarily because of the availability of training at a nearby community college. For the time being, she would aspire to this occupation, but she recognized that the future might provide opportunities in the field of dentistry. She had for the first time in her life developed a potential career direction.

Summary

In this chapter, we discussed using combinations of assessment results to help individuals consider their characteristics and traits during career counseling. We emphasized that assessment results should not be used in isolation; counselors and clients should consider the totality of individual needs. Assessment results taken from different types of tests and inventories provide useful information in the career decision-making process. Consider the model for comparing suggested occupations from various assessments.

Potential Occupations to Pursue

SDS	MIV	ASVAB	CACG	CARD SORT	OTHER
1.	1.	1.	1.	1.	1.
2.	2.	2.	2.	2.	2.
3.	3.	3.	3.	3.	3.
4.	4.	4.	4.	4.	4.
5.	5.	5.	5.	5.	5.

Occupations to Avoid

SDS	MIV	ASVAB	CACG	CARD SORT	OTHER
1.	1.	1.	1.	1.	1.
2.	2.	2.	2.	2.	2.
3.	3.	3.	3.	3.	3.
4.	4.	4.	4.	4.	4.
5.	5.	5.	5.	5.	5.

Once the client has filled out the chart, she or he can look for common occupations to consider in more depth. In addition, counselor and client can discuss the potential reasons certain occupations kept turning up on the "avoid" list, thus turning the process full circle again as self-knowledge is clarified.

Questions and Exercises

1. Following the steps of the conceptual model for using assessment results discussed in Chapter 2, develop a counseling case that illustrates each step.

2. How would you determine which instruments to use if you were requested to recommend tests and inventories for a group of tenth-graders interested in career exploration?

3. Defend the following statement: Multidimensional assessment results are more effective in career counseling than are the results of only one instrument.

4. How would you explain to an individual the differences in norms when using a combination of assessment results, some of which are based on local norms and others on national norms?

5. Illustrate how assessment results from two different instruments can support each other and how they can point out conflicts.

6. Micanel, a middle school student has come in for career counseling and has taken the middle school version of the Self-Directed Search, Career Explorer. In addition, he completed the values section of SIGI Plus, the Career Decision Profile, and a card sort. The card sort results indicated that his strongest skills that he most enjoyed using were analyzing, generating ideas, and teaching or training. His weakest skills that he strongly disliked using included making decisions, making arrangements and physical agility. He rated himself as highly competent at entertaining, reading for information and negotiating, but also rated these as strongly dislike using. Finally, he rated his ability to sell, design, and carpentry skills as minimal, which matched his strong dislike in using those skills. His other profiles are shown in Figure 14-3 through 14-5. How would you interpret his results? What next steps might you recommend? Do you have any concerns about the tests he took? Are there others you would have suggested, and if so, why?

7. Adriana Kedrick, a ninth-grade student was referred to you by several of her teachers. They have commented to you that although Adriana performs well on her written assignments, she does not participate very often in class. When they praise her achievements, she shrugs it off as "I just got lucky." As part of the school testing program, all ninth graders took the Career Planning Survey Report, which is a comprehensive career assessment program. Adriana's results are shown in Figure 14-6a and b. Before taking the inventory, she identified medical specialties/technology as a career area she thought she'd be interested in exploring. What do her results suggest? What about the discrepancy between her tested abilities and her ability self-estimates? Seeing that medical specialties and technologies is the only area that is not highlighted, how might you discuss this with her? On her interests, her number one rank is art, and yet that was not her trial job choice. What might you make of this? Her World-of-Work Map Regions for interests are in 8, 9, and 10, while her ability self-estimates fall in Region 99 (the center of the map). How might you interpret this? What other things might you like to plot on the world-of-work map, besides interests and self-estimates? In reviewing her profile, what other concerns seem to emerge? How might you structure the counseling session? What type of interventions and follow up activities might you suggest?

8. Pull together all of the assessment inventories you have taken. Pretend that you are a counselor, and that this information has been presented to you. How would you go about organizing the information in a way that would make sense? Create a form or chart that would allow you to concisely show the results.

Counting Your Answers

1. Activities

Go to page 4. Count how many times you marked **Y** (YES) for the **R** Activities only. Write that number above the R on the line to the right. Do the same thing for the **I, A, S, E,** and **C** Activities (pp. 4-5).

4	6	8	9	11	4
R	I	A	S	E	C

2. Skills

Go to page 6. Count how many times you marked **Y** for the **R** Skills only. Write that number above the **R**. Do the same thing for the **I, A, S, E,** and **C** Skills (pp. 6-7).

4	5	7	10	5	8
R	I	A	S	E	C

3. Careers

Go to page 8. Count how many times you marked **Y** for the **R** Careers only. Write that number above the **R**. Do the same thing for the **I, A, S, E,** and **C** Careers (pp. 8-9).

2	7	9	11	9	3
R	I	A	S	E	C

4. Rating Your Abilities

Go to page 10. Put the numbers you circled for **R, I, A, S, E,** and **C** on the lines to the right.

3	6	7	7	3	7
R	I	A	S	E	C

4	5	6	7	2	6
R	I	A	S	E	C

5. Total Scores

Add your five **R** scores and write that number above the **R**. Do the same thing for the other scores.

17	29	37	44	30	28
R	I	A	S	E	C

6. Holland Code

Enter the letter with the highest total score in the box marked Highest. Enter the letter with the next highest number in the box marked 2nd. If two letters are tied, put them in any order.

These letters make up your Holland code. For example, if your two highest letters are **E** and **I**, your Holland code is **EI.**

Highest   2nd

| S | A |

Figure 14-3   SIGI Plus. Copyrighted by Valpar International Corporation and used with permission.

Summarizing Your Answers

Step 1
Go to page 1. Add your ratings for the two statements under "Decidedness,"
and write the sum in its box below:
Do the same thing for "Comfort."

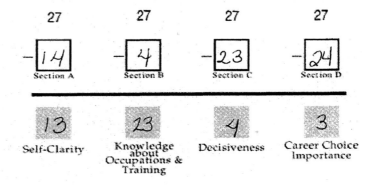

Step 2
For pages 2 and 3, add your ratings for each of the sections and write their sum
in the box below. Then subtract these sums from 27. Write the answer for each in
the shaded box.

Figure 14-4   SDS-CE. Adapted and reproduced by special permission of the Publisher, Psychological Assessment Resources, Inc., 16204 North Florida Avenue, Lutz, FL 33549, from the Self-Directed Search Career Explorer Self-Assessment Booklet by John L. Holland, Ph.D. and Amy B. Powell, Ph.D., Copyright 1970, 1973, 1977, 1979, 1985, 1990, 1994 by PAR, Inc. Further reproduction is prohibited without permission from PAR, Inc.

Your Career Decision Profile Scores

There are six scales on the Career Decision Profile. Two scales (Certainty and Comfort) assess how decided and how comfortable you are with your career choice-or with your process of making this choice. The four Reasons scales (Self-Clarity, Knowledge of Occupations and Training, Decisiveness, and Career Choice Importance) assess why you are undecided. If you are uncertain about your career, it is probably because you need more information aobut your personal characteristics, more information about occupations, better decision making skills, more interest in making a career decision, or some combination of the above. The CDP scores that follow will tell you why you are uncertain, and what you can do to become more certain.

Certainty and Comfort

How certain are you about your career choice? Scores on this scale range from 2 to 16. An average score for college students is 10 to 13.

Your Certainty score is: 2

How comfortable are you with your progress in making a career choice? Scores on the Comfort Scale range from 2 to 16. An average score for college students is 9 to 11.

Your Comfort score is: 2

You are uncertain about your career choice, and uncomfortable with your progress in making a career decision. It is probably time for you to get to work on career issues. Your discomfort is a sign that you need to address the
Decisiveness

This scale measures how capable you believe you are in making decisions. Scores range from 3 to 24.

Your Decisiveness score is: 10

If your score is 10 or less, you may have difficulty making decisions without unnecessary delay, difficulty or reliance on others, and you would benefit from completing some of the exercises described on the Decisiveness Action Plan.

If your score is 11 or more, you may be uncertain about your career, but it is probably not due to poor decision-making skills. Still you might frind the excercies on the Decisiveness Action Plan helpful in providing a model for making your career decision.   For more information about Decisiveness, review Decisiveness.

Career Choice Importance

Your Career Choice Importance score is: 21

This is an average score, suggesting that you are as concerned as most undergraduates about selecting a career. People with average scores typically are uncomfortable if they are undecided, and want to develop a clearer career plan. You may want to complete most of the tasks associated with your lower scores described in this web site. You are probably qiute motivated and are likely to find the tasks timely, informative, and rewarding.

Your Knowledge of Occupations and Training score is: 9

If your score is 10 or less, you probably need more information about occupations and training and you would benefit from completing some of the excercises described in the Knowledge of Occupations and Training Action Plan.

If your score is 11 or more, you probably know enough about occupations and training to make an informed career decision without doing much more research   For more information about Knowledge of Occupations & Training, review Knowledge of Occupations & Training.

Decisiveness

This scale measures how capable you believe you are in making decisions. Scores range from 3 to 24.

Your Decisiveness score is: 10

If your score is 10 or less, you may have difficulty making decisions without unnecessary delay, difficulty or reliance on others, and you would benefit from completing some of the exercises described on the Decisiveness Action Plan.

If your score is 11 or more, you may be uncertain about your career, but it is probably not due to poor decision-making skills. Still you might frind the excercies on the Decisiveness Action Plan helpful in providing a model for making your career decision.   For more information about Decisiveness, review Decisiveness.

Career Choice Importance

Your Career Choice Importance score is: 21

This is an average score, suggesting that you are as concerned as most undergraduates about selecting a career. People with average scores typically are uncomfortable if they are undecided, and want to develop a clearer career plan. You may want to complete most of the tasks associated with your lower scores described in this web site. You are probably qiute motivated and are likely to find the tasks timely, informative, and rewarding.

Figure 14-5   Career Decision Profile. Reproduced by permission of the author, Lawrence K. Jones.

![World-of-Work Map and Career Planning Survey Report]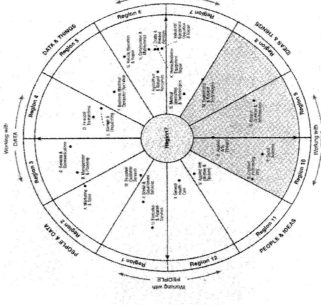

CAREER PLANNING SURVEY REPORT
Side 1

For: **KEDRICK, ADRIANA**
Preview Report, Grade 9
Date: **August 01, 2000**
About: **Jobs You May Wish to Consider**

The World-of-Work Map to the right arranges 23 Career Areas (groups of similar jobs) according to primary work tasks:

Working with—

● PEOPLE (care, services, leadership, sales, etc.)

● DATA (facts, numbers, files, business procedures)

● THINGS (machines, living things, materials such as food, wood, metal)

● IDEAS (knowledge, insights, new ways of expressing something)

Together, these Career Areas include all jobs in the work world. The Map is divided into 12 regions—like slices of pizza! Unlike pizza, each "slice" (map region) has a different work task "flavor."

Your Trial Job Choice

When you completed the Career Planning Survey, we asked you to make a trial job choice. You told us that it best fit Career Area:

Medical Specialties/Technologies
Please circle this Career Area on the Map (see Region 7).

Any job involves some work with People, Data, Things, and Ideas. As the Map shows, jobs in the Career Area you selected mainly involve working with Things.

Is this what you expected? Is it in line with the interests and abilities you reported? See below!

Your Work-Relevant Interest and Abilities

When you completed the Career Planning Survey, you told us about everyday activities that interest you—and about your abilities. The World-of-Work Map regions that best fit what you told us are shaded on the map. (See the Map's color key.)

Because interests and abilities are different, their map regions may not overlap. If they don't, you will need to decide which to emphasize as you explore your job possibilities. Please turn to side 2 of this report.

Figure 14-6a ACT Career Planning Survey. Reproduced by permission of the American College Testing Program.

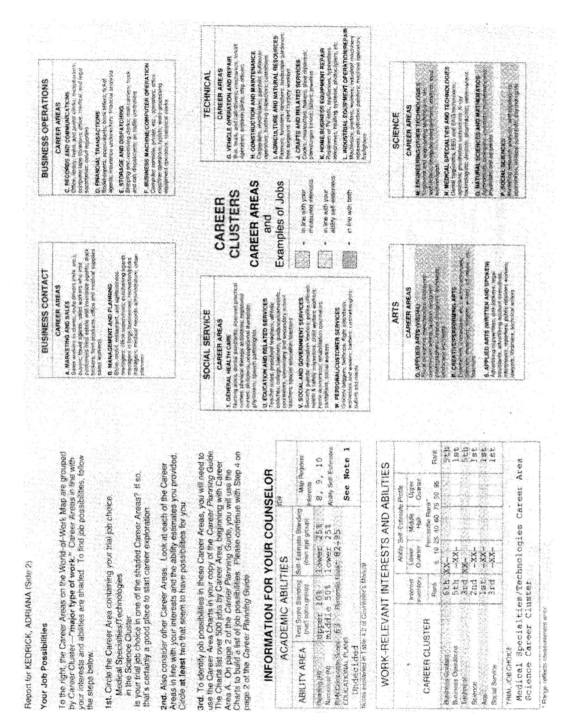

Figure 14-6b   ACT Career Planning Survey. Reproduced by permission of the American College Testing Program.

1 5 Ethics and Assessment

As a profession, those involved in career counseling are bound by a set of ethical standards. These standards help define what we should and should not be doing. They serve as reminders, but also rules for appropriate behavior with respect to the many aspects of counseling, such as individual and group counseling, confidentiality, diversity, testing, and advertising. As career counselors, our professional boards include the American Counseling Association and the National Career Development Association. If you are a nationally certified counselor, then you must adhere to the NBCC code of ethics as well. In addition, the Association for Assessment in Counseling (www.aac.ncat.edu) has published the *Standards for Multicultural Assessment* (2003). Even if a career counselor is not a member of a professional association, they are still responsible to act within the boundaries of those standards, and their actions held up against the standards of these professional associations. ACA, NCDA, NBCC and AAC standards are included in Appendix C.

Competence

As a counselor, you agree that you will act within your own "boundaries of competence" (BOC). Every counselor has areas of expertise, and other areas in which they do not have the skills or necessary training. Multiple areas of counseling foci exist, including: family counseling, marital counseling, career counseling, eating disorders, depression, anxiety, sexual abuse, and g/l/b/t issues, to name a few. With hundreds of assessments in existence, it is probable that a counselor will not be aware of or skilled in using every one. In order to become competent in an area or with an assessment, a counselor must have training and supervised experience. The ethical standards state that a counselor should not provide services or assessments that exceed the counselor's existing training and skills. With assessments, counselors should first take the assessment themselves and receive an interpretation of their inventory results prior to administering it to a client. Counselors should read the manual, and practice administering/interpreting the results on a peer or another counselor to build competence and confidence. In addition, knowing the validity, reliability and normative information about the assessment will help the counselor determine if the inventory is appropriate for a given client.

Client needs

Any intervention that a counselor selects should be based on the client's characteristics, needs and the stated goals for counseling. A common expectation of clients regarding career counseling is that they will take a test (Galassi et al., 1992), while many prefer reading about careers or other activities over testing. In some cases, administering an inventory might not be appropriate. The counselor should take into consideration a client's comfort/desire to engage in any intervention before recommending it. Some clients, being more "Social" in nature, will prefer to rely more on conversation. A counselor who is aware of Holland types might ask directed questions and then suggest looking a list of "S" occupations. Or, if a client is more in deciding between two occupations, giving an interest inventory would not be the logical next step, but helping the client to evaluate the options, either through the provision of more information, or a pro/con analysis, would be a better intervention.

Cultural Differences

Career counselors should strive to be culturally competent. Sensitivity to cultural differences should also be displayed by counselors when suggesting, administering and interpreting tests. According to Flores, Spanierman and Obasi (2003), career assessment that is culturally appropriate has the following components:

- "it integrates culturally relevant information about the client;

- attempts to understand the client in his or her cultural, personal and career contextual realities; and

- takes into account the limitations of traditional assessment and assessment tools" (p. 80).

Other considerations should include:

- *Norm groups for a test.* (If the client's norm group was not included, the results should be interpreted with caution. If there is a certain population that has a higher percentage of representation at a counselor's site, the counselor should consider developing local normative data on the test results for comparison. This would require masking identifiable information about the client. In addition, counselors should not just assume that because a particular ethnic group is mentioned in the normative data, e.g., Asian females, that the results of the norm group are comparable to all Asian females. For example, many times test developers will use college students as a large base for their norming sample. It would be wrong to assume that the results of a college-educated sample are generalizable to those even in the same ethnic group but who are not college-educated (Flores et al., 2003).

- *Incorporating standardized and non-standardized, formal and informal assessment approaches.*

- *Equivalence.* This includes linguistic, conceptual, scale and normative equivalency associated with an inventory (Fouad, 1993; Marsella & Leong, 1995).

- *Test security* (Flores et al., 2003).

- *Using appropriate self-disclosure* (Flores et al., 2003).

- *Above all else, focus on the therapeutic relationship.* If the client senses there is a strong working alliance, the client would have been involved in the decision to incorporate the assessment into the counseling session, and might be more willing to state concerns or disagreement with the results if the results did not seem to correspond with what the client expected. In some cultures, disagreement is seen as a sign of disrespect, and the counselor should be alert to this possibility, and even model some healthy questioning of the results.

COUNSELOR: So, what did you think about the inventory you completed?

LI: It was good. It showed me things I should do and things I shouldn't do.

COUNSELOR: Do you think that a test like this one should be the ultimate authority on whether or not you choose one career or another?

LI: I don't know – you talked about how this was a valid test – so the answers must be right. Maybe the test picked up on something I didn't know myself.

COUNSELOR: You make a good point there – maybe the results grouped your interests together in a way you hadn't seen them grouped before. So were there any surprises?

LI: Well, I would have never considered myself to be a politician, and it's listed in there. So is salesperson and fundraiser. I would have never thought of any of these. Maybe I should learn a little more about these jobs and consider changing my major?

COUNSELOR: I think you're wise to consider each of the options carefully before discarding them. However, remember, this inventory was a measure of your interests. There's a lot more to you than what was on that inventory – your personality, your values, your skills, and goals – all of these also play a part. You know, one of the inventories I took had physician listed as an option. It was picking up on the fact that I like to problem-solve and help people. What the inventory didn't pick up on was that I didn't want to spend that much time in college, I didn't really like the site of blood, and I didn't want to work on-call. What do you think the inventory might have been tapping into, in terms of your interests, when listing politician and those other occupations?

LI: Maybe that I'm a good leader? I guess I also can be persuasive if there's something I really believe in. But, I don't like to be pushy, and I think some of that has to come out if you're in those occupations.

COUNSELOR: OK. So you can see how those might fit some of your interests and skills, but is not such a good match in other areas. What were some of the occupations that were on your list that you felt good about?

LI: There was a project manager listed, and a small business owner. I liked those.

COUNSELOR: I can see you highlighted some others as well. Instead of focusing on the ones that you already feel are not a good fit for you, why don't we spend some time on the ones that seem to be better fits?

In this conversation, the counselor modeled the appropriateness of questioning the results of the inventory, without negating the results altogether. In addition, the counselor used self-disclosure as a way to demonstrate how the inventory might not pick up on all aspects of a person. By asking what interests the inventory might have found that resulted in some "surprising" occupations being listed, the counselor gave Li the opportunity to strengthen her self-knowledge, in that she re-stated her interests and clarified some of her work values.

Gender Issues

The Self-Directed Search, Strong Interest Inventory and Kuder Occupational Interest Survey continue to yield different results for women as compared to men. The questions of sex bias within an instrument and in the results of an inventory, as well as the way in which the data is reported by norm group appear to be the primary issues of concern with respect to gender issues and assessment. A counselor should read the manual of any assessment prior to administering it, to gain a better understanding of the assumptions made by the test developer and to determine if it is an appropriate inventory to administer to a particular client (considering client needs and psychometric properties, including norm group data).

While using same-sexed norms is often recommended (Whiston & Bouwkamp, 2003) especially with interest inventories, not all assessments report different results for women and men. Betz (1992; 2000) suggested that the counselor help the client evaluate suggested options with respect to opportunity and socialization. For example, did a client score lower in mechanical interests or skills because she actually has no interests or skills in that area, or could it be because she was never given the opportunity to develop those interests/skills, and was even socialized against those interests/skills, because those activities were seen as being more "boyish"?

Consider including non-standardized approaches, such as a values clarification exercise (Hackett & Lonborg, 1994), an ideal day exercise, and card sorts. In addition, given the research that shows that women tend to have lower self-efficacy, especially with respect to math skills (Betz & Hackett, 1997), counselors should not just accept it when a female client says, "I'm not good at math," but should be prepared to gently challenge that statement. For example, "What makes you think that you aren't good at math?"

Finally, Whiston and Bouwkamp (2003) bring up the findings that women do have a higher prevalence of mental disorders such as depression and anxiety, and that the possibility of these symptoms should not be overlooked when engaging in career counseling with women. In fact, Fassinger and O'Brien (2000) state that it is most likely unethical to ignore this possibility for women seeking career counseling.

Sexual Orientation Issues

Normative data on assessments do not generally include information on the sexual orientation of the norm group. This may stem from an assumption that career interests and skills do not differentiate according to a person's sexual orientation. While limited research has been conducted on this topic, Chung (2003) has outlined some ethical considerations associated with testing and lesbian, gay and bisexual (LGB) clients. For example, testing that includes information about barriers may bring up concerns of discrimination, victimization, and harassment. LGB clients may lean toward stereotypically appropriate LGB careers, or may lean for stereotypically heterosexual careers. While a counselor should not discourage a client from pursuing a career that is a real interest, the counselor might want to help the client evaluate how their perception of their career options are "related to social pressure, internalized stereotypes, or perceptions of limited occupational opportunities" (p. 100).

A counselor might also want to include the LGB person's significant other, parents, families and friends in the assessment/career counseling process as the client desires. Before choosing an inventory to use with a LGB client, the counselor should review the inventory to make sure that there is no evidence of heterosexist bias. For example, if a counselor wants to help the client identify potential barriers to making a career choice, does the inventory include an item such as "My spouse disapproves of my current choice" versus the more inclusive term of "partner"? Another consideration is that given the lack of standardized inventories for LGB, a counselor might use non-traditional assessment methods (Chung, 2003), such as card sorts or an ideal day, as described in other chapters of this book.

Confidentiality

Part of the power of counseling comes from the trust that develops between a client and the counselor. The client is free to share hopes and dreams, fears and doubts, with the confidence that the information shared is confidential, with a few caveats. Confidentiality also extends to test results. For example, test results can only be released with the client's consent (or client's legal representative), and then can only be shared with other professionals that are able to interpret the results. In addition, if a client uses a computer-assisted career guidance program or a computer inventory, the counselor is required to make sure that the data stored on the computer is confidential and that the records are periodically destroyed.

Orientation

If you follow the model described in Chapter 2, the client and the counselor should both know why a certain assessment is being suggested. You have discussed the client's needs, and working collaboratively, have decided that a certain inventory would best help achieve the next step towards meeting a goal. Even so, prior to administering an assessment, you should review why the assessment is occurring, and how the results will be used.

COUNSELOR: "Sandy, do you remember the reason that you are taking this interest inventory today?"

SANDY: "Yes, it's going to show me what career I should follow."

COUNSELOR: "Well, not quite. The results are going to help give us an idea of where your main interests lie. You'll also receive a list of occupations, but it won't do the work of narrowing down for you. That will be our next step, taking the suggested occupations, brainstorming from it, and getting some information to narrow those down so you can make a good choice about a career path. How does that sound to you?"

One of the common misperceptions by clients is that they can take one test that will tell them what they should be. In the example above, Sandy and the counselor had already discussed why an inventory would be useful, but as is often the case, Sandy had kept the misperception that the result would be an almost magical appearance of THE occupation that will satisfy her forever. Instead of beginning the assessment by simply reviewing the purpose, the counselor chose to let Sandy describe the purpose to gauge how accurate her perceptions were, and then reinforced the purpose and made a link between what she was about to do (take an assessment), the next step, and how that would help accomplish the overall goal. In addition to correcting a faulty perception, the counselor also demonstrated ethical behavior by accurately describing the purpose for and expected results of the assessment.

Along with confirming that the client and the counselor are on the same page about how the assessment will fit into the overall career counseling goals, the counselor needs to determine that the client is emotionally and mentally able to complete the administration. Someone who is feeling down, or having a great deal of negative thoughts, might approach an interest inventory with all negative responses, and thus skew the results. A vicious cycle can begin, starting with negative thoughts, that lead to negative responses on the inventory, which leads to poor options being suggested, which then leads back into negative thoughts again ("I knew there wouldn't be any good options for me"). Obviously, the validity of responses from a client who is under the influence of alcohol or drugs, or someone who is experiencing mania, paranoia, depression, anxiety, etc., will be questionable.

Computer-Based Test Interpretation (CBTI)

When a client completes an inventory, a common expectation is to see, as a result, some type of written interpretation of the results, along with a list of suggested occupations. A computer-based test interpretation report is an efficient and many times, effective, way to deliver a general interpretation and to pull a list of occupations from a database that match specific items endorsed by the client on the test. However, very rarely do you see validity information in an inventory manual about the interpretive report. Sampson, Purgar and Shy (2003) summarized the opinions of several authors about the role of CBTI. In a nutshell, they stated that CBTI should never be used as a replacement for a counselor, or as a "data dump" from a stand-alone computer or an online inventory, but should be used in a consultative manner between counselor and client. Sampson et al. (2003) provide an 8-step sequence for integrating

CBTI into career counseling and five competencies for using CBTI in an ethical manner, and several strategies for establishing and evaluating the validity of CBTI.

The 8–step sequence is similar to the model described in Chapter 2, in that they recognize that test results should be part of the overall counseling process, related to career theory, appropriate to the client' needs and contributing to the overall plan of action. To use CBTI ethically, a counselor should thoroughly understand the construct being tested (such as career indecision, interests, etc.); psychometric properties of the inventory; how to interpret the results and make appropriate interventions; and supervised experience with the CBTI. For more specifics on these steps and strategies, the reader is referred to Sampson et al. (2003).

Online Assessment

A keyword search on the phrase "career test" on a popular search engine yielded 23,000 hits/results. Alongside the many high quality online assessments are thousands with questionable psychometric properties. Even those that are valid and reliable have to face certain ethical concerns. For example, if a person takes the online Self-Directed Search and ends up with a list of suggested occupations that don't seem like a good fit, who is there to offer possible explanations or inquiries to determine if a high skill set (such as conventional skills) might have inflated the total score on one typology? Similarly, a person with limited reading skills might begin to complete a computer-assisted career guidance program online, only to find that they don't understand the directions. Some may not read the instructions or descriptions of the test purposes or norm group information at all, and then misapply or misinterpret the results.

Barak (2003) has outlined several ethical concerns associated with online assessment, including:
- the effects of a person's computer and Internet skills (or lack thereof);
- lack of preliminary screening – does this person need to take an inventory, and is this particular inventory the one they need to take);
- uncontrolled intervening personal psychological factors (technophobia, reading level, etc.);
- risk of cultural bias;
- secrecy of personal information and assessment results;
- unprotected, unregulated use of assessment results;
- lack of monitoring;
- technical failures;
- lack of contracted relationship between test-taker and test owner;
- lack of relevant information on a test;
- improper use of an online assessment by professional unaware of limitations;
- lack of assessment standardization;
- questionable construct validity;
- effects of digital divide (those who have regular access to a computer/Internet versus those who do not);
- lack of information on test-taking behavior;
- common use of a single assessment method;
- problems relating to test interpretation;
- the use of non-professional tests on the net;
- outdated tests;
- easy violation of test copyrights (a criminal act);
- lack of qualifications of test administrators;
- lack of personal assistance and support relating to assessment results;
- implementation and use of assessment results; and
- existence of hidden commercial agenda (gaining personal information to add to mailing or spam lists).

Some clients will come to career counseling with results from an online inventory in hand, or memories of having taken an online inventory. The career counselor should be cautious about giving too much credibility to questionable sources, but could use the results as a starting point for discussion. The career counselor should also model "Internet savvy" by sharing with the client a checklist and/or resources such as the Mental Measurements Yearbook that the career counselor uses to evaluate such inventories.

A sample checklist, created with the NCDA/ACSCI standards, as well as the criteria used in a recent special issue of the Journal of Career Development for online assessments is shown here:.

Table 15-1	Sample Career Website Evaluation Form

Name of Career Website:		
Standard/Guideline	Yes	No

Does the site follow NCDA's "Guidelines for the Use of Internet for Provision of Career Information and Planning Services, as well as the ethical guidelines for Internet-based counseling services endorsed by ACA & NBCC:
 	
    • www.ncda.org/about/polnet.html#guidelines (NCDA Guidelines)
    • www.counseling.org/gc/cybertx.htm (ACA's Ethical Guidelines for
      Online Counseling)		

Does the site contain a clear identification of the name and address of the organization for which the website was developed?		
Does the site have the title of the website prominently displayed near the top of the page?		
Does the site include a short statement about the purpose of the site?		
Does the site contain an index near the beginning of the site which can be internally linked back (e.g., return to index, return to top) to various locations on the page?		
Does the site have correct grammar, punctuation, and spelling throughout?		
Does the site contain a link to the home page (if any) of the organization for which the web site was developed?		
Does the site include enough images to be attractive but not so many that the page takes excessive time to load when using modems?		
Are the graphics used appropriate?		
Is an email address listed for further questions or comments and/or a link to Frequently Asked Questions (FAQ)?		
Is the target audience clearly identified (e.g., adults, children, international, school, businesses)?		
Is the career development content up-to-date and accurate?		
Would the content hold the attention of the target audience?		
Does it appear to be free from bias or stereotyping (e.g., gender, ethnic, age)?		
Does it appear to be user-friendly (i.e., easy to use and navigate by target audience)		
Does it include a date when the site was last updated?		
Does the site provide information about the qualifications of the developer of the content for the web site and/or persons who provide services?		
Is the content concise and use a clear vocabulary?		
Is information provided for user support and/or technical assistance?		
Does the site provide access to persons with disabilities?		
Is an evaluation plan of the site included?		
Is information provided on how user feedback is incorporated?		
Is data security and confidentiality addressed?		

Summary

As ethical, culturally competent counselors, we must be aware of and adhere to the ethical codes of our profession. This extends to career counseling as well as career testing. Gender and racial bias, the use of the Internet, and other ethical concerns affect not only counseling, but testing as well. We must know and educate other counselors as to the ethics associated.

Questions and Activities

1. Create a table comparing and contrasting the ethical standards for testing as set forth by ACA, NCDA and NBCC. For example:

Standard	ACA	NCDA	NBCC	AAC
Orientation to testing	Prior to testing, counselor gives an explanation as to the purpose, in language the client can understand – unless an explicit exemption has been agreed upon in advance.	Counselor must provide orientation to the client prior to and following test administration, describing the purpose of the test and how the results will be used.	Must provide instrument specific orientation prior to and following testing, so the results can be placed in context. Clients must know before they take the assessment the purpose for testing and how the results will be used.	Prior to assessment, counselors explain the nature and purposes of assessment and the specific use of results in language the client (or other legally authorized person on behalf of the client) can understand, unless an explicit exception to this right has been agreed upon in advance.

2. Choose 2 websites that provide online testing. One test should be a well-known inventory, such as the Self-Directed Search, Career Key, Kiersey, etc. and the other test should be one that you identify via an online search. First, evaluate the two sites on two general factors: what you liked and what you disliked. Then, complete an in-depth analysis of the two sites on some of the ethical criteria identified in this chapter.

3. A student comes into session with the results of an online inventory summarizing interests and a list of possible careers to consider. You have not seen this inventory before. How do you proceed?

4. A client who is an ethnic minority has been seeing you to help her make a career choice is interested in taking an interest inventory. However, the interest inventory that is available at your site (school, agency, center) does not include the normative information by racial distribution. What should you do?

5. How do the ethical standards relating to gender, diversity and sexual orientation compare and contrast?

6. A client wants to take a well-known inventory with which you have not had experience administering and interpreting. What should you do?

7. Many times, computer based programs allow students to save their data. What steps can you do to ensure confidentiality for students who choose this option at a computer terminal in your setting?

**National Career
Development Association
*Ethical Standards (Revised 2003)***

These Ethical Standards were developed by the National Board for Certified Counselors (NBCC), an independent, voluntary, not-for-profit organization incorporated in 1982. Titled "Code of Ethics" by NBCC and last amended in February 1987, the Ethical Standards were adopted by the National Career Development Association (NCDA) Board of Directors in 1987 and revised in 1991, with minor changes in wording (e.g., the addition of specific references to NCDA members).

Preamble: NCDA is an educational, scientific, and professional organization dedicated to the enhancement of the worth, dignity, potential, and uniqueness of each individual and, thus, to the service of society. This code of ethics enables the NCDA to clarify the nature of ethical responsibilities for present and future professional career counselors.

Section A: General

NCDA members influence the development of the profession by continuous efforts to improve professional practices, services, and research. Professional growth is continuous through the career counselor's career and is exemplified by the development of a philosophy that explains why and how a career counselor functions in the helping relationship. Career counselors must gather data on their effectiveness and be guided by their findings.

1. NCDA members have a responsibility to the clients they are serving and to the institutions within which the services are being performed. Career counselors also strive to assist the respective agency, organization, or institution in providing the highest caliber of professional services. The acceptance of employment in an institution implies that the career counselor is in agreement with the general policies and principles of the institution. Therefore, the professional activities of the career counselor are in accord with the objectives of the institution. If, despite concerted efforts, the career counselor cannot reach agreement with the employer as to acceptable standards of conduct that allow for changes in institutional policy that are conducive to the positive growth and development of clients, then terminating the affiliation should be seriously considered.

2. Ethical behavior among professional associates (e.g., career counselors) must be expected at all times. When accessible information raises doubt as to the ethical behavior of professional colleagues, the NCDA member must make action to attempt to rectify this condition. Such action uses the respective institution's channels first and then uses procedures established by the American Counseling Association, of which NCDA is a division.

3. NCDA members neither claim nor imply professional qualifications which exceed those possessed, and are responsible for correcting any misrepresentations of these qualifications by others.

4. NCDA members must refuse a private fee or other remuneration for consultation or counseling with persons who are entitled to their services through the career counselor's employing institution or agency. The policies of some agencies may make explicit provisions for staff members to engage in private practice with agency clients. However, should agency clients desire private counseling or consulting services, they must be apprised of other options available to them.

Figure 15-1   NCDA Ethical Codes. Reprinted from the NCDA Code of Ethics' copyrighted by the National Career Development Association. Reprinted with permission from NCDA.

NATIONAL BOARD FOR CERTIFIED COUNSELORS
CODE OF ETHICS

PREAMBLE

The National Board for Certified Counselors (NBCC) is a professional certification board which certifies counselors as having met standards for the general and specialty practice of professional counseling established by the Board. The counselors certified by NBCC may identify with different professional associations and are often licensed by jurisdictions which promulgate codes of ethics. The NBCC code of ethics provides a minimal ethical standard for the professional behavior of all NBCC certificants. This code provides an expectation of and assurance for the ethical practice for all who use the professional services of an NBCC certificant. In addition, it serves the purpose of having an enforceable standard for all NBCC certificants and assures those served of some resource in case of a perceived ethical violation.

The NBCC Ethical Code applies to all those certified by NBCC regardless of any other professional affiliation. Persons who receive professional services from certified counselors may elect to use other ethical codes which apply to their counselor. Although NBCC cooperates with professional associations and credentialing organizations, it can bring actions to discipline or sanction NBCC certificants only if the provisions of the NBCC Code are found to have been violated.

The National Board for Certified Counselors, Inc. (NBCC) promotes counseling through certification. In pursuit of this mission, the NBCC:

- Promotes quality assurance in counseling practice

- Promotes the value of counseling

- Promotes public awareness of quality counseling practice

- Promotes professionalism in counseling

- Promotes leadership in credentialing

Section A: General

1. Certified counselors engage in continuous efforts to improve professional practices, services, and research. Certified counselors are guided in their work by evidence of the best professional practices.

2. Certified counselors have a responsibility to the clients they serve and to the institutions within which the services are performed. Certified counselors also strive to assist the respective agency, organization, or institution in providing competent and ethical professional services. The acceptance of employment in an institution implies that the certified counselor is in agreement with the general policies and principles of the institution. Therefore, the professional activities of the certified counselor are in accord with the objectives of the institution. If the certified counselor and the employer do not agree and cannot reach agreement on policies that are consistent with appropriate counselor ethical practice that is conducive to client growth and development, the employment should be terminated. If the situation warrants further action, the certified counselor should work through professional organizations to have the unethical practice changed.

3. Ethical behavior among professional associates (i.e., both certified and non-certified counselors) must be expected at all times. When a certified counselor has doubts as to the ethical behavior of professional colleagues, the certified counselor must take action to attempt to rectify this condition. Such action uses the respective institution's channels first and then uses procedures established by the NBCC or the perceived violator's profession.

4. Certified counselors must refuse remuneration for consultation or counseling with persons who are entitled to these services through the certified counselor's employing institution or agency. Certified counselors must not divert to their private practices, without the mutual consent of the institution and the client, legitimate clients in their primary agencies or the institutions with which they are

Figure 15-2   NBCC Ethical Codes. Reprinted with the permission of the National Board for Certified Counselors, Inc. ™ and Affiliates; 3 Terrace Way, Suite D, Greensboro, NC 27403-3660.

List of Tests and Publishers

Adaptive Behavior Assessment
System – 2nd Edition

Harcourt Assessment
19500 Bulverde Road
San Antonio, Texas 78259
Phone: (800) 211-8378
Fax: (800) 232-1223
Website: www.harcourtassessment.com

Adolescent Personality
Inventory

Institute for Personality and Ability Testing, Inc.
1801 Woodfield Drive
Savoy, IL 61874
Phone: (800) 225-4728
Fax: (217) 352-9674
Website: www.ipat.com

Adult Career Concerns
Inventory

VOCIPHER
Website: www.vocopher.com

Adult Personality Inventory

Institute for Personality and Ability Testing, Inc.
1801 Woodfield Drive
Savoy, IL 61874
Phone: (800) 225-4728
Fax: (217) 352-9674
Website: www.ipat.com

American College Testing
(ACT)

American College Testing Program
500 ACT Drive
P.O. Box 168
Iowa City, Iowa 52243-0168
Phone: (800) 498-6068
Website: www.act.org

Armed Services Vocational
Aptitude Battery

ASVAB Career Exploration Program
Defense Manpower Data Center
400 Gigling Road
Seaside, CA 93955
Phone: (831) 583-2400
Website: www. asvabprogram.com/

Basic Achievement Skills
Individual Screener

Harcourt Assessment
19500 Bulverde Road
San Antonio, Texas 78259
Phone: (800) 211-8378
Fax: (800) 232-1223
Website: www.harcourtassessment.com

California Occupational
Preference Survey

Educational and Industrial Testing Service
Phone: (800) 416-1666
Website: www.edits.net

Campbell Interest and Skill
Survey

Pearson Assessments
PO Box 1416
Minneapolis, MN 55440
Phone: (800) 627-7271
Fax: (800) 632-9011
Website: www.pearsonassessments.com

Career Ability Placement Survey

Educational and Industrial Testing Service
Phone: (800) 416-1666
Website: www.edits.net

Career Assessment Inventory – Enhanced	Pearson Assessments PO Box 1416 Minneapolis, MN 55440 Phone: (800) 627-7271 Fax: (800) 632-9011 Website: www.pearsonassessments.com
Career Attitudes and Strategies Inventory	Psychological Assessment Resources, Inc. 16204 North Florida Avenue Lutz, FL 33549 Phone: (800) 331-8378 Fax: (800) 727-9329 Website: www.parinc.com
Career Beliefs Inventory	CPP 1055 Joaquin Rd., Suite 200 Mountain View, CA 94043 Phone: (800) 624-1765 Fax: (650) 969-8608 Website: www.cpp-db.com/
Career Decision Making-Revised Harrington/O'Shea	American Guidance Service, Inc. 4201 Woodland Road Circle Pines, Minnesota 55014-1796 Phone: (800) 328-2560 Fax: (800) 471-8457
Career Decision Profile	Lawrence K. Jones North Carolina State University Department of Counselor Education 520 Poe Hall Box 7801 Raleigh, NC 27695-7801 Phone: ((919) 515-6359
Career Decision-Making Self Efficacy Scale	Nancy Betz
Career Development Inventory	VOCIPHER Website: www.vocopher.com
Career Exploration Inventory-2nd Edition	JIST Publishing 8902 Otis Avenue Indianapolis, IN 46216-1033 Phone: (800) 648-5478 Website: www.jist.com
Career Factors Inventory	2000 Career/Lifeskills Resources, Inc. 116 Viceroy Road, Unit B1 Concord, Ontario, L4K 2M2 Phone: (905) 760-0111 Fax: (905) 750-0113 Website: www.career-lifeskills.com
Career Key, The	Lawrence K. Jones North Carolina State University Department of Counselor Education 520 Poe Hall Box 7801 Raleigh, NC 27695-7801 Phone: ((919) 515-6359

Career Maturity Inventory-R and Career Developer	Bridges Transition Company 33637-B Hwy 97 N. Oroville, WA 98844 Phone: (800) 281-1168 Fax: (888) 349-3437 Website: www.bridges.com
Career Orientation Placement and Evaluation Survey	Educational and Industrial Testing Service Phone: (800) 416-1666 Website: www.edits.net
Career Planning Survey?	American College Testing Program American College Testing Program 500 ACT Drive P.O. Box 168 Iowa City, Iowa 52243-0168 Phone: (800) 498-6068 Website: www.act.org
Career Thoughts Inventory	Psychological Assessment Resources, Inc. 16204 North Florida Avenue Lutz, FL 33549 Phone: (800) 331-8378 Fax: (800) 727-9329 Website: www.parinc.com
Career Values Card Sort Planning Kit	Career Trainer 3629 W. MacArthur Blvd. #201 Santa Ana, CA 92704 Phone: (800) 888-4945
Children's Personality Questionnaire	Institute for Personality and Ability Testing, Inc. 1801 Woodfield Drive Savoy, IL 61874 Phone: (800) 225-4728 Fax: (217) 352-9674 Website: www.ipat.com
CHOICES/CHOICES CT	Bridges Transition Company 33637-B Hwy 97 N. Oroville, WA 98844 Phone: (800) 281-1168 Fax: (888) 349-3437 Website: www.bridges.com
COIN/COIN JR.	Coin Educational Products 3361 Executive Parkway Suite 302 Toledo, Ohio 43606 Phone: (800) 274-8515 Fax: (419) 536-7056 Website: www.coin3.com
Differential Aptitude Test and Career Interest Inventory DAT/CII	Harcourt Assessment 19500 Bulverde Road San Antonio, Texas 78259 Phone: (800) 211-8378 Fax: (800) 232-1223 Website: www.harcourtassessment.com

DISCOVER for College and Adults	ACT 500 ACT Drive P.O. Box 168 Iowa City, Iowa 52243-0168 Phone: (800) 498-6068 Website: www.act.org/discover/index.html
Early School Personality Questionnaire	Institute for Personality and Ability Testing, Inc. 1801 Woodfield Drive Savoy, IL 61874 Phone: (800) 225-4728 Fax: (217) 352-9674 Website: www.ipat.com
Edwards Personal Preference Schedule (EPPS)	Harcourt Assessment 19500 Bulverde Road San Antonio, Texas 78259 Phone: (800) 211-8378 Fax: (800) 232-1223 Website: www.harcourtassessment.com
Flanagan Aptitude Classification Test	Pearson Reid London House 3361 Rouse Road Suite 225 Orlando, FL 32817 Phone: (800) 922-7343 www.pearsonreidlondonhouse.com
Geist Picture Interest Inventory	Western Psychological Services 12031 Wilshire Blvd. Los Angeles, CA 90025-1251 Phone: 800-648-8857 Fax: (310) 478-2061 Website: www.wpspublish.com
Guide for Occupational Exploration Inventroy-2nd Edition	JIST Publishing 8902 Otis Avenue Indianapolis, IN 46216-1033 Phone: (800) 648-5478 Website: www.jist.com
Guilford-Zimmerman Temperament Survey	Pearson Assessments PO Box 1416 Minneapolis, MN 55440 Phone: (800) 627-7271 Fax: (800) 632-9011 Website: www.pearsonassessments.com
Interest Determination, Exploration and Assessment System (IDEAS)	Pearson Assessments PO Box 1416 Minneapolis, MN 55440 Phone: (800) 627-7271 Fax: (800) 632-9011 Website: www.pearsonassessments.com
Iowa Test of Basic Skills	Riverside Publishing Company 425 Spring Lake Drive Itasca, IL 60143-2079 Phone: (800) 323-9540 Fax: (800) 630-467-7192 Website: www.riverpub.com

Jackson Vocational Interest Survey	Sigma Assessment Systems P.O. Box 610984 Port Huron, MI 48061-0984 Phone: (800) 265-1285 Fax: (800) 361-9411 Website: www.sigmaassessmentsystems.com
Kuder Occupational Interest Survey (KOIS)	National Career Assessment Services, Inc. 210 N. 10th Street PO Box 277 Phone: (800) 314-8972 Fax: (515) 993-5422 Website: www.kuder.com/
MicroSkills IV	The California Career Information System P.O. Box 647 Richmond, CA 94808-9900 Phone: (888) 463-2247 Fax: (510) 669-0992 Website: www.eurekanet.org
Minnesota Importance Questionnaire	Vocational Psychology Research University of Minnesota N657 Elliott Hall 75 East River Road Minneapolis, MN 55455-0344 Phone: (612) 625-1367 Fax: (612) 626-0345 Website: www.psych.umn.edu/psylabs/vpr/default.htm
Motivated Skills Card Sort	Career Trainer 3629 W. MacArthur Blvd. #201 Santa Ana, CA 92704 Phone: (800) 888-4945
My Vocational Situation	Psychological Assessment Resources, Inc. 16204 North Florida Avenue Lutz, FL 33549 Phone: (800) 331-8378 Fax: (800) 727-9329 Website: www.parinc.com
Myers-Briggs Type Inventory	CPP 1055 Joaquin Rd., Suite 200 Mountain View, CA 94043 Phone: (800) 624-1765 Fax: (650) 969-8608 Website: www.cpp-db.com/
NEO4	Psychological Assessment Resources, Inc. 16204 North Florida Avenue Lutz, FL 33549 Phone: (800) 331-8378 Fax: (800) 727-9329 Website: www.parinc.com
O*NET Career Values Inventory	JIST Publishing 8902 Otis Avenue Indianapolis, IN 46216-1033 Phone: (800) 648-5478 Website: www.jist.com

O*NET CCI	JIST Publishing 8902 Otis Avenue Indianapolis, IN 46216-1033 Phone: (800) 648-5478 Website: www.jist.com
Occupational Aptitude Survey and Interest Schedule – 3	PRO-ED 8700 Shoal Creek Boulevard Austin, TX 78757-6897 Phone: (800) 897-3202 Fax: (800) 397-7633 Website: www.proedinc.com
Occupational Interests Card Sort Planning Kit	Career Trainer 3629 W. MacArthur Blvd. #201 Santa Ana, CA 92704 Phone: (800) 888-4945 Fax: (714) 668-1100 Website: www.careertrainer.com
Occ-U-Sort	Lawrence K. Jones North Carolina State University Department of Counselor Education 520 Poe Hall Box 7801 Raleigh, NC 27695-7801 Phone: ((919) 515-6359
PAES	Talent Assessment, Inc. P.O. Box 5087, Jacksonville, FL 32247 Phone: (800) 634-1472 Fax: (904) 292-9371 www.talentassessment.com
Peabody Individual Achievement Test –R-NU	American Guidance Service, Inc. 4201 Woodland Road Circle Pines, Minnesota 55014-1796 Phone: (800) 328-2560 Fax: (800) 471-8457
PIC DV2000	Talent Assessment, Inc. P.O. Box 5087, Jacksonville, FL 32247 Phone: (800) 634-1472 Fax: (904) 292-9371 www.talentassessment.com
Pictorial Inventory of Careers DV-2000	Talent Assessment, Inc. P.O. Box 5087 Jacksonville, FL 32247 Phone: (800) 634-1472 Website: www.talentassessment.com
Purdue Pegboard	Psychological Assessment Resources, Inc. 16204 North Florida Avenue Lutz, FL 33549 Phone: (800) 331-8378 Fax: (800) 727-9329 Website: www.parinc.com

Reading-Free Vocational
Interest Inventory-II

Harcourt Assessment
19500 Bulverde Road
San Antonio, Texas 78259
Phone: (800) 211-8378
Fax: (800) 232-1223
Website: www.harcourtassessment.com

Rokeach Values Survey

CPP
1055 Joaquin Rd., Suite 200
Mountain View, CA 94043
Phone: (800) 624-1765
Fax: (650) 969-8608
Website: www.cpp-db.com/

Self-Directed Search (SDS)

Psychological Assessment Resources, Inc.
16204 North Florida Avenue
Lutz, FL 33549
Phone: (800) 331-8378
Fax: (800) 727-9329
Website: www.parinc.com

SIGI PLUS

VALPAR International Corporation
2450 W. Ruthrauf Road, Suite 180
Tuscon, AZ 85705
Phone: (800) 633-3321
Fax: (262) 797-8488
Website: www.valparint.com

Sixteen Personality Factor
Questionnaire (16PF) and
Personal Career Development
Profile (PCD)

Institute for Personality and Ability Testing, Inc.
1801 Woodfield Drive
Savoy, IL 61874
Phone: (800) 225-4728
Fax: (217) 352-9674
Website: www.ipat.com

SkillScan

SkillScan Online
Phone: 800-587-1262
www.skillscan.net

Stanford Achievement Test –
10th Edition

Harcourt Assessment
19500 Bulverde Road
San Antonio, Texas 78259
Phone: (800) 211-8378
Fax: (800) 232-1223
Website: www.harcourtassessment.com

Stanford Diagnostic
Mathematics Test

Harcourt Assessment
19500 Bulverde Road
San Antonio, Texas 78259
Phone: (800) 211-8378
Fax: (800) 232-1223
Website: www.harcourtassessment.com

Strong Interest Inventory (SII)

CPP
1055 Joaquin Rd., Suite 200
Mountain View, CA 94043
Phone: (800) 624-1765
Fax: (650) 969-8608
Website: www.cpp-db.com/

Survey of Interpersonal Values	Pearson Reid London House 3361 Rouse Road Suite 225 Orlando, FL 32817 Phone: (800) 922-7343 www.pearsonreidlondonhouse.com
Survey of Personal Values	Pearson Reid London House 3361 Rouse Road Suite 225 Orlando, FL 32817 Phone: (800) 922-7343 Website: www.pearsonreidlondonhouse.com
Talent Assessment Program	Talent Assessment, Inc. P.O. Box 5087, Jacksonville, FL 32247 Phone: (800) 634-1472 Fax: (904) 292-9371 www.talentassessment.com
TerraNova Achievement Test	CTB-McGraw-Hill 20 Ryan Ranch Road Monterey, CA 93940 Phone: (800) 538-9547 Fax: (800) 383-0366 Website: www.ctb.com
Tests of Adult Basic Education	CTB-McGraw-Hill 20 Ryan Ranch Road Monterey, CA 93940 Phone: (800) 538-9547 Fax: (800) 383-0366 Website: www.ctb.com
Transition to Work Inventory	Harcourt Assessment 19500 Bulverde Road San Antonio, Texas 78259 Phone: (800) 211-8378 Fax: (800) 232-1223 Website: www.harcourtassessment.com
Values Arrangement List	Harcourt Assessment 19500 Bulverde Road San Antonio, Texas 78259 Phone: (800) 211-8378 Fax: (800) 232-1223 Website: www.harcourtassessment.com
Values Driven Work	NOVA Connect Business Service Center 465 S. Mathilda Avenue Site 300 Sunnyvale, CA 94086 Phone: (408) 730-7830 Fax: (408) 773-9054 www.novaworks.org
Values Scale, The	CPP 1055 Joaquin Rd., Suite 200 Mountain View, CA 94043 Phone: (800) 624-1765 Fax: (650) 969-8608 Website: www.cpp-db.com/

VIP JR	Talent Assessment, Inc. P.O. Box 5087, Jacksonville, FL 32247 Phone: (800) 634-1472 Fax: (904) 292-9371 www.talentassessment.com
VISTA Life/Career Cards	Passport to Purpose www.PassportToPurpose.com Phone: (805) 496-5654 Fax: (805) 496-8983
Vocational Exploration and Insight Kit	Psychological Assessment Resources, Inc. 16204 North Florida Avenue Lutz, FL 33549 Phone: (800) 331-8378 Fax: (800) 727-9329 Website: www.parinc.com
Vocational Preference Inventory	Psychological Assessment Resources, Inc. 16204 North Florida Avenue Lutz, FL 33549 Phone: (800) 331-8378 Fax: (800) 727-9329 Website: www.parinc.com
Wide Range Achievement Test- Revision 3	Wide Range PO Box 3410 Wilmington, DE 19804 Phone: (800) 221-9728 Fax: (302) 652-1644 Website: www.widerange.com
Wide Range Interest Opinion Test	Wide Range PO Box 3410 Wilmington, DE 19804 Phone: (800) 221-9728 Fax: (302) 652-1644 Website: www.widerange.com
Wiesen Test of Mechanical Aptitude	Ramsay Corporation Boyce Station Offices 1050 Boyce Road Pittsburgh, PA 15241 Phone: (412) 257-0732 Fax: (412) 257-9929 www.ramsaycorp.com
Woodcock Johnson III	Riverside Publishing Company 425 Spring Lake Drive Itasca, IL 60143-2079 Phone: (800) 323-9540 Fax: (800) 630-467-7192 Website: www.riverpub.com

Code of Fair Testing Practices in Education

Prepared by the Joint Committee on Testing Practices

The Code of Fair Testing Practices in Education (Code) is a guide for professionals in fulfilling their obligation to provide and use tests that are fair to all test takers regardless of age, gender, disability, race, ethnicity, national origin, religion, sexual orientation, linguistic background, or other personal characteristics. Fairness is a primary consideration in all aspects of testing. Careful standardization of tests and administration conditions helps to ensure that all test takers are given a comparable opportunity to demonstrate what they know and how they can perform in the area being tested. Fairness implies that every test taker has the opportunity to prepare for the test and is informed about the general nature and content of the test, as appropriate to the purpose of the test. Fairness also extends to the accurate reporting of individual and group test results.   Fairness is not an isolated concept, but must be considered in all aspects of the testing process.

The Code applies broadly to testing in education (admissions, educational assessment, educational diagnosis, and student placement) regardless of the mode of presentation, so it is relevant to conventional paper-and-pencil tests, computer based tests, and performance tests. It is not designed to cover employment testing, licensure or certification testing, or other types of testing outside the field of education. The Code is directed primarily at professionally developed tests used in formally administered testing programs. Although the Code is not intended to cover tests made by teachers for use in their own classrooms, teachers are encouraged to use the guidelines to help improve their testing practices.

The Code addresses the roles of test developers and test users separately. Test developers are people and organizations that construct tests, as well as those that set policies for testing programs. Test users are people and agencies that select tests, administer tests, commission test development services, or make decisions on the basis of test scores. Test developer and test user roles may overlap, for example, when a state or local education agency commissions test development services, sets policies that control the test development process, and makes decisions on the basis of the test scores.

Many of the statements in the Code refer to the selection and use of existing tests. When a new test is developed, when an existing test is modified, or when the administration of a test is modified, the Code is intended to provide guidance for this process.

1

---

1 The Code is not intended to be mandatory, exhaustive, or definitive, and may not be applicable to every situation. Instead, the Code is intended to be aspirational, and is not intended to take precedence over the judgment of those who have competence in the subjects addressed.

The Code provides guidance separately for test developers and test users in four critical areas:

A. Developing and Selecting Appropriate Tests
B. Administering and Scoring Tests
C. Reporting and Interpreting Test Results
D. Informing Test Takers

The Code is intended to be consistent with the relevant parts of the Standards for Educational and Psychological Testing (American Educational Research Association [AERA], American Psychological Association [APA], and National Council on Measurement in Education [NCME], 1999). The Code is not meant to add new principles over and above those in the Standards or to change their meaning. Rather, the Code is intended to represent the spirit of selected portions of the Standards in a way that is relevant and meaningful to developers and users of tests, as well as to test takers and/or their parents or guardians. States, districts, schools, organizations and individual professionals are encouraged to commit themselves to fairness in testing and safeguarding the rights of test takers. The Code is intended to assist in carrying out such commitments.

The Code has been prepared by the Joint Committee on Testing Practices, a cooperative effort among several professional organizations. The aim of the Joint Committee is to act, in the public interest, to advance the quality of testing practices. Members of the Joint Committee include the American Counseling Association (ACA), the American Educational Research Association (AERA), the American Psychological Association (APA), the American Speech-Language-Hearing Association (ASHA), the National Association of School Psychologists (NASP), the National Association of Test Directors (NATD), and the National Council on Measurement in Education (NCME).

A.   Developing and Selecting Appropriate Tests

TEST DEVELOPERS	TEST USERS
Test developers should provide the information and supporting evidence that test users need to select appropriate tests.	Test users should select tests that meet the intended purpose and that are appropriate for the intended test takers.
A-1. Provide evidence of what the test measures, the recommended uses, the intended test takers, and the strengths and limitations of the test, including the level of precision of the test scores.	A-1. Define the purpose for testing, the content and skills to be tested, and the intended test takers. Select and use the most appropriate test based on a thorough review of available information.
A-2. Describe how the content and skills to be tested were selected and how the tests were developed.	A-2. Review and select tests based on the appropriateness of test content, skills tested, and content coverage for the intended purpose of testing.
A-3. Communicate information about a test's characteristics at a level of detail appropriate to the intended test users.	A-3. Review materials provided by test developers and select tests for which clear, accurate, and complete information is provided.
A-4. Provide guidance on the levels of skills, knowledge, and training necessary for appropriate review, selection, and administration of tests.	A-4. Select tests through a process that includes persons with appropriate knowledge, skills, and training.
A-5. Provide evidence that the technical quality, including reliability and validity, of the test meets its intended purposes.	A-5. Evaluate evidence of the technical quality of the test provided by the test developer and any independent reviewers.
A-6. Provide to qualified test users representative samples of test questions or practice tests, directions, answer sheets, manuals, and score reports.	A-6. Evaluate representative samples of test questions or practice tests, directions, answer sheets, manuals, and score reports before selecting a test.
A-7. Avoid potentially offensive content or language when developing test questions and related materials.	A-7. Evaluate procedures and materials used by test developers, as well as the resulting test, to ensure that potentially offensive content or language is avoided.
A-8. Make appropriately modified forms of tests or administration procedures available for test takers with disabilities who need special accommodations.	A-8. Select tests with appropriately modified forms or administration procedures for test takers with disabilities who need special accommodations.
A-9. Obtain and provide evidence on the performance of test takers of diverse subgroups, making significant efforts to obtain sample sizes that are adequate for subgroup analyses. Evaluate the evidence to ensure that differences in performance are related to the skills being assessed.	A-9. Evaluate the available evidence on the performance of test takers of diverse subgroups. Determine to the extent feasible which performance differences may have been caused by factors unrelated to the skills being assessed.

B.   Administering and Scoring Tests

TEST DEVELOPERS	TEST USERS
Test developers should explain how to administer and score tests correctly and fairly.	Test users should administer and score tests correctly and fairly.
B-1. Provide clear descriptions of detailed procedures for administering tests in a standardized manner.	B-1. Follow established procedures for administering tests in a standardized manner.
B-2. Provide guidelines on reasonable procedures for assessing persons with disabilities who need special accommodations or those with diverse linguistic backgrounds.	B-2. Provide and document appropriate procedures for test takers with disabilities who need special accommodations or those with diverse linguistic backgrounds. Some accommodations may be required by law or regulation.
B-3. Provide information to test takers or test users on test question formats and procedures for answering test questions, including information on the use of any needed materials and equipment.	B-3. Provide test takers with an opportunity to become familiar with test question formats and any materials or equipment that may be used during testing.
B-4. Establish and implement procedures to ensure the security of testing materials during all phases of test development, administration, scoring, and reporting.	B-4. Protect the security of test materials, including respecting copyrights and eliminating opportunities for test takers to obtain scores by fraudulent means.
B-5. Provide procedures, materials and guidelines for scoring the tests, and for monitoring the accuracy of the scoring process. If scoring the test is the responsibility of the test developer, provide adequate training for scorers.	B-5. If test scoring is the responsibility of the test user, provide adequate training to scorers and ensure and monitor the accuracy of the scoring process.
B-6. Correct errors that affect the interpretation of the scores and communicate the corrected results promptly.	B-6. Correct errors that affect the interpretation of the scores and communicate the corrected results promptly.
B-7. Develop and implement procedures for ensuring the confidentiality of scores.	B-7. Develop and implement procedures for ensuring the confidentiality of scores.

C.   Reporting and Interpreting Test Results

TEST DEVELOPERS	**TEST USERS**
Test developers should report test results accurately and provide information to help test users interpret test results correctly.	Test users should report and interpret test results accurately and clearly.
C-1. Provide information to support recommended interpretations of the results, including the nature of the content, norms or comparison groups, and other technical evidence. Advise test users of the benefits and limitations of test results and their interpretation. Warn against assigning greater precision than is warranted.	C-1. Interpret the meaning of the test results, taking into account the nature of the content, norms or comparison groups, other technical evidence, and benefits and limitations of test results.
C-2. Provide guidance regarding the interpretations of results for tests administered with modifications. Inform test users of potential problems in interpreting test results when tests or test administration procedures are modified.	C-2. Interpret test results from modified test or test administration procedures in view of the impact those modifications may have had on test results.
C-3Specify appropriate uses of test results and warn test users of potential misuses.	C-3 Avoid using tests for purposes other than those recommended by the test developer unless there is evidence to support the intended use or interpretation.
C-4. When test developers set standards, provide the rationale, procedures, and evidence for setting performance standards or passing scores. Avoid using stigmatizing labels.	C-4. Review the procedures for setting performance standards or passing scores. Avoid using stigmatizing labels.
C-5. Encourage test users to base decisions about test takers on multiple sources of appropriate information, not on a single test score.	C-5. Avoid using a single test score as the sole determinant of decisions about test takers. Interpret test scores in conjunction with other information about individuals.
C-6 Provide information to enable test users to accurately interpret and report test results for groups of test takers, including information about who were and who were not included in the different groups being compared, and information about factors that might influence the interpretation of results.	C-6 State the intended interpretation and use of test results for groups of test takers. Avoid grouping test results for purposes not specifically recommended by the test developer unless evidence is obtained to support the intended use. Report procedures that were followed in determining who were and who were not included in the groups being compared and describe factors that might influence the interpretation of results.
C-7. Provide test results in a timely fashion and in a manner that is understood by the test taker.	C-7. Communicate test results in a timely fashion and in a manner that is understood by the test taker.
C-8. Provide guidance to test users about how to monitor the etent to which the test is fulfilling its intended purposes.	C-8. Develop and implement procedures for monitoring test use, including consistency with the intended purposes of the test.

D. Informing Test Takers

Under some circumstances, test developers have direct communication with the test takers and/or control of the tests, testing process, and test results. In other circumstances the test users have these responsibilities.

Test developers or test users should inform test takers about the nature of the test, test taker rights and responsibilities, the appropriate use of scores, and procedures for resolving challenges to scores.
D-1. Inform test takers in advance of the test administration about the coverage of the test, the types of question formats, the directions, and appropriate test-taking strategies. Make such information available to all test takers.
D-2. When a test is optional, provide test takers or their parents/guardians with information to help them judge whether a test should be taken—including indications of any consequences that may result from not taking the test (e.g., not being eligible to compete for a particular scholarship) — and whether there is an available alternative to the test.
D-3. Provide test takers or their parents/guardians with information about rights test takers may have to obtain copies of tests and completed answer sheets, to retake tests, to have tests rescored, or to have scores declared invalid.
D-4. Provide test takers or their parents/guardians with information about responsibilities test takers have, such as being aware of the intended purpose and uses of the test, performing at capacity, following directions, and not disclosing test items or interfering with other test takers.
D-5. Inform test takers or their parents/guardians how long scores will be kept on file and indicate to whom, under what circumstances, and in what manner test scores and related information will or will not be released. Protect test scores from unauthorized release and access.
D-6. Describe procedures for investigating and resolving circumstances that might result in canceling or withholding scores, such as failure to adhere to specified testing procedures.
D-7. Describe procedures that test takers, parents/guardians, and other interested parties may use to obtain more information about the test, register complaints, and have problems resolved.

Note: The membership of the Working Group that developed the Code of Fair Testing Practices in Education **and of the Joint Committee on Testing Practices that guided the Working Group is as follows:**

Peter Behuniak, PhD	**Stephanie H. McConaughy, PhD**
Lloyd Bond, PhD	**Julie P. Noble, PhD**
Gwyneth M. Boodoo, PhD	**Wayne M. Patience, PhD**
Wayne Camara, PhD	**Carole L. Perlman, PhD**
Ray Fenton, PhD	**Douglas K. Smith, PhD (deceased)**
John J. Fremer, PhD (Co-Chair)	**Janet E. Wall, EdD (Co-Chair)**
Sharon M. Goldsmith, PhD	**Pat Nellor Wickwire, PhD**
Bert F. Green, PhD	**Mary Yakimowski, PhD**
William G. Harris, PhD	
Janet E. Helms, PhD	**Lara Frumkin, PhD, of the APA served as staff liaison.**

The Joint Committee intends that the Code be consistent with and supportive of existing codes of conduct and standards of other professional groups who use tests in educational contexts. Of particular note are the Responsibilities of Users of Standardized Tests (Association for Assessment in Counseling and Education, 2003), APA Test User Qualifications (2000), ASHA Code of Ethics (2001), Ethical Principles of Psychologists and Code of Conduct (1992), NASP Professional Conduct Manual (2000), NCME Code of Professional Responsibility (1995), and Rights and Responsibilities of Test Takers: Guidelines and Expectations (Joint Committee on Testing Practices, 2000).

Assessment Related Web Sites Including Ethical Standards

American Counseling Association
http://www.counseling.org/

American School Counselor Association
http://www.schoolcounselor.org/

American Mental Health Counselors Association
http://www.amhca.org/

American Psychological Association
http://www.apa.org/

Association for Assessment in Counseling
http://aac.ncat.edu/

Association of Computer-Based Systems for Career Information
http://www.acsci.org/

National Career Development Association
http://ncda.org/

Services by Telephone, Teleconferencing and Internet: A Statement by the Ethics Committee
of the American Psychological Association
http://www.apa.org/ethics/stmnt01.html

The Practice of Internet Counseling (NBCC's Statement)
http://www.nbcc.org/webethics2

Codes of Ethical Standards

American Counseling Association

National Career Development Association

NBCC

ACA Code of Ethics Preamble

The American Counseling Association is an educational, scientific, and professional organization whose members are dedicated to the enhancement of human development throughout the life-span. Association members recognize diversity in our society and embrace a cross- cultural approach in support of the worth, dignity, potential, and uniqueness of each individual.

The specification of a code of ethics enables the association to clarify to current and future members, and to those served by members, the nature of the ethical responsibilities held in common by its members. As the code of ethics of the association, this document establishes principles that define the ethical behavior of association members. All members of the American Counseling Association are required to adhere to the Code of Ethics and the Standards of Practice. The Code of Ethics will serve as the basis for processing ethical complaints initiated against members of the association.

ACA Code of Ethics (eff. 1995)

Section A: The Counseling Relationship
Section B: Confidentiality
Section C: Professional Responsibility
Section D: Relationships With Other Professionals
Section E: Evaluation, Assessment, and Interpretation
Section F: Teaching, Training, and Supervision
Section G: Research and Publication
Section H: Resolving Ethical Issues

Section A: The Counseling Relationship

A.1. Client Welfare

Primary Responsibility. The primary responsibility of counselors is to respect the dignity and to promote the welfare of clients.

Positive Growth and Development. Counselors encourage client growth and development in ways that foster the clients' interest and welfare; counselors avoid fostering dependent counseling relationships.

Counseling Plans. Counselors and their clients work jointly in devising integrated, individual counseling plans that offer reasonable promise of success and are consistent with abilities and circumstances of clients. Counselors and clients regularly review counseling plans to ensure their continued viability and effectiveness, respecting clients' freedom of choice. (See A.3.b.)

Family Involvement. Counselors recognize that families are usually important in clients' lives and strive to enlist family understanding and involvement as a positive resource, when appropriate.

Career and Employment Needs. Counselors work with their clients in considering employment in jobs and circumstances that are consistent with the clients' overall abilities, vocational limitations, physical restrictions, general temperament, interest and aptitude patterns, social skills, education, general qualifications, and other relevant characteristics and needs. Counselors neither place nor participate in placing clients in positions that will result in damaging the interest and the welfare of clients, employers, or the public.

A.2. Respecting Diversity

Nondiscrimination. Counselors do not condone or engage in discrimination based on age, color, culture, disability, ethnic group, gender, race, religion, sexual orientation, marital status, or socioeconomic status. (See C.5.a., C.5.b., and D.1.i.)

Respecting Differences. Counselors will actively attempt to understand the diverse cultural backgrounds of the clients with whom they work. This includes, but is not limited to, learning how the counselor's own cultural/ethnic/racial identity impacts her or his values and beliefs about the counseling process. (See E.8. and F.2.i.)

A.3. Client Rights

Disclosure to Clients. When counseling is initiated, and throughout the counseling process as necessary, counselors inform clients of the purposes, goals, techniques, procedures, limitations, potential risks, and benefits of services to be performed, and other pertinent information. Counselors take steps to ensure that clients understand the implications of diagnosis, the intended use of tests and reports, fees, and billing arrangements. Clients have the right to expect confidentiality and to be provided with an explanation of its limitations, including supervision and/or treatment team professionals; to obtain clear information about their case records; to participate in the ongoing counseling plans; and to refuse any recommended services and be advised of the consequences of such refusal. (See E.5.a. and G.2.)

Freedom of Choice. Counselors offer clients the freedom to choose whether to enter into a counseling relationship and to determine which professional(s) will provide counseling. Restrictions that limit choices of clients are fully explained. (See A.1.c.)

Inability to Give Consent. When counseling minors or persons unable to give voluntary informed consent, counselors act in these clients' best interests. (See B.3.)

A.4. Clients Served by Others

If a client is receiving services from another mental health professional, counselors, with client consent, inform the professional persons already involved and develop clear agreements to avoid confusion and conflict for the client. (See C.6.c.)

A.5. Personal Needs and Values

Personal Needs. In the counseling relationship, counselors are aware of the intimacy and responsibilities inherent in the counseling relationship, maintain respect for clients, and avoid actions that seek to meet their personal needs at the expense of clients.

Personal Values. Counselors are aware of their own values, attitudes, beliefs, and behaviors and how these apply in a diverse society, and avoid imposing their values on clients. (See C.5.a.)

A.6. Dual Relationships

Avoid When Possible. Counselors are aware of their influential positions with respect to clients, and they avoid exploiting the trust and dependency of clients. Counselors make every effort to avoid dual relationships with clients that could impair professional judgment or increase the risk of harm to clients. (Examples of such relationships include, but are not limited to, familial, social, financial, business, or close personal relationships with clients.) When a dual relationship cannot be avoided, counselors take appropriate professional precautions such as informed consent, consultation, supervision, and documentation to ensure that judgment is not impaired and no exploitation occurs. (See F.1.b.)

Superior/Subordinate Relationships. Counselors do not accept as clients superiors or subordinates with whom they have administrative, supervisory, or evaluative relationships.

A.7. Sexual Intimacies With Clients

Current Clients. Counselors do not have any type of sexual intimacies with clients and do not counsel persons with whom they have had a sexual relationship.

Former Clients. Counselors do not engage in sexual intimacies with former clients within a minimum of 2 years after terminating the counseling relationship. Counselors who engage in such relationship after 2 years following termination have the responsibility to examine and document thoroughly that such relations did not have an exploitative nature, based on factors such as duration of counseling, amount of time since counseling, termination circumstances, client's personal history and mental status, adverse impact on the client, and actions by the counselor suggesting a plan to initiate a sexual relationship with the client after termination.

A.8. Multiple Clients

When counselors agree to provide counseling services to two or more persons who have a relationship (such as husband and wife, or parents and children), counselors clarify at the outset which person or persons are clients and the nature of the relationships they will have with each involved person. If it becomes apparent that counselors may be called upon to perform potentially conflicting roles, they clarify, adjust, or withdraw from roles appropriately. (See B.2. and B.4.d.)

A.9. Group Work

Screening. Counselors screen prospective group counseling/therapy participants. To the extent possible, counselors select members whose needs and goals are compatible with goals of the group, who will not impede the group process, and whose well-being will not be jeopardized by the group experience.

Protecting Clients. In a group setting, counselors take reasonable precautions to protect clients from physical or psychological trauma.

A.10. Fees and Bartering (See D.3.a. and D.3.b.)

Advance Understanding. Counselors clearly explain to clients, prior to entering the counseling relationship, all financial arrangements related to professional services including the use of collection agencies or legal measures for nonpayment. (A.11.c.)

Establishing Fees. In establishing fees for professional counseling services, counselors consider the financial status of clients and locality. In the event that the established fee structure is inappropriate for a client, assistance is provided in attempting to find comparable services of acceptable cost. (See A.10.d., D.3.a., and D.3.b.)

Bartering Discouraged. Counselors ordinarily refrain from accepting goods or services from clients in return for counseling services because such arrangements create inherent potential for conflicts, exploitation, and distortion of the professional relationship. Counselors may participate in bartering only if the relationship is not exploitative, if the client requests it, if a clear written contract is established, and if such arrangements are an accepted practice among professionals in the community. (See A.6.a.)

Pro Bono Service. Counselors contribute to society by devoting a portion of their professional activity to services for which there is little or no financial return (pro bono).

A.11. Termination and Referral

Abandonment Prohibited. Counselors do not abandon or neglect clients in counseling. Counselors assist in making appropriate arrangements for the continuation of treatment, when necessary, during interruptions such as vacations, and following termination.

Inability to Assist Clients. If counselors determine an inability to be of professional assistance to clients, they avoid entering or immediately terminate a counseling relationship. Counselors are knowledgeable about referral resources and suggest appropriate alternatives. If clients decline the suggested referral, counselors should discontinue the relationship.

Appropriate Termination. Counselors terminate a counseling relationship, securing client agreement when possible, when it is reasonably clear that the client is no longer benefiting, when services are no longer required, when counseling no longer serves the client's needs or interests, when clients do not pay fees charged, or when agency or institution limits do not allow provision of further counseling services. (See A.10.b. and C.2.g.)

A.12. Computer Technology

Use of Computers. When computer applications are used in counseling services, counselors ensure that (1) the client is intellectually, emotionally, and physically capable of using the computer application; (2) the computer application is appropriate for the needs of the client; (3) the client understands the purpose and operation of the computer applications; and (4) a follow-up of client use of a computer application is provided to correct possible misconceptions, discover inappropriate use, and assess subsequent needs.

Explanation of Limitations. Counselors ensure that clients are provided information as a part of the counseling relationship that adequately explains the limitations of computer technology.
c. Access to Computer Applications. Counselors provide for equal access to computer applications in counseling services. (See A.2.a.)

Section B: Confidentiality

B.1. Right to Privacy

Respect for Privacy. Counselors respect their clients right to privacy and avoid illegal and unwarranted disclosures of confidential information. (See A.3.a. and B.6.a.)

Client Waiver. The right to privacy may be waived by the client or his or her legally recognized representative.

Exceptions. The general requirement that counselors keep information confidential does not apply when disclosure is required to prevent clear and imminent danger to the client or others or when legal requirements demand that confidential information be revealed. Counselors consult with other professionals when in doubt as to the validity of an exception.

Contagious, Fatal Diseases. A counselor who receives information confirming that a client has a disease commonly known to be both communicable and fatal is justified in disclosing information to an identifiable third party, who by his or her relationship with the client is at a high risk of contracting the disease. Prior to making a disclosure the counselor should ascertain that the client has not already informed the third party about his or her disease and that the client is not intending to inform the third party in the immediate future. (See B.1.c and B.1.f.)

Court-Ordered Disclosure. When court ordered to release confidential information without a client's permission, counselors request to the court that the disclosure not be required due to potential harm to the client or counseling relationship. (See B.1.c.)

Minimal Disclosure. When circumstances require the disclosure of confidential information, only essential information is revealed. To the extent possible, clients are informed before confidential information is disclosed.

Explanation of Limitations. When counseling is initiated and throughout the counseling process as necessary, counselors inform clients of the limitations of confidentiality and identify foreseeable situations in which confidentiality must be breached. (See G.2.a.)

Subordinates. Counselors make every effort to ensure that privacy and confidentiality of clients are maintained by subordinates including employees, supervisees, clerical assistants, and volunteers. (See B.1.a.)

Treatment Teams. If client treatment will involve a continued review by a treatment team, the client will be informed of the team's existence and composition.

B.2. Groups and Families

Group Work. In group work, counselors clearly define confidentiality and the parameters for the specific group being entered, explain its importance, and discuss the difficulties related to confidentiality involved in group work. The fact that confidentiality cannot be guaranteed is clearly communicated to group members.

Family Counseling. In family counseling, information about one family member cannot be disclosed to another member without permission. Counselors protect the privacy rights of each family member. (See A.8., B.3., and B.4.d.)

B.3. Minor or Incompetent Clients

When counseling clients who are minors or individuals who are unable to give voluntary, informed consent, parents or guardians may be included in the counseling process as appropriate. Counselors act in the best interests of clients and take measures to safeguard confidentiality. (See A.3.c.)

B.4. Records

Requirement of Records. Counselors maintain records necessary for rendering professional services to their clients and as required by laws, regulations, or agency or institution procedures.

Confidentiality of Records. Counselors are responsible for securing the safety and confidentiality of any counseling records they create, maintain, transfer, or destroy whether the records are written, taped, computerized, or stored in any other medium. (See B.1.a.)

Permission to Record or Observe. Counselors obtain permission from clients prior to electronically recording or observing sessions. (See A.3.a.)

Client Access. Counselors recognize that counseling records are kept for the benefit of clients, and therefore provide access to records and copies of records when requested by competent clients, unless the records contain information that may be misleading and detrimental to the client. In situations involving multiple clients, access to records is limited to those parts of records that do not include confidential information related to another client. (See A.8., B.1.a., and B.2.b.)

Disclosure or Transfer. Counselors obtain written permission from clients to disclose or transfer records to legitimate third parties unless exceptions to confidentiality exist as listed in Section B.1. Steps are taken to ensure that receivers of counseling records are sensitive to their confidential nature.

B.5. Research and Training

Data Disguise Required. Use of data derived from counseling relationships for purposes of training, research, or publication is confined to content that is disguised to ensure the anonymity of the individuals involved. (See B.1.g. and G.3.d.)

Agreement for Identification. Identification of a client in a presentation or publication is permissible only when the client has reviewed the material and has agreed to its presentation or publication. (See G.3.d.)

B.6. Consultation

Respect for Privacy. Information obtained in a consulting relationship is discussed for professional purposes only with persons clearly concerned with the case. Written and oral reports present data germane to the purposes of the consultation, and every effort is made to protect client identity and avoid undue invasion of privacy.

Cooperating Agencies. Before sharing information, counselors make efforts to ensure that there are defined policies in other agencies serving the counselor's clients that effectively protect the confidentiality of information.

Section C: Professional Responsibility

C.1. Standards Knowledge

Counselors have a responsibility to read, understand, and follow the Code of Ethics and the Standards of Practice.

C.2. Professional Competence

Boundaries of Competence. Counselors practice only within the boundaries of their competence, based on their education, training, supervised experience, state and national professional credentials, and appropriate professional experience. Counselors will demonstrate a commitment to gain knowledge, personal awareness, sensitivity, and skills pertinent to working with a diverse client population.

New Specialty Areas of Practice. Counselors practice in specialty areas new to them only after appropriate education, training, and supervised experience. While developing skills in new specialty areas, counselors take steps to ensure the competence of their work and to protect others from possible harm.

Qualified for Employment. Counselors accept employment only for positions for which they are qualified by education, training, supervised experience, state and national professional credentials, and appropriate professional experience. Counselors hire for professional counseling positions only individuals who are qualified and competent.

Monitor Effectiveness. Counselors continually monitor their effectiveness as professionals and take steps to improve when necessary. Counselors in private practice take reasonable steps to seek out peer supervision to evaluate their efficacy as counselors.

Ethical Issues Consultation. Counselors take reasonable steps to consult with other counselors or related professionals when they have questions regarding their ethical obligations or professional practice. (See H.1.)

Continuing Education. Counselors recognize the need for continuing education to maintain a reasonable level of awareness of current scientific and professional information in their fields of activity. They take steps to maintain competence in the skills they use, are open to new procedures, and keep current with the diverse and/or special populations with whom they work.

Impairment. Counselors refrain from offering or accepting professional services when their physical, mental, or emotional problems are likely to harm a client or others. They are alert to the signs of impairment, seek assistance for problems, and, if necessary, limit, suspend, or terminate their professional responsibilities. (See A.11.c.)

C.3. Advertising and Soliciting Clients

Accurate Advertising. There are no restrictions on advertising by counselors except those that can be specifically justified to protect the public from deceptive practices. Counselors advertise or represent their services to the public by identifying their credentials in an accurate manner that is not false, misleading, deceptive, or fraudulent. Counselors may only advertise the highest degree earned which is in counseling or a closely related field from a college or university that was accredited when the degree was awarded by one of the regional accrediting bodies recognized by the Council on Postsecondary Accreditation.

Testimonials. Counselors who use testimonials do not solicit them from clients or other persons who, because of their particular circumstances, may be vulnerable to undue influence.

Statements by Others. Counselors make reasonable efforts to ensure that statements made by others about them or the profession of counseling are accurate.

Recruiting Through Employment. Counselors do not use their places of employment or institutional affiliation to recruit or gain clients, supervisees, or consultees for their private practices. (See C.5.e.)

Products and Training Advertisements. Counselors who develop products related to their profession or conduct workshops or training events ensure that the advertisements concerning these products or events are accurate and disclose adequate information for consumers to make informed choices.

Promoting to Those Served. Counselors do not use counseling, teaching, training, or supervisory relationships to promote their products or training events in a manner that is deceptive or would exert undue influence on individuals who may be vulnerable. Counselors may adopt textbooks they have authored for instruction purposes.

Professional Association Involvement. Counselors actively participate in local, state, and national associations that foster the development and improvement of counseling.

C.4. Credentials

Credentials Claimed. Counselors claim or imply only professional credentials possessed and are responsible for correcting any known misrepresentations of their credentials by others. Professional credentials include graduate degrees in counseling or closely related mental health fields, accreditation of graduate programs, national voluntary certifications, government-issued certifications or licenses, ACA professional membership, or any other credential that might indicate to the public specialized knowledge or expertise in counseling.

ACA Professional Membership. ACA professional members may announce to the public their membership status. Regular members may not announce their ACA membership in a manner that might imply they are credentialed counselors.

Credential Guidelines. Counselors follow the guidelines for use of credentials that have been established by the entities that issue the credentials.

Misrepresentation of Credentials. Counselors do not attribute more to their credentials than the credentials represent, and do not imply that other counselors are not qualified because they do not possess certain credentials.

Doctoral Degrees From Other Fields. Counselors who hold a master's degree in counseling or a closely related mental health field, but hold a doctoral degree from other than counseling or a closely related field, do not use the title "Dr." in their practices and do not announce to the public in relation to their practice or status as a counselor that they hold a doctorate.

C.5. Public Responsibility

Nondiscrimination. Counselors do not discriminate against clients, students, or supervisees in a manner that has a negative impact based on their age, color, culture, disability, ethnic group, gender, race, religion, sexual orientation, or socioeconomic status, or for any other reason. (See A.2.a.)

Sexual Harassment. Counselors do not engage in sexual harassment. Sexual harassment is defined as sexual solicitation, physical advances, or verbal or nonverbal conduct that is sexual in nature, that occurs in connection with professional activities or roles, and that either (1) is unwelcome, is offensive, or creates a hostile workplace environment, and counselors know or are told this; or (2) is sufficiently severe or intense to be perceived as harassment to a reasonable person in the context. Sexual harassment can consist of a single intense or severe act or multiple persistent or pervasive acts.

Reports to Third Parties. Counselors are accurate, honest, and unbiased in reporting their professional activities and judgments to appropriate third parties including courts, health insurance companies, those who are the recipients of evaluation reports, and others. (See B.1.g.)

Media Presentations. When counselors provide advice or comment by means of public lectures, demonstrations, radio or television programs, prerecorded tapes, printed articles, mailed material, or other media, they take reasonable precautions to ensure that (1) the statements are based on appropriate professional counseling literature and practice; (2) the statements are otherwise consistent with the Code of Ethics and the Standards of Practice; and (3) the recipients of the information are not encouraged to infer that a professional counseling relationship has been established. (See C.6.b.)

Unjustified Gains. Counselors do not use their professional positions to seek or receive unjustified personal gains, sexual favors, unfair advantage, or unearned goods or services. (See C.3.d.)

C.6. Responsibility to Other Professionals

Different Approaches. Counselors are respectful of approaches to professional counseling that differ from their own. Counselors know and take into account the traditions and practices of other professional groups with which they work.

Personal Public Statements. When making personal statements in a public context, counselors clarify that they are speaking from their personal perspectives and that they are not speaking on behalf of all counselors or the profession. (See C.5.d.)

Clients Served by Others. When counselors learn that their clients are in a professional relationship with another mental health professional, they request release from clients to inform the other professionals and strive to establish positive and collaborative professional relationships. (See A.4.)

Section D: Relationships With Other Professionals

D.1. Relationships With Employers and Employees

Role Definition. Counselors define and describe for their employers and employees the parameters and levels of their professional roles.

Agreements. Counselors establish working agreements with supervisors, colleagues, and subordinates regarding counseling or clinical relationships, confidentiality, adherence to professional standards, distinction between public and private material, maintenance and dissemination of recorded information, work load, and accountability. Working agreements in each instance are specified and made known to those concerned.

Negative Conditions. Counselors alert their employers to conditions that may be potentially disruptive or damaging to the counselor's professional responsibilities or that may limit their effectiveness.

Evaluation. Counselors submit regularly to professional review and evaluation by their supervisor or the appropriate representative of the employer.

In-Service. Counselors are responsible for in-service development of self and staff.

Goals. Counselors inform their staff of goals and programs.

Practices. Counselors provide personnel and agency practices that respect and enhance the rights and welfare of each employee and recipient of agency services. Counselors strive to maintain the highest levels of professional services.

Personnel Selection and Assignment. Counselors select competent staff and assign responsibilities compatible with their skills and experiences.

Discrimination. Counselors, as either employers or employees, do not engage in or condone practices that are inhumane, illegal, or unjustifiable (such as considerations based on age, color, culture, disability, ethnic group, gender, race, religion, sexual orientation, or socioeconomic status) in hiring, promotion, or training. (See A.2.a. and C.5.b.)

Professional Conduct. Counselors have a responsibility both to clients and to the agency or institution within which services are performed to maintain high standards of professional conduct.

Exploitative Relationships. Counselors do not engage in exploitative relationships with individuals over whom they have supervisory, evaluative, or instructional control or authority. l. Employer Policies. The acceptance of employment in an agency or institution implies that counselors are in agreement with its general policies and principles. Counselors strive to reach agreement with employers as to acceptable standards of conduct that allow for changes in institutional policy conducive to the growth and development of clients.

D.2. Consultation (See B.6.)

Consultation as an Option. Counselors may choose to consult with any other professionally competent persons about their clients. In choosing consultants, counselors avoid placing the consultant in a conflict of interest situation that would preclude the consultant being a proper party to the counselor's efforts to help the client. Should counselors be engaged in a work setting that compromises this consultation standard, they consult with other professionals whenever possible to consider justifiable alternatives.

Consultant Competency. Counselors are reasonably certain that they have or the organization represented has the necessary competencies and resources for giving the kind of consulting services needed and that appropriate referral resources are available.

Understanding With Clients. When providing consultation, counselors attempt to develop with their clients a clear understanding of problem definition, goals for change, and predicted consequences of interventions selected. d. Consultant Goals. The consulting relationship is one in which client adaptability and growth toward self-direction are consistently encouraged and cultivated. (See A.1.b.)

D.3. Fees for Referral

Accepting Fees From Agency Clients. Counselors refuse a private fee or other remuneration for rendering services to persons who are entitled to such services through the counselor's employing agency or institution. The policies of a particular agency may make explicit provisions for agency clients to receive counseling services from members of its staff in private practice. In such instances, the clients must be informed of other options open to them should they seek private counseling services. (See A.10.a., A.11.b., and C.3.d.)

Referral Fees. Counselors do not accept a referral fee from other professionals.

D.4. Subcontractor Arrangements

When counselors work as subcontractors for counseling services for a third party, they have a duty to inform clients of the limitations of confidentiality that the organization may place on counselors in providing counseling services to clients. The limits of such confidentiality ordinarily are discussed as part of the intake session. (See B.1.e. and B.1.f.)

Section E: Evaluation, Assessment, and Interpretation

E.1. General

Appraisal Techniques. The primary purpose of educational and psychological assessment is to provide measures that are objective and interpretable in either comparative or absolute terms. Counselors recognize the need to interpret the statements in this section as applying to the whole range of appraisal techniques, including test and nontest data.

Client Welfare. Counselors promote the welfare and best interests of the client in the development, publication, and utilization of educational and psychological assessment techniques. They do not misuse assessment results and interpretations and take reasonable steps to prevent others from misusing the information these techniques provide. They respect the client's right to know the results, the interpretations made, and the bases for their conclusions and recommendations.

E.2. Competence to Use and Interpret Tests

Limits of Competence. Counselors recognize the limits of their competence and perform only those testing and assessment services for which they have been trained. They are familiar with reliability, validity, related standardization, error of measurement, and proper application of any technique utilized. Counselors using computer-based test interpretations are trained in the construct being measured and the specific instrument being used prior to using this type of computer application. Counselors take reasonable measures to ensure the proper use of psychological assessment techniques by persons under their supervision.

Appropriate Use. Counselors are responsible for the appropriate application, scoring, interpretation, and use of assessment instruments, whether they score and interpret such tests themselves or use computerized or other services.

Decisions Based on Results. Counselors responsible for decisions involving individuals or policies that are based on assessment results have a thorough understanding of educational and psychological measurement, including validation criteria, test research, and guidelines for test development and use.

Accurate Information. Counselors provide accurate information and avoid false claims or misconceptions when making statements about assessment instruments or techniques. Special efforts are made to avoid unwarranted connotations of such terms as IQ and grade equivalent scores. (See C.5.c.)

E.3. Informed Consent

Explanation to Clients. Prior to assessment, counselors explain the nature and purposes of assessment and the specific use of results in language the client (or other legally authorized person on behalf of the client) can understand, unless an explicit exception to this right has been agreed upon in advance. Regardless of whether scoring and interpretation are completed by counselors, by assistants, or by computer or other outside services, counselors take reasonable steps to ensure that appropriate explanations are given to the client.

Recipients of Results. The examinee's welfare, explicit understanding, and prior agreement determine the recipients of test results. Counselors include accurate and appropriate interpretations with any release of individual or group test results. (See B.1.a. and C.5.c.)

E.4. Release of Information to Competent Professionals

Misuse of Results. Counselors do not misuse assessment results, including test results, and interpretations, and take reasonable steps to prevent the misuse of such by others. (See C.5.c.)

Release of Raw Data. Counselors ordinarily release data (e.g., protocols, counseling or interview notes, or questionnaires) in which the client is identified only with the consent of the client or the client's legal representative. Such data are usually released only to persons recognized by counselors as competent to interpret the data. (See B.1.a.)

E.5. Proper Diagnosis of Mental Disorders

Proper Diagnosis. Counselors take special care to provide proper diagnosis of mental disorders. Assessment techniques (including personal interview) used to determine client care (e.g., locus of treatment, type of treatment, or recommended follow-up) are carefully selected and appropriately used. (See A.3.a. and C.5.c.)

Cultural Sensitivity. Counselors recognize that culture affects the manner in which clients' problems are defined. Clients' socioeconomic and cultural experience is considered when diagnosing mental disorders.

E.6. Test Selection

Appropriateness of Instruments. Counselors carefully consider the validity, reliability, psychometric limitations, and appropriateness of instruments when selecting tests for use in a given situation or with a particular client.

Culturally Diverse Populations. Counselors are cautious when selecting tests for culturally diverse populations to avoid inappropriateness of testing that may be outside of socialized behavioral or cognitive patterns.

E.7. Conditions of Test Administration

Administration Conditions. Counselors administer tests under the same conditions that were established in their standardization. When tests are not administered under standard conditions or when unusual behavior or irregularities occur during the testing session, those conditions are noted in interpretation, and the results may be designated as invalid or of questionable validity.

Computer Administration. Counselors are responsible for ensuring that administration programs function properly to provide clients with accurate results when a computer or other electronic methods are used for test administration. (See A.12.b.)

Unsupervised Test Taking. Counselors do not permit unsupervised or inadequately supervised use of tests or assessments unless the tests or assessments are designed, intended, and validated for self-administration and/or scoring.

Disclosure of Favorable Conditions. Prior to test administration, conditions that produce most favorable test results are made known to the examinee.

E.8. Diversity in Testing

Counselors are cautious in using assessment techniques, making evaluations, and interpreting the performance of populations not represented in the norm group on which an instrument was standardized. They recognize the effects of age, color, culture, disability, ethnic group, gender, race, religion, sexual orientation, and socioeconomic status on test administration and interpretation and place test results in proper perspective with other relevant factors. (See A.2.a.)

E.9. Test Scoring and Interpretation

Reporting Reservations. In reporting assessment results, counselors indicate any reservations that exist regarding validity or reliability because of the circumstances of the assessment or the inappropriateness of the norms for the person tested.

Research Instruments. Counselors exercise caution when interpreting the results of research instruments possessing insufficient technical data to support respondent results. The specific purposes for the use of such instruments are stated explicitly to the examinee.

Testing Services. Counselors who provide test scoring and test interpretation services to support the assessment process confirm the validity of such interpretations. They accurately describe the purpose, norms, validity, reliability, and applications of the procedures and any special qualifications applicable to their use. The public offering of an automated test interpretations service is considered a professional-to-professional consultation. The formal responsibility of the consultant is to the consultee, but the ultimate and overriding responsibility is to the client.

E.10. Test Security

Counselors maintain the integrity and security of tests and other assessment techniques consistent with legal and contractual obligations. Counselors do not appropriate, reproduce, or modify published tests or parts thereof without acknowledgment and permission from the publisher.

E.11. Obsolete Tests and Outdated Test Results

Counselors do not use data or test results that are obsolete or outdated for the current purpose. Counselors make every effort to prevent the misuse of obsolete measures and test data by others.

E.12. Test Construction

Counselors use established scientific procedures, relevant standards, and current professional knowledge for test design in the development, publication, and utilization of educational and psychological assessment techniques.

Section F: Teaching, Training, and Supervision

F.1. Counselor Educators and Trainers

Educators as Teachers and Practitioners. Counselors who are responsible for developing, implementing, and supervising educational programs are skilled as teachers and practitioners. They are knowledgeable regarding the ethical, legal, and regulatory aspects of the profession, are skilled in applying that knowledge, and make students and supervisees aware of their responsibilities. Counselors conduct counselor education and training programs in an ethical manner and serve as role models for professional behavior. Counselor educators should make an effort to infuse material related to human diversity into all courses and/or workshops that are designed to promote the development of professional counselors.

Relationship Boundaries With Students and Supervisees. Counselors clearly define and maintain ethical, professional, and social relationship boundaries with their students and supervisees. They are aware of the differential in power that exists and the student's or supervisee's possible incomprehension of that power differential. Counselors explain to students and supervisees the potential for the relationship to become exploitive.

Sexual Relationships. Counselors do not engage in sexual relationships with students or supervisees and do not subject them to sexual harassment. (See A.6. and C.5.b)

Contributions to Research. Counselors give credit to students or supervisees for their contributions to research and scholarly projects. Credit is given through coauthorship, acknowledgment, footnote statement, or other appropriate means, in accordance with such contributions. (See G.4.b. and G.4.c.)

Close Relatives. Counselors do not accept close relatives as students or supervisees.

Supervision Preparation. Counselors who offer clinical supervision services are adequately prepared in supervision methods and techniques. Counselors who are doctoral students serving as practicum or internship supervisors to master's level students are adequately prepared and supervised by the training program.

Responsibility for Services to Clients. Counselors who supervise the counseling services of others take reasonable measures to ensure that counseling services provided to clients are professional.

Endorsement. Counselors do not endorse students or supervisees for certification, licensure, employment, or completion of an academic or training program if they believe students or supervisees are not qualified for the endorsement. Counselors take reasonable steps to assist students or supervisees who are not qualified for endorsement to become qualified.

F.2. Counselor Education and Training Programs

Orientation. Prior to admission, counselors orient prospective students to the counselor education or training program's expectations, including but not limited to the following: (1) the type and level of skill acquisition required for successful completion of the training, (2) subject matter to be covered, (3) basis for evaluation, (4) training components that encourage self-growth or self-disclosure as part of the training process, (5) the type of supervision settings and requirements of the sites for required clinical field experiences, (6) student and supervisee evaluation and dismissal policies and procedures, and (7) up-to-date employment prospects for graduates.

Integration of Study and Practice. Counselors establish counselor education and training programs that integrate academic study and supervised practice.

Evaluation. Counselors clearly state to students and supervisees, in advance of training, the levels of competency expected, appraisal methods, and timing of evaluations for both didactic and experiential components. Counselors provide students and supervisees with periodic performance appraisal and evaluation feedback throughout the training program.

Teaching Ethics. Counselors make students and supervisees aware of the ethical responsibilities and standards of the profession and the students' and supervisees' ethical responsibilities to the profession. (See C.1. and F.3.e.)

Peer Relationships. When students or supervisees are assigned to lead counseling groups or provide clinical supervision for their peers, counselors take steps to ensure that students and supervisees placed in these roles do not have personal or adverse relationships with peers and that they understand they have the same ethical obligations as counselor educators, trainers, and supervisors. Counselors make every effort to ensure that the rights of peers are not compromised when students or supervisees are assigned to lead counseling groups or provide clinical supervision.

Varied Theoretical Positions. Counselors present varied theoretical positions so that students and supervisees may make comparisons and have opportunities to develop their own positions. Counselors provide information concerning the scientific bases of professional practice. (See C.6.a.)

Field Placements. Counselors develop clear policies within their training program regarding field placement and other clinical experiences. Counselors provide clearly stated roles and responsibilities for the student or supervisee, the site supervisor, and the program supervisor. They confirm that site supervisors are qualified to provide supervision and are informed of their professional and ethical responsibilities in this role.

Dual Relationships as Supervisors. Counselors avoid dual relationships such as performing the role of site supervisor and training program supervisor in the student's or supervisee's training program. Counselors do not accept any form of professional services, fees, commissions, reimbursement, or remuneration from a site for student or supervisee placement.

Diversity in Programs. Counselors are responsive to their institution's and program's recruitment and retention needs for training program administrators, faculty, and students with diverse backgrounds and special needs. (See A.2.a.)

F.3. Students and Supervisees

Limitations. Counselors, through ongoing evaluation and appraisal, are aware of the academic and personal limitations of students and supervisees that might impede performance. Counselors assist students and supervisees in securing remedial assistance when needed, and dismiss from the training program supervisees who are unable to provide competent service due to academic or personal limitations. Counselors seek professional consultation and document their decision to dismiss or refer students or supervisees for assistance. Counselors ensure that students and supervisees have recourse to address decisions made to require them to seek assistance or to dismiss them.

Self-Growth Experiences. Counselors use professional judgment when designing training experiences conducted by the counselors themselves that require student and supervisee self-growth or self-disclosure. Safeguards are provided so that students and supervisees are aware of the ramifications their self-disclosure may have on counselors whose primary role as teacher, trainer, or supervisor requires acting on ethical obligations to the profession. Evaluative components of experiential training experiences explicitly delineate predetermined academic standards that are separate and do not depend on the student's level of self-disclosure. (See A.6.)

Counseling for Students and Supervisees. If students or supervisees request counseling, supervisors or counselor educators provide them with acceptable referrals. Supervisors or counselor educators do not serve as counselor to students or supervisees over whom they hold administrative, teaching, or evaluative roles unless this is a brief role associated with a training experience. (See A.6.b.)

Clients of Students and Supervisees. Counselors make every effort to ensure that the clients at field placements are aware of the services rendered and the qualifications of the students and supervisees rendering those services. Clients receive professional disclosure information and are informed of the limits of confidentiality. Client permission is obtained in order for the students and supervisees to use any information concerning the counseling relationship in the training process. (See B.1.e.)

Standards for Students and Supervisees. Students and supervisees preparing to become counselors adhere to the Code of Ethics and the Standards of Practice. Students and supervisees have the same obligations to clients as those required of counselors. (See H.1.)

Section G: Research and Publication

G.1. Research Responsibilities

Use of Human Subjects. Counselors plan, design, conduct, and report research in a manner consistent with pertinent ethical principles, federal and state laws, host institutional regulations, and scientific standards governing research with human subjects. Counselors design and conduct research that reflects cultural sensitivity appropriateness.

Deviation From Standard Practices. Counselors seek consultation and observe stringent safeguards to protect the rights of research participants when a research problem suggests a deviation from standard acceptable practices. (See B.6.)

Precautions to Avoid Injury. Counselors who conduct research with human subjects are responsible for the subjects' welfare throughout the experiment and take reasonable precautions to avoid causing injurious psychological, physical, or social effects to their subjects.

Principal Researcher Responsibility. The ultimate responsibility for ethical research practice lies with the principal researcher. All others involved in the research activities share ethical obligations and full responsibility for their own actions.

Minimal Interference. Counselors take reasonable precautions to avoid causing disruptions in subjects' lives due to participation in research. f. Diversity. Counselors are sensitive to diversity and research issues with special populations. They seek consultation when appropriate. (See A.2.a. and B.6.)

G.2. Informed Consent

Topics Disclosed. In obtaining informed consent for research, counselors use language that is understandable to research participants and that (1) accurately explains the purpose and procedures to be followed; (2) identifies any procedures that are experimental or relatively untried; (3) describes the attendant discomforts and risks; (4) describes the benefits or changes in individuals or organizations that might be reasonably expected; (5) discloses appropriate alternative procedures that would be advantageous for subjects; (6) offers to answer any inquiries concerning the procedures; (7) describes any limitations on confidentiality; and (8) instructs that subjects are free to withdraw their consent and to discontinue participation in the project at any time. (See B.1.f.)

Deception. Counselors do not conduct research involving deception unless alternative procedures are not feasible and the prospective value of the research justifies the deception. When the methodological requirements of a study necessitate concealment or deception, the investigator is required to explain clearly the reasons for this action as soon as possible.

Voluntary Participation. Participation in research is typically voluntary and without any penalty for refusal to participate. Involuntary participation is appropriate only when it can be demonstrated that participation will have no harmful effects on subjects and is essential to the investigation.

Confidentiality of Information. Information obtained about research participants during the course of an investigation is confidential. When the possibility exists that others may obtain access to such information, ethical research practice requires that the possibility, together with the plans for protecting confidentiality, be explained to participants as a part of the procedure for obtaining informed consent. (See B.1.e.)

Persons Incapable of Giving Informed Consent. When a person is incapable of giving informed consent, counselors provide an appropriate explanation, obtain agreement for participation, and obtain appropriate consent from a legally authorized person.

Commitments to Participants. Counselors take reasonable measures to honor all commitments to research participants.

Explanations After Data Collection. After data are collected, counselors provide participants with full clarification of the nature of the study to remove any misconceptions. Where scientific or human values justify delaying or withholding information, counselors take reasonable measures to avoid causing harm.

Agreements to Cooperate. Counselors who agree to cooperate with another individual in research or publication incur an obligation to cooperate as promised in terms of punctuality of performance and with regard to the completeness and accuracy of the information required.

Informed Consent for Sponsors. In the pursuit of research, counselors give sponsors, institutions, and publication channels the same respect and opportunity for giving informed consent that they accord to individual research participants. Counselors are aware of their obligation to future research workers and ensure that host institutions are given feedback information and proper acknowledgment.

G.3. Reporting Results

Information Affecting Outcome. When reporting research results, counselors explicitly mention all variables and conditions known to the investigator that may have affected the outcome of a study or the interpretation of data.

Accurate Results. Counselors plan, conduct, and report research accurately and in a manner that minimizes the possibility that results will be misleading. They provide thorough discussions of the limitations of their data and alternative hypotheses. Counselors do not engage in fraudulent research, distort data, misrepresent data, or deliberately bias their results.

Obligation to Report Unfavorable Results. Counselors communicate to other counselors the results of any research judged to be of professional value. Results that reflect unfavorably on institutions, programs, services, prevailing opinions, or vested interests are not withheld.

Identity of Subjects. Counselors who supply data, aid in the research of another person, report research results, or make original data available take due care to disguise the identity of respective subjects in the absence of specific authorization from the subjects to do otherwise. (See B.1.g. and B.5.a.)

Replication Studies. Counselors are obligated to make available sufficient original research data to qualified professionals who may wish to replicate the study.

G.4. Publication

Recognition of Others. When conducting and reporting research, counselors are familiar with and give recognition to previous work on the topic, observe copyright laws, and give full credit to those to whom credit is due. (See F.1.d. and G.4.c.)

Contributors. Counselors give credit through joint authorship, acknowledgment, footnote statements, or other appropriate means to those who have contributed significantly to research or concept development in accordance with such contributions. The principal contributor is listed first and minor technical or professional contributions are acknowledged in notes or introductory statements.

Student Research. For an article that is substantially based on a student's dissertation or thesis, the student is listed as the principal author. (See F.1.d. and G.4.a.)

Duplicate Submission. Counselors submit manuscripts for consideration to only one journal at a time. Manuscripts that are published in whole or in substantial part in another journal or published work are not submitted for publication without acknowledgment and permission from the previous publication.

Professional Review. Counselors who review material submitted for publication, research, or other scholarly purposes respect the confidentiality and proprietary rights of those who submitted it.

Section H: Resolving Ethical Issues

H.1. Knowledge of Standards

Counselors are familiar with the Code of Ethics and the Standards of Practice and other applicable ethics codes from other professional organizations of which they are member, or from certification and licensure bodies. Lack of knowledge or misunderstanding of an ethical responsibility is not a defense against a charge of unethical conduct. (See F.3.e.)

H.2. Suspected Violations

Ethical Behavior Expected. Counselors expect professional associates to adhere to the Code of Ethics. When counselors possess reasonable cause that raises doubts as to whether a counselor is acting in an ethical manner, they take appropriate action. (See H.2.d. and H.2.e.)

Consultation. When uncertain as to whether a particular situation or course of action may be in violation of the Code of Ethics, counselors consult with other counselors who are knowledgeable about ethics, with colleagues, or with appropriate authorities.

Organization Conflicts. If the demands of an organization with which counselors are affiliated pose a conflict with the Code of Ethics, counselors specify the nature of such conflicts and express to their supervisors or other responsible officials their commitment to the Code of Ethics. When possible, counselors work toward change within the organization to allow full adherence to the Code of Ethics.

Informal Resolution. When counselors have reasonable cause to believe that another counselor is violating an ethical standard, they attempt to first resolve the issue informally with the other counselor if feasible, providing that such action does not violate confidentiality rights that may be involved.

Reporting Suspected Violations. When an informal resolution is not appropriate or feasible, counselors, upon reasonable cause, take action such as reporting the suspected ethical violation to state or national ethics committees, unless this action conflicts with confidentiality rights that cannot be resolved.

Unwarranted Complaints. Counselors do not initiate, participate in, or encourage the filing of ethics complaints that are unwarranted or intend to harm a counselor rather than to protect clients or the public.

H.3. Cooperation With Ethics Committees

Counselors assist in the process of enforcing the Code of Ethics. Counselors cooperate with investigations, proceedings, and requirements of the ACA Ethics Committee or ethics committees of other duly constituted associations or boards having jurisdiction over those charged with a violation. Counselors are familiar with the ACA Policies and Procedures and use it as a reference in assisting the enforcement of the Code of Ethics.

 **National Career Development Association**
Ethical Standards (Revised 2003)

These Ethical Standards were developed by the National Board for Certified Counselors (NBCC), an independent, voluntary, not-for-profit organization incorporated in 1982. Titled "Code of Ethics" by NBCC and last amended in February 1987, the Ethical Standards were adopted by the National Career Development Association (NCDA) Board of Directors in 1987 and revised in 1991, with minor changes in wording (e.g., the addition of specific references to NCDA members).

Preamble: NCDA is an educational, scientific, and professional organization dedicated to the enhancement of the worth, dignity, potential, and uniqueness of each individual and, thus, to the service of society. This code of ethics enables the NCDA to clarify the nature of ethical responsibilities for present and future professional career counselors.

Section A: General

NCDA members influence the development of the profession by continuous efforts to improve professional practices, services, and research. Professional growth is continuous through the career counselor's career and is exemplified by the development of a philosophy that explains why and how a career counselor functions in the helping relationship. Career counselors must gather data on their effectiveness and be guided by their findings.

1. NCDA members have a responsibility to the clients they are serving and to the institutions within which the services are being performed. Career counselors also strive to assist the respective agency, organization, or institution in providing the highest caliber of professional services. The acceptance of employment in an institution implies that the career counselor is in agreement with the general policies and principles of the institution. Therefore, the professional activities of the career counselor are in accord with the objectives of the institution. If, despite concerted efforts, the career counselor cannot reach agreement with the employer as to acceptable standards of conduct that allow for changes in institutional policy that are conducive to the positive growth and development of clients, then terminating the affiliation should be seriously considered.

2. Ethical behavior among professional associates (e.g., career counselors) must be expected at all times. When accessible information raises doubt as to the ethical behavior of professional colleagues, the NCDA member must make action to attempt to rectify this condition. Such action uses the respective institution's channels first and then uses procedures established by the American Counseling Association, of which NCDA is a division.

3. NCDA members neither claim nor imply professional qualifications which exceed those possessed, and are responsible for correcting any misrepresentations of these qualifications by others.

4. NCDA members must refuse a private fee or other remuneration for consultation or counseling with persons who are entitled to their services through the career counselor's employing institution or agency. The policies of some agencies may make explicit provisions for staff members to engage in private practice with agency clients. However, should agency clients desire private counseling or consulting services, they must be apprised of other options available to them.

Career counselors must not divert to their private practices, legitimate clients in their primary agencies or of the institutions with which they are affiliated.

5. In establishing fees for professional counseling services, NCDA members must consider the financial status of clients and the respective locality. In the event that the established fee status is inappropriate for the client, assistance must be provided in finding comparable services of acceptable cost.

6. NCDA members seek only those positions in the delivery of professional services for which they are professionally qualified.

7. NCDA members recognize their limitations and provide services or only use techniques for which they are qualified by training and/or experience. Career counselors recognize the need, and seek continuing education, to assure competent services.

8. NCDA members are aware of the intimacy in the counseling relationship, maintain respect for the client, and avoid engaging in activities that seek to meet their personal needs at the expense of the client.

9. NCDA member do not condone or engage in sexual harassment which is defined as deliberate or repeated comments, gestures, or physical contacts of a sexual nature.

10. NCDA members avoid bringing their personal or professional issues into the counseling relationship. Through an awareness of the impact of stereotyping and discrimination (e.g., biases based on age, disability, ethnicity, gender, race, religion, or sexual preference), career counselors guard the individual rights and personal dignity of the client in the counseling relationship.

11. NCDA members are accountable at all times for their behavior. They must be aware that all actions and behaviors of a counselor reflect on professional integrity and, when inappropriate, can damage the public trust in the counseling profession. To protect public confidence in the counseling profession, career counselors avoid public behavior that is clearly in violation of accepted moral and legal standards.

12. NCDA members have a social responsibility because their recommendations and professional actions may alter the lives of others. Career counselors remain fully cognizant of their impact and are alert to personal, social, organizational, financial, or political situations or pressures which might lead to misuse of their influence.

13. Products or services provided by NCDA members by means of classroom instruction, public lectures, demonstrations, written articles, radio or television programs, or other types of media must meet the criteria cited in Sections A through F of these Ethical Standards.

Section B: Counseling Relationship

1. The primary obligation of NCDA members is to respect the integrity and promote the welfare of the client, regardless of whether the client is assisted individually or in a group relationship. In a group setting, the career counselor is also responsible for taking reasonable precautions to protect individuals from physical and/or psychological trauma resulting from interaction within the group.

2. The counseling relationship and information resulting from it remains confidential, consistent with the legal obligations of the NCDA member. In a group counseling setting, the career counselor sets a norm of confidentiality regarding all group participants' disclosures.

3. NCDA members know and take into account the traditions and practices of other professional groups with whom they work, and they cooperate fully with such groups. If a person is receiving

similar services from another professional, career counselors do not offer their own services directly to such a person. If a career counselor is contacted by a person who is already receiving similar services from another professional, the career counselor carefully considers that professional relationship and proceeds with caution and sensitivity to the therapeutic issues as well as the client's welfare. Career counselors discuss these issues with clients so as to minimize the risk of confusion and conflict.

4. When a client's condition indicates that there is a clear and imminent danger to the client or others, the NCDA member must take reasonable personal action or inform responsible authorities. Consultation with other professionals must be used where possible. The assumption of responsibility for the client's behavior must be taken only after careful deliberation, and the client must be involved in the resumption of responsibility as quickly as possible.

5. Records of the counseling relationship, including interview notes, test data, correspondence, audio or visual tape recordings, electronic data storage, and other documents are to be considered professional information for use in counseling. They should not be considered a part of the records of the institution or agency in which the NCDA member is employed unless specified by state statute or regulation. Revelation to others of counseling material must occur only upon the expressed consent of the client; career counselors must make provisions for maintaining confidentiality in the storage and disposal of records. Career counselors providing information to the public or to subordinates, peers, or supervisors have a responsibility to ensure that the content is general; unidentified client information should be accurate and unbiased, and should consist of objective, factual data.

6. NCDA members must ensure that data maintained in electronic storage are secure. The data must be limited to information that is appropriate and necessary for the services being provided and accessible only to appropriate staff members involved in the provision of services by using the best computer security methods available. Career counselors must also ensure that electronically stored data are destroyed when the information is no longer of value in providing services.

7. Data derived from a counseling relationship for use in counselor training or research shall be confined to content that can be disguised to ensure full protection of the identity of the subject/client and shall be obtained with informed consent.

8. NCDA members must inform clients, before or at the time the counseling relationship commences, of the purposes, goals, techniques, rules and procedures, and limitations that may affect the relationship.

9. All methods of treatment by NCDA members must be clearly indicated to prospective recipients and safety precautions must be taken in their use.

10. NCDA members who have an administrative, supervisory, and/or evaluative relationship with individuals seeking counseling services must not serve as the counselor and should refer the individuals to other professionals. Exceptions are made only in instances where an individual's situation warrants counseling intervention and another alternative is unavailable. Dual relationships with clients that might impair the career counselor's objectivity and professional judgment must be avoided and/or the counseling relationship terminated through referral to another competent professional.

11. When NCDA members determine an inability to be of professional assistance to a potential or existing client, they must, respectively, not initiate the counseling relationship or immediately terminate the relationship. In either event, the career counselor must suggest appropriate alternatives. Career counselors must be knowledgeable about referral resources so that a satisfactory referral can be initiated. In the event that the client declines a suggested referral, the career counselor is not obligated to continue the relationship.

12. NCDA members may choose to consult with any other professionally competent person about a client and must notify clients of this right. Career counselors must avoid placing a consultant in a conflict-of-interest situation that would preclude the consultant's being a proper party to the career counselor's efforts to help the client.

13. NCDA members who counsel clients from cultures different from their own must gain knowledge, personal awareness, and sensitivity pertinent to the client populations served and must incorporate culturally relevant techniques into their practice.

14. When NCDA members engage in intensive counseling with a client, the client's counseling needs should be assessed. When needs exist outside the counselor's expertise, appropriate referrals should be made.

15. NCDA members must screen prospective group counseling participants, especially when the emphasis is on self-understanding and growth through self-disclosure. Career counselors must maintain n awareness of each group participant's welfare throughout the group process.

16. When electronic data and systems are used as a component of counseling services, NCDA members must ensure that the computer application, and any information it contains, is appropriate for the respective needs of clients and is nondiscriminatory. Career counselors must ensure that they themselves have acquired a facilitation level of knowledge with any system they use including hands-on application, search experience, and understanding of the uses of all aspects of the computer-based system. In selecting and/or maintaining computer-based systems that contain career information, career counselors must ensure that the systems provide current, accurate, and locally relevant information. Career counselors must also ensure that clients are intellectually, emotionally, and physically compatible with the use of the computer application and understand its purpose and operation. Client use of a computer application must be evaluated to correct possible problems and assess subsequent needs.

17. NCDA members who develop self-help, stand-alone computer software for use by the general public, must first ensure that it is initially designed to function in a stand-alone manner, as opposed to modifying software that was originally designed to require support from a counselor. Secondly, the software must include program statements that provide the user with intended outcomes, suggestions for using the software, descriptions of inappropriately used applications, and descriptions of when and how counseling services might be beneficial. Finally, the manual must include the qualifications of the developer, the development process, validation data, and operating procedures.

Section C: Measurement and Evaluation

1. NCDA members must provide specific orientation or information to an examinee prior to and following the administration of assessment instruments or techniques so that the results may be placed in proper perspective with other relevant factors. The purpose of testing and the explicit use of the results must be made known to an examinee prior to testing.

2. In selecting assessment instruments or techniques for use in a given situation or with a particular client, NCDA members must evaluate carefully the instrument's specific theoretical bases and characteristics, validity, reliability, and appropriateness. Career counselors are professionally responsible for using unvalidated information with special care.

3. When making statements to the public about assessment instruments or techniques, NCDA members must provide accurate information and avoid false claims or misconceptions concerning the meaning of psychometric terms. Special efforts are often required to avoid unwarranted connotations of terms such as IQ and grade-equivalent scores.

4. Because many types of assessment techniques exist, NCDA members must recognize the limits of their competence and perform only those functions for which they have received appropriate training.

5. NCDA members must note when tests are not administered under standard conditions or when unusual behavior or irregularities occur during a testing session and the results must be designated as invalid or of questionable validity. Unsupervised or inadequately supervised assessments, such as mail-in tests, are considered unethical. However, the use of standardized instruments that are designed to be self-administered and self-scored, such as interest inventories, is appropriate.

6. Because prior coaching or dissemination of test materials can invalidate test results, NCDA members are professionally obligated to maintain test security. In addition, conditions that produce most favorable test results must be made known to an examinee (e.g., penalty for guessing).

7. NCDA members must consider psychometric limitations when selecting and using an instrument, and must be cognizant of the limitations when interpreting the results. When tests are used to classify clients, career counselors must ensure that periodic review and/or re-testing are conducted to prevent client stereotyping.

8. An examinee's welfare, explicit prior understanding, and agreement are the factors used when determining who receives the test results. NCDA members must see that appropriate interpretation accompanies any release of individual or group test data (e.g., limitations of instrument and norms).

9. NCDA members must ensure that computer-generated assessment administration and scoring programs function properly, thereby providing clients with accurate assessment results.

10. NCDA members who are responsible for making decisions based on assessment results, must have appropriate training and skills in educational and psychological measurement—including validation criteria, test research, and guidelines for test development and use.

11. NCDA members must be cautious when interpreting the results of instruments that possess insufficient technical data, and must explicitly state to examinees the specific purposes for the use of such instruments.

12. NCDA members must proceed with caution when attempting to evaluate and interpret performances of minority group members or other persons who are not represented in the norm group on which the instrument was standardized.

13. NCDA members who develop computer-based interpretations to support the assessment process must ensure that the validity of the interpretations is established prior to the commercial distribution of the computer application.

14. NCDA members recognize that test results may become obsolete, and avoid the misuse of obsolete data.

15. NCDA members must avoid the appropriation, reproduction, or modification of published tests or parts thereof without acknowledgment and permission from the publisher.

Section D: Research and Publication

1. NCDA members will adhere to relevant guidelines on research with human subjects. These include:

    a. Code of Federal Regulations, Title 45, Subtitle A, Part 46, as currently issued.

b. American Psychological Association. (1982). Ethical principles in the conduct of research with human participants. Washington, DC: Author.

c. American Psychological Association. (1981). Research with human participants. American Psychologist, 36, 633-638.

d. Family Educational Rights and Privacy Act. (Buckley Amendment to P. L. 93-380 of the Laws of 1974)

e. Current federal regulations and various state privacy acts.

2. In planning research activities involving human subjects, NCDA members must be aware of and responsive to all pertinent ethical principles and ensure that the research problem, design, and execution are in full compliance with the principles.

3. The ultimate responsibility for ethical research lies with the principal researcher, although others involved in research activities are ethically obligated and responsible for their own actions.

4. NCDA members who conduct research with human subjects are responsible for the subjects' welfare throughout the experiment and must take all reasonable precautions to avoid causing injurious psychological, physical, or social effects on their subjects.

5. NCDA members who conduct research must abide by the following basic elements of informed consent:

a. A fair explanation of the procedures to be followed, including an identification of those which are experimental.

b. A description of the attendant discomforts and risks.

c. A description of the benefits to be expected.

d. A disclosure of appropriate alternative procedures that would be advantageous for subjects.

e. An offer to answer any inquiries concerning the procedures.

f. An instruction that subjects are free to withdraw their consent and to discontinue participation in the project or activity at any time.

6. When reporting research results, explicit mention must be made of all the variables and conditions known to the NCDA member that may have affected the outcome of the study or the interpretation of the data.

7. NCDA members who conduct and report research investigations must do so in a manner that minimizes the possibility that the results will be misleading.

8. NCDA members are obligated to make available sufficient original research data to qualified others who may wish to replicate the study.

9. NCDA members who supply data, aid in the research of another person, report research results, or make original data available, must take due care to disguise the identity of respective subjects in the absence of specific authorization from the subject to do otherwise.

10. When conducting and reporting research, NCDA members must be familiar with, and give recognition to, previous work on the topic, must observe all copyright laws, and must follow the principles of giving full credit to those to whom credit is due.

11. NCDA members must give due credit through joint authorship, acknowledgment, footnote statements, or other appropriate means to those who have contributed significantly to the research and/or publication, in accordance with such contributions.

12. NCDA members should communicate to others the results of any research judged to be of professional value. Results that reflect unfavorably on institutions, programs, services, or vested interests must not be withheld.

13. NCDA members who agree to cooperate with another individual in research and/or publication incur an obligation to cooperate as promised in terms of punctuality of performance and with full regard to the completeness and accuracy of the information required.

14. NCDA members must not submit the same manuscript, or one essentially similar in content, for simultaneous publication consideration by two or more journals. In addition, manuscripts that are published in whole or substantial part in another journal or published work should not be submitted for publication without acknowledgment and permission from the previous publication.

Section E: Consulting

Consultation refers to a voluntary relationship between a professional helper and help-needing individual, group, or social unit in which the consultant is providing help to the client(s) in defining and solving a work-related problem or potential work-related problem with a client or client system.

1. NCDA members acting as consultants must have a high degree of self-awareness of their own values, knowledge, skills, limitations, and needs in entering a helping relationship that involves human and/or organizational change. The focus of the consulting relationship must be on the issues to be resolved and not on the person(s) presenting the problem.

2. In the consulting relationship, the NCDA member and client must understand and agree upon the problem definition, subsequent goals, and predicted consequences of interventions selected.

3. NCDA members must be reasonably certain that they, or the organization represented, have the necessary competencies and resources for giving the kind of help that is needed or that may develop later, and that appropriate referral resources are available to the consultant.

4. NCDA members in a consulting relationship must encourage and cultivate client adaptability and growth toward self-direction. NCDA members must maintain this role consistently and not become a decision maker for clients or create a future dependency on the consultant.

5. NCDA members conscientiously adhere to the NCDA Ethical Standards when announcing consultant availability for services.

Section F: Private Practice

1. NCDA members should assist the profession by facilitating the availability of counseling services in private as well as public settings.

2. In advertising services as private practitioners, NCDA members must advertise in a manner that accurately informs the public of the professional services, expertise, and counseling techniques available.

3. NCDA members who assume an executive leadership role in a private practice organization do not permit their names to be used in professional notices during periods of time when they are not actively engaged in the private practice of counseling.

4. NCDA members may list their highest relevant degree, type, and level of certification and/or license, address, telephone number, office hours, type and/or description of services, and other

relevant information. Listed information must not contain false, inaccurate misleading, partial, out-of-context, or otherwise deceptive material or statements.

5. NCDA members who are involved in partnership or corporation with other professionals must, in compliance with the regulations of the locality, clearly specify the separate specialties of each member of the partnership or corporation.

6. NCDA members have an obligation to withdraw from a private-practice counseling relationship if it violates the NCDA Ethical Standards; if the mental or physical condition of the NCDA member renders it difficult to carry out an effective professional relationship; or if the counseling relationship is no longer productive for the client.

Procedures for Processing Ethical Complaints

As a division of the American Counseling Association (ACA) the National Career Development Association (NCDA) adheres to the guidelines and procedures for processing ethical complaints and the disciplinary sanctions adopted by ACA. A complaint against an NCDA member may be filed by any individual or group of individuals ("complainant"), whether or not the complainant is a member of NCDA. Action will not be taken on anonymous complaints.

For specifics on how to file ethical complaints and a description of the guidelines and procedures for processing complaints, contact:

ACA Ethics Committee
c/o Executive Director
American Counseling Association
5999 Stevenson Avenue
Alexandria, VA 22304
(800) 347-6647

NCDA Administrative Offices: 10820 E. 45 Street, Suite 210
Tulsa, OK 74146
http://ncda.org

Reviewed annually by the NCDA Ethics Committee

NCDA opposes discrimination against any individual on the basis of race, ethnicity, sex, gender identity, sexual orientation, age, religion, socioeconomic status, mental/physical disability, creed, or any other characteristics not specifically relevant to job performance.
(NCDA Board of Directors – January 2003)

NATIONAL BOARD FOR CERTIFIED COUNSELORS
CODE OF ETHICS

PREAMBLE

The National Board for Certified Counselors (NBCC) is a professional certification board which certifies counselors as having met standards for the general and specialty practice of professional counseling established by the Board. The counselors certified by NBCC may identify with different professional associations and are often licensed by jurisdictions which promulgate codes of ethics. The NBCC code of ethics provides a minimal ethical standard for the professional behavior of all NBCC certificants. This code provides an expectation of and assurance for the ethical practice for all who use the professional services of an NBCC certificant. In addition, it serves the purpose of having an enforceable standard for all NBCC certificants and assures those served of some resource in case of a perceived ethical violation.

The NBCC Ethical Code applies to all those certified by NBCC regardless of any other professional affiliation. Persons who receive professional services from certified counselors may elect to use other ethical codes which apply to their counselor. Although NBCC cooperates with professional associations and credentialing organizations, it can bring actions to discipline or sanction NBCC certificants only if the provisions of the NBCC Code are found to have been violated.

The National Board for Certified Counselors, Inc. (NBCC) promotes counseling through certification. In pursuit of this mission, the NBCC:

- Promotes quality assurance in counseling practice

- Promotes the value of counseling

- Promotes public awareness of quality counseling practice

- Promotes professionalism in counseling

- Promotes leadership in credentialing

Section A: General

1. Certified counselors engage in continuous efforts to improve professional practices, services, and research. Certified counselors are guided in their work by evidence of the best professional practices.

2. Certified counselors have a responsibility to the clients they serve and to the institutions within which the services are performed. Certified counselors also strive to assist the respective agency, organization, or institution in providing competent and ethical professional services. The acceptance of employment in an institution implies that the certified counselor is in agreement with the general policies and principles of the institution. Therefore, the professional activities of the certified counselor are in accord with the objectives of the institution. If the certified counselor and the employer do not agree and cannot reach agreement on policies that are consistent with appropriate counselor ethical practice that is conducive to client growth and development, the employment should be terminated. If the situation warrants further action, the certified counselor should work through professional organizations to have the unethical practice changed.

3. Ethical behavior among professional associates (i.e., both certified and non-certified counselors) must be expected at all times. When a certified counselor has doubts as to the ethical behavior of professional colleagues, the certified counselor must take action to attempt to rectify this condition. Such action uses the respective institution's channels first and then uses procedures established by the NBCC or the perceived violator's profession.

4. Certified counselors must refuse remuneration for consultation or counseling with persons who are entitled to these services through the certified counselor's employing institution or agency. Certified counselors must not divert to their private practices, without the mutual consent of the institution and the client, legitimate clients in their primary agencies or the institutions with which they are

affiliated.

5. In establishing fees for professional counseling services, certified counselors must consider the financial status of clients. In the event that the established fee status is inappropriate for a client, assistance must be provided in finding comparable services at acceptable cost.

6. Certified counselors offer only professional services for which they are trained or have supervised experience. No diagnosis, assessment, or treatment should be performed without prior training or supervision. Certified counselors are responsible for correcting any misrepresentations of their qualifications by others.

7. Certified counselors recognize their limitations and provide services or use techniques for which they are qualified by training and/or supervision. Certified counselors recognize the need for and seek continuing education to assure competent services.

8. Certified counselors are aware of the intimacy in the counseling relationship and maintain respect for the client. Counselors must not engage in activities that seek to meet their personal or professional needs at the expense of the client.

9. Certified counselors must insure that they do not engage in personal, social, organizational, financial, or political activities which might lead to a misuse of their influence.

10. Sexual intimacy with clients is unethical. Certified counselors will not be sexually, physically, or romantically intimate with clients, and they will not engage in sexual, physical, or romantic intimacy with clients within a minimum of two years after terminating the counseling relationship.

11. Certified counselors do not condone or engage in sexual harassment, which is defined as unwelcome comments, gestures, or physical contact of a sexual nature.

12. Through an awareness of the impact of stereotyping and unwarranted discrimination (e.g., biases based on age, disability, ethnicity, gender, race, religion, or sexual orientation), certified counselors guard the individual rights and personal dignity of the client in the counseling relationship.

13. Certified counselors are accountable at all times for their behavior. They must be aware that all actions and behaviors of the counselor reflect on professional integrity and, when inappropriate, can damage the public trust in the counseling profession. To protect public confidence in the counseling profession, certified counselors avoid behavior that is clearly in violation of accepted moral and legal standards.

14. Products or services provided by certified counselors by means of classroom instruction, public lectures, demonstrations, written articles, radio or television programs or other types of media must meet the criteria cited in this code.

15. Certified counselors have an obligation to withdraw from the practice of counseling if they violate the Code of Ethics, or if the mental or physical condition of the certified counselor renders it unlikely that a professional relationship will be maintained.

Section B: Counseling Relationship

1. The primary obligation of certified counselors is to respect the integrity and promote the welfare of clients, whether they are assisted individually, in family units, or in group counseling. In a group setting, the certified counselor is also responsible for taking reasonable precautions to protect individuals from physical and/or psychological trauma resulting from interaction within the group.

2. Certified counselors know and take into account the traditions and practices of other professional disciplines with whom they work and cooperate fully with such. If a person is receiving similar services from another professional, certified counselors do not offer their own services directly to such a person. If a certified counselor is contacted by a person who is already receiving similar services from another professional, the certified counselor carefully considers that professional relationship as well as the client's welfare and proceeds with caution and sensitivity to the therapeutic issues. When certified counselors learn that their clients are in a professional relationship

with another counselor or mental health professional, they request release from the clients to inform the other counselor or mental health professional of their relationship with the client and strive to establish positive and collaborative professional relationships that are in the best interest of the client. Certified counselors discuss these issues with clients and the counselor or professional so as to minimize the risk of confusion and conflict and encourage clients to inform other professionals of the new professional relationship.

3. Certified counselors may choose to consult with any other professionally competent person about a client and must notify clients of this right. Certified counselors avoid placing a consultant in a conflict of interest situation that would preclude the consultant serving as a proper party to the efforts of the certified counselor to help the client.

4. When a client's condition indicates that there is a clear and imminent danger to the client or others, the certified counselor must take reasonable action to inform potential victims and/or inform responsible authorities. Consultation with other professionals must be used when possible. The assumption of responsibility for the client's behavior must be taken only after careful deliberation, and the client must be involved in the resumption of responsibility as quickly as possible.

5. Records of the counseling relationship, including interview notes, test data, correspondence, audio or visual tape recordings, electronic data storage, and other documents are to be considered professional information for use in counseling. Records should contain accurate factual data. The physical records are property of the certified counselors or their employers. The information contained in the records belongs to the client and therefore may not be released to others without the consent of the client or when the counselor has exhausted challenges to a court order. The certified counselors are responsible to insure that their employees handle confidential information appropriately. Confidentiality must be maintained during the storage and disposition of records. Records should be maintained for a period of at least five (5) years after the last counselor/client contact, including cases in which the client is deceased. All records must be released to the client upon request.

6. Certified counselors must ensure that data maintained in electronic storage are secure. By using the best computer security methods available, the data must be limited to information that is appropriate and necessary for the services being provided and accessible only to appropriate staff members involved in the provision of services. Certified counselors must also ensure that the electronically stored data are destroyed when the information is no longer of value in providing services or required as part of clients' records.

7. Any data derived from a client relationship and used in training or research shall be so disguised that the informed client's identity is fully protected. Any data which cannot be so disguised may be used only as expressly authorized by the client's informed and uncoerced consent.

8. When counseling is initiated, and throughout the counseling process as necessary, counselors inform clients of the purposes, goals, techniques, procedures, limitations, potential risks and benefits of services to be performed, and clearly indicate limitations that may affect the relationship as well as any other pertinent information. Counselors take reasonable steps to ensure that clients understand the implications of any diagnosis, the intended use of tests and reports, methods of treatment and safety precautions that must be taken in their use, fees, and billing arrangements.

9. Certified counselors who have an administrative, supervisory and/or evaluative relationship with individuals seeking counseling services must not serve as the counselor and should refer the individuals to other professionals. Exceptions are made only in instances where an individual's situation warrants counseling intervention and another alternative is unavailable. Dual relationships that might impair the certified counselor's objectivity and professional judgment must be avoided and/or the counseling relationship terminated through referral to a competent professional.

10. When certified counselors determine an inability to be of professional assistance to a potential or existing client, they must, respectively, not initiate the counseling relationship or immediately terminate the relationship. In either event, the certified counselor must suggest appropriate

alternatives. Certified counselors must be knowledgeable about referral resources so that a satisfactory referral can be initiated. In the event that the client declines a suggested referral, the certified counselor is not obligated to continue the relationship.

11. When certified counselors are engaged in intensive, short -term counseling, they must ensure that professional assistance is available at normal costs to clients during and following the short-term counseling.

12. Counselors using electronic means in which counselor and client are not in immediate proximity must present clients with local sources of care before establishing a continued short or long -term relationship. Counselors who communicate with clients via Internet are governed by NBCC standards for Web Counseling.

13. Counselors must document permission to practice counseling by electronic means in all governmental jurisdictions where such counseling takes place.

14. When electronic data and systems are used as a component of counseling services, certified counselors must ensure that the computer application, and any information it contains, is appropriate for the respective needs of clients and is non -discriminatory. Certified counselors must ensure that they themselves have acquired a facilitation level of knowledge with any system they use including hands-on application, and understanding of the uses of all aspects of the computer-based system. In selecting and/or maintaining computer-based systems that contain career information, counselors must ensure that the system provides current, accurate, and locally relevant information. Certified counselors must also ensure that clients are intellectually, emotionally, and physically compatible with computer applications and understand their purpose and operation. Client use of a computer application must be evaluated to correct possible problems and assess subsequent needs.

15. Certified counselors who develop self-help/stand-alone computer software for use by the general public, must first ensure that it is designed to function in a stand-alone manner that is appropriate and safe for all clients for which it is intended. A manual is required. The manual must provide the user with intended outcomes, suggestions for using the software, descriptions of inappropriately used applications, and descriptions of when and how other forms of counseling services might be beneficial. Finally, the manual must include the qualifications of the developer, the development process, validation date, and operating procedures.

16. The counseling relationship and information resulting from it remains confidential, consistent with the legal and ethical obligations of certified counselors. In group counseling, counselors clearly define confidentiality and the parameters for the specific group being entered, explain the importance of confidentiality, and discuss the difficulties related to confidentiality involved in group work. The fact that confidentiality cannot be guaranteed is clearly communicated to group members. However, counselors should give assurance about their professional responsibility to keep all group communications confidential.

17. Certified counselors must screen prospective group counseling participants to ensure compatibility with group objectives. This is especially important when the emphasis is on self -understanding and growth through self-disclosure. Certified counselors must maintain an awareness of the welfare of each participant throughout the group process.

Section C: Counselor Supervision

NCCs who offer and/or provide supervision must:

a. Ensure that they have the proper training and supervised experience through contemporary continuing education and/or graduate training

b. Ensure that supervisees are informed of the supervisor's credentials and professional status as well as all conditions of supervision as defined/outlined by the supervisor's practice, agency, group, or organization

c. Ensure that supervisees are aware of the current ethical standards related to their professional practice

d. Ensure that supervisees are informed about the process of supervision, including supervision goals, paradigms of supervision and the supervisor's preferred research based supervision paradigm(s)

e. Provide supervisees with agreed upon scheduled feedback as part of an established evaluation plan (e.g., one (1) hour per week)

f. Ensure that supervisees inform their clients of their professional status (i.e., trainee, intern, licensed, non-licensed, etc)

g. Establish procedures with their supervisees for handling crisis situations

h. Render timely assistance to supervisees who are or may be unable to provide competent counseling services to clients and

i. Intervene in any situation where the supervisee is impaired and the client is at risk

In addition, because supervision may result in a dual relationship between the supervisor and the supervisee, the supervisor is responsible for ensuring that any dual relationship is properly managed.

Section D: Measurement and Evaluation

1. Because many types of assessment techniques exist, certified counselors must recognize the limits of their competence and perform only those assessment functions for which they have received appropriate training or supervision.

2. Certified counselors who utilize assessment instruments to assist them with diagnoses must have appropriate training and skills in educational and psychological measurement, validation criteria, test research, and guidelines for test development and use.

3. Certified counselors must provide instrument specific orientation or information to an examinee prior to and following the administration of assessment instruments or techniques so that the results may be placed in proper perspective with other relevant factors. The purpose of testing and the explicit use of the results must be made known to an examinee prior to testing.

4. In selecting assessment instruments or techniques for use in a given situation or with a particular client, certified counselors must carefully evaluate the specific theoretical bases and characteristics, validity, reliability and appropriateness of the instrument.

5. When making statements to the public about assessment instruments or techniques, certified counselors must provide accurate information and avoid false claims or misconceptions concerning the meaning of the instrument's reliability and validity terms.

Counselors must follow all directions and researched procedures for selection, administration and interpretation of all evaluation instruments and use them only within proper contexts.

7. Certified counselors must be cautious when interpreting the results of instruments that possess insufficient technical data, and must explicitly state to examinees the specific limitations and purposes for the use of such instruments.

8. Certified counselors must proceed with caution when attempting to evaluate and interpret performances of any person who cannot be appropriately compared to the norms for the instrument.

9. Because prior coaching or dissemination of test materials can invalidate test results, certified counselors are professionally obligated to maintain test security.

10. Certified counselors must consider psychometric limitations when selecting and using an

instrument, and must be cognizant of the limitations when interpreting the results. When tests are used to classify clients, certified counselors must ensure that periodic review and/or retesting are made to prevent client stereotyping.

11. An examinee's welfare, explicit prior understanding, and consent are the factors used when determining who receives the test results. Certified counselors must see that appropriate interpretation accompanies any release of individual or group test data (e.g., limitations of instrument and norms).

12. Certified counselors must ensure that computer -generated test administration and scoring programs function properly thereby providing clients with accurate test results.

13. Certified counselors who develop computer-based test interpretations to support the assessment process must ensure that the validity of the interpretations is established prior to the commercial distribution of the computer application.

14. Certified counselors recognize that test results may become obsolete, and avoid the misuse of obsolete data.

15. Certified counselors must not appropriate, reproduce, or modify published tests or parts thereof without acknowledgment and permission from the publisher, except as permitted by the fair educational use provisions of the U.S. copyright law.

Section E: Research and Publication

1. Certified counselors will adhere to applicable legal and professional guidelines on research with human subjects.

2. In planning research activities involving human subjects, certified counselors must be aware of and responsive to all pertinent ethical principles and ensure that the research problem, design, and execution are in full compliance with any pertinent institutional or governmental regulations.

3. The ultimate responsibility for ethical research lies with the principal researcher, although others involved in the research activities are ethically obligated and responsible for their own actions.

4. Certified counselors who conduct research with human subjects are responsible for the welfare of the subjects throughout the experiment and must take all reasonable precautions to avoid causing injurious psychological, physical, or social effects on their subjects.

5. Certified counselors who conduct research must abide by the basic elements of informed consent:

   a. fair explanation of the procedures to be followed, including an identification of those which are experimental

   b. description of the attendant discomforts and risks

   c. description of the benefits to be expected

   d. disclosure of appropriate alternative procedures that would be advantageous for subjects with an offer to answer any inquiries concerning the procedures

   e. an instruction that subjects are free to withdraw their consent and to discontinue participation in the project or activity at any time

6. When reporting research results, explicit mention must be made of all the variables and conditions known to the investigator that may have affected the outcome of the study or the interpretation of the data.

7. Certified counselors who conduct and report research investigations must do so in a manner that minimizes the possibility that the results will be misleading.

8. Certified counselors are obligated to make available sufficient original research data to qualified others who may wish to replicate the study.

9. Certified counselors who supply data, aid in the research of another person, report research results, or make original data available, must take due care to disguise the identity of respective subjects in the absence of specific authorization from the subjects to do otherwise.

10. When conducting and reporting research, certified counselors must be familiar with and give recognition to previous work on the topic, must observe all copyright laws, and must follow the principles of giving full credit to those to whom credit is due.

11. Certified counselors must give due credit through joint authorship, acknowledgment, footnote statements, or other appropriate means to those who have contributed to the research and/or publication, in accordance with such contributions.

12. Certified counselors should communicate to other counselors the results of any research judged to be of professional value. Results that reflect unfavorably on institutions, programs, services, or vested interests must not be withheld.

13. Certified counselors who agree to cooperate with another individual in research and/or publication incur an obligation to cooperate as promised in terms of punctuality of performance and with full regard to the completeness and accuracy of the information required.

14. Certified counselors must not submit the same manuscript, or one essentially similar in content, for simultaneous publication consideration by two or more journals. In addition, manuscripts that have been published in whole or substantial part should not be submitted for additional publication without acknowledgment and permission from any previous publisher.

Section F: Consulting

Consultation refers to a voluntary relationship between a professional helper and a help needing individual, group, or social unit in which the consultant is providing help to the client(s) in defining and solving a work related problem or potential work-related problem with a client or client system.

1. Certified counselors, acting as consultants, must have a high degree of self awareness of their own values, knowledge, skills, limitations, and needs in entering a helping relationship that involves human and/or organizational change. The focus of the consulting relationship must be on the issues to be resolved and not on the person(s) presenting the problem.

2. In the consulting relationship, the certified counselor and client must understand and agree upon the problem definition, subsequent goals, and predicted consequences of interventions selected.

3. Certified counselors acting as consultants must be reasonably certain that they, or the organization represented, have the necessary competencies and resources for giving the kind of help that is needed or that may develop later, and that appropriate referral resources are available.

4. Certified counselors in a consulting relationship must encourage and cultivate client adaptability and growth toward self-direction. Certified counselors must maintain this role consistently and not become a decision maker for clients or create a future dependency on the consultant.

Section G: Private Practice

1. In advertising services as a private practitioner, certified counselors must advertise in a manner that accurately informs the public of the professional services, expertise, and techniques of counseling available.

2. Certified counselors who assume an executive leadership role in a private practice organization do not permit their names to be used in professional notices during periods of time when they are not actively engaged in the private practice of counseling unless their executive roles are clearly stated.

3. Certified counselors must make available their highest degree (described by discipline), type and level of certification and/or license, address, telephone number, office hours, type and/or description of services, and other relevant information. Listed information must not contain false, inaccurate, misleading, partial, out-of-context, or otherwise deceptive material or statements.

4. Certified counselors who are involved in a partnership/corporation with other certified counselors and/or other professionals, must clearly specify all relevant specialties of each member of the partnership or corporation.

Appendix: Certification Examination

Applicants for the NBCC Certification Examinations must have fulfilled all current eligibility requirements, and are responsible for the accuracy and validity of all information and/or materials provided by themselves or by others for fulfillment of eligibility criteria.

Approved on July 1, 1982 Amended on February 21, 1987, January 6, 1989, October 31, 1997, and June 21,

Acknowledgment Reference documents, statements, and sources for development of the NBCC Code of Ethics were as follows: The Ethical Standards of the American Counseling Association, Responsible Uses for Standardized Testing (AAC), codes of ethics of the American Psychological Association and the National Career Development Association, Handbook of Standards for Computer -Based Career Information Systems (ACSCI) and Guidelines for the Use of Computer Based Information and Guidance Systems (ACSCI).

References

Abe, C., & Holland, J. L. (1965). *A description of college freshmen—I. Students with different choices of major field.* (ERIC Reproduction Service No. ED 0147 742)

Abu-Hilal, M. M. (2000). A structural model of attitudes towards school subjects, academic aspiration and achievement. *Educational psychology: An international journal of experimental educational psychology, 20*,75-84.

ACT, Inc. (2005). DISCOVER (Windows) [Computer software]. Hunt Valley, MD: Author.

Adelman, P. B., & Vogel, S. A. (1990). College graduates with learning disabilities: Employment attainment and career patterns. *Learning Disability Quarterly, 13*(3), 154–166.

Aiken, L. R. (1988). *Psychological testing and assessment.* Boston: Allyn & Bacon.

Albritton, F. R. (1996, Oct. 17, 29). Personal communication. Tallahassee, FL.

Allis, M. (1984). Review of the Career Decision Scale. *Measurement and Evaluation in Counseling and Development, 17,* 98–100.

Alston, R. J., & Burkhead, E. J. (1989). Computer-assisted career guidance and the career indecision of college students with physical disabilities. *Rehabilitation Counseling Bulletin, 32*(3), 248–253.

American College Testing Program. (1989). *DISCOVER for colleges and adults* [Computer program]. Hunt Valley, MD: Author.

American Counseling Association. (1995). *Code of ethics and standards of practice.* Alexandria, VA: Author.

American Psychological Association. (1985). *Standards for educational and psychological tests.* Washington, DC: Author.

American Psychological Association. (1986). *Guidelines for computer-based tests and interpretations.* Washington, DC: Author.

American Psychological Association. (2002). *Ethical guidelines of the American Psychological Association.* Washington, DC: Author.

Anastasi, A. (1988). *Psychological testing* (6th ed.). New York: Macmillan.

Aros, J. R., Henly, G. A., & Curtis, N. T. (1998). Occupational Sextype and Sex Differences in Vocational Preference-Measured Interest Relationships. *Journal of Vocational Behavior, 53*(2), 227–242.

Association for Assessment in Counseling (2003). *Standards for Multicultural Assessment.* Alexandria, VA: Author.

Atkinson, M. J. (2003). Review of the California Psychological Inventory Third Edition. In B.S. Plake, J.C. Impara, and R.A. Spies (Eds.), *The fifteenth mental measurements yearbook.* Lincoln, NE: Buros Institute of Mental Measurements. Retrieved December 15th, 2004, from Mental Measurements Yearbook database. Accession number: 15122723

Baker, H. E. (2002). Reducing adolescent career indecision: The ASVAB career exploration program. *Career Development Quarterly, 50,* 359-70.

Bahns, T. M.. (2001). Review of the NEO4. In B.S. Plake and J.C. Impara (Eds.), *The fourteenth mental measurements yearbook.* Lincoln, NE: Buros Institute of Mental Measurements. Retrieved December 15th, 2004, from Mental Measurements Yearbook database. Accession # 14122273.

Barak, A. (2003). Ethical and professional issues in career assessment on the Internet. *Journal of Career Assessment, 11,* 3-21.

Barak, A., & LaCrosse, M. B. (1975). Multidimensional perception of counselor behavior. *Journal of Counseling Psychology, 22,* 471–476.

Barnes, J. A., & Herr, E. L. (1998). The effects of interventions on career progress. *Journal of Career Development, 24*(3), 179–193.

Barrick, M. R., & Mount, M. K. (1991). The big five personality dimensions and job performance: A meta-analysis. *Personnel Psychology, 44,* 1–26.

Becker, R. L. (1988). *The Reading-Free Vocational Interest Inventory.* Columbus, OH: Elbern Publications.

Bennet, G. K., Seashore, H. G., & Wesman, A. G. (2002). Review of the Differential Aptitude Tests (DAT) & Career Interest Inventory (CII). In J.T. Kapes, & E. A. Whitfield (Eds.), *A counselor's guide to career assessment instruments* (pp. 123–131). Alexandria, VA: National Career Development Association.

Ben-Porath, Y. S., & Waller, N. G. (1992). "Normal" personality inventories in clinical assessment: General requirements and potential for using the NEO-PI. *Psychological Assessment, 4,* 4–19.

Benson, A. R. (1985). Minnesota Importance Questionnaire. In D. J. Keyser & R. C. Sweetland (Eds.), *Test critiques II* (pp. 481–489). Kansas City, MO: Test Corporation of America.

Bergeron, L. M., & Romano, J. L. (1994). The relationships among career decision-making self-efficacy, educational indecision, vocational indecision, and gender. *Journal of College Student Development, 35*(1), 19–24.

Betz, N. E. (1992). Career assessment: A review of critical issues. In S. D. Brown & R. W. Lent (Eds.), *Handbook of counseling psychology* (pp. 453–484). New York: Wiley.

Betz, N. E. (1993). Issues in the use of ability and interest measures with women. *Journal of Career Assessment, 1,* 217–232.

Betz, N. E. (1994). Basic issues and concepts in career counseling for women. In W. B. Walsh & S. H. Osipow (Eds.), *Career counseling for women: Contemporary topics in vocational psychology* (pp. 1–41). Hillsdale, NJ: Erlbaum.

Betz, N. E. (1997). What stops women and minorities from choosing and completing majors in science and engineering? In D. Johnson (Ed.), *Minorities and girls in school: Effects on achievement and performance* (pp. 105–140). Thousand Oaks, CA: Sage.

Betz, N. E. (2000a). Contemporary issues in testing use. In C. E. Watkins, Jr., & V. L. Campbell (Eds.), *Testing and assessment in counseling practice,* (481–516). Mahwah, NJ: Erlbaum.

Betz, N. E. (2000b). Self-efficacy theory as a basis for career assessment. *Journal of Career Assessment, 8,* 205-222.

Betz, N. E., Borgen, F. H., & Harmon, L. W. (1996). *Skills Confidence Inventory*. Palo Alto, CA: Consulting Psychologists Press.

Betz, N. E., Borgen, F. H., Kaplan, A., & Harmon, L. W. (1998). Gender and Holland type as moderators of the validity and interpretive utility of the Skills Confidence Inventory. *Journal of Vocational Behavior, 53*(2), 281–289.

Betz, N. E., & Gwilliam, L. R. (2002). The utility of measures of self-efficacy for the Holland themes in African American and European American college students. *Journal of Career Assessment, 10,* 283-300.

Betz, N. E., & Hackett, G. (1997). Applications of self-efficacy theory to the career assessment of women. *Journal of Career Assessment, 5,*383-402.

Betz, N. E., & Klein, K. L. (1996). Relationships among measures of career self-efficacy, generalized self-efficacy, and global self-esteem. *Journal of Career Assessment, 4,* 285-298.

Betz, N. E., Klein, K. L., & Taylor, K. M. (1997). Evaluation of a short form of the Career Decision-Making Self-Efficacy Scale. *Journal of Career Assessment, 4*(1), 47–57.

Betz, N. E., & Luzzo, D. A. (1996). Career assessment and the Career Decision-Making Self- Efficacy Scale. *Journal of Career Assessment, 4*(4), 413–428.

Betz, N. E., Schifano, R, & Kaplan, A. (1999). Relationships among measures of perceived self-efficacy with respect to basic domains of vocational activity. *Journal of Career Assessment, 7*(3), 213–226.

Betz, N. E., & Voyten, K. K. (1997). Efficacy and outcome expectations influence career exploration and decidedness. *Career Development Quarterly, 46*(2), 179–189.

Bingham, W. C. (1978). Review of the Career Development Inventory. In O. K. Buros (Ed.),*The eighth mental measurement yearbook* (Vol. 2). Highland Park, NJ: Gryphon.

Black, J. D. (1978). Review of the Survey of Interpersonal Values. In O. K. Buros (Ed.), *The eighth mental measurement yearbook* (Vol. 1). Highland Park, NJ: Gryphon.

Blackman, M. C. (2003). Personality comparison of airline pilot incumbents, applicants, and the general population norms on the 16PF. *Psychological Reports, 92,*773-780.

Blackwell, T. L., & Lutyhe, T. D. (2003). Test review: Review of Occupational Aptitude Survey and Interest Schedule – third edition. *Rehabilitation Counseling Bulletin, 46,*247-50.

Bloxom, B. M. (1978). Review of the Sixteen Personality Factor Questionnaire. In O. K.

Buros (Ed.), *The eighth mental measurement yearbook* (Vol. 1). Highland Park, NJ: Gryphon.

Boggs, K. R. (2002). Review of the Campbell Interest and Skill Survey. In J.T. Kapes, & E. A. Whitfield (Eds.), *A counselor's guide to career assessment instruments. Fourth Edition* (pp. 195–201). Alexandria, VA: National Career Development Association.

Bolles, R. N. (2000). What color is your parachute? Berkeley, CA: Ten Speed Press.

Bolles, R. N., & Bolles, M. E. (2005). What color is your parachute? 2005: A practical manual for job-hunters and career changers. Berkeley, CA: Ten Speed Press.

Bouffard, T., Markovitz, H., Vezeau, C., Boisvert, M., & Dumas, C. (1998). The relation between accuracy and self-perception and cognitive development. *British Journal of Educational Psychology, 68(3),* 321–330.

Brandel, I. W. (1982). Puzzling your career: A self-responsibility, self-acceptance approach to career planning. *Personnel and Guidance Journal, 61,* 225–228.

Brew, S. (1987). *Career development guide for use with the Strong Interest Inventory.* Palo Alto, CA: Consulting Psychologists Press.

Bridges (2005). Choices. [Computer Program]. Ontario, Canada: Author.

Brooke, S. L., & Ciechalski, J. C. (1994). Review of the Minnesota Importance Questionnaire. In J.T. Kapes, M. M. Mastie, & E. A. Whitfield (Eds.), *A counselor's guide to career assessment instruments* (pp. 222–225). Alexandria, VA: National Career Development Association.

Brown, D. (1996). Brown's values-based, holistic model of career and life-role choices and satisfaction. In D. Brown & L. Brooks (Eds.), *Career choice and development* (3rd ed.) (pp. 337–368). San Francisco: Jossey-Bass.

Brown, D. (Ed.). (2002). The role of work values and cultural values in occupational choice, satisfaction and success. In D. Brown's (Ed.), *Career choice and development* (4th ed.) (pp. 465-590). San Francisco: Jossey-Bass.

Brown, F. G. (1982). Kuder Occupational Interest Survey—Form DD. In J. T. Kapes & M. M. Mastie (Eds.), *A counselor's guide to vocational instruments* (pp. 77–81). Falls Church, VA: National Vocational Guidance Association.

Brown, F. G. (1993). Stanford Achievement Test. In J. J. Kramer & J. S. Conoley (Eds.), *The eleventh mental measurement yearbook* (pp. 861–863). Lincoln: Buros Institute of Mental Measurement, University of Nebraska.

Brown, R. P., & Josephs, R. A. (1999). A burden of proof: Stereotype relevance and gender differences in math performance. *Journal of Personality and Social Psychology, 76(2),* 246–257.

Buboltz, W. C., Jr., Johnson, P., Nichols, C., Miller, M. A., & Thomas, A. (2000). MBTI personality types and SII Personal Style Scales. *Journal of Career Assessment, 8*(2), 131–145.

Cairo, P. C. (1983). Evaluating the effects of computer-assisted counseling systems: A selective review. *Counseling Psychologist, 11,* 53–59.

Cairo, P. C., Kritis, K. J., & Myers, R. M. (1996). Career assessment and the Adult Career Concerns Inventory. *Journal of Career Assessment, 4*(2), 189–204.

Campbell, D. P. (1992). *Campbell Interest and Skill Survey (CISS).* Minneapolis: National Computer Systems.

Campbell, D. P. (2002). The history and development of the Campbell Interest and Skill Survey. *Journal of Career Assessment, 10,* 150-168.

Campbell, D. P., Hyne, S. A., & Nilsen, D. (1992). *Manual for the Campbell Interest and Skill Survey.* Minneapolis: National Computer Systems.

Campbell, V. C., & Raiff, G. W. (2002). Review of Harrington O'Shea Career Decision-Making System Revised (CDM). In J.T. Kapes, & E. A. Whitfield (Eds.), *A counselor's guide to career assessment instruments. Fourth Edition* (pp. 230–234). Alexandria, VA: National Career Development Association.

Cantwell, Z. M. (1994). Review of the Reading-Free Vocational Interest Inventory–Revised. In J. T. Kapes, M. M. Mastie, & E. A. Whitfield (Eds.), *A counselor's guide to career assessment instruments* (pp. 326–330). Alexandria, VA: National Career Development Association.

Careerware: ISM Corporation. (2000). *Choices/Choices CT* (USA version) [Computer program]. Ottawa, Ontario: Author.

Carlson, J. G. (1989). Affirmative: In support of researching the Myers-Briggs Type Indicator. *Journal of Counseling and Development, 67*(8), 484–486.

Carpraro, R. M., & Carpraro, M. M. (2002). Myers-Briggs Type Indicator score reliability across studies: A meta-analytic reliability. *Educational and Psychological Measurement, 62,* 590-602.

Carson, A. D., & Cartwright, G. F. (1997). Fifth generation computer-assisted career guidance systems. *Career Planning and Adult Development Journal, 13*(1), 19–40.

Carson, A.D, Stalikas, A., & Bizot, E. B. (1997). Correlations between the Myers-Briggs Type Indicator and measures of aptitudes. *Journal of Career Assessment, 5*(1), 81–104.

Cattell, R. B., Eber, H. W., & Tatsuoka, M. M. (1970). *Handbook for the Sixteen Personality Factor Questionnaire (16PF)*. Champaign, IL: Institute for Personality and Ability Testing.

Chang, D. H. F. (2002). The past, present, and future of career counseling in Taiwan. *Career Development Quarterly, 50*, 218-225.

Chartrand, J. M., Borgen, F. H., Betz, N. E., & Donnay, D. (2002). Using the Strong Interest Inventory and the Skills Confidence Inventory to explain career goals. *Journal of Career Assessment, 10*, 169-189.

Chartrand, J. M., and Nutter, K. J. (1996). The Career Factors Inventory: Theory and applications. *Journal of Career Assessment, 4*(2), 205–218.

Chartrand, J. M., Robbins, S. B., & Morrill, W. H. (1989). *The Career Factors Inventory.* Concord, Ontario: 2000 Career/LifeSkills Resources.

Chartrand, J. M., & Rose, M. L. (1996). Career interventions for at-risk populations: Incorporating social cognitive influences. *Career Development Quarterly, 44*, 341–353.

Ciechalski, J. C. (2002). In J.T. Kapes, & E. A. Whitfield (Eds.), *A counselor's guide to career assessment instruments. Fourth Edition* (pp. 282–287). Alexandria, VA: National Career Development Association.

Chung, Y. B. (2003). Ethical and professional issues in career assessment with lesbian, gay and bisexual persons. *Journal of Career Assessment, 11*, 96-112.

Clyde, J. S. (1979). *Computerized career information and guidance systems.* Columbus: Ohio State University, ERIC Clearinghouse on Adult, Career, and Vocational Education. (ERIC Document Reproduction Service No. ED 179 764)

Cooper, D. (1990). Factor structure of the Edwards Personal Preference Schedule in a vocational rehabilitation sample. *Journal of Clinical Psychology, 46*, 421–425.

Cooper, H., Lindsay, J. J., Nye, B., & Greathouse, S. (1998). Relationships among attitudes about homework, amount of homework assigned and completed, and student achievement. *Journal of Educational Psychology, 90*(1), 70–83.

Costa, P. T., Jr., & McCrae, R. R. (1985). *The NEO Personality Inventory.* Odessa, FL: Psychological Assessment Resources.

Crewe, N. M. (2000). A 20–year longitudinal perspective on the vocational experiences of persons with spinal cord injury. *Rehabilitation Counseling Bulletin, 43*(3), 122–133.

Crites, J. O. (1978). *The Career Maturity Inventory* (2nd ed.). Monterey, CA: CTB/McGraw-Hill.

Crites, J. O. (1982b). The self-directed search. In J.T. Kapes & M. M. Mastie (Eds.), *A counselor's guide to vocational guidance instrument* (pp.88–92). Falls Church, VA: National Vocational Guidance Association.

Crites, J. O., & Savickas, M. L. (1995b). *The Career Maturity Inventory–Revised Form.* Clayton, NY: Careerware: ISM.

Crites, J. O., & Savickas, M. L. (1996). Revision of the Career Maturity Inventory. *Journal of Career Assessment, 4*, 131–138.

Cronbach, L. J. (1979). The Armed Services Vocational Aptitude Battery—A test battery in transition. *Personal and Guidance Journal, 57*, 232–237.

Cronbach, L. J. (1984). *Essentials of psychological testing* (4th ed.) New York: Harper & Row.

Crouteau, J. M., & Slaney, R. B. (1994). Two methods of exploring interests: A comparison of outcomes. *Career Development Quarterly, 42*, 252–261.

Cummings, W. H. III. (1995). Age group differences and estimated frequencies of the Myers-Briggs Type Indicator preferences. *Measurement and Evaluation in Counseling and Development, 28*(2), 69–77.

Daniels, M. H. (1985). Review of the Social and Prevocational Information Battery, Revised. In J. V. Mitchell, Jr. (Ed.), *The ninth mental measurement yearbook* (Vol. 1) (p. 739). Lincoln: Buros Institute of Mental Measurement, University of Nebraska.

Darcy, M., & Tracey, T. J. G. (2003). Integrating abilities and interests in career choice: Maximal versus typical assessment. *Journal of Career Assessment, 11,* 219-237.

Davison Aviles, R. M., & Spokane, A. R. (1999). The vocational interests of Hispanic, African American, and White middle school students. *Measurement & Evaluation in Counseling & Development, 32*(3), 138–148.

Dawis, R. V. (2002). Person-environment-correspondence theory. In D. Brown's (Ed.), *Career choice and development* (4th ed.) (pp. 427-464). San Francisco: Jossey-Bass.

Dawis, R. V., & Lofquist, L. (1984). *A psychological theory of work adjustment: An individual differences model and its application.* Minneapolis: University of Minnesota.

Day, S. X., & Rounds, J. (1997). "A little more than kin, and less than Kind": Basic interests in vocational research and career counseling. *Career Development Quarterly, 45*(3), 207–220.

Diamond, E. E. (1975). Overview. In E. E. Diamond (Ed.), *Issues of sex bias and sex fairness in career interest measurement.* Washington, DC: National Institute of Education.

Diamond, E. E. (1982). Review of the AAMDBecker Reading-Free Vocational Interest Inventory. In J. T. Kapes & M. M. Mastie (Eds.), *A counselor's guide to vocational guidance instruments* (pp. 162–165). Falls Church, VA: National Vocational Guidance Association.

Dolliver, R. H. (1978). Review of the Strong- Campbell Interest Inventory. In O. K. Buros (Ed.), *The eighth mental measurement yearbook* (Vol. 2). Highland Park, NJ: Gryphon.

Domino, G. (1988). Review of the Reading-Free Vocational Interest Inventory, Revised. In J. T.Kapes & M. M. Mastie (Eds.), *A counselor's guide to career assessment instruments* (2nd ed.). Alexandria, VA: National Career Development Association.

Donnay, D. A. C. (1997). E. K. Strong's legacy and beyond: 70 years of the Strong Interest Inventory. *Career Development Quarterly, 46*(1), 2–22.

Donnay, D. A. C., & Borgen, F. H. (1996). Validity, structure, and content of the 1994 Strong Interest Inventory. *Journal of Counseling Psychology, 43,* 275–291.

Donnay, D. A. C., & Borgen, F. H. (1999). The incremental validity of vocational self-efficacy: An examination of interest, self-efficacy, and occupation. *Journal of Counseling Psychology, 46*(4), 432–447.

Droege, R. C. (1984). The Career Decision-Making System. In D. J. Keyser & R. C. Sweetland (Eds.), *Test critiques I* (pp. 322–327). Kansas City, MO: Test Corporation of America.

Drucker, P. F. (1992). *Managing for the future.* New York: Truman Talley Books/Dutton.

Drummond, R. J. (2004). *Appraisal procedures for counselors and helping professionals* (5th ed.).Upper Saddle River, NJ: Merrill.

Dumenci, L. (1995). Construct validity of the Self- Directed Search using hierarchically nested structural models. *Journal of Vocational Behavior, 47,* 21–34.

Edwards, A. L. (1959/1985). *Edwards Personal Preference Schedule manual.* New York: Psychological Corporation.

Einarsdottir, S., Rounds, J., AEgisdotter, S., & Gerstein, L. H. (2002). The structure of vocational interests in Iceland: Examining Holland's and Gati's RIASEC models. *European Journal of Psychologicla Assessment, 18,* 85-95.

Elmore, P. B., & Bradley, R. W. (1994). Review of the ASVAB. In J. T. Kapes, M. M. Mastie, & E. A. Whitfield (Eds.), *A counselor's guide to career assessment instruments* (pp. 73–77). Alexandria, VA: National Career Development Association.

Enright, M. S. (1996). The relationship between disability status, career beliefs, and career indecision. *Rehabilitation Counseling Bulletin, 40*(2), 134–152.

Fabian, E. S., Luecking, R. G., & Tilson, G. P. (1995). Employer and rehabilitation personnel perspectives on hiring persons with disabilities: Implications on job development. *Journal of Rehabilitation, 61,* 42–49.

Farmer, H., Rotella, S., Anderson, C., & Wardrop, J. (1998). Gender differences in science, math and technology careers: Prestige level and Holland interest type. *Journal of Vocational Behavior, 53(1),* 73–96.

Fassinger, R. E., & O'Brien, K. M. (2000). Career counseling with college women: A scientist practitioner-advocate model of intervention. In D. A. Luzzo (Ed.), *Career counselor of college students* (pp. 253-265). Washington, DC: American Psychological Association.

Feather, N. T. (1998). Attitudes toward high achievers, self-esteem, and value priorities for Australian, American, and Canadian students. *Journal of Cross-Cultural Psychology, 29*(6), 749–759.

Field, T. F., & Field, J. (1992). *Classification of jobs.* Athens; GA: Elliott & Fitzpatrick.

Fitzgerald, L. F., & Betz, N. E. (1994). Career development in cultural context: The role of gender, race, class, and sexual orientation. In M. L. Savickas & R. W. Lent (Eds.), *Convergence in career development theories* (pp. 103–177). Palo Alto, CA: Consulting Psychologists Press.

Fiitzpatrick, A. R. (1992). Adult Basic Learning Examination (ABLE). In J. J. Kramer & J. S.Conoley (Eds.), *The eleventh mental measurement yearbook* (pp. 19–21). Lincoln: Buros Institute of Mental Measurement, University of Nebraska.

Fleenor, J. W. (2001). Review of the Myers Briggs Type Inventory Form M. In B.S. Plake and J.C. Impara (Eds.), *The fourteenth mental measurements yearbook.* Lincoln, NE: Buros Institute of Mental Measurements. Retrieved August 15th, 2004, from Mental Measurements Yearbook database. Accession number: 14122331

Fletcher, J. M., Friedman, L., & Pasnak, R. (1998). The validation of the Transition-to-Work Inventory: A job placement system for workers with severe disabilities. *Journal of Developmental & Physical Disabilities, 10*(1), 1–22.

Flores, L. Y., Spanierman, L. B., & Obasi, E. M. (2003). Ethical and professional issues in career assessment with diverse racial and ethnic groups. *Journal of Career Assessment, 11,* 76-95.

Fouad, N. A. (1999). Validity evidence for interest inventories. In M. L. Savickas & A. R. Spokane (Eds.), *Vocational interests: Meaning, measurement, and counselinguse* (pp. 193–209). Palo Alto, CA: Davies-Black.

Fouad, N. A., & Mohler, C. J. (2004). Cultural validity of Holland's theory and the Strong Interest Inventory for five racial/ethnic groups. *Journal of Career Assessment, 12,* 423-439.

Fouad, N. A., & Spreda, S. L. (1995). Use of interest inventories with special populations. *Journal of Career Assessment, 3,* 453–468.

Fouad, N. A., & Walker, C. M. (2005). Cultural influences on responses to items on the Strong Interest Inventory. *Journal of Vocational Behavior, 66, 104-123.*

Frary, R. B. (1984). The Career Maturity Inventory. In D. J. Keyser & R. C. Sweetland (Eds.), *Test critiques I* (pp. 164–167). Kansas City, MO: Test Corporation of America.

Fretz, B. R. (1981). Evaluating the effectiveness of career interventions. *Journal of Counseling Psychology Monograph, 28,* 77–90.

Friedman, L., Cameron, C., & Fletcher, J. (1995). *Transition-to-Work Inventory: A job placement system for workers with severe disabilities.* San Antonio, TX: Psychological Corporation.

Fuller, B. E., Holland, J. L., & Johnston, J. A. (1999). The relation of profile elevation in the Self-Directed Search to personality variables. *Journal of Career Assessment, 7*(2), 111–123.

Fuqua, D. R., & Newman, J. L. (1994a). An evaluation of the Career Beliefs Inventory. *Journal of Counseling and Development, 72,* 429–430.

Fuqua, D. R., & Newman, J. L. (1994b). Review of the Campbell Interest and Skill Survey. In J. T.Kapes, M. M. Mastie, & E. A. Whitfield (Eds.), *A counselor's guide to career assessment instruments* (pp. 139–143). Alexandria, VA: National Career Development Association.

Galassi, J. P., Crace, R. K., Martin, G. A., James, R. M., & Wallace, R. L. (1992). Client preferences and anticipations in career counseling: A preliminary investigation. *Journal of Counseling Psychology, 39,*46-55.

Garcia, V., Zunker, V. G., & Nolan, J. (1980). *Analysis of a pre-vocational training program.*Unpublished manuscript, Southwest Texas State University.

Gati, I., Kleiman, T., Saka, N., & Zakai, A. (2003). Perceived benefits of using an Internet-based interactive career planning system. *Journal of Vocational Behavior, 62,*272-86.

Geist, H. (1964). *The Geist Picture Inventory.* Beverly Hills, CA: Western Psychological Publishers. (ERIC Document Reproduction Service No. ED 5005 9234) Gianakos, I. (1999). Patterns of career choice and career decision-making self-efficacy. *Journal of Vocational Behavior, 54*(2), 244–258.

Gillies, R. M., Knight, K., & Baglioni, A. J., Jr. (1998). World of work: Perceptions of people who are blind or vision impaired. *International Journal of Disability, Development & Education, 45*(4), 397–409.

Goldman, L. (1972). *Using tests in counseling* (2nd ed.). New York: Appleton-Century-Crofts.

Goldman, L. (1983). The vocational card sort technique: A different view. *Measurement and Evaluation in Guidance, 16,* 107–109.

Goldman, L. (1995). Comment on Crouteau and Slaney (1994*). Career Development Quarterly, 43,* 385–386.

Goodman, J. (1993, April 29). Using non-standardized appraisal tools and techniques. Presentation to Michigan Career Development Association Annual Conference. Kalamazoo, MI.

Gordon, L. V. (1967). *Survey of Personal Values. Examiner's manual.* Chicago: Science Research Associates.

Gordon, L. V. (1975). *The measurement of interpersonal values.* Chicago: Science Research Associates.

Gordon, L. V., (1976). *Survey of Interpersonal Values, revised examiner's manual.* Chicago: Science Research Associates.

Gottfredson, G. D. (1996). The assessment of career status with the Career Attitudes and Strategies Inventory. *Journal of Career Assessment, 4,* 363–381.

Gottfredson, G. D. (2002). Interests, aspirations, self-estimates and the Self-Directed Search. *Journal of Career Assessment, 10,* 200-208.

Gottfredson, G. D., & Holland, J. L. (1989). *Dictionary of Holland occupational codes* (2nd ed.). Odessa, FL: Psychological Assessment Resources.

Gottfredson, L. (1980). Construct validity of Holland's occupational typology in terms of prestige, census, Department of Labor, and other classification systems. *Journal of Applied Psychology, 651,* 697–714.

Gough, H. G., & Heilbrun, A. B., Jr. (1983). *The Adjective Checklist manual.* Palo Alto, CA: Consulting Psychologists Press.

Guilford, J. P. (1954). *Psychometric methods* (rev. ed.). New York: McGraw-Hill.

Hackett, G., & Byars, A. M. (1996). Social cognitive theory and career development of African American women. *Career Development Quarterly, 44,* 322–340.

Hackett, G., & Lonborg, S. D. (1993). Career assessment for women: Trends and issues. *Journal of Career Assessment, 3,* 197–216.

Hackett, G., & Lonborg, S. D. (1994). Career assessment and counseling for women. In W. B. Walsh & S. H. Osipow (Eds.), *Career counseling for women* (pp. 43–85). Hillsdale, NJ: Erlbaum.

Halpern, A., Raffeld, P., Irvin, L., & Link, R. (1986). *Social and Prevocational Information Battery–Revised.* Monterey, CA: CTB- /McGraw-Hill.

Hambleton, R. K. (1985). Review of Differential Aptitude Tests: Forms V & W. In J. V. Mitchell, Jr. (Ed.), *The ninth mental measurement yearbook.* Lincoln: Buros Institute of Mental Measurement, University of Nebraska.

Hansen, J. C. (1985b). *User's guide for the SVIB/SII.* Palo Alto, CA: Consulting Psychologists Press.

Hansen, J. C. (1990). Interpretation of the Strong Interest Inventory. In W. B. Walsh & S. H. Osipow (Eds.), *Career counseling for women.* Hillsdale, NJ: Erlbaum.

Hansen, J. C. (1994). Review of the Salience Inventory. In J. T. Kapes, M. M. Mastie, & E. A. Whitfield (Eds.), *A counselor's guide to career assessment instruments* (pp. 233–235). Alexandria, VA: National Career Development Association.

Hansen, J. C. (2000). Interpretation of the Strong Interest Inventory. In C. E. Watkins, Jr., & V. L. Campbell (Eds.), *Testing and assessment in counseling practice.* 2nd ed. (pp. 227–262). Mahwah, NJ: Erlbaum.

Hansen, J. C., Collins, R. C., Swanson, J. L., & Fouad, N. A. (1993). Gender differences in the structure of interests. *Journal of Vocational Behavior, 42,* 200–211.

Hansen, J-I C., & Neuman, J. L. (1999). Evidence of concurrent prediction of the Campbell Interest and Skill Survey (CISS) for college major selection. *Journal of Career Assessment, 7*(3), 239–247.

Hansen, J-I C., Neuman, J. L., Haverkamp, B. E., & Lubinski, B. R. (1997). Comparison of user reaction to two methods of Strong Interest Inventory administration and report feedback. *Measurement and Evaluation in Counseling and Development, 30*(3), 115–127.

Hanser, L. M., & Grafton, F. C. (1983). *Predicting job proficiency in the Army: Race, sex, and education.* Arlington, VA: United States Army Research Institute for the Behavioral and Social Sciences.

Harmon, L. W. (1994). Review of the Career Decision Scale. In J. T. Kapes, M. M. Mastie, & E. A. Whitfield (Eds.), *A counselor's guide to career assessment instruments* (pp. 259–262). Alexandria, VA: National Career Development Association.

Harmon, L. W., Hansen, J-I. C., Borgen, F. H., & Hammer, A. L. (1994). *Strong Interest Inventory: Applications and technical guide.* Palo Alto, CA: Consulting Psychologists Press.

Harmon, L. W., & Meara, N. M. (1994). Contemporary developments in women's career counseling: Themes of the past, puzzles for the future. In W. B. Walsh & S. H. Osipow (Eds.), *Career counseling for women: Contemporary topics in vocational psychology* (pp. 355–367). Hillsdale, NJ: Erlbaum.

Harrell, T. H. (1992). The Sixteen Personality Factor Questionnaire. In J. J. Kramer & J. S. Conoley (Eds.), *The eleventh mental measurement yearbook* (pp. 830–831). Lincoln: Buros Institute of Mental Measurement, University of Nebraska.

Harrington, T. F., & O'Shea, A. J. (2000). *The CDM 2000 manual.* Circle Pines, MN: American Guidance Service.

Harris, J. (1974). The computer: Guidance tool of the future. *Journal of Counseling Psychology, 21,* 331–339.

Harris-Bowlsbey, J. (1984). The computer and career development. *Journal of Counseling and Development, 63,* 145–148.

Harris-Bowlsbey, J. (1990). Computer-based career guidance systems: Their past, present and a possible future. In J. P. Sampson, Jr., & R. C. Reardon (Eds.), *Enhancing the design and use of computer-assisted career guidance systems: Proceedings of an international teleconference on technology and career development* (pp. 10–19). Alexandria, VA: National Career Development Association.

Hattrup, K. (2003). Review of the California Psychological Inventory Third Edition. In B.S. Plake, J.C. Impara, and R.A. Spies (Eds.), *The fifteenth mental measurements yearbook*. Lincoln, NE: Buros Institute of Mental Measurements. Retrieved December 15th, 2004, from Mental Measurements Yearbook database. Accession number: 15122723

Hartung, P. J. (1995). Developing a theory-based measure of career decision-making: The Decisional Process Inventory. *Journal of Career Assessment, 3*(3), 299–313.

Hartung, P. J. (1999). Interest assessment using card sorts. In M. L. Savickas & A. R. Spokane (Eds.), *Vocational interests: Meaning, measurement, and counseling use*. Davies-Black Publishing/Consulting Psychologists Press, Inc, Palo Alto, CA: 235-252.

Hartung, P. J., & Marco, C. D. (1998). Refinement and further validation of the Decisional Process Inventory. *Journal of Career Assessment, 6*(2), 147–162.

Hay, I., Ashman, A. F., & Van Kraayenoord, C. E. (1998). Educational characteristics of students with high or low self concepts. *Psychology in the Schools, 35(4),* 391–400.

Healy, C. C. (1989). Negative: The MBTI: Not ready for routine use in counseling. *Journal of Counseling and Development, 67*(8), 487–489.

Healy, C. C. (1994). Review of the Career Maturity Inventory. In J. T. Kapes, M. M. Mastie, & E.A. Whitfield (Eds.), *A counselor's guide to career assessment instruments* (pp. 269–272). Alexandria, VA: National Career Development Association.

Healy, C. C., & Woodward, G. A. (1998). The Myers-Briggs Type Indicator and career obstacles. *Measurement and Evaluation in Counseling and Development, 31*(2), 74–85.

Hegenauer, M., & Brown, S. (1990). Testing the test: A review of the Social and Prevocational Information Battery. *Journal of Counseling and Development, 68,* 338–340.

Helwig, A. A., & Myrin, M. D. (1997). Ten-year stability of Holland codes within one family. *Career Development Quarterly, 46*(1), 62–71.

Henkels, M. T., Spokane, A. R., & Hoffman, M. A. (1981). Vocational identity, personality, and preferred mode of interest inventory feedback. *Measurement & Evaluation in Guidance, 14,* 71–76.

Henington, C. (2001). Review of the NEO4. In B.S. Plake and J.C. Impara (Eds.), *The fourteenth mental measurements yearbook*. Lincoln, NE: Buros Institute of Mental Measurements. Retrieved December 15th, 2004, from Mental Measurements Yearbook database. Accession # 14122273.

Heppner, M. J., Fuller, B. E., & Multon, K. D. (1998). Adults in involuntary career transition: An analysis of the relationship between psychological and career domains. *Journal of Career Assessment, 6*(3), 329–346.

Herman, O. D. (1985). Review of the Career Decision Scale. In J. V. Mitchell, Jr. (Ed.), *The ninth mental measurement yearbook,* (Vol. II) (p. 270). Lincoln: Buros Institute of Mental Measurement, University of Nebraska.

Herr, E. L. (1989). Kuder Occupational Interest Survey. In J. S. Conoley & J. J. Kramer (Eds.), *The tenth mental measurement yearbook* (pp. 425–427). Lincoln: Buros Institute of Mental Measurement, University of Nebraska.

Herringer, L. G. (1998). Relating values and personality traits. *Psychological Reports, 83*(3, Pt 1), 953–954.

Hilton, T. L. (1982). Career Development Inventory. In J. T. Kapes & M. M. Mastie (Eds.), *A counselor's guide to vocational guidance instruments* (pp. 118–122). Falls Church, VA: National Vocational Guidance Association.

Hitchings, W. E., Luzzo, D. A., Retish, P., Horvath, M., & Ristow, R. S. (1998). Identifying the career development needs of college students with disabilities. *Journal of College Student Development, 39*(1), 23–32.

Holden, R. H. (1984). Review of the Reading-Free Vocational Interest Inventory, Revised. In D. J.Keyser & R. C. Sweetland (Eds.), *Test critiques II* (pp. 627–630). Kansas City, MO: Test Corporation of America.

Holland, J. L. (1985). *Making vocational choices: A theory of vocational personalities and work environments* (2nd ed.). Englewood Cliffs, NJ: Prentice-Hall.

Holland, J. L. (1992). *Making vocational choices: A theory of vocational personalities and work environments* (2nd ed.). Odessa, FL: Psychological Assessment Resources.

Holland, J. L. (1994a). *The occupations finder.* Odessa, FL: Psychological Assessment Resources.

Holland, J. L. (1994b). *The Self-Directed Search: Professional user's guide.* Odessa, FL: Psychological Assessment Resources.

Holland, J. L. (1997). *Making vocational choices: A theory of vocational personalities and work environments.* Odessa, FL: Psychological Assessment Resources.

Holland, J. L., Daiger, D. C., & Power, P. G. (1980). *My Vocational Situation.* Palo Alto, CA: Consulting Psychologists Press.

Holland, J. L., Fritzsche, B. A., & Powell, A. B. (1994). *The Self-Directed Search: Technical manual.* Odessa, FL: Psychological Assessment Resources.

Holland, J. L., Johnston, J. A., & Asama, N. F. (1993). The Vocational Identity Scale: A diagnostic and treatment tool. *Journal of Career Assessment, 1,* 1–12.

Holland, J. L., Powell, A., & Fritzsche, B. (1994). *The Self-Directed Search (SDS): Professional user's guide.* Odessa, FL: Psychological Assessment Resources.

Hoppock, R. (1976). *Occupational information.* New York: McGraw-Hill.

Hornaday, J. A., & Gibson, L. A. (1995). *The Kuder book of people who like their work.* Adel, IA: National Career Assessment Services.

Hoyt, K. B. (1972). *Career education: What it is and how to do it.* Salt Lake City: Olympus.

Hsu, L. M. (1985). Review of the Wide Range Interest Opinion Test. In J. V. Mitchell, Jr.(Ed.), *The ninth mental measurement yearbook.* Lincoln: Buros Institute of Mental Measurement, University of Nebraska.

Ihle-Helledy, K., Zytowski, D. G., & Fouad, N. A. (2004). .Kuder Career Search: Test-retest reliability and consequential validity. *Journal of Career Assessment, 12,* 285-297.

Jastak, J. F., & Jastak, S. (1979). *The Wide Range Interest-Opinion Test (WRIOT).* Wilmington, DE: Jastak Associates.

Johnson, R. W. (1978). Review of the Strong- Campbell Interest Inventory. In O. K. Buros (Ed.), *The eighth mental measurement yearbook* (Vol. 2). Highland Park, NJ: Gryphon.

Johnson, S. D. (1985). Review of the Career Development Inventory. In D. J. Keyser & R.C. Sweetland (Eds.), *Test critiques IV.* Kansas City, MO: Test Corporation of America.

Jones, K. H., & Womble, M. N. (1998). At-risk students' perceptions of work and careerrelated issues. *Journal for Vocational Special Needs Education, 20*(2), 12–25.

Jones, L. K. (1980). Issues in developing an occupational card sort. *Measurement and Evaluation in Guidance, 12,* 200–213.

Jones, L. K. (1983). A comparison of two self-directed career guidance instruments: Occ-U-Sort and Self-Directed Search. *The School Counselor*, 204–211.

Jones, L. K. (1986). *The Career Decision Profile.* Raleigh, NC: Author.

Jones, L. K. (1989). Measuring a three-dimensional construct of career indecision among college students: A revision of the Vocational Decision Scale—The Career Development Profile. *Journal of Counseling Psychology, 36,* 477–486.

Jones, L. K. (1990). The Career Key: An investigation of the reliability, and validity of its scales

and its helpfulness among college students. *Measurement and Evaluation in Counseling & Development, 23,* 67–76.

Jones, L. K. (1993). Two career guidance instruments: Their helpfulness to students and effect on students' career exploration. *School Counselor, 40,* 191–200.

Jones, L. K. (1997, March 14). Personal communication.

Jones, L. K., & DeVault, R. M. (1979). Evaluation of a self-guided career exploration system: The Occ-U-Sort. *The School Counselor,* 334–341.

Jones, L. K., Gorman, S., & Schroeder, C. G. (1989). A comparison between the Self- Directed Search and the Career Key among career undecided college students. *Career Development Quarterly, 37,* 334–344.

Jones, L. K., & Lohmann, R. C. (1998). The Career Decision Profile: Using a measure of career decision status in counseling. *Journal of Career Assessment, 6*(2), 209–230.

Jones, L. K., Sheffield, D., & Joyner, B. (2000). Comparing the effects of the Career Key with Self-Directed Search and Job-OE among eighth grade students. *Professional School Counseling, 3*(4), 238–247.

Judge, T. A., Higgins, C. A., Thoresen, C. J., & Barrick, M. R. (1999). The big five personality traits, general mental ability, and career success across the life span. *Personnel Psychology, 52*(3), 621–652.

Jung, C. G. (1971). Psychological types (H. G. Baynes, Trans., revised by R. F. C. Hull). In *The collected works of C. G. Jung* (Vol. 6). Princeton, NJ: Princeton University Press. (Original work published 1921)

Kahn, J. H., Nauta, M. M., Gailbreath, R., D., Tipps, J., & Chartrand, J. M. (2002). The utility of career and personality assessment in predicting academic progress. *Journal of Career Assessment, 10,* 3-23.

Kapes, J. T., Mastie, M. M., & Whitfield, E. A. (1994). *A counselor's guide to career assessment instruments* (3rd ed.). Alexandria, VA: National Career Development Association.

Kaplan, R., & Saccuzzo, D. (1993). *Psychological testing.* Pacific Grove, CA: Brooks/Cole.

Katz, L., Joiner, J. W., & Seaman, N. (1999). Effects of joint interpretation of the Strong Interest Inventory and the Myers-Briggs Type Indicator in career choice. *Journal of Career Assessment, 7*(3), 281–297.

Katz, M. R. (1982). Career Maturity Inventory. In J. T. Kapes & M. M. Mastie (Eds.), *A counselor's guide to vocational guidance instruments* (pp. 122–126). Falls Church, VA: National Vocational Guidance Association.

Katz, M. R. (1984). Computer-assisted guidance: A walk through with comments. *Journal of Counseling and Development, 63,* 158–161.

Kelly, K. R. (2002). Concurrent validity of the Kuder Career Search Activity Preference Scales and career clusters. *Journal of Career Assessment, 10,* 127-144.

Kelly, K. R., & Nelson, R. C. (1999). Task-Specific Occupational Self-Efficacy Scale: A predictive validity study. *Journal of Career Assessment, 7*(4), 381–392.

Klemp, G. L., & McClelland, D. C. (1986). What constitutes intelligent functioning among senior managers. In R. J. Sternberg & R. K. Wagner (Eds.), *Practical intelligence: Nature and origins of competence in the everyday world* (pp. 31–50). New York: Cambridge University Press.

Knefelkamp, L. L., & Slepitza, R. (1976). A cognitive-developmental model of career development model of career development: An adaptation of the Perry scheme. *Counseling Psychologist, 6*, 53–58.

Knowdell, R. L. (1995a). *Career Values Card Sort Planning Kit.* San Jose, CA: Career Research and Testing.

Knowdell, R. L. (1995b). *Motivated Skills Card Sort Planning Kit.* San Jose, CA: Career Research and Testing.

Krumboltz, J. D. (1985). Presuppositions underlying computer use in career counseling. *Journal of Career Development, 12*, 165–170.

Krumboltz, J. D. (1991). *The Career Beliefs Inventory.* Palo Alto, CA: Consulting Psychologists Press.

Krumboltz, J. D., & Vosvick, M. A. (1996). Career assessment and the Career Beliefs Inventory. *Journal of Career Assessment, 4*(4), 345–361.

Kuder, G. F. (1963). A rationale for evaluating interests. *Educational and Psychological Measurement, 23*, 3–10.

Kuder, G. F. (1979). *Kuder Occupational Interest Survey: General manual.* Chicago: Science Research Associates.

Kurtz, J. E., Lee, P. A., & Sherker, J. L. (1999). Internal and temporal reliability estimates for informant ratings of personality using the NEO PI-R and IAS. *Assessment, 6*(2), 103–113.

Lachar, B. (1992). Review of the Minnesota Importance Questionnaire. In J. J. Kramer & J.C. Conoley (Eds.), *The eleventh mental measurement yearbook.* Lincoln: Buros Institute of Mental Measurement, University of Nebraska.

Lancaster, B. P., Rudolph, C. E., Perkins, T. S., & Patten, T. G. (1999). The reliability and validity of the Career Decision Difficulties Questionnaire. *Journal of Career Assessment, 7*(4), 393–413.

Larson, L. M., & Majors, M. S. (1998). Applications of the Coping with Career Indecision instrument with adolescents. *Journal of Career Assessment, 6*(2), 163–179.

Larson, L. M., Rottinghaus, P. .J., & Borgen, F. H. (2002). Meta-analyses of big six interests and big five personality factors. *Journal of Vocational Behavior, 61*, 217-39.

Larson, L. M., Toulouse, A. L., Ghumba, W. E., Fitzpatrick, L. A., & Heppner, P. P. (1994). The development and validation of Coping with Career Indecision. *Journal of Career Assessment, 2*(2), 91–110.

Lattimore, R. R., & Borgen, F. H. (1999). Validity of the 1994 Strong Interest Inventory with racial and ethnic groups in the United States. *Journal of Counseling Psychology, 46*(2), 185–195.

Laurence, J. H., Wall, J. E., Barnes, J. D., & Dela Rosa, M. (1998). Recruiting effectiveness of theASVAB career exploration program. *Military Psychology, 10 (4)*, 225–238.

LaVoie, A. L. (1978). Review of the Survey of Interpersonal Values. In O. K. Buros (Ed.), *The eighth mental measurement yearbook* (Vol. 1). Highland Park, NJ: Gryphon.

Layton, W. L. (1992). Review of the Minnesota Importance Questionnaire. In J. J. Kramer & J.C. Conoley (Eds.), *The eleventh mental measurement yearbook.* Lincoln: Buros Institute of Mental Measurement, University of Nebraska.

Lenz, J. G. (1993). Holland's theory and effective use of computer-assisted career guidance systems. *Journal of Career Development, 19*, 245–253.

Lenz, J. G., Reardon, R. C., & Sampson, J. P., Jr. (1990). *Holland's theory and effective use of computer-assisted career guidance systems* (Tech. Rep. No. 12). Tallahassee: Florida State University, Center for the Study of Technology in Counseling and Career Development. (ERIC Document Reproduction Service No. ED 340 971) Leong, F. T. L., & Dollinger, S. J. (1991). Review of the NEO-PI. In D. J. Keyser & R. C. Sweetland (Eds.), *Test critiques VIII* (pp. 527–539). Austin, TX: PRO-ED.

Leung, S. A. (1998). Vocational identity and career choice congruence of gifted and talented high school students. *Counselling Psychology Quarterly, 11*(3), 325–335.

Leung, S. A. (2002). Career counseling in Hong Kong: Meeting the social challenges. *Career Development Quarterly, 50,* 218-225.

Leung, S. A., Conoley, C. W., Scheel, M. J., & Sonnenberg, R. T. (1992). An examination of the relation between vocational identity, consistency and differentiation. *Journal of Vocational Behavior, 40,* 95–107.

Levin, A. (1991). *Introduction to the Strong for career counselors.* Palo Alto, CA: Consulting Psychologists Press.

Levinson, E. M. (1994). Current vocational assessment models for students with disabilities. *Journal of Counseling and Development, 73,* 94–101.

Levinson, E. M., Rafoth, B. A., & Lesnak, L. A. (1994). Relationship between the OASIS-2 Aptitude Survey and grades in college English and psychology classes. *Journal of Employment Counseling, 31 (2),* 60–68.

Levinson, E. M., Zeman, H. L., & Ohler, D. L. (2002). A critical evaluation of the web-based version of the Career Key. *Career Development Quarterly, 51,* 26-35.

Lewin, M, & Wild, C. L. (1991). The impact of the feminist critique on tests, assessment, and methodology. *Psychology of Women Quarterly, 15*(4), 581–596.

Lewis, D. M., & Savickas, M. L. (1995). Validity of the Career Factors Inventory. *Journal of Career Assessment, 3*(1), 44–56.

Lindley, L. D., & Borgen, F. H. (2002). Generalized self-efficacy, Holland theme self-efficacy and academic performance. *Journal of Career Assessment, 10,* 301-314.

Linn, R. L. (1982). Differential Aptitude Tests/DAT career planning program. In J. T. Kapes & M. M. Mastie (Eds.), *A counselor's guide to vocational guidance instruments* (pp. 37–42). Falls Church, VA: National Vocational Guidance Association.

Locke, D. C. (1988). Review of the Career Development Inventory. In J. T. Kapes & M.M. Mastie (Eds.), *A counselor's guide to career assessment instruments* (2nd ed.). Alexandria, VA: National Career Development Association.

Lofquist, L. & Dawis, R. V. (1984). Research on work adjustment and satisfaction: Implications for career counseling. In S. Brown & R. Lent (Eds.), *Handbook of counseling psychology* (pp. 216–237). New York: Wiley.

Lowman, R. L. (1991). *The clinical practice of career assessment: Interests, abilities, and personality.* Washington, DC: American Psychological Association.

Lucas, E. B., Gysbers, N. C., Buescher, K. L., & Heppner, P. P. (1988). My Vocational Situation: Normality, psychometric, and comparative data. *Measurement and Evaluation in Counseling and Development, 20,* 162–170.

Lucas, J. L, & Wanberg, C. R. (1995). Personality correlates of Jones' three-dimensional model of career indecision. *Journal of Career Assessment, 3*(3), 315–329.

Lucas, M. S. (1999). Adult career changers: A developmental context. *Journal of Employment Counseling, 36*(3), 115–118.

Lundberg, D. J., Osborne, W. L., & Miner, C. U. (1997). Career maturity and personality preferences of Mexican-American and Anglo- American adolescents. *Journal of Career Development, 23*(3), 203–213.

Lunneborg, P. W. (1978). Review of the Strong- Campbell Interest Inventory. In O. K. Buros (Ed.), *The eighth mental measurement yearbook* (Vol. 2). Highland Park, NJ: Gryphon.

Luzzo, D. A. (1995). The relative contributions of self-efficacy and locus of control to the prediction of career maturity. *Journal of College Student Development, 36*(1), 61–66.

Luzzo, D. A. (1996). A psychometric evaluation of the Career Decision-Making Self-Efficacy Scale. *Journal of Counseling & Development, 74*(3), 276–279.

Luzzo, D. A., Hitchings, W. E., Retish, P., & Shoemaker, A. (1999). Evaluating differences in college students' career decision making on the basis of disability status. *Career Development Quarterly, 48*(2), 142–156.

Luzzo, D. A., & Pierce, G. (1996). Effects of DISCOVER on the career maturity of middle school students. *Career Development Quarterly, 45*(2), 170–172.

MacGregor, C. J. (2002). Personality differences between online and face-to-face students. *Journal of Continuing Higher Education, 50,* 14-23.

Manuelle, C. A. (1985). Review of the Wide Range Interest Opinion Test. In J. V. Mitchell, Jr.(Ed.), *The ninth mental measurement yearbook.* Lincoln: Buros Institute of Mental Measurement, University of Nebraska.

Manuelle-Adkins, C. (1989). Review of the Self- Directed Search: 1985 revision. In J. C. Conoley & J. J. Kramer (Eds.), *The tenth mental measurement yearbook.* Lincoln: Buros Institute of Mental Measurement, University of Nebraska.

Marsh, H. W., & Yeung, A. S. (1998). Longitudinal structural equation models of academic self-concept and achievement: Gender differences in the development of math and English constructs. *American Educational Research Journal, 35(4),* 705–738.

Mastrangelo , P. M. (2001). Review of the Myers Briggs Type Inventory Form M. In B.S. Plake and J.C. Impara (Eds.), *The fourteenth mental measurements yearbook.* Lincoln, NE: Buros Institute of Mental Measurements. Retrieved August 15th, 2004, from Mental Measurements Yearbook database. Accession number: 14122331

Mau, W. (1999). Effects of computer-assisted career decision making on vocational identity and career exploratory behaviors. *Journal of Career Development, 25*(4), 261–274.

Mazurek, N., & Shumaker, A. (1997). *Career selfefficacy in college students with disabilities: Implications for secondary and post-secondary service providers.* Iowa. (ERIC Document Reproduction Service No. ED 412 708)

McCaulley, M. H. (1990). The Myers-Briggs indicator: A measure of individuals and groups. *Measurement and Evaluation in Counseling and Development, 22,* 181–195.

McCray, P. (1982). *Vocational evaluation and assessment in school settings.* Menomonie: Research and Training Center, Stout Vocational Rehabilitation Institute, University of Wisconsin–Stout.

McDivitt, J. (2002). Review of the Career Maturity Inventory. In J.T. Kapes, & E. A. Whitfield (Eds.), *A counselor's guide to career assessment instruments. Fourth Edition* (pp. 336–342). Alexandria, VA: National Career Development Association.

McKee, L. M., & Levinson, E. M. (1990). A review of the computerized version of the Self-Directed Search. *Career Development Quarterly, 38,* 325–333.

McKinlay, B. (1990). *Developing a career information system.* Eugene, OR: Career Information System.

Mealor, D. J. (1991). Review of the Social and Prevocational Information Battery. In D. J.Keyser & R. C. Sweetland (Eds.), *Test Critiques VIII.* Austin, TX: PRO-ED.

Meyers, C. E. (1978). Review of the Social and Prevocational Information Battery. In O. K.Buros (Ed.), *The eighth mental measurement yearbook* (Vol. 2). Highland Park, NJ: Gryphon.

Michaels, C. A., & Risucci, D. A. (1993). Employer and counselor perceptions of workplace accommodations for persons with traumatic brain injury. *Journal of Applied Rehabilitation Counseling, 24*(1), 38–46.

Miller, R. J. (1992). Review of the Reading-Free Vocational Interest Inventory, Revised. In J. J.Kramer & J. C. Conoley (Eds.), *The eleventh mental measurement yearbook.* Lincoln: Buros Institute of Mental Measurement, University of Nebraska.

Mitchell, L. K., & Krumboltz, J. D. (1990). Social learning approach to career decision making: Krumboltz's theory. In D. Brown & L. Brooks (Eds.), *Career choice and development: Applying contemporary theories to practice* (pp. 145–197). San Francisco: Jossey-Bass.

Monahan, C. J. (1987). Construct validation of a modified differentiation index. *Journal of Vocational Behavior, 30,* 217–227.

Mueller, D. J. (1985). Survey of Interpersonal Values. In D. J. Keyser & R. C. Sweetland (Eds.), *Test critiques II* (pp. 759–763). Kansas City, MO: Test Corporation of America.

Murray, H. A. (1938). *Exploration in personality.* New York: Oxford University Press.

Myers, J. B., & McCaulley, M. H. (1985). *Manual: A guide to the development and use of the Myers-Briggs Type Indicator.* Palo Alto, CA: Consulting Psychologists Press.

National Institute of Education. (1974). *Proposed guidelines for assessment of sex bias and sex fairness in interest inventories.* Washington, DC: Author.

National Occupational Information Coordinating Committee (NOICC), U.S. Department of Labor. (1992). *The National Career Development Guidelines Project.*Washington, DC: U.S. Department of Labor.

Neuman, J. L., Gray, E. A., & Fuqua, D. R. (1999). The relation of career indecision to personality dimensions of the California Psychological Inventory. *Journal of Vocational Behavior, 54*(1), 174–187.

Niles, S. G., Anderson, W. P., Jr., Hartung, P. J. & Staton, A. R. (1999). Identifying client types from adult career concerns inventory scores. *Journal of Career Development, 25*(3), 173–185.

Niles, S. G., & Goodnough, G. E. (1996). Life-role salience and values: A review of recent research. *Career Development Quarterly, 45*(1), 65–86.

Noel, N. M., Michaels, C., & Levas, M. G. (2003). The relationship of personality traits and self-monitoring behavior to choice of business major. *Journal of Education for Business, 78,*153-57.

Ohler, D. L., Levinson, E. M., & Barker, W. F. (1996). Career maturity in college students with learning disabilities. *Career Development Quarterly, 44*(3), 278–288.

Okiishi, R. W. (1987). The genogram as a tool in career counseling. *Journal of Counseling and Development, 66,*139-143..

Oliver, L. W., & Zack, J. S. (1999). Career assessment on the Internet: An exploratory study.*Journal of Career Assessment, 7*(4), 323–356.

Olson, G. T., & Matlock, S. G. (1994). Review of the 16PF. In J. T. Kapes, M. M. Mastie, & E. A.Whitfield. *A counselor's guide to career assessment instruments* (3rd ed.) (pp. 302–305). Alexandria, VA: National Career Development Association.

Organist, J. E. (1985). Review of the Wide Range Interest-Opinion Test. In D. J. Keyser & R. C. Sweetland (Eds.), *Test critiques IV* (pp. 673–676). Kansas City, MO: Test Corporation of America.

Osborn, D. S., Peterson, G. W., Sampson, J. P., Jr., & Reardon, R. C. (2003).Client anticipations about computer-assisted career guidance outcomes. *Career Development Quarterly, 51,*356-67.

Osipow, S. H. (1980). *Manual for the Career Decision Scale.* Columbus, OH: Marathon Consulting and Press.

Osipow, S. H. (1987). *Manual for the Career Decision Scale.* Odessa, FL: Psychological Assessment Resources.

Osipow, S. H., Carney, C. G., & Barak, A. (1976). A scale of educational-vocational undecidedness: A typological approach. *Journal of Vocational Behavior, 27,* 233–244.

Osipow, S. H., Carney, C. G., Winer, J. L., Yanico, B. J., & Koeschier, M. (1987). *Career Decision Scale* (3rd rev.). Odessa, FL: Psychological Assessment Resources.

Osipow, S. H., & Gati, I. (1998). Construct and concurrent validity of the career decisionmaking difficulties questionnaire. *Journal of Career Assessment, 6*(3), 347–364.

Osipow, S. H., & Temple, R. D. (1996). Development and use of the Task-Specific Occupational Self-Efficacy Scale. *Journal of Career Assessment, 4*(4), 445–456.

Osipow, S. H., Temple, R. D., & Rooney, R. A. (1993). The short form of the Task-Specific Occupational Self-Efficacy Scale. *Journal of Career Assessment, 1*(1), 13–20.

Osipow, S. H., & Winer, J. L. (1996). The use of the Career Decision Scale in career assessment. *Journal of Career Assessment, 4,* 117–130.

Osipow, S. H., Winer, J. L., & Koschier, M. (1976). *Career Decision Scale.* Odessa, FL: Psychological Assessment Resources.

Overton, T. (1992). Social and Prevocational Information Battery (SPIB). In J. J. Kramer & J.S. Conoley (Eds.), *The eleventh mental measurement yearbook* (pp. 834–836). Lincoln: Buros Institute of Mental Measurement, University of Nebraska.

Paige, B. E. (2000). Psychological types of dental hygiene students. *Journal of Psychological Type, 52,* 32–35.

Parish, L. H., & Lynch, P. S. (1988). Review of the Pictorial Inventory of Careers. In J. T. Kapes & M. M. Mastie (Eds.), *A counselor's guide to career assessment instruments* (2nd ed.). Alexandria, VA: National Career Development Association.

Parish, P. A., Rosenberg, H., & Wilkinson, L. (1979). *Career information resources, applications, and research, 1950–1979.* Boulder: University of Colorado.

Parsons, F. (1909). *Choosing a vocation.* Boston: Houghton Mifflin.

Parsons, E., & Betz, N. E. (1998). Test-retest reliability and validity studies of the Skills Confidence Inventory. *Journal of Career Assessment, 31*(3), 150–163.

Pennock-Roman, M. (1988). Differential Aptitude Test. In J. T. Kapes & M. M. Mastie (Eds.), *A counselor's guide to career assessment instruments* (2nd ed.). Alexandra, VA: National Career Development Association.

Peterson, G. W. (1998). Using a vocational card sort as an assessment of occupational knowledge. *Journal of Career Assessment, 6*(1), 49–67.

Peterson, G. W., & Lenz, J. G. (1992). *Using card sorts: A cognitive mapping task.* Unpublished manuscript. Tallahassee, FL.

Peterson, G. W., Ryan-Jones, R. E., Sampson, J. P., Jr., Reardon, R. C., & Shahnasarian, M. (1987). *A comparison of the effectiveness of three computer-assisted career guidance systems on college students' career decision making processes* (Tech. Rep. No. 6). Tallahassee: Florida State University, Center for the Study of Technology in Counseling and Career Development.

Peterson, G. W., Ryan-Jones, R. E., Sampson, J. P., Jr., Reardon, R. C., & Shahnasarian, M. (1994). A comparison of the effectiveness of three computer-assisted career guidance systems: DISCOVER, SIGI, and SIGI PLUS. *Computers in Human Behavior, 10,* 189–198.

Peterson, G. W., Sampson, J. P., Jr., & Reardon, R. C. (1991). *Career development and services: A cognitive approach.* Pacific Grove, CA: Brooks/Cole.

Peterson, G. W., Sampson, J. P., Jr., Reardon, R. C., & Lenz, J. G. (2002). A cognitive information processing approach to career problem solving and decision making. In D. Brown (Ed.), *Career choice and development* (4th ed.) (pp. 312-372). San Francisco: Jossey- Bass.

Peterson, S. L., & delMas, R. C. (1998). The component structure of Career Decision-Making Self-Efficacy for underprepared college students. *Journal of Career Development, 24*(3), 209–225.

Petrill, S. A., & Wilkerson, B. (2000). Intelligence and achievement: A behavioral genetic perspective. *Educational Psychology Review, 12(2),*185–199.

Pinkney, J. W. (1985). A card sort strategy for flat profiles on the Strong-Campbell Interest Inventory. *Vocational Guidance Quarterly, 33,* 331–339.

Pinkney, J. W., & Bozik, C. M. (1994). Review of the Career Development Inventory. In J. T. Kapes, M. M. Mastie, & E. A. Whitfield (Eds.), *A counselor's guide to career assessment instruments. Third Edition* (pp. 265–267). Alexandria, VA: National Career Development Association.

Pitz, G. F., & Harren, V. A. (1980). An analysis of career decision making from the point of view of information processing and decision theory. *Journal of Vocational Behavior, 16,* 320–346.

Pope, M. (2002). Review of the Kuder General Interest Survey, Form E. In J.T. Kapes, & E. A. Whitfield (Eds.), *A counselor's guide to career assessment instruments. Fourth Edition* (pp. 258-264). Alexandria, VA: National Career Development Association.

Powell, D. F., & Luzzo, D. A. (1998). Evaluating factors associated with the career maturity of high school students. *Career Development Quarterly,47*(2), 145–158.

Prediger, D. J. (1980). The marriage between tests and career counseling: An intimate report. *Vocational Quarterly, 28,* 297–305.

Prediger, D. J. (1994). Tests and counseling: The marriage that prevailed. *Measurement and Evaluation in Counseling, 26*(4), 227–234.

Prediger, D. J. (1995). *Assessment in career counseling.* Greensboro, NC: ERIC Counseling and Student Services Clearinghouse, University of North Carolina.

Prediger, D. J., & Swaney, K. B. (1992). Career counseling validity of Discover's job cluster scales for the revised ASVAB score report (Report No. 92–2). Iowa City, IA: American College Testing Program.

Prediger, D. J., & Swaney, K. B. (1995). Using the UNIACT in a comprehensive approach to assessment for career planning. *Journal of Career Assessment, 3,* 429–452.

Railey, M.G., & Peterson, G. W. (2000). The assessment of dysfunctional career thoughts and interest structure among female inmates and probationers. *Journal of Career Assessment, 8*(2), 119–129.

Ralston, C. A., Borgen, F. H., Rottinghaus, P. J., & Donnay, D. A. C. (2004). Specificity in interest measurement: Basic Interest Scales and major field of study. *Journal of Vocational Behavior, 65, 203-216.*

Rangappa, K. T. (1994). Effect of self-concept on achievement in mathematics. *Psycho-Lingua, 24(1),* 43–48.

Rayman, J., & Atanasoff, L. (1999). Holland's theory and career intervention: The power of the hexagon. *Journal of Vocational Behavior, 55*(1), 114–126.

Reardon, R. C., & Lenz, J. G. (1998). *The Self- Directed Search and related Holland materials: A practitioner's guide.* Odessa, FL: Psychological Assessment Resources.

Reardon, R. C., Shahnasarian, M., Maddox, E. N., & Sampson, J. P., Jr. (1984). Computers and student services. *Journal of Counseling and Development, 63,* 180–183.

Ree, M. J., & Carretta, T. R. (1995). Group differences in aptitude factor structure on the ASVAB. *Educational and Psychological Measurement, 55,* 268–277.

Ricks, J. H. (1978). Review of the Career Development Inventory. In O. K. Buros (Ed.),*The eighth mental measurement yearbook* (Vol. 2). Highland Park, NJ: Gryphon.

Robbins, S. B. (1985). Validity estimates for the Career Decision-Making Self-Efficacy Scale.*Measurement & Evaluation in Counseling & Development, 18*(2), 64–71.

Rogers, J. E. (2002). Review of the Armed Services Vocational Aptitude Battery Career Exploration Program (ASVAB). In J.T. Kapes, & E. A. Whitfield (Eds.), *A counselor's guide to career assessment instruments* (pp. 93–101). Alexandria, VA: National Career Development Association.

Rojewski, J. W. (1996). Occupational aspirations and early career-choice patterns of adolescents with and without learning disabilities *Learning Disability Quarterly, 19*(2), 99–116.

Rokeach, M. (1973). *The nature of human values.* New York: Free Press.

Rosen, D., Holmberg, M. S.., & Holland, J. L. (1994). *Dictionary of educational opportunities.*Odessa, FL: Psychological Assessment Resources.

Rounds, J. B., Jr., Henly, G. A., Dawis, R. V., & Lofquist, L. H. (1981). *Manual for the Minnesota Importance Questionnaire: A measure of needs and values.* Minneapolis: Vocational Psychology Research, University of Minnesota.

Sampson, J. P., Jr. (1984). Maximizing the effectiveness of computer applications in counseling and human development: The role of research and implementation strategies. *Journal of Counseling and Development, 63,* 187–191.

Sampson, J. P., Jr. (1994). *Effective computer assisted career guidance* (Occasional paper No. 1). Tallahassee: Florida State University, Center for the Study of Technology in Counseling and Career Development.

Sampson, J. P., Jr., & Johnson, C. S. (1993). *Helping you help people find their way: Training resource guide (SIGI PLUS).* Princeton, NJ: Educational Testing Service.

Sampson, J. P., Jr., & Norris, D. S. (1995). *An evaluation of the effectiveness of Florida CHOICES implementation in high schools* (Tech. Rep. No. 20). Tallahassee: Florida State University, Center for the Study of Technology in Counseling and Career Development.

Sampson, J. P., Jr., & Peterson, G. W. (1984). *Evaluation standard: Computer-assisted career guidance systems.* Unpublished manuscript, Florida State University, Project LEARN— Phase II.

Sampson, J. P., Jr., Peterson, G. W., Lenz, J. G., & Reardon, R. C. (1992). A cognitive approach to career services: Translating concepts into practice. *The Career Development Quarterly, 41,* 67–74.

Sampson, J. P., Jr., Peterson, G. W., Lenz, J. G., Reardon, R. C., & Saunders, D. E. (1996). *The Career Thoughts Inventory.* Odessa, FL: Psychological Assessment Resources.

Sampson, J. P., Jr., Peterson, G. W., Lenz, J. G., Reardon, R. C., & Saunders, D. E. (1998). The design and use of a measure of dysfunctional career thoughts among adults, college students, and high school students: The Career Thoughts Inventory. *Journal of Career Assessment, 6*(2), 115–134.

Sampson, J. P., Jr., Peterson, G. W., & Reardon, R.C. (1989). Counselor intervention strategies for computer-assisted career guidance: An information-processing approach. *Journal of Career Development, 16,* 139–154.

Sampson, J. P., Jr., Peterson, G. W., Reardon, R. C., Lenz, J. G., Shahnasarian, M., & Ryan-Jones, R. E. (1992). The social influence of two computer-assisted career guidance systems: DISCOVER and SIGI. *The Career Development Quarterly, 41,* 75–83.

Sampson, J. P., Jr. Purgar, M. P., & Shy, J. D. (2003). Computer-based test interpretation in career assessment: Ethical and professional issues. *Journal of Career Assessment, 11,* 22-39.

Sampson, J. P., Jr., & Pyle, K. R. (1983). Ethical issues involved with the use of computer-assisted counseling, testing and guidance systems. *Personnel and Guidance Journal, 61,* 283–287.

Sampson, J. P., Jr., Reardon, R. C., Lenz, J. G., Peterson, G. W., Shahnasarian, M., & Ryan-Jones, R. (1987). *The impact of two computerassisted career guidance systems on college students' perceptions of the counseling dimensions of computer interaction.* Tallahassee, FL: Florida State University, Center for the Study of Technology in Counseling and Career Development.

Sampson, J. P., Jr., Reardon, R. C., Lenz, J. G., Ryan-Jones, R. E., Peterson, G. W., & Levy, F.C. (1993). *The impact of DISCOVER for adult learners and SIGI PLUS on the career decision making of adults* (Tech. Rep. No. 9). Tallahassee: Florida State University, Center for the Study of Technology in Counseling and Career Development. (ERIC Document Reproduction Service No. ED 363 824)

Sampson, J. P., Jr., Reardon, R. C., Norris, D. S., Greeno, B. P., Kolodinsky, R. W., Herbert, S.,

Sankofa-Amammere, K. T., Epstein, S., Odell, J., Wright, L., Radice, M., Peterson, G. W., & Lenz, J. G. (1996). *A differential feature-cost analysis of twenty-one computer-assisted career guidance systems* (Tech. Rep. No. 10, 7th ed.). Tallahassee: Florida State University, Center for the Study of Technology in Counseling and Career Development.

Sampson, J. P., Jr., Reardon, R. C., Shahnasarian, M., Peterson, G. W., Ryan-Jones, R., & Lenz, J. G. (1987). *The impact of DISCOVER and SIGI on the career decision making of college students* (Tech. Rep. No. 5). Tallahassee: Florida State University, Center for the Study of Technology in Counseling and Career Development.

Sampson, J. P., Jr., Shahnasarian, M., & Reardon, R. C. (1987). Computer-assisted career guidance: A national perspective on the use of DISCOVER and SIGI. *Journal of Counseling and Career Development, 65,* 416–419.

Sander, D. (1985). Review of Differential Aptitude Tests: Form V & W. In J. V. Mitchell, Jr. (Ed.), *The ninth mental measurement yearbook.* Lincoln: Buros Institute of Mental Measurement, University of Nebraska.

Saunders, D. E., Peterson, G. W., Sampson, J. P., & Reardon, R. C. (2000). Relation of depression and dysfunctional career thinking to career indecision. *Journal of Vocational Behavior, 56*(2), 288–298.

Savickas, M. L. (2000). Assessing career decision making. In C. E. Watkins, Jr., & V. L. Campbell (Eds.), *Testing and assessment in counseling practice* (pp. 429–477). Mahwah, NJ: Lawrence Erlbaum Associates.

Savickas, M. L., Briddick, W. C., & Watkins, C. E., Jr. (2002). The relations of career maturity to personality type and social adjustment. *Journal of Career Assessment, 10,* 24-41.

Savickas, M. L., & Hartung, P. (1996). The Career Development Inventory in review: Psychometric and research findings. *Journal of Career Assessment, 4 (2),* 171–188.

Saxon, J. P., & Spitznagel, R. J. (1995). Transferable skills and abilities profile: An economical assessment approach in the vocational placement process. *Vocational Evaluation and Work Adjustment Bulletin,* 61–67.

Schuerger, J. M. (2000). The Sixteen Personality Factor Questionnaire (16PF). In C. E. Watkins, Jr., & V. L. Campbell (Eds.), *Testing and assessment in counseling practice*(2nd ed.) (pp. 73–110). Mahwah, NJ: Erlbaum.

Seal, B. C. (2004). Psychological testing of sign language interpreters. *Journal of Deaf Studies & Deaf Education, 9,* 39-52.

Sharf, R. S. (1992). *Applying career development theory to counseling.* Pacific Grove, CA: Brooks/Cole.

Simon, S. B., Howe, L. W., & Kirschenbaum, H. (1972). *Value clarification.* New York: Hart.

Slaney, R. B. (1980). Expressed vocational choice and vocational indecision. *Journal of Counseling Psychology, 27,* 122–129.

Slaney, R. B. (1985). Relation of career indecision to career exploration with reentry women: A treatment and follow-up study. *Journal of Counseling Psychology, 32,* 355–362.

Slaney, R. B., & MacKinnon-Slaney, F. (1990). The use of vocational card sorts in career counseling. In C. E. Watkins, Jr. & V. L. Campbell (Eds.), *Testing in counseling practice* (pp. 317–371). Hillsdale, NJ: Erlbaum.

Slaney, R. B., Moran, W. J., & Wade, J. C. (1994). Vocational card sorts. In J. T. Kapes, M. M. Mastie, & E. A. Whitfield (Eds.), *A counselor's guide to career assessment instruments* (pp. 347–360). Alexandria, VA: National Career Development Association.

Slaney, R. B., Palko-Nonemaker, D., & Alexander, R. (1981). An investigation of two measures of career indecision. *Journal of Vocational Behavior, 18,* 92–103.

Slate, J. R., Jones, C. H., Sloas, S., & Blake, P. C. (1998). Scores on the Stanford Achievement Test – 8 as a function of sex: Where have the sex differences gone? *High School Journal, 81(2),* 82–86.

Sowers, J., Cotton, P., & Malloy, J. (1994). Expanding the job and career options for people with significant disabilities. *Developmental Disabilities Bulletin, 22*(2), 53–62.

Spokane, A. R., & Catalano, M. (2000). The Self- Directed Search: A theory driven array of self-guiding career interventions. In C. E. Watkins, Jr., & V. L. Campbell (Eds.), *Contemporary topics in vocational psychology* (2nd ed.) (pp. 339–370). Mahwah, NJ: Erlbaum.

Spokane, A. R., & Holland, J. L. (1995). The Self- Directed Search: A family of self-guided career interventions. *Journal of Career Assessment, 3,* 373–390.

Stilwell, N. A., Wallick, M. M., Thal, S. E., & Burleson, J. J. (2000). Myers-Briggs type and medical specialty choice: A new look at an old question. *Teaching & Learning in Medicine, 12*(1), 14–20.

Stoker, H. (1993). Stanford Achievement Test. In J. J. Kramer & J. C. Conoley (Eds.), *The eleventh mental measurement yearbook* (pp. 863–865). Lincoln: Buros Institute of Mental Measurement, University of Nebraska.

Stone, E. (1993). *The Career Interest Inventory: A review and critique.* (ERIC Document Reproduction Service No. ED 356 255) Strong, E. K., Jr. (1943). *Vocational interests of men and women.* Stanford, CA: Stanford University Press.

Sullivan, B. A., & Hanse, J-I. C. Evidence of construct validity of the interest scales on the Campbell Interest and Skill Survey. *Journal of Vocational Behavior, 65,*179-202.

Super, D. E. (1980). A life-span, life-space approach to career development. *Journal of Vocational Behavior, 16,* 282–298.

Super, D. E. (1983). Assessment in career guidance: Toward truly developmental counseling. *Personnel and Guidance Journal, 61,* 555–567.

Super, D. E. (1990). A life-span, life-space approach to career development. In D. Brown & L. Brooks (Eds.), *Career choice and development: Applying contemporary theories to practice* (pp. 197–261). San Francisco: Jossey-Bass.

Super, D. E., & Nevill, D. D. (1985). *The Salience Inventory.* Palo Alto, CA: Consulting Psychologists Press.

Super, D. E., Osborne, W., Walsh, D., Brown, S., & Niles, S. (1992, Sept./Oct.). Developmental career assessment and counseling: The C-DAC model. *Journal of Counseling and Development, 71,* 74–79.

Super, D. E., Thompson, A. S., Lindeman, R. H., Jordaan, J. P., & Myers, R. M. (1981). *Career Development Inventory, College and University Form.* Palo Alto, CA: Consulting Psychologists Press.

Swanson, J. L. (1999). Stability and change in vocational interests. In M. L. Savickas & A. R.

Spokane (Eds.), *Vocational interests: Meaning, measurement, and counseling use,* 135–158. Palo Alto, CA: Davies-Black.

Symes, B. A., & Stewart, J. B. (1999). The relationship between meta-cognition and vocational indecision. *Canadian Journal of Counselling, 33*(3), 195–211.

Tak, J. (2004). Structure of vocational interests for Korean college students. *Journal of Career Assessment, 12,*298-311.

Takigasaki, T. & Fujimura, K. (2004). Correlations between personal preferences and age for a sample of Japanese Open University students. *Psychological Reports, 94,* 771-774.

Taylor, K. M. & Betz, N. E. (1983). Applications of Self-Efficacy Theory to the understanding and treatment of career indecision. *Journal of Vocational Behavior, 21*(1), 63–81.

Taylor, K. M., & Popma, J. (1990). An examination of the relationships among career decision-making self-efficacy, career salience, locus of control, and vocational indecision. *Journal of Vocational Behavior, 37*(1),17–31.

Te Nijenhus, J., Evers, A., & Mur, J. P. (2000). Validity of the Differential Aptitude Test for the assessment of immigrant children. *Educational Psychology: An international journal of experimental educational psychology, 20,* 99-115.

Tenopyr, M. L. (1989). Kuder Occupational Interest Survey. In J. S. Conoley & J. J. Kramer (Eds.), *The tenth mental measurement yearbook* (pp. 427–429). Lincoln: Buros Institute of Mental Measurement, University of Nebraska.

Thompson, A. R., & Dickey, K. D. (1994). Self-perceived job search skills of college students with disabilities. *Rehabilitation Counseling Bulletin, 37*(4), 358–370.

Thomas, S. W. (1994). Review of the WRIOT. In J. T. Kapes, M. M. Mastie, & E. A. Whitfield (Eds.), *A counselor's guide to career assessment inventories* (pp. 342–345). Alexandria, VA: National Career Development Association.

Thompson, B., & Ackerman, C. M. (1994). Review of the MBTI. In J. T. Kapes, M. M. Mastie, & E. A. Whitfield (Eds.), *A counselor's guide to career assessment instruments.* Alexandria, VA: National Career Development Association.

Tittle, C. K., & Hecht, D. (1994). Review of the Social and Prevocational Information Battery–Revised. In J. T. Kapes, M. M. Mastie, & E. A. Whitfield (Eds.), *A counselor's guide to career assessment inventories* (pp. 332–335). Alexandria, VA: National Career Development Association.

Tokar, D. M., Fischer, L. R., & Subich A. M. (1998). Personality and vocational behavior: A selective review of the literature, 1993–1997. *Journal of Vocational Behavior, 53*(2), 115–153.

Toossi, M. (2004). Labor force projections to 2012: The graying of the U.S. workforce. *Monthly Labor Review, 127,* 37-57.

Tuel, B. D., & Betz, N. E. (1998). Relationships of career self-efficacy expectations to the Myers-Briggs Type Indicator and the Personal Styles Scales. *Measurement and Evaluation in Counseling and Development, 31*(3), 150–163.

Tyler, L. E. (1961). Research explorations in the realm of choice. *Journal of Counseling Psychology, 8,* 195–201.

U.S. Bureau of the Census (1990). Projections of the population of states, by age, sex and race: 1989–2010. *Current population representations: Series P-25, no. 1053.* Washington, DC: U.S. Government Printing Office.

U.S. Department of Defense. (1994). *Technical manual for the ASVAB 18/19 career exploration program.* Washington, DC: U.S. Government Printing Office.

U.S. Department of Defense. (1995). *The interest finder.* Washington, DC: U.S. Government Printing Office.

U.S. Department of Defense. (2005). *Exploring careers: The ASVAB career exploration guide.* Washington, DC: U.S. Government Printing Office.

U.S. Department of Labor. (2004-2005). *Occupational outlook handbook.* Washington, DC: U.S. Government Printing Office.

Vacc, N. A., & Newsome, D. W. (2002). In J.T. Kapes, & E. A. Whitfield (Eds.), *A counselor's guide to career assessment instruments* (pp. 123–131). Alexandria, VA: National Career Development Association.

VALPAR, International. Sigi Plus. [Computer program]. Tuscon, AZ: Author.

Vansickle, T. R. (1994). Review of the Harrington- O'Shea Career Decision-Making System–Revised. In J. T. Kapes, M. M. Mastie, & E. A. Whitfield (Eds.), *A counselor's guide to career assessment instruments* (pp. 174–177).Alexandria, VA: National Career Development Association.

Wall, J. E. (1994). Review of the CBI. In J. T. Kapes, M. M. Mastie, & E. A. Whitfield (Eds.), *A counselor's guide to career assessment inventories.* Alexandria, VA: National Career Development Association.

Wall, J. E., & Baker, H. E. (1997). The Interest- Finder: Evidence of validity. *Journal of Career Assessment, 5 (3),* 255–73.

Walls, R. T., & Fullmer, S. L. (1997). Competitive employment: Occupations after vocational rehabilitation. *Rehabilitation Counseling Bulletin, 41*(1),15–25.

Walsh, B. D., Thompson, B, & Kapes, J. T. (1997). The construct validity of scores on the Career Beliefs Inventory. *Journal of Career Assessment, 5*(1), 31–46.

Walsh, J. A. (1978). Review of the Sixteen Personality Factor Questionnaire. In O. K. Buros (Ed.), *The eighth mental measurement yearbook* (Vol. 1). Highland Park, NJ: Gryphon.

Walsh, W. B. (1972). Review of the Kuder Occupational Interest Survey. In O. K. Buros (Ed.), *The seventh mental measurement yearbook.* (Vol. 2). Highland Park, NJ: Gryphon.

Walsh, W. B., & Betz, N. E. (1995). *Tests and assessment,* 3rd ed. Englewood Cliffs, NJ: Prentice-Hall.

Walter, V. (1984). *Personal Career Development Profile.* Champaign, IL: Institute for Personality and Ability Testing.

Wang, L. (1993). *The Differential Aptitude Test: A review and critique.* (ERIC Document Reproduction Service No. ED 56 257).

Wang, L., Ye, M., & Tao, J. (2002). Mental health status, coping style, and personality characteristics of college students. *Chinese Journal of Clinical Psychology, 10,* 208-209.

Ward, C. M., & Bingham, R. P. (1993). Career assessment of ethnic minority women. *Journal of Career Assessment, 1,*246-257.

Weiss, D. J. (1978). Review of the Armed Services Vocational Aptitude Battery. In O. K. Buros (Ed.), *The eighth mental measurement yearbook* (Vol. 1). Highland Park, NJ: Gryphon.

Welsh, J. R., Kucinkas, S. K., & Curran, L. T. (1990). *Armed Services Vocational Battery (ASVAB): Integrative review of validity studies* (Report No. AFHRL-TR-90–22). Brooks Air Force Base, TX: Air Force Human Resources Laboratory.

Westbrook, B. W. (1983). Career maturity: The concept, the instrument, and the research. In W. B. Walsh & S. H. Osipow (Eds.), *Handbook of vocational psychology* (Vol. 1) (pp. 263-304). Hillsdale, NJ: Erlbaum.

Whiston, S. C. (2000). *Principles and applications of assessment in counseling.* Pacific Grove, CA: Brooks/Cole.

Whiston, S. C., & Bouwkamp, J. C. (2003). Ethical implications of career assessment with women. *Journal of Career Assessment, 11,* 59-75.

Whiston, S. C., Brecheisen, B. K., & Stephens, J. (2003). Does treatment modality affect career counseling effectiveness? *Journal of Vocational Behavior, 62,*390-410.

Williams, R. T. (1992). Adult Basic Learning Examination (ABLE). In J. J. Kramer & J. S. Conoley (Eds.), *The eleventh mental measurement yearbook* (pp. 21–23). Lincoln: Buros Institute of Mental Measurement, University of Nebraska.

Williams, R. T. (1994). Review of Adult Basic Learning Examination (ABLE) (2nd ed.). In J.

T. Kapes, M. M. Mastie, & E. A. Whitfield (Eds.), *A counselor's guide to career assessment inventories* (pp. 59–62). Alexandria, VA: National Career Development Association.

Williamson, E. G. (1939). *How to counsel students: A manual of techniques for clinical counselors.* New York: McGraw-Hill.

Williamson, E. G. (1949). *Counseling adolescents.* New York: McGraw-Hill.

Williams-Phillips, L. J. (1983). *Five career decidedness scales: Reliability, validity, and factors.* Unpublished master's thesis, North Carolina State University at Raleigh.

Willis, C. G. (1982). The Harrington-O'Shea Career Decision-Making System. In J. T. Kapes & M. M. Mastie (Eds.), *A counselor's guide to vocational guidance instruments* (pp. 57–61). Falls Church, VA: National Vocational Guidance Association.

Willson, V. L., & Stone, E. (1994). Review of the Differential Aptitude Test and the Career Interest Inventory. In J. T. Kapes, M. M. Mastie, & E. A. Whitfield (Eds.), *A counselor's guide to career assessment instruments* (pp. 93–98). Alexandria, VA: National Career Development Association.

Wircenski, J. L. (1994). Review of the Pictorial Inventory of Careers. In J. T. Kapes, M. M. Mastie, & E. A. Whitfield (Eds.), *A counselor's guide to career assessment instruments* (pp. 316–319). Alexandria, VA: National Career Development Association.

Wright, L. K., Reardon, R. C., Peterson, G. W., & Osborn, D. S. (2000). The relationship among constructs in the Career Thoughts Inventory and the Self-Directed Search. *Journal of Career Assessment, 8*(2), 105–117.

Wulff, M. B., & Steitz, J. A. (1999). A path model of the relationship between career indecision, androgyny, self-efficacy and self-esteem. *Perceptual & Motor Skills, 88*(3, Pt 1), 935–940.

Zmud, R. W., Sampson, J. P., Reardon, R. C., Lenz, J. G., & Byrd, T. A. (1994). Confounding effects of construct overlap. An example from IS user satisfaction theory. *Information Technology and People, 7,* 29–45.

Zunker, V. G. (2002). *Career counseling: Applied concepts of life planning* (6th ed.). Pacific Grove, CA: Brooks/Cole.

Zunker, V. G. (2005). *Career counseling: Applied concepts of life planning* (7th ed.). Pacific Grove, CA: Brooks/Cole.

Zytowski, D. G. (1978). Review of Wide Range Interest-Opinion Test. In O. K. Buros (Ed.), *The eighth mental measurement yearbook* (Vol. 2). Highland Park, NJ: Gryphon.

Zytowski, D. G. (1999). How to talk to people about their interest inventory results. In M. L. Savickas & A. R. Spokane (eds.), *Vocational interest: Meaning, measurement, and counseling use,* pp. 277–293. Palo Alto, CA: Davies- Black/Consulting Psychologists Press.

Zytowski, D. G., & England, R. J. L. (1995). Indices of interest maturity in the Kuder Occupational Interest Survey. *Measurement and Evaluation in Counseling and Development, 28,* 148-151.

Name Index

Subject Index